The Folkgames of Children

Publications of the American Folklore Society
Bibliographical and Special Series
General Editor, Wm. Hugh Jansen
Volume 24   1972

The Folkgames of Children

BY BRIAN SUTTON-SMITH

PUBLISHED FOR THE AMERICAN FOLKLORE SOCIETY BY THE
UNIVERSITY OF TEXAS PRESS · AUSTIN AND LONDON

Library of Congress Cataloging in Publication Data

Sutton-Smith, Brian.
   The folkgames of children.

   (Publications of the American Folklore Society.
Bibliographical and special series, v. 24)
   Bibliography: p.
   1. Games—New Zealand—Addresses, essays, lectures.
2. Games—United States—Addresses, essays, lectures.
3. Play—Addresses, essays, lectures. I. Title.
II. Series: American Folklore Society. Bibliographical
and special series, v. 24.
GV1204.91.S79   793.4   72-413
ISBN 0-292-72405-5

Composition by G&S Typesetters, Austin
Printing by Capital Printing Company, Austin
Binding by Universal Bookbindery, Inc., San Antonio

THE BOOK IS DEDICATED TO MY WIFE, SHIRLEY,

AND TO MY CHILDREN, KATHERINE, MARK, LESLIE,

MARY, AND EMILY, WHO HAVE ALLOWED ME TO

IMPOSE MY WILLFUL PLAYFULNESS UPON

THEIR BREAKFAST DAYS.

North
Auckland

AUCKLAND

Bay of Plenty

NORTH ISLAND

Auckland

Taranaki

GISBORNE

NEW PLYMOUTH

Hawkes

WANGANUI

NAPIER

PALMERSTON
NORTH

Bay

Wellington

Golden Bay

NELSON

WESTPORT

WELLINGTON

Nelson

Marlborough

Westland

Canterbury

CHRISTCHURCH

SOUTH ISLAND

TIMARU

Otago

OAMARU

Southland

DUNEDIN

INVERCARGILL

Map of New Zealand

CONTENTS

Foreword xi

Introduction xiii

SECTION I: HISTORICAL APPROACHES 1

  1. The Games of New Zealand Children 5

  2. Sixty Years of Historical Change in the Game
     Preferences of American Children
     (with B. G. Rosenberg) 258

  3. The Two Cultures of Games 295

SECTION II: ANTHROPOLOGICAL APPROACHES . . . 313

  4. The Meeting of Maori and European Cultures and Its
     Effects upon the Unorganized Games of Maori
     Children 317

  5. The Cross-Cultural and Psychological Study of
     Games (with John M. Roberts) 331

  6. Strategy in Games and Folk Tales (with John M.
     Roberts and Adam Kendon) 341

  7. Studies in an Elementary Game of Strategy (with
     John M. Roberts, Robert M. Kozelka, Vaughn J.
     Crandall, Donald M. Broverman, Abraham Blum,
     and Edward L. Klaiber) 359

SECTION III: PSYCHOLOGICAL APPROACHES . . . 401

  8. Development of Sex Differences in Play Choices dur-
     ing Preadolescence (with B. G. Rosenberg and E. F.
     Morgan) 405

  9. Role Replication and Reversal in Play . . . 416

 10. The "It" Role in Children's Games
     (with P. V. Gump) 433

 11. The Game as a School of Abstraction . . . 442

SECTION IV: UNIFIED APPROACHES   451
    12. Marbles Are In   455
    13. The Kissing Games of Adolescents in Ohio .   .   .   465
    14. A Formal Analysis of Game Meaning   .   .   .   491
    15. The Sporting Balance   506
    16. The Expressive Profile   521
A Chronological Bibliography   541
Index   547

FOREWORD

As its editorial staff can feelingly testify, the American Folklore Society does not have to beat the bushes seeking manuscripts for its publication series. Yet for this volume we did solicit Dr. Brian Sutton-Smith, and we are proud that we did.

A surprisingly long time ago—surely it must have been the first performance in the States by the precocious scholar—our Society in its annual meeting was entranced by the wit, youthful exuberance, and faint down-under accent with which a paper was delivered on children's games. The years that followed have been marked by a series of provocative articles (see the bibliography as well as the table of contents in this volume) in folklore journals across the land, and in many other journals, too.

As folklorists we would be proud to claim Dr. Sutton-Smith for our profession, but we must recognize a prior claim from another discipline. Head of Columbia University's Teachers College's Department of Developmental Psychology, Dr. Sutton-Smith looms very large in modern child psychology, and his research in children's games and children's play can therefore, I suppose, be called in the very best and most admirable sense applied folklore.

I want to thank Dr. Sutton-Smith for having complied with our request to make easily accessible to folklorists his own selection of his articles on children's folkgames. And I want to thank Dr. Roger Abrahams for inspiring me to make that request.

W. H. J.

INTRODUCTION

It is hardly possible to present this collection of fifteen articles and an entire book on games without raising some serious questions about one's own persistent pursuit of such "nonserious subject-matter." The roots for the persistence undoubtedly lie within my own personal life and are perhaps documented in my novels *Our Street* and *Smitty Does a Bunk*. I like to think, however, that my own early struggles for autonomy within the somewhat monotonous post-Victorian social environment of New Zealand during the 1930s and the 1940s have relevance for the inevitably crowded bureaucracies of the future. Playfulness and gamesmanship are not as trivial and nonserious as our puritan forebears opined, though they are ephemeral, postponable, and capable of much neglect. They can be forgotten when the urgencies of the group ethos or the group survival are given paramount value. Yet in play, and in its more immortal issue, art, each individual differentiates himself from his own entrapment and in so doing becomes, momentarily at least, a free spirit. An environment which would allow for and even encourage such uniqueness might be enriching regardless of the surrounding circumstances. I would like to think that my studies contribute to that type of sanity and have increasing relevance in the days of the population explosion.

For me play is what a person does when he can choose the arbitrariness of the constraints within which he will act or imagine. In its most primordial form, it is an attempt to control the circumstances of habitual action by reversing the direction of control. It may be, therefore, the ultimate source of all voluntary behavior on the levels of action and thought. The player substitutes his own conventions and his own urgencies for those of society and nature.

Affectively speaking, being in control engenders a relaxed freedom from customary tension, as well as the possibility of creating parallel or alternative tensions within the proscribed setting. This mixture of lowered tension in external relations and induced arousal within the novel constraints is probably the euphoric state we call fun. Cognitively speaking, being in control means a reversal of life structures. It is as if the usually reinforced "set" of having to accomplish one's objectives in terms of the requirements of others and of the external world is replaced now by another "set" within which one can control all the important contingencies. It is this new "set" that changes the direction of the structures of action and thought and also allows them to be modified or transformed. Thus we can speak of play in terms of novel behaviors, novel combinations, and novel consequences.

Once play has commenced, however, even this play "set" can be put to one side. Perhaps because play itself can become taxing, the players often seek further excitement in breaking it down. Thus, after a long period of concentrated blockbuilding, the young associates will gain great enjoyment from destroying their own efforts. What we describe as playfulness is often a state in which a further escalation of "sets" takes place and the play involvement gives way to wild invention, hilarity, and sometimes complete nonsense. It is as though play rode like a satire on the back of work, and playfulness, like a series of satires, on the back of play. Each contends there can be both a distance from and an alternative to the earlier more committed forms.

Since voluntary controls are hard to achieve, play takes place most easily in a setting established for that purpose and with scaled-down objects; i.e., dolls, which allow small players to more readily assume the guise of mastery. It is for such reasons that we can speak of play as a form of micro-knowing and the precursor to all later forms of imagination.

In *games*, where the rules are based on mutual agreement, there is no reversal of the orders of convention and nature. They are mirrored rather than put aside. The functional intent of games is limited. What games do promise is to reverse a man's fate within these orders, though only in terms of the testing of powers over fate, nature, and others. There are many types of play, such as imitation, exploration, and construction, which are only moderately assimilated into the game format; they find more adequate representation in drama, magic, and museums; while games give primary place to the play of contest. As well as rules, games also involve an opposition of forces and a disequilibrial outcome. The earliest games take place between mother and infant where there is a playful opposition and the outcome differs for the two parties. Thus the mother throws a blanket over the four-month-old baby's head, and the latter pulls it off. The action is repeated and there is much hilarity. It is clear that games can take place only between people who have confidence in each other, at least to some extent. Games and sports imply a higher level of agreement among the antagonists than exists between those who do not have games. Those activities that are usually called pastimes, such as "Ring a Ring of Roses," are in fact the earliest form of games in which a contest takes place between the players and the forces of anarchy. The question is whether the players can sufficiently organize themselves to maintain a rule-governed stability over time. More typically, however, games are contests between players to see who will be the winner in terms of the accomplishments lauded in the major culture. Here games are a microcosm of cultural fate, but one in which the customary order of superiority is, if not reversed, at least temporarily open for rectification. This book is mainly about games and their role in symbolizing human attempts to gain such leeway within particular forms of social order.

Naturally this material is a quite personal work and does not deal with the study of games in general, nor with my parallel concern for the nature of play. Both interests are covered in a more detailed fashion in previously published works.[1] However this republication of some of my work does provide an opportunity to include a selection of articles that will illustrate the various approaches toward games that I have used. The sections that follow

[1] See the *Study of Games* coauthored with Elliott Avedon (New York: John Wiley & Sons, 1971) and *Child's Play* coauthored with Robin Herron (New York: John Wiley & Sons, 1971). *The Study of Games* contains a number of approaches to games and analyses games according to various disciplines. The numerous bibliographies cover the literature on games in such fields as the military, business, education, recreation, and in professional therapy. In *Child's Play*, the play theory and play data of the past fifty years have been reviewed and interpreted.

deal, in turn, with historical, anthropological, psychological, and "unified" approaches. There is inevitably some overlap between them. The reader will detect a continual struggle for adequate counterbalance among the varying claims of the humanist and the social scientist, the folklorist and the psychologist, the claims of the formalist and the claims of the functionalist. In the last section, Unified Studies, I indicate my attempts to resolve these dilemmas.

SECTION I
HISTORICAL APPROACHES

Traditionally a folklore approach was one concerned with the origins of games. The hope was expressed that games could be used to restore an understanding of earlier historical levels of culture. This view was gradually replaced by the notion that the understanding of origins is in itself a form of explanation. There is some partial truth to this contention as the historically oriented works of Newell, Gomme, Bett, and Daiken attest, but it has not been a motivating force among folkgame theorists of recent years.[1] This view survives rather interestingly in the conviction of the Opies (*Lore and Language of Schoolchildren* and *Children's Games in Street and Playground*) that the parallels between games in earlier times and games today are evidence of the universality of the human motives underlying these games.[2] A brief glimpse at Section II, Anthropological Approaches, would not seem to support their thesis entirely. The type of game appears to be relative to the type of culture, even though many game forms are indeed widespread.

By contrast, my own historical approach has been focused on changes in games rather than constancies, and I have also sought to compare game changes with changes in other areas of child behavior. It makes sense to me that historical changes in the family as recorded by writers like Philippe Ariès in *Centuries of Childhood* and J. H. van den Berg in *The Changing Nature of Man* would be paralleled by changes in the nature of children's games.

[1] See Elliott M. Avedon and Brian Sutton-Smith, *The Study of Games* (New York: John Wiley & Sons, 1971), pp. 159–223, for these and other references.

[2] Peter and Iona Opie, "The Tentacles of Tradition," *The Advancement of Science* 22 (1963–1964): 9–17.

Admittedly the task of supplying historical parallels is a highly speculative venture, but once again the endeavor (if perhaps not the outcome) gains validity from the evidence for such parallels in the cross-cultural studies that follow. The interest for me has been to look at these changes as a way of finding out where indeed the larger culture is heading in its dealings with children. For a developmental psychologist there is also a parallel to be sought between a consideration of historical change and the more customary study of change in the individual's development.

The present section includes a book and two articles. The book, *The Games of New Zealand Children*, was originally published by the University of California Press in 1959 and is republished here with their kind permission. Work for this study was carried out during 1949–1950. Work on the second study, an article entitled "Sixty Years of Historical Change in the Game Preferences of American Children," was completed during 1959–1960 and afforded the opportunity to parallel the New Zealand game changes with those that had taken place in the United States. The final article in this section, "The Two Cultures of Games," published in 1969, reflects my more recent reconsideration of these historical changes.

1. The Games of New Zealand Children

PREFACE

The primary purpose of this work is to put on record the games of New Zealand children. A secondary but no less important purpose is to record the changes which have taken place in these games over the past one hundred years. As this is a work about childhood, a subsidiary purpose is so to arrange and classify the material as to illuminate the record of child nature that it contains. The organization and assessment of the data presented in the following pages were carried out while the author was a Research Fellow at the Institute of Child Welfare in the University of California at Berkeley. It could not have been carried out but for the aid of a United States Government Fulbright Travel Grant and a Smith-Mundt Research Fellowship. Nor would the original data collection have been possible without the ready coöperation of many people, including those surprised New Zealanders I confronted in their homes, schoolteachers, physical education instructors, teachers' college and university staff members and students; my mother, my wife, and Miss Jean MacLeod, who did much of the arduous recording; and my many friends in the United States, whose warm sympathy brought this volume into existence, in particular, Professor Archer Taylor of the University of California at Berkeley.

CONTENTS

Part One

The Collection 9
Historical Synopsis 10
Arrangement and Classification 15

Part Two

Singing Games: Category A 18
Dialogue Games: Category B 46
Informal Games: Category C 54
Leader Games: Category D 66
Chasing Games: Category E 75
Rhythmic Games: Category F 99
Games of Chance: Category G 120
Teasing Activities: Category H 122
Parlor Games: Category J 139
Games of Skill: Category K 152

Part Three

Developmental Synopsis 212
Epilogue 215

Appendix I. Additional Game Names: Category L . . 222
Appendix II. Historical Summary of Game Names . . 222
Appendix III. Sources of Information 226

Bibliography 234

Index of Game Names 240
Index of Rhymes 254

PART ONE

The Collection

This study is concerned with the games that children play of their own free will, without the assistance or leadership of adults. Originally, of course, these games may have been learned from relatives, schoolteachers, or recreation-club leaders. In general, the children involved were those between the ages of six and twelve years, but occasionally there is a historical reference to those older children of thirteen and fourteen years who attended school in earlier times. Information about these games was collected as follows. The research was widely advertised in all the national newspapers, a variety of weekly and monthly magazines, and through a series of radio talks. As a result, about a hundred manuscripts of varying lengths and value were received. Some two hundred and sixty-five persons, including a large number of aged people, were interviewed in many parts of the country. Six hundred and fifty-five teachers' college and university students from all parts of the country contributed information, and more than one hundred of these answered questionnaires. Nineteen schools in different parts of the country sent in reports on their present-day games. Thirty-two schools were visited in Dunedin, North Otago, Christchurch, Golden Bay, West Coast, Wellington, Wairarapa, and Auckland.[1] At the schools the children listed their games, wrote essays about them, and demonstrated the manner in which they were played. Observations were made on one particular school playground, Island Bay, Wellington, over a two-year period, 1949 and 1950.[2] As the material was collected it was filed in a number of

Source: *The Games of New Zealand Children*, Folklore Studies: 12 (Berkeley and Los Angeles: University of California Press, 1959). This book is reprinted in its entirety by permission of The Regents of the University of California.

[1] Further details are given in Appendix III.

[2] In New Zealand the school year is included within the calendar year, because the cold months there are the months identified with the summer season in the Northern Hemisphere.

ways. First, a summary of material from each informant was filed under the decade and place to which that material referred. This summary later permitted generalizations to be drawn about the differences obtaining between different historical periods and different places. Secondly, the details of the various games were classified into appropriate categories, so that, for example, all singing games could be treated together.

The study of the games of the nineteenth century was limited by the facts that oral reminiscence could take the record back only to about 1870 and there were few written reports of games which referred to an earlier period. Nevertheless, the eighty years that could be adequately surveyed did provide a clear picture of historical change. Naturally, the sample of games taken from various parts of the country was weighted in favor of those areas from which more information was received, in particular from the South Island of New Zealand. However, it was found that in respect to the games played and manner of playing them, the differences between districts in any parts of the country were nearly always slight. This fact, together with the known ethnic homogeneity of the New Zealand population, is believed to be sufficient grounds for accepting the study as representative.[3]

Historical Synopsis

The history of planned British settlement in New Zealand dates from 1840. Records of childhood in the first decades of settlement suggest that because children were an economic asset in the pioneering economy, they often had little spare time to play. Where they did have spare time, they tended to use it, especially the boys, in exploring the wild life and in adventures offered by the natural environment, rather than in playing traditional games. That is,

---

[3] Ninety-three percent of the population are of British origin. This was a study of New Zealand European games, not of the games of the Maoris, who comprise 6 percent of the population. For a restricted study of Maori games, see Brian Sutton-Smith, "The Meeting of Maori and European Cultures and Its Effects upon the Unorganized Games of Maori Children," *Journal of the Polynesian Society*, LX (1951), 93–107.

they spent their time swimming, climbing trees, exploring the bush, bird-nesting (finding and taking birds' nests), making shanghais (catapults), fishing, eeling, and hunting for berries and other natural edibles. With the consolidation of settlement, however, there arose more regular opportunities for children to play at and to develop formal games. For example, singing games and tagging games became an established part of the annual community picnics which were held from the earliest years. These picnics increased in number and popularity in the latter years of the nineteenth century and continued to grow in importance until after the First World War. Parlor games, too, were in abundance as a form of home recreation in the early years, although mainly restricted to the homes of the well-to-do. During the last decade of the nineteenth century, the use of these parlor games in Bible-class and church socials brought them to a much wider section of the population. The most important place in which the children of the day learned their games was, undoubtedly, the school playground. From the beginning of settlement in the 1840's, but more particularly after the institution of compulsory education in the 1870's, the school became the most important center for children's play. Before the establishment of the local school there was seldom a general community center where all the children could and did play regularly. Now, by the compulsion of school attendance, children were brought for five days a week into an environment conducive to common play. In these circumstances games proliferated. Many informants on the early years have stressed that the only place at which they ever played formal games was on the school playground, but this is a generalization which was true more particularly of rural than of urban children.

The nature of the collected data for the period between 1870 and 1900 admits of the following generalizations. This period was the heyday of traditional games in New Zealand; there was a greater variety of these games being played than in any subsequent period. All the games of the playground were managed entirely by the children themselves; there was no adult organization of play and little playground supervision. The greater part of the children's play apparatus was made by themselves. There were many very boisterous games, and rough play and fighting were a recurrent feature of school life then to a degree which does not exist today.

Apart from this stern note, the play was on the whole less sophisticated than it is today. Older children played at games which now are played, if at all, only by younger children: for example, Horses, Marbles, Tops, singing games, Hoops, and Kites. Secluded from the boys, often by a concrete wall, the girls carried on games of a more stationary nature than the games played by their counterparts today—for example, Knucklebones, singing games, and Cat's Cradle. Organized sports competitions between schools had hardly begun, even in the high schools. Shinty was better known than Rugby Football, and Rounders was more often played than Cricket. The school play year was divided into many play seasons rather than into two major ones, as it tends to be at present for Rugby and Cricket. There was much more group intolerance about the limits of these minor seasons than there is now. Today organized sports and the laws of commercial supply and demand have ridden roughshod across these earlier and more arbitrary group customs.

Between 1900 and 1920 there was an increase in playground supervision and teacher coaching of children in organized sports, with the result that there was a decrease in the number of rougher games and practices of earlier years. This period also witnessed a heightening of activity for girls and the beginnings of that widespread commercial influence upon children's play which was to have so much importance after the First World War. Taken as a whole, there were slightly fewer traditional games than before 1900. Some of the games which had been played less frequently in the nineteenth century were not heard of again in this period. Among the rougher games that faded from the playground were Tip Cat, with "cats" that were a danger to eye and window in a crowded space; Buck Buck, with its backbreaking potentialities, especially on asphalt; Duckstones, with its stone-throwing; punching forms of Bar the Door; and Fly the Garter, also a danger on hard grounds. Many boisterous running games lost importance because the skills they required were now adequately utilized in Football and Cricket practice; for example: Bull in the Ring, Hares and Hounds, Cockfighting, Paper Chase, French and English, Prisoner's Base, Tip Cat, Cunning Joe, and Egg Cap.[1] But if some of these games disappeared

---

[1] A complete summary of the names of games which were played in each period, 1870–1900, 1900–1920, 1920–1950, is to be found in Appendix II.

from the boys' playground and others waned in importance, this was, in part, counterbalanced by the fact that there was now much better provision for equipping and coaching the older boys in Rugby and Cricket. There was in many places a new opportunity to play those sports without there being as yet that sportsmania which militated against playing anything else. Out of school, of course, many of these rougher games continued to be played beyond the supervision of adults. The playground of these years saw also the introduction, in ever greater numbers, of swapping games, scrapbooks, transfers, prick books, post cards, and pastimes derived from an interest in the children's columns of the weekly journals. The important fact about these informal activities was that they were all incidents in the taming of the playground. They reflected the increasing introduction into the playground of games which were of a quieter hue; they represented also the first steps in the transference of children's play interests from the world of their own play objects to a world of play objects contrived by adults, partly out of a realization of the needs of children and partly for commercial purposes.

From 1920 onward the tremendous influence of the toy business on children's free activities, the great importance attributed to organized sports and recreation for children, and the urban structure of the modern world, all led to the speedy demise of the great majority of the older traditional games. Practically all the play activity of children of eleven or more years of age was now channeled into organized sports, whereas in earlier days children in this age group had maintained the more complex traditional games. This did not mean that there was no spontaneous play amongst these older children; on the contrary, they spent more time playing at their own unorganized variations of the major sports than they did at playing the sports themselves. However, these variations seldom led to new games; they normally led back into the major sports themselves. Younger children, on the other hand, maintained and extended the older traditional games which had been played by their predecessors. This was particularly true of the girls, who now had a much greater freedom to play than young girls had had in the nineteenth century.[2]

In general, three major characteristics differentiate today's play-

[2] See the chapters on tagging and leader games, Categories D and E.

ground from the nineteenth-century playground. The modern players are more sophisticated in their play. On the playground of today movement is swifter. The children of today are less turbulent in the way in which they play. For example, practically all the old games have slipped down the age scale; they are played by younger children than formerly. On the playground it is noticeable that, whereas in the eighteen-nineties twelve-year-old children played at Horses, Tops, Hoops, and Marbles, now only the very young will do these things. Play objects and toys are, on the whole, of a more artificial, commercial nature. The construction of homemade play objects, bows and arrows, pea-shooters, whips, catapults, and kites, although it still continues, is the work of the under-tens only. Singing games are no longer played by teen-age girls; they are restricted to the girls of seven, eight, and nine years. At the same time the modern playground presents a picture of constant movement. Not that there was no movement in the nineteenth-century playground, but there was less of it. There was little in the girls' section of the playground, and what movement there was in the boys' section was interrupted from time to time by the many important seasons concerned with such static pursuits as Marbles, Stagknife, Tops, Buttons, and Bells. Even the rhyming games of the girls reflect the change. Most of the game rhymes of yesterday were attached to the slow-moving singing games. Today the most important rhymes are used by the girls in their active skipping and ball-bouncing games. The play object of today is the ball. In its variegated shapes and sizes, it has replaced practically all the other play objects used in unorganized games. The swiftness and motility of the ball, as contrasted with the static qualities of stagknives, pocket knives, knucklebones, marbles, buttons, Cat's Cradles, "bells," and the "cats" of Tip Cat, are an index of the increase in playground speed. In quite another respect, too, the modern playground exhibits more swiftness than its predecessor: that is, in its greater amount of intellectual "slickness." Fewer conventional rhymes and sayings are repeated on set occasions, and there is a greater use of impromptu slanging, smart answers, smart sayings, teasing expressions, and teasing rhymes. These relatively mild symbolic expressions of aggressive feelings indicate another characteristic of the modern playground as compared with the playground of former days, namely, that it is freer from physical aggression and hence a calmer place in which to play. There is neither the roughness in the playground nor the fighting outside it that there used to be. In the main, of course, this playground quietness is but a reflection of the more ordered and peaceful nature of life in the home community.

In Part Two (except in the chapter on dialogue games), the subject matter is arranged chronologically in two sections, so as to bring out in detail the historical differences outlined in this synopsis. The two sections in each chapter cover, respectively, the period from about 1870 until the end of the First World War, and the period from 1920 until the time when the data for this research were collected, namely, 1949–1950. The 1870–1900 period and the 1900–1920 period are best dealt with together, because most of the games of the earlier period carried on into the second, but had disappeared by the modern period, 1920–1950.[3]

Arrangement and Classification

The problem of classifying play and games into appropriate categories has presented serious difficulties because games are complex group behaviors deriving their nature from many sources. Therefore, whether a classificatory system be based on the psychological, historical, educational, or structural characteristics of the games, there is bound to be a certain arbitrariness in any approach, as well as a great deal of overlapping between categories. The system of classification offered here is not above criticism on these points. To offset this handicap the games recorded have been given classificatory letters and numbers throughout, and also arranged in an alphabetical Index of Game Names at the end of the work. This makes the names and descriptions of the games more easily available to other workers in this field using other systems of classification.

[3] An attempt was made to interpret the psychological and educational significance of these games in my doctoral thesis, entitled "The Historical and Psychological Significance of the Unorganized Games of the New Zealand Primary School Children." See a copy in the Victoria University Library, Wellington, N.Z.

The system chosen rests partly on structural and partly on developmental considerations. That is, in distinguishing between different types of games two criteria are employed. First, does this group of games exhibit some unique characteristic which marks it off from other games? Singing games, for example, have singing as part of their structure. Secondly, is this group of games played by one particular age group or sex? Dialogue games are, for example, played predominantly by girls between the ages of seven and nine years. In the categorizing of the plays and games, either one or both of these criteria may be decisive. For example: It will be noted that girls rather than boys play the games of ritual and rhythm (Categories A, B, and C: singing, dialogue, and rhythm); that girls rather than boys prefer the games in which one player acts in a dominating "mother" role in relation to other players (Category D, leader games); that girls prefer the indoor games (Category J, parlor games). On the other hand, skill games are, by and large, the games of boys (Category K). Again, although make-believe, tagging, chance, and teasing games (Categories C, E, G, and H) are shared by both sexes at all ages, they contain "motifs" which, in my opinion, entitle them to separate treatment. In the chapters that follow, the order of treatment is roughly "developmental," that is, it begins with games played by younger children of six and seven years and ends with games more characteristic of twelve- and thirteen-year-olds.

Each type of game dealt with below is given a separate letter of the alphabet; singing games are all in Category A, dialogue games in Category B, and so on. Within each category the games are numbered consecutively: A-1, A-2, A-3, . . . If there is a large body of information about a game, that game is given a separate paragraph, but if only names or scraps of information about a game are available this is not done. The game index number (A-1, B-4, or F-9, for example) is placed in parentheses directly following the name of the game when it is first mentioned in the series; and also, as a rule, wherever it is discussed at length in connection with other games, or where further examples of it are given. In all cases the best-known game name is given the index number, the alternative names being listed with it in the appropriate chapter, but separately in the Index of Game Names.

In the Index of Rhymes, the rhymes are assigned the category letter and number of the type of game with which they are usually associated, but are indexed by page number also.

Those parts of chapters mentioning borderline play activities which are not, strictly speaking, games (for example, in the chapter on make-believe play) do not employ index numbers. These activities are included to complete the historical and developmental picture. Considerations of space have required that details be given only about New Zealand children's minor competitive games, their ritualistic singing and dialogue games, and their noncompetitive pastimes, such as pranks and teasing phenomena, Category H. Many of the more common of these have been only named or referred to briefly. Children's major sports, their homemade play with play objects, and their make-believe play have been named only. To have described all these activities would have made the volume unwieldy.

Footnote references to comparative sources are given in the text only when these have some special relevance to the game being described; for example, in the chapter on singing games a reference to Lady Gomme's *Traditional Games* is often necessary in order to indicate the appropriate music for the game. In the Index of Game Names, however, references for a number of the games are noted. Only those few British texts which indicate probable origins for the New Zealand games are used for these comparisons. As the main concern of this work is to put on record the games of New Zealand children, it has not been thought desirable to make comparisons with the games of other countries,[1] many of the sources for which are not available in New Zealand libraries.

The accompanying map of New Zealand (see frontispiece) provides a key to the various place names mentioned in the text. Only the provinces and major towns are indicated in this way. In the text, other local names are followed by the province in which they are situated, so that they can be located, approximately, on the map.

---

[1] An exception is made in the case of two American works on games by Paul G. Brewster. These two references are provided because there are a number of game names, particularly the more modern ones, for which there is an American parallel, but no British one, suggesting, perhaps, an American source for the New Zealand game.

PART TWO

Singing Games: Category A

The collection of singing games presented here and numbered from A-1 through A-42 contains three distinct subgroups. Numbers A-1 through A-26 are games of low organization, played most extensively by young girls of the age of six to nine years. This group includes circle unison games; circle games concerned with marriage, funerals, and pantomimic actions; circle games with an "It" player; and arch and winding games, many of which are also concerned with marriage. In all these games, all or the majority of players sing the song and carry out the movements in unison. The only exception occurs when one central player holds a special limelight or competitive role in relation to the others. In Poor Sally Is a-Weeping, for example, Sally is in a limelight role; the game movements and the other players revolve about her, and she is of central and cynosural importance. In Drop the Handkerchief the central player is an "It" who competes in a chase against another player in order to lose her central position. The second group of games, numbered A-27 through A-29, are the line games, in which the players are arranged in two opposing team lines. Most of these games are concerned with marriage. In the days in which they were played regularly, they seem to have been maintained by the girls of eleven, twelve, and thirteen years of age rather than by the younger ones. The third group of games, numbered A-30 through A-35, are the couple games, which were played originally by youths and adults. There are two types: the circle couple games, in which all the players aim to capture a partner; and the processional games, in which each player goes through prescribed movements with a partner chosen beforehand. There is a further group of singing games, A-36 through A-41, about which there is insufficient information for purposes of classification. The names alone are listed here.

§ I: 1870–1920

In the nineteenth-century playground the girls were usually segregated from the boys in their play. Protected by a wooden or con-

crete wall, they were able to carry on their tranquil singing games *
undisturbed. In the main, the games they played were ones they
had seen played at picnics and parties. The four singing games
most universally known were: Oranges and Lemons, Nuts and
May, Green Gravels, and The Jolly Miller. Others that appeared
frequently in the playground were The Jingo Ring, Draw a Pail of
Water, Pretty Little Girl of Mine, Ring a Ring a Roses, Farmer in
the Dell, Sally Waters, Poor Sally Is a-Weeping, Drop the Handkerchief, and Bobby Bingo. Those often played in the presence of
adults at picnics and parties, but also occasionally in the playground, were The Jolly Miller, The Three Dukes, London Bridge,
and The Grand Old Duke of York. The practice of playing singing
games differed from place to place. Generally they were played in
school playgrounds, although there are records of their being
played only in the public reserve (park), or at home. Nevertheless,
all the singing games mentioned below were reproduced by girls at
some time in some playground. The great majority of boys played
these games only at parties or picnics, except perhaps when they
were very young. Even this generalization has its exceptions, however, for boys at some small country schools played these games
until they were in their teens.

In detail, the games of the day were as follows. There were one
or two simple unison games that were probably improvised by the
children themselves and contained, in embryonic form, the essence
of all the traditional choral games. For example, at Stillwater, Nelson, in 1885, the children used to join hands on a very cold day and
gallop round and round sideways, playing what they called *Merry
Go Rounds* (A-1). At Putoka, Hawkes Bay, at a later date, 1920,
children carried out the same actions in a circle on a hilltop, singing
as they did so an infant school song, the first two words of which
were the name of their game, *Bell Horses* (A-2). The verse they
sang was:

> Bell horses, bell horses,
> What time of day?
> One o'clock, two o'clock
> Three and away.

And at "away," all the children would fling loose their hands and
fly off in all directions.

An equally simple form of unison game was the traditional *Ring a Ring a Roses* (A-3). This was played mainly by younger children. Today children often play it while holding hands and jumping up and down in the water at the seaside. The rhyme was:

> Ring a ring a rosie,
> Pop down a posie,
> A tishoo, a tishoo,
> We all fall down,

or

> Ring a ring a roses,
> Pop goes the weasel.

The players joined hands and skipped round in a circle, and at "A tishoo" put their hands upon their heads, and at the last line, "We all fall down," they all crouched down. When the second rhyme was used, the game was often called Pop Goes the Weasel.

Oka Ball (A-4), a similar game, is reported only once (Christchurch, 1875). In this game the children danced round in a circle, singing[1]

> Oka Ball Day,
> The twenty-seventh of May,
> If we don't get a holiday,
> We'll all run away.

A more complex unison game was *Baloo Baloo Balight* (A-5). A ring of children held hands and performed the appropriate actions as they sang:

> Baloo baloo balight,
> All on a Saturday night.
> Put your right hand in,
> Put your right hand out.
> Shake it a little, a little,
> And turn right about.

After they had turned, the children did the same actions with the other hand, then with each foot in turn, and finally with the head. The game was known as Lubyloo at Christchurch in 1904 and at Auckland in the late 1870's. At a private school in Auckland it was

---

[1] For an explanation of the name, see H. Bett, *The Games of Children* (London, 1924), p. 36.

played as follows: All the players held hands in a circle. The song
was sung, and after each time through, one player turned outward.
At the very end of the game, when all were facing outward, the
song was sung once more, and they all turned inward together. The
first verse was:

> Here we come lubyloo,
> Here we come lubylay,
> Here we come lubyloo,
> All on a summer's day.

Pointing to the player who was to turn about, the other players
chanted:

> Shake your right hand a little,
> Shake your left hand a little,
> Shake your right foot a little,
> And turn you round about.

At this the player, having carried out these instructions, turned
about. A form of the same game was revived in the 1940's in New
Zealand dance halls under the name of Hoki Toki.

Chain singing games, in which the children danced around,
usually in circles, with their hands together, were the most widespread of all singing games. They are said to have been the oldest
form of singing in Europe and to date back to medieval
times. In England these dances were first known as "carols," but
later simply as country dances.[2] The circle games of marriage played
in the early playgrounds were Pretty Little Girl of Mine, Poor Sally
Is a-Weeping, Sally Waters, The Jingo Ring, Farmer in the Dell,
Oats and Beans and Barley, Lady on the Mountain, and Down in
the Valley. Of these the first two were undoubtedly the most important. The many very slight variations in the words of these
games cannot be given here.

Pretty Little Girl of Mine (A-6), which was known in all the
provinces, contains all the essential characteristics of these marriage games. As the children march round in a circle with their
hands linked and sing, the "pretty little girl" in the middle performs actions to suit their words. In the more complete New Zea-

[2] D. Kennedy, *England Dances: Folk Dancing Today and Yesterday* (London,
1949), p. 34.

land versions there are three verses,[3] the first two of which are widely established.

1) Oh this pretty little girl of mine,
   She's cost me many a bottle of wine.
   A bottle of wine or anything too,
   To see what my little girl can do.

2) Down on the carpet she shall kneel,
   While the grass grows in the field.
   Stand upright upon your feet,
   And choose the one you love so sweet.

Here the "pretty little girl" chooses a partner and they stand in the center holding each other's hands. In one version the third verse is:

3) Now you're married you must obey,
   You must be true to all you say.
   You must be kind, you must be good,
   And help the wife to chop the wood. [Tahataki, Otago, 1875]

This is the only report, however, in which these lines are given as the third verse. In a number of nineteenth-century reports (Dunedin, Christchurch, Nelson) the last verse reads:

3) Now you're married we wish you joy,
   First a girl and then a boy.
   Seven years after, seven years to come,
   Pray young couple kiss and be done. [Christchurch, 1880]

At Nelson in 1890 the last two lines were:

Seven years after a son and daughter,
Pray young couple kiss together.

In Hawkes Bay, in 1920, there was a modernized version of the last line, in which the children sang:

Play and cuddle and kiss together.

Reports of the same game from Wellington and Auckland contain

[3] The music of this game is to be found in A. B. Gomme, *The Traditional Games of England, Scotland and Ireland* (Vol. I, London, 1894; Vol. II, 1898 [the Maxey version]), II, 69. This work is cited hereafter in the notes as Gomme.

only the first two verses. Occasionally the game led to an unexpected "transfer of training." One informant reports: "I played
this game at school when seven years old. The kissing was done
quite unselfconsciously in the game, but I got in for a whale of a
row for kissing the same girl 'goodbye' after school the same day."

Poor Sally Is a-Weeping (A-7) was also known in all the provinces. The usual name in Auckland Province was Poor Jenny Is a-
Weeping, which agrees with the name in Dublin. Moreover, one
version reported from the Bay of Plenty is identical with a certain
Dublin version.[4] The game had such other names as Poor Alice Is
a-Weeping (Christchurch) and Poor Mary Is a-Weeping (Palmerston North). There were usually four verses; in one typical
version these were:

1) Poor Alice is a-weeping,
   A-weeping, a-weeping.
   Poor Alice is a-weeping,
   On a bright summer's day.

2) Pray what is she weeping for,
   Weeping for, weeping for?
   Pray what is she weeping for,
   On a bright summer's day?

3) She is weeping for a sweetheart,
   A sweetheart, a sweetheart.
   She is weeping for a sweetheart,
   On a bright summer's day.

4) Then pray stand up and choose one,
   And choose one, and choose one,
   Then pray stand up and choose one,
   On a bright summer's day. [Amberley, Canterbury, 1890]

In this version Alice knelt throughout, while the others walked
slowly round singing their song. At the end she chose another
player to take her place in the middle. There were many small
variations; for example, sometimes she was weeping on a "fine
summer's day," at others she wept for her "true love" rather than
her sweetheart. In some versions Sally sang the last two verses
alone. In verse three, she sang, "I am weeping for my true love,"
and in verse four, "For Georgie is my true love" (Wellington,

---

[4] L. Daiken, *Children's Games Throughout the Year* (London, 1949), p. 75.

1900). In a Hawkes Bay version, having found out that Jenny was weeping for her true love, the players sang in the fourth verse, "Then we'll go and find him," after which Jenny chose her man. In other versions Sally did not kneel down until the commencement of the second verse, beginning "And on the carpet she shall kneel" (Taranaki, 1890). In certain Taranaki and Auckland versions an additional fifth verse was sung. The two lovers stood in the middle for the duration of the verses and performed the appropriate actions:

> 5) And now you're married you must be good,
>   And help your wife to chop the wood.
>   Chop it fine and bring it in,
>   Kiss the one in the silver ring. [Auckland]

Or:

> 5) Now you're married I wish you joy,
>   First a girl and then a boy.
>   Seven years after a son and daughter,
>   Pray young couple kiss together. [Taranaki]

In these versions from North Island towns of Taranaki and Auckland, the fifth verse of Poor Sally Is a-Weeping is the same as the last verse in the South Island versions of Pretty Little Girl of Mine (A-6). Generally, then, this last verse ("And now you're married . . .") went with the game of Pretty Little Girl of Mine in the South Island, and with the game of Poor Sally Is a-Weeping in the North Island. This verse which belongs to the two games is similarly confused in English records.

In *Sally Waters* (A-8) the action and words were much the same as in Poor Sally Is a-Weeping, but although there are reports of it from all provinces, the game was not played frequently.[5] The words in Dunedin in the 1890's were:

> 1) Sally, Sally Waters, sprinkle in the pan,
>   Rise Sally, rise Sally, for a young man.
>   Look to the East and look to the West,
>   Look to the very one that you love best.

When Sally had chosen her partner and the two were in the middle, the other children sang while the two carried out the actions described:

5 Gomme, II, 149.

2) Now you're married we wish you joy,
   Every year a girl or boy [sometimes "and boy"].
   Loving each other like sister and brother,
   Pray young couple to kiss together.

Sometimes the one chosen would be the next Sally; at other times a "grownup" would nominate her. Other versions show only minor differences; for example, at Christchurch in 1870, Sally bowed to the East and West, and bowed to the one that she loved best.

The Jingo Ring (A-9) appears to have been played only in Otago and South Canterbury.[6] It was sung in Moeraki, Otago, in the 1890's, as follows:

1) Here we go round a jinga-ring,
   A jinga-ring, a jinga-ring.
   Here we go round a jinga-ring,
   Around the marry ma tanza.

2) The last time's the catching time,
   The catching time, the catching time.
   The last time's the catching time,
   Around the marry ma tanza.

According to other reports, only the first verse was known. The manner in which the game was played is uncertain. Some reports mention it in association with Circle Tig, others as connected with the game of Tug-o'-War; still others say that it was definitely a marriage game, in which case it was probably just a remnant of a much longer English marriage game known as Marry Ma Tanza. This seems likely, as there are reports that a game of this name had been played in Otago, on the West Coast, and in Canterbury. In Christchurch the game was known as Merry Go Tansy.

Few other marriage games appear to have been important in the period 1870–1920. There is an occasional report, without details, of *Farmer in the Dell* (A-10), *Lady on the Mountain*[7] (A-11) or There Stands a Lady on the Mountain, *Oats and Beans and Barley* (A-12), and *Down in the Valley* (A-13).

A few children's circle chain games were concerned with death and funerals. Of these the most important was undoubtedly *Green*

---

[6] *Ibid.*, I, 284.
[7] *Ibid.*, I, 320.

Gravels (A-14), which is said to contain, in imaginative form, relics of old burial ceremonies.[8] There were reports of the game from all provinces. The most complete version was the following:

1) Green gravels, green gravels,
   The grass is so green.
   The fairest young lady that
   Ever was seen.

2) We'll wash her in milk,
   Or dress her in silk.
   And write down her name,
   With a gold pen and ink.

3) Dear Mary, dear Mary,
   Your true love is dead.
   He sends you a letter,
   To turn round your head.

4) Now you're married we wish you joy,
   First a girl then a boy.
   Seven years old and seven years young.
   Pray young couple kiss over again. [Fordell, Wanganui, 1900]

Here again is the floating fourth verse which has been recorded twice already, once attached to Pretty Little Girl of Mine and once to Poor Sally Is a-Weeping. Most versions did not include all four verses. Two reports—one from Christchurch and one from Nelson —contained the first three verses, but most of the other reports gave only two verses. In Canterbury and Otago districts, verses one and three were usually reported, and in Nelson and Wellington areas, verses one and two. Methods of play varied. In some versions the children danced round singing the song, and as each player's name was called she turned outward in the circle, but continued to hold the hands of those next to her. When all were facing outward the game was finished. In other versions, when all had turned outward the process was repeated in reverse till all were facing inward again. In yet other versions, when all the players were turned outward, the circle broke at one point and the players went "jingo-ringing round" in an eight formation, that is, as if running around a figure eight traced on the ground, until they were all turned inward again. In one version only, the four-verse form from Fordell,

8 *Ibid.*, I, 170.

given above, a center player chose another player at verse two and that player then turned about for the duration of verse three. In verse four, however, these two held hands in the center of the circle. As it was unusual to have a center player in Green Gravels, it is probable that this Fordell version, with its unusual fourth verse, was a mixture of Green Gravels and some other marriage game. Of all the singing games, Green Gravels probably had the most plaintive melody. Many players may well have felt as did the girl in Betty Smith's *A Tree Grows in Brooklyn*: "All the while her heart beat in rhythm to the poignant sadness of the song the children sang while walking round the ring with hands joined."[9] The game could strike deep chords in a child's mind. One informant recalls: "I saw it once played by some children as I passed and they sang 'Dear Molly, Dear Molly, now turn round your head.' The rest I never quite heard, but I remember that I was most concerned as my name was Molly, and being very young I never knew whether I was meant or whether it was a game" (Nelson, 1880).

The game of *Jenny Jones* (A-15), which also included elements of marriage and burial, was not so widely known.[10] All the players were in a circle, and at the appropriate verse the one chosen turned outward to signify her death. At Rockville, Nelson, in 1885, the words of the song were:

1) We've come to see Jenny Jones, Jenny Jones,
   How is she now, how is she now?
   Jenny Jones is ill in bed, ill in bed,
   Can't see her now [Jenny turns about].

2) What shall we dress her in, dress her in?
   Shall it be blue, shall it be blue?
   No, blue's for the sailors, the sailors,
   That will not do.

3) What shall we dress her in, dress her in?
   Shall it be red, shall it be red?
   No, red's for soldiers, the soldiers,
   That will not do.

4) What shall we dress her in, dress her in?
   Shall it be black, shall it be black?

[9] Betty Smith, *A Tree Grows in Brooklyn* (Penguin Books, Inc., 1951), p. 96.
[10] Gomme, I, 260.

No, black's for mourners, the mourners,
Black will not do.

5) What shall we dress her in, dress her in?
Shall it be white, shall it be white?
Yes, white's for the dead people, the dead people,
And that will just do.

At Wellington in 1890 the first verse was:

1) Jenny Jones is dead and gone,
Jenny Jones is dead and gone.
Everyone comes to see Jenny Jones,
But Jenny Jones is dead and gone.

In *Wallflowers* (A-16), also, the chosen player turned outward at the end of the second verse.[11] At Palmerston North, in 1900, the verses were:

Wallflowers, wallflowers,
Growing up so high.
And all the pretty maidens,
Have got to die.
Except [Mary],
For she's the fairest flower.
For she can dance and she can sing,
And she can turn round in a ring.

Whereupon the chosen girl turned round and thereafter danced and sang no more.

The next largest group of chain circle games were the pantomime games in which the children imitated, or rather, mimicked, the actions of adults. In *The Mulberry Bush* (A-17), or Here We Go Round the Mulberry Bush, the most widespread of the pantomime games, the players danced round together with their hands held,[12] singing the first lines. When they came to the words indicating actions, however, the circle stopped, and each player portrayed the subject matter of the song. The dancing verse was:

Here we go round the mulberry bush,
The mulberry bush, the mulberry bush,

---

[11] *Ibid.*, II, 329.
[12] *Ibid.*, I, 404.

> Here we go round the mulberry bush,
> So early on [Monday] morning.

The action verses alternated with the dancing chorus, and as each succeeding chorus referred to the following day, the actions also proceeded through the week. The first action verse was:

> This is the way we scrub the floor,
> Scrub the floor, scrub the floor.
> This is the way we scrub the floor,
> So early on Monday morning.

The first lines of other verses were "comb our hair," "wash our hands," "clean our shoes," "go to school," "clean our teeth," "wash our clothes," and "go to church." There are no reports of the game before 1900, but there are several for the period between 1900 and 1920, and many reports for the years since 1920.

When I Was a Lady (A-18) was played in Dunedin in the 1890's. The action was the same as in The Mulberry Bush.[13] First came the choral verse, then the actions:

1) When I was a lady, a lady, a lady,
   When I was a lady a lady was I.
   It was this way [curtseying to the left], and that way [to right],
   And this way [curtseying to the left], and that way [to right],
   When I was a lady, a lady was I.

2) When I was a gentleman, a gentleman, a gentleman,
   When I was a gentleman a gentleman was I.
   It was this way [bowing left], and that way [to right],
   And this way [bowing left], and that way [to right],
   When I was a gentleman, a gentleman was I.

In succeeding verses, it was the gardener who dug with an imaginary spade, the soldier who fired an imaginary rifle, the washerwoman who rubbed imaginary clothes vigorously, first on the left side and then on the right side. The game proceeded through as many occupations as could be thought of, until the players tired.

Cobbler, Cobbler, Mend My Shoe (A-19) was a similar game. It is mentioned as having been played in Auckland as early as 1880 and at Christchurch in 1900.

The other circle games of the day were slightly more complex.

---

[13] *Ibid.*, II, 363.

In *Drop the Handkerchief* (A-20), the players sat down in a ring while a "He" (or "It") player walked round outside the ring with a handkerchief in her hand.[14] When she dropped the handkerchief behind some person, that person had to rise and race round the circle in the opposite direction, in an effort to get back to her place in the circle first, and thus avoid becoming He. When the He person walked round the circle she sang a rhyme. One rhyme used for this purpose was:

> I sent a letter to my love,
> And on the way I dropped it.
> One of you has picked it up,
> And put it in your pocket.
> It wasn't you, it wasn't you, . . . [etc.],
> It was you!

And at "you," there was a screech and the chase began. This version was the most widely known. Occasionally the central player sang that she "wrote a letter" to her love. At East Taieri, Otago, she said:

> I had a little dog,
> And it won't bite you,
> And it won't bite you,
> But it will bite *you.*

At Collingwood:

> Lucy Locket,
> Lost her pocket,
> On the way to school.
> Someone else has picked it up,
> And it wasn't you, . . . [etc.].

In some versions no warning was given to the seated players. The He went on saying "it wasn't you" even after she had dropped the handkerchief. This game has been more often played without the words than with them, and has had the names Space Ring, Fill the Gap, and Rotten Egg. In these latter games, simple hand-tagging or tagging with a piece of stick or strap was sometimes used instead

---

[14] *Ibid.*, I, 109.

of dropping the handkerchief. The same game was played at picnics under the name of Kiss in the Ring.[15] There, however, it was played mainly by youths, and the aim of the tagged player was to catch and kiss the "He" player, not merely to race her back to a space in the ring. It is said that youths from thirteen to eighteen years old greatly enjoyed playing this game, as writers of the day put it, in the "shades of evening."

Another widely known circle game with a "He" player was Bingo, or *Bobby Bingo* (A-21).[16] This was a game of alertness. Unless a player was alert and able to give the correct letter in the spelling of Bobby Bingo she became Bingo herself and had to go into the center of the circle. It is said to have been played regularly at hop sprees and tea parties in Nelson in the first decades of this century. The version known there was:

> A farmer's dog lay on the mat,
> And Bingo was his name-oh.
> B-I-N-G-O [spelled out],
> B-I-N-G-O,
> B-I-N-G-O,
> And Bingo was his name-oh.

Games similar to the chain circle games were the chain games in which players held on to each other's hands and wound in and out among the standing players, filed under arches, or took hold of other players within the joined arms of two players. The most important of these—in fact, the most popular and widespread of all singing games in all periods—was *Oranges and Lemons* (A-22).[17] Two girls stood facing each other with their hands joined and arms held upwards in an arch. All the rest filed through underneath their extended arms while the archmakers sang:

> Oranges and lemons,
> The bells of St. Clements,
> I owe you five farthings,
> And when will you pay me,
> Tomorrow or the next day?
> Here is a light to light you to bed,

[15] *Ibid.*, p. 306.
[16] *Ibid.*, p. 29.
[17] *Ibid.*, II, 25.

> Here is a chopper to chop off your head.
> Chip, chop, chip, chop. [Avonside, Christchurch, 1876]

On the last "chop" the arch-makers enclosed a girl in their arms and then asked her which of two things she preferred, for example, a gold watch or a gold key, or simply oranges or lemons. The girl made her choice and then stood behind the arch-player who had previously chosen that particular article as her symbol. When all the players had chosen oranges or lemons and were behind their respective arch-players, a tug-of-war ensued. There were slight variations in the words; for example:

> Oranges and lemons,
> Said the bells of St. Clements,
> I'll give you five farthings,
> Said the bells of St. Martins.
> Then I'll be rich,
> Said the bells of Shoreditch.
> Here comes a candle to light you to bed,
> Here comes a chopper to chop off your head. [Dunedin, 1890]

Most New Zealand versions were the same as the first one given above, except that the fifth line was the more euphonious "Today or tomorrow."

London Bridge (A-23) resembled Oranges and Lemons.[18] Players filing round in a circle were enclosed between the arms of two arch-players. In London Bridge, however, the players so enclosed were prisoners. The game was known also as Here's a Prisoner, and What Have the Robbers Done to You? When all the players had been made prisoners (and tortured—by ear-twisting, etc.) they lined up behind the arch-players and joined in a tug-of-war. There are very few reports of the game before 1900. The choral accompaniment of Here's a Prisoner, as played at Collingwood, Nelson, in 1895, was sung as follows:

> 1) Here's a prisoner we have got,
>   Here's a prisoner we have got,
>   Here's a prisoner we have got,
>   Bright young lady.
>
> 2) She stole my watch and broke my chain,

---

[18] *Ibid.*, I, 333.

> She stole my watch and broke my chain,
> She stole my watch and broke my chain,
> Nice young lady.

3) Off to prison she must go,
   Off to prison she must go,
   Off to prison she must go,
   Nice young lady.

After verse three the nice young lady took her place behind one of the arches. A 1905 Onehunga, Auckland, version of What Have the Robbers Done to You? was:

1) What have the robbers done to you,
   Done to you, done to you?
   What have the robbers done to you,
   My fair lady?

2) Stole my watch and broke my chain,
   Broke my chain, broke my chain,
   Stole my watch and broke my chain,
   My fair lady.

3) Off to prison you must go,
   You must go, you must go,
   Off to prison you must go,
   My fair lady.

4) Pull her ears and let her go,
   Let her go, let her go.
   Pull her ears and let her go,
   My fair lady.

In the only game of London Bridge reported before 1900 the third and fourth of the verses given above were preceded by:

1) London Bridge is broken down,
   Broken down, broken down,
   London Bridge is broken down,
   Who's going to mend it? [Tahataki, Otago, 1875]

The first and second verses of What Have the Robbers Done to You? were omitted. There are many other verses in modern versions of this game, but there are no other reports of verses used before 1900.

Next in importance to Oranges and Lemons in these open chain

games was a game variously known as *In and Out the Windows*
(A-24), Follow Me to London, Follow Her to London, Round and
Round the Village, and In and Out the Village.[19] In all these variations, one player walked in and out amongst the other players, who
stood in a circle. Finally, that player chose one from the circle, after
which this chosen player led off, with the first player following her.
The procedure was then repeated while all the players sang the
verses. Finally, there were no players left in the circle, as they
were all winding round in serpentine fashion behind the last-
chosen player. In most versions there were only four verses. The
following, from Moeraki, Otago, had four:

1) In and out the windows,
   In and out the windows,
   In and out the windows,
   As we have done before.

2) Round and round the village,
   Round and round the village,
   Round and round the village,
   As we have done before.

3) Go and face your lover,
   Go and face your lover,
   Go and face your lover,
   As we have done before.

4) Follow her to London,
   Follow her to London,
   Follow her to London,
   As we have done before.

In the variant from Fordell, Wanganui (1900), the first lines were:

1) Walking round the village
2) Stand and face your lover
3) Follow me to London

The version sung at Palmerston North in 1910 had the following
first lines:

1) In and out the windows
2) Stand and face your lover
3) March her off to London

[19] Daiken, *op. cit.*, p. 76.

The same game is often played by children today under the name of In and Out the Dusty Bluebells. Some of the old verses, however, contained slight, and sometimes more stimulating, variations in method, and these are worth recording. In a Petone version of the first decade of this century, the player winding about was blindfolded and led by another player. At the end of the rhyme she would kiss the player she faced. In a Palmerston North game of the same period, the last player left in the circle then played Hen and Chickens with the line of players who were holding on behind the leading player (see B-5).

A game somewhat similar to In and Out the Windows, but apparently less well known, since it was reported only once, was *Rushes and Reeds* (A-25). In this game the players were divided into two groups. One group stood in a line and the other group wound in and out along the line, accompanying their progress with a curtsey at the appropriate word to the standing players. They sang:

> Rushes and reeds are bending,
> Rushes and reeds are bowing,
> My mother sits a-mending,
> My father goes a-plowing.
> In and out and all about,
> And curtsey as we go. [Auckland, 1900]

There was only one game in which the players moved in a spiral formation. This was *The Eely Ily Oh* (A-26),[20] which was played in Nelson about 1870 and at Christchurch around 1900. The Nelson version is described as follows:

> We used to join hands in a long line, with the head of the line putting her spare hand on a wall or post, making an arch. Then while all sang, the tail threaded through the arches beginning at the head. The line followed through until all the players were standing cross-armed, turned about by the tail going through the arch. When all were turned, the head and tail joined arms and we circled still singing our chant. Next the head and tail unjoined. The head joined back to the post again and we unthreaded from the tail end.

The chant was simply:

[20] Gomme, I, 119.

The big ship sails
Through the Eely Ily Oh,
On the nineteenth of December.

The last type of chain games consists of the team-line chain games, which involved two lines of players advancing and retiring from each other. It was naturally more difficult for young children to manage a game of this type than the circle and winding formations for which only one line of players was required. It has been said that these two-line formations occurred in a later historical period than the ring games.[21] The circle and winding games contain events occurring within one group; the line-chain games include a conflict between two different groups.

The chain line game of greatest importance was *Nuts and May* (A-27),[22] which was the great picnic game of all periods. In this game two lines of players danced forward to meet each other and backward again. The lines of players sang alternate verses. After the verses were sung there was a tug-of-war between two players. The player who managed to pull the other across the dividing line between the two teams won that player for her team. The verses at Palmerston North in 1900 were:

1) Here we go gathering nuts and may, nuts and may, nuts and
   may,
   Here we go gathering nuts and may,
   On a cold and frosty morning.

2) And who will you have for your nuts and may, nuts and may,
   nuts and may,
   And who will you have for your nuts and may,
   On a cold and frosty morning?

3) We will have [Sally] for our nuts and may, nuts and may,
   nuts and may,
   We will have [Sally] for our nuts and may,
   On a cold and frosty morning.

4) And who will you have to take her away, take her away, take
   her away,
   And who will you have to take her away,
   On a cold and frosty morning?

[21] C. Sachs, *World History of the Dance* (London, 1938), p. 144.
[22] Gomme, I, 424.

5) We will have [Johnny] to take her away, take her away, take
   her away,
   We will have [Johnny] to take her away,
   On a cold and frosty morning.

Johnny and Sally had their tug-of-war and one line gained a player. In the end the side which had won all the players was declared
winner. Although the original English title of this game is Nuts in
May, it has been generally known in New Zealand as Nuts *and*
May. There were only very slight variations in the verses. For
example, some versions contained verses beginning:

Here we come gathering nuts and may

and

Who will you take for your nuts and may?

and, as the final line of the verses,

So early in the morning.

The Three Dukes (A-28) was not as well known as Nuts and
May. It was played in all the provinces, but under various names:
Saucy Duke, Two Dukes (Dunedin, 1880), Saucy Jack (Nelson,
1920), The Duke (Nelson, 1890), Here Comes a Duke a-Riding
(Amberley, Canterbury, 1890), Here Comes a Lusty Wooer
(Avondale, Christchurch, 1875), Here Comes Three Dukes a-Riding (Wellington, 1890; Brightwater, Nelson, 1890; Bay of Plenty,
1885), and A Duke a-Riding (Auckland, 1900; Hawkes Bay,
1920).[23] Again, two lines of players dance backward and forward,
one line representing the Duke who has come to ask for a spouse:

1) Here comes a Duke a-riding,
   A-riding, a-riding.
   Here comes a Duke a-riding,
   To court your daughter Jane.

2) My daughter Jane is yet too young,
   To be controlled by such a one.
   Go back and back, you saucy Jack,
   And clean your spurs for they are black.

3) My spurs are bright and richly wrought,
   And in this town they were not bought.

[23] *Ibid.*, II, 233.

And in this town they'll not be sold,
Neither for silver nor for gold.

4) Go through the kitchen, go through the hall,
And choose the fairest one of all.
The fairest one that I can see,
Is [Sally Jane]; you come to me.

This Nelson version of 1890, unlike the majority of these games, was played in Hen and Chickens formation. The father stood in front of his children, who hung on behind him. (See B-5.) After the father and the Duke had said the verses, the Duke attempted to snatch a child from behind the father. The Duke's aim was to get a swaying tail of children behind himself. In some versions there was a tug-of-war at the end, and in others only a choice. In one version, when the suitor had made his choice he threaded his way in and out of the other line until he met his bride. This action represented going "through the kitchen" and "through the hall." Sometimes the verses were divided between the Duke and the mother. The words show only slight variations. The Saucy Jack was sometimes a Dirty Jack. Sometimes he had to peep through the hall, and sometimes he said, "Pretty Mary, come to me." The main difference between New Zealand and British versions was in the second line of the second verse. The New Zealand versions invariably had, "My daughter Jane is yet too young/To be controlled by such a one," whereas the majority of English versions had, "She can't abide your flattering tongue." It was strange that this element alone—the flattering tongue—should *not* have been incorporated in the New Zealand versions. Perhaps the change is significant in terms of national outlook. The "flattering tongue" was connected with foreigners and aristocracy, relatively rare experiences for young New Zealand girls imagining marriage; whereas "to be controlled by such a one" was an easily understood fate.

Surrender the Tower (A-29) was reported as having been played at only one place: Auckland, 1900.[24] It was not a marriage game. The conflict was between soldiers, not between prospective partners in marriage. One side represented the guardians of the tower, the other side the Queen and her soldiers. The two sides alternated singing the verses; and, after repeated dialogues alternated with

[24] *Ibid.*, I, 18.

more singing, they resorted to a tug-of-war. The games began with the challenging of the tower by one soldier:

1) Surrender the tower,
   Surrender the tower,
   To the Queen of Babylon.

2) We won't surrender,
   We shan't surrender,
   To the Queen of Babylon.

3) I'll go and complain,
   I'll go and complain,
   To the Queen of Babylon.

4) You may go and complain,
   You may go and complain,
   To the Queen of Babylon.

One of the soldiers then marched off to where the Queen stood with her other soldiers, some distance away. After a number of curtseys this dialogue took place:

"Good day, great Queen [Annie], I've come to complain to you."
"What's the matter?"
"They won't surrender."
"Well, take two of my soldiers."

And the first player proceeded back to the tower with two of the Queen's soldiers. The three soldiers and the guardians of the tower then repeated the song given above. The soldiers returned to the Queen and the whole procedure was repeated several times, until the Queen had no more soldiers left. Then, after saying, "I'll come myself to the tower," she chanted with her soldiers:

5) Surrender the tower,
   Surrender the tower,
   To the Queen of Babylon.

The intransigent tower soldiers replied as usual:

6) We won't surrender,
   We won't surrender,
   To the Queen of Babylon.

Whereupon the Queen and her soldiers took an age-old way out of the problem:

7) Then we'll break down your tower,
   Then we'll break down your tower,
   For the Queen of Babylon.

8) You may break down our tower,
   You may break down our tower,
   For the Queen of Babylon.

After this there was the customary tug-of-war.

The singing games mentioned thus far have all been either chain singing games, circle, winding, or line-chain singing games, which were essentially the games of children. We come now to the couple singing games, which were really the games of youths and adults and were played at picnics, socials, and parties, rather than spontaneously by children on their playgrounds.

The most widely known of these couple games was *The Jolly Miller* (A-30). It was played in all the provinces before 1900. At Wanganui the procedure was as follows: "The partners walked in opposite directions around in a circle. There was an odd man out in the centre of the circle. The song was a lively romp to a merry tune." It went:

There was a jolly miller,
And he lived by himself.
As his wheel went round,
He made his wealth.

One hand on the hopper,
And the other in the bag,
As the wheel went round,
He made his grab.

At this point all the players, including the one in the center, made a grab for a partner. Those that succeeded then marched round the circle arm in arm with their partners, singing:

A-hunting we will go,
A-hunting we will go.
We'll catch a fox,
And put him in a box,
And a-hunting we will go.

This version was also known at Napier and Nelson in the 1890's, but in all other versions, as in the British versions, only the first verse was known.[25] There were a few slight variations in the words. Sometimes the miller had his hand in his pocket or in the locker rather than in the hopper; he lived alone rather than by himself, and he made his pelf, not his wealth.

Would You Lend My Mother a Saucepan? (A-31), of which there is only one report, was played in the same manner as The Jolly Miller. The words at Rockville, Nelson, in 1885 were:

> Would you lend my mother a saucepan?
> Would you lend my mother a spoon?
> Because she's going to have
> Some friends to tea this afternoon.
>
> Would you lend my mother a half crown?
> This morning, Mrs. Burke?
> She'll pay you back on [Wednesday],
> When my father gets some work.

At this point the marching players and the center person each grabbed at a partner and then they sang while marching round arm in arm:

> A-hunting we will go,
> A-hunting we will go.
> We'll catch a fox,
> And put him in a box,
> A-hunting we will go.

Fire on the Mountains (A-32) is reported only for South Clutha, Southland, 1875. Half of the couples knelt while the other half and one extra player ran round them singing:

> Fire on the mountains,
> Lit by the sun.
> Fire on the mountains,
> Run, boys, run.

This was repeated several times, until the leader suddenly said "Stop!" Then every standing player attempted to place a hand on the head of a kneeling player. One player was left over and was therefore out.

25 *Ibid.,* I, 289.

All the other New Zealand couple games, unlike those mentioned thus far, were played with the participants arranged in two team lines. The best known of these was *The Grand Old Duke of York* (A-33), in which one couple danced up and down in between the players while all players sang the first verse, and then led their respective lines off round the hall and back during the second verse. The other players went through the arch of the couple's upraised arms, thus leaving that couple at the bottom of the lines instead of at the head. Another couple now took their place. The verse was:

1) The grand old Duke of York,
   He had ten thousand men,
   He marched them up to the top of the hill,
   And he marched them down again.

2) And when they're up, they're up,
   And when they're down, they're down,
   And when they're only half way up,
   They're neither up nor down.

No other processional couple games were as important as The Grand Old Duke of York, but there is occasional mention of one or two others. *Thread the Needle* (A-34) is reported, without details, as having been played at Dunedin in 1875. *How Many Miles to Babylon?* (A-35) is reported for Christchurch, 1875. Only three lines of the rhyme for the latter were known:

   How many miles to Babylon?
   Three score and ten.
   Half way up and half way down again.

There is mention of a number of other singing games which were played in these early years; not enough is known about them, however, to permit exact classification. They can only be names and numbers here: *Carry My Lady to London* (A-36), *Bold Jolly Lads* (A-37), *Green Grow the Leaves* (A-38), *My Fair Young Lady* (A-39), *I've Come to See Poor Mary Jane* (A-40), and *Babbity Bowster* (A-41).

§II: 1920–1950

Of the forty-one games mentioned above, seventeen dropped out

of regular play after 1900.[26] Another fifteen fell into desuetude between 1900 and 1930.[27] Only nine of these original forty-one games
were regularly reported for the period from 1930 to 1950.[28] All the
games that have survived, except Nuts and May, belong to the first
group of games described above (A-1 through A-26). Ring a Ring a
Roses, Nuts and May, and Oranges and Lemons are today the only
singing games which are known in all schools. Farmer in the Dell
and Poor Sally Is a-Weeping are still widespread. The Mulberry
Bush, In and Out the Windows, and Drop the Handkerchief are
still played in a few districts. Singing games, introduced by means
of the New Zealand Education Department's Infant Syllabus of the
1920's, have occasionally been carried over into the spontaneous
play of the children. Farmer in the Dell and The Alley Alley Ooh
(known earlier as the Eely Ily Oh, see A-26) were old games given
some added impetus by the Syllabus. More recently, during the
1940's, a singing game called *Punchinello* (A-42), introduced into
schools by physical education specialists, has become widespread
in children's spontaneous play. In this, a central-person circle
game, the person in the center performs pantomimic actions while
the others walk around singing, with their hands linked. The verses
are:

1) Look who is here,
   Punchinello, funny fellow.
   Look who is here,
   Punchinello, funny man.

2) What can you do,
   Punchinello, funny fellow?
   What can you do,
   Punchinello, funny man?

At this point the walking circle stops and Punchinello carries out
some performance such as skipping. The others then all imitate
him while singing:

3) We'll do it too,

[26] Numbers A-4, A-5, A-8, A-9, A-11 through A-13, A-16, A-19, A-29, A-31,
A-32, A-35 through A-38, and A-41.
[27] Numbers A-1, A-2, A-6, A-14, A-15, A-18, A-21, A-23, A-25, A-28, A-30,
A-33, A-34, A-39, and A-40.
[28] Numbers A-3, A-7, A-10, A-17, A-20, A-22, A-24, A-26, and A-27.

Punchinello, funny fellow.
We'll do it too,
Punchinello, funny man.

The circling players join hands again and walk around singing:

4) Who do you choose,
   Punchinello, funny fellow?
   Who do you choose,
   Punchinello, funny man?

Punchinello chooses another player and that player becomes the next Punchinello.

In sum, children today play far fewer games than their predecessors (a decrease from forty-one to nine in eighty years). Naturally the couple games have gone from children's play, because the teenagers who once maintained those games no longer play singing games. Such sedate and fairy-tale-like pastimes have little relevance in the world of active games, sports, and sophisticated entertainments in which they now live and play. For the same reasons, even the younger children of today play fewer singing games. But the play situation of these younger children is more complex, because some of their games have been conserved and one or two have even gained in popularity. It may be, as some writers have averred, that these children have kept some of their games because young children are so conservative.[29] As long as this concept of "conservatism" is defined in terms of our broader knowledge of child behavior it certainly provides one "reason" why the games are retained. For example, group life is very precarious amongst young children six to nine years of age; in their game organizations these youngsters can rise above the limitations of their own relatively unorganized personalities; the structure of their games makes group activity possible amongst them when there might otherwise be none; their games provide the first behavior patterns that (as a group of children reaching toward *social* organization) they can readily comprehend, enjoy, and maintain; and finally, most of their games are learned from older children, who, in the eyes of the smaller ones, have prestige and authority, and whose dictates are, therefore, not readily altered. In other words, the children's "con-

[29] I. and P. Opie, eds., *The Oxford Dictionary of Nursery Rhymes* (Oxford, 1951), p. 2.

servatism" (their jealous regard for the rules of the game) has its basis in their need for "structure" in social relationships and in their method of learning games from elders whom they hold in esteem. We are saying, in effect, that children conserve some games because these games satisfy their social needs.

Such an argument, however, still does not explain why particular games have gained in popularity, others have been merely conserved, and yet others have been forgotten. For an answer to this sort of question we need to discover the ways in which these various games correspond to the children's interests. Unfortunately, it is almost impossible to do this in any convincing detail. In general, of course, we can reason that the games they favor are the ones characterized by very simple organization such as they can comprehend and control by themselves, the games that include in their content such themes as marriage and mimicry, which attract the young girl players of this age group. But such general reasons cannot tell us why, say, Farmer in the Dell has been retained and a game of similar organization and motif, Pretty Little Girl of Mine, has not; why Punchinello thrives and When I Was a Lady is heard of no more. There is nothing in the organization or content of these games to indicate why one should be favored and the other not.

The reason for the children's likes and dislikes, therefore, may rest instead in those intangible qualities of rhythm, rhyme, and melody which distinguish one game from another. (It is noticeable, for example, that the funeral games of yesteryear have gone. Perhaps the present is a less morbid age than its predecessor and young girls reflect this fact in their game choices.) But if the success of singing games depends upon such intangible qualities as rhythm, rhyme, and melody, then their success is as difficult to analyze as that of a "hit" tune. Thus we may enumerate the reasons why young children *should* like a game; its organization must be comprehensible to them, its themes must be relevant to their experience, its relationships must mirror their psychological understanding; but we cannot determine merely from these criteria whether or not in its total impact it will finally appeal to them.

Dialogue Games: Category B

Dialogue games contain traditional dialogues, involve central players, and are played by young girls between the ages of six and nine years. There are two types of dialogue games. In the first, the central player represents a fearsome person, such as a witch or a ghost, who captures and steals children (numbers B-1 through B-5); in the second, the central player represents an old woman who is teased by the other players (B-6 and B-7).

§§ I AND II: 1870–1920 AND 1920–1950

Since these games have been widespread throughout the entire period encompassed by this study, it is convenient to deal with nineteenth-century and twentieth-century examples together. In the main, recent samples are drawn upon, because their details are more complete than those in the examples reported for earlier years. These games have probably maintained themselves successfully because they have been played by young girls, who have been little affected by modern organized games.

One of the most important early dialogue games was *Ghost in the Garden* (B-1). There are several reports of the game before 1900 (Dunedin, Nelson, Wellington), and, according to the reports, it is still played occasionally today. It was in a very active state in 1949 in several Dunedin schools, namely, in Forbury and North East Valley; and also in Waikouaiti, North Otago. In the Forbury version the mother smacks her children and tells them to go and wash their hands. The children run out into the garden, see a ghost, and come running back crying:

"Oh Mummy, there's a ghost in the garden."
"It's only my pink pants on the line. Go and wash your hands," the mother replies. The children do this, but once again come running back with the same cry as before:
"Oh Mummy, there's a ghost in the garden."
"It's only Daddy's white pants on the line," replies the mother once more. Again she sends them into the garden and again they return complaining. This time she instructs them to bring Daddy's white pants in to her. They run back crying:

"Oh, it got fur on it, Mummy."

"Come with me and I'll go and see," says the mother. She marches out with the children behind her. Confronting the ghost she says:

"What are you doing in my garden?"

"Picking up sticks," says the ghost.

"What do you want sticks for?" asks the mother.

"To light a fire."

"What do you want a fire for?"

"To boil a pot."

"What do you want the pot for?"

"To boil a stone."

"What do you want a stone for?"

"To sharpen a knife." [At this the children scream.]

"What do you want the knife for?"

"To cut off your head."

The ghost then chases mother and children. The player who is caught becomes the next ghost. In the North East Valley and Wai-kouaiti versions there is an additional element which appears to have been borrowed from the game of Mother, Mother, the Pot Boils Over (see B-2). In these, when the ghost catches a child, it takes the child to the ghost's shop, where the child becomes a fruit or a vegetable. When several children have been caught the mother goes to the ghost's shop and asks what wares the ghost has. The mother says, "Are there any oranges?" If none of the captured children has been named an orange by the ghost then nothing happens. If one has, then the ghost says "Yes" and that captured child puts its foot between the legs of the ghost from behind. The mother looks at the foot, saying, "Too dirty," or "Must be rotten." Next the child puts its head between the ghost's legs. The mother says, "This will do" (in the Waikouaiti version, "Why, this is one of my children!"), and then, "Poke out your tongue and spit on the ground, then stamp on the place you spat on. Now get home, you naughty girl." It is of some interest that in this account of the game most of the girls (North East Valley) did not want the spitting part to go on record. One of their number had learned it from her Grandma, and with some coaxing she gave the information. No version cited by Lady Gomme includes all the dialogue recorded above. All dialogue, however, is recorded separately in two different games.[1] In

---

[1] Gomme, I, 149, and II, 15.

a version from Dunedin, 1890, only the first part of the Forbury game (see above) takes place, and in this Dunedin version there is no ghost at all, as the mother finds out when she goes into the garden. She chases the children and gives those she can catch a whipping.

Mother, Mother, the Pot Boils Over (B-2) was (and is) a more widely known game than Ghost in the Garden. It was known at Richmond, Nelson, in 1885; Wakefield, Nelson, 1875; Arahura, Westland, 1900; Waitara, Taranaki, 1900; Birchfield, Westland, 1915; Granity, Westland, 1895; and Marton, Wellington, 1890. It has been known under various other names: Mother, Mother, the Kettle's Boiling Over (Dunedin, 1880); Blackman (Waikari, Dunedin, 1920); Fox and Family (Nelson, 1890); Rotten Eggs (Ohau, Wellington, 1910); Old Digley Bones (Bay of Plenty, 1885); Witch (Pakawau, Nelson, 1949); Blacksmith (Kaitaia, Westland, 1949); Pancakes (Millerton, Westland, 1949); and Witch and the Jam Pots (Wellington, 1949). The English folklorist Lady Gomme says:

> In this game the chorus [of the singing game] has disappeared; the principal characters tell the story in dialogue, the minor characters only acting when the dialogue necessitates it, and then in dumb show. ... It is a complete drama of domestic life at a time when child stealing and witchcraft were rife. A mother goes out to work, and returns to find one of her seven children missing. The game describes the stealing of them, one by one, by the witch, but the little drama tells even more than this. It probably indicates some of the practices and customs connected with fire worship and the worship of the hearth. ... After the children are stolen the mother has evidently a long and troublesome journey in search of them; obstacles are placed in the path quite in the manner of the folktale.[2]

As is true of Ghost in the Garden, the versions received are fluid. Some include elements that others do not. Some versions name the children by the days of the week or by the names of fruits, or mention a mother and a housemaid, or elder sister. Before the mother goes out to do some shopping or on some other errand she tells the maid to look after the children. While she is gone the maid calls out (Ohau, Wellington, 1910):

[2] *Ibid.*, I, 396.

"Mother, Mother, the kettle's boiling over."
"Get a spoon and stir it," says the mother.
"The spoon's broken," says the maid.
"Get the tinker."
"Tinker's dead."
"Oh well, I'll be home in a minute."

In the version played at Nelson in 1890, the same conversation goes as follows:

"Mother, Mother, the pot boils over."
"Get a spoon and stir it."
"Can't reach."
"Stand on a chair."
"The chair's broken."
"Use the table."
"The table's gone to be mended."
"Well, I'll be home in a minute."

And in the version at Ngapara, North Otago, 1949:

"Mother, Mother, the kettle's boiling over."
"Lift the lid."
"It's too hot."
"Get the dish cloth."
"It's down the drain. Mother, Mother, come home."

When the mother comes home she finds that one of her children has gone. In some versions the witch comes and steals the child silently away. In others the witch talks to the housemaid. In the version played at Waikari, Dunedin, in 1920, a blackman comes to the door and says:

"I want a match."
"Spit on the floor and take one," says the maid.
The blackman takes one of the children, whereupon the maid shouts, "Mother, Mother, the pot's boiling over."

In the variant played at Pakawau, Nelson, in 1949, the witch says:

"I want a child for my stew."
Then the mother comes home. "Where's my Peach?" she says to the maid.
"I was just going upstairs," replies the maid [and makes up some long story], ". . . and when I came down Peach was gone."

According to another report, "It was thrilling when the mother found the child gone. She whacked the maid with a stick and the maid yelled blue murder" (Ohau, Wellington, 1910). In this version the maid says:

"Old Digley Bones came and took her."
"What did he give you?" asks the mother.
"A bottle of wine and my big toe."
"Where is my share?"
"Upstairs."
"How am I to get up?"
"Sticks and chairs and broken stairs."
"Suppose I fall down and break my nose?"
"I don't care."

Then the mother whips the maid (Bay of Plenty, 1885). This sequence of events is repeated several times until all the children are gone. The mother then sets off to find them. She goes to Digley, who has all the children sitting in a row with their pinnies (pinafores) over their heads. She says to Digley:

"Have you seen my Monday?"
He answers, "No, but I have some jam," and names the jam.
The mother pretends to taste it and says, "Why, this jam is just like my Monday." She pulls the pinny off and says, "It *is* my Monday!"

Whereupon she whips her back home (Bay of Plenty, 1885).

The version reported to have been played at Ohau in 1910 contains a still different element. The mother goes to the tinker to buy some meat.

"I want a nice leg of beef," she says.
The tinker pulls a girl's foot through his legs.
The mother exclaims, "Naughty girl, where have you been?"

Peach and the other girls then squat on the ground holding their legs, with their arms about their knees. The mother and the tinker swing them by the arms. If the children let go their hold on their legs before three swings they are "rotten eggs." In some versions the children sitting in this position are called honey pots or pots of jam, and their weight or value is the number of times they can let themselves be swung without letting go of their legs.

In the Kaitaia, Westland, 1949 version, the mother goes to the blacksmith and the following conversation takes place:

"I want to go inside," says the mother.
"Your shoes are too dirty," says the blacksmith.
"I'll take my shoes off."
"Your feet are too dirty."
"I'll cut my feet off."
"The blood will drip on my new carpet."
"I'll wrap a blanket round them."
"The blood will soak through."
"I'll put glass slippers on."
"Come in."

In some versions the game ends with a game of Fox and Geese, in which the mother tries to retrieve her children from the witch (Nelson, 1890; Millerton, 1949; Waikari, 1920). In all the others the children get a good thrashing.

The game of *Honey Pots* (B-3) seems to have been a fragment of Mother, Mother, the Pot Boils Over that has become a game in its own right. This development is suggested by the fact that, although it was widely known in early years, Honey Pots seems to have been known only where Mother, Mother, the Pot Boils Over was not known. It was played as follows:

The players sat against a wall and clasped their hands tight around their legs below their knees. A man would come in to buy honey. He would pat a stick on top of their heads, as if tasting the honey. Finally he would say to the shopkeeper, "I'll take that, how many pounds is it?" The shopkeeper and buyer would then swing the honeypot by the arms until the honeypot let go her hold. The number of swings made before the hold was released was said to be the number of pounds of honey in the pot. The buyer would pay that amount in stones to the shopkeeper. [Dunedin, 1890]

In a Tahataki, Otago, version of 1875, if the player who was swung lost her hold within a given number of swings she paid a forfeit. "It was played for the benefit of the little ones," says an informant from Otago, referring to the year 1895.

In an Auckland version of 1900 the swingers sang a little ditty as they swung the honey pot:

> Honey pots, honey pots,
> All in a row,

Honey pots, honey pots,
All in a row.

In *Who Goes Round My Stone Wall?* (B-4), also, children were stolen. There were various names for this game: Jack a Lingo (Waikouaiti, Otago, 1890), Poor Old Tom (Canterbury, 1900), Bobby Bingo (Palmerston North, 1910; Wellington, 1910), Who Goes Round My Stony Wall? (Waitara, Taranaki, 1900), Who Goes Round My Garden Wall? (Rakaia, Canterbury, 1910), Old Tom (Bainham, Nelson, 1949). The description of Who's That Walking Round My House Tonight? from Moutere, Nelson (1900), is as follows: Two players are chosen, one for the mother and one for Tom. All the other players, any number, sit on the grass in a circle. The mother stands in the middle. Tom walks round the outside, and the mother asks:

"Who's going round my house tonight?"
"Only poor old Tom," replies Tom.
"Don't touch any of my poor chickens."
"Only this little one."

The chicken touched falls backward. The mother attempts to rescue her by taking both of the chicken's hands, placing her right foot below the chicken's feet, and pulling. If the chicken can be pulled to her feet without bending her knees, she sits in the ring again. If the knees bend she is left lying dead. The dialogue is repeated until all have been saved or are dead. Tom then chases the lot of them, and the first two caught are Tom and the mother for the next game. In other versions, it is simply a matter of whether Bobby Bingo can snatch a player out of the circle before the mother can seize her back (Bainham, Nelson, 1949). Sometimes the game includes a form of Fox and Geese. All the players hold on behind the mother and the fox tries to seize the player at the end of the file, while the mother, holding out her arms and whirling about, tries to stop the fox.

Hen and Chickens (B-5), or Fox and Geese, was universally known. When played for its own sake, it was simply a game of skill as just described. It seems, however, to have been originally a part of a dialogue game. In Wolf and Geese (Putoki, Auckland, 1920), for example, the mother goose kept shouting ,"You won't get any of my fat geese."

The dialogue games of caricature included *The Old Lady* (or Old Woman) *from Botany Bay* (B-6), sometimes referred to simply as Botany Bay. In this game the children were not to laugh at the old lady, although she did her best to provoke them to do so by asking some questions which tricked them into saying the words they were not supposed to. The old woman said:

> There came an old woman from Botany Bay,
> And what have you got to give me today?
> And you musn't say
> Yes, no or nay, black, white or gray.

The game was also known as Diggley Bones (Auckland, 1900), An Old Man from Botany Bay (Palmerston, 1910), and An Old Lady from Poverty Bay (Wellington, 1900). It has been widely reported in the last twenty years.

There are no early reports of *Old Mother Gray* (B-7). Lady Gomme says,[3] "There seems to be no other object in the game as now played except the pleasure of teasing and showing defiance to the mother's commands and trying to escape the consequences of disobedience by flight." As reported at Wellington, Nelson, and Dobson (Westland), in 1949, it was played as follows: The players include one He, who is Old Mother Gray, and a group of children. The children come up to her and recite the verse,

> Old Mother Gray,
> Can we go out to play?
> We won't go near the water
> To shoo the ducks away.

Old Mother Gray then replies either yes or no. If she says no, the children go away and come back later to ask again. When she says yes, they immediately go and shoo the ducks away until the Old Mother calls out:

"Children, where have you been?"
"To Grandmother's house," they reply.
"What did she give you?"
"Strawberries and cream."
"Where's my share?"
"Up in the air."

[3] *Ibid.*, p. 390.

"How shall I get it?"
"Table and chair."
"What say I fall?"
"I don't care."

Then the Old Mother chases the children, and the one she catches becomes He in the next game.

It would be impossible to explain in full the reasons for the ordinary, the ludicrous, and the horrific details of these games, although the standard works on folklore contain a great deal of material that is helpful. The folklorists demonstrate that many of the elements in these games came down to us from times when the same elements (witches, pots boiling over, and "blackmen") had a greater relevance to the lives of the players, for in those days the participants were often youths and adults rather than children. But such historical explanations of the origin of these elements cannot explain why the games persist today. We need to know as well how these things are relevant to the lives of modern children. Observation of the girls at play quickly suggests an answer. It is apparent that the girls use these games to play out their feelings about the relationships between children and adults. Sometimes they choose to be "good" mothers, solicitous for the welfare of their lost children; sometimes, domineering mothers chastising naughty girls for being stolen; or out-and-out "bad" adults in the form of devouring witches, ghosts, blackmen, and blacksmiths. They also play at being "good," "naughty," "scared," or "cheeky" children.

Given these very basic motives for enjoying the actions of the game, it is probable that the girls are "conservatively" (in the sense given on p. 44) contented to take for granted the abracadabra of boiling pots, bloody feet, and honey pots; though on occasions, too, there may be Freudian reasons for delight in some of these special features.

Informal Games: Category C

As one of the subsidiary purposes of this work is to present material relevant to an understanding of child development, it is necessary to include some reference to children's informal, as distinct from their formal, games, particularly since their informal games, their make-believe, their imitations,[1] and their toy play probably account for a larger proportion of their childhood playtime than any other single category reported here. Several types of informal games are described: imitative games, pack games, battle games, play activities with play objects, outdoor activities, and seasonal activities.

§I: 1870–1920

In the fifty years from 1870 to 1920 it was acceptable for children between ten and twelve to play imitative games that would be regarded as unsophisticated today. Those which occurred again and again in the play of boys were: Horses, Coaches, Bullock Teams, Trains, Miniature Ploughing Matches, Circuses, and Bands. Girls played: Houses, Dolls, Dressing Up, Shops, Concerts, and Schools. There is record of several rhymes used in playing Schools, as well as for general satirical purposes.[2] Two of these were:

> Mr. Low is a very good man,
> Who tries to teach us all he can.
> Singing, spelling, arithmetic,
> He never forgets to give us the stick.

> Mr. Low is a very good man,
> He goes to church on Sunday,
> He prays to God to make us good,
> And gives us the cuts on Monday. [Moeraki, Otago, 1900]

> Ole Pa Watson's a very good man,
> He goes to church on Sunday.
> He prays to God to give him strength
> To whack the kids on Monday. [Palmerston North, 1910]

Most important of all the boys' make-believe games were the cowboy-and-Indian type of "pack" games. These are called pack games because they involve two roughly equal groups (or "packs") of children playing out a drama of conflict under the impetus of some leading idea. These are the cultural counterparts in boys' play of the leader games of girls, which will be discussed in the next

---

[1] Imitative plays do not receive category numbers.
[2] See further Category H.

chapter. They absorbed as much of boys' time as was taken up by
the girls in playing their singing, dialogue, and leader games. The
largest number of these pack games belong under the heading of
Cowboys and Indians (C-1). Children seldom seem to have realized
that these men had their counterparts in New Zealand in the Pakehas and the Maoris.[3] At the end of the nineteenth century, children's literature in New Zealand was filled with the exploits of
American Indians. After 1870 the adventures of the arrow-shoot-
ing, scalping West were spread across the world. New Zealand, on
the other hand, has been shamefaced rather than proud of the
militant relationships of Pakehas and Maoris. But there were exceptions, and occasionally these relationships became the subject
matter for children's play, as in *Maoris* (C-2), or Pakehas and
Maoris. "During the Maori Wars, the Red Indians became Maoris,
though it was the same game of hiding and stalking" (Waipu,
North Auckland, 1860's).

The boys of Thorndon Flat would go out on the warpath, stripped
to the waist and dubbed with whale oil (stolen) and red ochre, and
armed with sticks. Their great ambition was to catch the Te Aro Flat
boys unawares, which was seldom. A great encounter would take place
and there would be a regular fight. This was a favourite game and
borrowed from the Maoris. The ring leaders would be threatened pa-
rentally with the stocks."[4] [Wellington, 1840's]

Another leading idea for these games was provided by the activities
of the notorious Australian Kelly gang of the 1870's. Children
throughout New Zealand formed themselves into rival outlaw
gangs of *Bushrangers* (C-3), which then would fight make-believe
wars with one another.

When pack games were played by the older boys of the school,
as they were in the nineteenth century, they were sometimes developed into more formalized team *Battle Games* (C-4), with improvised rules and a rough-and-ready contest that was decided as
much by skill as by imagination. The clashing of the Thorndon
and Te Aro Flat boys, made vivid in the foregoing account, is
probably of this sort, although it may have been realistic gang war-

[3] "Pakeha" is the Maori term for white man.
[4] G. MacMorran, *Some Schools and Schoolmasters of Early Wellington* (London, 1900), p. 7.

fare, an activity of a more dangerous sort. The latter could only by a stretch of the imagination be called play. Some examples of Battle Games are as follows:

... there had been a bit of blood working up for days between two factions of boys. After holding a League of Nations meeting (although not called that then) we decided to settle it with the sword. Buck Wilson was the captain of one side and I of the other. Some thought Wilson's side won and some thought it didn't. During the fight Porky was pressing Whirlie McNaughton very hard until Whirlie forgot the League of Nations rules and hit Porky round the ears with his sword. I think that ended the fight. [Waianiwa, Otago, 1880]

The personal and arranged individual fighting in our school [was] dwarfed by the mass fighting of the Reds and the Blues. Can you imagine twenty Blues, making use of straps with buckles on them, with waddies and six foot manuka stocks, confronting one another in real battle array and at a signal, and with the use of rallying calls, entering the fray determined to overcome and rout the enemy? Blood flowed, heads and bodies suffered, until one or other side was overcome through sheer exhaustion and casualties. This section fighting assumed such ugly proportions that authority, in the shape of the Headmaster, stepped in and prohibited it. [Queenstown, Otago, 1880]

Play objects included the whole class of miscellaneous objects which children used in their informal play. A striking fact about the play of children in the nineteenth century is that, to a remarkable extent, they improvised their own play materials. As play object itself and the means of bringing countless other play objects into existence, the *Knife* (C-5) was the most versatile piece of children's (especially boys') equipment, the factotum of the play-object world. It was used in school for erasing ink blots, sharpening slate pencils, and carving initials. Out of school it was used for making Catapults, called *Shanghais* (C-6), and *Slings* (C-7), with which the boys went *Bird-Nesting* (C-8), *Target-Shooting* (C-9), Rabbiting or *Rabbit-Hunting* (C-10), *Hive-Hunting* (C-11), and even *Fishing* (C-12). The knife was also used in the construction of *Bows and Arrows* (C-13), *Clay-Shooters* (C-14), elderberry *Popguns* (C-15), *Spring Guns* (C-16), *Pea-Shooters* (C-17), and *Water-Shooters* (C-18)—objects which in turn were variously used for hunting, make-believe play, and target-firing. Also, the knife had a part in creating those play objects which were projected through space: *Darts* (C-19), *Kites* (C-20), *Whips* (C-21), and *Hoops* (C-22); in those objects with which children propelled themselves: *Sledges* (C-23) (sleds) and *Stilts* (C-24); in those with which they made noise: *Whistles* (C-25), *Bull-Roarers* (C-26), *Flax-Flappers* (C-27), and *Snory-Bones* (C-28) (button and string, twisted); and in those in which they laid their schemes: forts, dens, manuka houses, and raupo whares (reed huts of the Maori type). The knife was needed also when they went into the bush looking for natural foods such as broom shoots, the young stems of the briar rose, elder-berries, and *Giggies* (C-29) (giggy or Kei Kei flowers). Practically all these outdoor play objects were used by boys. Girls had few out-door play objects. However, there are reports of their playing imag-inative *Flower Games* (C-30) with the pansy, the periwinkle, the hawthorn, with daisy chains, and with briarberry necklaces. Grass, too, was used in imaginative games for girls (*Grass Games*, C-31), in which each player selected a husband or a future by pulling off ears of the rye grass, as in Tinker Tailor Grass, saying as she did:

> Tinker, tailor, soldier, sailor,
> Richman, poorman, beggarman, thief.

Or she chose her clothes for the wedding, saying:

> Silk, satin, cotton, rags.

Or the vehicle in which she would ride:

> Horse, carriage, wheel-barrow, cart.

There were many more variations in this series, but they have more often been reported in connection with skipping games than grass games.[5] Animals and insects also came in for their share of play activity (*Animal Play*, C-32; *Insect Play*, C-33), as pets and as objects for teasing. Dogs had tins tied to their tails, and frogs were inflated through straws. Children kept cats, opossums, ferrets, guinea pigs, weasels, stoats, livestock, and silkworms for pets.

The most universal insect play in the North Island and in parts of the South Island was a game known as *Butcher Bats* (C-34), Butcher Boys, or Penny Doctor Beetles. In this game a straw, suit-ably moistened at the end with spittle, was pushed down the hole made by a certain (unknown) insect and flicked out when the in-

---

[5] See F-1.

sect bit the end of the straw. The player won who could flick out the first beetle.

Sometimes children amused themselves with *Food Play* (C-35). There is much talk of hungry children chewing wheat in school, and of children in North Auckland chewing and swapping kauri gum. There was a rhyme to be said while twisting the stem of an apple:

> Apple pip, apple pip,
> Fly over my head.
> Bring me another apple,
> Before I go to bed. [Blenheim, Marlborough, 1911]

When a child had something to give away he put his hands behind his back and said:

> Navy navy nick nack,
> Whit hand will yee tak?
> Tak the right or tak the wrong,
> And I'll beguile yee if I can. [Amberley, Canterbury, 1890]

In the period between 1900 and 1920 an increasing number of commercial play objects became more generally available. In the reports there are many references to *Scrapbooks* (C-36), *Transfers* (C-37), cigarette-card *Collections* (C-38), Painting, Claywork, *Beads* (C-39), Soldiers, Dolls, Blocks, and so forth. The children also had their own homemade toylike objects, which increased in importance during these years. *Pin Dips* (C-40) had been known earlier, but now reached a new importance. The players each paid a pin and earned a look at a book or at a glass front displaying pretty colors. The owner of the Dip said:

> A pin or a bull or a button,
> To see a rary rary show, show, show. [Tahataki, Otago, 1875]

A "bull" was, in this case, a marble. These Dips were also known as Poppy Shows. The *Prick Book* (C-41), which is seldom reported for the years before 1900, but often during the first decades of the twentieth century, was probably a development from the Pin Dip mentioned above. In this game a player actually pushed a pin into another player's book containing pretty pictures and post cards. The first player took the picture from the page at which her pin pricked. She then had to surrender her book for the other player to have a prick at. The progress of a particularly coveted picture from one book to another is said to have been watched with great interest, and the girl who had it for the time being was besieged with requests to be allowed to prick her book. *Fairy Gardens* (C-42), and collections of stamps, birds' eggs, sea shells, flowers, and grass should not pass unmentioned. They were of considerable importance in this era. *Smudographs* (C-43) were a school pastime in which an ink blot was smeared by folding over the page. Fancy designs sometimes resulted.

Many important outdoor activities like hunting or Bird-Nesting have already been mentioned above in connection with the children's play objects. Another was *Horse-Riding* (C-44), which often took the form of Horse Races, and there is talk of Bows and Arrows on Horseback, and also of *Polo* (C-45). *Swimming* (C-46) was the major summer sport for boys, and was also shared in, though less freely, by girls. The adult attitude to girls' swimming may perhaps have been expressed in the somewhat ambiguous rhyme:

> Mother, may I go out to swim?
> Yes, my darling daughter.
> Hang your clothes on the gooseberry bush,
> And don't go near the water. [Palmerston North, 1900]

Another swimming rhyme was:

> Down in the duckpond,
> Learning how to swim.
> First he does the overarm,
> Then he does the side.
> Now he's under water,
> Swimming against the tide. [Palmerston North, 1900]

Water Play (C-47) with homemade flax boats, rafts, and dams had its importance. In the winter, especially in the South Island, there were the play activities which went with snow and ice. There is much report of *Snowballing* (C-48), making *Snowmen* (C-49), *Tobogganing* (C-50), and *Skating* (C-51). From all localities come reports of *Tree-Climbing* (C-52), Treetop Races (races across the treetops), and the like.

Certain of the informal play activities of the past went with special seasons, times, or dates. Until the death of Queen Victoria, for example, the *Queen's Birthday* (C-53) was always a holiday, a fact celebrated in rhyme:

> Hip, hip, hooray,
> For the Queen's birthday,
> If you don't give us a holiday,
> We'll all run away. [Dunedin, 1890]

Or:

> Hip, hip, hooray,
> For the Queen's birthday,
> On the twenty-fourth of May. [Charleston, Westland, 1890]

The celebration of Guy Fawkes Day (*Guy Fawkes Play*, C-54), on November the fifth, was practiced from the very first days of settlement, although throughout much of the nineteenth century only the bonfire was known in most districts. The firecrackers came later. From all accounts it was a riotous evening. For example: "Guy Fawkes day was a battle royal. Different parts of the village clashed together with flax whips and rotten eggs. Later all would combine to burn the guy" (Collingwood, Nelson, 1895). In those days, as today, children had their rhymes and their stuffed "Guys" with which to entice coins from adults. One of their rhymes was:

> Git up, good wives, and shake your feathers,
> Dinna think that we are beggars.
> Only bairnies come to play,
> Git up and gi' us hog manay. [Dunedin, 1875]

Here the Scottish custom of letting children go about on New Year's Eve to receive a dole of cakes and small gifts (hog manay) has become a part of the Guy Fawkes celebrations.

Another Guy Fawkes rhyme was:

> Please to remember the fifth of November,
> The gunpowder treason and plot.
> I see no reason why the gunpowder treason
> Should ever be forgot.
> Four and twenty barrels lain down below
> To blow old England overflow,
> Happy was the night,
> Happy was the day.

See old Guy Fawkes going to his den,
With a dark lantern and a candle in his hand.
Get out, get out you dirty ole man.
Holla Holla boys, make the bells ring,
Holla Holla boys, God save the King.
A pound of cheese to choke him,
A bottle of beer to wash it down,
A jolly good fire to roast him.
Christmas is coming, the pigs are getting fat,
Please to put a penny in the old man's hat.
If you haven't got a penny a hapenny will do,
If you haven't got a hapenny, God bless you. [Christchurch, 1920]

This latter rhyme, which was inaccurately remembered by the informant, was, nevertheless, the longest of its kind reported. Most of the Guy Fawkes rhymes used in the last few decades have been only fragments of these older rhymes. The most general were:

Guy Fawkes Guy, stick him up on high,
Stick him on a lamp post and there let him die.

A penny for the guy,
A hapenny will do.
If you haven't got a hapenny,
You're a mingy Jew.

This last line could be varied, becoming "God bless you," or "Nothing will do."[6]

April the first, April Fools' Day, seems to have been a day of pranks taken more seriously by adults and children alike in the last century (*April Fools' Play*, C-55). There is much report of adult hoaxes on the whole community.[7] Today, if someone tries to trick a child after the limit hour of twelve noon, that child may reply:

April Fools' Day is past,
And you're the April Fool at last.
Four farthings make a penny,
And you're a bigger fool than any.

---

[6] This festival is reported on more fully in B. Sutton-Smith, "Declining Festival," *The New Zealand Listener*, XXV (1951), 8.

[7] I have reported on this festival more fully in "Traditional Frolics on April Fool's Day," *The New Zealand Standard*, Wellington, N.Z., XVIII (1952), 23.

Sentiments may be expressed in terms of playground scribble:

A duck in the pond,
A fish in the pool,
Whoever reads this
Is a big April Fool.

In addition to these traditional occasions there were other special times that always evoked a response from the children. Children tried to fortify themselves against examinations with this:

Shivery grass will make you pass
A rusty nail will make you fail. [Moutere, Nelson, 1900]

The last day of school was traditionally an occasion for letting off steam. The following rhymes were widespread:

Two more weeks and we shall be,
Out of the gates of misery.
No more writing, no more French,
No more sitting on a hard board bench.
No more walking two by two,
Like the monkeys in the Zoo,
No more spelling, no more sums,
No more teachers to whack our bums.
Or:
No more spelling, no more books,
No more teachers' dirty looks.
Or:
No more spelling, no more French,
No more sitting on a hard board bench.

§II: 1920–1950

Imitative games have slipped down the age scale. The game of Horses, for example, is no longer to be seen outside the infant playground, and when played there, it is generally a part of Cowboys, rather than an imitation of horses. The game of Schools continues and still contains its old rebellious note. The children are usually excessively naughty and the teacher excessively strict. The following widely known rhymes express this attitude of the children:

Four and four are twenty-four,
Kick the teacher out the door.

If she squeals, bring her in.
Hang her on a safety pin.

When asked, "What is the date?" the children reply:

Thirty days has September,
All the rest I can't remember.
The calendar is hanging on the wall.
Why bother me with this at all?

Most of the other imitative games are still played at home, although
unusual ones like Ploughing Matches have gone. And new ones
like Social Security, Post Offices, Libraries, Factories, and School
Dentists have come to take their place.

Pack games of Cowboys and Indians seem to have increased in
number. The films and the radio have done much to provide modern children with ideas which are the stimulus and the framework
for pack games. There was far less mention of these games in earlier
years, when the stimulus to such group ideas was often to be found
in a literature that only few had read. The battle games (see C-4)
have gone from the playground. Perhaps they have been institutionalized in Rugby Football, with its notoriously rough scrim-
maging and tackling.

Play objects are on the whole of a commercially made or mechanical sort. Boys still construct kites, shanghais, bows and arrows, pea-shooters, sledges, and stilts, but ordinarily it is the
younger ones (seven to nine) who do it, and even they spend much
less time at such tasks than their predecessors did. However, the
modern world has brought new opportunities in the form of model
aeroplanes, meccano, carpenters' tools, innumerable hobby kits
and toys, *Trolley Wheels* (C-56), automobile *Tyres* (C-57), and
Bicycles (C-58). There are more mechanical guns than there used
to be; toy guns, cap guns, and water pistols. The *Elastic Gun* (C-
59) is a modern invention; in many schools quite complicated guns
are made with triggers which release taut elastic bands. The *Parachute* (C-60), made of a handkerchief, a string, and a stone weight,
is a new play object; so also is the wooden propeller; and both are
obvious representations of aspects of the modern world of flight.
Also characteristic today are the paper play objects (often trick
objects) for which there was less scope in the days of the slate.
These have played an essential part in the domestication of the

playground by helping to turn children's hostility from solely physical outlets into a variety of symbolic concerns. Civilization is spared a little violence, for example, when, instead of torturing a classmate, a child says:

"Guess what happened to Bailey?"
"What?"
"This!"

Whereupon the first child pulls out the fold in a piece of paper upon which Bailey has been drawn with his neck in a noose. When the fold is pulled out the neck is stretched out several inches in length. This widespread trick is known as *Hanging Bailey* (C-61). Another rather recent contrivance is used in *Fortune-Telling* (C-62), a complex paper object that tells a child's fortune in answer to his choice: he chooses this flap or that, and when it is turned up he has yet another choice. Other paper objects are: ticket-butt *Cinematographs* (C-63), matchbox *Cameras* (C-64), shoe-box *Peep Shows* (C-65), treacle-tin *Telephones* (C-66), and *Tractor Cotton Reels* (C-67).

Considerations of space have permitted only the briefest enumeration or description of the manifold informal play activities of children yesterday and today. This record is sufficient, however, to demonstrate the important point that children may be both experimental and original in their play activities. In seeking to understand children at play, therefore, we must hold in mind the dual fact that children are *innovative* as well as *conservative* (the latter being the point made in the chapter on singing games).

In general, younger children tend to be more conservative than older ones. Though inventive in informal play they may still set up firm routines, and in rule games they may demand strict adherence to the rules. But, through their lack of social understanding and the preponderant importance, to themselves, of their own personal fantasies, they do not always abide closely either by their own routines or the rules. Still, this does not alter their basic trust in the rules, which are seldom changed by them except through misunderstanding. Older children, with their greater social confidence, both abide by the rules more adequately and feel freer to modify or alter the rules when they think that a change is likely to result in more fun for all the players. In consequence, older players are the main source of those changes which endure through the generations. Such changes occur most frequently when play takes place in a small group of close friends, where the children feel sufficiently secure with one another to make socially creative variations during group activity. Larger and more heterogeneous groups must adhere more closely to the known rules so that all players (being less certain of one another), may be guaranteed a "fair" share of the game's advantages.

Leader Games: Category D

Leader games are central-person games in which the central person is a leader who directs the course of the game and the moves that the other players are allowed to make. The other players compete with one another to take the leader's place, but, as has been stated, the leader exercises a strong control over their competition. To a limited extent the players also compete with the leader and the leader with the players. These games are played almost entirely by girls of seven to nine years.

§ I: 1870–1920

Leader games are only occasionally reported for the fifty-year period 1870 to 1920. The following games are mentioned as having been played between 1890 and 1920: Giant Steps, Butcher's Bat, Steps and Stairs, Names, Steps, Alla Balla, Here Come Two Nuns, I Am a Turkey Merchant, Trading, and Colours. But none of these, with the possible exception of Giant Steps (Steps, or Steps and Stairs), was widespread.

§ II: 1920–1950

The great growth of leader games in recent years is further evidence of the growing freedom that modern girls have had for active play. All the games mentioned below are widespread. There are several types of leader games, which will be called commanding games (D-1 through D-4), statue games (D-5), creeping games (D-6), treasure games (D-7), guessing games (D-8 through D-15), team games (D-16), organized leader games (D-17 through D-23), and skill games (D-24 and D-25).

In the commanding games (as in most of the others) one player, the central person or leader, stands out in front of the other players and gives them commands. The group of players stand in a line at one end of a prearranged space, and the leader takes a position at the other end (usually of a school shelter shed). The aim of each of the players is to move up to the leader. The first player to reach the leader becomes the new leader herself. But the players can only move when the leader so commands them. Within the bounds of her commands they compete among themselves.

In *Letters* (D-1), the leader faces the players and calls out certain letters. She says, in effect, "All those with the letter A in their name take a stride towards me." Actually, the leader simply calls A, or Z or B or any other letter, at random. The players know that each one who has that letter in her name is then to take a stride forward. The rule is, generally, that, if the letter called out is an "ordinary" (i.e., small) letter in the player's name, the player takes one step forward for every occurrence of the letter in her name. If the letter called is a capital letter in her name, she takes two steps forward. Sometimes the game is speeded up by letting the players take more strides for each letter that is called. For example, the players may take three strides when an ordinary letter is called, and six strides for a capital. Sometimes only the first and last names of the players are counted. In other versions, the players assume fictitious names: for example, the names of trees. The leader may often favor certain players by calling out letters she knows to be in their names. The players may have to move only up to the leader, or may have to go back again as well. The game is also known as Initials, Alphabets, and Names.

A variant is *Colours* (D-2). In this game all the players who are wearing an article of clothing in which there is a certain color, take a step forward when that color is called out. If a player is wearing two articles of clothing in which the color occurs, she may take two steps forward. This variant is also known as Clothes, Cauliflowers, Cabbages, Vegetables, and Red and Blue.

In the action type of commanding game, known most widely as *Steps and Strides* (D-3), but also as Giant Steps, Steps, Giant Strides, and Steps and Stairs, the element of chance, which may play a part in the letter leader games, is missing. Here there is no haphazard choice of a letter. Instead, the leader chooses the actions that each player shall make and tells the players in turn what they are to do. As in the games described above, the first player to cover the distance from the group starting place to the leader, becomes leader herself. In these action leader games a complete terminology for the movements has arisen. Generally the players in any one school know from six to a dozen different types of actions that can be commanded by the leader. In 1940 the names of the movements at Waikouaiti, Otago, and their meanings were: needle (put the heel of one foot just ahead of the toe of the other foot, and move the hind foot up alongside the front one); pin (move forward half a foot-length); lamppost (go down on the hands, the feet remaining constant, the hands stretching as far out in front as possible, and then stand up on the point to which the outstretched fingers reach); umbrella (whirl round and forward until the command to stop); motorcars (run up and back until the leader says stop); caterpillar (go down on the hands and bring the feet up to the hands); scissors (astride jump, then jump forward with legs crossing, astride jump and bring feet together); and steps, strides, hops, jumps, and skips (which are self-explanatory). The terms often have different meanings at different schools. The following were some of the terms used at other schools in 1949: Hokitika, Westland—cabbages, lettuces, ladder, carrot, needle, pin, strides; Forbury, Otago—stride, cabbage, pin, needle, lamppost, banana skin, caterpillar, cauliflower, giant strides, and carrots.

In the action type of commanding games the omnipotence of the leader is more obvious than in the other central-person games. In the game of *May I?* (D-4) the arbitrariness of the leader is made quite explicit. In this game the players request the moves which they wish to make. A player requests, for example, "May I take two banana skins, please?" But she must be careful to begin with "May I" and to finish with "please," or else the leader may refuse the request with an imperious "No." If, on the other hand, the leader replies, "Yes, you may," then the requesting player must be sure to say "Thank you," or the privilege will be withdrawn because of the player's lack of courtesy. It is not surprising that in these games there is some report of cheating on the part of the group of players. Cheating is described by various children as follows: (*a*) "You can cheat by edging up when the leader is not looking." (*b*) "They're supposed to be fair but they often favour their own friends." (*c*) "A person who favours is only allowed to favour once." Such cheating and unfairness as exist in these games are usually offset somewhat by the fact the games are played by a small group of friends who can accept such behavior without anger.

In the statue leader games (*Statues*, D-5), the leader decides which postures the other players must assume. She throws them into these postures, then judges whether they maintain the postures adequately or not. There are numbers of minor variations: The leader may decide what the children must do. It is stated beforehand that they are to stop in an ugly or a beautiful posture. The leader judges which player performs best, and that player becomes the next leader. Sometimes the manner in which they shall move when swung by the leader is prescribed, for example, gracefully or slowly. Sometimes each player may name her own position after she has landed. "If someone lands hunched up and staring fixedly at the ground she may be a scientist looking at a flea" (Karori, Wellington, 1949). Or, "The leader shuts her eyes and counts sixty to a hundred while they take up positions" (Takaka, Nelson, 1935). "When they cry 'break-away' she lets them go" (Rakaia, Canterbury, 1910). Some statue games are of longer duration. "The player picked as the best the first time helps the leader the next time. Both nominate positions in turn, and the next best player becomes one of the leaders also. The players left gradually have to pass through more and more actions as these are nominated by the increasing number of leaders. If the last player left cannot remember all the actions which she must do, she becomes a donkey or an ass" (Karori, Wellington, 1950). "The leader does everything possible to make the players laugh or lose their statue position. If she succeeds that player falls out. The last player left becomes leader for the next game" (Waikouaiti, Otago, 1949). Some forms are more like "He" games. "The first player to move becomes He for the next swing" (Waikouaiti, 1949). The same game could be played to music as Musical Statues (see J-37), but in that case the "leader" element was less important, as it was a game of elimination in which the players who moved when the music stopped were eliminated.

In the "creeping-up" type of leader game (*Creeping Up*, D-6), the leader has her back turned and the other players endeavor to creep up and tag her. A player who succeeds in tagging her takes her place. But the leader keeps turning round. If she catches any of them moving she sends those players back to the base line. Sometimes the leader counts aloud from one to ten, then turns round; for example, in Steps (Rakaia, Canterbury, 1910). Sometimes the players only go back one step when they are seen moving, as in Creepy Crawly (North East Valley, Dunedin, 1949). The game has many names, but Creeping Up is the most widespread. Other names are Creepy (Brooklyn, Wellington, 1948; Christchurch, 1920); Victoria (Hokitika, Westland, 1949); Creeping Jack (Stoke, Nelson, 1949); Creeping or Creep the Curtain (Aohunga, Wairarapa, 1949); Peep Behind the Curtain (Te Hapara, Gisborne, 1949); Grandmother's Footsteps (Waingake, Wairarapa, 1935); and Go, Go, Stop (Bainham, Nelson, 1949; Woodville, Wairarapa, 1949).

In the treasure types of leader games, the leader stands with her back to the players and with the treasure—a stone, tin, or ball—behind her. The players creep up and try to steal her treasure before she turns round and catches them moving. These games are similar in form to Creeping Up, except for the treasure element. The player who succeeds in getting the treasure then tries to escape with it. If she escapes to the safety of the base, the leader must continue to be He. This game has a variety of differing names and slight variations. Examples: *The Giant and His Treasure* (D-7) (Onekaka, Nelson, 1949); Giant's Treasure (Dunedin, Wellington, and Westland, 1949); Creeping Jack (Nelson, 1949); Steps and Stairs (Karori, Wellington, 1949); Get the Keys (Northland, Wellington, 1949); and Find the Key (Wairarapa, 1949).

The guessing leader games include *Queenie* (D-8). In this game the leader again has her back to the players. She throws the ball over her head. If any player catches the ball that player takes Queenie's place. If no player catches the ball, whoever gets hold of it first hides it behind her back. Queenie then turns round and tries to guess who has her ball. If she guesses correctly she gets her ball back again and remains the leader. If she does not guess correctly the player who is hiding the ball becomes leader. The players generally call out "Queenie" when they want her to turn round and guess who has the ball. At Nelson, a player who catches Queenie's ball in the air calls out "Butcher" and takes Queenie's place. The game is generally known as Kiwi in the Otago District and Alla Balla or Ella Bella in Christchurch. In one Christchurch version all the players line up behind Alla Balla and chant:

> Alla Balla, who has got the ball?
> See, I haven't,
> See, I haven't,
> See, I haven't at all.

And as they chant this rhyme they show each hand alternately. Alla Balla must then make her guess (Christchurch, 1905).

In a variation known as *Folding Arms* (D-9), played at Wellington in 1949, the leader, who has the ball, faces the other players, who stand opposite to her in a line. The other players have their arms folded. The leader throws, or pretends to throw, the ball at one of them. If she actually throws and the intended receiver misses the ball that player is out. If she only pretends to throw (that is, if she feints) and the intended receiver unfolds her arms, that player is out. The last player left in the line becomes the next leader.

Other similar types of guessing leader games are always appearing. For example: "One person stands up in front of a row of others and picks up some small object while the others have their back turned. Then the people are told what letter the object begins with and they have to guess what it is. The first person to guess right goes out in the front and the game begins again" (*Guessing*, D-10) (Auckland, 1949).

In the other types of guessing leader games, acting and chasing are also involved. The leader (an individual or "group") acts generally at workaday occupations—dustmen, firemen, housewives—and the players who are the chasers, try to guess what the leaders are acting. When the chasers guess what the leaders are acting, they chase the actors and try to take their place by tagging them before these leaders can reach a certain boundary. Among the various forms of these acting games is one that is very like an ordinary tagging game. In this type the group of players do the acting and one player is Chaser (not a leader, because no one wants her position: all want to avoid it). The one player chases and tries to tag the others when she guesses what they are acting.

In *Johnny in the Inkpot* (D-11),

Johnny stands at the end of the hall or shed with his back turned. The rest of the players think of something to do such as paint a picture. They are at the other end of the hall. When they have thought what to do, they run towards Johnny saying "Johnny in the Inkpot, what do we have to do today?" Johnny turns round and says "Set to work." They do what they have thought of and if Johnny guesses he tags one of the players, who then goes Johnny the next time. [Brooklyn, Wellington, 1948]

A game of the same type is *Busy Bees* (D-12) (Karori, Wellington, 1949). The dialogue in this game is:

"Here come some busy-bees to do some work."
"What sort?"
"All sorts."
"Do it, then."

Another is *Jack of All Sorts* (D-13) (Millerton, Westland, 1949). In this version the "He" stands with her back to the players.

The greatest number of these acting games, however, have the following formation. One or two players act (these are the leaders), and the rest of the players, the group, attempt to guess the leaders' act and then chase, tag, and replace them. Games of this sort include: *Here Come Two Nuns* (D-14) (Ohau, Wellington, 1912); Colours (Woodville, Wairarapa, 1950); Film Stars (Wanganui, 1950; Dunedin, 1949); Cripple Jack (Millerton, Westland, 1949); Shops (Karori, Wellington, 1944); I Sent My Son (North East Valley, Dunedin, 1949); Shopping (Brooklyn, Wellington, 1948); Ivory (Caversham, Dunedin, 1949); and I Am a Turkey Merchant (Marton, Wellington, 1890).

In another group of much the same type there is a runner as well as the leader-actor. When the members of the group guess the action of the leader-actor, they chase the runner, and not the actor, and thus give the runner a better chance to escape. Games of this type are: *Times* (D-15) (Mangitainoka, 1949); Busy Bees (Oxford, Canterbury, 1949; Mangitainoka, Wairarapa, 1949; Wellington, 1949); and Sticks (Kotinga, Westland, 1949).

The team leader games represent a development of the guessing games. In these games one group acts and the other group chases the acting team, after guessing the nature of the act. The dialogue of *Trades* (D-16) (Granity, Westland, 1949) is:

"Here we come."
"Where from?"
"New York."
"What's your trade?"
"Find out."
"Set to work."

A game known as Trades was also played at Brooklyn, Wellington, in 1949. Other names for games of the same type are: New York (Kapuka, Southland, 1930); Trading (North Canterbury, 1890); Colours (Ohau, Wellington, 1912); Bum, Bum, Here We Come (Bainham, Nelson, 1949); Grocers (Waikouaiti, Otago, 1949); and Buzz, Buzz, Busy Bee (Ratapiko, New Plymouth, 1950).

Many other games have a similar leader formation. Some played under the supervision of adults have a leader formation (the adult taking the part of the leader) and occasionally carry over into children's play. They are not true leader games, however, since the leader is an outside organizer rather than one of the players. Typical games of this sort are *Man the Ship* (D-17); *Cannon Balls* (D-18); *Rats and Rabbits* (D-19) or Rabbits and Rips; *In the Pond and Out of the Pond* (D-20); *Ducks in the Pond* (D-21); *Dog and Bone* (D-22); and *Fish in the Pond* (D-23).

In the skill type of leader game, the leader is a player with a bat. The players try to catch the ball which the leader hits with her bat. Although it has variations, there is only one game of this type. It was widely known in earlier times and was, in the main, a girls' game. In *Butcher's Bat* (D-24), "The batter stood about nine feet away from the others and hit the ball into the air. The players stood around about and the one who caught the ball became the next batter" (Amberley, Canterbury, 1890; Rakaia, Canterbury, 1910; Palmerston North, 1900). More often the same game was played as *Tuppenny Catches* (D-25) (Dunedin, 1915), or Penny Catches (Collingwood, Nelson, 1949), or as Pounds, Shillings, and Pence (Wellington; Ngapara, Otago; Dunedin, 1949). In these games the catchers cannot become batter until they have made a certain amount of money. Each time the batter hits a ball she calls an amount of money, and the player who catches that ball has that amount of money to her credit. It is known also as Catcher (Whare-toa, Gisborne, 1930). "It was a nice game for summer" (Waikato, Auckland, 1910).

Girls' acrobatics often adopt the same type of leader formation. At several Dunedin schools in 1949 I found girls playing at the game of standing on their hands (*Handstands*, D-26). The leader told the girls when to go up on their hands. She then judged which was the winner; or, rather, the winner was the player who stayed up the longest, and the leader announced the verdict. The winner then became the new leader. It is noticeable that girls' games of skipping and their informal activities often fall into this leader type of organization, with one player taking a commanding role over all the others.

Among children in the seven- to nine-year age group, the organization of these leader games is as distinctive of girls' play as the organization of pack games (described in the preceding chapter) is of the play of boys. Anyone who would seek to understand children's games, therefore, must determine why it is that girls spontaneously adopt the leader pattern in so many of their games and why boys spontaneously choose to fashion their games after the style of Cowboys and Indians.

It is obvious to us that when girls play at being mothers they are representing the characteristics of the women they know. Perhaps it should be equally obvious that in these leader games they are representing the type of social relationship which, in their experience, is most characteristic of women in association with children. In the game of "May I?" (see D-4), this relationship has been made explicit. According to the game, women are creatures given to queenly partiality in their dealings with inferiors. One cannot believe that this pattern of relationships could have so much importance in girls' play unless there were something in their *real* relationships with women to support it.

But, following the same line of argument, what possible aspect of the male cultural role can the boys be imitating in their pack games? One possible explanation is as follows. Boys see so much less of their fathers in the workaday environment than girls see of their mothers and a mother's daily routine, and are therefore so much less able to form a clear idea of what their role in life should be, that they are less sure about how to model their own (distinctively masculine) behavior. As a result, they are driven to a greater dependence upon one another for support and security than are the girls, and are more given to representing the heroic roles (cowboys, spacemen) of the mass-media fantasy. In cowboys the boys find a masculine role whose characteristics are clear-cut and definite, and in the equality of their packs they find a reassuring and companionable solidarity to make up for the lack of clear-cut guidance about the male life-pattern. In the play of girls, it will be noted, there seems to be far less need to play at "unreal" characters (girls play at mothers or teachers, not at spacemen or bandits). Girls seem to have a clearer idea of what the future holds for them, and of what they should be like, themselves.

Such "reasons" as these, with which we seek to understand what children are representing in their leader and pack play, are, of course, of a highly speculative sort. These children's play activities do challenge us to gain further insight into the nature of our own society.[1]

[1] Current psychological research along these lines is described in two current articles: B. G. Rosenberg and B. Sutton-Smith, "A Revised Conception of Masculine-Feminine Differences in Play Activities," *The Journal of Genetic Psychology*, XCVI (1960), 165–170; and B. Sutton-Smith and B. G. Rosenberg, "Manifest Anxiety and Game Preferences in Children," *Child Development*, XXXI (1960), 307–311.

Chasing Games: Category E

In this category two types of chasing games are described: central-person chasing games and team chasing games. The central-person chasing games of childhood involve one player in a competitive relationship with all the other players. In all these games the central player chases and attempts to tag or capture the other players. These chasing games are the most universal of games the world over and the games most frequently played by children of all ages.[1]

[1] For discussions of psychological research on these games, see: B. Sutton-Smith, "The Psychology of Games," Parts 1 and 2, *National Education*, Welling-

All chasing games have certain essential characteristics. The central player is called a "He" or an "It." (In New Zealand this player is most often called a "He.") The other players try to avoid being captured by the He. Usually they do this by running from him, retreating into a safe base or "home," holding on to some safe object, as in Touchwood (*Tiggy Tiggy Touchwood*, E-1), or by hiding, as in *Hide and Seek* (E-2). The He can represent a fearsome creature and have awesome names (Hairy Man). Sometimes the He is blindfolded, and in these cases it is easier to taunt him, which the runners may do as they please and at their own risk. When the game is played at dusk or in darkness the He is thought to be more frightening. As one child said, "You never know when he is about to seize you." There can also be something dangerous about the He's power. In some games if he tags a player he "poisons" that player or makes him "lame." The He must be carefully chosen, and for this the mysterious counting-out rhymes may be used. Despite his powers, the potency of the He may be reduced in games in which the players work together against him, as in *Kick the Tin* (E-3).

Team chasing games involve two teams in a competitive relationship in which one team chases the other or the two teams chase each other at the same time. Some of the acting team leader games of the last chapter are of this sort (see D-16).

§ I: 1870–1920

Before 1900 there appears to have been less playing of, and perhaps fewer of, these He games. Some informants say that they never played *Tag* (E-4), or Tig, as it is more often called in the South Island, in its present haphazard form, but only in circle formations, as in *Cat and Mouse* (E-5), known also as Cat and Rat, and *Twos and Threes* (E-6). And it can be expected that the circle would have been a more general form in earlier days because children would imitate it from picnics and adult practice. It may have been more suitable to the starched and heavy garments of the time, particularly those of the girls. However, if greater attention was given

---

ton, N.Z., XXXVI (1955), 228–229 and 261–263; P. V. Gump and B. Sutton-Smith, "The 'It' Role in Children's Games," *The Group*, XVII (1955), 3–8; and B. Sutton-Smith and P. V. Gump, "Games and Status Experience," *Recreation*, XLVIII (1955), 172–174.

to formal tag games it can only have been a matter of emphasis. Many of the chief tag games were played then as they are today. Tiggy Tiggy Touchwood and Hide and Seek had a loose structure. In addition, *Fox and Geese* (E-7), *Bar the Door* (E-8), *Tom Tiddler's Ground* (E-9), *Prisoner's Base* (E-10), *French and English* (E-11), and *Puss in the Corner* (E-12) were all common. There are also traces of other games of a more formless type. For example: "In Tig around the school, you 'jinked' and turned back. We played it to warm us up but it was a dangerous game" (Taieri, Otago, 1875). There is also mention of *Trip and Go* (E-13) (Tahataki, Otago, 1875); *Chase* (E-14) (Naseby, Otago, 1900); and "a lot of random tagging" (Christchurch, 1870).

Let us consider some of these He games:

The universal game of *Puss in the Corner* (E-12), with the He player in the middle trying to get himself a corner and the other four players exchanging corners and at the same time taunting him with "Puss, Puss," was particularly suited to the school shelter sheds throughout New Zealand. On any wet day, even today, there is always a revival of Puss in the Corner in the shelter shed among children much older than those who usually play it.

Hide and Seek (E-2), or Hideygo, was also particularly well suited to the playgrounds of the very early days. One informant says, "We used to play Hide and Seek amongst the flax bushes and nigger heads during our lunch hour" (Blenheim, Marlborough, 1890).

Occasionally rather unusual types of Hide and Seek were played. For example, in *All In* (E-15), as played at Taranaki in 1890, there were two teams and a home base. One team, the "outs," went and hid, while the home team, the "ins," counted. When the counting was over the "ins" went and looked for the hiding "outs." As soon as an "in" spied an "out" he shouted the name of the player he had seen, saying, "All in for Tommy Jones." At that cry all the "in" players raced for home, and all the "out" players emerged from their hiding places and tried to tag them. Now if all the "in" players could get home without being tagged, then the person seen, Tommy Jones, was considered captured and he had to come and sit in the home base. The "in" team went on trying to sight "out" players and then get home without being tagged. In that way, one by one, they caught all the "out" players. When they were very

near the end and had all the "out" players except one or two, they
would naturally send out only their very good players. They did
not want one of their own players to be tagged; because if this happened to an "in" player while he was running back to the home
base he was said to be "cut-off." This meant that all the captured
"out" players could go free again and hide. Then the "in" team
had to start from scratch and capture the "outs" all over again. It
was quite popular and suited to the smaller play spaces of the day,
where there were a number of buildings and bushes to provide
hides, from which "outs" could dart to tag unwary "ins" trying to
spy them.

A favorite time for playing "He" games was in the dusk, and certain of these games, for example, *Twilight Tig* (E-16), were specially adapted to the half-light.

Twilight Tig was a game played on our cousins' lawn and garden,
which was dotted with shrubs. We played it before we went home
after spending a day with them. It was played at dusk in complete
silence after the first counting-out, so that it was difficult to tell who
was He until perhaps you felt a touch on your shoulder and knew then
that it was yourself. The effect of the silent figures flitting and dodging in and out among the bushes in the half dark was eerie in the
extreme, and I can feel it still. [Dunedin, 1890]

Perhaps the commonest of the outdoor dusk He games was
Moonlight, Starlight (E-17), which began with a chanting of the
rhyme:

> Moonlight, starlight,
> Bogey won't come out to-night.

One informant reports: "We had several paddocks divided off by
hedges and the neighbouring children always congregated for
games after their chores were done. We usually ended with Moonlight, Starlight. As the bogey was at liberty to move round one
never knew where the next pounce was coming from" (Nelson,
1910).

In some chasing games the He's tag represented a dangerous
power. In *Touch Touch* (E-18), "When one was touched the hand
had to be kept on the place until the touched person tagged another.
Perhaps we had sides for I remember us, one with a hand on seat,

another with a hand on the head, running round and convulsed with laughter when some unfortunate was touched low on the leg and had to hobble" (Nelson, 1890). The same game was known elsewhere as French Tag and at a later date as Poison Tag or Poisoned Stag. "In Poisoned Stag the aim was to tag them on the foot in order to thoroughly incapacitate them" (Rakaia, Canterbury, 1910). Occasionally it was not the He's tag that was poisonous, but some special object, as in the parlor game of *Jack-a-balan* (E-19), as played in North Canterbury in 1890.

On winter nights we sat round the fire playing Jack-a-balan. Someone took a stick from the fire with a glowing end and said to his neighbours "Will yae hae Jack-a-balan?" And the neighbour said "What if he dies in my hand?" The answer was:

> "You shall bear the saddle-ban,
> Thro moss, thro moor,
> Thro a' the lan,
> Take him safe oot o' my han."

And so the burning stick went on round, each player saying the curse until finally the stick went out. The player who held the stick when the fire went out had to pay a forfeit and go through all sorts of tortures.

Although the He represented a dangerous power, he could also be taunted and pushed about, as in *Blindman's Buff* (E-20). In some games the players seemed to love challenging him; for example, in the variant of *Bar the Door* (E-8) known as King Caesar.

King Caesar was a running game and very lively too. In late afternoons in a quiet suburb, the area we loved was the street outside our homes. The property frontages set the boundaries. King Caesar was He and he roamed the road. We had to keep moving or he'd be after us. We crossed from footpath to footpath. Once off the path we had to get to the other side without being tagged or go He. We sang derisively:

> King King Cae—ree,
> You'll stay He—ee!

and then ran parallel to the road dodging across and taking risks with the He. [Nelson, 1890]

And in Heathcote Valley, Canterbury, in 1899, when the children were playing the similar game of *Bar the Door* (E-8), they would dart out from the base yelling at the He:

> Here I come full sail,
> Cock—on—ee—bru—ah!

In a few tagging games the players joined hands with the He when they were caught and helped him to catch the other players. These games were known as *The Bellahonie* (E-21) (Wellington, 1910), Kick Post One (Hampden, Otago, 1880), and Ballyhooley (Wellington, 1920). More popular were those games in which the players helped one another to fight the He, and of these the most widespread was the game known as *Kick the Tin* (E-3), Kick the Boot, Kick the Block, or Homaiacky.

In this game the He was put on guard of a jam tin placed inside a small circle marked on the ground. The He stood by the tin, closed his eyes and counted to one hundred. The other players hid. The He then stood near the tin or cautiously extended his circle of enquiry beyond it, trying to spy the other players. Anyone he could see he called by name and tapped on the tin three times, "One, two, three, for Betty Smith." That put that person out and she had to come and wait by the base. Meanwhile the other hiders were peeping from their hide-aways in order to discover a suitable moment to rush the tin and kick it out of the ring. If the tin was kicked out in this fashion all those already caught were free again to run and hide while the He rushed to replace his tin. A He had to call in all the players before his duties were finished. He sometimes had a long session. The last player called in became the next He, though sometimes there were volunteers for the job.

Another game of a similar nature was *Bedlam* (E-22) (Christchurch, 1920). It has been known more often since as Relievo. In this game the He tapped an appointed spot when he saw the hidden players and cried, "One, two, three, Jacky is He." But Jacky or any other uncaught player could release the captured players by avoiding the He, tagging the base, and crying "Release," which was another name for the game.

In general, circle tagging games were played at picnics. This is certainly true of *Twos and Threes* (E-6), in which all but two of the players stood round in a ring in couples, and one of these two players chased the other in and out among them. When the chased player went in front of a pair of standing players, then the back person in that pair ran off and was chased by the He. This game was widely known as Teazle in Nelson and Wellington provinces. A game played by younger children, and therefore more often played in the school grounds, was *Fill the Gap* (E-23). In this game the players stood in a ring. One player ran round outside the ring and tagged a standing player, who then had to run round in the opposite direction and try to get back into the gap before the tagger. The player who failed to get back first was the next tagger. In the Otago area the game was known also as Space Ring, Circle Tig, and Space to Space; and elsewhere as Drop the Handkerchief or Rotten Egg (see A-20).

The most widely known and most popular tagging game in all historical periods—in fact, the most popular game in New Zealand —was undoubtedly the game known variously as: *Bar the Door*[2] (E-8); All Over; Barbadoor; Barley; Barley Goats; Bar the Gate; Black Bull Bee; Blackthorn; Broken Barley; By the Door; Caesar; Father Door; Free Pass; Goosey; Goosey Up and Down; Holding; Horney; Julius Caesar; King Caesar; King's Den; King Dick; King O'Seenie; King O'Weenie; King Seenie; King Seize-Her; King-a-Sene; Last Man Over; Last Over Call; Pass Over; Punch King; Punch King Seenio; Red Rover; and Running Through the Middle. The game was played at Anderson's Bay, Dunedin, in 1870, as follows:

Another game was Bar the Door, sometimes called Prisoner's Base. Two lines were drawn across the playground any suitable distance apart. One boy stood on guard midway between the lines and called a boy from behind one of the lines to run across. The boy on guard endeavoured to catch the runner and pat him three times on the back. If he succeeded the runner stood beside his captor and in turn called on a boy to run. Should a boy succeed in crossing he called out "Bar the Door" and all the boys ran, as many as were caught taking their place between the lines. Naturally, the first boy called on was the weakest runner.

Generally, the player who managed to pass the He in the middle

2 This game of Bar the Door is used as a vehicle for my discussion of game theory in "A Formal Analysis of Game Meaning," *Western Folklore*, XVIII (1959), 13–24.

called out as the "cry" whatever the name of the game was: for example, "Red rover all over" or "Pass over." Sometimes the crowd of players rushing through the middle was named the Holy Mob or the Bull Rush. The He player in the middle did not always merely tag the players on the back; there were much rougher practices in some towns. One of the most important of these was the crowning ceremony. "The fellow in the middle had to catch one of the runners and having done so, hold him, while he chanted a crowning ceremony" (Gisborne, 1900). In the form of the game called Sinio, "He was required to crown the captive three times on the head crying 'One, two, three, Sinio'" (Granity, Westland, 1900). At Collingwood, Nelson, in 1900, the cry was "King Caesar, one–two–three," but in this case the running player could avoid being tagged by holding his hand on his head. A similar practice is reported from South Clutha, Otago, 1875. "When King Seenie attempted to crown the player with the cry 'one–two–three, you're the man for me,' the player attempted to escape by punching and biting the He's hands in an effort to keep them off his head." The best example of a crowning ceremony is one called Kinging. In this ceremony the captive was patted on the head while he lay flat on the ground with other players astride him. If he managed to escape during the ceremony, the rhyme had to be said again:

> King-seenie, one, two, three,
> You're the very man for me.
> Keep him quiet,
> Hold him down,
> Pat him thrice upon the crown.
> Blackball, blackball,
> One, two, three.
> Joseph Jackson,
> You are He. [Canterbury]

There are no reports of elaborate crowning ceremonies later than 1900. Crowning was probably displaced by Rugby tackling, or frowned upon when playgrounds were supervised. The practice may also have lost some of its significance as the custom of wearing school caps waned. It would be of some importance not to have the dirty hand of another boy on this symbol of your dignity. Undoubtedly one reason for the popularity of Bar the Door in New Zealand was its adaptability to the Rugby code. It was almost inevitable that the tackling in Rugby Football would carry over into Bar the Door. And in many schools where the ground was suitable, forms of tackling (not always very orthodox) were substituted for tagging. It was often a general practice in these games to let some disliked player run across last and then the whole crowd of players in the middle would "down" him, piling on top like Sacks on the Mill. Thus, if a running player fended too hard on his earlier trips, he would generally meet a time of reckoning later on, when the mass of players in the middle would combine to return the injuries. Sometimes the tagging was done with three punches. This is said to have led to many fights, especially when running players felt they had been punched too exuberantly. Tackling forms of the game were often known to the participants as Scragging or Collaring and to mothers as the "clothes-tearing game." Other variants of Bar the Door were Gag or No Gag and Punch King. In *Gag or No Gag* (E-24), sometimes known as Gag or Geg or Smuggling the Geg, there were two teams. One of the players of one team hid on his person some object, such as a pocket knife or a stone, and when his team ran over in Bar the Door fashion, the other team tried to guess which player had the object and catch him. When they succeeded, it became their turn to carry the object, the "gag."

Punch King (E-25) was a more boisterous game than Bar the Door, but similar to it in some ways. In its mildest forms it was virtually the same as Bar the Door except that the middle players punched (instead of tagging) the running players three times on the back. In its proper form, the game was more violent. It was played at Wellington by secondary school boys in 1876 as follows:

The game was called Punch King Sinny Oh. Five were left "un-crowned." The five had their backs to the wall, and woe betide any luckless mite who dared to come within reach of their punches, so indiscriminately were they delivered. Any punch was legal, rabbit or otherwise. Many retired hurt in silence to nurse their bruises; not a few were placed hors-de-combat by blows below the belt. As soon as the five showed the least signs of exhaustion, the pack exultingly rushed in, and all was over. It was really the only regular outlet for boyish exuberance we had.

The game began by one team lining up with their backs to a wall, and the other team attempting to pull them out over a line placed about one yard from the wall. The pulling team could only pull, but the defending team could punch. It was known in Otago in the early days under the name of Goosey.

One of the most interesting sidelights on these He games of yesterday was a development which took place within their forms across the age levels. In the most elementary type of He games each player was in direct and individual relationship with the He while in the midst of other children. At this stage, the only form of combination experienced by the participants was with the He. Occasionally the players joined hands with the He and helped him to catch the other independent players, as in *Chain Tag* (E-26). This was, and is, a type of game frequently played by infants. Its form fits in with the way in which children of that age level will side with an adult rather than with their age-mates. By about the age of eight, nine, or ten, however, children were beginning to play games like Bedlam and Kick the Boot, in which players occasionally helped each other. Here was occasional, although real, experience of coöperation. And then, rising in importance at the same age level and afterwards, came Bar the Door, in which the players gained momentary experience of team formations. It will be remembered that at one stage in that game half of the players were in the middle trying to catch the other team of players running through the middle.

There are records of other forms of Bar the Door in which the two-team basis was more clearly defined, showing that in some areas the children of that day had an opportunity to develop through experience in "He"-like games to the team game proper. Here are some examples of Bar the Door games in which there were definitely two teams and at the same time an individual He player in the middle. A game played at Timaru, Canterbury, in 1880, is described as follows:

This was a very popular game before football was general. There were two sides with a captain for each side. Each team lined up on opposite sides of a space, for example, a street or playground with boundaries marked with stones. The captain on one side would go out into the middle and call one person from the opposite side. That person would run across and attempt to avoid capture. If he succeeded the whole team would come after him. Everybody caught joined the team of this captain in the middle. Now the other captain would have his turn and see how many he could catch for his team.

At Rakaia, Canterbury, 1910:

There were two lines of children facing each other at some distance with one in the middle. The one in the middle called children singly, in which case they were required to run across the ground and back to their own base. Players were called alternately from each side. Failing to catch anyone, the player in the middle could call "Bar the Door," and both teams were required to run across the playground and back to their bases. This was a competition between teams to keep their numbers intact.

A similar game was known as Black Bull Bee at Waitara, New Plymouth, 1899.

In yet another class of Bar the Door games, there were only the two teams. For example, *Horney* (E-27) (Wakefield, 1875)

was played outside the school along a cutting with banks eight to ten feet high on each side. One team joined hands so that the players, usually about six a side, advanced side by side up the cutting, crying out "Horney," "Horney." The opposite team would race down the cutting in an attempt to get through or around the ends of this barrier. They would break their way through the closed hands if they could, or alternatively scramble up the steep side of the cutting in an attempt to go round the end of the line. Those caught would join on the end of the line until it stretched right across the road and up the bank. Those who broke through were safe. They stood behind the line and waited for the time when the line would turn round and, crying "Horney," "Horney," advance towards them.

Games of this type were rather widely known. They are reported as King Seenie (Dunedin, 1875), Horney (Waianiwa, Otago, 1885), Blackthorn (Carterton, Wairarapa, 1895), King O'Weenie (Takaka, Nelson, 1910), and King's Den (Kapuka South, Southland, 1929).

Next in line, in the child's development through chasing games, came the fluid team running games played by the twelve- and thirteen- and fourteen-year-olds: French and English, Prisoner's Base, King's Peg, Chevvy Chase, Chibby, Tallyho, Hares and Hounds, and the Paper Chase.[3] Here, then, was a course of develop-

---

[3] These are dealt with under Category K, numbers K-62 through K-70.

ment which carried children through from the He games of immature years to the "He"-like team games of a later age level.

To folklorists, one of the most interesting characteristics of all
tagging and other "He" games is the way in which the He player
was chosen, or the first pick decided upon. The commonest method
in early years was to use a counting-out rhyme. But there were
other methods: Players drew lots with sticks or straws, and the
player with the longest (or shortest) stick was the He; rye grass
was used and the He was chosen by "tinker-tailoring" (see *Grass
Games*, C-31); or a coin was tossed, or, more often, a board or bat.
One informant writes: "I see our captain of a once notable rounders team spit on the bat as, calling 'Wet or Dry,' she tosses it high
in the air. Wet wins the toss and our leader assembles the players
behind the den with a final warning to anyone who dares give a
twopenny catcher or a miss ball in the batting" (Dunedin, 1890).
Sometimes the He was chosen simply by common consent. "Last
in's lousy," they cried at Dunedin in 1875, and the last in became
He. Another favorite was "plum pudding." It was more often used
by team captains, to pick who would have first choice of the other
players for his team. "Two boys advanced towards each other, foot
after foot heel to toe, saying 'plum pudding, plum pudding' to each
step. The player who put down the last whole foot, leaving not
enough room for his opponent to do so, won the decision." The
Rules of Contrary, another method of picking out a player for a
special role, is referred to later.

It will be noticed that the majority of the rhymes recorded below
include numbers or distorted numerals. Many of these numbers are
said to have their origin in superstitious rites in which magicians
chanted the doggerel of the counting-out rhymes as a part of their
mysterious practices. It is clear, however, that what was important
to the children was not this ancient origin, but the fact that nonsense words themselves gave a sense of mystery. Also the cumula-
tive effect of the mounting jumble, the "Inky pinky fidgety fell,
Ell dell drom and ell," suggested that something mysterious was
impending, that something "unknown" was about to occur. And,
of course, that is exactly what was happening. When the person
was chosen to be He, that person was transformed into a creature
with strange and dangerous powers. The counting, as it were, sym-

bolized the process whereby the He arose as a mysterious personage from among the players.

The best-known counting-out rhymes before 1900 were "Ickle Ockle," "Eenie Meenie," and "Onery Twoery." Between 1900 and 1930, "One, Two, Three" rose to equal importance. The commonest counting-out rhyme in all historical periods was known as either "Eenah Deenah Dinah Doe" or "Eenie Meenie Minie Moh." On the whole, "Eenah Deenah" was the more usual form before 1900 and "Eenie Meenie" after that date. Its usual form was:

Eena deena dina doe,
Catch a nigger by the toe,
If he squeals, let him go,
Eena deena dina doe,
O-U-T spells out.

But there were variations on the theme:

Eena deena dina doe,
Catla weela wila woe,
Each peach pear plum,
Out goes old Tom Thumb.
O-U-T spells out. [Moeraki, Otago, 1900; Charleston,
    Westland, 1895]

Eena deena dina doe,
Catch a nigger by the toe,
If he squeals let him go,
Iggly piggly, dina doe. [Waikouaiti, Otago, 1880]

Eena dena dina doh,
Cotched a nigger by the toe.
Why did you let him go?
'Cos he bit my finger so. [Wellington, 1870]

Eenah deena dinah doh,
Catla weela wila woe,
Spit spot must be done,
Twiddlum, twaddlum, twenty-one,
O-U-T spells out and out you must go.

"For some reason which I now fail to see," reports one informant, "the last rhyme was regarded as a highly amusing rhyme which convulsed us all with laughter. It was not in common use, but was

taught to me by my father as having been used by him in his childhood. He was born in 1864 and lived at Kaiapoi, Dunedin" (Waitara, Taranaki, 1900). One version began "Eeny meeny minney
mo" and then in the second line went on to "Eena deenah dinah
doh," and ended with the last three lines of the first example given
above (Nelson, 1895).

The commonest form of "Ickle Ockle" was the following:

> Ickle ockle black bottle,
> Ickle ockle out,
> If you come in my house,
> I will kick you out.

But there were slight variations. At Waikari, Otago, in 1900, when
the children wanted a very quick rhyme they would simply say:

> Ickle ockle black bottle,
> Ickle ockle out.

Others almost the same were:

> Ickle ockle black bottle,
> Ickle ockle out.
> O-U-T spells out,
> And out you must go. [Wellington, 1915]

> Ickle ockle black bottle,
> Ickle ockle out.
> Turn the dirty dishcloth,
> Inside out. [Palmerston, 1910]

"Onery, Twoery" had various forms, all of them interesting and
no doubt provocative of much mirth in their day:

> Onery twoery dickery seven,
> Allerby crackerby tanerby eleven.
> Pin pan Musky Dan,
> Tweedledum twoddledum twenty-one. [Dunedin, 1875]

> Onery, twoery, tickery, seven,
> Alerby, crackerby, tenerby, eleven.
> Tin pan, Whiskey Dan,
> Twiddlum, twaddlum, twenty-one.
> Black fish, white trout,
> Irry, orry, you are out. [Dunedin, 1910]

Or:

> Black fish, white trout,
> Irrie, orrie, you are right out. [Wellington, 1865]

> Onerie awrie, Ickery Ann,
> Filsie, falsie, dicklie, Jan,
> Quirbie, quorbie, Irish Mary,
> Tickle 'em, tackle 'em, buck. [Waikouaiti, Otago, 1895]

The popularity of this last rhyme may have been partly explained by the presence of Irish in Waikouaiti at the time.

The commonest of the "heaven" rhymes was:

> One, two, three, four, five, six, seven,
> All good children go to heaven.
> Penny in the water, twopence in the sea,
> Threepence on the railway,
> Out goes He.

"I may say that this was rather frowned upon by our Victorian parents as being 'not nice.' " (Waitara, Taranaki, 1900). At Nelson, in 1890, only the last three lines were known. Another version was:

> One, two, three, four,
> Five, six, seven,
> All good children go to heaven.
> Open the gate and let them in,
> One, two, three, four, five, six, seven. [Amberley, Canterbury, 1900]

Others dependent on numbers for their "sense" were:

> One, two, three,
> Mother caught a flea,
> Flea died, mother cried,
> Out goes she. [Waikouaiti, Otago, 1895]

> Two, four, six, eight,
> Mary at the cottage gate,
> Eating cherries off a plate. [North Canterbury, 1890]

"This one is my best. For years I believed it was pure Chinese. Naturally I have guessed at the spelling":

Anna, manna, mona, mike,
Borcelona, bonus, stike,
Care, ware, fro, frack,
Aleka, baleka, wee woe WHACK,
Whack put that one well out. [Nelson, 1895]

The following rhyme was one of the most popular about 1910 in
the Manawatu (Wellington Province):

A monkey came into my shop one day
And asked for a bottle of beer.
Where is your money?
In my pocket.
Where is your pocket?
I left it at home.
Well, please walk out.

"Paddy [or Piggy] on the Railway" was well known by the first
decades of the twentieth century:

Paddy on the railway,
Picking up stones,
Along came an engine,
And broke Paddy's bones.
Oh, said Paddy,
That's not fair,
Oh, said the engine-driver,
I don't care.
O-U-T spells out and out you must go.

One that we thought was very daring in the 1890's and sang well
away from adult ears, began:

"Cups and saucers, plates and dishes,
There goes Sally in calico britches . . ." [Taranaki]

The following counting-out rhyme was used in a game of Rounders, when someone had made a rounder and two or more were out.
The person who was "brought" back with the rounder was counted
in, not chosen. There seem to have been two versions:

Go hearty, fearty, hally go lum,
An old man went out to get some fun.
He got some fun and hurt his shin,
Go hearty, fearty, hally go in.

Or:

> Go heerty, feerty, hally go lum,
> The fox went out to get some fun.
> He got some fun and tore his skin,
> Go heerty, feerty, hally go in. [Nelson, 1890]

Then there were the other slightly obscene counting-out rhymes which nice young girls will repeat for you only with a blush even today. There was the truncated and respectable version:

> Inky pinky penny wink,
> Out goes she [Rockville, Nelson, 1895],

and its source:

> Ink pink, I smell a big stink,
> And it comes from Y-O-U.

One of the most interesting of the old ones, but one of which only a fragment remains, is:

> Zintie tintie tetherie metherie,
> Bamferie oorie over dover
> Dicky dell on tan toosh . . . [South Clutha, Southland, 1875]

§ II: 1920–1950

In the modern playground there has been an increase in the number of active girls' games. Girls have tended to develop their own versions of *Bar the Door* (E-8). These have a "feminine" ring to them, because they demand a much greater attention to colors, names, and guessing, all of which are things in which girls rather than boys delight. All these games are widespread.

In *Colours* (E-28), for example, the runners at the end of the ground pick colors and the He player in the middle calls out the name of a color at random. The player who has chosen the color which is called then runs across and tries to avoid the He in the middle. Other games of a similar kind are Vegetables, Fruits, and Initials, in which the players at the end make a similar choice and run across when it is called.

In *Please, Jack, May We Cross Your Golden River?* (E-29), Jack, who is the He in the middle, answers inquirers who ask the question, with: "Yes, you may cross my golden river [a crack or a line on the playground], if you have [say, red] on you." Those with that color then walk across the playground to the safe base at the other end. Those without the color must run across while Jack attempts to catch them. The caught players join Jack in the middle.

In *Nigger Boys* (E-30), the He nominates the number of "nigger boys" he wants to come across the playground at a time; and in Cross the Bar, the players who are caught by the He do not stay in the center, but fall out. They are called back into the center only when the He finds it too difficult to catch the last players. This makes it easier for the smaller girls who play this game with older ones to run across. For most of the game there is only one He in the middle whom they must pass.

In *Charlie over the Water* (E-31), the game proceeds along the same lines as Bar the Door, until there are three players in the center. These players then turn their backs to the rest. They put out their hands, stand at arm's distance from one another, and drop their hands. The other players now try to creep up behind the He players and run between them. But if the He players manage to raise their hands quickly and touch the runners on the way through, the runners are out. If any get through, the He players turn round the opposite way, and the runners try to come through again. It goes on this way until all are caught. The first player caught running through is He for the next game. Black Peter is the same. Others of a similar nature are Chase the Leader, Farmer and the Lion, Fishes and Whales.

Perhaps the widest known of these girls' variations of Bar the Door is *Sheep, Sheep* (E-32), known also as Run Sheepie Run and Wolf, Wolf, Go Home. This game was also widely played in early days. The wolf stands in the middle, the sheep at one end of the play space, and the mother sheep at the other end. When the sheep run across and are caught by the wolf they are out. A dialogue is carried on between mother and children, as follows:

"Sheep, sheep, come home."
"Afraid, afraid."
"What of?"
"The wolf."
"The wolf's gone to Devonshire and won't be back for seven years. Sheep, sheep, come home."

Whereupon they all run across. This version was played at Nelson in 1900 and is played at Bainham, Nelson, today. Similar though abbreviated versions have been played in most places. For example, at Hampden, Otago, today, the dialogue is:

"Sheep, sheep, come home."
"The wolf is there."
"The wolf has gone to Rattrey town, so sheep, sheep, come home."

In some versions the wolf is away for "one hundred years," in others till "nine o'clock" or till "ten tonight." Much shorter versions, such as the following, seem to be more common.

"Sheep, sheep, come home."
"I'm afraid."
"What are you afraid of?"
"The wolf."

The increased speed on the modern playground is reflected in an increase of tagging games. Some of these are: *Beware the Bear* (E-33), *Black Peter* (E-34), *Bogies* (E-35), *Broken Barley* (E-36), *Burglars* (E-37), *Bush Tiggy* (E-38), *Colours* (E-39), *Donkey Tag* (E-40), *Ghosts* (E-41), *I Saw You* (E-42), *I Spy* (E-43), *Keys or Pads* (E-44), *Kikeri* (E-45), *Murder* (E-46), *Odd Man Out* (E-47), *Opossum* (E-48), *Pebbles and Stones* (E-49), *Penny Under the Chair* (E-50), *Point to the Bell* (E-51), *Poisonous Ball* (E-52), *Policeman* (E-53), *Running Waters* (E-54), *Sardines* (E-55), *Seat Tig* (E-56), *Shadow Tig* (E-57), *Sharky* (E-58), *Snakes* (E-59), *Stone Tag* (E-60), *Tiki Tiki Touchwood* (E-61), *Tip Tap* (E-62), *Toes off the Counter* (E-63), *Tree Tig* (E-64), *Ups and Downs* (E-65), *Wet and Dry* (E-66), *Whales in the Ocean* (E-67), *Who Steps in the Dark?* (E-68), *Witch's Tig* (E-69), and *Wolfie* (E-70).

Of these new games, *Tip the Finger* (E-71) is worth fuller treatment. In some versions a rhyme is used in it:

Draw a snake down your back,
This is the way it went,
North, south, east, west,
Who tipped your finger?

The players stand behind the He player, who stands with her back to them and holds one finger outstretched behind her. The players then chant the rhyme and one of the players tips the He's finger. The He turns round and tries to guess who did it. Before being told by the players whether she has guessed correctly, the He player tells the player whom she suspects what that player must do as a penalty. If the He player has guessed wrongly, she must carry out the penalty herself while the other players go and hide. The game then turns into Hide and Seek, and the first player caught becomes He for the next game. Though called Tip the Finger in Brooklyn and Island Bay (Wellington, 1935), the game is known by a number of other names. For example: Draw the Snake (this name is common in the Golden Bay area); Round and Round the Mulberry Bush (Collingwood, Nelson, 1949; Dannevirke, Hawkes Bay, 1930); Round and Round the Merry Go Round (Stockton, Westland, 1949; Palmerston North, 1910); Here We Go Round the Merry Go Round, and I Tipped the Finger (Onehunga, Auckland, 1905); This Is the Way the World Goes Round, and Somebody Must Tig (this is the common name in the Otago area); This Is the Way the Windmill Goes Round, and Who's the One to Touch It? (Christchurch, 1930); Who Tipped Your Finger Last? (Marton, Wellington, 1944); and Crown (Ratapiko, Wairarapa, 1949).

The popularity and increased number of these running games can be attributed to the lighter clothing and shoes of children today, and to the encouragement which children are given to play actively. These games are mainly played and developed by the children in the lower half of the primary school, who are relatively free to play and are at the same time old enough to develop games of some formal complexity.

The most popular counting-out rhymes of today are "Ickle Ockle" and the much simpler "One Potato, Two Potato." Others of some importance are: "Eenie Meenie"; "Ink Pink"; "One, Two, Three—Heaven"; "Piggy on the Railway"; "My Mother and Your Mother." Apart from "One Potato, Two Potato," and "My Mother and Your Mother," all these rhymes have been used in earlier years. The fact that the rhyme

> One potato, two potato,
> Three potato, four,
> Five potato, six potato,
> Seven potato more,

is the most important one today, suggests the present state of counting-out rhymes. Clearly it is very simple when compared with "Onery Twoery" and "Eenah Deenah," the favorite rhymes of the nineteenth-century playground. This has come about because such rhymes tend today to enter only into the play of the younger children (the under-nines), whereas previously they were also used by older children. Modern children's most popular rhymes are also very brief. Such rhymes are intended not to delay the game for any length of time while the He is chosen. This does not imply that counting-out rhymes are necessarily disappearing. Many new ones are now in use, and, in addition, the class of counting-out rhymes in which the players have a more active part to play in their own fate has now much greater importance than it previously had. All the following rhymes are widespread. The very brief rhymes are:

Icky acky chew the baccy,
Icky acky out.

Each peach pear plum,
Out goes old Tom Thumb. [A relic of Eenah Deenah]

One, two, sky blue,
All out but [or, except] you.

Wellington City Council, W. C. C. [or Auckland City Council],
Wellington City Council, you're not he.

Christchurch City Council, see, see, see,
Christchurch City Council, you're not he.

Call lummy koo,
Out goes you.

O-U-T spells out,
And out you must go.

Umpa umpa,
Stick him up the bumpa,
You are out.

Look up, sky blue,
All out but you.

Pig snout,
Walk out.

It's quite fair that
You should go he.

The longer rhymes in which the players have a "say" as the rhyme progresses are mainly used by girls, as indeed are all counting-out rhymes. In all of them the players have the right to name either a number or a color. There is only one record of this type before 1900, and this is:

Once I had a box of colours,
What colour do you think was in it? [Amberley, Canterbury, 1890]

Today's rhymes are:

Old Mother Ink,
Fell down the sink.
How many think
She went . . . [say, five]
F-I-V-E spells five,
And out you must go,
If I say so.

Engine, engine, on the line,
Wasting water all the time.
How many gallons does it waste?

As the words are said the players are pointed to. The last player pointed to must give a number—say, two:

T-W-O spells two,
And O-U-T spells out.
My mother and your mother
Were hanging out clothes.
My mother gave your mother
A punch on the nose.
And what colour do you think the blood ran? [Say, blue.]
B-L-U-E.

The word is spelled out round the circle, and the last person pointed to is out. Or:

Blue spells B-L-U-E,
And out spells O-U-T.

Or:

B-L-U-E spells blue,
So out you go for saying so.

My mother and your mother
Had a fiddle.
My mother and your mother
Chopped it in the middle.
How many strings did it have then?

My mother bought me a dress,
What colour is it?

My mother bought me a box of new ribbons,
And what colour do you think they were?
B-L-U-E spells blue,
And as you haven't got
It on you,
You must go out.

As I was going down piggy wiggy track,
I met some piggy wiggy children.
They asked me this,
They asked me that,
They asked me the colour of my best hat.

Counting-out rhymes of today which are either relics or transformations of earlier rhymes are listed below. (Not all the old
rhymes have become counting-out rhymes; some have become
skipping rhymes.)

Eeny meeny miny mo,
Catch a nigger by the toe,
If he squeals let him go,
Eeny meeny miny mo.
O-U-T spells out.

In some versions it is "Eena meena mina moh." In others, the
"nigger" doesn't squeal; he "hollers." The following rhymes have
dropped the "Mary" of the older one. Perhaps she has gone into
the ball-bouncing rhymes listed in Category F.

Two, four, six, eight,
Swinging on the cottage gate,
Eating cherries off the plate,
Two, four, six, eight.

Two, four, six, eight,
Eating cherries at the gate,
Eat up, don't wait.

The monkey version has changed from a series of questions to a
rhyme:

Monkey, monkey, draw the beer,
How many monkeys are there here?

Two, four, six, eight,
Out goes my best mate.

The quick counting-out rhyme "Ickle Ockle" is still widely used, in the various forms that have been already mentioned. At Dunedin the children say:

Ickle ockle black bottle,
Ickle ockle out.
O-U-T spells out,
Out you must go,
If I say so.

At Foxton, Wellington:

Ickle ockle black bottle,
Ickle ockle out.
Turn the dirty dishcloth
Inside out.

Many rhymes collected from children today have been culled from magazines and other written sources, and may not, therefore, be "relics" of a local oral tradition. Two odd-sounding ones from Wellington are:

Inky pinky fidgety fell,
Ell dell drom and ell,
Anki panki torri nook,
Ell dell juicy jook.

Ina mina ping pong,
Ching chong,
Isa visa vacka tu,
Vi va veck.

And one from Auckland:

Esa vesa vacka vesa
Mink monk mow,
Esa vesa vacka vesa,
Ve vi vow.

Others are:

As I was going over London bridge,
I met a dead rat,
I one it, you two it . . . [etc.].

The one who ate it was out.

Hibberty bibberty I salliberty,
Pompalary jig,
Every man who has no hair
Ought to [or: Is bound to] wear a wig.

Old Father Christmas, guess what he did,
Upset the cradle,
Out fell the kid.
The kid began to bubble,
So he hit him with a shovel.
O-U-T spells out,
And out you must go for saying so.

The peanut sat on the railway track,
Its heart was all a-flutter.
The train came roaring round the bend,
Toot, toot. Peanut butter.

Did you ever see a bear
Walk a tightrope in the air?
If you did it was all a dream,
So out you must go for saying so.

Oliver Cromwell lost his shoe,
In the battle of Waterloo.

These He games seem to involve the playful representation of fear and pursuit by threatening and powerful adult-like figures. As children in most cultures seem to experience real and imaginary fears about their actual parents, it is not surprising that they find enjoyment in these He games. Perhaps this is one of the reasons for the universality of chasing games.

Rhythmic Games: Category F

This category includes games in which rhythmic movements are essential. They are predominantly the games of girls of all ages. They can be divided into skipping (rope-jumping) games and rhymes (F-1); games involving rhythmic movements accompanied by chants (F-2 through F-6); hand-clapping games (F-7 and F-8); and ball-bouncing games and rhymes (F-9). The skipping and ball-bouncing games involve skills which appeal to girls up to the age of twelve years.

§ I: 1870–1920

In this section, the nineteenth-century forms of skipping only are dealt with. The twentieth-century examples and all the other games in this category—chants, hand-clapping, and ball-bouncing —are dealt with in § II, since they do not show clear historical differences.

It appears probable that the girls of the nineteenth century were not as skilled as their modern counterparts in the art of *Skipping* (F-1). Their clothing and the rough playgrounds of the day would certainly have militated against a superior performance. Skipping was the major winter game of girls before 1900, and it still rivals Basketball for that position today. It continues to be the major winter game of the younger girls. Both in New Zealand and in England, few rhymes were used in skipping games before 1900.[1] After that year, however, rhymes appeared in ever-increasing numbers. The only generally known early rhyme was:

> House to let, apply within,
> Jennie go out and Mary jump in [Dunedin, 1900],

or

> House to let, apply within,
> People turned out for drinking gin.
> Smoking pipes is a terrible sin,
> So Annie runs out and Mary runs in. [Wellington, 1900]

A rhyme which appeared in the first decade of the century was:

---

[1] A. Uttley, in *Country Things* (London, 1946), mentions only one skipping rhyme ("A.B.C., silk satin"). A. B. Gomme, who records hundreds of singing game rhymes, mentions only thirteen skipping rhymes. F. Thompson in her *Lark, Rise to Candleford* (Oxford, 1945), does not mention any skipping rhymes, although she records many singing games. But writing of London after 1900, Norman Douglas, in his *London Street Games* (London, 1916), records many of them, perhaps suggesting that they are both a twentieth-century and a metropolitan phenomenon. They are certainly a play form that has thrived in the cramped play space and playgrounds of the modern age.

> Andy pandy, sugary candy,
> French almond nuts [Auckland, 1910]

or:

> Anzy, panzy, sugary canzy,
> French almond nuts. [Ohau, Wellington, 1910]

The actions to go with the rhymes are described: "We played with a skipping rope turned by two children and sang the above jingle; the last word was always shouted with great gusto. We skipped to the jingle and at the word 'nuts' bobbed down and the rope was turned above our heads while the words were repeated at a faster tempo. At the word 'nuts' we again skipped and so went on alternately until we tripped and went out" (Auckland, 1900). And: "This was a young kids' game. The rope was swung [swayed] backwards and forwards and turned right over at 'French,' then swung as before" (Ohau, Wellington, 1910). Another rhyme used as early as 1903 was:

> Pounds, shillings and pence,
> The monkey jumped the fence;
> He went so high, he reached the sky,
> Pounds, shillings and pence. [Collingwood, Nelson]

Two other rhymes are reported from Dunedin (1910):

> Old Mother Mason,
> Broke her basin,
> Travelling down to the railway station.
> How much do you think it cost?
> Penny, twopence, . . .

In this rhyme the prices were skipped "Pepper," that is, at double speed. In "Cross the Bridge," players skipped across the rope in opposite directions, saying:

> Cross the bridge,
> Cross the bridge,
> Cross the bridge
> To London.

As other informants mentioned rhymes of the early days that they did not recollect, it is probable that some of the later rhymes were known also in this period. Some of the skipping activities known in the nineteenth century have been described as follows: "Skipping with a big rope, with one player at each end twirling. This was known as ca'ing or cawing in Otago. The children asked, 'Who'll caw?' A line of children skipped through. First running directly through, then running through with one skip, then with two skips and so on. Those who tripped fell out" (Dunedin, 1890). "Sometimes the trippers went to the bottom of the line and those who were successful had the first turns" (Amberley, Canterbury, 1890). "In 'Bake the Bread' the skipper had a stone about the size of a penny bun in her hand. She skipped three times with the stone in her hand. Then she crouched and put the stone on the ground while the rope was turned high in the air above her head. Then she seized the stone and rose to skip three times in the normal position. And so on, until she was tired" (Moeraki, Otago, 1900). "In 'Chase the Fox' the children stood one behind the other, then they jumped in and skipped once or twice by arrangement and ran out at the other end of the queue" (Moeraki, 1900). "In 'Double Dutch' two ropes were turned, one after the other, inwards; usually the right hand, then the left. This necessitated the skippers jumping twice as quickly over the rope nearest them and under the one up in the air at the same time" (Moeraki, 1900). "You had to be good at Double Dutch, otherwise you would get a clout in the ear" (Waikouaiti, Otago, 1890). "With dresses down to our ankles it wasn't easy" (Catlins, Otago, 1895).

With single ropes, often cow ropes, the children of the day did "Pepper," skipped backwards and forwards, and folded their arms.

§ II: 1920–1950

There is much evidence to suggest that in recent decades the greater encouragement given girls to play actively has resulted in an increase in the number of their games. The host of skipping games and rhymes and ball-bouncing games and rhymes recorded below tends to support this generalization. The more static chanting and hand-clapping games (numbers F-2, F-3, F-7, and F-8) may well have been played more frequently in the nineteenth century, but that is uncertain. Those reported for the present century only are numbers F-5 and F-6 below.

These rhymes can be classified in a number of ways. In the first place, all skipping games are tests of skill and alertness. In many of them the players skip throughout the rhyme, and then at the end

of the rhyme the "chorers" (rope-turners) turn the rope doubly
fast for "Pepper," to see which one player can stay in the longest.
In All in Together, the players all skip in together, but at the end
of the verse when the players skip out one at a time, the last player
left in must do a "Pepper" by herself. If she trips she takes a rope.
The verse is:

> All in together,
> This fine weather,
> Trip stays out,
> And the last pepper.
> One, two, three,
> Busy, busy bee,
> Nineteen, twenty,
> Leave the rope empty.

Or:

> All in together,
> All sorts of weather,
> I spy Jack,
> Peeping through a crack,
> Bang, shot, fire.

Or:

> All in together,
> This fine weather,
> I saw a peacock,
> Sitting on the window.
> Fish, bang fire out.

In other games in which the speed of the skipping is gradually increased in an attempt to trip the players, the rhymes used are:

> One to make ready,
> And two to prepare,
> Good luck to the rider,
> And away goes the mare.
> Salt, mustard, vinegar, pepper.

> Baker, baker,
> Bake your bread [side-to-side swinging],
> Salt, vinegar, mustard, pepper.

> Onery, twoery, threery, same,
> Bottle of vinegar,

Who'll be game.
Salt, mustard, vinegar, pepper.

Mabel, Mabel,
Set the table,
Don't forget your
Salt, vinegar, mustard, pepper.

Bluebells, cockleshells,
Evy ivy over,
You buy salt,
And I'll buy flour.
And we'll bake a pudding
In half an hour,
With salt, mustard, vinegar, pepper.

Bluebells, cockleshells,
Evy ivy over,
Up the ladder,
And down the wall,
A penny an hour
Will serve us all,
You buy butter,
And I'll buy flour,
Salt, mustard, vinegar, pepper.

The test of skill differs from game to game. Sometimes only the rhyme has to be skipped through in turn, and there is no Pepper at the end, but the tripper is nearly always penalized and must take a rope end:

Bake a pudding,
Bake a pie,
Did you ever
Tell a lie?
Yes, you did,
I know you did,
You broke your mother's
Teapot lid.
O-U-T spells out,
And out you must go,
Right in the middle
Of the deep blue sea.

Others are:

One, two, three,
Red, white, and blue,
Ten, twenty, thirty . . . [the first to get to one hundred with
　　Pepper wins].

I want a teddy bear,
With blue eyes and curly hair,
Up among the Eskimoes,
Having a game of dominoes [the player skips until tripped].

Cinderella at a ball,
Cinderella had a fall,
When she fell she lost her shoe,
Cinderella, Y-O-U [three "bumps" are skipped on Y-O-U].

Calling in, calling out,
I call Mary in and out [one calls in another, who stays
　　when the former one goes out].

Five, ten, fifteen, twenty,
Nobody leaves the rope empty.
If they do, they shall suffer,
Take an end and be a duffer [players run through singly].

January, February, . . . [etc.].

The children run through in succession, and the child who is in at
December must do a Pepper from January to December. If she
trips she takes an end.

Other skipping rhymes involve slightly more complicated actions. For instance:

Bread and butter,
For my supper,
That is all my mother's got.

The player skips in the rope the first time the rhyme is said. Then
the rope is turned over her head while the rhyme is said once more,
and finally she skips in it again. The following rhyme is skipped
with two pairs in the rope at the same time:

Crossing the bridge
To London town,
One jumps up,
And the other down.
If you jump,

> Win ten peppers
> And run right through.

In the following rhymes the player must end with one foot on each side of the rope or take a rope end:

> There was an old woman,
> And her name was Pat.
> And when she died
> She died like *that*.

Or:

> Crackers, crackers,
> Penny a cracker,
> When you pull them,
> They go *bang*.

In the following rhyme the same action is repeated several times:

> There was an old woman and her name was Pat,
> And when she died, she died like *that*.
> They put her in a coffin
> And she fell through the bottom,
> Just like *that*.
> They put her in a bed,
> And she bumped her head,
> Just like *that*.

Sometimes there are two ropes. In Over the Garden Wall, the player hops over one rope swung from side to side and holds another which is stretched more tightly between the chorers. At the word "over," the two ropes are turned in opposite directions.

> Over the garden wall
> I let the baby fall,
> My mother came out,
> And gave me a clout,
> Over the garden wall.

Other skipping rhymes are of a divinatory nature. The skipping player learns, when she catches her foot, the initial letter of her lover's name, whether he will marry her, how many kisses she will get, and a host of other things, which the following rhymes illus-trate.

Bluebells, cockleshells,
Evy ivy over,
I saw a blackbird kissing Mary.
How many kisses did she get?
One, two, three . . . [and Pepper].

A game rhyme having innumerable verses is:

1) Raspberry, strawberry,
   Blackberry jam,
   Tell me the name
   Of your young man.
   [Pepper], A, B, C . . .

2) What is his surname?
   [Pepper], A, B, C . . .

3) Does he like you?
   [Pepper], yes, no, yes, no . . .

4) Is he going to marry you?
   [Pepper], yes, no, yes, no . . .

5) What is he going to marry you in?
   Silk, satin, cotton, rags [repeat until the skipper trips].

6) What kind of shoes are you going to wear?
   Clogs, slippers, boots, shoes [repeat].

7) How are you going to the church?
   Taxi, wheelbarrow, cart, horse [repeat].

8) What kind of church are you going to get married in?
   Church, steeple, barnyard, inn [repeat].

9) What are you going to live in?
   Small house, big house, pigsty, barn [repeat].

10) How many children are you going to have?
    One, two, three . . . [Pepper].

In many cases these rhymes begin:

Apple jelly, my jam tart,
Tell me the name of your sweetheart.

Other beginning verses are:

I like coffee,
I like tea,

I like the boys,
And the boys like me.
What is your boy friend's name?
A, B, C . . . [Pepper].

Charlie Chaplin
Sat on a pin.
How many inches
Did it go in?
One, two, three . . . [Pepper].

I like coffee,
I like tea,
I like sitting
On Hitler's knee.

My little sister,
Dressed in pink,
She washed the dishes
In the sink.
How many dishes
Did she break?
One, two, three, four . . . [etc.].

Father is a butcher,
Mother cuts the meat.
Pussy rocks the cradle,
While baby goes to sleep.
How many hours does baby sleep?
One, two, three, four . . . [etc.].

Father is a butcher,
Mother cuts the meat.
Baby's in the cradle
Fast asleep.
How many hours does she sleep?
Two, four, six, eight . . . [etc.].

Dancing Dolly
Has no sense,
She bought some eggs
For fourteen pence.
The eggs went bad,
The dolly went mad.
A, B, C, D . . . [etc.].

Polly on the railway,
Picking up stones,
Along came an engine
And broke Polly's bones.
Oh, said Polly,
That's not fair.
Oh, said the engine driver,
I don't care.
How many bones did Polly break?
One, two, three, four . . . [etc.].

How many miles to London town,
How many miles up and down?
Two, four, six, eight . . . [etc.].

Cups and saucers, plates and dishes,
Here comes the man with calico breeches.
How many stitches in his britches?
One, two, three . . . [Pepper].

Early one morning, about eight o'clock,
What should I hear but the postman's knock.
Up jumps Mary to open the door,
See how many letters on the floor?
One, two, three . . . [etc., until she trips].
Boy, girl . . . [etc., until she trips].
A, B, C . . . [etc., until she trips; the letter at which
   she trips gives the initial of the writer's Chris-
   tian name].
A, B, C . . . [etc., initial of surname].

In the rhyme just given there are two skippers; the second one enters at "Up jumps Mary."

Grace, Grace, dressed in lace,
Went upstairs to powder her face.
How many boxes did she use?
Five, ten, fifteen . . . [etc.].

The butcher and the baker,
And the candlestick-maker,
They all jumped over
A rotten potato.
I'll tell your mother
I saw a black boy,
Kiss you in the gutter.

How many kisses did you get?
One, two, three . . . [etc.].

Mother, Mother, I feel ill,
Send for the doctor over the hill.
Doctor, doctor, shall I die?
Yes, my dear, but do not cry.
How many days shall I live?
Five, ten, fifteen . . . [etc.].

Granny, Granny, I am ill,
Send for the doctor to give me a pill.
Doctor, doctor, shall I die?
Yes, you shall and so must I.
How many carriages shall I have?
Ten, twenty, thirty, forty . . . [etc.].

On some occasions the other players will try to confuse the skipper
by crying "Trip, trip, trip!"

In another class of skipping rhymes the players imitate the various actions of the rhyme as they skip; for example, in "Teddy
Bear, Teddy Bear," which is one of the most widespread of skipping rhymes and has innumerable slight variations. Most of the
rhymes of this class are similar to the following one, in which the
skipper carries out the actions mentioned:

I had a teddy bear dressed in green,
I didn't want it so I gave it to the Queen.
The Queen didn't want it so she gave it to the King,
And the King said:
Teddy bear, teddy bear, touch the ground,
Teddy bear, teddy bear, turn around,
Teddy bear, teddy bear, show your foot,
Teddy bear, teddy bear, take your hook,
Teddy bear, teddy bear, run upstairs,
Teddy bear, teddy bear, say your prayers,
Teddy bear, teddy bear, read a big book,
Teddy bear, teddy bear, take your hook.

When the bear takes her hook, she gives a pull up above her at an
invisible hook. Another version finishes:

Teddy bear, teddy bear, look to the sky,
Teddy bear, teddy bear, wink one eye,

> Teddy bear, teddy bear, touch your toes,
> Teddy bear, teddy bear, out you goes.

Another very popular one is "Girl Guide Dressed in Blue":

> I am a Girl Guide dressed in blue,
> These are the actions I can do.
> Stand at ease, bend my knees,
> Salute to the King, bow to the Queen,
> Never turn my back on the Union Jack,
> Under the archway,
> One, two, three . . . [Pepper].

Sometimes, however, the players actually say "Turn my back on the Union Jack," or, with less flagrance to patriotic sentiment:

> Turn your back on the sailor Jack.
> Sailor Jack is very funny,
> That's the way he makes his money,
> Salt, mustard, ginger, pepper.

In other versions they turn their back on Sergeant Jack or the Old Tom Cat. Other rhymes in which the skippers enact the verses are the following:

> Madam Morel,
> She went to the well,
> She never forgets her soap or towel,
> She washes her hands,
> She dries and dries,
> She combs her hair,
> She jumps up high,
> And touches the sky,
> Then twirls around
> Until she drops.

> Ladybird, ladybird, drop your purse [a piece of wood],
> Ladybird, ladybird, pick it up.
> Ladybird, ladybird, go up stairs,
> Ladybird, ladybird, say your prayers.
> Ladybird, ladybird, read your book,
> Ladybird, ladybird, take your hook.

The rhyme just above is sometimes chanted as "Lady, lady, drop your purse . . ."

Charlie Chaplin walks like this,
Charlie Chaplin throws a kiss.
Charlie Chaplin winks one eye,
Charlie Chaplin waves good-bye.

Charlie Chaplin went to France,
To show the French girls how to dance.
First your heel then your toe,
Round and round and out you go.

Mother Brown went to town,
She gave me a nickel to buy me a pickle.
The pickle was sour, she gave me a flower,
The flower was yellow, it got me a fellow.
The fellow was lazy, I gave him a slap,
The slap was hard, he gave me a card.
On the card it said:
Spanish dancer does high kick,
Spanish dancer does low split.
Spanish dancer does low bow,
Spanish dancer that will do now.

One, two, touch my shoe,
Three, four, touch the floor,
Five, six, billy kicks,
Seven, eight, don't be late.
Salt, mustard, pepper, vinegar.

Doctor Foster went to Gloucester
In a shower of rain.
He stepped in a puddle
Right up to the middle,
And never went there again.

Girls also report skipping to popular songs and imitating the actions as they go. In some schools the collection of skipping rhymes by eight-year-old girls was something of a fetish, and brought with it continual changes. Most of these rhymes are used with the long single rope. Often, however, they are said by a player skipping singly or by two players skipping together with a rope held by one of them.

Skipping is varied not only by using different themes and variations of rhymes, like those given above, but also in a number of other ways. Players can skip singly, crossing the arms backwards and forwards, or doing double jumps, leaps with one foot, or "bumps," in which they spin the rope twice for every single jump. In the following rhyme the players "bumped" at the end of every line.

> What-oh, she bumps,
> See how she jumps,
> She jumps so high
> She nearly reaches the sky.

Most of the following terms, used with the long rope, were known in earlier days: In Bluebells, the rope is swung backward and forward from side to side, but is not turned over. In Double Dutch, two ropes are turned inward alternately. Duck Skipping is carried out in the crouch position. In French, two ropes are turned inward alternately. In High Water, the rope is turned so that it either does not touch the ground, or turns above the skippers' heads. The latter movement is sometimes known as Over or Under the Water. Mustard and Vinegar signify intermediate speeds. Over the Moon is said to apply when a player runs into a rope that is turning away from her. Pepper means turning the rope very fast; Salt, slowly. In Snakes and Ladders, the players skip backward and forward across a rope that is writhing on the ground. The expression Under the Moon applies when the rope is turning toward the skipper.

One of the most interesting practices in children's skipping today is that of having skipping "exams," which were not known in earlier times. In these the two rope-holders secretly decide what skipping activities they may call for—say, eight High Waters, five Bluebells, and six Peppers. The candidates are then taken individually. The chorers count aloud and then suddenly change activities at predetermined intervals. The skipper must attempt to keep going, and the player who continues the longest wins.

How are the first chorers chosen? In addition to the usual methods of selection (see p. 86), there is Loops. The rope is wound into loops, and every player seizes one of them. The players who take hold of an end must begin as chorers (Dunedin, 1949).

In the next group of games rhythmic movements are accompanied by the chanting of verses in a singsong voice. *Draw a Bucket of Water* (F-2) was played by four players standing in pairs with hands joined. The pairs stood at right angles to each other, with the arms of one pair crossed above those of the other. While the words were said the players made a seesaw motion with their arms and bodies. The words were:

> Draw a bucket of water,
> For a lady's daughter.
> One in a bush,
> Two in a bush,
> This little lady goes under. [Leeston, Canterbury, 1910]

At the last line, one of the players went inside the arms of the opposing pair but continued to hold hands with her partner. At the end of the second time through the verse, her partner came in with her. At the end of the third time a member of the other pair went under the arms of the enclosed pair, but without removing her arms from around them. Finally the last player came in, so that at the finish all the players were huddled together enclosed in one another's arms. The verse was then repeated and the players stepped out, one at a time, after each repetition of the verse. In a report for 1900 from Auckland this game was combined with Oranges and Lemons. It began with the players lined up as in Oranges and Lemons. Two players joined hands in front of the queue and chanted the following verses. At the end of these verses, the front player in the queue went under their arms and chose "cherries or plums" or another fruit object. When all had made their choices, there was a tug of war. The verses were:

1) Draw a bucket of water,
    For a lady's daughter.
    Milk the cow,
    And feed the sow,
    And drive the ducks to water.

2) One in a rush,
    Two in a bush,
    Pray young lady,
    Creep under the bush.

In some versions the players jumped round and round as they sang a verse. In others they played the game while sitting on the ground, feet to feet, with hands joined. The game is still well known today.

It is rarely known by the foreign-sounding name of Draw a Pail of Water.

Although widely reported in the last twenty years, *Wash the Dishes* (F-3) does not seem to have been played before 1900. It involved two children chanting the words and turning about each other. They faced each other with arms outstretched and hands joined, and said, "Wash the dishes,/Dry the dishes,/Turn the dishes over." At "over" they turned outward while still holding hands. The chant was repeated and they resumed their original position.

There is only one report of *Skip a Basket* (F-4) (Levin, Wellington, 1930), and no details are given.

There is only one report of *Hooks and Eyes* (F-5). It needed only two players. The girls stood side by side facing in opposite directions, with their inside arms linked. In this manner they trotted around like the spokes of a wheel while chanting:

Hooks and eyes,
Joined together,
You're a book,
And I'm a feather. [Dunedin, 1915]

There is only one report also of *American Jump* (F-6), and that from the same source. The rhyme is:

American jump, American jump,
One, two, three.
Down in the deep blue sea,
Catching fishes for your tea.

American Jump was usually played by two girls of unequal size. They faced each other, and the smaller one put her hands on the other's shoulders. On the word "three" she leaped up, winding her legs around the other's waist. The taller girl took hold of the hands of the smaller one, and the latter leaned back until her head almost touched the ground. On the word "tea" the tall girl jerked the smaller one, who jumped backwards onto her feet. A "swifter" could also be performed in this game. In this the girls joined hands and spun round as fast as possible, their feet close together and their bodies leaned back and apart.

Hand-clapping Games (F-7) were a form of unison game played occasionally by girls in pairs. One of the best known was My Mother Said:

This was a game we played on cold and frosty mornings to get our hands warm. The actions were as follows. The players hit each other's hands together, clapped their own hands, and hit their sides. This was the order of procedure, except for the last two lines in each verse, in which only the two hand-clapping actions were employed, that is, they hit each other's hands and then clapped their own. Two of these sequences were accomplished in each line. The verses were:

1) My mother said, I never should
   Play with the gypsies in the wood,
   If I did, she would say,
   Naughty girl to disobey.
   Disobey, disobey,
   Naughty girl to disobey.

The first four lines were then repeated, and the following verse was added, with only the two hand-clapping actions throughout:

2) Pease pudding hot,
   Pease pudding cold,
   Pease pudding in a pot,
   Nine days old.
   Some like it hot,
   Some like it cold,
   Some like it in a pot,
   Nine days old. [Palmerston, 1910]

Parts of these verses, as well as verses with other words, were known elsewhere. For example, in Nelson, in 1890, the first four lines of the first verse above (1) were the first verse. The second Nelson verse comprised the first two lines from that same verse (1), together with:

If I did, she'd break my head
With the big black boiler lid.

Yet another version, played in Palmerston North in 1900, has the first verse above, and as a second verse repeats the first four lines of the first verse and continues (after "disobey") with:

Your hair won't curl,
Your shoes won't shine,

Naughty girl,
You won't be mine.

The third verse goes on with:

I came to a river,
Couldn't get across,
Paid ten bob,
For an old lame horse.
Jumped on its back,
Gave it a crack,
Said lame horse,
You'll never get back.

In Christchurch, in 1900, there was yet another hand-clapping game. The accompanying rhyme was unusual, and there is no report of the way in which this game, called *There Was a Man* (F-8), was played:

There was a man and he went mad,
He jumped into a biscuit bag.
The bag it was so full,
He jumped into a roaring bull.
The bull it was so fine,
He jumped into a bottle of wine.
The bottle of wine it was so clear,
He jumped into a barrel of beer.
The barrel of beer it was so thick,
He jumped into a walking stick.
The walking stick broke,
And gave him a poke.
And that's the end
Of my gentleman's joke.

Ball-Bouncing (F-9) is a game which has come into its own on the asphalt playgrounds of modern schools. It is played in a large number of schools throughout the country. There are no records of the game before 1900, but many for the years between 1900 and 1920, with such names as Fives, Tens, Sevens, and Walls. It has been recorded often recently as O'Leary or Sevens. There is only one early report of Ball-Bouncing being played with a rhyme. This rhyme was more often used in skipping:

Charlie Chaplin went to France
To teach the ladies how to dance,
And this is the way he taught them:
Heel, toe, and over we go,
Heel and toe and over we go,
Heel and toe and over we go.

During the first three lines a ball was bounced on the ground. Then, while continuing to bounce the ball, the player tapped the ground with her heel, her toe, and finally bounced the ball under her leg (Dunedin, 1915). One of the more recent rhymes is:

[1] One, two, three, o'leary,
[2] One, two, three, o'leary,
[3] One, two, three, o'leary,
[4] One, o'leary postman.

At line 1: three bounces under the right leg from the outside. Line 2: three bounces under the right leg from the inside. Line 3: three bounces under left leg from outside. Line 4: three bounces under left leg from inside.

Another recent bouncing rhyme is:

Open the gate and let me through, sir,
Open the gate and let me through, sir,
Open the gate and let me through, sir,
Early in the morning. [Wellington, 1950]

The skirt is held in the left hand and the ball is bounced off the ground, coming up through the gap between the arm and the skirt.
Others are:

Bounce, bounce, ball, ball, twenty lassies on the wall,
One boy among them all, bounce, bounce, ball, ball. [Westport, Westland, 1950]

One, two, three, o'leary,
Throw the ball to Sister Mary,
Way down in Canterbury,
Eating mandarines. [Widespread]

Two, four, six, eight,
Mary's at the garden gate,
Eating cherries off a plate,
Two, four, six, eight. [North Auckland, 1950]

This North Auckland version is played as follows:

The first time the rhyme is said, the ball is bounced on the ground. The second time the back of the right hand is raised to touch the forehead between the third and fourth beats of each line. The interval between those beats is lengthened to allow this movement. Thus: "Two, four, s-i-i-i-x-x, eight." In the third round the left hand touches the head though the ball is bounced with right hand. In the fourth, the left hand both bounces ball and touches head. In the fifth, the left hand holds the skirt at the side to form a gap and the ball is patted as before, but on the third beat the ball passes through this gap on its downward flight from the front of the body to the rear. In the sixth movement the same action is performed except that the ball comes up through the gap as it passes from the rear of the body to the front. In movements seven and eight a similar movement is made, only the ball must go through a gap made by the left hand placed on the head, not on the skirt.

This game is said to be common in the Bay of Islands and Whangarei, North Auckland areas. A player falls out when she misses a turn. In most places the game is played against a wall and known as Sevens. For example, at Lawrence, Otago, the children throw the ball and catch it with both hands for seven, bounce it on the ground and against the wall for six, bounce it under the right leg and against the wall for five, under the left leg for four, between both legs facing for three, between both legs with back to the wall for two, and finally while standing sideways behind the back for one. Then, all these actions are repeated as before, descending from seven to one, first with the right hand, then with the left hand, while clapping both hands between movements. Finally, the ball is thrown to the accompaniment of the mimicry outlined in the following verse. On the last line the player faces the wall, throws the ball, touches the ground, and catches the ball. The first time through the players say the verse and do the mimicry while throwing the ball and catching it with both hands as in the very first action above. The players then proceed through all the other actions mentioned above, but saying the verse and adding its mimicry as they do. The verse is:

> Mademoiselle,
> She goes to the wall.
> She never forgets

Her soap or towel.
She washes her hands.
She dries them down.
She twirls her hands.
She touches the ground.

If we are to judge by the games in this chapter, and by those in the chapters on singing and dialogue games, in childhood, girls are the creatures of rhythm, rhyme, and ritual.

Games of Chance: Category G

Category G consists of games in which the outcome is determined by chance factors beyond the control of the players. Distinct games clearly dependent on chance do not have a great place in children's play, although chance factors enter incidentally into many games, especially those played by girls, such as counting-out rhymes, divinatory skipping rhymes, guessing leader games, and some parlor games. Guessing is the most important way in which chance operates in childhood games, and guessing games are mainly the games of girls.

§ I: 1870–1920

There are records of only a few gambling games, for the school authorities frowned upon them. However, in the unsupervised playgrounds of the day, boys sometimes managed to gamble for marbles and matchsticks with miniature gambling wheels. The *Pop 'Em Down, Gents* (G-1), for example, "was a miniature Monte Carlo Wheel. It would last at school only a few days before the teacher stopped it" (Taieri, Otago, 1870). "We played with a wheel for matches. There was a number on the wheel and the number which stopped opposite your pin stuck in the ground was the number of matches you won. The teacher said it was gambling and stopped it" (Oamaru, Otago, 1905).

A combination of gambling and skill was *Ring-a-let* (G-2): "We also had the game of Ring-a-let, which was played like Hoopla.

Bangles or horse bridle rings of any sort were used. You paid a match per shot and won three if you ringed a peg" (Oamaru, 1905). The commonest form of gambling throughout the country was played with a *Marble Board* (G-3). The players shot marbles at the numbered holes in the board, and whenever a boy's marble went through a hole he won that number of marbles. Naturally the biggest holes were numbered one and two and were near the center of the board, whereas the smallest holes were numbered four or five and were at the extremities of the board, where it was easier for the player to miss the board altogether. Marbles were also used in other games. Sometimes they were the stakes in games of Pitch and Toss. There is a record of their being used as stakes in games of *Dice* (G-4). In one game, for example, a die was placed on top of a stick. "All the players had turns at knocking this dice [*sic*] off the stick from a distance with their marbles. Whatever the dice turned up when it was knocked off, the owner of the stick and dice had to pay in marbles to the player who had knocked it off. If a player missed the stick with his marble, he lost the marble to the owner. The boys would pocket the dice if they heard the master coming" (Rockville, Nelson, 1895).

Perhaps the most widely known guessing game was *How Many Eggs in the Bush?* (G-5), also known as Eggs in the Nest and Eggs in the Basket. The game was played with counters, buttons, stones, marbles, or aniseed balls and was in fact a gambling game. Two players began with an equal number of articles, and in turn they asked each other, "How many eggs in the bush, bush, bush?" One informant says of this game:

If the guesser guessed correctly, the eggs were handed over to him, but if he guessed incorrectly he had to pay the difference between the number actually hidden and the number he had guessed. It was considered a low trick to make the number one. The game was also played sometimes with karaka and tawa berries. As a child I was puzzled to know why the eggs were in a "bush," and I remember asking my mother the reason. She, however, said she didn't know, but it always had been bush, so bush it remained. [Taranaki, 1902]

The widespread game of guessing in which hand the other player held a certain article was *Nivy Nivy Nick Nack* (G-6), which was accompanied by the following rhyme:

Nivy nivy nick nack,
Which hand will you take?
The right or the wrong,
Or the old blind man?

Sometimes the player had to guess how many articles the person had in his hand, as in *Hickety Bickety* (G-7) (or Ickety Bickety), in which he said:

Hickety bickety, my black hen,
She lays eggs for gentlemen.
Sometimes one, sometimes two,
Hickety bickety, my black hen. [Tahataki, 1875]

Hot Cockles (G-8), which is a very ancient boys' game, is reported only once. The He was blindfolded and held out his hand. The other players then proceeded to hit the flat of his palm. He had to guess who had hit him. If he succeeded, then the hitter became He. His hand became very hot with being hit, so it was called a Hot Cockle (South Clutha, 1875).

§ II: 1920–1950

Eggs in the Nest is the only one of the games described in § I which is played today, and even this game is not played frequently. But, as has been mentioned above, chance continues to have an important part in play, particularly in girls' games, in the form of counting-out rhymes, skipping rhymes, and leader and parlor games. While boys prefer to win games by outright tests of skill, girls apparently feel safer when their fortunes are in the more impersonal, if magical, hands of Lady Luck.

Teasing Activities: Category H

There are innumerable ways by which children playfully express their feelings of aggression. Because some of these expressions take on a stereotyped form and become a part of group custom they are a legitimate subject matter for folklore study. In this chapter we include physical and verbal tricks, initiation tricks, teasing rhymes, teasing expressions, smart answers, smart sayings, and slanging.

§I: 1870–1920

The evidence suggests that there was more physical aggression, as well as serious teasing, in this earlier period than there has been in the modern period. There are many reports, for example, of individual and intergroup hostilities, fighting on the way to school, between schools, and on the school playground. There are records, too, that some schools had a special fighting arena to which boys retired out of sight and fought out their battles. Often these fights were arranged for the entertainment of the older boys. For them, at least, such fights had the character of play. One informant tells us: "Fighting was arranged for us in a paddock. If one funked it he was crowned. The victor patted him three times on the back and spat over his head, usually aiming too low. I never remember seeing any boy consent to crowning even when threatened. Sometimes he was held. Otherwise it was the ultimate humiliation which no one could stand and retain his self-respect" (Petone, Wellington, 1900). Our concern here, however, is with more conventionalized forms of expression.

One of the common ways in which children of the day, both boys and girls, expressed their hostility was in teasing tricks. As one informant has it, "It was always essential that tricks involving pain or ridicule for other boys should be staged by the more expert barbarian warrior so that there should be no subsequent 'thumping,' 'bashing,' 'lamming,' or 'neckscrewing' handed out by the victim."

Some of the widely known tricks of the day are described below under numbers H-1 through H-11.

Kick, Donkey, Kick (H-1): This was a game in which the scapegoat player was blindfolded, led around, and allowed to kick other children. Finally he was led up to a door and left there to kick at it until someone came out (Moeraki, Otago, 1895).

What's a Ship to Do? (H-2): "We would ask: 'What's a ship to do when it comes into harbour?'

" 'It ties up!'

"Then we would flip out their tie" (Dunedin, 1915).

The Golden Rule (H-3): "We would get a boy to play the Golden Rule. In this game we would all put our caps down and then race around the building. One boy lagged behind and removed all the caps except the cap of the newcomer, who was allowed to win the race. When he arrived at the starting place once more, he found his school cap full of horse dung" (Dunedin, 1870).

Animated Oats (H-4): "We would put the seed of the oat down other persons' necks. These seeds we called Animated Oats" (Dunedin, 1875).

You Have Things in Your Head (H-5): "One child would look closely at another's hair and then say in a shocked voice: 'You have things in your head. They are white and they bite.'

" 'Oh, I haven't,' the other child would most certainly reply.

" 'Oh, you haven't any teeth?' the first would jeer" (Palmerston, 1910).

In the trick of *Skin a Rabbit* (H-6), one child would take hold of another's arm and, rubbing it, would say:

> Skin a rabbit,
> Skin a rabbit,
> Chop him off here.

And at the word "here" he would deal that child a blow on the inside of the arm opposite the elbow (Rockville, Nelson, 1895). Variations of this were Skin a Hare and Skin a Snake.

In *Knick Knock* (H-7), the children knocked on some innocent person's door, then ran away. There was a more elaborate version known as Tick Tack or Tip Tap. A pin was stuck in the middle sash of a window. A button was suspended from this pin by cotton (thread) so that it hung onto the windowpane. Then a longer piece of cotton was attached to the smaller and led away to the gate. A person hiding behind the gate could, by pulling this longer piece of cotton, make the button tap on the window. "This was done at night time. Folks would pull up the blind and peer out. Some more adventurous spirits would come out and investigate and would maybe get entangled with the cotton. Then the culprit would run away to some other house" (Moeraki, Otago, 1900).

In *Jingle the Penny* (H-8), a piece of string was tied to a penny with a hole in it. "The trickster then hid behind a hedge or on top of a verandah. He let the penny lie in front of passers by and jingled it as they went. Then as they stooped to pick it up he whisked it away from in front of them" (Ngakawau, Westland, 1895). Sometimes the same trick was played with a button, or by throwing a nail from a height so that it sounded like money and caused passers to look for a coin. The trick was not always a roaring success. Sometimes the scapegoats found the disappointment a little too much for them. As one informant says, "Once a lady took to us and beat us with her umbrella" (Palmerston, 1914).

A related trick was called *Rats* (H-9). In this trick a piece of fur or rag was left to lie or was suspended in front of passers-by. People would jump because they thought it was a rat. "Men would strike at it with their walking sticks and ten to one would break them" (Charleston, Westland, 1890).

The *Dummy Parcel* (H-10) was a lure. "There was a practice of making neat parcels and dropping them around the roads. Some of these were over a foot long. Those who made them would then hide and see who took them home. I don't know what the finder said when he found that the parcel contained dry grass, stones, mud, and cow dung" (Moeraki, 1895).

A similar but more dangerous trick was known as *Ooh! My Toe!* (H-11). A Wellington boy of the 'nineties would put a brick in an old bun hat and wait for an idle foot to kick it. Then the trickster would wait to hear the victim cry out the name of the game, "Ooh! My toe!" More often this gag took the form of putting a stone in a brown paper bag. One informant reports that his toes are bent to-day because he kicked at such a bag with his bare foot.

Besides these tricks, there were in many schools initiation pranks to play on newcomers. Ducking children under the tap (*Ducking*, H-12) was the most widespread of these activities. Others were of an obscene nature and can only be named; they included: *King of the Golden Sword* (H-13), *Pee Wee Some More Yet* (H-14), *Spitting* (H-15), *Horse's Piss* (H-16) or Under the Horse, and the *Cap-Tug* (H-17).

The most characteristic method of attack was through the use of *Teasing Rhymes* (H-18). The most universal of them was:

> Giddy giddy gout,
> Your shirt's hanging out.
> Five miles in,
> And ten miles out.

It is reported: "Every effort was made, at the first sign of disaster, to make the relative distances more or less correct. We would pull their shirt out as far as we could get it. A whole mob would rush around after the boy chanting aloud the rhyme" (Wellington, 1900). In such a situation there was only one effective response. This was also universal:

> Sticks and stones
> May break my bones,
> But names
> Will never hurt me.

Most of the teasing rhymes of that day, as well as of this, were aimed at the children's appearance or habits. The following were widespread:

> Skin a ma links,
> And lanky legs,
> And big banana feet,
> Jammy face. [Thompson]

> Green eyes, greedy eyes.
> Brown eyes, pick the pies.
> Blue eyes tell lies.

> Baby, baby, bunting,
> Set a cat a-hunting,
> Round and round the porridge pot,
> To get a bit of dumpling.

> Tell, tale, tit,
> Your tongue shall be split.
> And all the little puppy dogs
> Shall have a little bit.

> Cowardy, cowardy, custard,
> You ate your father's mustard.

Religious differences, especially those between Protestants and Catholics, were regarded as legitimate grounds for teasing rhymes. For example:

> Catholic dogs
> Jump like frogs [or, stink like dogs],
> Don't eat meat on Friday.

The victims would reply in kind:

> Protestant dogs
> Jump like frogs,
> Do eat meat on Fridays.

Or the taunt might be:

> Catholic, Catholic,
> Ring the bell.

And the retort:

> Proddy dog, Proddy dog,
> Go to hell.

Adults, particularly foreigners, were also regarded as legitimate targets for children's pranks and teasing rhymes. Several of the tricks mentioned above were most appropriately played upon adults: H-7, H-8, H-9, H-10, H-11. Unlike insults directed towards other foreigners, which were mainly of an aggressive and physical kind (throwing stones onto roofs, letting the air out of tires, jeering, and catcalling), insults to Orientals were often of a symbolic nature. For example, one spat through crossed fingers and then rubbed the spittle into the ground with one's foot (*Spitting Through Crossed Fingers*, H-19). This insult would, it was said, bring down dire Oriental vengeance if performed in the presence of the local greengrocer (Wellington, 1920). Alternatively, one threw one's cap on the ground, and then, clasping the hands in front and bowing the head, trotted round it on tiptoe in the shuffling manner which was supposed to characterize the Chinaman's gait (*Chinese Walking*, H-20) (Wellington, 1910). If this did not suffice, then the following insult in schoolboy Chinese (see *Teasing Rhymes*, H-18) would "most certainly bring the 'Chink' on your trail":

> Tu la marnie,
> Dubble I tite tie.

Girls could combine veiled insults with skipping:

> Ching Chong Chinaman,
> Bought a toy doll.
> Washed it, dyed it,
> Then he caught a cold.

> Sent for the doctor,
> Doctor couldn't come,
> Because he had a pimple,
> On his tum, tum, tum.

Or children could shout, as boys still do today:

> Ching Ching Chinaman,
> Born in a jar.
>
> Christened in a teapot,
> Ha, ha, ha!
>
> A cabbage, a carrotie,
> Turnie up the lettucie.

The Jews had their share of banter, and the prejudice against them was perpetuated in a skipping jingle:

> Iky Moses, king of the Jews,
> Sold his wife for a pair of shoes [bought his wife a
>   new . . .],
> When the shoes began to wear,
> Iky Moses began to swear.
> When the swearing began to stop
> Iky Moses bought a shop.
> When the shop began to sell,
> Iky Moses went to H-E-L-L.

The same rhyme has sometimes been attributed to Nebuchadnezzar and sometimes to Pontius Pilate. Another rhyme was:

> Get a bit of pork,
> And stick it on a fork,
> And give it to
> The Jew boy, Jew.

"Unusual" adults sometimes were the objects of children's teasing: old spinsters, bachelors, or inebriates—in fact, anyone a little unorthodox.

> Follow old Mummy to market,
> To buy a silver basket.
> When she comes home,
> She'll break our bones,
> But follow old Mummy to market.

In the 1890's the Salvation Army, a new institution in the community, came in for its share of teasing.

The Salvation Army had many a rotten trick played on it. The older toughs of the township would throw rotten eggs and old cabbages. We boys would imitate their band. We would parade back and forth, ten to fifteen of us, with kerosene tins for drums, tops of tins for tambourines or cymbals, hollow cones of brown paper, several combs wrapped in tissue paper and squeakers. The band played a number of tunes and shouted over and over again words that sometimes parodied the original words. For example:

> Oh, you must be a lover of the Lord, of the Lord,
> Or you won't go to heaven when you die, when you
>   die.
> Oh, you must wear a collar and a tie, and a tie,
> Or you won't go to heaven when you die. [New
>   Plymouth, 1890]

§ II: 1920–1950

Children in modern playgrounds are less given to activities involving physical aggression than were their predecessors. There does, however, seem to have been an increase in symbolic forms of aggression. Modern children use many more smart sayings, smart answers, and teasing rhymes. This increase in the verbal slickness of the modern playground is partial evidence of its increased sophistication.

Children's tricks reflect the times. Sometimes children have actually posted *Dummy Parcels* (H-21). More frequently, they make false *Telephone Calls* (H-22). In one trick, for example, the children ring up the local greengrocer (usually Chinese or Hindu) and ask:

> "Is your shop on the tramline?"
> "Yes," the greengrocer replies.
> "Well, shift it, because there's a tram coming."

The prank *My Father Has Cut My Finger Off* (H-23) has been reported only for the years since 1930, but is probably of much older origin. In this trick one boy secretly shows another boy a finger. He has the finger lying in a tobacco tin and says either that it is his and that his father cut it off, or that he found it lying on the road. The finger lies on cotton wool and appears to be covered with blood. In fact, there is a hole in the bottom of the tin through which the owner pushes his own finger amply splashed with red ink or cochineal. Sometimes a piece of string is tied around the base of the finger to give it a "drawn" look.

Although it is very probable that some of the rhymes listed below were known earlier, but were not reported, there definitely seem to be more of them in use now (*Teasing Rhymes*, H-18). "Sticks and Stones" and "Giddy Gout" appear to be as important as they ever were. Personal characteristics and habits are still the main targets for scorn, particularly fatness.

> Big fat hog,
> You look like a fish,
> And stink like a dog.

> How long ago,
> Did you cut your wig,
> You big fat pig?

> Fatty in the teapot,
> Skinny in the spout.
> Fatty blew off,
> And blew Skinny out.

> Jenny funny, Jenny fat,
> Hit her in the tummy
> With a baseball bat.

Thinness:

> Jenny penny,
> Stick, stenny,
> Cry old bobtail,
> Skinny old Jenny.

Eyes:

> Green eyes, greedy eyes,
> Brown eyes, pick the pies,
> Blue eyes, tell lies.

Perhaps the most typical teasing rhymes are those which are directly provocative, their main object being to provoke, to tease. When someone throws a stone, for example, you say:

Good shot, never miss,
When you've got a girl to kiss.

Others are:

Ole Tommy Finlayson,
Is a bit of rusty tin,
So stick him in the rubbish bin,
And there'll be nothing more of him.

One, two, three,
[Ronny] caught a flea,
Put it in a teapot,
To make a cup of tea.
Flea jumped out,
[Ronny] gave a shout,
In came [Ronny] with
His shirt hanging out.

Inky pinky ponky,
You're a dirty donkey.

[Diane Carson] is no good,
Chop her up for fire wood.
If she is no good for that,
Give her to the old Tom cat.

Go on, you big bumble bee,
You couldn't catch a flea.

You're the biggest drip,
If ever there was a drop.

Clear the track
For the maniac.

Hop, skip, and jump,
Hop, skip, and jump,
If you cannot do this
You are punk.

Here's sulky Sue,
What shall we do,
Turn her face to the wall,
Until she comes to.

The supposedly reprehensible actions of other children are causes for teasing, as, for example, in "Tell, Tale, Tit":

Tell, tale, tit,
Your mother's in a fit,
Your father's in the washing tub,
Tell tale tit.

Cry, baby, cry,
Put your finger in your eye,
And tell your mother,
It wasn't eye.

Stare, stare,
Like a bear,
Sitting on a monkey's chair.

Cowry, cowry, custard,
Your mother's made of mustard.

Beg your pardon, grouchy Grace,
Hope the cat will spit in your face.

Hey you copy cat,
You dirty rat.

Have a good stare,
By the way, you remind me of a bear.

Sometimes a child can be teased by disparaging references to his or her mother:

Mrs. B. went to town,
With her britches upside down.

Mrs. Brown went to town,
To buy a pair of britches,
When she came home,
She tried them on,
And "bang" went the stitches.

To make your mother dance,
Put ants in her pants.

Mrs. Martin fell down barking,
Got up blinking,
Ran away thinking.

Beg your pardon, Mrs. Arden,
There's a nigger in your garden.

Mrs. Barton, Mrs. Barton,
There's a devil in your garden.

You're mad, you're barmy,
Your mother's in the army.
She wears black britches,
With pink and white stitches.

Or:

She wears brown britches,
With a hundred and twenty stitches.

One, two, three,
Mother caught a flea,
She put it in the teapot.
When she put the milk in,
It rose to the top.
When she put the sugar in,
It went off pop.

Or:

One, two, three,
Mother caught a flea,
Put it in the teapot,
And made a cup of tea.
The flea jumped out,
And made mother shout,
One, two, three,
Hee, hee, hee!

Sometimes it is "old men" who are the subject of the rhymes. And most important of these is "Dirty Dan."

Dan, Dan, the dirty man,
Washed his face in a frying pan,
Combed his hair with the leg of a chair,
Dan, Dan, the dirty man.

Baldy's teeth were long,
Baldy's teeth were strong.
It would be no disgrace,
To Baldy's face,
If Baldy's teeth were gone.

It's raining, it's pouring,
The old man's snoring.
He went to bed to mend his head,
And couldn't get up in the morning.

Poor old Ernie's dead,
He died last night in bed.
They put him in a coffin,
He fell through the bottom,
Poor old Ernie's dead.

Little Michael Finnigan,
Grew whiskers on his chinnagin.
The wind came along,
And blew them innagin,
Poor old Michael Finnigan.

There are special times for certain teasing rhymes. April Fool rhymes have been mentioned in Category C. At the end of the month any child feels justified in saying, with appropriate actions:

A pinch and a punch,
For the end of the month.

Some teasing rhymes play on boy-girl differences:

Boy, boy, boy,
You big saveloy.

Young Jean lies over the ocean,
Young Jean lies over the sea.
Young Ann lies just round the corner,
Oh what liars these women can be.

Little boys are made of slugs and snails,
And puppy dogs' tails.
Little girls are made of sugar and spice,
And all things nice.

Occasionally teasing rhymes are based on school "House" or 'Club" intraschool hostility and emphasize the colors of the group. Thus:

Green, green,
You're the best ever seen.
Red, red,
You don't go to bed.
Yellow, yellow,
You dirty fellow.
Black and white,
You dirty skite.

Older children tend to prefer the more impromptu smart verbal tricks, smart sayings, and smart answers to the formal teasing rhymes. Some *Verbal Teasing Tricks* (H-24) are as follows:

> You tap a finger on a child's head and say, "Head."
> Tap on the left eye and say, "Chicken."
> Tap on the right eye and say, "Rooster."
> Pull the nose and say, "Pullet."

> "Oh, look, there's a spider on you!" [child points, subject looks].
> "That made you look!" [says the questioner, scornfully].

> "Do you like lollies?"
> "Yes," is the reply.
> "Then go upstairs and kiss your dollies."

> "Just saved you" [give the subject a sudden push and as
>   suddenly pull him back to safety].

> "Smell the cheese!" [extend hand towards the subject].
> "Smell!" [as subject stoops to smell, slide fist of the other hand
>   along the first hand into the subject's face].

> "See my finger" [hold finger up].
> "See my thumb" [hold thumb up].
> "Watch my fist" [hold fist up].
> "Here it comes!" [punch subject].

> "Do you know the latest out?"
> "No. What?"
> "Your shirt" [with appropriate actions].

Some *Teasing Expressions* (H-25) are:

> Go and play trains in a wheelbarrow.

> Go and tell your mother she wants you.

> Put your head out and see if you're awake [when someone
>   forgets].

> You can't knock a flea off a piece of sticky paper.

> I can pick your face,
> But I can't pick your nose.

> Good story, bad grammar,
> Now then, stop the clamour.

> Do you want to come to my party?
> There'll be apples and jelly,
> And a kick in the belly.
>
> Half a dollar,
> And I'll give you my life story [to the inquisitive].
>
> You've got a medal [when a trouser button is showing].
>
> Your father's coming out of prison [when a child's toe is
> poking out of his sock].

In addition to these verbal "plays" there are innumerable possible *Smart Answers* (H-26). They constitute a sort of intellectual game and were not unknown earlier, as the following examples indicate. When a child said, "Don't care!" the other child replied:

> Don't care was made to care,
> Don't care was hung.
> Don't care was put in a pot,
> And boiled till he was done. [Palmerston, 1900]

When two children met one might say:

> "What ho! She bumps." To which the other would reply:
> "When she bumps she bruises." [Waitara, Taranaki, 1899]

There are many more of these smart answers today. Perhaps the most common of these is:

> "You know what?"
> "What?"
> "You're a nigger and I'm not."

In the following examples, the smart answer follows the original and naïve statement:

> "Heh!"
> "In the next paddock."
>
> "What?"
> "Before my time."
>
> "You're mad."
> "I know you are."
>
> "Heh!"
> "Good for donkeys."

"You'll get in trouble."
"Why?"
"For sitting on a rusty bubble."

"Joan!" [Christian name of person addressed].
"Yes?" [her reply].
"Joan Smith" [Christian and surname of person addressed].

"Say 'why.' "
"Why?"
"Because I want you to."

"How?"
"Not so bad, thanks" [the original question is interpreted as
    if it were an Indian salutation].

"Why? Why? Why? Why?"
"He's on first base."

"Know what?"
"What?"
"You're mad and I'm not."

"Why?"
"Because Y's a crooked letter and Z's no better."

"I'll throw you one."
"You couldn't throw as far as I can spit."

"Well!"
"Yes, you find water in it."

"What's the time?"
"Half past nine, hang your britches on the line."
"What's the time?"
"Ten to ten. Time to bring them in again."

"What's the clock say?"
"Tick tock."

"What's the time?"
"Daytime."

"Shut-up."
"I wasn't shut-up. I was brought up."

When one child outsmarts a second, the second may take a piece
of paper and write upon it:

2 Y's U R,
2 Y's U B,
I C U R
2 Y's 4 me.

It seems likely that slang has also increased in the playground today and that children occasionally use it to get the better of one another. Sometimes there are vigorous *Slanging Contests* (H-27), in which the contestants try to outdo each other using phrases like the following:

"You're up the shoot."
"Oh, bullswool!"
"Go jump in the lake."
"That's a tall one."
"Go and take a running jump at yourself."
"Shivery dick."
"Shiver me timbers."
"You nincompoop!"
"Oh, phooey!"
"You're telling I."
"You've got it on the brain."
"Like smoke in a wheelbarrow!"
"I'll bounce you."
"Go hang yourself."
"You've ants in your pants."
"You're bats."
"Greetings gruesome; who dented your beak?"
"Ya big lug!"
"You'll get a kick in the chops."
"Go bite your back."
"Nerts to you."
"Mole balls to you."
"Shut your face."
"Go have a roll."
"Dronk!"
"Drongo!"
"Dill!"
"Dippy!"
"Drip!"

A perhaps more sophisticated way of annoying one's peers is simply to talk *Nonsense* (H-28) to them:

Yesterday at three o'clock in the morning,
An empty house full of furniture caught light.
The fire brigade came and put it out before it started,
Ran over a dead cat and half killed it.
Two naked men came running down the stairs,
With their hands in their pockets.
Two dead men went to hospital all right.

It is reasonable to conclude that the most rapidly expanding type of folk phenomena in the modern world is of the verbal sort outlined in this chapter. The increased verbal sophistication of today's adults, adolescents, and children, the homogeneity of their backgrounds brought about by radio, television, newspapers, comics, and magazines, has made them much more responsive to jokes, smart sayings, verbal tricks, and slang expressions, which are shared by all.[1]

Parlor Games: Category J

This category includes miscellaneous games distinguished by certain characteristics: most of them are games for special social occasions; they are played indoors (usually at home or at parties); they are quite often played by girls and boys together, but are mainly girls' games. In general they tend to be played by children from the age of eleven years up into the early teen ages. They are among the games that have been hit the hardest by the new modes of modern recreation for young children, particularly radio, cinema, and television.

§ I: 1870–1920

In this period girls played the following games both at home and at school. It was possible for them to practice these games in the school playgrounds because of their seclusion from the boys. Boys sometimes shared in these games at home, but seldom played them at school.

[1] This phenomenon is illustrated in my article, "Shut-Up and Keep Digging— The Cruel Joke Series," *Midwest Folklore*, X (1960), 11–22.

Many of the better-known games need only be named in the following account. Girls played various types of dramatic parlor games, among which *Charades* (J-1) was undoubtedly the best known. Another game of a similar nature was *Do As I Do* (J-2), in which the players imitated one central player, who acted in a ridiculous manner. "There was a great amount of stamping, pushing, and general amusement" (Wakefield, Nelson, 1875). In *Imitations* (J-3), a person came into the room expecting to be told what to do, but instead everyone set about the task of imitating her (Rockville, Nelson, 1885). *Dumb Crambo* (J-4) was a game very much like Charades. There were two sides. One side went out of the room, and while they were out the other side chose a word. When the first side came back they were told something that rhymed with that word and they had to guess it. They then acted in dumb show the word they thought might be the chosen one, and, if their guess was incorrect, proceeded to act out more words in an effort to strike upon the right one. If they were wrong the audience hissed at them. If right, the audience applauded them.

Perhaps the most uproarious of these imitative parlor games was a game variously known as *Mrs. McKenzie's Dead* (J-5) (Otago), Mother Mumby's Dead (Canterbury), and Queen Anne's Dead (Wanganui).

The leader stood or sat at the head of the row and said to the person on her left, "Mother Mumby is dead." To which the person replied "How did she die?" The leader answered "With one shut eye," or "Standing on one leg," or any other absurd way she could think up, and at the same time acted out what she had said. The second player then repeated the tale to the player on her left and so it went down the line. Anyone who could not repeat what the leader had said was out or paid a forfeit. [Amberley, Canterbury, 1890]

At Taieri, Otago, the formula was:

> Mrs. McKenzie's dead.
> How did she die?
> With her right eye,
> Le kai, le kai,
> With her right eye,
> Le kai, le kai.
> Mrs. McKenzie's dead.

"And we all sat round roaring with laughter as each person bowing to the next said her bit." In the similar game of Queen Anne's Dead the leader addressed each player in turn. They sat in a circle and the leader addressed each one:

> "Queen Anne's dead!" said the leader.
> "How did she die?" responded the player.
> "One finger up," said the leader.

Then all the players put one finger up in turn, each time a new action being added. All the players did all the actions, old and new (Fordell, Wanganui, 1900).

Another farcical action game was *My Aunt Sally Has Gone to Paris* (J-6), reported to have been played at an Auckland private school as early as 1868:

All the players sat in a ring and one player said to the next, "My Aunt Sally has gone to Paris." The neighbour said, "What did she bring you?" "A fan," the first one replied. "A fan," everybody said and made fanning actions with their hands. Then the first neighbour turned to the player next to her and the dialogue was repeated, but this time the player said that her Aunt Sally had bought her a fan and a pair of scissors, making appropriate actions to both. Everybody else imitated her, and so it went, until Aunt Sally had bought a fan, scissors, rocking horse, treadle machine and cuckoo clock and everybody was trying to perform all these actions at once.

Blindfold games were always popular, and of these *Blindman's Buff* (J-7) was the best known. This game has been played in school sheds and corridors almost as much as at home. In the former environment it was generally played in haphazard fashion, the blindman being taunted by the others and chasing them everywhere. At home, however, it was played in a more formal manner. "All the players sat round the room and the blindfolded one sat in the centre. The sitting persons each took the name of some town. The controller of the game called, say, 'Foxton to Nelson,' and those two players had to exchange seats. This they did as quietly as possible in order to avoid helping the blind man, who tried to catch them as they crossed."

Another blindfold game with a more formal pattern was *Isaac and Rebecca* (J-8). "Isaac, who was blindfolded, went into the centre of the ring. Rebecca went there also, but Isaac did not know where she was. He called for her. She answered in a falsified voice. When he caught her, Isaac had to guess who Rebecca was" (Palmerston, 1910). A game of a similar type was *The Queen of Sheba* (J-9), in which a player covered with a rug had to guess the identity of another player who sat on her knees (Rockville, Nelson, 1885).

Indoor treasure games like *Hunt the Slipper* (J-10), Hunt the Thimble or *Hide the Thimble* (J-11), and *Treasure Hunts* (J-12) were universal. The cries of "Hot!" "Cold!" "Boiling!" and "Freezing!" need no elaboration. Girls would sometimes sit on the grass in a circle and pass a slipper around behind them. The He in the middle would have to guess who had the slipper. Alternatively the game would be played with a button or a ring, in a circle or in a row. Sometimes the object would be a ring on a string, and the game was then called *Slip the Ring* (J-13); or, if it were a button, Slip the Button. The form of the game known as *Buttons* (J-14) has been described in some detail; it

could be played with any number of players sitting in a straight row with their palms pressed together between their knees. A leader stood in front. The leader took a stone or any tiny article: it was supposed to be very precious and was called the button. This she placed between her palms with the fingers close together and the fingers pointing straight before her. She drew her hands in that position between the palms of the player at one end of the line and proceeded to the next and the next all down the line. She left the button in one person's hands. She then named a player and asked her "Who has got the button?" If that player's guess was correct she became leader, and the leader sat down in her place. The game could be started by "ickling" for a leader but it more often arose spontaneously. If a row of girls were sitting on the edge of the verandah on a sunny winter day it was quite sufficient for a girl to place her palms together and point to raise a general cry of "Button, Button." [Lower Moutere, Nelson, 1900]

Some games included the "hot and cold" element of Hide the Thimble, but in singing form, as, for example, in *John Brown's Body* (J-15): "One person went out of the room. The rest decided what the absent person should do, such as taking a certain book out of the bookcase and handing it to a person in the room. Those who remained in the room sang a tune, soft or loud, according to whether the newcomer was hot or cold. The tune we sang was 'John Brown's Body' " (Fordell, Wanganui, 1900).

A chasing game widely known in the early years at Sunday School picnics and parties was *Race for a Wife* (J-16), or Last Couple Out or Last Pair Out. "The couples lined up one behind the other with the odd man out in front. He called 'Last couple out,' and the last couple separated, going each side of a line of players in an effort to reach the top of the line without being tagged. Whoever was tagged became the He, regardless of whether she was really a He or not" (Kohinui, Wairarapa, 1900).

Two other chasing games of the day of which no description was given were *What Colour's the Sky?* (J-17) and *There Was an Old Woman Who Lived in a Shoe* (J-18).

General Post (J-19) was a universally known parlor and party game.

Each child became a part of a coach such as the step, the whip or the dashboard. The player who was He started to tell the story of the coach and its journey from one town to another and as he went along he mentioned the various parts of the coach. Each player who was mentioned had to get up, turn around, and resume her seat. But while she was doing this the He would try to take her seat. Every now and then the He would order a "general post" and everyone had to change their seats. In the ensuing confusion the He and everyone else would attempt to get a seat. The player left over became the new He. [Christchurch, 1904]

Today the game is more often known as *Family Coach* (J-20).

Some parlor games gained their humor from the distortion of the normal that occurred in the course of the game. In *Whispers* (J-21), for example, the message which went round the circle was always transformed. In *Consequences* (J-22), "odd" consequences sometimes occurred. In this game each player had a piece of paper, wrote something on it, then handed his paper on to the next player. The story to be written was that of two lovers. First, every player wrote the lovers' names on his piece of paper. He folded the paper down (so that the names were covered) and passed it on. Each player now wrote on the piece of paper he had received, where the lovers met. This was also folded under and passed on. Thus in turn was written what the lovers said, what they did, where they went, what happened to them afterward. At the end all the players unfolded the pieces of paper in their possession and read them aloud.

The game of *Heads, Bodies, and Legs* (J-23) was similar, but in it each player had to draw a piece of a body on paper without seeing the other pieces that had already been drawn. *Trim the Hat* (J-24) was a task more often given to boys, who were expected to be duffers at this sort of thing and might, in consequence, produce some queer creations. They were given old hats and materials and had to make them into something new and fashionable. Here the girls and women had fun at the boys' expense. Another game that showed the human being in an absurd light was *Dooking for Apples* (J-25), in which the player had to dip his head into a bucket of water and take hold of an apple with his teeth.

Various parlor games derived their amusement from some trick that they embodied. In *I See a Ghost* (J-26), everyone stood in a straight line, generally graduated in size, with tall children at the top end. The leader began by saying to his neighbor, "I see a ghost." The neighbor answered, "Where?" The leader said, "There," and pointed with his hand. This question and answer went right down the line till all were pointing. The last player made her statement to the leader. With further questions and answers down the row, the leader pointed with the other hand, knelt on one knee, then knelt on both knees. For the last question the leader said, "I see a ghost." "Where?" "There," said the leader and gave his neighbor a hard shove, and if everyone was sufficiently unaware the whole line toppled over (Nelson, 1885).

In *The Queen of Sheba* (J-27), prospective victims were sent out of the room.

The King and Queen, those who had already played the game, and any suspicious or shy members remained behind. The King and Queen, suitably attired, sat on chairs side by side and upon a rug spread tightly over the seats of the chairs which served to obscure the fact that there was a gap of two or three feet between the chairs. One of the players outside was then invited to an interview. After an elaborate introduction and proper paying of respects, as a mark of honour, this player was invited to sit on the regal throne in between the King and Queen. The royal pair had to time their rise so that they stood up as the player sat down. His collapse and consternation were enjoyed by all present. A cushion generally eased the fall, though the game has been played with a bucket of water underneath. The last victim then took his place with the onlookers and gloated over the "loss of face" of the next victim. [Taranaki, 1895]

Another widely known game, called *Black Magic* (J-28), was a guessing game in which one player, who had been outside the room, had to guess an object that everyone inside the room was thinking about. The leader pointed to various objects and the player had to guess which object was the one thought of. As if by magic, the player was always able to guess. In actual fact he was in conspiracy with the leader, who always gave him some prearranged signal before pointing to the object agreed upon by the other players, such as scratching his nose or crossing fingers or the like.

Some games, paradoxically enough, gained their humor from the fact that the players were supposed not to laugh. The best known of these was *Poor Pussy* (J-29). All the players would sit down, one would be the pussy. In turn, Pussy went to the various players, who had to stroke her head and say "Poor Pussy, poor Pussy," without laughing. A player who laughed became Pussy herself. In other games the humor lay in the barring of certain words. In *Pork and Beans* (J-30), questions were fired at the different players in turn, but they had to answer "Pork and beans." If they said anything else they were out.

In *Forfeit Games* (J-31), or Forfeits, the players underwent some penalty if they lost the game. Unfortunately, many different games went by the name of Forfeits, although that name actually described only an aspect common to many games. It is, therefore, difficult to say which of all the games played under that name most deserved the title. Perhaps the commonest was *Here's a Thing* (J-32), a game in which the players put some article that belonged to them into a hat. One person held the hat, and then another person knelt down in front of it with her head bowed so that she could not see it. The holder of the hat took one article from the hat and said:

> Here's a thing,
> A very pretty thing.
> What's to be done
> With this very pretty thing?

The kneeling person made up some onerous task, which the person who owned the article had to perform. Unfortunately for the kneeler, the article might be her own. This possibility exercised a controlling influence on the penalties she meted out. In some variations, if the player failed to carry out the penalty, she forfeited the article she had put into the hat. If she performed the penalty she won her property back. The tasks were sometimes unpleasant, such as biting an inch off a candle or singing in a corner. Forfeits were usually articles like handkerchiefs or thimbles.

Some of the most popular parlor games involved a romantic interest. No child of the day missed the vicissitudes of *Postman's Knock* (J-33).

All sit down in a room. There is a doorkeeper. One boy goes out of the room. There is a knock on the door. The doorkeeper announces that there are two letters for Miss Jones. Miss Jones leaves the room and goes out into a darkened hall or room to receive her letters (kisses). The first boy now returns and she knocks and calls a master to get his letters. Of course no one inside the room could be sure that the well-recognised rules were properly carried out. It was difficult to assess the popularity of the game. Many of the boys (and girls too) behaved as though they thought the whole thing was like washing their ears. Something that perhaps ought to be done but was a bit of a bother. Others no doubt enjoyed it. [Nelson, 1890]

In a modern version the child outside presents the letter and asks, "Do you want a punch or a kick, or a tickle or a kiss?"

Winks (J-34) was another well-known game with a romantic flavor. The girls sat round in a circle, a boy standing behind each girl's seat. One of the standing players had no partner. He endeavored to entice sitting players to his vacant seat by winking at them. Their partners tried to prevent them from leaving by seizing hold of them just as they appeared about to slip away. *Come and Sit in My Chair* (J-35) was much the same, but also had an element of guessing. All the girls sat on alternate chairs and each chose a boy partner after all the boys had left the room. The boys were then invited in, one at a time. As a boy came in he had to sit in the vacant chair belonging to the girl he thought had chosen him. Meanwhile all the other girls enticed him by saying "Come and sit in my chair," at the same time patting their chairs. If a boy sat in the correct chair he was applauded and remained sitting there. If he sat in the wrong one he was hissed and in some discomfort hurried from the room. The next boy then tried his luck. All these romantic games seem to have been calculated to make the adolescent romancer play his hand.[1] Games like the last may have been contrived by the girls to test their hopes. Little wonder that many of the boys of the day had little taste for these pastimes.

Probably the parlor games that appealed most to boys were more clearly action games demanding physical skill, where a little brute force did not go amiss. Consider *Musical Chairs* (J-36) in this light. *Tableaux* (J-37), or Musical Statues, which was Statues to music, was similar. *Spin the Trencher* (J-38) was another that called for speed. A dish was spun in the middle of the seated circle, a player's name was called, and that player had to rise, rush over, and catch the spinning trencher before it hit the floor, otherwise he was out or paid a forfeit. A milder action game was *Donkey* (J-39), in which the players in turn attempted to balance cotton reels one on top of another. Every time the player knocked down the pile he took a letter of the donkey's name.

Undoubtedly the most important of all the indoor games were the intellectual games, which were sometimes played with paper, pencil, cards, boards, and slates. These could be played in school, at home on wet days, or anywhere there were one or two children with time to fill in. Many were guessing games, such as *Animal, Vegetable, or Mineral* (J-40), or *I Spy* (J-41) or I Love My Beau with an A. "Sometimes we played these at parties, but more often just in small groups at a picnic or a Saturday afternoon play, each person in turn thinking of the thing to be guessed" (Dunedin, 1890). Other games of a similar nature were games known as Cum Je Cum, Fruits, and Clumps.

Many games involved *Word-Making* (J-42) and word-taking. For example:

Letters were plainly printed on cards and these turned over in the middle of the table. The players sitting round took turns at turning a card the right side up. The first player to see a word of not less than three letters, that could be made by these upturned letters, collected

---

[1] The role of kissing games in child development is dealt with more fully in my article, "The Kissing Games of Adolescents in Ohio," *Midwest Folklore*, IX (1959), 189–211.

all the cards in that word and placed them in front of herself. By the addition of a letter or letters to an opponent's word a player could turn it into another word and annex it for herself. The player won who had the most words when all the letters had been turned up. [Wellington, 1900]

Another word-making game was *Constantinople* (J-43):

Players sat round, each with a pencil and paper. A word with a good number of letters was chosen, for example, Constantinople. For a given time, generally two minutes, players wrote as many words beginning with "C" as could be made from the letters of the chosen word, using any letter no more times than in occurred in the word. For the next two minutes words beginning with "O" were made up, and so on. At the end of the allotted time the player with the most words called out his words in order. Those who had failed to write the first word said "No." The "Noes" were counted and all the players who had had that particular word on their list wrote down beside the word the number of people who had said "No." Scores were taken at the end of each two minutes. The highest score at the end was the winner. [Taranaki, 1890]

A similar type of game was *Telegrams* (J-44), in which one person called out twelve letters and the other players had to make up a telegram (Wellington, 1910). Another was *Geography* (J-45), in which each player had to find a place name beginning with the last letter of a place name mentioned by the previous player.

There is a record of girls' turning these word games into outdoor pastimes. "At Rakaia, 1910, all the girls would sit round in a circle on the grass while the He wandered round. When the He threw a handkerchief at a player she would say 'Earth, one two three . . .' and she would gabble quickly to ten. If that player could not nominate a denizen of the earth before the He reached ten, then she went He. The He proceeded through earth, fire, water, air in this fashion trying to catch out different players." The game was known as *Elements* (J-46) and also as Fire, Air, and Water. Most of these games demanded speed. Some did so more explicitly. In *Buzz* (J-47), for example, all the players had to shout "Buzz" when a certain number or multiples of that number were mentioned. If they failed to do this, they were out. In the simpler forms of the game the numbers to which the players must react were the same for everyone and all the players counted aloud together. In more complicated games the players had different numbers. There is a report that a publican at Rockville, Nelson, was fined in the 1920's when the occupants of his hotel were playing the game round the bar. In this version all the players put in a forfeit to begin with, and the player who lasted the longest took the lot. Unfortunately their efforts were attended by a great amount of noise, which attracted the local constable.

The Priest of the Parish (J-48) required similar alertness. Each player had a number. The priest in the middle recited, "The priest of the Parish has lost his considering cap; some say this and some say that, but I say number . . ." The priest mentioned a number and then gabbled "One two three, down." If the player whose number was called did not respond quickly enough he became the priest, and the late priest took his place and number. The response required from the player was:

> "What, I, sir?"
> "Yes, you, sir."
> "No, not I, sir."
> "Who then, sir?"

And the questioned player snapped out another number and said quickly, "One two three, down," but if that numbered player said "What, I, sir?" in time, then the procedure was repeated, and so on. A variation of this was known as The Parson's Cat.

Other *Intellectual Games* (J-49), such as Observation, tested the player's ability to observe and remember things. These games were later made much of by Scouts and Guides.

Slates provided scope for indoor games, either at home or at school. *Noughts and Crosses* (J-50) was the most universal of these. One informant claims that this game could be detected in school from the noises that were made on the slates. Apparently it was not always the cleanest of pastimes. "Boys could clean their slates by licking their hands and then rubbing off the crosses. The slates, not to mention their hands, became filthy" (Ngakawau, Westland, 1895). Another and similar diversion was *Noughts and Dots* (J-51), in which the players had turns at joining together a number of noughts that had been drawn in triangular formation on the slate, to see who could join the greatest number of dots without being blocked. Each player's line went from one dot to another each time he played. The lines were not to go outside the triangle or across another line.

Ric Tic Toe (J-52) (Taieri, Otago), Tic Tac Toe (Nelson), Tip Tap Toe (Clutha, Otago), or Tit Tat Toe (Hampden, Otago) was another slate game. The slate was marked out in a circle which was divided into compartments like a dart target, each of which was numbered. The players took turns. They were blindfolded, spoke the rhyme, and then took a stab with a pencil or pin at the target. Their scores were tallied. Several rhymes are recorded, as follows:

> Tic, tac, toe,
> My first go,
> Three jolly nigger boys,
> All in a row. [Nelson]

> Rick, rick, toe,
> Here I go,
> If I miss
> I come to this. [Taieri]

> Tip, tap, toe,
> Here I go,
> And if I miss
> I stop on this. [Clutha]

> Tit, tat, toe,
> My first go,
> Three jolly butcher boys,
> All in a row.
> Stick one up,
> Stick one down,
> Stick one in the Ole Man's crown. [Hampden]

> Ickety, bickey, my black hen,
> She lays eggs for gentlemen,
> Sometimes nine and sometimes ten,
> Ickety, bickey, my black hen. [Rockville, Nelson]

Another slate game was called *Spiders* (J-53) and is described as follows:

Paper pellets were flicked onto one slate by two players. Our slates all had permanent lines scratched on one side for writing, so we used these lines for the game. Each player in turn flicked a pellet between the

lines. Each time a player landed in between any two lines he put a
stroke on the left hand (or right hand) side of the slate between these
two lines. The aim of each player was to add to the strokes on his side
of the slate so that he could make a spider out of them. It took eight
lines going through a central point and a blob on that central point to
make a spider. [Nelson, 1885]

The first to get a complete spider won. There is a report also of a
game called *Buttons* (J-54), played on slates on a diagram which
was marked out in concentric squares with straight lines across
from the mid-point on both sides and from corner to corner. There
were two sets of buttons and each player aimed to line his buttons
up in a row of three. Every time a player managed to get three buttons in a row he took one of the other player's buttons off. "We
played it mostly at home, but sometimes at school" (Nelson, 1895).

A variety of *Board Games* (J-55) also had a part to play in home
amusements. There were Snakes and Ladders, Ludo, Draughts,
Parcheesi, Halma, The Bicycle Game, Tiddlywinks, Dominoes,
Lotto, and Quartettes. In *Card Games* (J-56) there were: Old Maid,
Beggar My Neighbour, Grab, and Animal Grab. These were the
favorites. Youths might also play Vingt et Un, Cribbage, and
Euchre; adults, Whist, or, at a later date, Bridge. But, "We never
played for money and of course never cards on Sundays" (Dunedin, 1890).

In some schools attempts were made to provide girls with indoor
games to play during the winter. There is recorded that a box of
games, a "compendium" of games, was provided at a Wellington
school in the 1890's and at a Dunedin school between 1900 and
1910. It contained games like those listed in the first part of the preceding paragraph.

§ II: 1920–1950

Many games that have been mentioned are still played by children
today, but are not played as often and do not have the importance that was attached to them in the earlier period. The following games are often reported: Musical Chairs, Musical Statues,
Noughts and Crosses (also with chairs), Charades, Postman's
Knock, Blindman's Buff, Oranges and Lemons, Hide and Seek,
Hunt the Thimble or Hide the Key (see J-11), and Winks. A new

game which has become very popular is *Tail on the Donkey* (J-57), in which a blindfolded player attempts to pin the tail on a paper donkey fixed to the wall.

Games of Skill: Category K

Games of skill are predominantly the games of older children and boys. Boys of eleven years and older spend the major part of their playtime at these games. As this category is a lengthy one, § I, on the earlier period (1870–1920), is subdivided according to particular types of physical activity. The subdivisions are: hitting games (K-1 through K-14); throwing games (K-15 through K-20); pitching games (K-21 through K-30); manipulative and catching games (K-31 through K-47); hopping games (K-48 through K-53); jumping games (K-54 through K-61); running games (K-62 through K-70); and athletic games (K-71 through K-86).

§ I: 1870–1920

In the period 1870–1900 there were no major sports as we know them today, though there were many team games. Some team games were more important to the children than others, but none commanded the attention which is commanded by Rugby, Cricket, Basketball, and Softball, the major school sports of today. The year brought an ever-changing round of seasonal activities, including games of all types. The most widespread summer game of both boys and girls was Rounders. In some areas boys played Cricket, in which case Rounders was mainly played by girls. Shinty, or Hockey, was the most important winter game for boys. In the last twenty years of the nineteenth century, however, Rugby and Cricket grew in importance, particularly in the larger townships. Rounders continued to be the mainstay of girls' summer play, even after the advent of Tennis about the time of the First World War. Softball finally began to take its place in the 1940's. Girls had no major winter sport until Basketball became established in the 1920's, although they did have a major winter game in Skipping. Most of the skill games were boys' games. Skill games such as Skipping, Hopscotch, Knucklebones, which were distinctively girls' games, could be numbered on one hand. In general the girls played quieter games and home games like singing, dialogue, rhythm, leader, parlor, and tagging games.

The major sports seasons were not the only ones. Almost as definite and important were the school play seasons of other games, distributed through the year more or less as follows: In winter—Shinty; Skipping; Hopscotch; Whip Tops; King Seenie; Prisoner's Base; Hoops; Stilts; Cockfighting; Duckstones; and parlor games. In spring—Follow the Leader; Egg Cap; Soldiers; Fly the Garter; Leap Frog; Buck Buck; Peg Top; Bows and Arrows; and Kites. In summer—Rounders; Tip Cat; Swimming; Hares and Hounds; Paper Chase; Chevvy Chase; Shanghais; Butcher's Bat; Cat's Cradle; and Fishing. In autumn—Athletics; Foot Races; Pole-Vaulting; Hop, Step, and Jump; Marbles; Knucklebones; Stagknife; Buttons; Conkers; Pitch and Toss; Pea-Shooters; Bells; Sledges; Rough and Tumble; Sacks on the Mill; and King of the Castle. But these special play seasons were not fixed; their positions in the yearly schedule can be only approximate. That is, most of the schools had their seasons at these times, but many did not.[1] Practically every game in the foregoing classification has been played at some other time of year than the one given here.

HITTING GAMES

A characteristic of the unorganized but important skill games was the manner in which the children improvised their own sports gear. Just as they manufactured their own play objects for the make-believe and less mature games (Category C), so they contrived play gear for their more complexly organized individual and team skill games.

In *Rounders* (K-1), for example, the first thing they had to do before they could play was to make some play gear. Here are some of the comments of various informants on the gear they made for themselves: "We didn't play with a tennis ball until the end of my time at school; usually it was an old stocking rolled up tight and

---

[1] The question of children's play "seasons" is dealt with in my article, "Marbles Are In: Some Observations on the 'Seasonal' Nature of Children's Games in New Zealand," *Western Folklore*, XII (1953), 186–193.

sewn together" (Hampden, Otago, 1885). "A common bat was the stem of the Korari, from the flax bush. It had to be still wet because it was brittle when dry. We called it a Kaladdy" (South Clutha, Otago, 1875). The early games of Rounders were, on the whole, more complex than their modern counterparts. The fielding team usually had to get the whole of the batting side out, a much more difficult feat than getting out only three players, which is the usual procedure today. In some versions the batting team could buy back its players who were out. One complete rounder, if canceled, would buy back one player. "It became an endless game" (Gladstone, Nelson, 1900). Further to complicate matters, the fielding team could also gain points in some games. For example, at the Arthur Street School, Dunedin, between 1890 and 1895, the fielding team got six points for a "fly," which was a catch on the full and put the whole batting team out, and one point if they hit a player between bases, or caught a player on the bounce, which put only that player out. The batting team scored three points for every rounder. The pitcher was from the batting team and the backstop from the opposing team. The batter had to run on any ball even if he missed, and in this case the backstop would try to put him out. At South Clutha, 1875, a full catch put only one player out, but a player could be put out if he had two bounce-catches against him. The first bounce-catch was called a "first-start," and the second catch a "whole-out." From all accounts, players were enthusiastic: "We practised every night after school in the summer. There were seventy-three boys in our class and we had one team. The class elected the captain and deputy and they picked the team. We played other classes and other schools" (Dunedin, 1890). The game is still played today in its various forms, and quite complex variations are occasionally heard of in rural areas.

If Rounders is reminiscent of girls, summer afternoons, and picnic fun, then *Shinty* (K-2), by contrast, reminds us of a primeval dark age.

One other pastime which accorded well with boys in spirit was Shinty, a prehistoric version of hockey, one in which boys of the cave-dwelling age would have revelled. It was played without restrictions as to the sticks used, or the height or direction of the swing made when swiping the ball. The popularity of the game would become a craze. In the heat of the vigorous contests someone would suffer serious damage and

Shinty would be proscribed. Few indeed escaped without hard knocks and losses of skin. But under the pressure of eager spirits the embargo would relax until another casualty imposed the ban. So it went on, and it was not till Rugby took hold that Shinty vanished from the playground. Shinty required sticks, any shape sufficed, and Black Jack's palings were very suitable, even if obtaining them involved encounters with Black Jack. Occasionally iron-shod sticks were used; the wonder is that more heads were not broken. The cry now rings in my ears, "Shinty one, Hockey two, Shinty three, and away." Sid Tarlton, though a duffer at spelling, was a demon with the stick, adding at least one opponent's finger to his war trophies. [Invercargill, Southland, 1880]

In most places Shinty was the roughest and least regulated game of Hockey that was played. Generally the two ends of the paddock, road, or playground, depending on the locus of the game, were goals enough. In some cases, however, Shinty was the more sophisticated game, with special goals and other rules, and Bang the Tin (Dunedin, 1875) and Hurling (South Clutha, Otago, 1875) were the haphazard forms of the game. In some areas in the North Island the name Hockey alone was known (Bay of Plenty, 1885). For Shinty, as for Rounders, the children made their own equipment. "We used manuka roots for sticks and macrocarpa nuts for balls" (Tua Marina, Marlborough, 1880). Sometimes children displayed even greater initiative. "I sawed the wooden end off the bedstead and filed down the rough edge. It was a great ball and lasted for a long time, even though I did get a hiding for it" (Colac Bay, Southland, 1909).

There is only one report of the use of the *Rules of Contrary* (K-3) in New Zealand. They were used as a part of the regular Shinty game at South Clutha, Otago, in 1875, in order to decide which captain would have the first pick of the players. The two captains caught hold of a bat and someone else said, "By the rules of contrary, when I say let go, hold fast, and when I say hold fast, let go." The captain who didn't do the contrary lost his choice of player.

Players in *Cricket* (K-4) also depended upon homemade equipment in the earliest years of the game.

At first all the material for the games was either the product of the boys or their parents or friends, made out of anything convertible such as staves of barrels trimmed off for bats, or rough palings or boards similarly shaped with a draw knife or spokeshave, or toned down by a pocket knife. "Punk" [a fungus] taken from trees was at hand everywhere in the bush, and was used for a ball. Large pieces of punk two or three pounds in weight would cut out three balls. Boys became quite expert in rounding these to make a ball resembling a polo ball. Gloves and pads were out of the question, so the boys knew how the hands stung when a faulty hit was made. [Carterton, Wairarapa, 1880]

Of all the hitting games the widely known *Tip Cat* (K-5) was without doubt the most important. In places where the ground was really not suitable for Cricket, boys varied their summer play at Rounders with some form of this game. There were individual and team games, and the latter were remarkably like Cricket. These Tip Cat games were, in fact, one of the forerunners of Cricket itself. It is perhaps not surprising, therefore, that such games readily gave way to Cricket when reasonable playing pitches (equivalent of Baseball diamond) and supplies of Cricket gear came to hand after the turn of the century. There were other reasons why Tip Cat gave way to Cricket. For example: "Tip Cat came in suddenly in seasons like Marbles, but it was nearly always stopped straight away because children were hit with flying 'cats' and windows were broken" (Carterton, 1890). "One boy received a nasty gash over the eye from one of the sticks" (Stratford, Taranaki, 1900). "In a crowded playground a lot were hurt" (Nelson, 1875). "It was later stopped because it was dangerous" (Seddon, Westland, 1910). However, the game had its harmless aspects. "Half the pleasure lay in whittling the sticks into shape" (Palmerston, 1900). Occasionally the game had other names: Kit Cat (Otago, 1900), Tip Tap (Palmerston North, 1930), Tippenny Tap (Carterton, 1895), Jackstick (Stratford, 1900), Cat (Charleston, Westland, 1889), Cat and Dog (Woolston, South Canterbury, 1900), and Peewees (Invercargill and Otaki, Wellington, 1940).

In the simplest form of Tip Cat the players competed to see who could hit the cat farthest. The cat was a thin, six-inch stick with pointed ends. Their bat (or dog) was a round stick about the size of a cricket wicket (two and a half feet long). The cat was placed on the ground, tapped on its point, and then as it jumped up into the air, hit once more. Most children who have played the game since 1920 know it only in this hitting form, but the further we go back into its history the more complex the game becomes. Sometimes the cat was tapped just as it lay on the ground. At other times it was placed across another stick, or propped diagonally in a hole, and tapped while in one of those positions, then hit again as it rose in the air. Another simple version introduced an element of chance. In this game the cat was rectangular with pointed ends, instead of cylindrical with pointed ends, and its four sides were numbered from one to four. The number that was uppermost when the cat landed after being hit was the player's score, or indicated the number of hits that that player was allowed to have. At this point many disputes arose, because the cat had a tendency to lie in the long grass with an edge uppermost, and then there was an altercation about which side was "really" the top side. An example of the first type was the Dunedin game in which the players flicked the cat up and then hit it out of a large circle marked on the ground. If they managed to get it outside the ring then the number which was uppermost on the cat was their score (1895). To the second type belonged the many games in which the players flicked the cat, then read from the number which turned up how many hits they would have. They had their number of hits, progressing away from the base, then measured in paces or in bat-lengths the distance they had hit the cat away from the base. The total number of these lengths was their score. In yet other versions the batsman had to *estimate* how many bat-lengths he had hit the cat away from the base. If he estimated too many, he was out. If he estimated short then he remained in, and the number he estimated was his score. More often the batsmen had to estimate how many jumps, steps, or hops it would take to reach the cat. For example:

There were two players; we began the game by throwing our cats up to a ring marked on the ground. The boy whose cat went the nearest had first turn, and the number his cat turned up indicated how many hits he could have. When he had had all his hits and had sent the cat as far away from the base as he could go, he would estimate the number of jumps it would take the other player to get to the cat. He could say, for example, "I'll give that ten," which meant that that player had to do it in ten jumps. Sometimes the other player would not try, in which case the first player gained 10 points, at others he would say "I'll tackle the jump." If he got there in ten jumps the batter was out with no score and the other player became batsman. If the player could not do it in ten, he could try again or give it to "stick" (the batter) to do. If the batter managed to do it, he scored ten and stayed in. If he could not do it, he was out. When there were more than two players, they often fell out or missed a turn when they made an incorrect estimation. Each man kept his score as the game proceeded and each player gained the bat as he put another player out. [Gisborne, 1895]

Another even more complex version was the following:

First the batter put his cat across a hole in the ground and flicked it out with his batting stick. If it was caught by the other player he was out. If he didn't go more than the length of one stick away from the hole he was out. The batter then placed his bat across the hole and the fielder threw the cat at it from where the cat had landed. If he hit the bat, the batter was out. If the batsman was still in, then the batsman held the cat in his hand and struck at it with his bat. If the fielder did not catch him the fielder then attempted to throw the cat back into the hole. If he got it into the hole the batsman was out. If it did not get into the hole, or the batsman was able to prevent it going in, then the batsman could go on with his innings. The batsman now propped the cat up on the inside of the hole, tapped its end so that it could rise into the air and then hit it. If he was not caught his score was the number of bat-lengths he had hit the cat. These three stages were repeated until the batsman was put out. [Bay of Plenty, 1910]

The team games of Tip Cat were similar to those already described, except that there were two definite teams in which the batsmen took turns and their individual scores were totaled. In a Tapanui version played in Otago in 1880, the fieldsmen were not permitted to catch the cat, but they could hit at it with their hands in an attempt to reduce the length of the hit. As the cat was sharp-pointed, this was a dangerous procedure. In other team games the resemblance to Cricket is marked.

Two holes were scraped in the ground. Two boys picked sides and tossed up for first play. A boy stood at one of the holes, batting stick in hand, while the other side went out fielding. The boy struck the cat on one end causing it to spring up from the ground. He then hit it as hard as he could and ran to and fro between the holes. Should the cat be caught he was out with all his side. Should he fail after three trials to hit the cat when it was in the air, he alone was out. [Dunedin, 1870]

There is a report of yet another game, called Cat and Bat, which was played in almost exactly the same manner as Rounders, except that when the fieldsmen picked up and read the number on the cat a corresponding number of batting players who had been out went back in once more (Wainui-o-mata, Wellington, 1910).

But the most interesting of all the team games was a small group team game variously known as *Cunning Joe* (K-6), Cunny, Conjure, Conjo, Cunny Joe, and Cronje. In this game the cat was sometimes called the Cunning Joe stick (Waikouaiti, Otago, 1900) or the kip (Dunedin, 1895). It was a game for four players.

Two rings were marked on the ground a short distance from each other with a square drawn in the middle of each. A boy armed with a short stick stood at each ring, a bowler behind him. One of the bowlers tossed a short piece of wood at the ring opposite. The striker hit it as hard as he could, then both boys ran as in cricket. If the piece of wood was caught the side was out. Should the boy miss his stroke and the stick fall in the ring without touching any line, the side was out. If, however, the wood should fall on a line the bowler picked it up, and both bowlers went a little distance away to "conjure" it, that is, one hid it under his coat. Coming back with one hand under his coat each boy knelt beside his own ring or base. The strikers stood, sticks in base, and were required to run, trying not to leave empty the ring at which knelt the boy who had the conjure, for immediately their stick was lifted clear off the ground, the conjure would promptly be thrust into the ring and the side would be out. Naturally there was a great deal of by-play on the part of the strikers in their endeavours to decide which bowler had the conjure. [Dunedin, 1870]

In this game at Waikouaiti (1900), "It was a gentleman's agreement for the wicket-keeper bowlers not to throw the stick from one hole to the other when the batsman ran." Elsewhere, "The circle was divided into quarters, which made it easier for the stick to go on the line and a cunjo to result. There were all sorts of dodges to make the bowlers reveal who had the kip. We would start to run, but leave the bat behind in order to fool the bowler into bringing his hand out of his pocket and revealing the kip" (Dunedin, 1895). "At any time the batsman removed his stick from the hole, he could be got out by the bowler thrusting the 'ball' into the hole accompanied by a loud yell of Cronje" (Paeroa, North Auckland, 1900). "All the other children watching were excited to see which player had the little stick and whether he could conjure it into the hole" (Moeraki, Otago, 1895). At Auckland in 1900, there was a further variation: "When the batsmen had hit the cat they had to run and say a rhyme as they did so. They had to finish the rhyme before the bowlers put the cat into the hole or they were out." The rhyme itself was not remembered. Cunning Joe was almost as widespread as Tip Cat before 1900.

Tip Cat is reported only occasionally in recent years. Nowadays it is a game which, like Cat's Cradle, some children play once or twice at home after learning it from a parent or grandparent. The modern version, called Peewees, may derive from the Laurel and Hardy film *Babes in Toyland*, in which such a game occurred.

A hitting game which was more widespread even than Tip Cat, but of less formal complexity, was *Soldiers* (K-7), a game played with plantain grass. It is still played by children today. "The grass or weed had dark brown flower heads which were called soldiers. We tried to strike off the heads of an opponent's soldiers, one strike at a time. Each started of course with the same number, ten or twelve" (Dunedin, 1890). "The thinner stalks were more durable than the thicker ones. There was plenty of scope for cheating. It was not an uncommon thing for a player to pick some extras when the other player wasn't looking" (Hawkes Bay, 1940). "The players were graded according to the number of heads they had hit off. The one with, say, twelve heads to his credit was a Duke, with fifteen heads a King, with twenty a Cardinal" (Moutere, Nelson, 1930). Sometimes the grass heads were known as rats' tails (Moutere) or as lambs' tongues (Rockville, Nelson, 1925) or nigger heads (Tikokino, Napier, 1940).

Conkers (K-8), one of the great English children's games, was played in New Zealand only where and when horse chestnuts were available. There are reports of the game only from Christchurch, Blenheim, and Nelson, and all are dated after 1900.

Each of two boys gets the nut of a horse-chestnut, bores a hole in it and threads it on a string fifteen inches long and knotted at the bottom. A strong string is very necessary. One of the boys suspends his conker at arm's length. The other takes the end of his [own] string between the thumb and finger of his right hand, and holds it at about chin level. He takes aim at his opponent's nut and then with a downward swipe knocks it as hard as possible. Each takes a turn at this. A miss swipe gives the other boy two swipes, until one of the nuts is broken on the string. The breaker's nut is then called a "One" conker. If that nut breaks yet another it is called a "Two" conker, and so on. The nut that conquers, acquires for itself the number of the nut it breaks. Thus a nut by breaking a two and then a five conker, becomes a seven conker. I have known them to come to eighty and one hundred before being broken. They are a great prize and pride to own. To get our conkers really hard for the game we used to bake them. The best method, however, was to carry them round in our trouser pockets as many weeks as possible. No doubt this had some chemical action, such as the hardening of a potato when carried in a rheumatic's pocket for cure. [Nelson, 1910]

This report is exceptional. In all other reports the informants had not the same science of the game. Usually the conkers were called only "One-ers," "Two-ers," "Three-ers," and so forth.

Spang-Weazling (K-9) was a rather odd hitting game and appeared in only one locality, namely, Denniston, a mining village on the West Coast. "In the same season as we blew up frogs we caught crawleys, put them on a small see-saw device, that is, a piece of wood balanced over a stone, and then before the crawley could crawl off the piece of wood, we threw a rock on the other end of the wood and the crawley was catapulted over the cliff to his doom on the rocks below" (Denniston, Westland, 1920). A later variant at Denniston was known as Hit the Crawley or Strike the Crayfish.

You go over the hills and catch as many crayfish as possible in the streams. You put them on the end of a stick, hit the other end of that stick with another stick and catapult them into the air. When they are in the air you hit them once again. If they fly into more than six pieces you are allowed another shot. You count the pieces and that is your score. Any number can play. It is difficult because the crayfish crawl off the stick very quickly. [Denniston, 1949]

A similar game, which was called Tip Cat, was played at Wakefield, Nelson, in 1875. "The Kingfishers would annoy us whirling around our ears, so we would get a nest of young ones, place them on the end of a stick, catapult them in the air, and hit them once more. They were dead when they came down."

Other hitting games only occasionally mentioned were: Croquet (K-10), Battledore or *Shuttlecock* (K-11) (Paeroa, North Auckland, 1900), and Bumble Puppy (K-12) (Palmerston, 1910), which was also known as Feather Ball or Spiral Pole (Hawkes Bay). There are no reports on the manner of playing of K-10 and K-11. "In Bumble Puppy, a ball was attached to a tall pole on a string. Two players with tennis racquets stood on each side hitting at the ball in order to get it twisted round the pole in the opposite direction to the other player."

Hoops (K-13) may be taken as the general name for a whole cluster of popular activities, for the hoop was a mobile play object around which many special games were built. Games with hoops included Hoop-Racing, Follow the Leader, Just Bowling Around, and Hoop-Flicking, in which the hoop was spun forwards and backwards in the same way as a serviette ring is often spun on the breakfast table. Team games played with hoops demonstrated once more how the children of the day developed unsophisticated kinds of play to higher levels of complexity. "There were evenings when the hoops were out and races or long rambles took place, a dozen or more boys participating. Even stunts were not barred, for hurdles, tournament clashes and bowling in and out of bottles often varied the program" (Nelson, 1900). "Every second Saturday a Hoop Race was held. It covered a distance of about three miles. The juniors were given a good start with their small hoops, but it was heartbreaking just when you thought you were doing well to see one of those six-foot hoops coming up in the rear; more heartbreaking still when one thought he would receive a prize and his hoop broke at the welded joint" (Waimate, Nelson, 1880).

A form of Tops that should be included among hitting games is *Whip Tops* (K-14), in which the players hit the tops with the strands of a whip. Races with tops were the main issue, and in the proper season tops were great rivals to hoops. "It was nothing to see dozens of youngsters whipping their tops to school, perhaps a mile or more away. Hurdles or targets, usually kerosene tins, were often called upon to vary the game. One unfortunate danger with Whip Tops was that they sometimes went through windows, particularly when they were undercut, and as the top usually carried the owner's name on it somewhere, it was useless to make a run for it" (Taranaki, 1880). These games disappeared, as traffic thickened on the roads and as the flax bush disappeared into the hinterland.

Whip Tops was the most highly esteemed of the early top games, being even more important than Peg Top. The whip top itself was a piece of wood about an inch and a half to two inches long, worked to a point into which an iron peg was inserted and driven flush with the wood, not projecting as with the peg top. It was usually varnished, and the upper surface was painted in target circles or some other design which suited the fancy of the owner. The tops were started by being spun with the hands and then whipped along with the whip. There was a special part of the top which had to be hit to get a maximum result in speed and distance. The ordinary whip tops were relatively slow-moving when compared with the racing whip tops. These latter were mushroom-shaped tops about one and a half inches across the upper surface and two and a half to three inches long. They could be hit fifteen yards or more and still retain their spin on good roads until the owner caught up with them. Such tops could be started in the same way as the ordinary whip tops, but the best start for a race was made by binding two soft strands of special whip flax around the stem of the top. The top was then lain carefully on the road so that the strands would not be loosened. It was pointed toward the winning post, and at the word "Go!" it was given a sharp flick forward. In this game the rule was that a top "going down" (that is, running down, failing to spin) must be restarted at the point of failure. There was no "creeping-up" allowed. The top whips were made from flax strips and had handles two and a half to three feet long. It is said that the "know-alls" always chose the back-edged flax and "skinned" it, that is, prepared the white fine fibers with a pocket knife. Whips often had extra strands wound round the handle as a reserve, because the whip might not retain its maximum effectiveness to the end of the game. The season for Whip Tops was the winter, beginning in autumn when the flax was in its best condition for the game. Whip Tops is still played occasionally, although mainly in isolated rural areas, particularly by Maoris in North Auckland settlements.

THROWING GAMES

Throwing games as well as hitting games were helpful, at least indirectly, in preparing children for the batting and bowling of the major sports.

The most important and also the most complex of throwing games was *Peg Top* (K-15). As Whip Tops decreased in importance, Peg Top gained in popularity, although Peg Top was at all times more widespread. The earliest tops used in Peg Top were ordinarily homemade. For example: "We made our tops out of big long cotton reels. The end was cut off and trimmed down. A peg of hard wood was pushed through the middle and then they were trimmed together. Care was necessary to make it balance. We would often cut notches out of the side to make it hum" (Tapanui, 1885). Cotton and linen reels were often used as a material for homemade tops. Some informants report that these reel tops were used only for spinning. Others mention making a peg top from willow, taking it "from the end of a turned chair," or winning it as a prize at picnics and parties, or having it made by their fathers on a lathe or by some local top-maker, at threepence or fourpence. After 1900 more and more bought tops were available, and of these the Australian hardwood top was apparently a favorite. After 1920, however, it was replaced by a light wooden top which could do much less damage in "pegging" but was much harder to spin.

Humming tops, which were imitations of the Maori humming top, described by Elsdon Best, were made by New Zealand children in the northern districts. Here is a description of a Taranaki child's humming top of 1880:

It was a top shaped like a plain whip top, but having a tapering wooden spindle from six to nine inches long protruding from the upper surface of the top and being of one piece with the rest of the top. The top was spun by a piece of string, usually a fishing line wound round the spindle beginning at the top. This string was pulled quickly through the eye of a wooden needle held firmly against the spindle just above the top. The needle was a round stick with one flat end pierced by a wide hole. Top and needle were held in the left hand and the string was pulled with the right. At the moment of pulling, the grip of the left hand on the spindle was released. The humming sound was produced by grooves down the body of the top and notches round its upper edges. The hum was quite definite but not as loud as that produced by a commercial tin humming top.

In most places the homemade humming top was merely an ordinary peg top with notches in it. A whistling top was made by cutting little square holes in the upper part of the top, but not entirely through it. Recently, homemade varieties have been replaced by the mechanical humming tops.

This [the manufactured humming top] was a type that usually appeared at Christmas, a metal top with its greatest width at the middle tapering to the top and bottom. It was spun with a thread round its axle. A swift pull on the thread set the axle spinning, and when placed on the floor the top spun in the direction opposite to the axle. Holes in the body caused a humming noise which was higher pitched when the top spun faster. We usually broke it in three days. We were tired of it by then. Another kind was a miniature humming top with a winder on top. Pressure on this released power and the top began spinning at a terrific rate. This kind required no skill to spin. Years later the gyroscopic top had a brief run, but, though clever and scientific, it too required no skill and was dropped quickly. [Petone, Wellington, 1910]

The plastic tops of the 1940's also aroused little but ephemeral interest.

Among the games played with tops, the most universal was undoubtedly Pegging. "There was a big ring about six feet in diameter. The aim was to spin your top in the ring in such a way to make it finally spin out again. If it didn't run out of the ring the next man had a chance to peg your top, which meant he threw, or rather spun his own top on to yours. Naturally he did his best to split your top, which had to stay in the circle till it was knocked out or split" (Dunedin, 1875). Sometimes the players fired at a halfpenny or something else placed on the ground rather than at each other's tops. But there is no doubt that more enjoyment arose from attempting to "puckeroo" a top owned by another player, than from smashing any other object. Nevertheless, it is reported that tops were not often smashed, even though some players sharpened the pegs of their tops in the hope that they would be better able to effect a split. Some present-day players speak of tops with screws for pegs, which apparently make them travel more quickly out of the ring. These particular tops are known as "commercials." There are several reports from the early years of team Pegging games, in which two sides of players strove to peg a top through an opponent's goal. "You could throw as well as spin your top at the dead top. Frequently our fingers were scalded with the heat of winding up the tops so quickly and so often" (Dunedin, 1875). A team game of a similar type was sometimes played with plain, heavy whip tops. The game of Dumpy "was played on a space about the size of a tennis court and divided into three sections. There were six (often more) players, two on each section. Each player had a whip and each pair had to stick to its own section. When the top was whipped over the back line, that gave a point to that team" (Taranaki, 1880). Top games today are only relics of those played formerly. Often the children play only Keep the Kettle Boiling, just spinning, or firing at a target, or picking up the top in the hand or with two pieces of string. One seldom hears now of knuckles' being skinned by picking up spinning tops. Top seasons have never been as important as marble seasons, although Tops, at least in the earlier period, enjoyed two seasons, a Whip Top season in late autumn and early winter and a Peg Top season in spring.

A game which was based directly upon children's interest in throwing stones was *Duckstones* (K-16). It was by no means as widely played as Tops, and there are only one or two reports from most districts. There were several forms of the game. In the simplest form, the players put one stone on top of a larger stone and then attempted to knock the top one off by throwing other stones at it. The player who knocked off the most stones won. Sometimes several stones with others on them were set up in a row (South Clutha, 1875; Stillwater, Nelson, 1885; Wakefield, Nelson, 1875). At Stoke, in 1949, I came across a game called *Fivestones* (K-17), which may have been relic of some form of Duckstones. In this game four stones were placed about a central stone and the players endeavored to knock the middle one out of the group by throwing a ball at it. Another variant, reported to have been played in Takaka in 1870, included bowling and "collaring" (tackling). All the players lined up and each had his turn at bowling his stone, called "the dub," at a heavy stone called "the duckstone." As soon as a player knocked the duckstone off, he and all the other players rushed to put it on again. It was a race, and every player attempted to impede every other player, and especially to impede the player who had knocked the stone off. The player who restored the stone had the first turn next time. In a West Coast version there was a He player whose job it was to guard the duckstone and see that no one

either knocked or hit it off. In this game the duckstone belonged to
the He. As soon as he put his duckstone on the big stone the game
commenced and the others began to fire their own "dubs" at the
duckstone. When a player had fired his stone he did not retrieve it
until all had finished their shots, unless it fell short of the duckstone. In this case he had to go up immediately and retrieve it, and
while doing so he could be tagged by the He or hit by flying stones.
But the He had to guard his stone, too, and he could only tag a
player while his duckstone was on its mount. As soon as it was
knocked off, or all the players had thrown their stones, they would
rush up and attempt to retrieve their stones without being tagged.
As soon as the He put his duckstone back in place a player would
throw at it. It was a dangerous game, and the player worst off was
the He (Granity, 1895, Seddonville, 1890, and Millerton, 1949, all
of Westland). In the Golden Bay the children had a team version
of the same game which was similar to Prisoner's Base. One side
guarded the duckstones and attempted to catch the other players;
the other side threw stones at the duckstones and attempted to
score runs. A throwing player could only score a run when he had
knocked the duckstone off, and a guarding player could only attempt to catch him when the duckstone was in position. The throwing players scored their runs between two bases. The runner was
assisted by his teammates, who would resume their throwing at the
duckstone as soon as it was put on again. When the throwing team
had all been captured, then the guarding team threw at the stone
and scored runs (Collingwood and Takaka, Nelson, 1890).

Another universal stone-throwing game was *Ducks and Drakes*
(K-18), or Skipping Stones, which consisted simply in "skipping"
flat stones across the water. There is report also of a stone game
called *Dead Man's Dive* (K-19), in which a large round stone was
thrown as high as possible above the water in order to make it enter
with very little splash (Nelson, 1880).

Throwing Hats (K-20) was another game. Informants talk of
boys' spinning their caps through the air in order to make the
heavy visors of the caps hit a target. However, the game played with
caps was more often as follows: "There were two sides with equal
numbers. The aim was to capture as many caps of the opponents as
possible and to recapture any caps that had been taken. Caps were

thrown to members of one's own side constantly on the move and away from opponents. The game was hard on caps" (Taranaki, 1890).

PITCHING GAMES

Pitching games were never as important in the play of New Zealand children as were hitting and throwing games. Nevertheless, they had their place, and the most important of all was undoubtedly *Egg Cap* (K-21), known also as Egg in Cap, Egg in the Nest, Egg Cup, Rotten Egg, and Mingle the Bonnets. It was a pitching, chasing, and ball-tagging game in which a ball was pitched into school caps or holes in the ground. Fortunately, the game is still played at Alexandra, Central Otago, and has been recorded in some detail.

Egg Cap is a game which has been played at Alexandra for generations. It is sometimes called Egg Pie, and is played enthusiastically by boys and girls. The "season" is usually the third term [Sept.-Dec.], and the playing area then becomes pitted with sets of "nests" which are regarded as the private property of definite parties, who vociferously defend their claims against other players. There are seven players in a normal game, although any number can play. The apparatus consists of a tennis ball, a supply of small stones, or "eggs," and an oval-shaped hole in the ground for each player. These holes or "nests" are four inches to six inches apart, and are named after the days of the week, the right hand nest being Monday. There is a line marked on the ground four feet away from the nest. Each player takes the name of a day in the week and lines up behind the line, opposite his proper nest. Monday takes the ball. He can stand on the line and roll it into one of the nests (this is an advantage unless the ball by some mischance rolls into his own nest), or stand at one end of the nests and throw the ball into one, or he can run up and place the ball in a nest (this last leaves him in a dangerous position). The player who owns the nest into which the ball has settled, runs out, takes the ball, and attempts to hit one of the other players (including Monday, who put the ball in) by throwing the ball. All players run as far as possible from the nests before the thrower can gain possession of the ball. The players can dodge in any manner. If the thrower hits one of the players, this player must "lay an egg," that is, he must put a stone egg in his nest. If the thrower misses, it is he who then must lay an egg in his own nest. If two or more players are hit by the ball they must all lay an egg. If the player throwing the ball into the nests (Monday, in this case) throws it into his own nest, he must get it and run up and down between the line and the nests four times before he can attempt to hit another player. If the player throwing the ball into the nests fails to put it into any nest in three attempts, he lays an egg in his nest and the next player, Tuesday, takes his turn. After Monday has thrown the ball into someone's nest, and the play has finished, and the eggs are laid, Tuesday has the next turn, and so on until Sunday has his turn. Then Monday begins again. This keeps on going until one player gets seven eggs in his nest, when he has to "cluck," that is, he drops out of the game. It goes on in this way until there is only one player left in. Instead of the player dropping out completely when he goes "clucky" there is a variation sometimes played where the "clucker" cleans out his nest and takes his eggs with him to the end nest, the Sunday nest. All the players below him take their eggs and move up one, the clucker starting in the bottom nest with no eggs. The aim of this version is to get as near the top, Monday nest, as possible, and "ganging-up" against players is common. [Alexandra, 1940's]

In some versions reported it is usually the player who is hit who has to pitch next. This puts players out of the game more quickly. In other versions the defeated player is maltreated. A great clamor is raised about his smell. "You are a rotten egg!" "Pooh! you stink!" His cap is thrown away (Naseby, Otago, 1900; Nelson, 1875; Dunedin, 1885). "If he mulled his throw the others would hurl his cap away" (Gisborne, 1890). "We would kick his hat out when he had three eggs against him. Three eggs were out" (Waikouaiti, Otago, 1895). "He was clapped out of the game for being a bad egg" (Auckland, 1890). The number of stones put in a player's cap before he was out varied from one to ten. It was the particular aim of the pitcher to feint, to fool the others in order to get them rushing towards their caps. There is a record of slightly variant types. For example, at Oamaru, Otago, in 1905, in a game called *Rotten Egg* (K-22), the players all put their caps down and then turned with their backs to the caps. One boy put the ball under one of the caps and at the given signal they all rushed to look under their caps. The person who found the ball under his hat threw it at the others, and the one who was hit became the rotten egg and the next player to hide the ball. There are early reports of degenerate forms of the game (Wakefield, Nelson, 1870; Charleston, Westland, 1890), in which the players merely bowled the ball into their caps to see who could get it in the greatest number of times.

Next in order of importance in the pitching games was *Bells* (K-23). This was based on the game of Pitch and Toss (see K-26), but had a more innocuous character. The coins for this game, that is, the "bells," were the round, flat tops of the cylindrical Bell Wax Vesta matchboxes. The head was the blue end with red flowers in the middle. The "sugaries" at the other end of the box (the spot on which the match was struck) were not often used, although there is one report in which they were said to represent half the value of the bell. There were several variants of the game. In one, the players threw the bells up to a line and the one whose bell landed nearest to the line took the lot (Palmerston, 1900). In another variant, the owner of the bell nearest to the line picked up all the bells, threw them in the air, and claimed all those that came down heads. The next nearest had the next throw with the remaining bells, and so on, until there were none left (Wellington, 1900). "You could say three up or six up, etc., according to the number of bell tops you intended to throw up to the line or wall" (Ohau, Wellington, 1910). "In some versions the game was played with marbles, which were thrown up to a peg, and the bells were used as coinage with which to pay the winner; and of course we tramped the gutters to get them" (Sumner, Canterbury, 1910). There are no New Zealand reports of Bells before 1890, although there are reports of a similar game known by the name of *Buttons* (K-24). In this game the players threw buttons up to a line and the one whose button came nearest took all. Naturally enough, it was a very unpopular game with parents, as the boys took the buttons off their own coats or trouser flies. The marble game of *Knock-Backs* (K-25), Span-'Em, Backits, or Leggings-Out was also sometimes played with buttons, and the rules were much the same as in the game just described. Players threw up to a wall and the one whose button fell nearest to the wall tried to "hand-span" from his own button to the others. If he could do this he took their buttons. "They would play it with buttons until there were no buttons left on their clothes and the game was put beyond the pale" (Kaikohe, North Auckland, 1910).

Pitch and Toss (K-26), or Chuckfarthing, with coins is more often mentioned as an adolescent than as an elementary school diversion for boys. One report refers to a game called *Shove Penny* (K-27), in which the boy who pitched nearest took all the pennies, lined them up in his hand, threw them up in the air, and kept all those he could catch on the back of his hand (Auckland, 1910). A variation of this was Shove Ha'penny. An odd pitching game was *Toodle-em-Buck* (K-28) (Richmond, Nelson, 1919), in which a piece of broomstick a foot in length was placed upright in a circle about two feet in diameter and a button was placed on top of the stick. Players pitched another piece of broomstick of the same size at the upstanding piece in an attempt to knock it over and send the button outside the circle. The game was played to the cry of "Roll up, tumble up, come and play the game of Toodle-em-buck." There is report also of *Quoits* (K-29), played with horseshoes. "The horseshoe was thrown at the stick and had to stay inside the ring drawn around that stick" (Epokongino, Wairarapa, 1915). Quoits are referred to more generally in Westland reports, where the game was a regular adjunct to hotel life for many years. Hoopla is occasionally mentioned. *Skittles* (K-30), or Ninepins, although not often mentioned, was also played in conjunction with hotel life before the days of billiards, and can be assumed to have had a place as one of the pitching games of pioneer childhood.

Manipulative and Catching Games

Manipulative and catching games are in many respects the unique games of childhood. Marbles, Knucklebones, Stagknife, and the others do not appear to "prepare" children for major sports in the way that throwing and hitting games so obviously do. Perhaps for this reason they seem to be the special preserve of children.

Stagknife (K-31), a universal game of nineteenth-century childhood, was important because it was played with the most treasured play object of all boys, the pocket knife. Although known in nearly all parts of New Zealand by the name of Stagknife, the game was also known as Bites, Jackknife, Stabknife, Knifey, Momley Peg, and Throwing a Knife. The numerous variations followed more or less closely this pattern: There were generally two players, sometimes three or four, who each sought to deflect the point of the pocket knife from certain parts of the body by a flick of the hand in such a way that the blade would stick firmly into the ground. All experts tried to make the knife stick in upright, and also showed their ability by slipping their flat hands under a leaning knife without disturbing it. Every movement had to be done three times.

Typical movements were: (1) Place the open pocket knife (loose) [name of movement] on the closed knuckles of the right hand, point the knife towards the thumb, then with a quick upward flick of the hand to the left, deflect the point of the knife into the ground. (2) The same as in movement 1, but with the left hand. (3) Hold the open knife in the right hand, parallel with the fingers, point outward, fingers tapered round the handle of the knife; then with a downward flick, release the knife and drive the blade into the ground. (4) Start with the knife in the right hand, as in movement 3, but this time with the point of the blade facing toward the wrist; then with a forward and upward flick cause the knife to "upend" and land on its point in the ground. (5) With the handle pointed to the left, and the knife blade resting on the forefinger of the right hand and with its point under the thumb, apply pressure with the thumb while raising the hand slightly upward and leftward to cause the knife to turn over and land on its point (called "tips"). (6) Place the point of the knife on the left elbow, with the left arm bent. Hold it there momentarily with the tip of the right-hand index finger. Then with a downward sweep draw the handle slightly toward the body and cause the knife to turn and land point downward. (7) Similarly, place the point of the knife on the left shoulder, hold it there with the right index finger, and flick it downward so that it turns over and sticks in the ground. Repeat this action off the right shoulder. (8) Repeat the same movement, but flick the knife off the knee. (9) Repeat the movement, but flick the knife from the chest off a button of the coat or vest. (10) Repeat the movement, flicking the knife from the cap or hat while the head is bent. (11) Finally, stick the knife into the ground at such an angle as to allow the flat hand, palm upwards, to pass under the handle. Then, strike the knife sharply upward and forward to cause it to come out of the ground, upend once or twice, and land on its point. This shot was known as the "somersault" or "leap the gate," and often caused the players to cut their hands. "The game was played almost exclusively by boys, though my sisters were fairly expert. The somersault generally only took one turn. More turns were permitted, but they were considered bad luck" (Taranaki, 1880). The winner in this game was, of course, the one who could go right through the series first. When a player failed a shot, the next player commenced, and the first player recommenced later at the stage at which he had failed. Other movements are reported. Throwing the knife: "Off the ear, from between the teeth, and between the fingers" (Waimate, Nelson, 1880). "Off the toe" (Heriot, Canterbury, 1920). "Off the coat lapel" (Nelson, 1875). At least one variation involved a penalty for the loser. "The winner took a peg and was allowed to hit it into the ground with three smacks of his knife. The loser had to pull it out again with his teeth" (Collingwood, Nelson, 1890).

In another type of Stagknife the game was played with the big blade half closed and the small blade open. The point of the big blade was then stuck into the ground (or board), and the handle, which was parallel to the ground, was given an upward flick with the finger. Points were awarded according to the way in which the knife landed. If the small blade stuck in and the whole knife stood up in a vertical position, that was worth four points. If both blades stuck in, that was three points. If the knife somersaulted and returned to its original position, that was one point (Nelson, 1895). The game is reported as having been played at Nelson in 1935. There is record of a similar game having been played with matchboxes at Lower Moutere in 1930. The matchbox was placed on the edge of the desk top so that it overlapped the desk. It was then flicked upward, and points were awarded according to the way in which it landed on the desk: ten points for the end, five for the side, and one for the flat. Another variation was a development of the action "leap the gate," of Stagknife (see movement 11, above). In this game the knife was stuck into the ground at an angle and driven along by blows with the hand. The winner was the player who could cover a set distance in the fewest shots (Christchurch, 1920).

Pegknife (K-32), a more savage game than Stagknife, was generally known by the latter name. It developed probably from a fusion of Stagknife and Pegging. "In this game the players toss up to see who will be the first to put his knife down. He throws it into the ring. The others then have a turn each to see whether they can split his knife handle by throwing their knives at it. It was not a popular game, as a good knife was easily spoilt, which was, after all, the aim of the game" (Nelson, 1875). At times, savage play with pocket knives went even further than this. "There was a passion for blood-letting rivalling that of the apothecaries of the old school.

The boys' amusement sometimes took the form of jabbing one another with the point of a pocket knife. Some queer carving was sometimes done in this way" (Invercargill, 1880).

We come next to *Marbles* (K-33), the greatest of all games within the children's play world. It would be possible to write a book on this game alone. Only selections of the collected material can be given here. The game was known in New Zealand from the earliest years. In certain North Auckland mining districts in the 1870's and 1880's, according to some reports, adults organized marble "schools," with gambling on the side.

Marbles had a language of its own. There were names for the marbles, the games, and all the various aspects of the play. There were terms for marbles such as "taw" or "shooter," referring to the marble used to fire with; "dubs," "dates," "stakes," "dukes," or "changers," referring to the marbles put down to be fired at. Then there were the terms referring to particular kinds of marbles: for example, agates, aggies, aggotties, American alleys, blood alleys, bomb-squashers, bonies, bonsers, bottlies, bull's eyes, bum-squashers, cat's eyes, chinkies, connies, duckies, eggies, glassies, Greeks, milkies, molly-bars, mulley-bars, peelies, peewees, pisswees, pretties, Scotties, Scottish alleys, smokies, stinkies, stonies, stripies, tom-bobblers, white-alleys, and in more recent years ball-bearings, chippies, plastics, and woodies. These, of course, had their respective exchange rates, which differed from one another and from place to place and changed with the passage of years. For example:

When I first went to school, bottlies were good currency, being classed as two-ers, but usually sodawaters and black-bottlies counted as the equivalent of six-ers. Rapidly this changed and first of all, bottlies were classed as two-ers and then two-ers were not acceptable as currency. There was just nothing you could do with them except use them in shanghais, a practice much discouraged by adults, especially those with windows on to a street. Strangely enough, as they went out of currency they were seldom seen in use as taws. [Petone, Wellington, 1913]

In the nineteenth century the ring game seems to have been the most popular marble game. (In more recent years marble games with holes have had the greater role.) There was Big Ring, in which a circle a yard or more in diameter was drawn on the ground; there was the mullibar variation, in which an outsize taw was catapulted amongst the marbles in this circle. There were Little Ring, Liney, Follows, Follow the Taw, Holey, and then, on a less important scale, Butcher's Board, in which the marbles were bowled through holes in a board, Eye-Drop, Knock-Backs, Leggings-Out (or Leggin's-Out), Span-'Em, and Backits. The last was more usually a girls' game.

Some of the typical terms used in marbles referred to the act of shooting and the movement of the marbles. Those related to ways of shooting marbles were cribbing, firsts, fudging, funks, funnicks, funnigans, flunks, forces, knee-high, knuckle-down-stiff, knuckles, and lasts. Terms connected with the movement of the marbles were: cannons, clears, dead-stick, double-hits, fires, funs, gees, haystacks, in smug, keeps, kills, kisses, lay-ups, manyes, ones, pink, ringer, rolls, scat, screws, skinned, skun, spiders, sported-off, stays, stops, tracks, throughs.

Here is Little Ring as played in Waitara, Taranaki, in 1899:

A team would consist of six to eight boys, and the first would say "I'll play you first big ring or last little ring!" The challenge being taken up for, say, Little Ring, the second boy would say "First to it," the third boy "Second to it," the fourth boy "Third to it," and so on till all were engaged; and the boy who had the last say as to position, would be required to "fire" first, and so on in reverse order down the line, till the one who said "Last little ring" would be of course the last to fire. An oval ring was described in the earth by means of a stick, and each player would "dub in" one marble (in this case suppose six players). A line was drawn some six or eight feet away, as the firing line, and the first player sang out "Fire!" as he fired the first shot. It was very necessary to say "Fire!" Otherwise, if he failed to do so, and a marble was knocked out of the ring by his first shot, he had to replace it. By saying "Fire!" he could, of course, retain it. Suppose, however, during the first round no marble was knocked out; then we would see six "taws" (as they were called) ranged in different positions near the ring, like approach shots in golf. The object of going "last" was to give the last player the opportunity of hitting not only the marbles in the ring but any of the five other "taws" which had been fired ahead of him. If he managed to hit one of these "taws" when "firing" he immediately had another shot. The boy who fired first would not have this added target, but merely the marbles in the ring. Suppose again, however, that the six have "fired" and no marbles were hit. Then the "taw" nearest the ring would have the right to fire the next shot, irrespective of the order in which he had at first played. He could either shoot at the "taw" lying nearest him, or at the marbles in the ring. If he hit the neighbouring "taw" he would endeavour to send it flying as far as possible from the ring, while his own would "stick" at the place of impact. This would give him another shot. That would be a good "taw" indeed. If it could "stick" well, it was called a "good stick" (i.e., sticker or stayer). A "taw" was usually an "alley" or "blood alley" made of agate. We used to take them home and burn them in a fire to convert them into "blood alleys." If there was an obstruction in the line of fire, the player who had the next shot, and was awaiting his turn, would wait until the last shot before his was fired and shout "everythings!" That gave him the right to clear away the obstruction. But he did not have it all his own way, because the others would be watching too, and ready to shout "nothings" as soon as, but not before, the last shot was fired. If, therefore, he was forestalled in the shout, he was not allowed to remove the obstruction. Many heated arguments arose as to who said "everythings" or "nothings" first. If a player's "taw" touched a marble and lay alongside it, the others would shout "knuckle down" just before his turn. He would endeavour to say "no knuckles," and if he got in first, he was allowed to withdraw his taw a short distance and shoot in comfort. "Knuckle down" meant that the player had to hold his taw close to the marble attacked and fire it in that very inconvenient position. Measuring distances was done by foot lengths (or boot lengths, if boots were worn). Many went to school barefooted, which was quite a common occurrence. When a boy lost all his marbles at play, he was "scat." If he wished to continue playing he could always ask a friend to "dub in" for him, and make repayments if he won again. If a player wished to improve his position nearer the ring, after having fired his first shot (or he may have been shot away by another taw) he could "lay-up," that is, toss the marble nearer the ring by holding it in the palm of his hand. This was not a shot, and if he knocked a marble out of the ring, he had to replace it. A "ringer" was a taw which, when fired at the commencement of the game, lodged in the track of the ring itself; that, and knocking a marble out when he "fired" were the perfect shots. A taw which lodged within the ring was not a "ringer" and had to yield pride of place to the "ringer" when the next turn came. To fire a shot while holding the hand nearer to the ring than where the taw had lain, was to "funk," an unforgiveable crime.

Knucklebones (K-34) was played in both Europe and Polynesia, independently at first. In the nineteenth century distinct European and Maori versions were known. More recently, the two types have merged, and today the Maori children, who are mainly responsible for perpetuating the game in New Zealand, include in their games movements borrowed from European tradition. We are concerned here, however, with the European rather than the Maori game. In most of the provinces the game was known as Knucklebones, and it is widely reported as having been played by New Zealand children of European origin until about 1900. Occasionally it was known as Chucks, Chuckstones, Chuckystones, Fingerstones, Hucklebones, Jacks, Jackstones, Knuckles, or Knucklestones. Children still played it here and there throughout the country in 1949, but they knew little about it until plastic knuckles were imported in 1954 in large quantities and revived the game. Before 1900 the game was particularly interesting for the ways in which children acquired and looked after the bones. For example:

My brother, sisters and schoolmates and I would search the paddocks and walk many miles in doing so, to find the decayed and bleached remains of a dead sheep. I shudder now when I recall how we would poke among the bones until we found the coveted knuckle, which upon arriving at our home we would scrub and polish. As the boys, yes and girls too, kept their marbles in marble bags, so we carried our knucklebones in bags made specially for that purpose. In those days children travelled from as far south as Glasnevin and Waipara by train to attend the Waikari public school. We wiled away our time playing knucklebones much to the train passengers' amusement. [Otago, 1880]

"They [the knuckles] were used plain or dyed brown with onion skin, yellow with wattle bark, pink with red ink or purple with indelible pencil. Handling year after year gave the bones the patina of old ivory, so the natural ones were really the lovely ones" (Napier, 1904). "They were carried in our pockets until they went white" (Wakefield, Nelson, 1870). "There was great competition to see who could have their sets dyed the prettiest colours. *Auckland Weekly* covers put in an old tin and boiled with bones were most popular" (Ross, Westland, 1910). "The bones were dyed red with red ink or cochineal and there was much careful swapping to build up a good set" (Nelson, 1875).

The game was generally played with five sheep's knucklebones, and at times with other objects such as ordinary stones (the usual object amongst the Maoris) or peach stones. In order to simplify the treatment of this often very complex game, it is convenient to classify its varieties in four major categories. (1) In the first type of movement the player throws the knucklebones into the air with his right hand and endeavors to catch them on the back of the same hand. (2) In the second type of movement, one or more stones are thrown up in the air by the right hand, and while they are in the air, one or more stones are picked off the ground by the right hand, and then the descending stones are caught in the same hand. In a very few complex Maori versions the left hand is also used in this movement, to catch and throw up some of the descending stones. This gives the whole movement the appearance of juggling. The Maoris use the left hand only in this movement and permit it to seize only what are called the "common stones." The leader stone (or taw) must be caught only by the right hand. (3) In the third type of movement, a stone is thrown up and caught by the right hand, while other stones are moved about, to form diamonds, squares, rows, and circles, on the ground and picked up by the same hand. (4) In the fourth type of movement, while stones are thrown up and caught with the right hand, other stones are moved by the right hand, underneath, over, and through the fingers of the left hand. The present investigation showed that originally the Maori versions of the game included only movements of the first three types. They were developed to a far greater degree of complexity and skill than the New Zealand European variants. The European games used the fourth or left-hand type of movement freely.[2]

Here is a description of an unusual version of the game played at Rakaia, Canterbury, in 1910, a province in which Knucklebones has always been popular and in which (at Oxford) it continues to flourish even today. In the first move the player attempted to see how many he could catch on the back of his right hand. First he tried to catch two, then three, four, and five, in that order. The movement was then repeated with the left hand, throwing them up and catching them on the back. (Any use of the left hand for throwing, handling, or catching in Knucklebones is highly exceptional.) If it seemed as though he were going to catch more than he

---

[2] B. Sutton-Smith, "The Meeting of Maori and European Cultures and Its Effects upon the Unorganised Games of Maori Children," *Journal of the Polynesian Society*, LX (1951), 93–107.

wanted he would shake his hand just at the moment of reception in order to get the right number. After they were caught on the back of the hand, they were tossed up from there and then caught on the palm. Everybody did this in turn. It was more fun for each person to have a turn. In the second move a knucklebone was thrown into the air, another bone was picked off the ground, and then the descending bone was caught in the same hand, the right hand. The same movement was repeated with the left hand. This movement was then repeated, alternating the right and left hands and picking up two, three, and four knucklebones in succession. Finally five bones were thrown up and caught by each hand in turn. If the bones were placed close together on the ground during this movement, they were easier to pick up. There was no third type of movement. In the fourth type of movement the left hand was placed on the ground with hand arched and fingers apart. Then, while the right hand threw up the bone, that hand also pushed the other bones, in turn, through the gaps between the fingers of the left hand. Next, while the bone was in the air, the other bones were pushed in turn under the left hand. Finally, while the bone was in the air, the other bones were hopped, in turn, over the left hand. In this version played at Rakaia, the movements had no names; elsewhere, those of type four were usually named. At Fernside, Wanganui, for example, in 1890, they were known as "jump the fence," "Postie's knock," and "put the chickens in." From Waikouaiti, Otago (1900), there are records of the third type of movement, for which there is no counterpart in the Rakaia version described above. One was for the right hand to throw a bone into the air and then to arrange other bones in a small circle and to place the fourth bone on top and in the center of these three bones as a pyramid. This was known as "Polly put the kettle on." In another movement the four bones were arranged in a row on the ground and were then jumped from side to side with the point of the index finger of the right hand. One bone was jumped each time the bone was in the air. This was known as "jump the ladder." An example of a difficult fourth movement is reported from Leeston, Canterbury, 1893.

If the player is right handed, he places his left hand flat on the ground and places a bone on the second knuckle of each finger of the left hand;

with the right hand one bone is thrown into the air and simultaneously the bone from the knuckle of the left forefinger is flicked into the air and the two descending bones caught in the right hand. When flicking the bones from the knuckles of one finger, the bones resting on the other knuckles must not be disturbed and the bone from each finger must be flicked off individually. (The third finger generally proved the Waterloo of champions.) The last and most difficult movement was to flick the bone from the little finger joint, throw the other four bones into the air and catch all five before reaching the ground.

The reporter of this extremely difficult movement says that it

was accomplished by only two boys in the school, but I think they were more or less freaks. One, in after life,was on the stage in the days of the old Gaiety Vaudeville Company in Wellington. There I remember seeing him perform this trick but instead of knucklebones he was using half-crown pieces. He was a good juggler and eventually left the country for overseas [!]. While at school he taught at least one other boy this last intricate movement. This particular boy was always inventing new movements in Knucklebones. For example, his movement to precede the above was as follows: the bones were placed on the first joints of the four fingers placed close together; all four bones were then flicked into the air together, the thumb only resting on the ground, a comparatively simple movement as the thumb acted as a fulcrum.

Such rhymes as

        Jack, be nimble, Jack, be quick,
        Jack, jump over the candlestick [Nelson, 1892],

and

        Sweep the floor, pick up the chair,
        Sweep under, place it there [Alexandra, Otago, 1910],

accompanied some movements, but do not appear to have been ordinarily used.

Although, in the first example from Rakaia given above, the players took turns after each movement, this was not generally the case. Usually a player went on until he missed a movement. Then the next player had a turn, and the first commenced later at the place where he had missed. In some versions the player who slipped had to begin all over again when his turn came round the next time. The game was played in wet or fine weather. Many associate it with sitting on the grass in summer or autumn, others with sitting on shelter-shed floors or indoors on a wet day. Sometimes the game was played merely to win, at other times "The successful player confiscated the bones of the losers or [took as forfeits their] pennies or marbles" (Leeston, Canterbury). Boys played the game occasionally at school and more often at home, but in the main it was a girls' game, at which some were surprisingly skilled.

Buttons (K-35) was a well-established game. Each player put his buttons in the ring and then took his turn at lifting them out again. "The hand was pressed down on the button and the button that stuck to the hand long enough for the owner to get it out of the ring, became the possession of the player" (Wellington, 1890). "We would wet our finger first in an attempt to make it stick" (Auckland, 1900). In another version the players put their buttons in a circle, then attempted to lift their "taw" buttons from a base mark into the circle. Once they did this they were free to lift as many out of the circle as they could, in a similar fashion. "But it was banned as a gambling game" (Christchurch, 1920). There are later reports of marbles played with buttons (Onehunga, Auckland), and *Button Hockey* (K-36) (Ratapiko, Wairarapa, 1949).

Hand games had an important part among the play activities of these years. In Stone, or *Stone, Scissors, and Paper* (K-37), the players displayed their hands together in certain positions. The player whose hand was in the "superior" position won the point. There were three positions. In "stone" the fist was closed; in "scissors" the hand was open with the thumb separated from the rest of the hand; in "paper" the hand was open and the thumb lay with the fingers. The order of superiority lay in the fact that "Stone grinds scissors cuts paper wraps stone" (Nelson, 1910). In a more recent version (Masterton, 1938), the winner was entitled to punish the loser by whacking him on the wrist with two fingers. In Wiggle Waggle also, a faulty action was punished by a rap over the fingers with a pencil. The usual form of Wiggle Waggle was *Simon Says* (K-38), played with the thumbs. In Simon Says a leader-player gave the various instructions, but only those prefaced by "Simon says" were to be followed by the others. Any instruction followed when the prefatory "Simon says" had not been said caused the player concerned to be eliminated. The last player left in the game was the winner. In Wiggle Waggle, players making a mistake were not eliminated, but were rapped over the fingers with a pencil (South Clutha, Otago, 1875). Another kind of Wiggle Waggle was Solomon Says.

In the widely known *Hands upon Hands* (K-39), the players placed their hands alternately on top of each other's, continually drawing out the bottom hand in order to put it on top.

Another hand game was *Peter and Paul* (K-40). A small piece of paper was dampened in the mouth and stuck on one fingernail of each hand. These two fingers rested on the edge of the table. The other fingers were kept below the table. Then, to the chant of

> Two little dicky birds sitting on a wall,
> One named Peter, one named Paul.
> Fly away Peter, fly away Paul,
> Come back Peter, come back Paul,

the two fingers were tapped on the table once or twice, each hand in turn was thrown quickly behind the back, and another two fingers were tapped down on the table to make it look in turn as if Peter and Paul had really flown away, much to the surprise of the innocents. But at "Come back . . ." the hands were again put behind the back, and this time the two papered fingers, or "Peter and Paul," were tapped down on the table (Karori, Wellington, 1949). In Nelson (1880) the game was known as Jack and Jill.

Another hand game was *Here's the Church* (K-41), in which the chant was:

> Here's the church, and here's the steeple,
> Look inside and see the people,
> Here's the parson going upstairs,
> Here's the parson saying his prayers.

In the first line the fingers of the two hands were interlocked with the knuckles uppermost. The first and little fingers of both hands were extended so that they met in points, each representing a steeple. To accompany the second line the hand was turned over and the fingers, retaining their locked position, were slipped inside the hand. They wiggled to represent the people. To accompany the third line, two fingers of one hand trotted outside the fingers of the other hand, that is, the parson went upstairs. To accompany the last line the thumb of the trotting hand was pushed up through the pulpit formed by the encircled thumb and forefinger of the other hand.

Another rhyme of the time, but one recited more often by parents or older children for the amusement of infants, was *Walk down the Path* (K-42):

Walk down the path [draw finger down child's hair parting],
Knock at the door [knock on the forehead],
Peep in the windows [lift the eyelids],
Lift up the latch [the nose],
And walk in [open mouth and put two fingers in].

To accompany another rhyme recited to infants, *This Little Pig* (K-43), the older person pointed to the infant's toes, beginning with the big one, and then at the end, after pointing to the little one, ran her hand all the way up the infant's leg. The rhyme was:

This little pig went to market,
This little pig stopped home,
This little pig had bread and cheese,
This little pig had none,
And this little pig went wee, wee, wee,
All the way home.

Shadows, or *Hand Shadows* (K-44), was a pleasant pastime well suited to being "played in bed" by children "just before going to sleep" (Palmerston, 1900). "Most of these we practised from those illustrated in Cole's Book Arcade, which was a great favourite, viz., finding hidden animals in the pictures, such as ducks, rabbits and butterflies."

In the *Mousetrap* (K-45), Crab-Hole, or Bird's Nest, "two first fingers of one hand were placed across two of the other hand at right angles. A boy was then invited to try the trap by putting one of his fingers down the hole. The trap was squeezed together and an underneath thumb, often long-nailed, bored into the intruding finger." In a more pleasant version the trap-setter chanted the rhyme:

Put your finger in Tabby's house,
Tabby's not at home,
Tabby's at the back door,
Picking at a bone,

"whereupon Tabby duly picked at the finger of the intruder"
(Oamaru, Otago, 1925).

Cat's Cradle (K-46), with string, was quite widely played, although never as often as Knucklebones or Hopscotch. "Cat's Cradle with string, I just remember among the older schoolgirls, so that was on the way out, too. I used to envy the girls their deftness, but I never learned to make the intricate patterns my mother knew. She told me children played it constantly in her own schooldays of the late 1860's and early 1870's" (Paeroa, North Auckland, 1900). Most informants reported only a half dozen versions. There are few reports of the game after 1900, except from those places where children have picked it up from Maori children. One report from Hawkes Bay, 1949, for example, mentioned specific figures: Cup and Saucer, One Diamond, Two Diamonds, Five Diamonds, Twenty Diamonds, Triangle, Complicated Square, and the Union Jack.

Other string tricks were practiced. One, for example, was *Threading the Needle* (K-47). A piece of string was wound round the left thumb and forefinger. The first end, which had been left long, was held in the right hand, and then, after one or two feints, the trickster threaded it through the loop by pulling the string round the end of the thumb very quickly. Wonderers were then challenged to "jump through the loop as quickly as that" (Horowhenua, Wellington, 1900).

Hopping Games

Up to this point I have dealt with hand games. I shall now deal with leg games, involving hopping, jumping, and running, that were, once again, mainly the games of boys. Girls had little more than Skipping and Hopscotch.

Boys' hopping games were naturally vigorous, especially the individual or team game (and it was more often a team game) of *Hopping Base* (K-48). Two sides were chosen by alternate picking. Two parallel lines were drawn, about twenty to forty-five feet apart, in some clear space. The length of the lines was dependent upon the number of the players and the size of the available space. Midway from the ends and three to five feet behind each base line an oblong prisoner's base was drawn, about eight feet by three. Each side stood behind its own line with the opponents' prisoners behind it. When the game began, players from each side hopped out from their respective bases into the playing area between, to engage the enemy's forces. There was no rule limiting the use of superior numbers. The object of the game was to force the opponents "down," which meant, to make them put both feet on the ground, or to step off instead of hopping off the hopping foot, or to collapse on the ground. A player was allowed to put down the tips of his fingers or the palms of his hands to help him recover his balance. Players attacked by pushing with their open hands, by heaving with an elbow or a shoulder, by cutting down fending arms with a downward push, and by hopping out of the way of a charge and giving the strenuous opponent a shove as he went past. Foot-tripping, kicking, and "clinging-on" were barred. "No cling on," was the cry. To get rid of an exceptionally big or expert player a small opponent might drop down on knees and elbows behind him, while a mate "in the know" would try to push him backwards over the obstacle. Players who were "down" must go to the prisoner's base behind the opponents' line. These prisoners could be released by their teammates coming out from the home base and hopping furiously against the determined pushing of the defenders, who were standing in front of the prisoners. These rescuers could be attacked too by opponents who were still hopping in the playing area. The rescuers must touch the prisoners' outstretched hands to save them. When in the playing area players could "rest" (while considering tactics and awaiting an opening), by placing the heel of the free foot on the instep of the hopping foot and the toe on the ground. They could also change feet while at rest, by a quick interchange of positions of the feet. This movement was always carefully watched; any shuffling constituted a "down." It could only be done while at rest. A player pushed off rest, or attacking from rest, would be "down" if he did not land on his hopping foot and thus took a step instead of a hop. Players could hop back to base to escape attack or have a rest. When all of a side were prisoners the game was won by the opponents. When all but a few were prisoners, the free members of a team could not remain long in their base to prevent defeat. Their own fellow players who were prisoners kept urging them to "risk it," and finally, if they showed a complete lack of enterprise, they would be counted out by the opponents and the game would be "claimed." Many of the boys who played this game were still attending elementary school at the age of sixteen years. It was, in consequence, an extremely vigorous activity. It was generally a bit too rough for the smaller boys (Taranaki, 1880). The game was reported also from Wakefield, Nelson, 1875, and Murchison, Westland, 1890.

The same type of game is mentioned in a variety of individual forms. One of these was known as *Bumpers* (K-49), in which the players kept their arms folded throughout (Fairton, Canterbury, 1915). The winning player took on all comers in turn. In some versions the hands were tied behind the back (Nelson, 1875), and in others one leg was tied to the other (South Clutha, Otago, 1875). In another form, both the hands and the legs were bound and the players knelt opposite each other and attempted to knock each other over in that position (South Clutha, Otago, 1875). Yet another variation was *Dunk and Davey* (K-50), reported to have been played at Denniston in 1925. This was a game of Bar the Door in which the He in the middle must bump "down" the other players as they hopped across. The He also hopped. If the He was knocked off his balance then the player who knocked him over took a free passage, and all the other players came hopping through and the He had to try to stop them. It is known today as Humpty Dumpty.

The game of *Hop-Peg* (K-51) was even harder on the legs than Hopping Base. It was played with three pegs. The first player took one hop from the base, reached forward, and stuck a peg in the ground as far ahead of himself as he could without losing his balance. He then hopped over it and in a similar manner pushed the second and, in turn, the third peg into the ground. The other players, using the same pegs, attempted to extend the distance of these pegs from the base. The game is reported from Takaka, Nelson, 1899, and Milton, Otago, 1910.

And, finally, there was *Hop the Hats* (K-52), a hopping game of more savage hue:

On wet days we played on the verandah a game called Hop the Hats. All the players put down their hats on the floor in a row, say three feet apart. The game was to hop along the length of the row and back, then in and out, as many times as was arranged. If any boy touched a hat during the operation he had to bear the penalty of being put through the mill. The "mill" consisted of a row of successful hoppers with their legs well apart, and the unfortunate boy had to crawl on hands and knees between the legs of this row of boys, who with hats and fists belaboured him on the part of anatomy where punishment is usually applied. [Waianiwa, Otago, 1870]

Hopscotch (K-53) was generally regarded as a girls' game. A boy might be stigmatized as a "sissy" if he played it too openly or too often. On the whole, the Hopscotch games of the nineteenth century were more complex than those now played by the younger children. However, when the older children of today play, they develop games of equal complexity. Before 1900 rectangular diagrams were the most important. The straight-avenue diagrams and the less frequent circle with a spiral within were both used more often than they are today. The game was universally unpopular with parents because of its effects upon the children's footwear. In those days children preferred to kick the block around the bases; they did not throw it into the bases and hop round after it.

In all hopping games certain rules were universal. If the tin or block did not land in the square, it was the next player's turn. If anyone hopped on a line by mistake, she was out. No person could hop on a square bearing a name other than her own. No one could stand in a square into which she had thrown a block.

Rectangular Hopscotch, sometimes known as Kick the Block, was played in a rectangular diagram, subdivided into six squares, of two rows, three squares in each, numbered up one row (1–3) and down the next (4–6). These squares were known as "dens," "beds," "steps," or "nests." The block was thrown into the first den and then kicked, den by den, through the rest. The block was then thrown into den two and the same procedure was followed. In turn the block was thrown into dens three to six until the player had been around.

After progressing successfully through the six dens, one then indulged in fancy rounds, some of which were: "miss-a-den," which was from one to three, three to four and four to six; "zig-zag," which was from one to six, six to five, five to two, two to three, three to four, four to five, five to two, two to one, one to six; "cut the cabbage," one to five, five to three, three to four, four to two, two to six. Then there were various rounds without the block, for example, blindfold. [Waitara, Taranaki, 1902]

A similar movement was "thread the needle," in which the player proceeded through bases one, six, five, two, three, four, five, two, and one (Onehunga, Auckland, 1905). In "sweep the den," the players made a backward sweep of the free foot at each hop (Millerton, Westland, 1920). In some rectangular games there were eight squares, that is, in two parallel rows of four each. One informant writes:

I have never seen Hopscotch played so well as we played it. There were rules for beginners who played separately, but the real game was very skilled and required years of practice. There were eight dens and a 3½" square wooden block. The block was thrown into the first square; the player then stepped in after it and shuffled it to the next square with one hop. Beginners were allowed many hops and shuffling, but experts had to hop into the correct position. The fourth den was a rest. The player shuffled the block from there into the fifth and then shot it down the remaining dens of that side with one kick. The block was then thrown into succeeding dens. In the next figure the player hopped round while the block was held on the outstretched hand. In the next the block was held on the palm, tossed and caught on the back of the hand, before the player hopped round. Finally, the block was held between the toe and ankle of the left foot while she hopped round. I can remember the feeling of anxiety mixed with determination as I took my turn and launched out into the big dens in front of the most critical group of spectators. [Ohau, Wellington, 1912]

In avenue Hopscotch there were four beds and "plum" at the end to turn round in. You threw the block into one, hopped and kicked it to four, put your feet down in plum and came back the same way. It had to go in each time with one kick. Next you threw into two and so on till four. Then you had to throw into each number as before, but this time you had to "scuff" it from base to base, that is, you had to jump, hop, and kick all in one action. When that was done the same first-time "scuffing" movement had to be done with both feet. [Dunedin, 1890]

Another form of Hopscotch was that known as Donkey (Blenheim, Marlborough, 1911), or French Hopscotch (Dunedin, 1890). The diagram was in the shape of a large rectangle with two bases side by side at each end and four bases enclosed in the arms of a diagonal cross in the center. The players either kicked their way through them all, doing two squares in the cross on the way up, and two others on the way back, or they hopped through doing astride jumping as they passed the diagonals. The cyclic Hopscotch game was known variously as Round the World Hopping, The

Snake, The Snail, Round the World and Back Again, and The Maze. The squares were placed end on end and spiraled inward to a central base. Sometimes the players simply hopped round the bases; at other times they kicked a block round.

It was simply an endurance test, as the diagram covered perhaps a chain width. Some of the bases were numbered and you were not allowed to tread on these. If you did you had that number of points against you. The player with the least number of points at the end of the game won the game. The biggest number was in the middle and if you stood on a line you were right out and with that middle number against you. If you rested you had to rest on a number. [Rakaia, Canterbury, 1910]

According to a report from Waitara, Taranaki (1902), "After accomplishing each journey one could put one's initials in any den, which was thereafter forbidden to the rest of the players. The object was to so group one's preserves as to make it difficult for the other players to jump over them."

Although these were the main types of the game, there are reports of endless variations. Clearly one reason for their persistence is found in the freedom that children have felt to vary and complicate the rules. In some places the children even played team Hopscotch. They tossed up for the first move and then scored points per player according to the distance which that player went without making any mistakes (Wakefield, Nelson, 1875). In those days most schools seem to have been limited to one or two varieties of the game, as is still true today.

JUMPING GAMES

Among jumping games *Leap Frog* (K-54) was, by all reports, a very popular game in the early days. It was played sometimes on the road to school, but more often round and round the school, a long line of boys jumping over each other's backs in turn. As the game progressed the backs became higher and higher, "until the game broke down because the little kids got sick of it" (Gisborne, 1890). Generally it was played "on a cold and frosty morning" (Nelson, 1895), or on a "cold winter's morning to warm ourselves up before school" (Takaka, Nelson, 1870). In a Charleston (Westland, 1890) variety, after the first jumper had gone over the first back, then the first jumper stooped down in front of the first back and became a back himself. The next jumper had to jump over the two backs, the following one over three backs, and so on, until one boy was unable to jump the distance, in which case he became the first back for another round. The same game was played at Collingwood, Nelson, in 1895. It is said that sometimes the girls played the game, and did so by jumping over the backs from the side rather than from the rear position.

Cap-It (K-55), or Cappon-Pie (Masterton, Wairarapa, 1905), or Cap-Oh (Wellington, 1900), was a variant of Leap Frog. Each player who went over the back put his cap on that back, and the next player had to jump over the cap as well as the back. When he had done so he also added his cap to the other, and so the pile of caps grew larger. The first to knock them off became the next back. A Nelson version of 1890, called Cap-It, was played as a team game with three players on each side. It is pointed out that in this game each jumping player had to place his cap on the back as he jumped over it, not afterward. If any player dallied in placing it there, or knocked the other caps off in doing so, then his team provided the back. One team provided one boy as a back as long as the other team of three players successfully jumped and placed their three caps on that back.

The most widespread leapfrog game of the nineteenth century was undoubtedly *Fly the Garter* (K-56).

There was a leader player in this game who went by the title of "Fly." He commenced by doing a two foot jump from the base line and marking the spot where he landed. At this spot the first back went down sideways. The Fly then nominated how everyone was going to go over the back. "I say one standing jump," or "I say one running jump." The other players proceeded to do this and Fly went last. If any player should fail he went down as the back. However, if a player thought that he couldn't do the jump and doubted whether Fly could do it either, he could say "I call on Fly," which was a challenge and meant that Fly had to do the jump first. Now if Fly failed then the challenger went Fly and Fly went the back. But if Fly succeeded then the challenger automatically became the back, which was a wise piece of legislation to say the least. When Fly had had his jump and succeeded in it, then the back moved forward to the spot where Fly landed and put his foot on that spot. This increased the distance of the back from the base. After each jump the distance increased still further which made it more difficult for Fly to estimate how much it would take to get there. He might say "Two hops and three jumps," but if any player got there in less than his estimation then Fly went down as the back and that player became Fly. [Waitara, Taranaki, 1899]

In a Gisborne version played in 1890, Fly the Garter was combined with Cap-It. After all the players had had their turn as described above, a cap was placed on the back, and they all had another turn. If no one knocked the cap off then another cap was placed on the back, and so it went on until the caps were knocked off. The player who knocked them off then became the back. It is reported that the player who was unfortunate enough to be chosen as the back had the right to choose who Fly would be (Granity, Westland, 1900). At Carterton (Wairarapa, 1890) the jumper was called "over." "You just about broke your neck trying to get across," says one informant (Palmerston, 1914). At Taranaki in 1880, the boys commenced by jumping a distance to see who would be Fly and who would be "down." The boy who did the best standing jump from a line became Fly and the boy who did the smallest jump was "down." The back was known as the "go down," and he was said to "give a back" to the players. "There was a great strictness about 'no over the mark' and 'no riding the donkey,' that is, perching on the 'go down' or knocking him over. But not much patience was shown to a 'go down' who wasn't stable." Although the game was known in all provinces as Fly the Garter, there is one report of it as Flying the Gap (Westport, 1890).

Team varieties of jumping games which were known throughout New Zealand had the names of Buck Buck; Saddle the Nag; Jump, Little Nag Tail; Monkey on the Bridge; and Humbug, Finger or Thumb.[3] Consider first the game of *Buck Buck* (K-57). All accounts of this game, in which it is given the name of Buck Buck, come from the southern half of New Zealand's South Island, where the early settlers were chiefly of Scottish and English origin. It was known in Clutha, South Otago, and Waikouaiti, North Otago, up to about 1900, but there are no reports of its having been played

---

[3] This material on team jumping games has been published previously in my article, "New Zealand Variants of the Game 'Buck Buck,'" *Folklore*, LXII (1951), 329–333.

there after that date. Here is a report from Adair, Canterbury, for the year 1890.

> We called the game "Buck Buck, How many fingers do I hold up?" We played it with about six boys. The first boy leans against the school wall with his arms horizontal against the school and his head and face looking towards the ground and his back in an horizontal position. The next boy leans up against him in the same way with his head down and his back horizontal; and so on back to the last boy. Then another [player] who is going to call the tune jumps on to the back of the boy at the end of the row . . . and works his way along the backs of all the boys until he gets to the [one] up against the school. When he gets there he says to the boy he is sitting on—"Buck Buck, How many fingers do I hold up?" For instance, he may be holding up two fingers on one hand and three fingers on the other, which makes five in all. The boy underneath says (for instance) "Seven," which is not right. The boy on top who called, then says, "Seven you say and five it is" and he immediately holds up another number of fingers and says as before "Buck Buck," etc. And so it goes on until the boy underneath guesses the right number. When this happens, the boy on top says, for example, "Six you say and six it is, buck, buck up," and the one underneath immediately bucks him off. The boy then who was bucked off goes to the end of the row of boys and joins up with his back down the same as the others. The boy who was up against the wall then pulls out and the next boy to him leans up against the school. The boy who has pulled out now calls the tune by jumping over the other backs, and so it goes on. A boy may have a lot of guesses before he strikes the right number or he may guess right first time. Of course we got most fun if we could get a good ride on his back by keeping him guessing. There are always other boys looking on. This is just as well because the boy calling the number can easily cheat, especially if the back calls the correct number too quickly before he has had a decent ride.

The same game was played in Dunedin, Otago, between 1870 and 1895.

In the Clutha versions mentioned above there was only one rider and one back, as was the case with Petronius Arbiter, in the Roman example cited by Gomme.[4] There is, however, another and team form of the game from Central Otago (Queenstown), known as *Saddle the Nag* (K-58):

----

[4] Gomme, I, 46.

There was a rough and tumble game which the bigger and stronger boys loved. We called it Saddle the Nag. Sides were chosen, say seven against seven. On the side which was "out" the seventh boy stood against the wall with his back to it, and the other six bent down in a row in front of him. Each boy clutched with his arms the coat of the boy in front of him and buried his head in that boy's rump. When they were well set in this position the word was given to "go," whereupon the riders—those on the other side—followed one after another with a run and a jump. Naturally the best flying jumper took the first run and jump. His object was to land on a boy's back as far as possible along the line of bent boys, so that those to follow would have a chance to land safely on the back of a nag or on top of one of their fellows. How sturdy those nags had to be, for they had to set themselves to bear up against the flying weight of a heavy opponent. The test was "No foot or part of a rider must touch the ground." The whole game was a gruelling one and usually the team with the most brawn and strategy won the bout and then took its turn as riders.

A team version of Buck Buck almost identical with the example given just above was played until about 1900 in the Nelson and Golden Bay districts (northern tip of South Island—settlers of predominantly English origin). It was called *Jump, Little Nag Tail* (K-59). In this game the backs each put their heads between the legs of the boys in front. When all the riders were on the backs, always one more rider than the number of backs, they chanted:

Jump, little nag tail, one, two, three,
Jump, little nag tail, one, two, three,
Jump, little nag tail, one, two, three,
Off! Off! Off!

and at the last "Off" they jumped off. The riders won if they could stay on till they had said their piece or if the backs collapsed underneath them before they had completed the verse. Imagine the pandemonium when a string of backs went down with their heads jammed between the legs in front of them and with riders on their necks! Naturally the riders jerked up and down as they said their verse and did their very best to collapse the horse. Often all the riders would pile up on the second or third back, which made it extremely difficult for that back to hold them up, but even more difficult for them to stay on without putting a foot down. This piling up of the players on one back was caused by the fact that in this version of the game the players were not allowed to crawl round on top of the backs once they had stopped their leapfrogging flight. There was of course the occasional and legendary boy who could leapfrog twice before coming spread-eagled to earth on a back. In the Adair and Dunedin version given above, the one rider was permitted to move along the back. This was known as "Riding the Buck," and the Buck or backs did their best to buck him off before he could get along to the end and ask his questions. In the team game, some riders were particularly valuable to their teams and would always ride first. They were often nicknamed according to their qualities, for example, "razor-arse"!

It will be noticed that in these team forms (Queenstown and Nelson), in contrast to the other forms, there is no guessing element. This distinction accords with the difference between Gomme's Buck Buck and Bung the Bucket.[5] There was another version of the game played in certain of the mining districts on the West Coast of the South Island (where a large proportion of the settlers were of Irish origin), in which the guessing and team elements were combined. This version was called *Monkey on the Bridge* (K-60), and it was the same as Jump, Little Nag Tail, except that there was no bobbing up and down on the back and no chanting of "Jump, little nag tail." Instead, the first rider on the backs said to the first back down, "Humbug, finger or thumb?" (which was also an alternative name for the game), and the back had to guess whether the rider was holding up his finger, his thumb, or a "humbug." The humbug was a circle made by holding the tips of the thumb and first finger of one hand together.

By 1900 these games had faded out of regular school playground play. But out of school, we can assume, these games were still played occasionally. For example, a version of Buck Buck (see K-57) under the name Jumbucks is played today by one of New Zealand's tramping clubs (hiking clubs) in its haunts near the snow line. It is said that the hobnailed boots of the players contribute strongly to the hazards of the game.

There is, however, one important exception to the generalization that Buck Buck has vanished. In the Westland mining districts of Ngakawau, Granity, Millerton, and Denniston, the game carried

---

[5] *Ibid.*, pp. 46 and 52.

on in the form of Monkey on the Bridge right up till the end of the depression in 1935. Several factors contributed toward its continuance in these areas. In the first place, these mining communities were far more homogeneous than any other community of comparable size in New Zealand. All the inhabitants were in some way connected with the work of the mines. And, obviously, a community of common occupations is more likely to share its recreation and create a common tradition of play than is an urban or other community in which the occupations are diverse. Furthermore, these homogeneous communities were situated, not only in an isolated province, but in even more isolated districts, some of them virtually on the tops of mountains. The only entrants to these districts tended to come, not from elsewhere in New Zealand, but from the British Isles. These immigrants would help to keep alive traditions extinct everywhere else in New Zealand but still alive in their former home communities. Again, until just after the depression years practically all the amenities of life in these districts had to be provided by the inhabitants themselves.

Consequently, while Buck Buck faded elsewhere, the homogeneity, isolation, and self-reliance of these communities kept alive a continuous tradition in which it could continue to thrive. During the depression years, in fact, traditional pastimes were revived. Every day large numbers of unemployed miners assembled on the mud patch at Millerton and whiled away their time playing the games of their boyhood like Monkey on the Bridge and its half-cousin Fly the Garter.

The better conditions which succeeded the depression years broke down the isolation of these communities and brought them much more into line with the rest of New Zealand in material prosperity. This has occurred only in the last twenty to twenty-five years. It is not surprising, therefore, that in 1949 I discovered just one "wee" remnant of the original Buck Buck still in existence in the mining district of Denniston, a district reached only after a winding and almost vertical six-mile trip up the side of a mountain. The game I discovered had the essential mark of all degenerations of rugged games: it was now more of a girls' game than a boys' game! It was called *Big and Wee* (K-61). One girl jumps upon the back of another and she cries "Big or Wee?" For "Big" she holds up her two thumbs; for "Wee" she holds up her two little fingers.

The back guesses whether she is holding up the "Big" or the "Wee." The rider must of course retain her balance or else she goes down.

RUNNING GAMES

Running is of great importance in New Zealand's major sport, Football, that is to say, *Rugby Football* (K-62). In this history the concern is not with the details of Football rules but with the general conditions of play and the way in which the players improvised their gear. Informants say: "The game was quite unknown to us. I never saw the game until long after I left school" (Lawrence, Otago, 1880). "We only once had a master who taught us. The rules were rafferty and we really had no idea of the game" (Waikouaiti, Otago, 1895). In some districts, however, the game was played much earlier than these quotations indicate, and was generally stimulated by the elementary school's association with a secondary department. Football was a college game from quite an early period. "The advent of the Grammar School's first football was a great event. It arrived in 1875, and was subscribed for by the boys collecting and selling bones, bottles and rubbish. Rugby was then unknown locally: no goal posts were used and aimless punting formed the sport. Severe restrictions on the housing of the precious ball were imposed" (Invercargill). "In winter we practised drop-kicking in the Basin Reserve; the use of punting was then unknown to us" (Wellington College, 1876). "The bullock's bladder was quite good when dried out. We would get it from Patrick's on a Saturday morning, blow it up with our mouths through a piece of straw and tie it with string" (Dunedin, 1885). In some country areas, boys continued to play Football with these animal bladders till after the First World War. There were other materials employed, although the animal bladders were always the most popular. "We used matagouri scrub in a sugar bag for football. It was light and bouncy but 'bust' very soon" (Hampden, Otago, 1880). "Our football was made of sea-weed wound round and round, plaiting it like the fender of a ship. The ends, tied with flax, never came undone" (Charleston, Westland, 1890). Even when proper footballs arrived there were still difficulties. If a football was punctured a new bladder had to be obtained. There were no materials for mending rubber.

The commonest running game of the day was, as we have seen, Bar the Door (see E-8). In addition to Bar the Door, the majority of schools had at least one and sometimes two other important running games played on marked-out areas with bases. The most important of these in the period before 1900 was undoubtedly *Prisoner's Base* (K-63). In all forms of the game there were two home bases and two prisoner's bases. The two home bases were adjacent to each other at one end of the playground, and the prisoner's bases were opposite each other at the other end of the playground. Team A placed all of its prisoners in its own prisoner's base, which was directly opposite its home base at the other end of the playground. Team B did the same. This meant that either team had to run from its base diagonally across the playground and in front of the opposing team's home, in order to retrieve prisoners from the opponent's base. The aim of the game was to place all the players of the other side in one's own prisoner's base by tagging them. The game began when one player from one team went out into the playing area and challenged the other team. In some early New Zealand versions this was done by one team's sending one of its members to its own prisoner's base. This was called sending one of its players "show." While he was going "show" he was immune from tagging. From this position at the prisoner's base the show player, having satisfied himself that his team was ready, loudly called out "Show!" and immediately raced back for home, whereupon members of the other side raced out to tag him, and members of his own side raced out to save him by tagging members of the other side. The rule for tagging was that a player could only be tagged by some player who had left the home base after he had. If the first team's "show" got safely back to his base without being tagged and none of the other runners were tagged, the second team would send out a "show." A player who could run across untagged to the enemy's prisoner's base and rescue one of his own teammates had a safe passage home with that prisoner. They were both "dead" while they returned. No player was able to run out and tag another player and also rescue a teammate, however; only one action was allowed at a time. The venturing player would have to return to home base between

actions. There would be much side play as one player and then another stepped in and out of their home base in order to be able to
tag a rival player who had stepped out of his home base an instant
before. In attempts to recover prisoners, players could "inch out"
of the base to try to gain some "distance" advantage or cut across
behind the opponents' base. But in so doing, by being out first, they
lost their tagging rights and also became open to attack from different vantage positions held by the other side. When the game was
won the sides changed places for another round. "It was an excellent game for both boys and girls, quite as good in my opinion as
some of the organised sports. It was as strenuous as the players
liked to make it and even the weakest players could find someone
to match, something effective they could do" (Horowhenua, Wellington, 1900). In one variety, called Peggy, "the prisoners linked
hands in a long line to make it easier for them to be saved. Only
one prisoner needed to have his feet in the prison" (Waikouaiti,
Otago, 1885). The game was known as Bell Block, in Taranaki, as
early as 1870, and as Scotch and English it is reported to have been
the only organized game at Akaroa, Christchurch, in 1880.

One of the most popular of all capturing games was *French and
English* (K-64), or Prisoners. Sometimes this was played in the
haphazard style of Cowboys and Indians. At other times it had
more definite features.

We played the game on a wet day in the off seasons between Rugby
and Cricket. The two teams lined up at opposite ends of the playshed,
each having a corner of the shed as their den. The aim was to capture
all the members of the other side and confine them to your den. When
the weather allowed, sorties would be made into the trees and grounds
surrounding the shed. To capture a member of the other side it was
only necessary to have the physical strength to drag him to your den.
On the other hand to release a prisoner of your own side from the den
of the enemy it was necessary to crown him on the head "One– two–
three." Boys were often hurt on the concrete floor of the shed while
struggling to avoid capture. [Outram, Otago, 1920]

King Pin (K-65) was also very much like Prisoner's Base, except
that the stealing of "treasure" was involved. It was played at Rockville, Nelson, in 1880, under the name of Stealing Grass. "Sides
were chosen and each side had a home base with a certain number
of stones in the nest. The game then followed the main principle of

Red Rover [see E-8], with each side trying to catch prisoners and to prevent them from getting across, but in this game the members of one side had to take a stone from the opposing side's nest and return uncaught." The game has also been known as Stones, Steal a Peg, Kingy, and King's Peg.

Chibby (K-66) was fundamentally the same as Prisoner's Base, except for one detail. The challenger who went out in front challenged from a post placed equidistant from both home bases and between the prison bases. Any player who chased the challenger was not permitted to tag until he had gone round or touched the post or tree. In some varieties only the first two players had to touch the post. In others all had to go round the post.

Chevvy Chase (K-67) was not any distinctive type of game. It was a name which in various places was used to refer to Prisoner's Base, Bar the Door, or Hares and Hounds. At South Clutha, in 1875, it was a cross-country run competition over difficult terrain; at Hampden, in 1880, a two-team form of Bar the Door. At Moeraki, Otago, in 1895, "All the children except one stood in a row side by side. The one approached and said 'Chevvy chevvy chase, the donkey's race, I call Tom Brown.' The one selected would run after the caller and try to tag him before he could reach a certain base. The one tug would go on with the game until all had been called."

The other major type of running game which was very popular in the earlier years was the type in which children ranged far and wide over a large and unspecified area. This game was generally played out of school time, but it was also played in school lunch hours. The game was stimulated by the rural surroundings of most of the early schools. One of the most rugged of these running games was *Follow the Leader* (K-68), which was also known as Steeplechasing. It was apparently one of the major aims in this game to lead the followers into all the most awkward and forbidden places that ingenuity could contrive. And the players had to do exactly as the leader did.

In my earliest years the leader had more scope for initiative. The countryside was, in effect, an unfenced no-man's land. As the years passed this freedom was more and more restricted and the game lost a great deal of its popularity. The event was mainly an obstacle harrier run in which the competition consisted, not in getting home first, but in sticking to the leader through thick and thin. The run extended over several miles, and following meant going over ditches and up banks, over and through streams, through fairly dense gorse, over and under gates and fences, up one side of a tree and down the other and even over a shed or two if the owners were known to be absent. Some of the smaller boys ran round some of the hurdles. [New Plymouth, 1880]

Hares and Hounds (K-69) was played as a change from Follow the Leader. Sometimes it was known as Fox and Hounds, and at others as Tallyho. There were usually two or three hares, who set off before the hounds and attempted to traverse a certain distance and then return home before the hounds could catch up to them. There are many reports.

It was an after-school game generally played on summer evenings. Two were selected as foxes. They took a horn with them which they blew every now and then at intervals. The foxes would dodge about anywhere, then when they thought the hounds were off the track they would give another blast. It was a great exercise for summer evenings, but because the hounds started to take too many short-cuts through people's gardens it eventually died out. [Waimate, Nelson, 1880]

"We played it round the city streets. The hares had to cry out 'Tallyho!' to let the others know where they were. The hounds would try to cut off exits by going the other way round street blocks. Cries of 'Here they are' would echo down the streets" (Palmerston, 1895). "Players were not loath to go in the front door of a house and out the back" (Sumner, Canterbury, 1905). Again and again in rural areas one meets the comment that half the satisfaction of Hares and Hounds, which started off in the school lunch hour over the surrounding country, was the fact that the players came back well after the afternoon school session had started. "Our main object was to stay away till it was about time to come out of school. Then we'd get a hiding but we used to reckon it was worth it" (Takaka, Nelson, 1900). "Perhaps we wouldn't get back at all. That came natural. The school master didn't learn you that" (Wakefield, Nelson, 1875).

Another popular way of letting the hounds know where you were was by laying a paper trail, in the game of *Paper Chase* (K-70). "The 1890's revived Paper Chase escapades, headed by ————, who piloted less venturesome souls through the mazes of

Howell's manuka to return reluctantly, tired and done, to the after-noon's work" (Waianiwa, Otago). At Oxford, Canterbury, there is report of paper steeplechases in the 1870's. The paper was gener-ally carried in sugar bags. Sometimes the hares would hide the bags of paper at strategic spots along a predetermined course before the race began. The hares generally had a start of three to five min-utes. Naturally enough, these Paper Chases were most often ar-ranged for free periods out of school time, particularly during the week ends. The advent of Harriers (see K-71) and Football in the 1890's and Boy Scout Tracking (see K-70) after the Boer War helped to replace these cross-country running pastimes.

The annual sporting events of the day had an effect on children's play in a way that they do not have today. There was a tendency for the children to imitate in their own play the athletic skills which were of most importance in these events. We hear much in these years about children practicing *Foot Races* (K-71), including Egg and Spoon Races, *Three-legged Races* (K-72), *Sack Races* (K-73), and *Wheelbarrow Races* (K-74), on the school grounds. They even took on *Pole-Vaulting* (K-75). "We made our own cross bar. We ran up and went over with the pole" (Waikouaiti, Otago, 1895). *Hop, Step, and Jump* (K-76) was universal, and the omnipresence of soft grass was an asset. Then there was the *Tug-o'-War* (K-77). "If we had no rope we took hold of each other round the waist and pulled in that fashion" (Dunedin, 1875). Around the turn of the century, when school games were first organized by adults, these athletic games had a standing equal to Rugby or Cricket. In the years that followed, however, athletic activities did not retain that status.

The playground was characterized not only by the more formal athletic games, but also by many athletic games of a more informal nature. Most of these were rough-and-tumble games or stunt ac-tivities. Consider, for example, the rough-and-tumble of Cockfight-ing, Bull in the Ring, No Man Standing, King of the Castle, Sacks on the Mill, Wrestling, Lazy Stick, Handstands, and various bal-ancing, sliding, and swinging stunts.

Perhaps the most recurrent and universal of rough games in the early period was *Cockfighting* (K-78). This was a free-for-all con-test in which a smaller boy mounted on the back of a bigger boy and the two endeavored to dislodge all other riders by pushing or pulling them over. There were no rules, except that tripping was usually barred. "Sometimes we had the same jockey day after day. We would challenge all comers. We tried to get up behind the other jockey with an arm round the neck from behind and tear him off his horse" (Nelson, 1875). "As we fought on the asphalt, and usually in the winter, there were plenty of skinned hands and skinned knees. The fights were en masse as well as of an individual nature, and the parents strongly objected because shirts and clothes were torn" (Dunedin, 1875). Sometimes the game was known as a Piggy-back Contest or as Pulling Off. "One trick of the game was to 'buck-jump' your rider, which consisted in jerking up your elbows so that the rider was lifted over your head" (Naseby, Otago, 1905). The proper form of Cockfighting, which was, in effect, an imitation of game-cock fighting, was not as widespread as the piggy-back variety. "Two players sat down facing each other in a ring. Each player had a stick, horizontally placed at the back of his knees. His arms were threaded under this stick and his two hands clasped in front of his legs. Rocking on their buttocks each player then attempted to push and kick the other player out of the ring, which had a radius of about five feet" (Palmerston, 1894). "Once your opponent was rolled over and helpless you were allowed to kick him out of the ring" (Nelson, 1875). Often, on a wet day, this game was played indoors in a ring chalked on the floor.

Bull in the Ring (K-79), in which one player tried to escape from a circle of players, was also a very boisterous game. "A big fellow in the middle would terrify the smaller ones when he began to bang and punch his way out of the ring holding his two hands together" (Naseby, Otago, 1895). The bull in the center tried to break out of the circle by rushing between two players to break their hold. "The 'chain hold' was considered particularly strong by the circle of players. When the bull was out he ran round the playground to avoid being captured. The player who tagged him first became the next bull. The bull was not allowed to dodge under the player's arms, though he could jump over the top. This was risky. It was only an odd game and not played very often" (Horowhenua, Wellington, 1900). At Waikouaiti (Otago, 1915), the player who let the bull out became the next bull. At Amberley (Canterbury, 1890), the group selected another bull, generally a big fellow, as that made it more realistic.

No Man Standing (K-80) was a matter of throwing everyone else off his feet, not just a matter of tagging those who were not squatting down, as it often is today. "A group of a dozen to twenty boys engaged in a rough and tumble. A boy thrown squarely on his back was out and the rest continued till only one was left. A variation was for all the players to continue until they stopped from sheer exhaustion. It was vigorous work and hard on the clothes" (Westport, Westland, 1895).

King of the Castle (K-81), in its rougher forms, was similar to No Man Standing. "I'm the king of the castle and you're the dirty rascal," was the cry of defiance with which the king challenged the rabble. Any hillock or pile of sods would do for the castle. There is record of a team form of the game, "in which a side of twenty fought to hold a platform of steps against the invading horde. The side of twenty wore caps and the invaders did not. It was the aim of the invaders to snatch the caps off the kings. It was an extremely dangerous game and after many had been bruised and broken and an eye nearly gouged out, the authorities stepped in and stopped the game" (Nelson, 1890).

There were in addition a variety of other more informal rough-and-tumble games. There was, for example, the universal *Sacks on the Mill* (K-82). "We would knock one boy down, and then pile one on top of another on his back until we all fell off" (Tahataki, Otago, 1875). The game was often called Stacks on the Mill, or Rough and Tumble, and had been known more succinctly and perhaps more aptly as Squash (Rangiotu, Auckland, 1920). In a variant, the player sat on the shed seat and the others piled one on top of another on his knees. A form of this was *Heave Ho* (K-83), which was also played in a school shed on a wet day. In this game one player, sitting sideways on the seat, faced the wall and braced his legs against it. The others, also sitting sideways on the seat but behind him, attempted to squash him flat against the wall.

Wrestling (K-84) was also popular: "We used to imitate the adult wrestling, then in vogue at all the sports meetings, namely the Cumberland style, Collar and Elbow and Catch as Catch Can" (Lawrence, Otago, 1890).

In what we imagined was the Cumberland style, boys took hold of each other with their arms "one over and one under." The hands were clasped behind the back. Then by tripping, drawing in the back, lifting off the ground or flinging over the shoulder, the player attempted to throw his opponent on to the ground on his back. In the Japanese hold, as we knew it, competitors seized each other at the shoulders at arm's length and then by tripping, jerking, pulling or swinging tried to throw the opponent on his back. [Taranaki, 1880]

"Our activities were stimulated by the fighting schools that half-pie men used to run on moonlit nights" (Takaka, Nelson, 1870).

In *Lazy Stick* (K-85), the two players sat opposite each other with their hands clasping the "lazy stick." This was a strong stick about four feet long. Each player pulled the stick towards him and by so doing attempted to lift his opponent off the ground. The game was played at home and at school by children, and at sports gatherings by men.

§ II: 1920–1950

The skill games which were dealt with under separate headings in § I will be dealt with together in this section.

In the last thirty years most of the skill games of the earlier period have either disappeared or are being played by younger children. As a result they are often executed with less skill. Older children in the early years devoted themselves to the development of these games, but the older children of today spend their time in other pursuits, in particular, playing in or watching major sports. Here and there, in isolated districts (as is true of examples K-60 and K-61, above), there are "pockets of tradition" in which some of the old individual skill games have continued. But with few exceptions all the older traditional team skill games have gone. Most children, for example, still know Bull in the Ring, Leap Frog, French and English, Follow the Leader, Sacks on the Mill, Cockfighting, King of the Castle, Paper Chase, Hoops, and Hop, Step, and Jump, but play them only infrequently or because they are encouraged to do so by recreationists or parents.

The general trend in skill games is reflected in the fate that has overtaken Tops and Marbles. Tops faded much earlier than Marbles. In one report it is stated that as early as 1910 the game seemed to be on the wane in Petone. As flax became less accessible and streets more populated, Whip Tops naturally departed from the scene. Today, where Tops is played it tends to be played by the younger boys of the ages of seven and eight. In a few areas there are exceptions, where the game is the practice of older boys as heretofore. Marbles has maintained a stronger hold, though it, too, has tended to be played by children in the lower rather than the upper school. Because of emergency transportation priorities and subsequent import restrictions, the Second World War seriously affected the playing of Marbles, and many children grew up without any knowledge of the game. Now that supplies have arrived again there are flickers of interest here and there in places where the game has been moribund. It is difficult to say whether the few boys to be seen playing the game where it has been thus revived will ever develop school Marbles seasons on a grand scale once more. Can a broken tradition of this sort be reëstablished? Elsewhere the tradition has continued unbroken (with "chippies" throughout the war), and strong seasons still flourish. The present position may be summarized as follows. Of 25 Wellington and Hutt City schools in 1949,

$$
\begin{array}{ll}
\text{for Tops} \quad \cdot \cdot \cdot \left\{ \begin{array}{l} \text{7 reported big season} \\ \text{2 reported a small sprinkling} \end{array} \right\} \cdot \cdot \cdot (9/25) \\[2ex]
\text{for Marbles} \quad \cdot \cdot \left\{ \begin{array}{l} \text{10 reported big season} \\ \text{5 reported a small sprinkling} \end{array} \right\} \cdot \cdot (15/25)
\end{array}
$$

Yet every elderly informant reported having played both Tops and Marbles in one fashion or another, and reported also the occurrence of large school seasons for these games.

Just as modern modes of recreation have affected the types of skill games played, so these modes of recreation have affected the old game "seasons." In the earlier period the seasonal boundaries within any one school were relatively rigid. But this was a state of affairs which could continue only so long as the children's play group was always the arbiter of its own play destiny, as was the case when its play objects were chiefly of its own manufacture and its play occasions under its own control. Today children's play groups are subject to the recurrent and unpredictable stimulation of novel play objects entering the toy market. The old seasons have been further upset by the fickleness of supply and demand in the economy of the twentieth century. In addition, modern adults have taken an educational, a psychological, and a commercial interest in the children's play world, and as a result have brought that world under the sway of laws other than those narrowly conservative peer-group laws which previously dominated it. The new major sports seasons have ridden roughshod across the old traditional boundaries at the same time as they have deprived those boundaries of their one-time paramount importance. Deviators from those old traditional boundaries are regarded more tolerantly than they used to be, not necessarily because there is more tolerance in modern playground life (though it seems as if this is probably the case), but because those traditional boundaries are now matters of trifling concern. It might be rash to conclude that that same tolerance exists for those who deviate from the major sports by refusing to play them. The pervasive influence of the modern sports is certainly much greater.

Yesterday the seasonal variations were initiated by children and ran their course more or less directly in accord with the laws of child nature. They arose spontaneously from the unorganized resources of child nature working upon a play-group tradition of great antiquity. Today the children's pattern of seasonal variation is responsive to many other influences which arise from outside the children's play group.

Merely because many of the old games have gone it does not necessarily follow that the modern playground is not a lively environment for children. In many respects children's play is much more active. Just as there is much more movement and speed in the modern world than there was in the relatively leisurely world of the nineteenth century, so in the modern playgrounds there is much more movement. The characteristic play object of the twentieth-century playground, for example, is the ball. It is a much swifter and more mobile play object than the characteristic play objects of the nineteenth century. Let us consider, briefly, some examples of modern games in which the ball plays an important part.

One of the most successful of modern games for children of ten and eleven years is *Longball* (K-86). It was originally taught to New Zealand children by school physical education specialists in the 1940's and has subsequently carried over into their spontaneous play. It is a game which combines elements of Rounders, Ball Tag, and Bar the Door, all of which are old games that have persisted into the modern period. The game is played on a rectangular field, as in Bar the Door, and the batting team runs back and forward between the two bases at opposite ends of the field. A ball is pitched to members of the batting team in turn. A batter may run on his own hit or on the hit of another player. Nobody may run on a hit that does not go straight up the field inside the side lines of the rectangular space. The fielders' aim is to get the ball and tag the members of the batting side as they run between bases. Three players tagged puts the batting team out. The batting side scores a run only when one of its batters returns to the home base. They may wait down at the far end until someone else is batting and then run. The bat is a small round stick about a foot in length and in inch in diameter.

Ball Tag (K-87), known also as Branding, is simply a game of chasing in which the players tag each other with the ball. A slightly more complex version is Kingy (Wellington South). In this game the players begin by standing round in a circle with their arms on one another's shoulders. The ball is dropped in the middle of the circle. When it touches someone's foot that person is He. He may then run after and ball-tag another player, who then joins his side. Once there are two of them, however, no player may run with the ball. This means that the game henceforth requires team passing as well as ball-tagging. Every player tagged helps the He players until the game finishes with one player trying to avoid being cornered by all the rest of the players, who pass the ball from one to another and only throw when they are near enough to tag him.

Prisoner's Base (see K-63) is an old game which has been revived as a result of the influence of school physical education specialists.

Echo (K-88) is an outdoor game widely known throughout Southland and in individual schools elsewhere. The children are divided into two teams, which line up on opposite sides of the playshed, each team unseen by the other. A ball is thrown by one member of Side A over the playshed to Side B. The B person catching it runs round the shed and attempts to hit one member of Side A before that person can run away and reach the nearby fence. If any A person is hit that person goes on the side of the ball-thrower, Side B. If no one is hit then the running side (A) must have a chance to receive the ball from B and, if successful in catching it, throw it at B. When a catching team misses the catch, then it throws the ball back over the shed and the other team has a chance to catch it and then throw it. The game goes on until all the players have been captured to one side, or "until the bell goes" (Kapuka

South, Southland, 1935). When the catching team catches the ball
they are supposed to cry "echo" so as to warn the other team, who
then begin running toward the nearest fence. I have seen this game
played without the presence of the intervening shed (Takaka, Nelson, 1949).

Rotten Egg (K-89), a game also known as Base or Donkey, is a
game similar to the old game of Egg Cap, but without the caps. A
ball is thrown into the air and a player's name is called. If the ball
is caught it is thrown up again. If it is missed the player whose
name was called tries to get the ball, and when she does, cries
"Stop!" or "Base!" The other players who have been running
away, now stop. The He player then takes a prearranged number
of steps toward one of the other players (the players may have
agreed before the game to allow, say, two steps) and attempts to hit
her with the ball. If that player is hit, then she is the rotten egg and
must fall out; if not hit, then the thrower is the rotten egg. Alternatively, the player who is hit or the unsuccessful thrower may be
the D of Donkey. The next time she fails she will be the DO of
Donkey, and so on. This game is widely known. Equally well
known is another game, also called *Donkey* (K-90), in which players have catches, throwing a ball round a circle. Each time a player
misses a catch that player takes one letter of Donkey until a player
is a complete Donkey. This game is known also as Sick, Dying,
Dead. In this variation any player who misses one catch is "sick"
and goes down on her knees. Any player who misses a second catch
is "dying" and sits down. The player who misses a third catch is
"dead" and lies down on her back. If a "dead" player misses a further catch she is eliminated, and the game goes on until only one
player is left. Pig in the Middle is similar, except that two players
attempt to keep the ball away from a third player in the middle.
The two throw it back and forth to each other. If the middle player
catches the ball, she takes the place of one of the others.

Balls are also used in the many variations of the organized sports
which have grown up since major sports came to have such importance in the playground.

Spontaneous variations of the major sports include, for Rugby:
Comp (K-91) (Nelson, 1949), a game in which several players,
taking turns, kick at the goal posts and receive points according to
the type of kicks with which they succeed; thus, three points for a

"place-kick," two points for a "drop-kick," and one point for a "punt." In *Kicks* (K-92) (Karori, Wellington, 1949), there are two teams of players at opposite ends of the playground. Each team kicks in turn, and if the other team fails to catch the ball they lose a point. In *Mark* (K-93) (Rangataua, 1950), the player who catches the ball must "Mark" it, in the Rugby sense, which means that just as he catches it, he must dig his heel in the air and at the same time cry "Mark." If he does this he gets to kick the ball undisturbed by the others. If he fails to catch and call "Mark," then all scramble for the ball and he who can get it kicks it. In *Scrag* (K-94) (North East Valley, Dunedin, 1949), or Scragging, and in Kick and Collar (Moutere, Nelson, 1949), everybody goes after the player who has the ball. It is a free-for-all, in which the player who has the ball attempts to dispose of it as quickly as he can. Quite often in these games players "wax" each other: that is, two players take turns at having kicks, and in this way one player in difficulties will pass the ball to his partner, who will get the kick in for him.

Cricket variations are *Tippenny Runs* (K-95) or Tip and Run, *French Cricket* (K-96), *Non-Stop Cricket* (K-97), *Country Cricket* (K-98), *Peg Ball* (K-99), and *Hot Rice* (K-100). All of these aim to speed up the normal game and, in a sense, constitute a commentary on the main weakness of Cricket from the elementary school child's point of view. Three of these games, Non-Stop Cricket, Country Cricket, and Peg Ball, are variations which have been introduced by teachers and tend to flourish only in those places where they have been thus encouraged. Tippenny Runs is one of the most widely reported of all cricket games. In this game the two batsmen must run between the wickets every time they tip a ball bowled to them. This greatly increases their chance of going out and accelerates the rotation of batting amongst all the players. French Cricket is a game of long standing in which the ball (usually a soft ball) is thrown at the batter's legs. If his legs are hit the batter is out. The batter must not move once a fielder has caught hold of the ball. While the ball is in flight, however, the batter does his best to get away from the prospective bowler. Bowlers may throw the ball to another fielder rather than bowl it, in an endeavor to catch the batsman napping. These other players then throw the ball straight at the batsman's legs, whether from the side or the back. At Waterloo, Wellington, in 1951, I observed boys playing an

even speedier version of French Cricket. In this game the batsman
batted in the normal way, holding the bat at his side rather than in
front of his legs. In this game the bowler had to bowl "through" the
batsman, that is, hitting his legs or going within a foot of either
side of him. Otherwise the rules were as in French Cricket, except
that the batsman had to be given a chance to square up before the
ball was bowled at him. In Hot Rice (Millerton, Westland, 1949),
known also as Hit and Out (Stockton, Westland, 1949), the players
aimed to hit the batsman with the ball anywhere on the body, not
simply on the legs as in French Cricket. As soon as the batter was
hit he had to drop the bat and pick up the ball. He could throw the
ball at the new batter as soon as that batter had the bat in his hand.

The most widespread of all cricket games is *Putting Out Goes In*
(K-101), in which each player bowls for himself. The players toss
up for the one batting position, and the ball. After that, whichever
player fields the ball, has the right to bowl it. Again, players often
"wax" with each other. It will be noticed that none of these variations of Cricket are team games. They are all individualistic games
in which each child plays for himself.

In Basketball there are variations known as *Defence* (K-102),
Sides (K-103), and *Goals* (K-104), all of which involve either a
competition over shooting at the goal or small-side team competitions. In Hockey there are *Stick Hockey* (K-105), *Hand Hockey*
(K-106), and *Handkerchief Hockey* (K-107), which are adult-
sponsored variations. In Rounders or Softball there are *Danish
Rounders* (K-108), *Dutch Rounders* (K-109), *Rivelea Rounders*
(K-110), *Hand Rounders* (K-111), *Peg Rounders* (K-112), and
Kat (K-113), which, again, are all games sponsored by school recreationists. In Tennis there is *Hand Tennis* (K-114). In Longball
there are *Shortball* (K-115) and *Flyball* (K-116).

It is probable that the increase in playground speed is connected
with the greater suppleness of modern players, a suppleness manifested, for example, in the never-ending acrobatic and handstand-
ing activities of girls. Girls in one school (St. Clair, Dunedin)
claimed that Handstands was their favorite game, "because we
haven't as many games as boys and ours aren't so exciting." It is
evident that the new physical education work in schools has played
a great part in encouraging girls to develop along these lines.

Girls' Hopscotch also reflects the trends of the times. The popular avenue diagram of earlier days has almost completely disappeared, but its place has been taken by a diagram shaped like an aeroplane —a not unnatural development. Rectangular and spiral diagrams continue. In addition a new variety of Hopscotch has arisen, *Ball Hopscotch* (K-117). One type of Ball Hopscotch is as follows: There are eight dens in two rows of four in a rectangular diagram. The ball is rolled into the first den; it is picked up and then bounced in each of the other dens as the child walks through them, putting only one foot in each den. In number eight den the ball is bounced eight times. The child then proceeds through as before, but uses the left hand to roll and bounce the ball. In subsequent rounds the child rolls and bounces the ball while: hopping on the right foot, hopping on the left foot, jumping with both feet, walking round and clasping with one hand the wrist of the bouncing hand, and walking round and clasping hands at back and front between bouncing. This last movement is known as "blue-bottle." A game of this nature was known in Wellington as early as 1910. Girls to-day often play a game of this sort in the spiral diagrams. In one school the girls were even playing a game of *Kicking Ball Hopscotch* (K-118). In that particular school they counted among their other Hopscotch games: *Bouncing Ball Hopscotch* (K-119), *Kicking Block Hopscotch* (K-120), and *Throwing Block Hopscotch* (K-121). In my experience, the younger children play more of the throwing variety and the older children more of the kicking type. There is a report too of *Blind Hopscotch* (K-122).

One well-known London game of which there have been only a few reports in New Zealand is *Flicks* (K-123), in which players pitch cigarette cards up to a mark and the owner of the nearest one takes all. This had some strength in the 1930's when cigarette cards were readily available, but does not seem to have survived the Second World War (Hutt, Wellington, 1935).

PART THREE

Developmental Synopsis

As the major purposes of this work have been folkloristic and historical, it has not been thought advisable to categorize games exclusively in terms of developmental criteria, though these have played a minor part in the choice of categories. To illuminate further the material presented, there follows a brief outline of the manner in which a thoroughgoing organization in developmental terms might proceed. There would be four major categories: (1) choral games; (2) central-person games; (3) individual-skill games; and (4) team games.

1) *Choral games.*—These are games in which all players carry out the same actions, to a choral accompaniment. Such games are popular with the six- to nine-year-olds. The ritualized content and simple form (usually circular) provide movements and motifs which young children can readily comprehend and through which they can gain a security in large-group social activity seldom to be matched outside of games (A-1 through A-5).

2) *Central-person games.*—The majority of games played by children up to eleven years of age are central-person games. They are games in which a number of players are related in special ways to one or more central players. (*a*) Sometimes the central player has a cynosural or *limelight* role in relation to the other players, in which case the games generally contain few competitive features, their movements being prescribed beforehand by song and ritual movement, as when the group dances round in a circle singing about the central person Sally, who is "a-weeping," or the "pretty little girl of mine," or Punchinello "the funny fellow" (Category A). (*b*) Sometimes the central person is a dominating maternal or *leader* figure, and in these cases competition plays some part, as in Mother, Mother, the Pot Boils Over, or May I? (Categories B and D). (*c*) Sometimes the central player is a *fearsome* "He" character, and here competition has an importance parallel with the dramatic features of the game, as, for example, in simple chasing (Category E).

At about the age of ten years two other types of central-person games become of increasing importance. The first type (*d*) consists of those games in which the central person has to maintain his position in the face of open competition from others, as in King of the Castle (K-81). In types *a*, *b*, and *c* of central-person games the group of players may be said to have been on the defensive against the central person. They are now on the attack, attempting to wrest the central person's role from him. These may be termed *attacking* central-person games. (*e*) At about the same age, *scapegoat* central-person games become popular with children. In these the central person is made a "goat" of by the group (A-30, J-8, J-9).

3) *Individual-skill games.*—Arising to importance at about the same time as the attacking central-person games mentioned above are the many games in which children compete as individuals against others in terms of a variety of skills, as in Marbles and Tops (Category K).

4) *Team games.*—The only other important game type of the seven- to nine-year age period are (*a*) the *pack-versus-pack* cowboy-and-Indian games of boys. These are, in effect, very early team games which emphasize dramatic details (capture, gunplay) to a greater extent than straight competition (Category C). By the time that the age of eleven and twelve years has been reached, most of these team games have been replaced by (*b*) *organized-sport* team games, or the children's simplified variations of such games (Category K), and by (*c*) *coöperative group* parlor games in which players work for a common result, as in Consequences (J-22), and on occasion by (*d*) the *team singing* games of Category A.

From this analysis it is clear that at about the age of nine or ten years there is a swing away from the more dramatic types of games to games which are predominantly a test of skill. I would like to suggest that the majority of the dramatic games contain play representations of relationships which children normally experience in their family life. The concern with central adults (parents) becomes in these games a concern with central persons. This is not surprising, as the relation to an adult (say, a dominating or admiring or fearsome one, to be rebelled against, obeyed, or flown from) is the most important social relationship which children have experienced in their early life. The form of the game, therefore, is one that is comprehensible to all the players. Although these players do not as yet have much experience in getting along with one another, they do have in common their experience of the relationships between inferior and superior beings. Such common experiences, when represented in the forms and fantasy content of these games, can bind the children into a group where other things might fail. The most immature central-person games, for example, portray the child in his narcissistic pre-oedipal role, as the center of the family circle. "What can you do, Punchinello, funny fellow?" In the leader and "He" games there is the more mature identification with parent figures seen as arbitrary and fearsome. All children have had the experience of contending, in fact or fantasy, against such figures. In these games they can explore these feelings, but can do so without the dangers that would be involved in exploring such feelings in real life. The games invite exploration (screaming with fear, roaring with rage), but with their rules and the agreement that this is only "play," they safeguard the children from the anxiety which might otherwise result from unguarded exploration and expression of impulse.

But this is only the subjective side of the children's activity. While they are thus recapitulating their personal history (between the ages of five and eight years) under the guise of play, they are also learning the strictly objective and arduous give-and-take of immediate social relations with their peers. These peers, who at first share little but a common plight and similar fantasies, in due course and by their very interaction, are sufficiently confident to shed these play "motifs" and compete equally in terms of physical and intellectual skills. In short, the early central-person games are a symbolic bridge between the child's primary ties to his parents and his secondary ties to his peers. The competitive individual and team games of later years do, of course, contain many vestiges of these early symbolisms (phallic objects, safe-enclosures, etc.), but these are subordinate now to the main cultural concern with effective competition and the chance of victory.

The major point of this very brief sketch is that games would not have their meaningfulness to children if they were not thus intrinsically related to the fabric of human development.

EPILOGUE

The changes in children's games are often interpreted as evidence of the increasing standardization of children's lives. In his recent book, *American Nonsinging Games*, Paul Brewster says, "Supervised play has taken the place of the earlier spontaneous and hence more enjoyable playing and has made participation in games a mechanical performance instead of the delight which it once was and which it should be still."[1] And Norman Douglas, in his minor classic, *London Street Games*, says:

My point . . ., my only point [about children's traditional games], was the inventiveness of the children. . . . one marvels at the stupidity of the social reformer who desires to close to the children the world of adventure, to take them from their birthright of the streets, and coop them up in well regulated and uninspiring playgrounds where under supervision of teachers, their imagination will decline, their originality wither.[2]

Many statements of similar import could be quoted.[3]

When one examines the picture in detail, however, it appears to be more complex than such generalizations indicate. The number of traditional games that children play spontaneously has sharply declined, but this does not mean that children were formerly more "spontaneous," "original," and "imaginative" than they are today.

Consider, for a moment, this question of originality in children's play. The plays in which children are most inventive and original are the informal make-believe and imitative games played by youngsters up to the age of seven and eight years. The evidence shows that there is just as much of this sort of play as there ever

[1] Paul G. Brewster, *American Nonsinging Games* (Norman, Okla., 1953), p. xx.

[2] Norman Douglas, *London Street Games* (London, 1931), p. xi.

[3] For example: C. Deslisle Burns, *Leisure in the Modern World* (London, 1932), p. 126; A. Gesell, *The Child from Five to Ten* (New York, 1946), p. 363; H. C. Lehmann and P. A. Witty, *The Psychology of Play Activities* (New York, 1927), p. 225; H. Marshall, "Children's Play, Games and Amusements," in C. Murchison, ed., *Handbook of Child Psychology* (London, 1933), p. 524.

was. The content of the games may have changed (yesterday's bandits may be today's spacemen), but the creative exercise of the imagination remains a primary function of the play. Further, as has already been pointed out, children in the next age group, the seven- to nine-year-olds, have developed many new leader and tagging games. They can hardly be said to be less original than their predecessors were. To be sure, the ten- to thirteen-year-olds who now spend so much time playing at the major sports appear to have fewer games than nineteenth-century children of those ages. Yet, when we observe modern children in their day-by-day play, we notice that a great proportion of their time is spent in playing their own unorganized variants or original adaptations of the major sports. At the most, only a few hours a week are spent in play activities which are directly refereed by supervising adults. Furthermore, in defense of the modern child it will be remembered that many children of the nineteenth century had only a fraction of the free time that children have today. At home they were often required to help with the very necessary family chores. Often they played games only when at school. The older children of today probably have a greater amount of time for their spontaneous adaptations than the children of the nineteenth century had for their original sports activities! Such a state of affairs is quite contrary to that suggested by other writers. Again, even when modern children do play at games directly refereed or controlled by adults, how true is it to say that these constitute a "mechanical performance"? I have never yet seen one game played in any recreation hall or playground anywhere which I could describe in these terms. Nearly all such games have been, to quote Brewster, but to reverse effect, "enjoyable playing" and a "delight" to the majority of the participants. It is true that children's play has at times been so rigorously controlled that the delight has been taken out of it, but such exceptions are phenomena notably related to the place of Rugby and Cricket in the English social class aspirations and patriotism of the late nineteenth and early twentieth centuries. In brief, there is every evidence that children spend as much time in original play as they ever did—if not more.

All this leads naturally to the question of just how truly original children ever are in their formal games, whether these be old traditional games or new sports. It is something of a paradox that some folklorists should believe that the great *diversity* of games played in the nineteenth century is in itself an indication of the originality of nineteenth-century play, because they have at the same time devoted much effort to showing how conservative children are, and how little originality they employ in their play. Some folklorists have said, for example, that children have inherited their innumerable games from the adult customs of former ages, and that, far from showing any originality in these games, they have handed them on from generation to generation practically unchanged.[4] We do not, of course, have to approve of this point of view, but it presents at the least a counterweight to the claims of those who would assert that the number of games alone constitutes a measure of originality. The truth seems to lie somewhere between these views.[5] Children do conserve group traditions, yet constantly and surely they whittle away at the edges of these traditions, altering them to suit their own ever-changing needs.[6] From this one may conclude that, so far as originality is concerned, the fact that children's play preserves many folkgames or only a few major sports may make little difference.

We usually think of children as being *original* in their play when they introduce novelty into it. Their ability to be novel, however, generally depends upon whether or not they are autonomous. And they are *autonomous* in their play activities to the extent that they are self-directed and self-controlled. A more helpful comparison of the differences between children yesterday and children today follows when we focus our attention on autonomy rather than originality. To what extent did children yesterday have scope for such autonomous activities? Has the situation changed?

At first sight, the completely unsupervised playgrounds of the nineteenth century, where all the games were directed by the children themselves, might seem to have offered greater scope for au-

4 For example: Gomme, II, 514; P. Opie, "Children's Links with Long Ago," *John O'London's Weekly*, 1949, p. 781.

5 Carl Withers, in *A Rocket in My Pocket* (New York, 1948), p. 204, presents views which contrast strongly with those presented by Gomme, Opie, and many others.

6 This process has been dealt with in my doctoral thesis, "The Historical and Psychological Significance of the Unorganized Games of the New Zealand Primary School Children."

tonomous activities. On the other hand, children today spend just as much and probably more time governing their own activities, although they may also spend much time in play organized by adults. Although present-day school play is always supervised by adults, for the greater part in New Zealand this is a distant supervision only. Generally schoolteachers do not interfere with the ongoing activity of the children unless it is unusually violent or dangerous. True, a number of dangerous games have been forced out of the playground by this supervision, but it might be argued that this change has made many children more rather than less autonomous. They are now freer from the fear of the dangerous or violent actions of their more powerful peers. In the more hostile, dangerous, and violent atmosphere of the nineteenth century, playground autonomy must have been, on many occasions, the preserve of the bullies and more powerful group members. For example, young children forced to fight in the school arena for the amusement of elder peers had on such occasions very little autonomy.

Objection may be made to the fact, however, that in the modern playground a comparatively small number of activities are available for the children. Although modern children may be sufficiently original and autonomous in the exercise of these few activities, they are restricted by the limitations indirectly placed upon their choice.[7] This limitation of their own play resources, together with the increased influence of adults on children's play (see p. 205), makes modern children more susceptible to the enthusiasms of their elders. If the latter are sufficiently single-minded, then it is true that they can increasingly manipulate children's preferences toward one-sided play pursuits. In New Zealand there have been a few monomaniacs, for example, who have insisted on training schoolboy Rugby footballers from the age of six years and upwards. Fortunately this has been exceptional. Either from wisdom or from indifference, most adults have left children very much to themselves in their own play hours. This has meant that the modern players are perhaps freer to choose from amongst their fewer ac-

[7] Elsewhere I have suggested ways in which the modern playground could be made to serve in promoting a wider range of potential competences than it does today; see the articles, "What Is a Junk Playground?" *National Education* (journal of the New Zealand Educational Institute), XXXIV (1952), 398–399; and "Postscript on Junk Playgrounds," *ibid.*, XXXV (1953), 8–9.

tivities. The nineteenth-century player seems to have been more rigorously limited to playing activity number one when everyone else did, under threat of physical attack or at least the "smuggin' " of his marbles if he did not.

Up to this point we have drawn an inconclusive picture, with the balance probably tipped in favor of the modern playground. When we consider the total range of children's activities, rather than games alone, the result is overwhelmingly in favor of the situation today. The modern child has many new fields in which he can be autonomous. In the family, instead of being firmly "disciplined" or suppressed, he is more and more being treated as a participant who has a right to make his own decisions about the use of pocket money, leisure time, dress, the decoration of his room, choice of companions, and the like. In the school, a fifty-year development of play theory has introduced innumerable new techniques of self-government in all subject matters. Modified democratic control of the classroom allows increased scope for originality as well as autonomy. Increased material prosperity and a vastly enlarged toy market mean for the child an increased range of consumer play objects and of potentially stimulating activities and hobbies. If he is a member of the middle class the same prosperity has brought him access to innumerable new opportunities for learning specialized leisure-time skills in dancing, music, gymnastics, and painting, which were formerly the preserve of the economically privileged members of the community. The child's voluntary mastery of these skills and his acquaintance with the arts of which they are a part has increased his autonomy. Even the large amount of leisure time spent in assimilating the products of the mass media—comics, radio, movies, and television—has brought new opportunities for the autonomic exchanging of values, preferences, tastes, and "know-how." This taste-exchanging is an active consequence of pastimes which we often think of erroneously as being entirely passive.[8] The effects of such assimilation are at their worst only when the other areas of child activity in family and school do not provide scope for autonomy.

From all of this I conclude that the child of today is a much more

[8] This concept of "taste-exchanging" is borrowed from David Riesman, *The Lonely Crowd* (Hartford, Conn., 1950).

autonomous person than the child of the past. And if this is true it makes nonsense out of any simple comparison between the games of the two centuries that leads to pessimistic conclusions about the children of today.

What seems to me to be a more fundamental contrast may be stated as follows. For the children of the nineteenth century in state schools, play was the only sphere in which they had any great scope for autonomy. It was the therapeutic clinic of the community of children, and in consequence, a "life-space" in which they expressed the *Realpolitik* of the larger world in which they lived. We notice, for example, that they worked at their play with all the intense individualism and earnest craftsmanship that their fathers displayed in the world of work. They spent long years sharpening the edges of their physical and mental competences. Their assiduous practice of, say, Stagknife was a moral counterpart in childhood to dependable application in adult life. Yet today the state-school child, in contrast, is typically a dilettante of games. He participates in innumerable social and physical games in the physical education class, in the recreation hall, and on the playground. Unless he is particularly gifted and destined to be a "sportsman" (and, therefore, in a sense, a professional), he does not spend long hours of assiduous training at any of these games. He is not required to. The requirement laid upon him is only the social one that he be capable of having fun with his peer group, class group, school group, and club group. For him the game is a test of social competence rather than physical or intellectual prowess. Usually the games are so matched with the children's general level of development that the physical and intellectual requirements do not unduly strain the players!

Some reasons for this remarkable change have already been suggested. The children of today find scope for originality and autonomy in too many places to require as much from their games as did the children of the nineteenth century. In consequence, they treat games far more lightly than earlier generations of children did. Douglas and Brewster and others have observed this fact, but, it seems, they have interpreted it incorrectly. Furthermore, they have not observed the compensatory and comparative ease with which modern children are able to flit from old game to new game, always observing the verities that "fun's the thing" and that winning, while extremely important, is not all. Nineteenth-century children showed no such ability to cross gamecraft barriers. Two other influences are important in interpreting this change. Although the puritan-minded of the nineteenth century thought games were trivial, the upper and privileged social classes insisted that sports were character-forming, that games had moral and patriotic qualities, and that play was a social duty. Toward the end of the nineteenth century psychologists began to stress the great importance of games in child development, particularly in social development. It was believed that infants would grow rightly if given sufficient freedom for group play, that delinquents would be redeemed if enlisted in organized sports programs. In other words, aristocrats and psychologists agreed that games had a "socializing" function in growth. When we add to these influences such general sociological changes as the swing from the individualistic society of the nineteenth century to the more socially conscious welfare society of the mid-twentieth century, we begin to see why, in the socially conscious schools and society of today, games have become an exercise of social rather than individual competence. A socially conscious society does not require its members to be entrepreneurs of outstanding play-skill, but expects them to be capable of participating in game fun of many sorts.

In brief, the society of today does not require that children be craftsmen of play; it requires, rather, that they be competent social mixers in play, or, to use a term of some current vogue, it requires that they be "gamesmen."

APPENDIX I

Additional Game Names: Category L

This category consists of the names of games reported as having been played in New Zealand, but concerning which the informants gave no details.

Beg o' My Neighbour (L-1)
Block, Hammer, and Nails (L-2)
Boys and Girls (L-3)
Brewer (L-4)
Brother Ebenezer (L-5)
Cocky Hole (L-6)
Duck Under Water (L-7)
Follow Old Mum to Market (L-8)
Fool, Fool, Come to School (L-9)
Hats (L-10)
Judge and Jury (L-11)
Mummy (L-12)
On and Off the Bridge (L-13)
Pat Ball (L-14)
Pinch (L-15)
Putting an Eye in the Peg (L-16)
Run a Mile (L-17)
Run the Ball (L-18)
Russian Scandal (L-19)
Sir Roger de Coverley (L-20)
There Was an Old Woman (L-21)
Three Little Ships (L-22)
Who's That Knocking at My Door? (L-23)

APPENDIX II

Historical Summary of Game Names

This appendix summarizes what has been reported about the distribution of children's games according to periods described in the text.

GAME NAMES WIDESPREAD BEFORE 1900 (1870–1900)

The following game names were widely known throughout New Zealand before 1900, but were seldom mentioned after that date. Buck Buck (Jump, Little Nag Tail, or Monkey on the Bridge); Buttons; Chevvy Chase; Chibby; Cunning Joe (Cronje, Conjo, or Cunny); Duckstones; Dumb Crambo; How Many Miles to Babylon?; Ickety Bickety; Jingo Ring; Last Pair Out (or Run); Lazy Stick; Pole-Vaulting; Punch King; Queen Anne's Dead; The Queen of Sheba; Sally Waters; Tip Tap Toe.

LOCAL GAME NAMES, 1870–1900

Game names which were known only in some provinces before 1900 and which were seldom mentioned after that date are the following.

OTAGO: Babbity Bowster; Carry My Lady to London; Cum Je Cum; Dooking for Apples; Follow Old Mum to Market; Hop the Hats; Horney; Hot Cockles; Jack a Lingo; Kick Post One; Marry Ma Tanza; Mingle the Bonnets; Nivy Nivy Nick Nack; Oats and Beans and Barley; Peggy; Pinch; Trip and Go; Wallflowers.

CANTERBURY: Baloo Baloo Balight; Block, Hammer, and Nails; Bold Jolly Lads; Boys and Girls; Down in the Valley; Green Grow the Leaves; Hop the Hats; Judge and Jury; There Was an Old Woman; Three Little Ships.

NELSON: Bumpers; Cap-It; Duck Under Water; Here's a Prisoner; Hop-Peg; Hopping Base; Horney; Would You Lend My Mother a Saucepan?

WELLINGTON: Blackthorn; Cap-Oh; Cocky Hole; Merry Go Rounds; Mummy; Run the Ball.

TARANAKI: All In; Dumpy; Flicks; Hats; Hopping Base; I Love My Beau with an A; Putting an Eye in the Peg.

HAWKES BAY: Brother Ebenezer; Fool, Fool, Come to School.

AUCKLAND: My Aunt Sally Has Gone to Paris; Wallflowers.

Game Names Widespread from 1870 until 1914

Game names which were widespread before 1900 and until the First World War but have been mentioned only infrequently thereafter are the following. Bells; Bingo; Butcher's Bat; Cat's Cradle; Croquet; Egg and Spoon Races; Egg Cap; Fill the Gap; Fly the Garter (Flying the Gap); General Post; Green Gravels; Honey Pots; The Jolly Miller; Knucklebones (Jacks, Knuckles, Chuckstones, Hucklebones); Lotto; Old Woman from Botany Bay; Pretty Little Girl of Mine; Quoits; Shinty; Skittles; Smuggling the Geg; Stagknife; Tip-Cat; Thread the Needle; The Three Dukes (or a Duke or Two Dukes or Saucy Duke).

Local Game Names, 1870–1914

Less generally known were the following game names.

OTAGO: Follow Her to London; Goosey; Holding; Hurling; Kit Cat; London Bridge; Round and Round the Village; Space Ring; Space to Space; When I Was a Lady; Wiggle Waggle.

CANTERBURY: Brewer; Chuckfarthing; The Parson's Cat; Trading; What Colour's the Sky?

GOLDEN BAY: Homaiacky; Jenny Jones; King Pin; Stealing Grass; Tallyho; Teazle.

Game Names Widespread between 1870 and 1950

This section includes the names of games which were played generally before 1900 and are still played today. Most of these games are seldom played as much today as formerly. The names of games that have retained their popularity are italicized: Animal, Vegetable, or Mineral; *Bar the Door* (or Red Rover, or King Seenie); Bedlam; Bird-Nesting; *Blindman's Buff*; Board Games; Bows and Arrows; Bull in the Ring; *Card Games*; Charades; *Circuses*; Cockfighting; Consequences; *Cricket*; *Daisy Chains*; Darts; Do As I Do; *Dolls*; *Draughts*; Draw a Bucket (Pail) of Water; Drop the Handkerchief; Ducks and Drakes; Eggs in the Basket; Family Coach; Fire, Air, and Water; Fishing; Follow the Leader; *Foot Races*; *Football*; Forfeits; French and English; Ghost in the Garden; *Giant Strides*; Hares and Hounds (Fox and Hounds); Hen and Chickens (Fox and Geese); *Hide and Seek*; *Hide the Thimble* (Key); Hoops; Hop, Step, and Jump; *Hopscotch*; Horses; *Houses*; *I Spy*; In and Out the Windows; Kick the Tin (or Boot); King of the Castle; Kiss in the Ring; Kites; Leap Frog; Marbles; Moonlight, Starlight; Mother, Mother, the Pot Boils Over; The Mulberry Bush; Musical Chairs; No Man Standing; *Noughts and Crosses*; Nuts and May; Odd Man Out; Oranges and Lemons; Paper Chase; Pat Ball; Pea-Shooters; Peep Shows; Pitch and Toss; Poor Sally (Jenny, Alice) Is a-Weeping; Prisoners; Prisoner's Base; Postman's Knock; *Puss in the Corner*; Rabbiting; Ring a Ring a Roses; Rotten Eggs; Rounders; Sacks on the Mill; *Schools*; Shanghais; Sheep, Sheep; *Shops*; Simon Says; *Skipping*; Skipping Stones; Sledges; Soldiers (Conkers); Spin the Trencher; *Statues*; *Steps and Strides*; Stilts; *Swimming*; *Tail on the Donkey*; Telegrams; *Tig or Tag*; *Tiggy Tiggy Touchwood*; *Tinker Tailor Grass*; Tip Tap; *Tip the Finger*; Tom Tiddler's Ground; Tops; Trading; Transfers; *Tuppenny Catches*; Twos and Threes; Whips; Whispers; Word-Making.

Game Names Appearing Between 1900 and 1914 of which There Is Little Earlier Record

Game names recorded for the period between 1900 and 1914 and little known before 1900 are as follows.

WEST COAST: Dunk and Davey; Spang-Weazling.

WELLINGTON: Beg o' My Neighbour; Bellahonie; Bumble Puppy; Colours; Fives; Here Come Two Nuns; Isaac and Rebecca; On and Off the Bridge; Run a Mile; Scrag; Who Goes Round My Stone Wall?

AUCKLAND: Ball Hopscotch; Ball-Bouncing; My Fair Young Lady; Rushes and Reeds; Solomon Says; Surrender the Tower; Walls.

HAWKES BAY: Wolf, Wolf, Go Home.

CANTERBURY: Gag; Poor Old Tom; Rabbits and Rips; Skin a Snake; Steal a Peg; Steps; Toodle-em-Buck.

NELSON: Branding; Creeping; O'Leary; Steps and Stairs; Who's That Walking Round My House Tonight?

OTAGO: Sir Roger de Coverley; Who's That Knocking at My Door?

Game Names Appearing More Frequently after than before 1914

Game names that appeared more often after the First World War are the following. The Alley Alley Ooh; Alphabets; Ball Hopscotch; Ball Tag; Base; Bedlam; Big and Wee; Black Peter; Broken Barley; Bum, Bum, Here We Come; Busy Bees; Cabbages; Cauliflowers; Comp; Country Cricket; Creeping (Creep the Curtain); Cripple Jack; Danish Rounders; Defence; Do As I Do; Donkey; Dutch Rounders; Echo; Farmer in the Dell; Flyball; French Cricket; Fruits; Giant Strides (Steps and Strides); Giant's Treasure; Go, Go, Stop; Goals; Hand Hockey; Hand Rounders; Handkerchief Hockey; Hideygo; Hot Rice; Initials; Ivory; Jack of All Sorts; Johnny in the Inkpot; Kat; Keys or Pads; Kicks; Letters; Longball; May I?; Names; Nigger Boys; Non-Stop Cricket; Odd Man Out; Opossum; Pat Ball; Pebbles and Stones; Peg Ball; Penny Under the Chair; Pig in the Middle; Please, Jack, May We Cross Your Golden River?; Point to the Bell; Pounds, Shillings, and Pence; Prisoners; Punchinello; Queenie; Rivelea Rounders; Rotten Egg; Sardines; Seat Tig; Sevens; Shadow Tig; Shortball; Sides; Spin the Trencher; Statues; Stick Hockey; Stone Tag; Tail on the Donkey; Telegrams; Tiki Tiki Touchwood; Tip Tap; Tip the Finger (Draw the Snake, Round and Round the Merry Go Round); Trading; Vegetables.

APPENDIX III

Sources of Information

In this appendix are listed the names of persons and schools that contributed to this research. The name of each informant is followed by
the place and the date to which his report refers. If the report was
written, the date is followed by the abbreviation "R" (Report); if oral,
by the abbreviation "I" (Interview). Among the persons interviewed,
however, were some who did not wish their names recorded, and the
entries on their contributions (giving place and time of the games
they described) are therefore labeled as anonymous, "Anon.," instead
of beginning with the informants' names. The names of the schools
visited are followed by the abbreviation "SV" (School Visit); and the
names of the schools mentioned by children but not visited by the investigator are followed by the abbreviation "SR" (School Report).

In order to show the geographical distribution of the reports, the
sources are listed according to provinces. The list proceeds from north
to south: North Auckland, Auckland, Taranaki, Hawkes Bay, Wellington, Wairarapa, Nelson, Marlborough, Westland, Canterbury, Otago,
and Southland. Under each province, personal sources are given first,
then the schools, if any. If the informants are all from different localities, there is a single list of personal sources, with the recorded names
alphabetically arranged and the anonymous contributors mentioned
last. But if there are any cities or townships from which two or more
contributions were received, the local groups of informants are listed
first, under their respective localities, and all other informants are
listed together under the subhead "Other Towns."

North Auckland Province

Mr. W. G. Johnston, North Auckland,   Mr. C. Spanahake, North Auckland,
  1910–1920 (R)   1940–1950 (R)
Mr. D. A. McPherson, Whangarei,   Mr. I. Sparks, Matamata, 1920–1930
  1896–1900 (R)   (R)

Auckland Province
AUCKLAND CITY

Mrs. W. D. Dodd, 1910–1915 (R)   Mr. Oates, 1915–1920 (I)
Mrs. James, Onehunga, 1905–1910 (I)   Mrs. Shand, 1900–1905 (I)
Mrs. I. Moore, 1905–1915 (R)   [Anon.], 1935 (I)

OTHER TOWNS

Mr. Anderson, Ohatu, 1920 (I)
Mrs. J. Beever, Glenn Massey, 1912–
  1925 (R)
Mr. J. Ching, Te Mawhai, 1930 (I)
Mr. J. Delahunty, Thames, 1890–1895
  (I)
Mr. Gillies, Maroa, 1949 (I)
Mr. Holyoake, Bay of Plenty, 1910–
  1915 (I)

Mrs. E. D. McIntosh, Bay of Plenty
  (R)
Mr. B. Palmer, Paroa, 1949 (I)
Mr. P. Wilson, Tauranga, 1933–1938
  (I)
[Anon.], Hamilton, 1935 (I)
[Anon.], Paerata, 1930–1935 (I)

SCHOOLS

Diocesan Girls' High (SR)
Intermediate Normal (SV)
Papakura Normal (SV)

Papatoetoe (SR)
St. Cuthbert's Girls' College (SR)

Taranaki Province
NEW PLYMOUTH

Mr. W. H. Clark, New Plymouth,
  1880–1890 (R)

Mrs. E. Vivian, Weston, 1885–1895
  (R)

WAITARA

Mr. N. M. Chappell, 1899–1905 (R)   Miss I. K. Wylie, 1902–1909 (R)

OTHER TOWNS

Mrs. M. Blampied, Mangopeetu, King
  Country, 1900–1910 (R)

Hawkes Bay Province

Mr. F. L. Combs, Gisborne, 1890–1895
  (I)
Mr. E. S. Harrison, Hastings, 1925–
  1930 (R)
Mrs. A. M. Isdale, Putoka, 1920–1924
  (R)
Mr. McGregor, Waikatea, 1910–1920
  (I)

Mr. T. McKenzie, Waingahe, 1930–
  1940 (I)
Mrs. H. Shaw, Napier, 1949 (R)
Mr. Turley, Otane, 1920–1930 (I)
Mrs. Verrier-Jones, Napier, 1949 (R)
[Anon.], Napier, 1890–1900 (I)

SCHOOLS

Napier Girls' High (SR)

Wellington Province
PALMERSTON NORTH

Mrs. G. C. Birch, 1932–1937 (R)
Mr. A. E. Campbell, 1915–1920 (I)

Mrs. Lewis, Terrace End, 1910–1920
  (I)

Mr. J. K. McKay, 1920–1940 (R)
Mrs. Murray, 1914–1920 (I)
Mr. J. Penketh, 1920–1940 (R)
Mr. Philpott, 1930–1935 (I)

Mrs. E. J. Sutton-Smith, 1905–1910 (I)
Mr. H. Wollerman, 1895–1900 (I)

WANGANUI

Mr. Pirdie, 1930–1936 (I)

Mrs. D. Singleton, Wanganui, 1900–1910 (R)

WELLINGTON CITY

Mr. N. Aitken, 1890–1900 (I)
Mr. P. Anderson, 1949 (I)
Professor C. L. Bailey, 1915 (I)
Mrs. B. Barcus, 1890–1900 (R)
Mr. J. Barnard, Johnsonville, 1949 (I)
Miss Burgess, 1949 (I)
Mr. W. Burgess, 1949 (I)
Mr. W. J. Clark, 1910–1920 (R)
Miss H. Crump, Lower Hutt, 1935–1940 (I)
Miss B. Dibble, Island Bay, 1935–1940 (I)
Mrs. Aileen Findlay, 1920–1925 (R)
Mr. A. E. Gell, 1905–1915 (I)
Mrs. E. Gillon, 1882–1892 (I)
Mr. E. B. Goddard, Petone, 1904–1913 (R)
Mrs. P. Hattaway, 1920–1925 (I)

Mr. D. Hempleman, 1935 (I)
Mrs. Innes, Wainui-o-mata, 1910–1920 (I)
Miss Muriel Kim, 1948 (R)
Mr. E. McDonald, Mount Cook, 1880 (R)
Mr. P. Mitchell, 1949 (I)
Mr. B. Piper, Eastern Hutt, 1935–1940 (I)
Mrs. J. C. Reid, 1918–1925 (R)
Mr. Rendall, Eastbourne, 1930–1935 (I)
Mrs. Rome, 1890–1900 (I)
Mrs. W. Sutton, Kaiwarra, 1905–1910 (I)
Mrs. D. Tooby, Karori, 1930–1935 (I)
Mr. William Toomuth, 1870–1880 (R)

SCHOOLS

Clifton Terrace (SR)
Island Bay (SV)
Karori (SV)

Mount Cook (SR)
Northland (SR)

Wairarapa Province

Mr. Barnes, Epokongiro, 1905–1910 (I)
Mrs. Catherine Gregory, Kohinui, 1900 (R)
Mr. Jonsen, Carterton, 1895–1900 (R)
Mr. D. H. Leitch, Ratapiko, 1949 (R)
Mrs. Manchester, 1949 (I)
Mrs. T. Muir, Carterton, 1930–1935 (I)

Mrs. J. Ponga, Masterton, 1925–1930 (R)
Mr. D. O'Connor, 1920–1925 (I)
Miss Oswin, South Featherston, 1903–1905 (I)
Mr. Roydhouse, 1900–1905 (I)
[Anon.], Aohunga, 1949 (I)
[Anon.], Ratapiko, 1900 (I)
[Anon.], Ratapiko, 1930 (I)

Aohunga (SV)   Mangitainoka (SV)
Eketahuna (SR)   Pongaroa (SV)
Horoeka (SV)   Rangapiko (SR)
Kohinui (SR)   Rangataua (SR)
Makuri (SV)   Woodville (SR)

Nelson Province
BRIGHTWATER

Mr. Bryant, 1920–1925 (R)   Mrs. M. Cameron, 1920–1925 (R)

COLLINGWOOD

Mr. Page, Sr., 1890–1895 (I)   Mrs. Wigsell, 1900–1905 (I)
Mr. Wigsell, 1895–1900 (I)

NELSON

Mrs. A. M. Anderson, 1894–1896 (R)   Mrs. H. S. Newbury, 1946 (R)
Mrs. C. M. Blackett, 1886–1890 (R)   Mr. Shand, 1875–1880 (I)
Mr. Goodyear, 1895–1900 (I)   Mr. A. B. Thompson, 1910–1915 (I)
Mrs. Goodyear, 1895–1900 (I)   Mrs. Win, 1935–1940 (I)
Mr. Hasse, 1890–1900 (I)

ONEKAKA

Miss M. Peterson, 1949 (R)   Miss Z. Thomas, 1949 (R)

ROCKVILLE

Mr. Berry, Sr., Rockville, 1895–1900   Mr. Berry, Jr., 1920–1925 (I)
    (I)   Mrs. Jamieson, 1894–1902 (I)

TAKAKA

Mrs. Hasse, 1900–1908 (I)   Mr. Lewis, 1900 (I)
Mr. Kirk, 1885–1890 (I)   Mr. Page, Jr., 1910–1920 (I)

OTHER TOWNS

Mrs. E. R. Edwards, Lower Moutere,   Mr. K. L. Sigglelow, Upper Moutere,
    1900 (R)   1930 (I)
Mrs. E. Hodgson, Richmond, 1885–   Mr. L. Whatman, Waimea, 1925–1930
    1895 (I)   (I)
Mr. Isdell, Stillwater, 1885–1895 (I) Mrs. M. Woodley, Lower Moutere,
Mr. L. R. Palmer, Waimate West,   1900 (R)
    1920 (I)

SCHOOLS

Aorere (SR)   Barrytown (SR)
Bainham (SR)   Brightwater (SR)

Collingwood (SV)   Stoke (SR)
Kotinga (SR)   Takaka (SV)
Manganakau (SR)   Takaka Convent (SR)
Motupipi (SR)   Tarakahe (SR)
Nelson Central (SV)   Upper Moutere (SV)
Onekaka (SR)   Upper Takaka (SR)
Pakawau (SR)

Marlborough Province

Mrs. A. A. Barton, Blenheim, 1911–
  1919 (R)

Westland Province
DENNISTON

Miss Innes, Denniston, 1930–1940 (I)   Mr. Shand, 1910–1920 (I)
Mr. T. Muir, 1930–1935 (I)

GRANITY

Mr. Kean, 1900–1905 (I)   Mr. D. G. Rogers, 1930–1934 (R)
Mr. Murry, 1895–1900 (I)   Mrs. Watson, 1895–1900 (I)
Mr. Prosser, 1930–1935 (I)

WESTPORT

Mr. James Merton, 1895–1900 (R)   Miss Strachan, 1920–1925 (I)
Mrs. Murry, 1895–1900 (I)

OTHER TOWNS

Mrs. G. Bleach, Ross, 1920–1925 (R)   Mr. I. Orman, Millerton, 1928–1936
Mrs. P. Dennahie, West Coast, 1910–   (I)
  1920 (I)   [Anon.], West Coast, 1930–1935 (I)
Mr. James, Murchison, 1890–1895 (I)   [Anon.], 1920–1925 (I)
Mr. Murry, Seddonville, 1890–1900
  (I)

SCHOOLS

Awatura (SR)   Hokitika (SV)
Barrytown (SR)   Hokitika Convent (SV)
Denniston (SV)   Kahatahi (SR)
Dobsen (SV)   Kaiata (SV)
Granity (SV)   Kaihinu (SR)
Granity Convent (SV)   Kanieri (SR)
Greymouth (SR)   Kumara (SR)
                                Lake Rotama (SR)
Greymouth Main (SR)   Lower Koiterangi (SR)
Harihari (SR)   Millerton (SR)

Paenga (SR)
Ross (SR)
Ruatapu (SR)
Seddonville (SV)
Sheffield (SR)

Stockton (SV)
Upper Koiterangi (SR)
Westport South (SR)
Woodstock (SR)

Canterbury Province
CHRISTCHURCH

Mr. R. de B. Adamson, Papanui, 1903–1904 (R)
Mrs. J. R. Allison, 1920–1925 (R)
Mr. J. Auten, Shirley, (I)
Mr. L. Cleveland, 1920–1925 (I)
Mr. Maffey, Sumner, 1905–1910 (I)
Miss I. Norwood, 1948 (R)
Miss B. Odell, 1928–1934 (I)
Miss F. Owens, 1893–1895 (R)
Mr. G. Parkin, 1919–1920 (I)

Miss Rackham, Beckenham, 1935–1940 (I)
Mr. E. Riach, 1904–1905 (R)
Mr. Thomson, 1925–1930 (I)
Mr. G. Van Haast, 1887–1880 (R)
Mrs. S. A. Watkins, 1870–1875 (R)
Mrs. P. Wilson, Akaroa, 1890–1900 (R)
[Anon.], 1875–1880 (I)
[Anon.], 1930 (I)

TIMARU

Mr. G. V. Gussell, Adair, 1895–1900 (R)

Mr. D. Hilary, 1935–1940 (I)
Mr. Malthus, 1880–1890 (I)

WAIMATE

Mr. Dewar, 1914–1918 (I)

Mr. McKenzie, 1890–1900 (I)

OTHER TOWNS

Mr. R. de B. Adamson, Heathcote Valley, 1899–1901 (R)
Miss Bowen, Ashburton, 1935–1940 (I)
Mr. W. H. Cartwright, South Canterbury, 1900–1910 (R)
Mrs. H. Chapman, Elmwood, 1913–1922 (R)

Mrs. McCatchy, Oxford, 1950 (R)
Mrs. Page, Rakaia, 1910–1920 (I)
Mrs. P. S. Phillips, Ashburton, 1949 (R)
Mrs. S. Rockell, Amberley, North Canterbury, 1890–1900 (R)
[Anon.], Akaroa, 1880–1890 (I)
[Anon.], Kaikoura, 1925–1930 (I)

SCHOOLS

Oxford (SR)

Christchurch Normal (SV)

Otago Province
DUNEDIN

Mr. C. R. Allen, 1870–1880 (R)
Mr. James Begg, 1880–1890 (R)
Mr. Chapman-Cohen, Forbury, 1915–1925 (I)

Mr. Crawford, 1930–1935 (I)
Mrs. Gubbins, 1880–1890 (I)
Mr. Harrison, 1930–1935 (I)
Mr. Hudson, 1930–1935 (I)

Mrs. Hutchison, 1890–1895 (I)

Mr. A. Lee, 1900–1905 (I)

Mr. Luke, Anderson's Bay, 1900–1915 (I)

Mr. A. McDavidson, 1920–1948 (I)

Mr. McGeorge, 1880–1885 (I)

Mrs. D. Malloch, 1900–1905 (I)

Mrs. T. Muir, 1905–1914 (I)

Mrs. T. Murray, 1910–1920 (I)

Mr. Nind, 1900–1905 (I)

Mr. Robertson, 1890–1895 (I)

Mr. Shand, 1900–1910 **(I)**

Mrs. M. Stronach, 1877 (R)

Professor Tennant, 1875–1880 (I)

Miss V. Turton, 1870–1880 (I)

Mr. Tyrell, 1905–1910 (I)

Miss A. Woodhouse, 1890–1896 **(R)**

[Anon.], 1925–1930 (I)

[Anon.], 1865–1890 (I)

[Anon.], 1870–1880 (I)

[Anon.], Kaitangata, 1927–1928 (I)

[Anon.], 1925–1930 (I)

[Anon.], 1935 (I)

[Anon.], 1905 (I)

[Anon.], Maori Hill, 1920–1930 (I)

[Anon.], 1890–1895 (I)

[Anon.], Mornington, 1948 (I)

[Anon.], Kensington, 1947 (I)

[Anon.], Tainui, 1935–1940 (I)

HAMPDEN

Mr. McCarrow, 1880–1885 (I)   Mrs. McCarrow, 1885–1890 **(I)**

WAIKOUAITI

Miss D. Black, 1880–1890 (I)

Mrs. Brown, 1880–1885 (I)

Mr. J. Brown, Sr., 1870–1875 (I)

Mr. J. Brown, Jr., 1915–1920 (I)

Mrs. Henderson, 1890–1900 **(I)**

Mr. D. Malloch, 1885–1890 (I)

Mrs. M. Racham, 1900 (I)

Mr. E. J. Sutton-Smith, 1890–1910 (I)

Mr. Templeton, 1895–1900 (I)

Mrs. Templeton, 1895–1900 (I)

OTHER TOWNS

Mr. Bathgate, Outram, 1927

Dr. J. Brugh, South Clutha, 1875–1880 (I)

Mrs. W. H. Cormack, North Otago, 1900–1910 (R)

Miss Fisher, Alexandra, 1930 (I)

Mr. R. Gray, Lawrence, 1880–1885 (I)

Mrs. Henderson, Catlin, 1895–1900 (I)

Mrs. Johnstone, Tahataki, 1877–1885 (I)

Mr. Marton, Milton, 1910–1915 (I)

Mr. G. O. Matheson, Palmerston South, 1896–1900 (I)

Mr. Patterson, Heriot, 1920–1930 (I)

Mrs. E. Percy, Alexandra, 1910–1920 (R)

Mrs. Reid, Salisbury, Taieri, 1860–1870 (I)

Mr. C. W. Ross, Queenstown, Central Otago, 1880 (R)

Mr. Searl, Oamaru, 1905–1910 (I)

[Anon.], Alexandra, 1930 (I)

[Anon.], Caversham, 1949 (I)

[Anon.], Clinton, 1940 (I)

[Anon.], Karitane, 1925 (I)

[Anon.], Karitane, 1951 (I)

[Anon.], Lauder, 1915 (I)

[Anon.], Taieri, 1870–1880 (I)

[Anon.], Taieri, 1930–1935 (I)

[Anon.], Tapanui, 1880–1885 (I)

[Anon.], Weddeburn, 1845 (I)

SCHOOLS

Caversham (SV)

Forbury (SV)

Hampden (SV)

MacAndrew Intermediate (SV)

North East Valley (SV)

Ngapara (SR)

St. Clair (SV)

Waikouaiti (SV)

Southland Province

WAIANIWA

Mr. William Grieve, 1870 (R)

Mr. George McDonald, 1870 (R)

OTHER TOWNS

Mrs. C. Duthrie, Waikari, 1925–1930 (R)

Miss Ford, Wyndam, 1940–1945 (I)

Mr. Hamilton, Southland, 1948 (R)

Mrs. E. M. Laing, Riverdale, 1900 (R)

Mr. McGibbon, 1920–1930 (R)

Mrs. P. McKenzie, 1880–1890 (R)

Mr. Phillips, Tuatapere, 1923–1924 (I)

Mrs. E. Scott, 1895–1900 (R)

Mr. Young, Isles Bank, 1945 (I)

[Anon.], Lumsden, 1948 (I)

[Anon.], Isles Bank, 1945 (I)

[Anon.], Southland, 1914–1918 (I)

[Anon.], Invercargill, 1925–1930 (I)

[Anon.], Invercargill, 1930 (I)

[Anon.], Ranfurly, 1948 (I)

[Anon.], Stirling, 1930–1935 (I)

[Anon.], Gore, 1930–1935 (I)

BIBLIOGRAPHY

This bibliography includes works published in New Zealand and a few British and American sources used for comparative purposes. The majority of the New Zealand references are available through the New Zealand National Library Service, Wellington, New Zealand.

I. School Jubilee Celebration Booklets

The following booklets were, for the most part, published and written by the schools mentioned in their titles. The only dates given are, in general, those that are part of the title. The later of these dates indicates the year of publication.

Albany Street School, 1874–1924.
Anderson's Bay School, Seventieth Anniversary, 1858–1928.
Auckland Grammar School, 1869–1929.
Balclutha Public School, Souvenir Booklet, 1863–1931.
Blenheim Borough School, 1859–1937.
Carterton District High School, 1861–1937.
Caversham School Sixty-fifth Anniversary Celebrations, 1861–1926.
Cheltenham School District Jubilee, *These Fifty Years*, 1886–1936.
College Street School, Palmerston North, 1893–1943.
Dannevirke North School, 1872–1936.
Dannevirke South School, 1900–1950.
The Elsthorpe School, Golden Jubilee, 1898–1948.
Gladstone School, Diamond Jubilee, 1898–1936.
Grovetown School, *The Early History of the School of the Big Bush.*
   (Dates not given.)
Hampstead School, Ashburton East, Jubilee Magazine, 1886–1936.
Invercargill Middle School Jubilee, 1873–1923.
Kaitangata School, Sixty-first Anniversary, 1866–1927.
Karamu School, 1889–1939.
Kopuaranga School, 1885–1935.
MacCandrew Road School, 1883–1933.
Manakau School, 1888–1948.
Manawaru Public School Jubilee, 1900–1950.
Mangapiko Te Awamutu, 1879–1939.
Mangatainoka School, 1889–1949.
Manuku School Jubilee, 1883–1933.
Mosgiel District High School, Diamond Jubilee, 1871–1931.

Newtown School, Jubilee Souvenir, 1879–1934.
North West Valley School, 1851–1932.
Oamaru South School, 1877–1929.
Ohakune District High School, *A Mountain and a School,* 1896–1940.
Ohaupo District High School, Waikato, 1869–1939.
Otaua School, Golden Jubilee, 1895–1941.
Opawa School, Seventy-seventh Jubilee Celebration, 1872–1949.
Otaki School, 1886–1946.
Otepopo Reunion, 1864–1929.
Owaka District High School, 1875–1935.
Paekakariki School, 1886–1946.
Papakura, 1877–1937.
Papatawa School, 1887–1937.
Paraparaumu, Jubilee Souvenir of School, 1889–1940.
Parks High Street School, 1864–1924.
Paterangi School, 1876–1936.
Pongaroa School, 1897–1947.
Porirua School, Seventy-fifth Anniversary, 1873–1948.
Port Chalmers District High School, 1856–1948.
Rangitumau School Jubilee Celebrations, 1893–1946.
Ravensbourne School Jubilee, 1877–1927.
Richmond School, 1875–1925.
Riwaka School Jubilee, 1848–1948.
Saint Albans School District Jubilee, 1873–1933.
Sawyer's Bay School, Seventieth Anniversary, 1861–1939.
Souvenir of the Jubilee of the Main School, Timaru, 1874–1929.
Union Street School, 1862–1929.
Waihou School Jubilee, 1880–1930.
Waikanae School, Jubilee Souvenir, 1896–1946.
Waianiwa Jubilee, Southland, 1863–1933.
West Christchurch School Jubilee, 1874–1924.
Whakaronga School, Stony Creek, Palmerston North, 1877–1937.
Wylie's Crossing School, Taieri Plain, Otago, 1894–1944.

II. Other New Zealand Sources

In the following references the abbreviation N.Z.C.E.R. indicates that this item is a manuscript in the possession of the New Zealand Council for Educational Research Library, in Brandon Street, Wellington, New Zealand.

Adams, J. J. "School Day Reminiscences, Papanui, 1875–1883." N.Z.C.-E.R.

Alexander, D. "Maori Hand Games," *The New Zealand Education Gazette*, XXV (1946), 123, 133, 155, 185.

Anderson, J. C. *Maori String Figures*, Board of Maori Ethnological Research (Wellington, N.Z., 1927).

Bannister, C. *Early History of Wairarapa* (Masterton, N.Z., 1940).

Barker, Lady. *Station Life in New Zealand* (London, 1870).

——— *Station Amusements in New Zealand* (London, 1875).

Best, Elsdon. *Games and Pastimes of the Maori*, Dominion Museum Bulletin, No. 8 (Wellington, N.Z., 1928).

——— "Scrapbook Number 3." MS in the possession of the Alexander Turnbull Library (Wellington, N.Z.).

Brereton, C. B. *No Roll of Drums* (Wellington, N.Z., 1947).

Campbell, F. C. "Some of My Educational Reminiscences." N.Z.C.E.R.

Chapman, F. R. "The Maori Game of Knuckle-Bone," *Journal of the Polynesian Society*, VIII (1898), 114.

Cohen, G. C. *Early Takaka and the Lower Takaka School, 1880–1949* (Nelson, N.Z., 1949).

Colec, W. C. "Reminiscences, Greendale, 1880." N.Z.C.E.R.

Cowan, J. *Settlers and Pioneers* (Wellington, N.Z., 1940).

Grindley, F. "Chibby," *New Zealand Physical Education Society Bulletin*, II (1947), 148.

Gump, P. V., and B. Sutton-Smith. "The 'It' Role in Children's Games," *The Group*, XVII (1955), 3–8.

Hall, A. M. *A History of the Tua-Marina School, 78th Anniversary, 1871–1949* (Blenheim, N.Z., 1949).

Harcourt, M. *The Day Before Yesterday* (Dunedin, N.Z., 1940).

Heenan, Sir Joseph. "Mount Cook School," *Evening Post*, Wellington, N.Z., June 10, 1950.

Katitata [pseudonym]. "Nostalgia," *Otago Daily Times*, Dunedin, N.Z., April 13 and 21, 1949.

Kempthorne, W. O. "Kempthorne Family History." MS in possession of the Early Settlers' Association (Dunedin, N.Z., 1947).

Leckie, F. M. *The Early History of Wellington College* (Wellington, N.Z., 1933).

Lee, J. A. *Children of the Poor* (London, 1949).

McKenzie, N. R. *The Gael Fares Forth* (Wellington, N.Z., 1933).

Maclean, S. "Knucklebones," *New Zealand Physical Education Society Bulletin*, II (1947), 105–106.

MacMorran, G. *Some Schools and Schoolmasters of Early Wellington* (London, 1900).

"New Zealand Centennial, 1840–1940," *The Press*, Christchurch, N.Z., March 19, 1940.

Rosenberg, B. G., and B. Sutton-Smith. "A Revised Conception of Masculine-Feminine Differences in Play Activities," *The Journal of Genetic Psychology*, XCVI (1960), 165–170.

Roydhouse, A. P. "Egg Cup," *New Zealand Physical Education Society Bulletin*, IV (1948), 181.

———— "Sevens," *ibid.*, p. 182.

Schofield, G. H. *The History of Tokomairiro District High School, 1856–1931* (Dunedin, N.Z., 1931).

Simpson, H. M. *The Women of New Zealand* (Wellington, N.Z., 1940).

Soper, E. L. *The Otago of Our Mothers* (Dunedin, N.Z., 1948).

Sutcliffe, J. R. "Reminiscences, Marton, 1903–1909." N.Z.C.E.R.

Sutton-Smith, B. "Children at Play Seventy Years Ago," and "Children at Play in the Twentieth Century," MSS of ten radio talks delivered in 1952 and 1955, and now in the possession of the New Zealand Broadcasting Service, Wellington, N.Z.

———— "Competitive Athletics for Primary School Children," *National Education*, Wellington, N.Z., XXXV (1953), 289–291.

———— "Declining Festival," *The New Zealand Listener*, XXV (1951), 8.

———— "The Fate of English Traditional Games in New Zealand," *Western Folklore*, XI (1952), 250–253.

———— "A Formal Analysis of Game Meaning," *ibid.*, XVIII (1959), 13–24.

———— "The Game Rhymes of New Zealand Children," *ibid.*, XII (1953), 14–24.

———— "The Historical and Psychological Significance of the Unorganized Games of New Zealand Primary School Children," doctoral thesis. MS, 900 pp. Copy in the Victoria University Library, Wellington, N.Z. Microfilm copy (positive, 2 reels), Ball State Teachers' College Library, Muncie, Indiana.

———— "The Kissing Games of Adolescents in Ohio," *Midwest Folklore*, IX (1959), 189–211.

———— "The Last Frontier," *National Education*, Wellington, N.Z., XXXVI (1954), 134–135.

———— "Marbles Are In: Some Observations on the 'Seasonal' Nature of Children's Games in New Zealand," *Western Folklore*, XII (1953), 186–193.

———— "The Meeting of Maori and European Cultures and Its Effects upon the Unorganised Games of Maori Children," *Journal of the Polynesian Society*, LX (1951), 93–107.

———— "New Zealand Variants of the Game 'Buck Buck,' " *Folklore*, LXII (1952), 329–333.

———— "Postscript on Junk Playgrounds," *National Education*, Wellington, N.Z., XXXV (1953), 8–9.

———— "The Psychology of Games," Part 1, *ibid.*, XXXVI (1955), 228–229; and Part 2, *ibid.*, pp. 261–263.

———— "Shut-Up and Keep Digging—The Cruel Joke Series," *Western Folklore*, X (1960), 11–22.

———— "Traditional Frolics on April Fool's Day," *The New Zealand Standard*, Wellington, N.Z., XVIII (1952), 23.

———— "Traditional Games of New Zealand Children," *Folklore*, LXIV (1953), 411–423.

———— "What is a Junk Playground?" *National Education*, Wellington, N.Z., XXXIV (1952), 398–399.

Sutton-Smith, B., and P. V. Gump. "Games and Status Experience," *Recreation*, XLVIII (1955), 172–174.

Sutton-Smith, B., and B. G. Rosenberg. "Manifest Anxiety and Game Preferences in Children," *Child Development*, XXI (1960), 307–311.

Thomson, J. M. *The Bush Boys of New Zealand* (London, 1905).

Wilkinson, J. R. "Early Reminiscences from 1886, Christchurch." N.Z.C.E.R.

III. General References, British and American

Since the works listed below are used as references in the Index of Game Names, the abbreviation for each is given here (in brackets, at the end of the item), as well as in the list of abbreviations at the head of that index. Each work in the County Folk-Lore series is designated by the letters CF plus the appropriate volume number. The preliminary phrases, *Printed Extracts . . . Examples of Printed Folk-Lore Concerning*, are omitted from the titles of books in this series.

Balfour, M. C., and N. W. Thomas. *Northumberland*, County Folk-Lore, Vol. IV (Publications of the Folk-Lore Society, Vol. LIII; London, 1904). [CF IV]

Black, C. F., and N. W. Thomas, comps. *The Orkney and Shetland Islands*, County Folk-Lore, Vol. III (Publications of the Folk-Lore Society, Vol. XLIX; London, 1901). [CF III]

Brewster, P. G. *American Nonsinging Games* (Norman, Okla., 1953). [Brewster]

———— "Children's Games and Rhymes," in N. I. White, ed., *The Frank C. Brown Collection of North Carolina Folklore*, I (Durham, N.C., 1952), 31–219. [Carolina]

Douglas, Norman. *London Street Games* (London, 1931). [Douglas]

Gomme, A. B. *The Traditional Games of England, Scotland and Ireland*, Vols. I (London, 1894) and II (1898). [Gomme]

Gurdon, E. C., comp. *Suffolk*, County Folk-Lore, Vol. I (Publications of the Folk-Lore Society, Vol. XXXVII, Pt. II; London, 1893). [CF I]

Gutch, Mrs. Eliza, comp. *The East Riding of Yorkshire*, County Folk-Lore, Vol. VI (Publications of the Folk-Lore Society, Vol. LXIX; London, 1912). [CF VI]

———, comp. *The North Riding of Yorkshire, York and the Ainsty*, County Folk-Lore, Vol. II (Publications of the Folk-Lore Society, Vol. XLV; London, 1901). [CF II]

Gutch, Mrs. Eliza, and Mable Peacock, comps. *Lincolnshire*, County Folk-Lore, Vol. V (Publications of the Folk-Lore Society, Vol. LXIII; London, 1908). [CF V]

Hardy, J. *The Denham Tracts*, Vols. I (London, 1892) and II (1895). [Hardy]

Maclagan, R. C. *The Games and Diversions of Argyleshire* (London, 1901). [Maclagan]

Simpkins, J. E., comp. *Fife, with Some Notes on Clackmannan and Kinross-Shires*, County Folk-Lore, Vol. VII (Publications of the Folk-Lore Society, Vol. LXXI; London, 1914). [CF VII]

INDEX OF GAME NAMES

The game names are arranged in alphabetical order and are each followed by one or more category numbers indicating the approximate position of the game in the text. For many of the games, references to comparative British and American texts on games are given, in abbreviated form. The name of the game referred to in the comparative texts, if different from the name which is most important in New Zealand, is recorded in parentheses.

The abbreviations used and the works to which they refer are listed immediately below. The reference works indicated by the abbreviations CF I through CF VII are all in the County Folk-Lore series. For more detailed bibliographical information on all the comparative texts mentioned here, see the last part of the Bibliography, General References, British and American.

Key to Abbreviations Used

Brewster   P. G. Brewster, *American Nonsinging Games*
Carolina   P. G. Brewster, "Children's Games and Rhymes"
CF I   E. C. Gurdon, comp., *Suffolk*
CF II   Mrs. Eliza Gutch, comp., *The North Riding of Yorkshire, York and the Ainsty*
CF III   C. F. Black and N. W. Thomas, comps., *The Orkney and Shetland Islands*
CF IV   M. C. Balfour and N. W. Thomas, comps., *Northumberland*
CF V   Mrs. Eliza Gutch and Mable Peacock, comps., *Lincolnshire*
CF VI   Mrs. Eliza Gutch, comp., *The East Riding of Yorkshire*
CF VII   J. E. Simpkins, comp., *Fife, with Some Notes on Clackmannan and Kinross-Shires*
Douglas   Norman Douglas, *London Street Games*
Gomme   A. B. Gomme, *The Traditional Games of England, Scotland and Ireland* (2 vols.)
Hardy   J. Hardy, *The Denham Tracts* (2 vols.)
Maclagan   R. C. Maclagan, *The Games and Diversions of Argyleshire*

All In, E-15
All Over, E-8
Alla Balla, D-8
Alley Alley Ooh, The, A-26. CF IV, 112 (All Hid) and 104 (Bedstocks); Gomme, II, 384 (Wind Up the Bush Faggot); Brewster, 174 (Twist Tobacco Twist)
Alphabets, D-1
American Jump, F-6. Douglas, 26

Animal Play, C-32
Animal, Vegetable, or Mineral, J-40. Gomme, I, 388
Animated Oats, H-4
April Fools' Play, C-55

Babbity Bowster, A-41. Maclagan, 136
Backits, K-25 (see also K-33)
Ball Hopscotch, K-117
Ball Tag, K-87
Ball-Bouncing, F-9
Ballyhooley, E-21
Baloo Baloo Balight, A-5. Gomme, II, 430 (Hulla-balloo-ballee)
Bang the Tin, K-2
Bar the Door, E-8, K-67 (see also E-24, E-25, E-27 through E-32, and K-50). Maclagan, 210; Brewster, 53 (Wolf over the Ridge)
Bar the Gate, E-8
Barbadoor, E-8
Barley, E-8. CF VII, 176 (Barley-Breaks); Gomme, I, 21; Brewster, 52 (Molly Bright)
Barley Goats, E-8
Base, K-89
Basketball. See K-102 through K-104
Battle Games, C-4
Battledore, K-11. Gomme, I, 25
Beads, C-39
Bedlam, E-22. Douglas, 19; Gomme, I, 25
Beg o' My Neighbour, L-1
Bell Horses, A-2
Bellahonie, The, E-21
Bells, K-23
Beware the Bear, E-33
Bicycles, C-58
Big and Wee, K-61
Big Ring, K-33. Gomme, II, 40 (Pig-Ring) and 113 (Ring-Taw)
Bingo, A-21
Bird-Nesting, C-8
Bird's Nest, K-45. Douglas, 18 (Finger in the Bird's Nest)
Bites, K-31

Black Bull Bee, E-8 (see also E-27)
Black Magic, J-28
Black Peter, E-31, E-34. Douglas, 24
Blackman, B-2
Blacksmith, B-2
Blackthorn, E-8, E-27. Gomme, I, 34
Blind Hopscotch, K-122
Blindman's Buff, E-20, J-7. CF I, 57; CF IV, 112; CF VI, 149; Gomme, I, 37; Brewster, 12
Block, Hammer, and Nails, L-2
Board Games, J-55
Bobby Bingo, A-21, B-4. CF VI, 149; Gomme, I, 29; Carolina, 154
Bogies, E-35. Douglas, 81 (Bogie Man)
Bold Jolly Lads, A-37
Botany Bay, B-6
Bouncing Ball Hopscotch, K-119
Bows and Arrows, C-13. Maclagan, 44
Bows and Arrows on Horseback, C-44
Boys and Girls, L-3
Branding, K-87
Brewer, L-4
Broken Barley, E-8, E-36
Brother Ebenezer, L-5
Buck Buck, K-57. CF I, 57; CF IV, 104; CF VI, 139; Douglas, 16; Gomme, I, 46; Maclagan, 42 (How Many Fingers Do I Hold Up); Brewster, 116 (Johnny on the Pony)
Bull in the Ring, K-79. CF VI, 149; Gomme, I, 50 (Bull in the Park, Bull in the Barn) and 143 (Fox in the Fold); Maclagan, 239 (Breaking through the Fence)
Bull-Roarers, C-26
Bum, Bum, Here We Come, D-16
Bumble Puppy, K-12. Gomme, I, 51 (Bummer), and II, 291 (Thunder Spell)
Bumpers, K-49. Douglas, 15
Burglars, E-37
Bush Tiggy, E-38

Bushrangers, C-3
Busy Bees, D-12, D-15
Butcher Bats, C-34
Butcher Boys, C-34
Butcher's Bat, D-24
Butcher's Board, K-33. Gomme, I, 45
  (Bridgeboard)
Button Hockey, K-36
Buttons, J-14, J-54, K-24, K-35. CF V,
  250; Douglas, 6; Gomme, I, 54;
  Maclagan, 118 (Mrs. McPherson's
  Ring); Brewster, 9 (Thimble)
Buzz, J-47. Douglas, 25
Buzz, Buzz, Busy Bee, D-16
By the Door, E-8

Cabbages, D-2
Caesar, E-8
Cameras, C-64
Cannon Balls, D-18
Cap-It, K-55. CF IV, 106 (Hatty);
  Douglas, 6; Gomme, I, 1 (Accro-
  shay); Maclagan, 145 (Hot Pies)
Cap-Oh, K-55
Cappon-Pie, K-55
Cap-Tug, H-17
Card Games, J-56
Carry My Lady to London, A-36
Cat, K-5
Cat and Bat, K-5
Cat and Dog, K-5. Gomme, I, 60
Cat and Mouse, E-5. Douglas, 56;
  Gomme, I, 64 (Cat after Mouse);
  Maclagan, 214; Brewster, 63
Cat and Rat, E-5
Catapults, C-6
Catcher, D-25. Gomme, I, 64 (Catch-
  ers)
Cat's Cradle, K-46. CF V, 255; Gom-
  me, I, 61; Maclagan, 190
Cauliflowers, D-2
Chain Tag, E-26. CF IV, 111 (Widdy-
  waddy-way); Douglas, 10 (Widdy);
  Gomme, I, 67; Maclagan, 208
  (Press Gang); Brewster, 67 (Link
  Tag)

Charades, J-1
Charlie over the Water, E-31 (see also
  E-8)
Chase, E-14
Chase the Leader, E-31
Chevvy Chase, K-67. Douglas, 83
Chibby, K-66
Chinese Walking, H-20. Gomme, II,
  40 (Pigeon Walking)
Chuckfarthing, K-26
Chucks, K-34
Chuckstones, K-34
Chuckystones, K-34
Cinematographs, C-63
Circle Tig, E-23 (see also A-20). Gom-
  me, II, 144 (Round Tag)
Clay-Shooters, C-14
Clothes, D-2
Clumps, J-41
Cobbler, Cobbler, Mend My Shoe, A-
  19. Douglas, 5
Cockfighting, K-78. Gomme, I, 73
  and 74 (Cockertie-hooie)
Cocky Hole, L-6
Collaring, E-8
Collections, C-38
Colours, D-2, D-14, D-16, E-28, E-39
  (see also E-8)
Come and Sit in My Chair, J-35
Comp, K-91
Conjo, K-6. Douglas, 9 (Cunjer)
Conjure, K-6
Conkers, K-8. CF III, 107 (Cob-Nut);
  CF IV, 106 (Handy Nut); Gomme,
  I, 71 and 77 (Cob-Nut)
Consequences, J-22. Brewster, 176
  (Where you are . . .)
Constantinople, J-43
Country Cricket, K-98
Cowboys and Indians, C-1. Douglas,
  66
Crab-Hole, K-45
Creep the Curtain, D-6
Creeping, D-6
Creeping Jack, D-6, D-7
Creeping Up, D-6
Creepy, D-6

Creepy Crawly, D-6
Cricket, K-4 (see also K-95 through K-101)
Cripple Jack, D-14
Cronje, K-6
Croquet, K-10
Cross the Bar, E-30
Crown, E-71
Cum Je Cum, J-41
Cunning Joe, K-6. Gomme, I, 84 (Cudgel); Maclagan, 14 (Cat and Dog)
Cunny, K-6
Cunny Joe, K-6

Danish Rounders, K-108
Darts, C-19
Dead Man's Dive, K-19
Defence, K-102
Dice, G-4
Diggley Bones, B-6
Do As I Do, J-2
Dog and Bone, D-22
Donkey, J-39, K-53, K-89, K-90
Donkey Tag, E-40
Dooking for Apples, J-25
Down in the Valley, A-13. Gomme, I, 99; Maclagan, 56
Draw a Bucket of Water, F-2. Gomme, I, 101; Carolina, 142
Draw a Pail of Water, F-2. CF II, 36; CF V, 250; Gomme, I, 100
Draw the Snake, E-71
Drop the Handkerchief, A-20, E-23. CF I, 108; CF II, 351; CF V, 250; Gomme, I, 109; Maclagan, 213; Carolina, 81
Duck Under Water, L-7
Ducking, H-12
Ducks and Drakes, K-18. CF II, 315; CF V, 257; Gomme, I, 114
Ducks in the Pond, D-21
Duckstones, K-16. CF V, 258; Douglas, 72; Gomme, I, 116; Maclagan, 241 (Duck and Drake)
Duke, The, A-28
Duke a-Riding, A, A-28

Dumb Crambo, J-4. CF I, 57; Gomme, I, 117, and II, 418
Dummy Parcel, H-10, H-21
Dumpy, K-15
Dunk and Davey, K-50
Dutch Rounders, K-109

Echo, K-88. Gomme, I, 53 (Burly Whush); Brewster, 84 (Anthony Over)
Eely Ily Oh, The, A-26. Gomme, I, 119
Egg and Spoon Races, K-71
Egg Cap, K-21. Gomme, I, 58 (Capie-Hole), 199 (Hats in Holes), and 389 (Monday, Tuesday); Maclagan, 9 (Bonnety); Brewster, 84 (Hat Ball) and 86 (Roley Holey)
Egg Cup, K-21
Egg in Cap, K-21. Douglas, 1
Egg Pie, K-21
Eggs in the Basket, G-5. CF VI, 142 (Eggs in a Bush); Gomme, I, 187 (Hairy My Bossie); Maclagan, 78; Brewster, 9
Egg(s) in the Nest, G-5, K-21
Elastic Guns, C-59
Elements, J-46
Ella Bella, D-8
Eye-Drop, K-33. Douglas, 63 (Bounce Eye)

Fairy Gardens, C-42. Douglas, 60
Family Coach, J-20. Brewster, 99 (Blow Out)
Farmer and the Lion, E-21
Farmer in the Dell, A-10. Gomme, II, 420 (The Farmer's Den); Carolina, 146
Father Door, E-8
Feather Ball, K-12
Fill the Gap, E-23 (see also A-20). Gomme, II, 144 (French Jackie) and 146 (Gap)
Film Stars, D-14
Find the Key, D-7
Fingerstones, K-34

Fire, Air, and Water, J-46

Fire on the Mountains, A-32. Gomme, II, 421

Fish in the Pond, D-23

Fishes and Whales, E-31

Fishing, C-12

Fives, F-9. CF II, 315

Fivestones, K-17. CF I, 57; Douglas, 71; Gomme, I, 122

Flax-Flappers, C-27

Flicks, K-123. Douglas, 68

Flower Games, C-30

Fly the Garter, K-56. Douglas, 6 (Under the Garter) and 13 (Cut-a-lump); Gomme, I, 129 and 133 (Foot and Over)

Flyball, K-116 (see also K-86)

Flying the Gap, K-56. CF IV, 106 (Foot-an'-a-half)

Folding Arms, D-9

Follow Her to London, A-24

Follow Me to London, A-24

Follow Old Mum to Market, L-8

Follow the Leader, K-13, K-68. CF I, 57; CF IV, 106 (Jock and Jock's Man); Douglas, 78; Gomme, I, 131; Maclagan, 213; Brewster, 169

Follow the Taw, K-33

Follows, K-33. Gomme, I, 44 (Boss-Out)

Food Play, C-35

Fool, Fool, Come to School, L-9

Foot Races, K-71

Football, K-62

Forfeit Games, J-31

Forfeits, J-31. Gomme, I, 137; Maclagan, 115

Fortune-Telling, C-62

Fox and Family, B-2

Fox and Geese, B-5, E-7 (see also B-2 and B-4)

Fox and Hounds, K-69. Douglas, 79

Free Pass, E-8

French and English, E-11, K-64. CF III, 218 (King-come-a-lay); Gomme, I, 144

French Cricket, K-96. Douglas, 2

French Hopscotch, K-53

French Tag, E-18. CF IV, 112; CF VI, 149; Douglas, 76 (French Touch); Maclagan, 207; Brewster, 63

Fruits, E-28, J-41

Gag, E-24

Gag or No Gag, E-24

Geg, E-24

General Post, J-19. CF IV, 112; Maclagan, 87 (Coach)

Geography, J-45

Get the Keys, D-7

Ghost in the Garden, B-1. Douglas, 24 (The White Shirt); Gomme, I, 149 (Ghost at the Well); Maclagan, 215

Ghosts, E-41

Giant and His Treasure, The, D-7

Giant Steps, D-3

Giant Strides, D-3

Giant's Treasure, D-7

Giggies, C-29

Go, Go, Stop, D-6

Goals, K-104

Golden Rule, The, H-3

Goosey, E-8, E-25

Goosey Up and Down, E-8

Grand Old Duke of York, The, A-33. CF VI, 149

Grandmother's Footsteps, D-6

Grass Games, C-31

Green Gravels, A-14. CF IV, 117; CF V, 251; Gomme, I, 170, and II, 426; Maclagan, 83; Carolina, 56

Green Grow the Leaves, A-38

Grocers, D-16

Guessing, D-10

Guy Fawkes Play, C-54

Hand Hockey, K-106

Hand Rounders, K-111

Hand Shadows, K-44

Hand Tennis, K-114

Hand-clapping Games, F-7 (see also F-8)

Handkerchief Hockey, K-107

Hands upon Hands, K-39. Gomme, I,

97 (Dish-a-loof); Brewster, 179 (Eleven Up)

Handstands, D-26

Hanging Bailey, C-61

Hares and Hounds, K-67, K-69. CF IV, 106 (Hunt the Hare); Douglas, 79; Gomme, I, 191; Maclagan, 213; Brewster, 77 (Fox)

Harriers, K-71

Hats, L-10

Heads, Bodies, and Legs, J-23

Heave Ho, K-83

Hen and Chickens, B-5 (see also A-24 and A-28). CF VI, 144 (Fox and Hen) and 183 (Shue-Gled-Wylie); Gomme, I, 139 (Fox and Goose) and 201 (Hen and Chicken); Maclagan, 132

Here Come Two Nuns, D-14

Here Comes a Duke a-Riding, A-28

Here Comes a Lusty Wooer, A-28

Here Comes Three Dukes a-Riding, A-28

Here We Go Round the Merry Go Round, E-71

Here We Go Round the Mulberry Bush, A-17

Here's a Prisoner, A-23

Here's a Thing, J-32

Here's the Church, K-41

Hickety Bickety, G-7. Gomme, I, 210

Hide and Seek, E-2 (see also E-3, E-15, E-22, and E-71). CF II, 315 (Felts); CF IV, 110 (Spinney-Wye); Gomme, I, 211; Maclagan, 211; Brewster, 43

Hide the Key, J-11

Hide the Thimble, J-11. Gomme, I, 214 (Hide and Seek [2]); Maclagan, 91 (Hide the Button); Brewster, 416 (I Spye)

Hideygo, E-2

Hit and Out, K-100 (see also K-4)

Hit the Crawley, K-9

Hive-Hunting, C-11

Hockey, K-96 (see also K-2 and K-105 through K-107). Gomme, I, 216

Hoki Toki, A-5

Holding, E-8

Holey, K-33. Douglas, 62 (Three Holes); Gomme, I, 51 (Bun Hole, Holey), and II, 256 (Three Holes)

Homaiacky, E-3

Honey Pots, B-3. CF I, 57; CF VI, 149; Douglas, 21; Gomme, I, 209 and 75 (Cockle-Bread)

Hooks and Eyes, F-5

Hoop-Flicking, K-13

Hoopla, K-29

Hoop-Racing, K-13

Hoops, K-13, C-22. Douglas, 62

Hop, Step, and Jump, K-76. CF IV, 112; Douglas, 13; Gomme, I, 187

Hop the Hats, K-52. Douglas, 5 (Hop o' My Thumb); Maclagan, 133 (Cutting the Cheese)

Hop-Peg, K-51

Hopping Base, K-48

Hopscotch, K-53 (see also K-117 through K-122). CF I, 57; CF II, 317 (Pally-ully, Pally-hitch); CF VI, 145; Douglas, 74; Gomme, I, 223, 26 (Beds), and 190 (Hap the Beds), and II, 145 (Pickie); Maclagan, 134 (Peaver)

Horney, E-8, E-27. Gomme, I, 237

Horse Races, C-44

Horse-Riding, C-44

Horse's Piss, H-16

Hot Cockles, G-8. CF I, 57; CF III, 217 (Handycrooper); CF IV, 112; Douglas, 15; Gomme, I, 229, and II, 429

Hot Rice, K-100 (see also K-4). Douglas, 1

How Many Eggs in the Bush? G-5. CF VI, 142; Gomme, I, 218 (Ho-Go) and 187 (Hairy My Bossie); Brewster, 8 (Hul Gul, Jack in the Bush)

How Many Miles to Babylon? A-35. Gomme, I, 231; Carolina, 74

Hucklebones, K-34. CF V, 259; Gomme, I, 239

Humbug, Finger or Thumb? K-60
Humpty Dumpty, K-50
Hunt the Slipper, J-10. CF I, 57;
   Gomme, I, 241
Hunt the Thimble, J-11
Hurling, K-2

I Am a Turkey Merchant, D-14
I Love My Beau with an A, J-41
I Saw You, E-42
I See a Ghost, J-26
I Sent My Son, D-14
I Spy, E-43, J-41. CF I, 47; Douglas,
   26; Maclagan, 212
I Tipped the Finger, E-71
Ickety Bickety, G-7
Imitations, J-3
In and Out the Dusty Bluebells, A-24.
   Douglas, 23 (Running In and Out
   the Bluebells)
In and Out the Village, A-24. Douglas,
   23 (Walking round the Village);
   Carolina, 119 (Marching Round the
   Levee)
In and Out the Windows, A-24. CF
   IV, 116; CF VI, 147
In the Pond and Out of the Pond,
   D-20
Initials, D-1, E-28
Insect Play, C-33
Intellectual Games, J-49
Isaac and Rebecca, J-8. Brewster, 69
   (Jacob and Rachel)
I've Come to See Poor Mary Jane,
   A-40
Ivory, D-14

Jack a Lingo, B-4. CF IV, 116
Jack and Jill, K-40. Maclagan, 224
Jack of All Sorts, D-13
Jack-a-balan, E-19. CF III, 216 (For-
   feits: "Whaul buy me Jocky-be-
   Laund?"); CF VI, 145 (Jack's
   Alive); Gomme, I, 256 (Jack's
   Alive)
Jackknife, K-31
Jacks, K-34. CF VI, 145

Jackstick, K-5
Jackstones, K-34
Jenny Jones, A-15. CF V, 251; Gom-
   me, I, 260, and II, 432; Carolina, 44
Jingle the Penny, H-8
Jingo Ring, The, A-9. CF VII, 180
   (Merry-Metanzie); Gomme, I, 284;
   Maclagan, 55
John Brown's Body, J-15
Johnny in the Inkpot, D-11
Jolly Miller, The, A-30. CF I, 109;
   CF II, 68; CF V, 251; Gomme, I,
   289; Carolina, 111 (Happy is the
   Miller, Boys)
Judge and Jury, L-11
Julius Caesar, E-8
Jumbucks, K-57
Jump, Little Nag Tail, K-59

Kat, K-113 (see also K-1)
Keep the Kettle Boiling, K-15
Keys or Pads, E-44
Kick and Collar, K-94
Kick, Donkey, Kick, H-1
Kick Post One, E-21. Douglas, 11
   (Widdy)
Kick the Block, E-3 (see also K-53).
   CF IV, 112; Gomme, II, 438
Kick the Boot, E-3
Kick the Tin, E-3. CF I, 57; Douglas,
   8 (Tin Can Copper, Kick Can Police-
   man); Gomme, I, 401 and 412
   (Mount the Tin, and New Squat);
   Brewster, 47 (Kick the Can)
Kicking Ball Hopscotch, K-118
Kicking Block Hopscotch, K-120
Kicks, K-92
Kikeri, E-45
King Caesar, E-8. Douglas, 83; Gom-
   me, I, 299, and II, 482
King Dick, E-8
King of the Castle, K-81. Gomme, I,
   300
King of the Golden Sword, H-13.
   Douglas, 12 (Touching the King's
   Sceptre)
King O'Seenie, E-8

King O'Weenie, E-8, E-27
King Pin, K-65. Brewster, 70 (Steal Sticks)
King Seenie, E-8, E-27
King Seize-Her, E-8. Gomme, I, 299
King-a-Sene, E-8
King's Den, E-8, E-27
King's Peg, K-65
Kingy, K-65, K-87. Douglas, 3 (King)
Kiss in the Ring, A-20. CF II, 316 (Mana Minetail); CF V, 259; Gomme, I, 306
Kit Cat, K-5
Kites, C-20
Kiwi, D-8
Knick Knock, H-7
Knife, C-5
Knifey, K-31. Maclagan, 142
Knock-Backs, K-25 (see also K-33). Gomme, I, 17 (Buttons)
Knucklebones, K-34. Gomme, I, 95 (Dibs), and II, 122 (Fivestones); Brewster, 136 (Jacks)
Knuckles, K-34
Knucklestones, K-34

Lady on the Mountain, A-11. CF I, 62; Gomme, I, 320
Last Couple Out, J-16
Last Man Over, E-8
Last Over Call, E-8
Last Pair Out, J-16
Lazy Stick, K-85. Gomme, II, 222; Maclagan, 218; Brewster, 175 (Pulling Swag)
Leap Frog, K-54. CF I, 57; CF IV, 112; Douglas, 13; Gomme, I, 327, and II, 440; Maclagan, 144; Brewster, 103
Leggings-Out, K-25 (see also K-33)
Letters, D-1
Liney, K-33. Gomme, II, 46 (Plum Pudding)
Little Ring, K-33. Gomme, I, 324 (Lag); Brewster, 144 (Lag Marbles)
London Bridge, A-23. CF IV, 113; CF VI, 149; Douglas, 55; Gomme, I, 333, and II, 441; Carolina, 137
Longball, K-86 (see also K-115 and K-116)
Lubyloo, A-5. CF II, 64 (How do you do, Luby Lue); Gomme, I, 352 (Lubin); Carolina, 156 (Looby Loo)

Man the Ship, D-17
Maoris, C-2
Marble Board, G-3. Douglas, 63 (Bridge Board)
Marbles, K-33. Douglas, 52, 63, 68; Gomme, I, 364; Maclagan, 152
Mark, K-93
Marry Ma Tanza, A-9. CF VII, 180 (Merry-Metanzie); Gomme, I, 369 (Merry-ma-tansa), and II, 443; Maclagan, 53 (The Gala Ship)
May I? D-4
Maze, The, K-53
Merry Go Rounds, A-1
Merry Go Tansy, A-9
Mingle the Bonnets, K-21. Gomme, I, 14 (Ball and Bonnets)
Momley Peg, K-31. Maclagan, 142; Brewster, 142 (Mumblepeg)
Monkey on the Bridge, K-60. CF VI, 146 (Long-Back); Gomme, I, 52 (Bung the Bucket)
Moonlight, Starlight, E-17
Mother, Mother, the Kettle's Boiling Over, B-2
Mother, Mother, the Pot Boils Over, B-2. Gomme, I, 396; Douglas, 24 (Light Mother's Copper Fire, or Old Devil in the Fire)
Mother Mumby's Dead, J-5
Mousetrap, K-45. Douglas, 18 (Mouse in Trap)
Mrs. McKenzie's Dead, J-5. Gomme, II, 13; Maclagan, 1 (The Afflicted); Brewster, 32 (Old Mother Hobble Gobble)
Mulberry Bush, The, A-17. CF V, 251; Douglas, 56; Gomme, I, 404; Carolina, 85

Mummy, L-12
Murder, E-46
Musical Chairs, J-36
Musical Statues, J-37 (see also D-5)
My Aunt Sally Has Gone to Paris, J-6
My Fair Young Lady, A-39
My Father Has Cut My Finger Off,
  H-23
My Mother Said, F-7. CF IV, 120
  (Hot Cross Buns)

Names, D-1
New York, D-16. Brewster, 14
Nigger Boys, E-30 (see also E-8)
Ninepins, K-30
Nivy Nivy Nick Nack, G-6. CF IV,
  107 (Neivy-neivy-nick-nack); Gom-
  me, I, 410; Maclagan, 127
No Man Standing, K-80. Douglas, 79
  (Last Man Standing)
Nonsense, H-28
Non-Stop Cricket, K-97
Noughts and Crosses, J-50. Gomme, I,
  420
Noughts and Dots, J-51
Nuts and May, A-27. CF V, 252; Gom-
  me, I, 424; Carolina, 109

Oats and Beans and Barley, A-12. CF
  V, 252; Douglas, 55; Gomme, II, 1;
  Carolina, 87
Observation, J-49
Odd Man Out, E-47. CF V, 252; Gom-
  me, II, 14 (Odd Man)
Oka Ball, A-4
Old Digley Bones, B-2
Old Lady from Botany Bay, The, B-6.
  Gomme, II, 24 (Old Soldier)
Old Lady from Poverty Bay, An, B-6
Old Man from Botany Bay, An, B-6
Old Mother Gray, B-7
Old Tom, B-4
Old Woman from Botany Bay, The,
  B-6
O'Leary, F-9. Douglas, 3 (One, two,
  three a-lairy)
On and Off the Bridge, L-13

Ooh! My Toe! H-11
Opossum, E-48
Oranges and Lemons, A-22. CF I, 57;
  CF V, 252; Douglas, 57; Gomme, II,
  27

Pakehas and Maoris, C-2
Pancakes, B-2
Paper Chase, K-70. Douglas, 1
Parachutes, C-60
Parson's Cat, The, J-48. Maclagan, 115
  (Parson's Mare Has Gone a-Mis-
  sing)
Pass Over, E-8
Pat Ball, L-14
Pea-Shooters, C-17
Pebbles and Stones, E-49
Pee Wee Some More Yet, H-14
Peep Behind the Curtain, D-6. Doug-
  las, 26
Peep Shows, C-65
Peewees, K-5
Peg Ball, K-99 (see also K-4)
Peg Rounders, K-112
Peg Top, K-15. Douglas, 4 (Pegging);
  Gomme, II, 38 (Peg in the Ring,
  Peg Top) and 186 (Gully)
Pegging, K-15
Peggy, K-63
Pegknife, K-32
Penny Catches, D-25
Penny Doctor Beetles, C-34
Penny Under the Chair, E-50
Peter and Paul, K-40. Maclagan, 224;
  Brewster, 166 (Jack and Jill)
Pig in the Middle, K-90. Douglas, 3
  (Catch, Teaser)
Piggy-back Contest, K-78
Pin Dips, C-40. Gomme, II, 41 (Pinny
  Shows)
Pinch, L-15
Pitch and Toss, K-26. Gomme, II, 43;
  Maclagan, 45 (Buttons)
Please, Jack, May We Cross Your
  Golden River? E-29 (see also E-8)
Point to the Bell, E-51
Poison Tag, E-18

Poisoned Stag, E-18
Poisonous Ball, E-52
Pole-Vaulting, K-75
Policeman, E-53
Polo, C-45
Poor Alice Is a-Weeping, A-7
Poor Jenny Is a-Weeping, A-7. Douglas, 55
Poor Mary Is a-Weeping, A-7. CF V, 252 (Poor Mary sits a-weeping); Gomme, II, 46 (Poor Mary sits a-weeping)
Poor Old Tom, B-4
Poor Pussy, J-29
Poor Sally Is a-Weeping, A-7 (see also A-6 and A-14). CF II, 66; CF VI, 146
Pop 'Em Down, Gents, G-1
Pop Goes the Weasel, A-3. Gomme, II, 63
Popguns, C-15
Poppy Shows, C-40. Douglas, 80; Gomme, II, 64 (Poppet Show); Maclagan, 173
Pork and Beans, J-30
Postman's Knock, J-33. Douglas, 77; Gomme, II, 404 (American Post); Brewster, 154 (Post Office)
Pounds, Shillings, and Pence, D-25
Pretty Little Girl of Mine, A-6 (see also A-7 and A-14). CF IV, 118; Gomme, II, 69
Prick Book, C-41. Gomme, I, 95 (Dab)
Priest of the Parish, The, J-48. CF I, 62; Douglas, 83 (Daddy Red Cap); Gomme, I, 301 (King Plaster Palacey), and II, 79; Brewster, 26 (The Priest Has lost his Cap)
Prisoners, K-64
Prisoner's Base, E-10, K-63, K-67. CF I, 57; CF IV, 112; Douglas, 19 (Release); Gomme, II, 79; Maclagan, 217
Pulling Off, K-78
Punch King, E-8, E-25
Punch King Seenio, E-8
Punch King Sinny Oh, E-25

Punchinello, A-42
Puss in the Corner, E-12. CF I, 57; CF IV, 112; Douglas, 83; Gomme, II, 88; Maclagan, 210 (King, King, Come Along, Change all Corners); Brewster, 96 (Puss Wants a Corner)
Putting an Eye in the Peg, L-16
Putting Out Goes In, K-101 (see also K-4)

Queen Anne's Dead, J-5
Queen of Sheba, The, J-9, J-27. CF V, 252; Gomme, I, 59 (Carrying the Queen a Letter), and II, 104; Brewster, 121 (King and Queen)
Queenie, D-8. CF V, 252 (Queen Anne); Douglas, 1
Queen's Birthday, C-53
Quoits, K-29

Rabbit-Hunting, C-10
Rabbiting, C-10
Rabbits and Rips, D-19
Race for a Wife, J-16
Rats, H-9
Rats and Rabbits, D-19
Red and Blue, D-2
Red Rover, E-8. Douglas, 77; Gomme, I, 286 (Johnny Rover)
Release, E-22. Douglas, 19; Maclagan, 218
Relievo, E-22. CF V, 252; Douglas, 10 (Point); Gomme, II, 107; Maclagan, 207
Ric Tic Toe, J-52
Ring a Ring a Roses, A-3. CF V, 252 (Ring a Ring o' Roses); Douglas, 59; Gomme, II, 108; Carolina, 150
Ring-a-Let, G-2
Rivelea Rounders, K-110
Rotten Egg(s), B-2, E-23, K-22, K-89 (see also A-20 and K-21). Douglas, 21; Gomme, I, 53 (Burly Whush); Maclagan, 8 (Cobs)
Rough and Tumble, K-82
Round and Round the Merry Go Round, E-71

Round and Round the Mulberry Bush, E-71
Round and Round the Village, A-24. CF V, 253; Gomme, II, 122
Round the World and Back Again, K-53
Round the World Hopping, K-53
Rounders, K-1 (see also K-108 and K-113). CF VI, 149; Douglas, 1; Gomme, II, 145; Maclagan, 22
Rugby Football, K-62. Gomme, I, 134
Rules of Contrary, K-3. Gomme, I, 79; Maclagan, 157
Run a Mile, L-17
Run the Ball, L-18
Run Sheepie Run, E-32
Running Through the Middle, E-8
Running Waters, E-54
Rushes and Reeds, A-25
Russian Scandal, L-19

Sack Races, K-73
Sacks on the Mill, K-82. Gomme, I, 390 (More Sacks to the Mill)
Saddle the Nag, K-58. CF VI, 146 (Longback); Gomme, I, 52, and II, 147
Sally Waters, A-8. CF V, 253; Gomme, II, 149 and 453; Maclagan, 58 (Down on the Carpet) and 63 (Here's a Poor Widow); Carolina, 130
Sardines, E-55
Saucy Duke, A-28
Saucy Jack, A-28
Scotch and English, K-63. CF IV, 109; CF VII, 182; Gomme, II, 183 (Scots and English); Hardy, I, 151
Scrag, K-94
Scragging, E-8, K-94
Scrapbooks, C-36
Seat Tig, E-56
Sevens, F-9. Gomme, II, 405 (Ball); Maclagan, 9
Shadow Tig, E-57
Shadows, K-44
Shanghais, C-6

Sharky, E-58
Sheep, Sheep, E-32 (see also E-8). Douglas, 57; Gomme, II, 187 (Shepherd and Sheep) and 396 (Wolf)
Shinty, K-2. CF IV, 109 (Shinney); CF V, 260; CF VI, 147; CF VII, 177; Gomme, II, 190; Maclagan, 24; Brewster, 158
Shopping, D-14
Shops, D-14
Shortball, K-115 (see also K-86)
Shove Ha'penny, K-27. Douglas, 17
Shove Penny, K-27
Shuttlecock, K-11. Gomme, I, 25, and II, 192 (Shuttlefeather)
Sick, Dying, Dead, K-90
Sides, K-103
Simon Says, K-38. Brewster, 25
Sinio, E-8
Sir Roger de Coverley, L-20
Skating, C-51
Skin a Hare, H-6
Skin a Rabbit, H-6. Douglas, 16
Skin a Snake, H-6
Skip a Basket, F-4
Skipping, F-1. Douglas, 26; Gomme, I, 200; Maclagan, 227
Skipping Stones, K-18
Skittles, K-30
Slanging Contests, H-27
Sledges (Sleds), C-23
Slings, C-7. Maclagan, 229
Slip the Button, J-13
Slip the Ring, J-13. Gomme, I, 96 (Diamond Ring) and 121 (Find the Ring), and II, 225 (Thimble Ring); Maclagan, 89; Brewster, 19 (Ring on a String)
Smart Answers, H-26
Smudographs, C-43
Smuggling the Geg, E-24. Gomme, I, 147 (Gegg), and II, 205 (Smuggle the Gig); Maclagan, 89 (Smuggle the Keg)
Snail, The, K-53
Snake, The, K-53
Snakes, E-59

Snory-Bones, C-28
Snowballing, C-48
Snowmen, C-49
Softball. See K-108 through K-113 (see also K-1)
Soldiers, K-7. CF II, 369 (Kemps); CF IV, 104 (Fighting Cocks); Gomme, I, 73 (Cock-Battler); Maclagan, 231
Solomon Says, K-38
Somebody Must Tig, E-71
Space Ring, A-20, E-23
Space to Space, E-23 (see also A-20)
Span-'Em, K-25 (see also K-33). Douglas, 63 (Hits and Spans); Gomme, II, 210 (Spangie)
Spang-Weazling, K-9
Spiders, J-53
Spin the Trencher, J-38. CF V, 253 (Turn Trencher) and 260 (Turn-Trencher); Gomme, II, 312 (Turn the Trencher); Brewster, 32
Spiral Pole, K-12
Spitting, H-15 (see also H-19)
Spitting Through Crossed Fingers, H-19
Spring Guns, C-16
Squash, K-82
Stabknife, K-31
Stacks on the Mill, K-82
Stagknife, K-31 (see also K-32)
Statues, D-5 (see also J-37)
Steal a Peg, K-65
Stealing Grass, K-65
Steeplechasing, K-68
Steps, D-3, D-6. Brewster, 164
Steps and Stairs, D-3, D-7
Steps and Strides, D-3
Stick Hockey, K-105
Sticks, D-15
Stilts, C-24
Stone, K-37. Brewster, 15
Stone, Scissors, and Paper, K-37
Stone Tag, E-60
Stones, K-65
Strike the Crayfish, K-9

Surrender the Tower, A-29. Gomme, I, 18
Swimming, C-46

Tableaux, J-37
Tag, E-4
Tail on the Donkey, J-57
Tallyho, K-69
Target-Shooting, C-9
Teasing Expressions, H-25
Teasing Rhymes, H-18
Teasing Tricks, Verbal, H-24
Teazle, E-6. CF V, 260 (Terzy)
Telegrams, J-44
Telephone Calls, H-22
Telephones, C-66
Tennis. See K-114
Tens, F-9
There Stands a Lady on the Mountain, A-11
There Was a Man, F-8
There Was an Old Woman, L-21
There Was an Old Woman Who Lived in a Shoe, J-18
This Is the Way the Windmill Goes Round, E-71
This Is the Way the World Goes Round, E-71
This Little Pig, K-43
Thread(ing) the Needle, A-34, K-47. CF V, 253; Gomme, II, 228; Carolina, 108
Three Dukes, The, A-28. CF IV, 115 (Two Old Jews); CF V, 253; Gomme, II, 233 and 455; Maclagan, 90 (Three Brothers Came from Spain); Carolina, 89
Three Little Ships, L-22
Three-legged Races, K-72
Throwing a Knife, K-31
Throwing Block Hopscotch, K-121
Throwing Hats, K-20
Tic Tac Toe, J-52. CF V, 260 (Tip, tap, toe); Maclagan, 240; Brewster, 130
Tick Tack, H-7

Tig, E-4. CF IV, 111; CF VI, 148; Gomme, II, 293; Maclagan, 207

Tiggy Tiggy Touchwood, E-1. CF IV, 112; CF V, 260 (Ticky-touch-wood); CF VI, 148; Douglas, 76 (Touchwood); Gomme, II, 292 (Ticky Touchwood); Brewster, 65 (Wood Tag)

Tiki Tiki Touchwood, E-61. CF V, 260 (Ticky-touch-wood); Gomme, II, 292 (Ticky Touchwood)

Times, D-15

Tinker Tailor Grass, C-31

Tip and Run, K-95 (see also K-4). CF II, 314 (Tip and Go)

Tip Cat, K-5. CF I, 58 (Kit Cat); CF IV, 107 (Kitty-Cat); CF V, 253; Douglas, 8 (Tippit and Tibby Cat); Gomme, I, 310 (Kit-Cat), and II, 294; Maclagan, 19; Brewster, 160 (Tippy)

Tip Tap, E-62, H-7, K-5

Tip Tap Toe, J-52. CF IV, 109 (Rittit-O); CF V, 260

Tip the Finger, E-71. Douglas, 15 (North South East West); Gomme, I, 229 (Hot Cockles); Brewster, 48 (Tap on the Back)

Tippenny Runs, K-95 (see also K-4). CF II, 314 (Tip and Go)

Tippenny Tap, K-5

Tit Tat Toe, J-52. CF V, 253; Gomme, II, 296 (Tit-tat-toe)

Tobogganing, C-5

Toes Off the Counter, E-63

Tom Tiddler's Ground, E-9. CF I, 57; Douglas, 56; Gomme, II, 298; Maclagan, 208

Toodle-em-Buck, K-28. CF IV, 103 (All in the Well); Gomme, I, 2 (All in the Well)

Tops. See K-14 and K-15. Gomme, II, 299; Maclagan, 242

Touch Touch, E-18

Touchwood, E-1

Tracking, Boy Scout, K-70

Tractor Cotton Reels, C-67

Trades, D-16. Douglas, 21 (Please, We've Come to Learn a Trade); Gomme, I, 117 (Dumb Motions), and II, 305; Maclagan, 140; Brewster, 4

Trading, D-16

Transfers, C-37

Treasure Hunts, J-12

Tree Tig, E-64

Tree-Climbing, C-52

Treetop Races, C-52

Trim the Hat, J-24

Trip and Go, E-13. Gomme, II, 308

Trolley Wheels, C-56

Tug-o'-War, K-77. Douglas, 82; Maclagan, 132; Brewster, 176

Tuppenny Catches, D-25

Twilight Tig, E-16

Two Dukes, A-28

Twos and Threes, E-6. CF V, 253 (Round Tag); Douglas, 25; Gomme, II, 144 (Round Tag); Maclagan, 86 (Wee Wee Man); Brewster, 93

Tyres, C-57

Under the Horse, H-16

Ups and Downs, E-65

Vegetables, D-2, E-28

Verbal Teasing Tricks, H-24

Victoria, D-6

Walk down the Path, K-42

Wallflowers, A-16. CF II, 67; CF V, 253; Gomme, II, 329; Maclagan, 84

Walls, F-9. Douglas, 3 (Wallie)

Wash the Dishes, F-3. Brewster, 164 (Wash the Dishrag)

Water Play, C-47

Water-Shooters, C-18

Wet and Dry, E-66

Whales in the Ocean, E-67

What Colour's the Sky? J-17

What Have the Robbers Done to You? A-23

What's a Ship to Do? H-2

Wheelbarrow Races, K-74

When I Was a Lady, A-18. CF IV, 117; Gomme, II, 363

Whip Tops, K-14. CF VI, 149

Whips, C-21

Whispers, J-21

Whistles, C-25. Maclagan, 170

Who Goes Round My Garden Wall? B-4

Who Goes Round My Stone Wall? B-4. CF II, 65; CF V, 253; Gomme, II, 375

Who Goes Round My Stony Wall? B-4

Who Steps in the Dark? E-68

Who Tapped Your Finger Last? E-71

Who's That Knocking at My Door? L-23

Who's That Walking Round My House Tonight? B-4

Who's the One to Touch It? E-71

Wiggle Waggle, K-38. CF I, 107; Gomme, II, 383

Winks, J-34. Brewster, 153

Witch, B-2

Witch and the Jam Pots, B-2

Witch's Tig, E-69

Wolf and Geese, B-5

Wolf, Wolf, Go Home, E-32

Wolfie, E-70

Word-Making, J-42

Would You Lend My Mother a Saucepan? A-31

Wrestling, K-84

You Have Things in Your Head, H-5

INDEX OF RHYMES

This index contains the first lines of the rhymes and rhythmic formulas given in this volume, including the first lines of many second and subsequent verses. The rhyme line is followed by the category with which the rhyme is classified, and, if given as a part of a game, by the category number of that game.

A cabbage, a carrotie, H-18
A duck in the pond, C-55
A farmer's dog lay on the mat, A-21
A monkey came into my shop one day, E
A penny for the guy, C-54
A pin or a bull or a button, C-40
A pinch and a punch, H-18
A-hunting we will go, A-30; A-31
All in together, F-1
Alla Balla, who has got the ball? D-8
American jump, American jump, F-6
Andy pandy, sugary candy, F-1
Anna, manna, mona, mike, E
Anzy panzy, sugary canzy, F-1
Apple jelly, my jam tart, F-1
Apple pip, apple pip, C-35
April Fools' Day is past, C-55
As I was going down piggy wiggy track, E
As I was going over London bridge, E

Baby, baby, bunting, H-18
Bake a pudding, F-1
Baker, baker, F-1
Baldy's teeth were long, H-18
Baloo baloo balight, A-5
Beg your pardon, grouchy Grace, H-18
Beg your pardon, Mrs. Arden, H-18
Bell horses, bell horses, A-2
Big fat hog, H-18
Black fish, white trout, E
Blue spells B-L-U-E, E
B-L-U-E spells blue, E
Bluebells, cockleshells, F-1

Bounce, bounce, ball, ball, twenty lassies on the wall, F-9
Boy, boy, boy, H-18
Bread and butter, F-1

Call lummy koo, E
Calling in, calling out, F-1
Catholic, Catholic, H-18
Catholic dogs, H-18
Charlie Chaplin, F-1
Charlie Chaplin walks like this, F-1
Charlie Chaplin went to France, F-1; F-9
Ching Ching Chinaman, H-18
Ching Chong Chinaman, H-18
Christchurch City Council, see E
Cinderella at a ball, F-1
Clear the track, H-18
Cowardy, cowardy, custard, H-18
Cowry, cowry, custard, H-18
Crackers, crackers, F-1
Cross the bridge, F-1
Crossing the bridge, F-1
Cry, baby, cry, H-18
Cups and saucers, plates and dishes, E; F-1

Dan, Dan, the dirty man, H-18
Dancing Dolly, F-1
Did you ever see a bear, E
Doctor Foster went to Gloucester, F-1
Don't care was made to care, H-26
Down in the duckpond, C-46
Draw a bucket of water, F-2
Draw a snake down your back, E-71

Each peach pear plum, E
Early one morning, about eight o'clock, F-1
Eena deena dina doe, E
Eena dena dina doh, E
Eenah deena dinah doh, E
Eeny meeny miny mo, E
Engine, engine, on the line, E
Esa vesa vacka vesa, E

Father is a butcher, F-1
Fatty in the teapot, H-18
Fire on the mountains, A-32
Five, ten, fifteen, twenty, F-1
Follow old Mummy to market, H-18
Four and four are twenty-four, C

Get a bit of pork, H-18
Giddy giddy gout, H-18
Git up, good wives, and shake your feathers, C-54
Go hearty, fearty, hally go lum, E
Go heerty, feerty, hally go lum, E
Go on, you big bumble bee, H-18
Good shot, never miss, H-18
Good story, bad grammar, H-25
Grace, Grace, dressed in lace, F-1
Granny, Granny, I am ill, F-1
Green eyes, greedy eyes, H-18
Green gravels, green gravels, A-14
Green, green, H-18
Guy Fawkes Guy, stick him up on high, C-54

Have a good stare, H-18
Here comes a Duke a-riding, A-28
Here I come full sail, E-8
Here we come lubyloo, A-5
Here we go gathering nuts and may, nuts and may, nuts and may, A-27
Here we go round a jinga-ring, A-9
Here we go round the mulberry bush, A-17
Here's a prisoner we have got, A-23
Here's a thing, J-32
Here's sulky Sue, H-18

Here's the church, and here's the steeple, K-41
Hey you copy cat, H-18
Hibberty bibberty I salliberty, E
Hickety bickety, my black hen, G-7
Hip, hip, hooray, C-53
Honey pots, honey pots, B-3
Hooks and eyes, F-5
Hop, skip, and jump, H-18
House to let, apply within, F-1
How long ago, H-18
How many miles to Babylon? A-35
How many miles to London town, F-1

I am a Girl Guide dressed in blue, F-1
I came to a river, F-7
I had a little dog, A-20
I had a teddy bear dressed in green, F-1
I like coffee, F-1
I sent a letter to my love, A-20
I want a teddy bear, F-1
Ickety, bickety, my black hen, J-52
Ickle ockle black bottle, E
Icky acky chew the baccy, E
Iky Moses, king of the Jews, H-18
In and out the windows, A-24
Ina mina ping pong, E
Ink pink, I smell a big stink, E
Inky pinky fidgety fell, E
Inky pinky penny wink, E
Inky pinky ponky, A-18
It's quite fair that, E
It's raining, it's pouring, H-18

Jack, be nimble, Jack, be quick, K-34
Jenny funny, Jenny fat, H-18
Jenny Jones is dead and gone, A-15
Jenny penny, H-18
Jump, little nag tail, one, two, three, K-59

King King Cae—ree, E-8
King-seenie, one, two, three, E-8

Ladybird, ladybird, drop your purse, F-1

Little boys are made of slugs and snails, H-18
Little Michael Finnigan, H-18
London Bridge is broken down, A-23
Look up, sky blue, E
Look who is here, A-42
Lucy Locket, A-20

Mabel, Mabel, F-1
Madam Morel, F-1
Mademoiselle, F-9
Monkey, monkey, draw the beer, E
Moonlight, starlight, E-17
Mother Brown went to town, F-1
Mother, may I go out to swim? C-46
Mother, Mother, I feel ill, F-1
Mr. Low is a very good man, C
Mrs. B. went to town, H-18
Mrs. Barton, Mrs. Barton, H-18
Mrs. Brown went to town, H-18
Mrs. Martin fell down barking, H-18
Mrs. McKenzie's dead, J-5
My little sister, F-1
My mother and your mother, E
My mother bought me a box of new ribbons, E
My mother bought me a dress, E
My mother said, I never should, F-7

Navy navy nick nack, C
Nivy nivy nick nack, G-6
No more spelling, no more books, C
No more spelling, no more French, C

Oh this pretty little girl of mine, A-6
Oh, you must be a lover of the Lord, of the Lord, H-18
Oka Ball Day, A-4
Old Father Christmas, guess what he did, E
Old Mother Gray, B-7
Old Mother Ink, E
Old Mother Mason, F-1
Ole Pa Watson's a very good man, C
Ole Tommy Finlayson, H-18
Oliver Cromwell lost his shoe, E
Once I had a box of colours, E

One potato, two potato, E
One to make ready, F-1
One, two, sky blue, E
One, two, three, E; F-1; H-18
One, two, three, four, E
One, two, three, four, five, six, seven, E
One, two, three, o'leary, F-9
One, two, touch my shoe, F-1
Onerie awrie, Ickery Ann, E
Onery, twoery, threery, same, F-1
Onery twoery dickery seven, E
Onery, twoery, tickery, seven, E
Open the gate and let me through, sir, F-9
Oranges and lemons, A-22
O-U-T spells out, E
Over the garden wall, F-1

Paddy on the railway, E
Pease pudding hot, F-7
Pig snout, E
Please to remember the fifth of November, C-54
Polly on the railway, F-1
Poor Alice is a-weeping, A-7
Poor old Ernie's dead, H-18
Pounds, shillings and pence, F-1
Proddy dog, Proddy dog, H-18
Protestant dogs, H-18
Put your finger in Tabby's house, K-45

Raspberry, strawberry, F-1
Rick, rick, toe, J-52
Ring a ring a rosie, A-3
Ring a ring a roses, A-3
Rushes and reeds are bending, A-25

Sally, Sally Waters, sprinkle in the pan, A-8
Shivery grass will make you pass, C
Skin a ma links, H-18
Skin a rabbit, H-6
Stare, stare, H-18
Sticks and stones, H-18
Surrender the tower, A-29

Sweep the floor, pick up the chair, K-34

Teddy bear, teddy bear, look to the sky, F-1
Tell, tale, tit, H-18
The big ship sails, A-26
The butcher and the baker, F-1
The grand old Duke of York, A-33
The peanut sat on the railway track, E
There came an old woman from Botany Bay, B-6
There was a jolly miller, A-30
There was a man and he went mad, F-8
There was an old woman, F-1
There was an old woman and her name was Pat, F-1
Thirty days has September, C
This little pig went to market, K-43
Tic, tac, toe, J-52
Tinker, tailor, soldier, sailor, C-31
Tip, tap, toe, J-52
Tit, tat, toe, J-52
To make your mother dance, H-18
Tu la marnie, H-18
Turn your back on the sailor Jack, F-1
Two, four, six, eight, E

Two little dicky birds sitting on a wall, K-40
Two more weeks and we shall be, C
T-W-O spells two, E
2 Y's U R, H-26

Umpa umpa, E

Wallflowers, wallflowers, A-16
Wash the dishes, F-3
Wellington City Council, E
We've come to see Jenny Jones, Jenny Jones, A-15
What have the robbers done to you, A-23
What-oh, she bumps, F-1
When I was a lady, a lady, a lady, A-18
Would you lend my mother a saucepan? A-31

Yesterday at three o'clock in the morning, H-28
You shall bear the saddle-ban, E-19
Young Jean lies over the ocean, H-18
You're mad, you're barmy, H-18
You're the biggest drip, H-18

Zintie tintie tetherie metherie, E

2. Sixty Years of Historical Change in the Game Preferences of American Children

The changes which have occurred in children's games during the past fifty years have not been studied extensively. These changes merit investigation because games are a genuine folk phenomenon, and they may reveal subtle changes in culture and in child nature. For a long time it has been taken for granted that traditional games are central to peer group activities. It has been assumed that certain games belong to girls, and that others belong to boys, and that the differences between them are clear-cut and unchangeable. This paper investigates both of these assumptions.

Previous attempts to gather material on historical change have involved, in the main, the use of reminiscence, as when Yoffie contrasted the singing games of her own childhood in St. Louis, Missouri, 1895, with collections which she made subsequently in the

SOURCE: Reprinted from the *Journal of American Folklore* 74, no. 291 (1961): 17–46, with the permission of the co-author B. G. Rosenberg, and the American Folklore Society.

same place in 1914 and 1944.[1] Sutton-Smith used interviews involving reminiscence together with extensive documentary materials to date the changes in the games of New Zealand children from 1870 through 1950.[2] In the present investigation it is proposed to approach the same problem by comparing the results of four large-scale studies of children's games which were made in the years 1896, 1898, 1921 and 1959. This method has the virtue that each of these studies is reasonably representative of the time and place at which it was taken. The four studies are: (A) in 1896 Crosswell presented a questionnaire to 1,929 children between the ages of six and eighteen years in Worcester, Massachusetts. The children were asked to write down their preferences for games, plays, toys, and amusements. This technique yielded a list of approximately 500 items.[3] (B) in 1898, McGhee furnished 8,718 children in South Carolina between the ages of six and eighteen years, with a 129 item check-list of games from which they were to choose the five games that they liked the most.[4] (C) in 1921, Terman presented a check-list of 90 games and activities to 474 children between the ages of six and seventeen years in the metropolitan area of San Francisco. The children were asked to check the things they had played, the things they could do well, the things they liked to do or play, and the things they liked very well.[5] (D) in 1959 Rosenberg and Sutton-Smith presented a check-list of 181 items to 2,689 children between the ages of 9 and 15, in seventeen townships in northwestern Ohio. The list was composed of games and activities and was derived from a preliminary survey of the written lists of 450 children throughout the same area. The children were asked to mark their preferences (like or dislike) for those games they recognized.[6]

[1] Leah Rachel Clara Yoffie, "Three Generations of Children's Singing Games in St. Louis," *JAF*, LX (1947), 1–51.

[2] Brian Sutton-Smith, *The Games of New Zealand Children* (Berkeley, California, 1959).

[3] T. R. Crosswell, "Amusements of Worcester School Children," *The Pedagogical Seminary*, VI (1898–99), 314–371.

[4] Zach McGhee, "A Study in the Play Life of Some South Carolina Children," *The Pedagogical Seminary*, VII (1900), 459–478.

[5] Lewis M. Terman, *Genetic Studies of Genius*, Vol. 1 (Stanford, 1926).

[6] B. G. Rosenberg and B. Sutton-Smith, "A Revised Conception of Masculine-

In Tables 1 and 2 the results of these four investigations are presented for boys and girls separately. The items are ranked in order of preference with each item being followed by the number of children checking it in the particular study. The differences between these rankings are the major basis for drawing conclusions about the changes in children's games during the period 1896 through 1959. In addition, further comparisons are made among the thirty-five items which the three check-lists (1898, 1921, 1959) have in common.

It would be naive to assume that all differences between these lists are due to historical change. In interpreting results a number of precautions need to be kept in mind: (a) Each of the studies was carried out in a different geographical locale. Differences between the lists, therefore, may be the results of sampling in different places, rather than due to historical change. Some check on this is possible. The 1896 and 1898 lists can be checked against each other for consistencies and inconsistencies. The 1921 collection can be checked against the large scale Kansas collection of games and activities by Lehmann and Witty also taken during the twenties.[7] Unfortunately, this latter collection cannot be used *in toto*, as the authors did not publish their data in full. There are, in addition, other small collections from that period.[8] The contemporary collection is derived from seventeen towns and cities in northwestern Ohio. It is not at present known how representative this current list is of the country as a whole. If games are as universally played and as similar from place to place, as has often been averred, these various sampling differences may well be unimportant.

(b) Each of the lists of games required the children to record their responses in a different way. The 1896 study had the children write down their own games. All the other investigations (1898, 1921 and 1959) had the children mark games on a prepared check list. This makes the latter lists more directly comparable in method,

Feminine Differences in Play Activities," *Journal of Genetic Psychology*, 1960, 96, 165–170.

[7] Harvey C. Lehmann and Paul A. Witty, *The Psychology of Play Activities* (New York, 1927).

[8] Josephine C. Foster, "Play Activities of Children in the First Six Grades," *Child Development*, I (1930), 248–254, and Norma Schwendener, "Game Preferences of 10,000 Fourth Grade Children," (New York, 1942).

so they alone are used in making the comparison of the thirty-five common items. The 1921 and 1959 lists are most directly comparable, since in each instance the children were asked to mark all the games that they wished; whereas in the 1898 list, they were asked to mark only five games. The different techniques are reflected in the different frequencies of response in these studies (see tables). The 1896 study required children to differentiate between the games played (frequency) and the games most preferred (popularity). The frequency responses were the larger of the two and were used for the rankings of the 1896 collection which is found in Tables 1 and 2. The 1898 study was based on the five most popular games. The 1921 authors combined both frequency and popularity counts into a combined index. The 1959 list was based on recognition and popularity. Terman claims that the method of response, frequency or popularity, makes little difference to over-all ranking. so this reported variety of techniques may not be too important.

(c) The composition of the different lists may have an effect upon the order of ranking. The 1896 list composed by the children themselves contained a wide assortment of games, plays, and pastimes. The 1898 list, however, contained only games. The 1921 and 1959 lists contain a mixture of games and pastimes. This means that the rank position of a game in the list may depend partly upon the nature of the other items which can be elected. In this respect the 1896, 1921, and 1959 lists are more alike than the 1898 list which is restricted to games alone. As the 1921 and 1959 lists are comparable, and the 1896 and 1898 can be checked against each other, it is possible to exercise some control over differences arising from this source. In addition, all the lists are of different length. It was decided therefore to include all the items from the three check lists [1898 (129 items), 1921 (90 items), 1959 (180 items)], but only the first 180 from the 1896 list (of approximately 500 items) as beyond that level of preference there were only one or two responses to each item on this list.

(d) There are some differences in the age of the respondents. The 1896, 1898 and 1921 investigations involve a wider age range than the 1959 investigation. However, in all these investigations the largest number of respondents is in the same age group, 9 through 15 years. The effect of the responses of those in the higher age levels presumably balanced the responses of those at the younger age levels in the averaging procedure which is used in the present comparisons. This procedure, rather than an age-by-age comparison, had to be followed as it was the method adopted in both the studies of the 1890's.

In sum, it will be seen that these many differences in the nature of the lists imply that the generalizations made about historical changes in this article must be accepted as tentative in nature.

RESULTS

In the results that follow, the matter of historical changes in sex preference for games is dealt with first. There follows a treatment of a variety of different types of plays and games. The games are arranged in groups according to certain obvious unitary characteristics which they have. The order of treatment is approximately "developmental," that is, games which tend to be played by younger children are dealt with first. The reasons for this classification and ordering of games have been dealt with elsewhere.[9]

Changes in boy-girl game preferences

A number of recent studies have demonstrated that differences between the sexes, as measured by check-list preferences, have been considerably reduced during the past 30 years. Jones reported that ninth grade boys and girls of today are more like each other in their attitudes towards heterosexual activities, religion, and sports.[10] Rosenberg and Sutton-Smith reported that fourth, fifth, and sixth grade girls of today are substantially more like boys in their game choices than was the case in 1921.[11] These and other studies have served to indicate that not only has there been a definite shift in attitudes and preferences of children over the last 25

[9] B. Sutton-Smith, "A Formal Analysis of Game Meaning," *Western Folklore*, XVIII (1959), 13–24; and B. Sutton-Smith, "The Historical and Psychological Significance of the Unorganized Games of New Zealand Primary School Children" (Ph. D. Thesis, University of New Zealand, 1953). A copy is in the library of Victoria University of Wellington, New Zealand, and a microfilm copy is in the library of Ball State Teachers College, Muncie, Indiana.

[10] Mary Cover Jones, "A Comparison of the Attitudes and Interests of Ninth Graders Over Two Decades," a paper presented at the 25th Anniversary Meeting of the Society for Research in Child Development, Bethesda, Maryland, 20 March 1959.

[11] B. G. Rosenberg and B. Sutton-Smith, *ibid.*

years, but in particular, the studies show the increasing incorporation of masculine preferences by females.[12] It seems reasonable to assume that this trend towards increasing similarity of the sexes has been occurring over a period greater than 30 years.

The thirty-five items which were common to the 1898, 1921 and 1959 lists are as follows: Baseball, Football, Basketball, Swimming, Hide and seek, Tag, Marbles, Checkers, Cards, Kites, Wrestling, Puzzles, Blindman's buff, Tennis, Dancing, Dominoes, Drop the handkerchief, Leapfrog, Simon says, Tiddleywinks, Store, Fox and geese, Chess, Jacks, Jumprope, Hopscotch, Parchesi, Fox and hounds, Houses, Spin tops, Charades, Prisoner's base, Snap, Puss in corner, Dolls. If these items are arranged by rank order of preference for boys and girls separately in each of the years 1898, 1921 and 1959, and rank-order correlations are run between the lists, there is evidence of increasing similarity between the sexes in game preferences. There is little relationship between the sexes in game preferences in 1898 (rho$=-.023$), which means that the sexes prefer quite different games. There is a slight relationship in 1921 (rho$=+.328$), and a moderate relationship in 1959 (rho$=+.451$) which means that the sexes have become increasingly similar in their game preferences.

When the rankings of each sex are treated separately, and rank order correlations run between each period, the following results obtain. Between 1898 and 1921 the rho correlation for boys is: $=+.672$. Between 1898 and 1959 the rho$=+.595$. Between 1921 and 1959 the rho$=+.707$. These results suggest a high similarity in game preferences among boys during this period. The same rank correlations for the girls are: 1898 to 1921, rho$=+.490$; 1898 to 1959, rho$=+.397$; 1921 to 1959, rho$=+.680$. These rank order correlations for the girls are smaller, suggesting that the increasing similarity between the sexes from 1898 to 1959 has been brought about more by changes in girls' play preferences than by changes in those of the boys. This finding is consistent with the other investigations of changes in boy-girl differences.

If we choose, arbitrarily, a change in ten rank points between these three separate studies as indicative of an historical change,

[12] Daniel G. Brown, "Sex Role Preference in Young Children," *Psychological Monographs*, LXX (1956), 1–19.

then those game choices which show a tendency towards increasing similarity between the sexes between 1898 and 1959 are:

Puss in the corner	Drop the handkerchief
Swimming	Dancing
Tag	Marbles
Leap frog	Kites
Fox and hounds	Tops

The games which remain fairly constant retaining their rank difference of less than ten points between the sexes from 1898 to 1959 are:

Parchesi	Dominoes
Charades	Prisoner's base
Hide and seek	Puzzles
Checkers	Tiddleywinks
Tennis	Snap
Blindman's buff	Simon says
Fox and geese	Chess
Cards	

The games which remain constant by continuing to hold more than ten rank point differences between the sexes throughout this period are:

Jackstones	Football
House	Wrestling
Hopscotch	

Closer examination of the items showing increasing similarity between the sexes with time reveals that there are a variety of reasons for these changes. In some cases, the increased similarity is due to the fact that the girls now favor these games less than they used to and have thus become more like the boys (e.g., Puss in the corner, Drop the handkerchief). Other games have gained in favor with the girls and made their choices more like those of the boys (e.g., Swimming, Tag and Kites). There are games that have lost favor with boys and now make their choices more like those of the girls (e.g., Fox and hounds, Tops); games that have lost favor with the boys and gained favor with the girls (e.g., Leapfrog and Marbles); and games that have lost favor with both sexes (e.g., Parchesi, Fox and geese, Prisoner's base). It should be noted, however, that although the sexes have become more similar in these respects, there are still statistically significant differences between them in their responses to some of these items. In particular, Football, Marbles, and Wrestling which are more preferred by the boys, and Dance, Dolls, Drop the handkerchief, Fox and geese, Hopscotch, Houses, Jacks, Jumprope, Leapfrog, Puzzles, Simon says and Store which are more preferred by the girls.[13]

Changes in types of games

It has seemd worthwhile to analyze the changes that have taken place in the children's preferences for games in terms of a variety of *types* of games. The types of games that are dealt with are as follows:

imitative or make-believe games	games of individual skill
singing games	skilled pastimes
dialogue games	undifferentiated team games
leader games	of skill
chasing games	indoor or backyard games
central person parlor games	of skill
undifferentiated team guessing	board and card games
and chasing games	major sports
central person games of low	co-operative parlor games
power	couple and kissing games

Imitative or make-believe games

It is noticeable that boys' make-believe games where two groups participate in dramatized conflict have remained remarkably stable over this period of time. Ranking high in choice within the first twenty in all periods are Play horse (1896), Buffalo Bill and Policeman (1898), Cowboys (Kansas, 1924, Lehmann and Witty's investigation reported in *The Psychology of Play Activities*), and Cops and robbers, Bow and arrows, and Soldiers (1959). Within the first forty ranked are War (1896) and Bandits (1959). The preferences of girls for these games has not changed appreciably from 1898 until present, their rank position ranging from the low second

---

[13] B. G. Rosenberg and B. Sutton-Smith, "The Measurement of Masculinity and Femininity in Children," *Child Development*, XXX (1959), 373–380.

fifty downwards. Apparently, in becoming more masculine, girls have not been concerned to identify themselves with these fantasy roles which are so important to boys. This raises an important question: Why should girls show an increasing preference for the minor and major sports of boys (e.g., Marbles and Swimming), but not for these dramatized male games? The simplest interpretation is that girls are following the lead of women, that while women have shown increased interest and participation in men's sports, they have not so extensively taken over the warrior-like activities of men (Soldiers, Cops, Cowboys). It would be of interest to know whether girls' play is similar in those cultures where the women have, in recent years, been assuming warriorlike functions (Israel and China). It has often been observed that boys follow fantasy models in their imitative play (Cowboys and Indians) and that girls follow realistic models in theirs (Mothers, Nurses, etc.); and it has been suggested that for boys this is due to their lack of clear-cut father models to imitate, their fathers being absent most of the time and involved in abstract and complex white collar functions.[14] If these imitative games do reflect such basic issues of sex-role identification, this would be an additional reason for the girls' avoidance of them.

The imitative games which are usually associated more with girls than with boys, seem to have decreased in importance for boys over the years. In the 1896 and 1898 lists, playing at School, House, and Store are in the first fifty ranked items for both boys and girls. They remain in the first fifty for girls through 1959. For the boys, they drop to the second fifty in preference in 1921 and to the third fifty (ranking lower than 100), in 1959. The marked change in the rank order of these games for boys is not a result of changes in the lists, or this would have been reflected in the girls' preferences also. It suggests rather the hypothesis that boys have lowered their liking for games of this sort because they are strongly preferred by girls. Further, it suggests that because girls have encroached upon the play preferences of boys, and appear therefore less separate from boys than they once were, boys have attempted to clarify their own distinctness, by lowering their preference for any games that are not obviously masculine. In an attempt to remain as sepa-

[14] T. Parsons, *Essays in Sociological Theory* (Glencoe, Illinois, 1949).

rate in their games from girls as they once were, boys have had to surrender interest in pursuits that were not completely and exclusively masculine. If this generalization is veridical, then it follows that in these respects at least the play of boys today is more circumscribed than it was at the end of the nineteenth century. This generalization is a refinement of the customary view which suggests that differences between the sexes has decreased over the years. Nominally differences may have decreased but apparently at the expense of variety in boys' role behaviors. We will note, as we proceed, other types of female-associated games in which the same tendency can be seen to operate. [For example, boys rank play at Dolls as 51st (1896), 87th (1898), 82nd (1921) but 171st (1959).] This indicates, we believe, that we are recording a genuine historical change, and not merely a change resulting from geographic locale or sample selection. Other changes in boys' imitative play refer more to obvious historical content than to fundamental changes in child behavior. In the 1890 collections we have mention of Steamboat, Buffalo Bill, Black Maria, and Robinson Crusoe, which are less familiar to children today. In their place are games like Spacemen and Inventors. It is not surprising, in view of the population shift from rural to urban areas, that playing at Horses has dropped some fifty rank positions.

The major girls' imitative games, Dolls, Houses, and Schools, may have lost rank to some extent but the change is relatively small. Dolls rank first in both 1896 and 1898, but in 1921 and 1959 it is 8th. More active games have taken Dolls' position of priority (Jump rope, Bicycle-riding, Roller-skating, etc.). Apparently modern girls play the more active games at an earlier age than used to be the case. These games have slipped down the age levels making today's children appear more sophisticated. Playing at Houses moves from 7th (1896) and 9th (1898) to 13th (1921) and 26th (1959). Playing at School goes from 9th (1896) to 14th (1921) and 20th (1959). It would be interesting to know whether the increasing masculinity of girls' choices has led to a decrease in their interest in more central feminine concerns as these shifts in game preferences seem to indicate. Perhaps the relatively greater interest in play at Dressing-up which is not found in the earlier lists but ranks as 15th (1921) and 16th (1959) reflects a shift in interest from the feminine domestic to the feminine glamor role. Some writers have suggested that one price women have paid for their emancipation has been increasing confusion about their own distinctive role behavior. The new situation has made it simpler for younger girls to identify with the more obvious "glamor" role than with the domestic sex roles once thought appropriate for women.[15]

Singing games

Yoffie found in her study of "Three Generations of Children's Singing Games in St. Louis" that children at the end of the last century played more traditional singing games than do children today.[16] This finding seems to be confirmed by the present investigation. The 1896 Worcester list in which the children wrote down their own responses contains some twenty-five games.[17] Very few of these games were written by children on the lists from which the 1959 check-list was originally derived. The games mentioned in the 1896 list, most of them with only one or two frequencies, were in order of popularity: Drop the handkerchief, On the green carpet, Grandmother Grey, Go in and out the windows, Lazy maid, lazy Mary, lazy Bessie, Water, water, wildflowers, Ring a round the rosy, Farmer in the dell, London bridge, Round the mulberry bush, Round the barley bush, Billy Billy button, Three kings, Bushel of wheat, bushel of rye, Fly Kitty through peals, Jenny a Jones, Jemima Jones, Poor Tommy is dead, Little Sally Water, Forty girls go round the ring, Merry girls, Draw a pail of water, Here comes an old woman from Farmerland (Cumberland), Here comes one king, Here's the way we wash our clothes, Have you bread and wine. No description is given of these games in the 1896 report.

Although not as many basic game items are listed in the 1921 investigation, the games that are listed seem as high in popularity as those listed in the 1896 and 1898 reports. This is also true in the 1924 report from Kansas,[18] which makes it appear as if the large change that has come about in the playing of girls' traditional singing games has, in the main, occurred after the 1920's. There may,

[15] Lawrence K. Frank et alia, "Personality Development in Adolescent Girls," *Monographs of the Society for Research in Child Development*, XVI (1951), 195.

[16] Leah Yoffie, p. 50.

[17] T. R. Crosswell, p. 320.

[18] Lehmann and Witty, p. 79.

however, have been fewer games known by the twenties, even though those played were very popular. Yoffie found this in St. Louis, and Sutton-Smith obtained similar results in New Zealand. It is further confirmed by the fact that a collection of approximately 600 games from 10,000 children in 1931 in the states of Massachusetts, Ohio, Michigan, Texas and Florida appears to have yielded no more singing games than the list above from Worcester alone.[19] (Only game names are listed so it is difficult to be definite about this point.) Contemporary girls have many rhyming interests, but these find their expression mainly in Jump rope, ranked number one in the 1959 list and ball bouncing, also ranked high (25th). Individual games reflect the above general picture. Drop the handkerchief has probably maintained its position of high rank in the first thirty because it is as much a chasing as a singing game. It ranked 24th (1896), 5th (1898), 19th (1921), 24th (1959). In and out the windows was 46th (1896), 33rd (1921), 82nd (1959). Ring a round the rosy was 54th (1896), 41st (1898), 25th (1921), 89th (1959). Farmer in the dell was 57th (1896), 16th (1921), 60th (1959). London Bridge dropped from 24th (1921) to 55th (1959). The Mulberry bush changes little from 90th (1896) to 93rd (1959). Several games popular in the Nineties are not on subsequent lists, namely, Little Sallie Water, 13th (1898); On the green carpet, 35th (1896); Lazy maid, 50th (1896) and Water wildflowers, 51st (1896). The boys' rankings of these games, although lower than the girls', reflect similar trends, except that they have dropped proportionately much lower than the girls' in the 1959 period. This is further evidence apparently of their increasing withdrawal from feminine pursuits.

Dialogue games

These are chasing games played by young girls which involve a traditional dialogue and a dramatization of conflict between an old witch or mother and her children. Several rank highly with girls in the earlier studies: Goosie, goosie, 17th, Mother may I pick a rose, 23rd, and Chick-a-my chick-a-my crany crow, 29th (all of 1898); Grandmother Grey, 38th, Old witch, 71st, Old Mother Goose, 89th (all of 1896). There is no mention, let alone high ranking of any

---

[19] Schwendener, pp. 38–45.

of these games in the 1921 and 1959 studies. The Kansas 1924 study, however, lists Old witch. And the Schwendener 1931 study in five states lists Old Mother witch with high frequency, but lists with only one frequency in ten thousand children, Grandmother Grey and Mother may I go out to play. We would assume that these dialogue games, like the singing games, have fallen into desuetude largely because of their inappropriate symbolism. On the other hand it seems hardly likely that dual-mother play is no longer important to young girls. Perhaps they get that sort of play representation while playing schools and at leader games.

Leader games

These games are usually played by young girls of seven to nine years and involve one girl taking a commanding position over others. She is part of the game but is also its arbiter. As far as can be judged games of this sort have increased in number. All earlier lists contain only one or two of these games, whereas the 1959 list has Mother may I (22nd), Follow the leader (27th), Simon says (31st), Statues (47th), I spy (49th), Initials (140th), Letters (142nd). The 1896 list has Steps (33rd) and this is similar to Mother may I. Simon says improves rank position from 84th (1898) to 38th (1921). Follow the leader and I spy maintain rank position from 1921 to 1959. Statuary is mentioned in the Kansas list, 1924. Schwendener mentions Follow the leader, Redlight and Initials as played in 1931. We can generalize, though the evidence is meager, that playing at this type of leader role-taking is more important to young girls than it used to be. Once again, we find that the boys' response to these girls' games is less favorable than it was. Whereas Follow the leader and Simon says retain rank position for girls, both descend in importance for boys, Follow the leader from 30th (1921) to 55th (1959), and Simon says from 57th (1921) to 86th (1959).

Chasing games

Chasing games have played an important part in the play of both boys and girls throughout the sixty years involved in this study. The physical activity of running and the themes of pursuit and capture are apparently very basic motifs in this culture. With few exceptions girls show higher rankings in more of these games in all historical periods. The games which have remained most constant over this period are Tag and Hide and seek. Girls rank Tag, 3rd (1896), 1st (1921) and 3rd (1959). Boys rank Tag, 7th (1896), 4th (1921) and 7th (1959). Girls rank Hide and seek 4th (1896), 5th (1921), 2nd (1959). Boys rank Hide and seek 10th (1896), 8th (1921), 4th (1959). Rather unexpectedly both of these games had much lower rankings in the 1898 list from South Carolina. Girls ranked Tag and Hide and seek respectively as 86th and 12th and boys ranked them respectively as 23rd and 17th. For girls the highest ranking chasing game in South Carolina was Drop the handkerchief (4th) and for boys Fox and geese (5th). Both of these are more formal chasing games than Tag or Hide and seek. In addition Tag is more popular with boys than girls in Carolina, which is not the case elsewhere. These differences, together with the higher ranking given to other formal chasing games in South Carolina to singing games, to parlor games and to dancing, suggest that play in that state at that time was more decorous and formal than it was at the other places sampled in this study.

Although chasing games are generally more popular with girls, exceptions occur for the following games which are more popular with boys: Relievo, Black Tom, Run sheep run (1896), Tag, Fox and geese (1898), Fox and geese, Pom pom pull away (1921), Ghosts, Kick the can, Poison tag, Pom pom pull away, Black Tom, Blackman (1959). The fact that there are still these distinctive and vigorous boys' chasing games probably accounts for the fact that boys' preferences for these games have not yet decreased. If the circumscription of the masculine role continues, however, it might be predicted that boys would show decreasing favor for girl associated chasing games in the years ahead. The tagging games which are preferred by girls today are Hide and seek, Tag, Stoop tag, Red Rover, Frozen tag, Fox and geese, Blindman's buff, Wood tag, Cat and mouse, Squirrel in tree, What time is it? and Two deep.

Central person parlor games

As in other central person games (chasing and leader games), these games contain one or two persons occupying central roles and steering the course of the game. These games can be played by the under tens because of their simple organization. They are games played at parties and on indoor social occasions and are preferred more by girls than by boys. Games of the Nineties which are not played today are Stagecoach, William my tremble toe, Guessing riddles, Geography, Jake grin at me, Proverbs, and Object Questions. Games played in 1898 which are still played today but preferred to a slightly lesser extent are, Find the ring or Ring on a string, Hide the thimble (also 1896), Twenty questions, and Forfeits. The only comparable game of today with a higher ranking is Musical chairs which is the same game as Walk to Jerusalem of 1898. The new but similar games of today are Tail on the donkey, I've got a secret, Name that tune, Black magic, and Poor pussy. These games seem still to be important, but perhaps not quite as important as they once were.

Undifferentiated team guessing and acting

In these games there are two teams or groups of loose formation. Characteristically, one group performs and the other must guess the nature of the performance. The games involve mainly dramatization and guessing. They are universally girls' games played by children nine years and over and often take place on formal indoor occasions such as parties. While all the lists contain one or two of these games, the largest number are in the South Carolina list, presumably further evidence of more formal social play in that state at that time, 1898. The games itemized in that list were Devil and angel, Clumps, Charades, Up jinks, Pretty maids country, Dumb scrambo, and Open the gates. Four of these were ranked in the first forty by the girls. None of the similar games in other lists, Trades (1896), Here I come, where from? (1924, Kansas and 1959), Charades (1959) have this rank importance.

Central person games of low power

In the leader, dialogue, central person parlor and chasing games, the person at the center of the action, the central person, has been given relatively high power by the nature of the game. He can choose whom to chase, when to run, and so on. At the ages of 9 to 10 years, children, especially boys, begin to play central person games in which the central person is not given great power by the game and must use his own skill to fight off the challenge of the other players. The most popular games of this sort today are Dodgeball, King on the mountain, and Wall dodge ball. In earlier lists, positions of similar importance were held by Snap the whip (1921), Duck on rock (1921 and 1896), Pig in the pen, and Bull in the pen (1898).

There seems to have been little historical change in the position of these games. Indeed the fact that there is so little change in chasing games which are games of high central person power, and so little change in these games of low central person power, suggests that these two types of game are the major stepping stones in game development. First, the child experiences games of high central person power, where the game provides support and protection for his own inadequacy; then there are these games at the later age where the child must face the other players without such protection. The transition from protected to unprotected game status is perhaps the major one that a child must be able to accomplish in his game development if he is to be a successful gamesman! This argument has been developed more fully elsewhere.[20] If and when games ever decrease in children's own spontaneous play it is reasonable to assume that recreationists will continue to use a game series of this sort for educational purposes.

Games of individual skill

Increasingly from 9 or 10 years of age onwards, boys and girls play games where all players are on equal terms, and they compete with each other to see who can win. Games of this sort were more varied in earlier years than they are today. For example, Mumble peg, Foot and a half, Five hundred, Philopoena, Green, Bean bags, Book, Roly poly, Hide the switch (1898), Jackknife, Pick knife and Horse chestnut (1896). A few of these games, however, have remained remarkably constant. For boys these are Marbles: 2nd (1896), 4th (1898), 7th (1921) and 8th (1959). For girls: Jump rope, 3rd (1896) [Omitted from Table 2. Frequency of 480.], 2nd (1898), 12th (1921), 1st (1959) and Jacks 10th (1896), 12th (1898), 46th (1921), 14th (1959). Some have lost popularity with boys, such as Spin tops 12th (1896), 10th (1898), 15th (1921) and 133rd (1959), and Leapfrog which was 41st (1896), 9th (1898),

---

[20] B. Sutton-Smith, "Peer Status and Play Status," *Recreation*, XLVIII (1955), 172–174; and P. V. Gump and B. Sutton-Smith, "The 'It' Role in Children's Games," *The Group*, XVII (1955), 3–8.

33rd (1921) and 69th (1959). Hopscotch has gained in popularity
with girls from 14th (1896), 45th (1898), 7th (1921) to 5th
(1959). Racing has gained popularity with both sexes. For the three
girls' games of Hopscotch, Jacks, and Jump rope, boys' preferences
have drawn further away from those of girls, especially since 1921.
For the three boys' games of Marbles, Leapfrog, and Spin tops,
however, the girls' preferences have drawn closer to those of the
boys over these years. This may be due, in part, to the fact that
boys' preferences for these games have decreased.

It is interesting to note that the older skill games with a penalty
written into their laws find few counterparts in modern play;
games such as Quaker meeting, Hat stack, Hide the switch, Foot
and a half, Club fists, Forfeits, Book, Knucks, Jake grin at me
(1898) and Duck on rock (1896). Modern children are apparently
less rough in their play, a finding which is consistent with the general view that the play of children has been increasingly supervised and controlled throughout this period of sixty years.[21]

Skilled pastimes

These are activities which are usually carried on by individuals
alone or among others. These activities may give rise to competitive, gamelike activities, but are not in themselves formally organized games. Bicycle riding, Horse riding, and Climbing are activities which have increased in importance for both sexes over this
period of time. The girls have narrowed the difference between
themselves and the boys in Climbing, and have erased the difference in Horse and Bicycle riding. Swimming, Kites, and Fishing
are activities which have remained fairly constant in rank for boys,
but girls have shown increased preference for these items, so that
they now show equal preference with the boys for Swimming and
much greater preference than formerly for the other two. The only
item in which the boys show a much greater preference than formerly and the girls do not, is Throwing snowballs. Boating remains
fairly constant for both sexes. Markedly decreased interest is shown
over the years in winter time activities such as Skating, Skiing, and
Tobogganing, and in the antique pastimes of Hoops, Stilts and Hik-

[21] B. Sutton-Smith, "Traditional Games of New Zealand Children," *Folk-
Lore*, LXIV (1953), 411–423.

ing. Roller-skating seems to have taken the place of some of the earlier winter pastimes, particularly with girls. This is partly a reflection of urbanization. Roller-skating ranked 10th with Brooklyn girls of the 1890's according to Crosswell. One must have open spaces to ski and toboggan.

Children's hobbies permit few comparisons with the earlier period except in terms of item content. Play with leaves and flowers, nuts, grass, etc., ranks high in the Nineties, but is unmentioned today. However, comparison with the 1921 list shows less interest for both sexes today in Model aeroplanes, Using tools, Machinery, Gardening, Sewing, and Knitting. The girls have held their rank position on Cooking, but the boys have decreased theirs greatly, apparently being once again less willing to be associated with a feminine type activity than in earlier times. It seems that hobby-type activities are less important than they were, their place perhaps being taken by the greater availability of movies, radio, TV, etc. The number of skilled activities in the first forty rank positions for boys does not change greatly in the 1896, 1921 and 1959 lists. The girls' list of 1896 contains fewer of these activities in the first forty than do the girls' lists of 1921 and 1959, another respect apparently in which the girls have become more like the boys. (The 1898 list was restricted to formal games, and as such cannot be used in this comparison.) As almost half of boys' preferences in the first forty are for skilled pastimes, and as the girls' preference for these activities is increasing, it follows that formal games are becoming less important in general. If this trend should continue with girls becoming more like boys, and boys tending to give up all formal games which have anything to do with girls, the time may come when neither sex shows any strong interest in most of the formal games of childhood (as distinct from the athletic and formal sports of adults). If it is true that such a trend is occurring in childhood away from formalized group activities, then it is interesting to speculate on the causes of this development. One argument might be that children who today live in more permissive, free-communicating, and equalitarian relationships with their parents, have less need for formalized relationships in play. This argument would suggest that the formalities of the traditional children's games, the prestige role-positions, and the power differences invested in the players by the game, were a representation of the hierarchically ordered societies in which the children found themselves. The games were modeled after the formal social interactions which were thought appropriate in the family and in society. Elements of this sort are most obvious in the singing games, team guessing and acting games, dialogue games, co-operative parlor games and couple parlor games, all of which have shown the most striking decrease in importance. When we remember that these games were originally created and played by adults to meet the needs of an older society, the fact of their decay is less surprising.

Today's children by contrast have relatively less need to understand formalized social relations, which makes it understandable that formal group play activities are less meaningful to them. Today's children are said to spend much more time in informal peer group activities both in and out of school. It follows that in their play they would be increasingly interested in such informal group activities as Swimming, Fishing, Hunting, Boating, Bicycle-riding, and Roller skating, which as we have seen, have widespread popularity but are not governed by set patterns of game rules. It has been observed that these children do not show increasing interest in the informal activities that are usually pursued by the individual on his own, such as hobbies.

If these speculations have any foundation, we would expect that the playing of formal games will be of ever decreasing importance in the spontaneous play of children.[22] No doubt numbers of the more competitive of such games will be retained by teachers and playground supervisors for recreational purposes and some will continue to be employed as a subsidiary means of training potential professional athletes. One would expect, too, that children will continue spontaneously to participate in some of these games, in particular chasing, and commercially sponsored board and skill games from time to time; but it is doubtful that a wide range of formal games will continue to be the foundation of peer group activity as it has been traditionally throughout the first forty years of this century.

[22] A similar interpretation of game-types as paralleling social life will be found in John M. Roberts, Malcolm J. Arth and Robert R. Bush, "Games in Culture," *American Anthropologist*, LXI (1959), 597–605.

Undifferentiated team games

These are formal games of skill in which the two "teams" are only slightly differentiated in terms of different role behaviors. Each group acts as a pack against the other pack. It is clear that this type of game played mainly by 11–12-year-old boys has decreased in importance. Presumably the greater modern attention to major sports has weakened interest in these games. The games that are directly comparable (Fox and hounds or Hare and hounds, Prisoner's base or Base, and Capture the flag or Stealing chips or Eggs) have all lost rank position. Several games, Battle, Stealing chips, Fox and hounds, and Base all have high rankings in the 1890's, whereas the only game today in the first 30 is Tug-o-war where the position is unchanged from 1921.

Indoor or backyard games of physical skill

The modern list contains a few more games of this sort. Of the comparisons possible, Pick up sticks (Jackstraws) retains about the same rank position today as in 1898. Tiddleywinks loses rank in 1898 and 1921. Billiards loses with both sexes from 1921, Pool loses with girls but holds constant for boys. Croquet seems to have lost importance from the 1890's to 1921 and is not in the 1959 list. Quoits also has lost rank position as between 1896 and 1959. Highest ranking games today are Darts, Ping pong, and Horseshoes, all favored by boys. Highest ranking in the early lists was Croquet, favored by girls. It seems likely that commercial sponsorship will keep some of these games alive for many years to come. The same may be said of the board and card games.

Board and card games

There is a tendency for games of this sort to have a slightly higher ranking in the early (1898) list. Old favorites which are not in the current list are Parchesi, Authors, Crokinole, and Lotto. New games of this sort are Bingo, Monopoly, Scrabble, and Clue. Dominoes is less highly ranked than it was. Chess and Snap have maintained their ranking. Checkers and Cards have been in the first twenty in most of the lists. They have been slightly more important to the boys until the 1959 list when they were ranked slightly higher by the girls. Puzzles and Tic Tac Toe have improved their rank positions, but this is more noticeable with the girls. Indications are that these types of games might be increasing in importance for girls and decreasing in importance for boys.

Major sports

In the major sports of Bowling, Football, Basketball, Wrestling and Boxing, the girls' preferences are closer to those of the boys in the 1921 list than they were in the earlier lists. However, in the 1959 list, the sexes are again farther apart in these preferences than in the 1921 list. There are several reasons for this. Some games have decreased markedly in popularity with girls since 1921 (or as between San Francisco, 1921 and Ohio, 1959). These are Football, Basketball, Baseball, Wrestling, and Boxing. Bowling has remained constant with the girls, but has improved rank position with the boys since 1921. The positions of Football and Basketball have improved with boys, while they have lost rank with the girls. Baseball, Wrestling and Boxing have lost rank position with the boys also, but not to the extent that they have with the girls. Tennis, Soccer, and Handball have lost rank position with both sexes, with the difference between the sexes (the boys showing slightly more preference) remaining more or less constant. Football has taken Baseball's place as the number one athletic game.

We might hypothesize that the increase in girls' interest between 1900 and 1920 was due to their greater freedom to play actively and be interested in boys' activities. But their unwillingness to get closer to boys in these particularly vigorous masculine sports since that time is due to the realization that these activities, like Cops and robbers, are distinctively masculine.

These trends would indicate that boys are spending more and more time on fewer sports. Bowling, Basketball, and Football improve in rank position, but all the other sports decline (Baseball, Wrestling, Boxing, Volleyball, Tennis, Soccer, Handball). These facts must be kept in mind when rating the disappearance of the undifferentiated team games of yesterday and the decline of the number of individual games of skill. This would appear to be further evidence of the increasing circumscription of the boys' play role.

Co-operative parlor games

Games of this sort are very important in the list of 1898, but not in subsequent lists. The games no longer found are: Cross questions, Old dame Wiggins, I see a ghost, Consequences, My father had a rooster, Gossip, Key, Table rapping, Borrowed property, Introducing the King and Queen. These games involved the co-operation of two or more players in order to produce a trick on some of the other players, or some absurd result, which was a source of hilarity to all. Apparently the youths of today occupy themselves in other activities as we have noted because these games do not appear on the more recent lists. The games were played mainly by teenagers or older persons in earlier times. They were more highly ranked by girls than by boys.

Couple and kissing games

Items that are comparable, Dance, Spin the plate (or bottle), and Post office show a decrease in rank position. These games are not as important as they were. Although Spin the bottle is the most favored of kissing games today,[23] its position in the second fifty cannot compare with the 4th ranking of Clap in clap out in 1898. Other games in the earlier lists were: Smiling angel, Goodnight, Pig in parlor, Kiss the pillow, and Last couple out. The rank position of the new kissing games in the 1959 list (Flashlight and Perdiddle) is much lower.

Conclusion

This survey of the changes in games over sixty years is based on game lists derived in 1896, 1898, 1921 and 1959. The differences in the sampling techniques used in these various studies implies that considerable caution must be exercised in interpreting differences between their results as differences of an historical sort. Nevertheless, the following conclusions appear warranted.

Some types of games are much less important to children of today than they were to children of the 1890's. These are children's

[23] B. Sutton-Smith, "The Kissing Games of Adolescence," *Midwest Folklore*, IX (1959), 189–211.

singing games, dialogue games, team guessing and acting games, co-operative parlor games, couple and kissing games, all of which are predominantly girls' games, and team games without role differentiation which are boys' games. Other types of games appear to be played as much today as they were earlier. These are imitative games, chasing games, and central person games of low power. There are other games where the trend is less clear, but that give some evidence of being played less than they used to be. These are individual games of skill, a wide range of organized sports, central person parlor games, and board and card games. Again there is slight evidence that the following types of games are played more often than they used to be: leader games, indoor and backyard games of physical skill, skilled pastimes, and a few selected organized sports.

Perhaps the most important generalizations arising out of this study concern the changing relationships between boys and girls. The finding that the responses of girls have become increasingly like those of the boys as the sixty years have passed is not unexpected, in the light of the well known changes in woman's role in American culture during this period of time. On the other hand, the finding that boys' play roles have become increasingly circumscribed with the passing of the years was unexpected. Yet there is little doubt that boys have been steadily lowering their preference for games that have had anything to do with girls' play. So that it is by implication much more deviant behavior for a modern boy to play at, say, Dolls, Hopscotch, Jacks, Houses, Schools, Cooking, Jump rope, Musical chairs, Simon says, and Singing games than it was for a boy to play at these things in the earlier historical periods covered by these studies. In another sense, too, boys' play is more circumscribed, for it would seem that they have greatly reduced the range of games of individual and team skill and the organized sports to which they will devote their time. This reduction in the range of boys' activities can, of course, be variously interpreted. It contributes to clear-cut role definition of appropriate boys' behavior and perhaps facilitates the development of those boys who have the particular skills required by the games that are in demand. On the other hand it must as surely penalize those many other boys who find that there is a discrepancy between their own abilities and those required in the play roles of their own age sex category.[24] Judging by the few activities that now clearly differentiate a boy from a girl, masculine roughplay (Football, Boxing, Wrestling) and masculine-like intrusiveness (Horseshoes, Throwing snowballs, Marbles, and Darts) have become the residual and central facets of the male sex role.[25]

Of a somewhat more speculative order is the attendant generalization that these historical changes imply that the majority of children's formal games may themselves in due course become anachronistic. The increasing preference of children is for informal group activities, a preference which would appear to be more in accord with the social world in which they now live. Formal games are vestiges of an earlier and more hierarchically arranged society, and they may pass out of spontaneous play as the formalities which they represent become increasingly meaningless to new generations of children. We would not expect such games to disappear completely, but we would expect them to become relatively less important parts of a child's development in this culture.

[24] Leonard S. Cottrell, "The Adjustment of the Individual to His Age and Sex Roles," *American Sociological Review*, VII (1942), 617–620.

[25] E. H. Erikson, "Sex Differences in the Play Configurations of American Pre-Adolescents," *American Journal of Orthopsychiatry*, XXI (1951), 667–692.

TABLE I: BOYS

No.	N.W. Ohio, 1959 N=1370	f	Bay Area, Cal, 1921 N=225	f	South Carolina, 1898 N=3958	f	Worcester, Mass, 1896 N=1000	f
1	Football	1221	Baseball	212	Baseball	2697	Ball	679
2	Throw Snowballs	1213	Ride Bicycle	197	Football	2216	Marbles	608
3	Bicycle Riding	1211	Fly Kites	195	Swimming	953	Sled	555
4	Hide and Seek	1181	Play Tag	190	Marbles	603	Skates	538
5	Basketball	1180	Do Garden Work	189	Fox and Geese	562	Football	455
6	Marbles	1140	Use Tools	187	Crokinole	437	Relievo	356
7	Tag	1137	Marbles	172	Checkers	398	Tag	356
8	Swimming	1136	Hide and Seek	172	Battle	387	Hockey, Shinny, Polo	313
9	Baseball	1117	Football	161	Leapfrog	370	Checkers	277
10	Cowboys	1116	Walk on Stilts	158	Spinning Tops	344	Hide and Seek	241
11	Checkers	1108	Racing or Jumping	157	Buffalo Bill	343	Dominoes	185
12	Cops and Robbers	1091	Basketball	156	Foot and a Half	300	Top	176
13	Cards	1090	Shoot	154	Policeman	278	Play Horse	166
14	Bows and Arrows	1089	Skate	143	Fox and Hounds	275	Cards	163
15	Shooting	1086	Spin Tops	143	Cards	260	Bicycle	160
16	Racing	1080	Volleyball	142	Croquet	250	Snowballing	123
17	Fly Kites	1070	Ride Horseback	139	Hide and Seek	233	Swimming	119
18	Climbing	1063	Boxing	139	Flying Kite	232	Kite, Parachute	107
19	Darts	1055	Wrestling	138	Mumble Peg	226	Black Tom, Black Jack	102
20	Soldiers	1050	Hunt	138	Punch and Judy	218	Horse Chestnuts, Horse Cobbles	85
21	Tic Tac Toe	1041	Cards	135	Parchesi	208	Books, Reading	83
22	Fish	1038	Tug-O-War	132	Tennis	191	Fishing	80
23	Tug-O-War	1028	Fish	125	Tag	190	Boats, Canoes, Rafts	78
24	Boating	1028	Snap the Whip	122	Drop the Handkerchief	187	Leaves	75
25	Horseshoes	1026	Checkers	121	Lotto	179	Hoop	71
26	Horseriding	1022	Swim	120	Basketball	179	Stilts	70
27	Camping	1017	Jump the Rope	118	Goosie Goosie Gander	178	Play School	69
28	Skating	1002	Hike	112	Jail	170	Hare and Hound	65
29	Make Model Aeroplanes	992	Bow and Arrows	111	Base	170	Snow Shovel	65
30	Dodgeball	983	Follow the Leader	109	I Spy	167	Guns, Rifles, Hunting	64

Rank	Item	No.
31	Wrestling	974
32	Building Forts	971
33	Bingo	969
34	Bandits	968
35	Hunt	966
36	Ping Pong	965
37	Seven Up	958
38	Roller Skating	944
39	Hunting	940
40	Use Tools	950
41	Boxing	928
42	King on the Mountain	928
43	Stoop Tag	899
44	Red Rover	892
45	Bowling	887
46	Monopoly	878
47	Building Snowmen	859
48	Crack the Whip	856
49	Frozen Tag	847
50	Pool	843
51	Volleyball	838
52	Puzzles	825
53	Raise Pets	821
54	Tennis	792
55	Follow the Leader	791
56	Work With Machines	784
57	Dice	776
58	Toy R. Trains	766
59	Shuffleboard	765
60	Fox and Geese	760
61	Dominoes	759

Item	No.
Work with Machinery	102
Roll Hoops	99
Leapfrog	98
Fox and Geese	96
Handball	89
Row a Boat	88
Drop the Handkerchief	87
Anty Over	86
Hopscotch	83
Farmer in the Dell	81
Puss in the Corner	79
Dominoes	78
Tennis	75
Cat and Mouse	73
Dare Base	69
Post Office	69
Ring Around the Rosy	64
London Bridge	63
Cook	62
Pom Pom Pull Away	61
Soccer	61
Pool	60
Play School	59
Shinny	59
Guessing Games	57
Blindfold	57
Simon Says	57
Solve Puzzles	57
Tiddleywinks	54
Play Store	54
Blackman	50

Item	No.
Circus	166
Dancing	163
Bull in the Pen	163
Authors	163
Clap in Clap Out	148
Steamboat	147
Wrestling	146
Stealing Chips	145
Shinny	138
Swinging	136
Open the Gates as High as the Sky	134
Dominoes	133
Dog on Wood	128
Up Jinks	127
Book	125
Hide the Switch	122
Jackstones	120
Ten Pins	116
Roly Poly	112
Pig in the Pen	110
Keeping Store	109
Blindman's Buff	109
Black Maria	105
Jump Rope	102
Bull Pen	100
One Hole Cat	95
Working Puzzles	94
Jackstraws	92
Kitty Wants a Corner	90
My Father Had a Rooster	89
Chick a My Chick a My Cranny Crow	86

Item	No.
Croquet	62
Shovel, Hoe	61
Play House	59
Run Sheep Run	58
Snow Shoes, Skiis	58
Pick Knife	57
Play War	55
Tenpins	53
Tennis	51
Racing	51
Leapfrog, Foot and Half	48
Nutting	48
Hill Dill	45
Jumping	44
Blindman's Buff	42
Bull in the Ring	42
Bar Up	42
Snap the Whip	41
Play Fire	41
Carpentry, Tools	41
Dolls	39
Old Maids	38
Duck on Rock	37
Snowman	36
Dog	36
Puss in Corner	35
Stealing Eggs	35
Tip Cat	33
Tents	33
Flowers	32
Messenger Boy, Errand Boy	31

(*Table I, continued*)

No.	N.W. Ohio, 1959 N=1370	f	Bay Area, Cal., 1921 N=225	f	South Carolina, 1898 N=3958	f	Worcester, Mass., 1896 N=1000	f
62	Ghosts	758	Play House	49	Little Sallie Walker	84	Grass	31
63	Stunts in Gym	757	In and Out the Window	47	Picking Eggs	82	Jackstones	28
64	Tail on the Donkey	755	Red Rover	46	Devil and Angel	82	Snow House	28
65	Cars	753	Duck on Rock	45	Having Show	81	Authors	28
66	Musical Chairs	742	Dance	44	Tiddley Winks	79	Chess	25
67	Wall Dodge Ball	740	Fox and Hounds	44	Hull Gull	67	Climbing Trees	25
68	I Spy	737	Anagrams	44	Pig in the Parlour	63	Drop the Handkerchief	22
69	Leap Frog	731	Jackstraws	42	Jack in the Bush	62	Tiddleywinks	22
70	Horses	730	Snap	41	Pillow Dex	61	Gymnasium	22
71	Drop the Handkerchief	723	Parchesi	36	Guessing Riddles	61	Drawing, Painting	22
72	Pick up Sticks	717	Croquet	35	Golf	59	Puzzles	21
73	Clay Modeling	714	Billiards	33	Anty Over	59	Lotto	21
74	Blind Man's Buff	703	History Cards	32	William My Tremble Toe	59	Sand, Dirt	21
75	Dance	702	Geography Cards	32	Walk to Jerusalem	58	Snow Fort	20
76	Spin the Bottle	698	Roly Poly	32	Spin the Plate	58	Playing in Hay	20
77	Wood Tag	696	Bowling	31	I See a Ghost	58	Musical Instruments	20
78	Spacemen	693	Sewing	29	Goodnight	58	Horseshoes, Quoits	19
79	Kick the Can	689	Jackstones	29	Knucks	57	Apples	18
80	Hide the Thimble	675	Coast or Toboggan	28	Cross Questions and Crooked Answers	55	Sticks	18
81	Hiking	668	Church	27	Mother May I Pick a Rose	54	Wheelbarrow	18
82	Make Collections	662	Dolls	24	Tit Tat Taw	53	Parchesi	17
83	Ball Tag	661	Dress-up	23	Keeping House	47	A Trip Around the World	17
84	Doctors	657	Authors	23	Club Fists	47	Cat	17
85	Walk on Stilts	650	Chess	22	Catcher	47	Hop Scotch	16
86	Simon Says	645	Knit	18	Old Dame Wiggins is Dead	44	Pillow Dex	16
87	Kissing	614	Crokinole	17	Dolls	44	Carriage, Sleigh, Buckboard, Tallyho	16

88	Chess 610	
89	Scrabble 600	Ski 15
90	Tiddleywinks 588	Backgammon ... 14
91	Poison Tag 586	Charades 11
92	Statues 579	
93	Soccer 578	
94	Make Scrapbook .. 576	
95	Dog and Bone 574	
96	Kick Dodge 567	
97	I've got a Secret . 566	
98	Jacks 566	
99	Draw or Paint 551	
100	School 548	
101	Hoops 548	
102	Cooking 541	
103	Post Office 538	
104	Jump Rope 536	
105	Make Radio 533	
106	Mother May I 523	
107	Hopscotch 506	
108	Handball 501	
109	Skiing 492	
110	Redlight 482	
111	Cat and Mouse ... 479	
112	Inventors 477	
113	Name That Tune .. 460	
114	Store 460	
115	Chicken 437	
116	Clue 435	
117	Garden 427	
118	Church 424	
119	Toboggan 419	
120	Farmer in the Dell .. 409	

Here we go Round the Rosy Bush ... 42	Berrying 16
Stagecoach 40	Hide the Thimble 15
Snap 40	Policeman 15
Five Hundred 40	Hide the Buttons 14
Chess 35	Walks 14
Hop Scotch 33	Pinch Me, Oh! 13
Thimble 31	Billiards, Pool 13
Having Parade 31	Swinging 13
Jake Grin at Me 30	Bear "When Younger" . 13
Green 30	Backgammon 12
Smiling Angel 29	Fish Pond 12
Sheepie 29	Stones 12
Quaker Meeting 28	Jack-knife 12
Introducing to K & Q . 28	Rake 12
Ring (on a String) ... 27	Go Bang 11
Teacher 25	Tic-Tac-Toe 11
Sting-a-Miree 25	Singing 11
Table Rapping 22	Indians 10
Bean Bags 22	Guessing Games 10
Simon Says Wig Wag . 19	Steps 9
Parlor Croquet 17	Birds 9
Geography 17	Tin Cans 9
Pretty Maids Country . 15	Farmer in the Dell ... 8
Borrowed Property ... 15	Tea Set 8
Making Play-House .. 14	Water 8
Key 14	Robinson Crusoe 8
Charades 14	Anagrams, Letters, Spelling ... 8
Rachel and Jacob 13	Horseback Riding 7
Stooping Catcher 11	Camera 7
Consequences 11	Talking 7
Proverbs 10	Lost Heir 7
Night Dodge 10	Chicopee 7
King-a-Mount 10	On the Green Carpet .. 6

(Table I, continued)

No.	N.W. Ohio, 1959 N=1370	f	Bay Area, Cal., 1921 N=225 f	South Carolina, 1898 N=3958	f	Worcester, Mass., 1896 N=1000	f
121	London Bridge	404		Selling Forfeits	9	Colors	6
122	Matching Coins	381		Philopoena	8	Trades	6
123	See-Saw	379		Twenty Questions	7	Old Witch	6
124	Actors	367		Hat Stack	7	Bonney	6
125	Steal the Bacon	330		Backgammon	6	Rachel and Jacob	6
126	Dressing-Up	330		Clumps (yes and no)	5	Chase the Squirrel	6
127	Handsprings	327		Object Guessing	4	Slate	6
128	Colors	320		Gossip	3	Piano	6
129	Black Magic	317		Dumb Scrambo	2	Gardening	6
130	Huckle Buckle	317				Snap	6
131	Beanstalk	316				Napoleon	6
132	Cartwheels	316				Yacht Race	5
133	Crochet	312				Quaker Meeting	5
134	Spin Tops	307				Grandmother Grey	5
135	Ring Around the Rosy	306				Ring Around the Rosy	5
136	In and Out the Windows	305				Billy, Billy Button	5
137	Capture the Flag	297				Doll Carriage	5
138	Houses	296				Pig Tail	5
139	Charades	294				Fire	5
140	Fox and Hounds	272				Violin	5
141	Pom Pom Pull Away	270				Fox and Geese	4
142	Squirrel in the Tree	265				Cuckoo	4
143	Here I Come, Where From?	261				Go In and Out the Window	4
	Flashlight	261					
144	Prisoner's Base	256				Horse	4
145	Snap	255				Lion in the Den	4
146	Black Tom	248				Pig, including Pig Pen	4
147	Poor Pussy	236				Salvation Army	4

148	Crows and Cranes	202
149	Find the Ring	202
150	What Time is It?	200
151	Blackman	199
152	Punt Back	199
153	Twenty Questions	196
154	Sewing	191
155	Bull in the Ring	190
156	Two Deep	189
157	Letters	183
158	Hoki Toki	179
159	Beast, Bird or Fish	176
160	Mulberry Bush	175
161	Initials	171
162	Buzz	155
163	Muffin Man	145
164	Roly Poly	142
165	Noughts and Crosses	141
166	Quoits	140
167	Four Square	138
168	Beater Goes Round	129
169	Knit	126
170	Puss in Corner	126
171	Dolls	125
172	Billiards	120
173	Kingsland	119
174	Forfeits	112
175	Actresses	109
176	Cobbler Cobbler	108
177	Oranges and Lemons	96
178	Perdiddle	93
179	Draw a Bucket of Water	85
180	Nuts in May	70

Santa Claus	4
Play Sunday School	4
Play Church	4
Rush	4
Bean Bag	4
Jackstraws	4
Trunk	4
Golf	4
Cricket	4
Matches	4
Dance	4
Paper, Paper Cutting, Colored Paper	4
Tell Stories	4
Riddles	4
Parties, Social	4
Dr. Busby	3
Cinderella	3
House that Jack Built	3
Jack the Giant Killer	3
U.S. Puzzle	3
Old Mother Goose	3
Cash	3
Innocents Abroad	3
Post Office	3
Doll Furniture	3
Toll Gate	3
Farmer	3
Dress Up	3
Acorns	3
Skip	3
Bells	3
Buttons	3
Pail	3

TABLE II: GIRLS

No.	N.W. Ohio, 1959 N=1319	f	Bay Area, Cal., 1921 N=249	f	South Carolina, 1898 N=4760	f	Worcester, Mass., 1896 N=1000	f
1	Jump Rope	1210	Tag	223	Dolls	1365	Dolls	621
2	Hide and Seek	1189	Do Plain Sewing	214	Jump Rope	1029	Sled	498
3	Tag	1170	Ride Bicycle	208	Croquet	923	Tag	442
4	Bicycle Riding	1162	Baseball	207	Clap In Clap Out	907	Hide and Seek	427
5	Hopscotch	1138	Hide and Seek	204	Drop the Handkerchief	778	Skates	412
6	Checkers	1116	Basketball	200	Dancing	732	Ball	409
7	Roller Skating	1115	Hopscotch	197	Crokinole	696	Play House	365
8	Dolls	1111	Play With Dolls	194	Parchesi	664	Jackstones	341
9	Bingo	1101	Skate	193	Keeping House	595	Play School	257
10	Cooking	1098	Cook a Meal	189	Open the Gates as High as the Sky	517	Teaset	242
11	Swimming	1096	Dance	189	Authors	516	Doll Carriage	233
12	Cards	1089	Jump the Rope	187	Hide and Seek	492	Relievo	194
13	Stoop Tag	1088	Play House	180	Little Sallie Walker	449	Checkers	189
14	Jacks	1082	Play School	172	Jackstones	406	Hopscotch	154
15	Red Rover	1077	Play "Dress-Up"	172	Checkers	384	Cards	151
16	Dressing-Up	1066	Farmer in the Dell	140	Cross Questions and Crooked Answers	378	Croquet	148
17	Tic Tac Toe	1065	Do Garden Work	138	Goosie Goosie Gander	378	Dominoes	133
18	Dance	1062	Volleyball	138	Tennis	370	Doll Cradle	131
19	Skating	1058	Drop the Handkerchief	136	Blind Man's Buff	366	Marbles	130
20	School	1054	Play Store	132	Fox and Geese	357	Leaves	112
21	Musical Chairs	1025	Racing or Jumping	131	Lotto	353	Hoop	110
22	Mother May I	1024	Cat and Mouse	130	Up Jinks	335	Books, Reading	108
23	Building Snowmen	1020	Cards	129	Mother May I Pick a Rose	326	Flowers	102
24	Drop the Handkerchief	987	London Bridge	124	Kitty Wants a Corner	318	Drop the Handkerchief	101
25	Seven Up	980	Ring Around Rosy	121	Stealing Chips	318	Snowballing	98
26	Houses	963	Guessing Games	115	Devil and Angel	313	Black Tom and Black Jack	97
27	Follow the Leader	958	Ride Horseback	121	Smiling Angel	303	Bicycle, Tricycle and Velocipede	91

28 Sewing 951
29 Horse Riding 939
30 Monopoly 938
31 Simon Says 937
32 Throw Snowballs 925
33 Frozen Tag 924
34 Puzzles 922
35 Store 912
36 Raise Pets 912
37 Racing 907
38 Pick Up Sticks 904
39 Basketball 902
40 Ping Pong 901
41 Dodgeball 890
42 Fly Kites 881
43 Actresses 874
44 Marbles 871
45 Boating 869
46 Crack the Whip 858
47 Statues 856
48 Hoops 854
49 I Spy 852
50 Blind Man's Buff 848
51 Clay Modeling 840
52 Fox and Geese 839

Follow the Leader 115
Knit 114
Puss in the Corner 111
Checkers 105
Walk on Stilts 103
In and Out the Windows 103
Dare Base or Prisoner's Base 99
Blindfold 99
Fox and Geese 94
Hike 92
Simon Says Thumbs Up 89
Post Office 86
Solve Puzzles 86
Snap the Whip 83
Swim 81
Fly Kites 81
Anty Over 80
Tennis 80
Jackstones 79
Dominoes 78
Leapfrog 72
Handball 71
Play Church 68
Tug-O-War 65
Roll Hoops 62

Cards 265
Chick-a-My Chick-a-My Cranny Crow 256
Baseball 245
Dominoes 240
Spin the Plate 239
Pretty Maids Country 232
Jackstraws 223
Introducing the King and Queen 216
Hide the Switch 216
I Spy 212
Guessing Riddles 211
Good Night 209
Walk to Jerusalem 208
Here We Go Round the Rosy Bush 204
Teacher 199
Swinging 194
Dog on Wood 182
Hopscotch 166
Base 157
Making Play House 154
Old Dame Wiggins is Dead 148
Thimble 147
Mumble Peg 145
Keeping Store 141
I See a Ghost 137

Lion in the Den 80
Doll Furniture 79
Old Maids 73
Puss in the Corner 73
Bean Bag 72
Steps 65
Blindman's Buff 64
On the Green Carpet 62
Musical Instruments 60
Hide the Buttons 55
Grandmother Grey 53
Piano 51
Authors 50
Snap the Whip 50
Hill Dill 47
Lotto 47
Play Horse 47
Colors 40
In and Out the Windows 40
Parchesi 40
Duck on the Rock 36
Run, Sheep, Run 36
Lazy Maid, Lazy Mary, Lazy Bessie 33
Water, Water, Wild Flowers 33
Tennis 31

(Table II, continued)

No.	N.W. Ohio, 1959 N=1319	f	Bay Area, Cal., 1921 N=249	f	South Carolina, 1898 N=4760	f	Worcester, Mass., 1896 N=1000	f
53	Camping	839	Pom Pom Pull Away	60	Consequences	134	Tiddleywinks	31
54	Climbing	834	Tiddleywinks	58	Football	132	Ring Around a Rosy	31
55	London Bridge	825	Blackman	54	Working Puzzles	127	Nutting	28
56	Spin the Bottle	815	Marbles	52	Punch and Judy	122	Boats, Canoes	27
57	Baseball	814	Fish	51	Quaker Meeting	121	Farmer in the Dell	26
58	Draw or Paint	812	Play Jackstraws	47	Book	120	Hide the Thimble	26
59	Leapfrog	809	Spin Tops	45	Tiddleywinks	120	Snowman	26
60	Farmer in the Dell	809	Row a Boat	45	Pillow Dex	114	Birds	25
61	Tug-O-War	808	Bow and Arrow	44	Pig in the Parlor	106	Walks	25
62	Volleyball	808	Fox and Hounds	44	Ring on a String	101	Snowhouse	23
63	I've Got a Secret	791	Anagrams or Word-Building	41	Basketball	95	London Bridge	23
					William My Tremble Toe	94	Trades	23
64	Wood Tag	784	Football	40	Pig in Pen	90	Carriage, Sleigh, Buckboard, Tallyho	22
65	Doctors	783	Snap	40	Bean Bags	90	Singing	22
66	Tennis	779	Red Rover	35	Proverbs	86	Swinging	22
67	Name That Tune	767	Duck on Rock	34	Parlor Croquet	84	Pillow Dex	21
68	Stunts in Gym	735	History Cards	34	Tit Tat Taw	83	Bar Up	20
69	Fish	727	Shoot	33	My Father Had a Rooster	83	Snow Shovel	19
					Rooster	82		
70	Horseshoes	723	Wrestling	31	Swimming	80	Old Witch	19
71	Horses	722	Geography Cards	31	Geography	79	Acorns	19
72	Dog and Bone	720	Authors	31	Borrowed Property	79	Sand, Dirt	18
73	Tail on the Donkey	719	Croquet	29	Sheepie	78	Playing in Hay	18
74	Make Collections	713	Parchesi	28				
75	Shuffleboard	712	Roly Poly	27	Jake Grin at Me	69	Pig Tail	18
76	Tiddleywinks	711	Hunt	26	Charades	69	Messenger Boys, Errand Boy	16
77	Redlight	708	Use Tools	25	Snap	66	Poison	16
78	Darts	707	Shinny	22	Table Rapping	62	Swimming	15
79	Make Scrapbook	706	Boxing	20	Selling Forfeits	59	Backgammon	15

80	Scrabble	700
81	Ghosts	696
82	In and Out the Windows	694
83	Bowling	691
84	See-Saw	668
85	Hide the Thimble	667
86	Church	666
87	Garden	647
88	Cowboys	635
89	Ring Around the Rosy	632
90	Cat and Mouse	627
91	Post Office	624
92	Walk on Stilts	619
93	Mulberry Bush	616
94	Dominoes	612
95	Kick Dodge	581
96	Wall Dodge Ball	577
97	Poison Tag	572
98	Bows and Arrows	571
99	Cops and Robbers	570
100	Clue	570
101	Kick the Can	563
102	Football	561
103	Hiking	554
104	Building Forts	553
105	Ball Tag	542
106	Actors	529
107	Kissing	528
108	Knit	521
109	Here I Come Where From	521
110	Bandits	517

Coast or Toboggan	19
Work With Machinery	17
Bowling	15
Chess	15
Charades	15
Pool	14
Crokinole	13
Ski	13
Soccer	11
Billiards	11
Backgammon	9

Having Show	59
Battle	59
Key	57
Hull Gull	57
Simon Says Wigwag	56
Marbles	56
Tag	53
Circus	53
Stage Coach	52
Ten Pins	51
One Hole Cat	51
Picking Eggs	49
Rachel and Jacob	47
Jack in the Bush	45
Club Fists	42
Green	41
Policeman	40
Anty Over	38
Leap Frog	37
Catcher	36
Buffalo Bill	36
Flying Kite	35
Gossip	34
Shinny	33
Lead, Leadman	33
Spinning Tops	31
Chess	30
Golf	29
Jail	26
Bull in the Pen	25
Roly Poly	23
Philopoena	23

Fish Pond	15
Slate	15
Dance	15
Peter Coddles	15
Stove	15
Doll Table	15
Tents	14
Show Fort	14
Fox and Geese	14
Old Mother Goose	14
Round the Mulberry Bush	14
Bull in the Ring	13
Puzzles	13
Bear "When Younger"	13
Stones	13
Blackboard	13
William Tell	13
Kite, Parachute	12
Stilts	12
Shovel, Hoe	12
Sticks	12
Tell Stories	12
Gypsy	12
Lead, Leadman	12
Last Couple Out	12
Top	11
Dog	11
Trees, Climbing Trees	11
Gymnasium	11
Go Bang	11
Jackstraws	11

(Table II, continued)

No.	N.W. Ohio, 1959 N=1319	f	Bay Area, Cal., 1921 N=249	f	South Carolina, 1898 N=4760	f	Worcester, Mass., 1896 N=1000	f
111	Charades	493			Backgammon	22	Snow Shoes, Skiis	10
112	Crochet	485			Black Maria	17	Tip Cat	10
113	King on the Mountain	454			Foot and a Half	16	Tic Tac Toe	10
114	Poor Pussy	451			Fox and Hounds	15	Quaker Meeting	10
115	Colors	451			Object Guessing	14	Play Sunday School	10
116	Dice	424			Twenty Questions	13	Stealing Eggs	9
117	Chess	410			Stooping Catcher	13	Cat	9
118	Squirrel in the Tree	405			Steamboat	13	Play Church	9
119	Huckle Buckle Beanstalk	402			Having Parade	11	Drawing, Painting, etc.	9
120	Hunting	399			Five Hundred	11	Hockey, Shinny, Polo	8
121	Pool	395			Clumps	11	Play War	8
122	Handball	390			Sting-a-Miree	10	Racing, Running	8
123	Hunt	386			King-a-Mount	8	Jumping	8
124	Shooting	376			Bull Pen	8	Grass	8
125	Use Tools	375			Dumb Scrambo	6	Apples	8
126	Soccer	369			Night Dodge	4	Snap	8
127	Snap	362			Knucks	3	Horse Chestnuts	7
128	What Time Is It?	347			Hat Stack	3	Fishing	7
129	Spin Tops	342			Wrestling	2	A Trip Around the World	7
130	Cars	341					Tin Cans	7
131	Black Magic	331					Robinson Crusoe	7
132	Skiing	312					Talking	7
133	Wrestling	311					Show, Circus, etc.	7
134	Inventors	299					Riddles	7
135	Handsprings	290					Hare and Hound, etc.	6
136	Flashlight	286					Tenpins	6
137	Soldiers	273					Berries, Berrying	6
138	Toy Trains	270					Gardening	6
139	Hoki Toki	268					Cuckoo	6
140	Initials	255					Salvation Army	6

Parties, Social		6
Post Office		6
Dress Up		6
Pound the Back		6
Anagrams, Letters, Spelling Game		5
Halma		5
Bible Game		5
Christmas Goose		5
Horseback Riding		4
Paper, Paper Cutting, Colored Paper		4
Steeple Chase		4
Three Kings		4
Jack and Jill		4
Tin Tin a Poppy Show, Pin Pin, etc.		4
Guns, Rifles, Hunting		3
Pick Knife		3
Play Fire		3
Carpentry, Tools, Toolbox, etc.		3
Rake		3
Water		3
Bonney		3
Rachel and Jacob		3
Horse		3
Pig, including "Pig Pen," etc.		3
Santa Claus		3
Trunk		3
Matches		3

141	Twenty Questions	248
142	Letters	247
143	Find the Ring	241
144	Pom Pom Pull Away	240
145	Steal the Bacon	240
146	Matching Coins	238
147	Two Deep	236
148	Buzz	233
149	Chicken	219
150	Black Tom	210
151	Fox and Hounds	198
152	Crows and Cranes	191
153	Boxing	191
154	Work with Machines	187
155	Puss in the Corner	186
156	Beast, Bird or Fish	184
157	Toboggan	184
158	Spacemen	182
159	Prisoner's Base	178
160	Muffin Man	176
161	Make Model Aeroplanes	175
162	Oranges and Lemons	167
163	Blackman	144
164	Roly Poly	126
165	Noughts and Crosses	125
166	Bull in the Ring	121
167	Four Square	116
168	Beater Goes Round	114

(Table II, continued)

No.	N.W. Ohio, 1959 N=1319	f	Bay Area, Cal., 1921 N=249	f	South Carolina, 1898 N=4760	f	Worcester, Mass., 1896 N=1000	f
169	Draw a Bucket of Water	101					Dr. Busby	3
170	Make Radio	100					Cinderella	3
171	Kingsland	100					Bells	3
172	Forfeits	98					Pails	3
173	Cobbler Cobbler	94					Baby	3
174	Capture the Flag	91					Bagatelle	3
175	Cartwheels	91					Studying	3
176	Billiards	75					Pencil	3
177	Quoits	69					Pussel	3
178	Perdiddle	60					Shopping Game	3
179	Nuts in May	58					Little Miss Muffit	3
180	Punt Back	53					Shouting Proverbs	3
							Milkman	3

Bowling Green State University
Bowling Green, Ohio

3. The Two Cultures of Games

Introduction

In this paper I wish to take the role of historian rather than the more familiar one of psychologist. Some recent research on children's play seems to suggest that children's imaginative play is not universal. When this is put together with an earlier finding of Roberts and mine, that competitive games are not universal, it leads to some basically new notions about the role of play, games and sports in society.

Let me highlight the significance of these contentions by pointing out that we are just emerging from the era of "universality" in games' scholarship. The systematic study of games at the end of the last century, for example, was devoted largely to demonstrating

SOURCE: Reprinted from *Sociology of Sport, The Proceedings of the Symposium* (Chicago: The Athletic Institute, 1969), pp. 135–147. The paper was originally presented as a lecture sponsored by the University of Wisconsin Lecture Committee.

the universal character of play and game forms throughout the world. Whether games were said by anthropologists to be diffused from some centers of civilization, or to have been autonomously invented, their parallelism was not in doubt. Again when games were studied as survivals of earlier customs, as in folklore, the devolutionary scheme was unilineal. In child psychology, likewise, children's play sequences were said to be atavistically reminiscent of the single evolutionary history of mankind. While each of these grand schemes in anthropology, folklore or psychology subsequently fell into theoretical desuetude, the habit persisted nevertheless of taking it for granted that, at least on the empirical level, children's play and children's games would be in most places much the same. Child psychologists continued to write about the language of play as if there were no foreign languages, while comparative psychologists sought for universal laws of exploration and playful behavior amongst varied species, paying little attention to the implications of species-specific differences. "Universalism" thus persisted as an empirical habit even though the theoretical superstructure had been discredited. Of course, the assumed triviality of the whole subject-matter made it difficult for most serious scholars to rise to new theoretical heights without some functional justification (Sutton-Smith, 1968).*

Nevertheless, an erosion of this older point of view has been going on apace over recent years. The fundamental import of Huizinga's *Homo Ludens: The Play Element in Culture* (1938), for example, was that the dualistic premise behind the older studies was no longer tenable. Huizinga set out to show that the play element permeates all of culture—that men, in law, business, war and politics act much of the time as do players at their games, with rules, with spatio-temporal confines, with secrecy, with intensity, with voluntariness and with a sense of difference. Which implied that the older view of games and sports as the cast-offs of culture was no longer relevant and had been sustained by the underlying puritan distinction between the serious and the non-serious, between the real and the unreal, between the important and trivial. Games and play could be vestiges only in a culture which degraded such expressive experiences. Huizinga's work implied that men

* Material within parentheses refers to sources listed at the end of this article.

had always been playing and gaming even when they did not recognize it. More recent studies by Szasz, Haley, Berne and Goffman which in various ways illustrate the permeation of gaming strategies throughout social behavior are an implementation and specification of the Huizinga viewpoint. An illustration is Goffman's recent statement that a game is a place where you can test out your courage, your gallantry, your integrity, your composure and your stage confidence without too great a cost. You can keep up your character as society demands, but without ruinous trial and error (1967).

Paradoxically, although Huizinga heralded a new era in thinking about play and games, in which their forms were treated as realities coeval with those of work, he still dealt with them primarily as universals. And it is this assumption that I most wish to protest in this paper.

Play and Game Deficits

In our cross-cultural work Roberts and I had reached the conclusion that the basic forms of competitive games with which we dealt, those of physical skill, chance and strategy and their various combinations were not universal (Roberts and Sutton-Smith, 1966). We found, indeed, that only in the most complex cultures were all forms present—and as these post-neolithic cultures were those that had been the chief focus of Western History and Scholarship, it was natural that some games would have been assumed to be universal. On the other hand if one dealt with less complex cultures, as we had, there were some which had no such games, some which had only games of physical skill and some which had mixtures of physical skill and chance, or physical skill and strategy. Furthermore these differences seemed to make sense in terms of the many correlates we were able to establish for them. The cultures with no competitive games, which were mainly Australian and South American, were kin homogeneous and very simple. There appeared to be few distinctions in small group life around which ludic contest could profitably develop. The groups with games of physical skill on the other hand were groups in which contesting over hunting and fishing skills were a part of the cultural pattern. The ludic contest seemed related to this function. Again groups with games of chance were nomadic and faced with considerable survival uncertainty. They used religious procedures for decision making (divinatory) purposes. Games of chance were an exercise of the same sort. Groups with strategy were more complex than all the others. There were both advanced technology and class stratification. The games appeared to have been a part of the learning of social diplomacy and military skills amongst the military or priestly elite groups. We saw the games as buffered models of power (character contests in Goffman's more recent terms), within which the child could acquire some of the basic performances required by the adult culture.

Whether or not our various analyses were correct in detail, I think we presented strong evidence for the view that games were cultural inventions (not biological universals). Given the circumstances of mankind their development may have been ethologically probable but it was, nevertheless, not essential. What this meant was that we were required to account for the presence of games in terms of the accidentals of learning, rather than the universals of biology and ecology.

In a way there was nothing strange in this. We are used to thinking of individual differences in play and sports habits and preferences. Yet we have paradoxically tended to combine this recognition with the older one, that play and games are yet universal in form throughout humanity.

My sense of the importance of the finding that games were not universal has been heightened by a new work published this year entitled *The Effects of Sociodramatic Play on Disadvantaged Pre-School Children* by Sara Smilansky (Wiley, 1968). For some time various psychologists working in Head Start programs have been pointing out that such children tend not to play imaginatively. Their play is dominated by sensory-motor and kinetic activity. Smilansky working in Israel with immigrant groups from Asia and North Africa has now documented this fact with these groups. Unlike middle class children, these children do not indulge extensively in role playing, dramatic play, or imaginative activity. They proceed from motor play to rule games without the symbolic activities which have usually been assumed to mediate between these. So, not only are competitive games not universal, it now appears that imaginative play is not universal either. This is quite a shock. Though we should add that Smilansky's findings need to be treated with tentativeness until further data are in hand. Questions have been raised about their generality.

In the rest of this paper, I would like to construct a hypothetical picture of what I have termed here the games of two cultures. From the work we have already done on physical game cultures, chance game cultures and strategy game cultures, it will be realized that I should actually be talking about the games of many cultures. I am opting for simplicity at this point, however, because I think there is something very important to be learned by so doing. We are at a point in history when two major cultural game schemes interpenetrate each other with considerable scholarly confusion as attempts are made to reduce one to the other.

ASCRIPTIVE GAME CULTURE

There is one type of game culture, which is the one we read about in Philippe Ariès' *The Centuries of Childhood*, which I will, following sociology, label as the ascriptive game culture. Here, as Aries describes, children are not separate from the surrounding adults. Life is always living in a crowd. The families tend to be extended rather than nuclear. The group is dominated by the arbitrary power and control of its leading individuals. Parents tend to give instructions and exact demands without reason or explanation ("Go get the bread. If you aren't home in five minutes I'll murder you." "Don't ask questions"). They expect the children to fight their own battles in the streets.

In these groups, if we can follow Smilansky, when children have grown beyond sensory-motor play (about the ages of two and three years), they imitate the activities of their adults. But their imitative play is not imaginative. They use realistic toy representations (rather than improvised ones), to imitate in very circumscribed ways the behavior of their parents. If they play together it is usually in terms of one child bossing the others. When the others refuse to be the subordinates, the play breaks down. Or the play is in parallel terms in which each child with the same toy does the same thing. In addition their play is strongly object-related; they cannot readily shift to something else, or improvise without the toy. Their spoken language tends to be power oriented or manipulative of others (bring me this, take that away). Words are act and object-oriented. Laughter is aggressive and has a ridiculing function.

Once we get to the age of five to nine years, then we can rely on
the record contained in folklore, because the materials that were
collected by Newall (1883), Gomme (1894) and the others as
survivals of an earlier cultural state, were actually current expressions of this ascriptive cultural state which was being followed by
ever fewer people. In this folklore record we find the play of this
age period for girls preoccupied with ritual dramatic games in
which, with song and dance, the girls enacted the practices of marriage, death and the working life. The majority of these games were
central person games. Although rule games, they were not the
games of players who were equal before the law, but of a group of
players contesting against the ascribed power of the central person.
Most customarily the power of the central person consisted in her
ability to choose or to exclude the others as marriage partners, the
next central player and the like. In parallel fashion the central person games of hiding, chasing, capture and attack played by the
boys, centered on the special powers of a central person, to call the
player he would chase, to immobilize him, etc. Players were defended from the dangers of identification with this aggressor
through counting-out formulae. Around the middle years, 9
through 12, these games gradually transformed into those where
the central person could maintain his centrality only through a
real exhibition of power (as in King on the Mountain or Bull in
the Ring) and later in early adolescence there developed in addition, central person games in which the central figure was a scapegoat to be tricked and made a fool of at the very moment he was
being made a King. In an old New Zealand game of the 1890's
called the King of the Golden Sword, the new boy who was appointed King, sat on a special perch, was blindfolded, given the
duty of knighting his followers, was told to draw the sword
through his hand with a flourish and then touch each warrior.
Unbeknown to him the sword had been dipped in the latrine. "The
Dozens" as played amongst Negro children is an excellent example
of the same form.

At about ten years of age also there arose those games of physical skill which were the most widespread of all games throughout
the variety of human cultures of which we have record; which
means everything from marbles, pitching, athletics, knife games, to
spear throwing and racing. As we move back over the past hundred

years, however, we do not find the team games as we currently know them (Strutt, 1801). There were team games but they were diffuse teams with few differentiated roles, and with sometimes a powerful leader on each team. They looked like central person games transformed into two teams. Amongst children the games might involve one group attempting to run through the joined hands of another group barring the route in a road cutting. Historically they have involved the members of one part of the village in a struggle for a ball with the members of another part of the village which is the precursor of modern football. A recent copy of the *New York Times* quotes a beautiful example still played in Afghanistan (October 24, 1968, 49):

"The King of Afghanistan sat on a brocade-covered sofa and sipped teas as he watched some of the fiercest, most agile horsemen in Central Asia play a form of mounted football with the carcass of a beheaded calf.

"This gentle pastime is played here every year at this time in honor of the birthday of the king, Mohammed Zahir Shah, who has now turned 54.

"To score in the game—known as buzkashi—all a rider has to do is snatch the carcass from the ground, gallop with it a quarter of a mile down the field, then gallop back and throw it in a chalked circle near the point where he started.

"Grabbing the carcass can be a bit tricky, however, for it weighs 75 to 100 pounds. Also, at the moment the rider leans from his saddle to hoist this weight, several of his opponents' powerful horses are likely to come slamming into his in an attempt to knock the carcass loose.

"For a moment the men and animals shove and heave like a wave on the verge of breaking. Then with shouts and a cracking of whips, one of the horsemen breaks loose from the pack at a hard gallop, somehow throwing a leg over the heavy carcass to hold it to the side of his mount.

"At that instant buzkashi has more than a touch of epic beauty as the horsemen stretch out across the landscape in thunderous pursuit.

"Often, when the lead rider is caught, a tug-of-war results with the carcass stretched between two galloping horses, their riders leaning away at angles of 45 degrees or more to break the opponent's hold.

"That's how buzkashi gets its name. Kashi means pull and buz means goat, calves being only one of several possibilities for the carcass.

"The buzkashi matches sponsored here by the National Olympic Federation for His Majesty's pleasure are as rugged and dangerous a sport spectacle as can be seen anywhere— except on the far side of the mountain barrier called the Hindu Kush, near the Soviet border, where Turkmen and Uzbek horsemen play it without any reference to the rule book the Olympic Federation has attempted to write.

"Here there are 10 men on a side playing on a field with marked boundaries under the supervision of a referee who is supposed to call a foul if one of the players uses such traditional buzkashi tactics as whipping an opponent across the face or pulling him from his horse.

"In the north, there can be 100 men on a side or, so it is said, there can even be no sides at all—each man pitted against the rest. That sounds like certain death, but apparently it isn't for the best horsemen, called chapandaz, survive to play before the King on his birthday.

"One of today's stars, Hakim Pahlavon, has only half of one ear, a minor example of the kinds of injuries a chapandaz can sustain."

Those who are familiar with descriptions of the play of children in the lower socioeconomic strata of this society will recognize similarities. W. F. Whyte in his classic *Street Corner Society*, gives an account of the way in which the dominance of the lower class gang leader affects the scores of the other players, so that while better than him at bowling, they never manage to consistently outscore him. Maas describes the hierarchical character of play relationships amongst lower class pre-adolescents as compared with the egalitarian character of those amongst middle class boys (1951, 1954). But in general accounts of gang life and gang play in modern civilization have focused on these phenomena as if they were rather peculiar reactions to modern circumstances of deprivation, whereas ethnological accounts would suggest that such age-graded and hierarchical play groups are a much older and more general cultural form than the more egalitarian peer groups of modern society. Again if the picture I have presented here makes any sense, it follows that the play patterning thus traced is of a systemic character. Because deprived children cannot play imaginative games, and instead prefer hierarchical relationships involving power and aggression does not mean they are outside of culture. It would seem to mean rather that they are still persisting with cultural forms of far greater antiquity and generality than those that have come to have influence in the Western world.

ACHIEVEMENT GAME CULTURES

In my own earlier studies of historical changes in children's games over the past 100 years first in New Zealand and then later in the United States, I reached the following conclusions:

1. Children today play fewer status games. There is less mention of roles for Kings, Queens, Priests, Aunt Sallys, Brother Ebenezers, Julius Caesars, Dukes, etc. There are fewer Singing Games, Dialogue Games and Parlor Games. While there are remnant circle games, the older line and couple games of marriage have disappeared.

2. Children today show more verbal slickness and smart answers. The verbal elements in games has increased as indicated by the proliferation of joke cycles (Sutton-Smith, 1960).

3. There is less physical aggression in both games and playground than was formerly the case. Fewer penalty games, fewer games prone to cause accidents. Less fighting.

4. Girls show increasing preference for boys' games (Rosenberg and Sutton-Smith, 1960).

5. There is more verbal freedom of expression including verbal aggression than was formerly the case (see 2 above) (Sutton-Smith, Morgan Rosenberg, 1961).

6. There is a greater emphasis on organized games and sports.

7. There is a changing trend away from formal sports and games to informal pursuits (swimming, boating, fishing, skating, etc.). Even the fairly ritualized play-party marriage games have given way to more informal kissing games. The ritualized singing games have been replaced by the more open jump rope games (Sutton-Smith, 1959).

Until recently I had interpreted these various historical changes in games in terms of the increasing use of psychological (symbolic) discipline within the family, the increased emphasis on achievement for girls, and the relatively egalitarian as compared with hierarchical structure of the modern family. These points are not negated by my present analysis, but they do need to be considerably amplified. I might add that in a return visit to New Zealand in 1967, on which I administered the same game lists to several of the same schools that had been used in 1949, one of my chief findings was that the children's responses were much more heterogeneous than had previously been the case.

To understand these historical changes one has to return again to the Ariès approach in *Centuries of Childhood*. He suggests, in effect, that childhood as we currently know it was created at the beginning of the modern era (in the Seventeenth Century or thereabout).[1] The development of the middle class family, the nuclear family, schools, and privacy in daily life were associated with the treatment of childhood as a distinctive period of life. Children became separated from the life going on around them. More recently in a book *The Changing Nature of Man*, J. H. Van den Berg (1964) has argued, in addition, that the child's segregation from the rest of society was also brought about by the scientific revolution in knowledge. The differentiation of knowledge he suggests meant that reality was no longer the same for all men. There were various canons of truth. Men could no longer make judgments in confidence and in terms of immediate perceptual information. The affairs and understanding of adults became increasingly invisible to children. As a result children were, in fact, increasingly innocent. If a child asked a question about green leaves, he could no longer be given an immediate answer in terms of the vernal spirit of Spring, but was given instead some mystifying information about chlorophyll and the conversion of carbon dioxide into carbohydrates. His innocence too was emphasized by his inability to read, his inability to follow adults into that private world of the mind's eye fostered by the development of printing (McLuhan) as well as the heresy of Martin Luther.

---

[1] One of my students, The Reverend Benedict J. Groeschel of Children's Village, Dobbs Ferry, New York, argues contrarily that the concept of childhood was rediscovered, not invented.

In these terms, of course, my playground changes recorded above simply meant that as time has passed, more and more children have acquired at earlier ages some of the symbolic masteries previously restricted to adults, and at some far distant time restricted even more completely to the priestly classes, or to those military leaders playing some form of chess in preparation for battle. So today's children play fewer status (or ascriptive) games, show less aggression, are more verbal, and girls are more interested in games of achievement.

But it would be wrong to pretend that we fully understand this transition to an achievement culture that has been going on these past several hundred years and is now upon us in mass form; although some of those who have studied cultural deprivation have acted as if the deprived had not only a resistance to acquiring middle class American culture, but also no culture of their own. These same scholars have shown a considerable inability to define the essence of that middle class culture itself.

Perhaps children acquire this culture, as Van den Berg implies, by not being given straight answers. Some remedial programs are based on this premise. One of the most successful of such programs has focused on having the children discuss situations which did not exist in front of them at the moment. On the other hand, a Freudian might well argue that the real change came with the historical shift from the extended to nuclear families and with the great changes in infant socialization that came about at that time. From the 1550's to the 1750's there was a great shift towards more restrictive forms of infant socialization (oral, anal, sex, dependency) (Ryerson, 1961). This might well imply that the total patterning of middle class reality became one that directed the child away from immediate impulse satisfaction, towards the fulfillment of distant abstractions ("good behavior") both in behavioral as well as linguistic terms.

If we turn from such possibilities to reports of the development of play and games in middle class Western children, there are some parallels, but the account is not entirely clear. If we follow Smilansky's account and enlarge upon it with Piaget's middle class observations, we get an outline of the development of play in Achievement Culture something along the following lines.

There is no systematic data on the sensory-motor play of infants in the two different game cultures we are here discussing. One's tendency is to grant that even if games and imaginative play are not universal, then at least motor play is everywhere the same. But this is probably not true. There are studies indicating (at least on the case level), that mothers vary a great deal in the extent to which they play with their infants. Some mothers play with their infants' fingers while feeding them, others do a great deal of tickling, lifting, laughing and peek-a-boo. We might expect that such activities would induce a readiness for playfulness; that the alternations, with humor, of motor position and social responses, might well be the precursor behaviors which are antecedent to a later readiness for flexibility on the role taking level. In a four month old baby, for example, laughter is readily evoked by suddenly placing the familiar person's head against the baby's stomach, rather than holding it in the customary position. Eibl-Eibesfeldt has contended that the essence of animal play is such a combination of normal behavior sequences in a novel manner (1967). And Hutt (1966) has described the same phenomenon amongst four year old children in terms of "transposition of function." One of the faults of Piaget's otherwise excellent account of infant play, is that too much attention is paid to the way in which the play episodes replicate the intellectual structures which they parallel, and not enough to the unique character of the novel combinations that are the essence of play. Though probably the greatest transformation at this age level, one that is discussed by Piaget, and the one to which Freud paid most attention, is the transformation from passivity to activity. What we need to know is whether the child is helped towards such ludic flexibility by similar manifestations in the doting parent. My hypothesis would be that the relationship is positive.

By the age of two years we have the ascriptive game children in motor play closely imitative of that of their elders. There is the ludic transformation from passive to active. They now carry it out—instead of just witnessing it. But this representative play follows in principle most of the sensory-motor play of the earlier motor period. It replicates, but does not transform. Or the transformation is affective rather than structural. Already by this time, as judged by Piaget's records, the middle class child is introducing into his play a greater variety of subject-object, object-object and self-other transformations. He uses a shell for a drinking cup, the same shell for a shovel and for a block. He imitates many people in his play, not just the power figure most immediate to him.

And by the third year the middle class child appears to have gone off into a new structural form in his solitary play—which if we read Smilansky correctly—is not found to any great extent in the ascriptive child's play. Namely, that he introduces various dialogues between characters who take different roles in his play. There are dyadic and plural social relations portrayed, and again there is flexibility as the members change over time. By four years imaginary characters enter the play activity, and in some cases even imaginary companions. A recent report from England indicated that middle class mothers felt that the presence of such companions was a good index of their children's developing imaginative powers, whereas working class mothers worried about the children's mental health when such characters made their appearance (*New York Times*, November 3, 1968, 97–99).

Some figures from Smilansky are useful at this point, so that we don't dichotomize these two game cultures too severely. Observing three to five year old children both from achievement oriented middle class groups and from tradition oriented asiatic groups (ascriptive), she scored their play in terms of the following categories:
1. Imitative role play
2. Make believe with objects
3. Make believe with actions and situations
4. Persistence
5. Interaction
6. Verbal communication
It is of some interest that whereas only three per cent of the achievement group showed no play at all, 69 per cent of the traditional group showed no play. The differences in imitative role play were not great with approximately 20 per cent of each group showing play of this sort. On the other hand when compared for sociodramatic play (which involves others, talking, and make believe with situations, etc.) only 11 per cent of the traditional group and 78 per cent of the achievement group participated. The verbalization differences were equally striking. The achievement group used more words, a greater variety of words, longer sentences, longer statements.

I should perhaps mention that the intent of Smilansky's work

was to induce sociodramatic play in traditional childen by participating with them and by encouraging them in this play. Her ascriptive group made considerable movement into sociodramatic
play as a result of her training procedures. If the relationships between play and cognition are fundamental, her finding has an important implication for Head Start programming (Sutton-Smith,
1967). But the readiness of the children to be triggered off by the
example of adults, also suggests that ludic tendencies have something of an innate character, but must be released by appropriate
external models.

By four years of age most children are playing alongside or with
others. Despite good descriptive accounts of this play by various
workers in the 1930's we do not have currently any systematic reports of the varieties and forms of this collective play. This is an
imperative need because it seems that increasingly children's later
play forms are an extension of this earlier informal play. Through
literature we are acquainted with the fact that this has been the
case with solitary and intelligent children for centuries. What is
now occurring is that a larger segment of the population is more
interested in its own solitary and imaginative social play for a longer chronological aged period than was previously the case. Fewer
children are jumping the cultural gap from imaginative play, to ascriptive central person play, than used to be the case.

It is not that children today no longer have any experience of
chase and capture and the like (though as I have mentioned many
of the varieties of these games have gone. There is no more Sally is
a-Weeping or Mother Mother the Pot Boils Over).

But these more rigid structures seem less important to children
whose relationships with parents are also more egalitarian. In traditional culture social life and games appear to have been largely
synonymous in early childhood. The cry of "Tag" mobilized and
structured social intercourse. The Achievement Culture children
by contrast have their social life structured by the group shared
fantasies of reading and of television. These children are capable
of dialogue. They are not restricted to group action. Verbal humor
plays a childlore role that was once taken by action.

The type of rule games with their considerable role complexity
which have developed over the past hundred years are apparently
the natural successor to this increasing flexibility. The team game

of several hundred years ago or of Afghanistan today was that of the mob and the emergent powerful individuals. The game of today (particularly football) is that of a complex organization. While professionals usually settled on particular roles, it is true that the course of development in games throughout childhood requires considerable role flexibility, role exploration and the understanding of the roles of others. This sort of shifting about is a far cry from the relatively fixed statuses of ascriptive cultures.

There was one other finding in my earlier historical study, however, which seems to have even more far-reaching implications, and this was the move away from sports towards informal and individual sports (cycling, fishing, etc.). This was also the major change I found in my New Zealand sample over the past 20 years. Their levels of response were not different, but their heterogeneity was. There were more differences, more diversity. It is already the case that fewer children are prepared to give themselves to modal activities like football and baseball. It perhaps follows that these team sports will continue to be sustained only as long as there is continued upward mobility of minority groups, but that in due course such modal pursuits of large population segments will give way to a relatively more differentiated picture of play and sports. It is not likely that team sports are doomed, but it is likely they will become the hobbies rather than the avocations of mankind.

Still I don't suppose we should protest if sports cease to be a form of national mania and become recreations.

CONCLUSION

I began by suggesting that at the beginning of our era game scholarship focused on the universality of forms of games and play. My approach and material today has indicated the untenability of that older approach. In addition, however, the data seems to imply that play and games are not as trivial as they were thought to be but are instead part and parcel of the cultural systems within which they function. In turn, the present account of two game cultures (while over-simplified), further modifies unilinear notions of development through play. There are instead a variety of cultural systems of psychological development through play and games.

REFERENCES

Ariès, P. *Centuries of Childhood*. New York: Knopf, 1962.

Eibl-Eibesfeldt, I. "Concepts of ethology and their significance in the study of human behavior." In Stevenson, H. W., Eckhard, H., and Rheingold, H. (Eds.) *Early Behavior*. New York: Wiley, 1967.

Goffman, E. *Interactional Ritual*. New York: Doubleday Anchor #596, 1967.

Gomme, A. B. *The Traditional Games of England, Ireland and Scotland*. London: Nutt, 1894.

Huizinga, J. *Homo Ludens*. London: Routledge, 1949.

Maas, H. S. "The role of members in clubs of lower class and middle class adolescents," *Child Development*, 1954, 25, 241–251.

Newall, W. W. *Games and Songs of American Children*. New York: Dover, 1963.

Piaget, J. *Play, Dreams and Imitation in Childhood*. London: Heinemann, 1951.

Roberts, J. M., and Sutton-Smith, B. "Cross cultural correlates of games of chance," *Behavior Science Notes*, 1966, 3, 131–144.

Rosenberg, B. G., and Sutton-Smith, B. "A revised conception of masculine-feminine differences in play activities," *Journal of Genetic Psychology*, 1960, 96, 165–170.

Ryerson, A. J. "Medical advice on child rearing 1550–1900," *Harvard Educational Review*, 1961, 31, 302–323.

Smilansky, S. *The Effects of Sociodramatic Play on Disadvantaged Preschool Children*. New York: Wiley, 1968.

Sutton-Smith, B. *The Games of New Zealand Children*. Berkeley: University of California, 1959.

———. "The kissing games of adolescents in Ohio," *Midwest Folklore*, 1959, 9, 189–211.

———. "The cruel joke series," *Midwest Folklore*, 1960, 10, 11–22.

———, and Rosenberg, B. G. "Sixty years of historical change in the game preferences of American children," *Journal of American Folklore*, 1961, 74, 17–46.

———, ———, and Morgan, E. "Historical changes in the freedom with which children express themselves on personality inventories," *Journal of Genetic Psychology*, 1961, 99, 309–315.

———. "The role of play in cognitive development," *Young Children*, 1967, 6, 361–370.

————. "Games, play and daydreams," *Quest*, 1968, 10, 47–58.

————. "The folkgames of the children." In Tristram P. Coffin (Ed.) *Our Living Traditions*. New York: Basic Books, 1968, 179–191.

Strutt, J. *The Sports and Pastimes of the People of England*. London: Methuen, 1801.

Van den Berg, J. H. *The Changing Nature of Man*. New York: Delta, 1961.

Whyte, W. F. *Street Corner Society*. Chicago: University of Chicago Press, 1931.

SECTION II

ANTHROPOLOGICAL APPROACHES

This section begins with my first published scholarly article, and I reprint it here more for the flavor of children's games that it contains than for any considerations of great anthropological weight. It is a reminder that part of the satisfaction of working with materials of this nature, irrespective of the historical or anthropological rationales in which we wrap them, is their intrinsic interest. They evoke a nostalgia for childhood that may be an important psychological origin for any such studies.

The subsequent group of articles coauthored with John M. Roberts, professor of anthropology at Cornell University, represents a body of work which has not yet been published in final form, although a considerable segment of our data and much of our reflection upon it is contained here. We worked together on these materials for four summers, from 1960 to 1963, and I am greatly indebted to my coauthor for the stimulation and excitement of those days. Whereas my appreciation of most childlore had been to that point humanistic and historical, it was after working with Roberts that I learned to ask the functional question concerning the cultural purposes that the continued persistence of this or that cultural form might serve. Accustomed as I had been to thinking in terms of individual behavior, sociogenic thinking was novel to me. Our conflict-enculturation theory of games reflected our diverse stances as well as an attempt to come to terms with the cross-cultural data with which we worked. I was more concerned with the games' origins in the lives of the players; Roberts was more concerned with the cultural effects of playing the games in question. Our data supported both points of view and suggested that one-sided psychogenic or sociogenic theorizing was insufficient. What we took for granted at that time, and what I now think is equally important, was the reconciliation of those sorts of empirical relationships with the structure-making capacities that we call the invention of games. Given certain states of motivation and given certain cultural requirements, we attempt to describe how these phenomena are reconciled within the symbol making operations of the persons concerned, so that a series of games emerges with all their lawfulness and inherent grammar.

4. The Meeting of Maori and European Cultures and Its Effects upon the Unorganized Games of Maori Children

In the past two years I have been investigating the psychological and historical significance of the unorganized (traditional) games of New Zealand Pakeha children. In the course of my investigations I have had cause to study the effects of Maori children's unorganized games upon the unorganized games of Pakeha children and *vice versa*. The information that I have received makes it clear that, despite the immense value of Elsdon Best's *Games and Pastimes of the Maori*, there is still a great deal of research to be carried out in this field. As my own study has not been directly concerned with the games of the Maori, and as I am not myself an expert in Maori lore, it is with some diffidence that I make any report whatsoever. I do so, however, in the hope that it will stimulate others, more expert than myself, to record similar data.

In general it can be said that the history of nineteenth century

SOURCE: Reprinted from the *Journal of the Polynesian Society* 60, nos. 2/3 (1951): 93–107, by permission of The Polynesian Society, Inc. (Wellington, New Zealand).

Maori-European conflict of cultures was, in effect, the history of the gradual submergence of Maori culture. To this submergence the disruptive effects of successive Maori wars, the repressive attitudes of the missionaries, the outlook of Europeans, and the policy of Government officials, all contributed.[1] In this article only those Maori children's games which have survived this process of cultural disintegration, are considered. Further, only those games are considered which have been retained spontaneously by children. This means that the organized games and pastimes which were encouraged by the Maoris themselves, especially after the rise of the Young Maori Party in the 1890's, and which were encouraged by the Education Department after 1930, are not considered.[2] Again, those games encouraged by the Physical Education Department after 1939 are only considered if they are still played spontaneously by Maori children.[3] My information is derived from correspondence and interviews with physical education specialists and others who have been educated, or have taught, in Maori schools; the information is derived also from interviews with members of the Maori Club at Ardmore Teachers' College in 1950.[4]

[1] See for example: Miller, H., *New Zealand*, p. 13; Beaglehole, J. C., *New Zealand, A Short History*, p. 18; Best, E., *Games and Pastimes of the Maori*, *N.Z. Dom. Museum Bull.*, No. 8, p. 11; Butchers, A. G., *Young New Zealand*, p. 120; Polack, J. S., *The Manners and Customs of the New Zealanders*, Vol. 1, p. 1.

[2] Sutherland, *The Maori People Today*, p. 40.

[3] After 1939, physical educationalists, stimulated by their Director, Mr. P. A. Smithells, saw the educational value in certain Maori rhythmic games and sought to revive these for use in both Maori and Pakeha schools. Most of their work was done with hand games and stick games. They collected these games from Maoris who still knew how to play them (generally the older Maoris). The games were then recorded and introduced to teachers at refresher courses and in Training Colleges. Some attention, but not as much, was paid to string games and knucklebones. See: *Education Gazette*, April, 1941, p. 58, October, 1941, p. 201. Records of hand games and knucklebones are in the possession of the physical education authorities at Ardmore and Auckland Teachers' Training Colleges. See also Beard, D., *The History of Physical Education in the Primary Schools of New Zealand*, p. 136.

[4] I am particularly indebted to Colin Spanhake and W. G. Johnston of North Auckland and Koro Dewes, Walker Kamata, and Whitu McGarve of the East Coast. I record their names out of gratitude only. I would not like them to be held responsible for any of the above interpretations of their reports. All the material quoted above refers to conditions within the last twenty years.

These sources indicate that the following games are still played by Maori children in some areas: Hand games, knucklebones, stilts, whip tops, string games. In addition there are many other games of a more informal nature which are still played. These include: Vine-swinging, hunting and fishing, sliding and sledging, throwing and skipping stones and pipi shells, slings, juggling, spears, skipping, sailing flax canoes, penny doctors, *putuputu*, *hotaka*, head-standing and acrobatics, swimming, mock-fights and racing. It is of some interest that hand games, string games, whip tops, stilts and knucklebones should be the *formal* games most generally retained by Maori children. All these games had their counterparts in the unorganized play of Pakeha children. The Europeans brought to New Zealand their own versions of all these five games. (The European hand games are known as stone, paper and scissors.) With a few possible exceptions all the above-mentioned *informal* games also had their counterparts in the European tradition.

The persistence of these particular Maori games suggests that the existence of the parallel games in the European culture acted as a permissive factor on the same games in the Maori culture; that the Maori children were implicitly encouraged to continue with these particular games in preference to others, because these particular games were intelligible to the European mode of life. Perhaps missionaries and others, who are said to have done such damage to Maori pastimes, even looked with a more lenient eye upon pastimes that they recognized as the pastimes of "civilised," and not just "heathen" children. There may be other reasons why these particular games have persisted. The hand games, for example, require no apparatus and can be played at any odd moment; they may have been carried on because of their inconspicuous nature and their convenience. They are reported as still being played by men and women at odd shearing sheds in the East Coast area. But, if there are any other reasons why hand games and the other games mentioned above have been carried on, and all the other original spontaneous Maori children's games not carried on, then these reasons are not known. It is certainly true that there are not any comparable number of distinctively Maori pastimes which have survived and which do not have their counterparts in the European tradition. In fact no evidence was received of any such Maori games which had survived and which were still of widespread importance.

It can be assumed, therefore, that with all the above-mentioned games, the respective traditions, European and Maori, served to confirm and re-emphasize each other. It is probable that in many cases the traditions of the two cultures combined so that features of both were preserved in the ultimate product. The most interesting example of the way in which this has happened is provided by the case of knucklebones. The fusion of Maori and European knucklebones in fact, is of some anthropological significance. It will therefore be reported in detail.

The claim has been made that knucklebones was introduced to the Maoris by the early whalers.[5] No evidence, however, has been provided to support this claim. All the information to hand suggests, on the contrary, that knucklebones was separately a part of both the European and the Maori traditions. It is known, for example, that knucklebones was an extremely ancient game; that it was played throughout the ancient world; and played throughout the Pacific area in pre-European times.[6] This information suggests that the European settlers brought their own tradition of knucklebones to New Zealand, and that the Maoris already had one of their own before those settlers arrived in New Zealand.

It is possible to classify all the types and varieties of Maori and Pakeha knucklebones into four main categories. Each of these categories refers to a broad type of movement which includes many subsidiary movements of that type. No description is given here of the subsidiary movements as they are irrelevant to the purpose at hand. Details of some of these subsidiary types can be acquired from the references given in the footnotes. All types of knucklebone games include the fundamental movement of throwing a knucklebone up into the air with the right hand and catching it with the same hand. While this is being done, that is while this knucklebone is still in mid-air, the four types of movements that are possible are: (a) catching the thrown knucklebone(s) on the back of the right hand when it falls; (b) arranging other knucklebones on the ground in various formations such as rows, circles,

[5] *Education Gazette*, December, 1942, p. 298.

[6] See the *Oxford Classical Dictionary*, *Astralgus*, p. 110; Tylor, E. B., *Primitive Culture*, Vol. II, p. 81; Lovett, E., "The Ancient and Modern Games of Astragals," *Folklore*, Vol. 12, Sept., 1901; Budd, E. G. and Newman, L. F., "Knucklebones—An Old Game of Skill," *Folklore*, Vol. LII, 1941, p. 8.

squares and diamonds with the right hand and then catching the knucklebone which has been previously thrown up with the same hand; (c) picking up other knucklebones off the ground with the right hand and then catching the thrown knucklebone; (d) moving knucklebones with the right hand on the ground, in, over and about the *left hand* and then catching the thrown knucklebone with the right hand.

An examination of the English and Maori games which have been recorded and which I have collected, suggests that where knucklebones was played in its most complete traditional form the European game often included all the four movements outlined above and the Maori game only the first three types. I have collected many early New Zealand reports of European knucklebones which contain all the four types and were played in areas in which there was no great contact with the Maori. In addition, reports of knucklebones as played in England contain references to all the four types.[7] On the other hand there are reports of early Maori knucklebones which do not contain references to the fourth type of movement. It can be reasonably certain that the Maoris playing the games contained in these reports were uninfluenced by the European tradition of play.[8] It is worthy of note also that in all the examples of knucklebones from other Polynesian islands which are mentioned by Elsdon Best, there is no reference to the fourth movement. It should, however, be mentioned in passing, that in all the reports of Maori knucklebones the movements of the first three types are developed to a far more advanced stage than are the same movements in the reports of European knucklebones which I have collected in this country. Some Maori games, for example, include juggling amongst the movements of (b) above.

More recent reports of Maori games also suggest that Maori knucklebones originally lacked the fourth type of movement. For example, two recent articles which record Maori knucklebones include movements of the fourth type, but these movements of the fourth type, unlike the movements of the other types in these games, are known by Pakeha terms, not by Maori terms.[9] Obvious-

[7] Lovett, E., *op. cit.*; Budd, E. G. and Newman, L. F., *op. cit.*

[8] Chapman, F. R., "Koruru, the Maori Games of Knucklebones," *Journal of the Polynesian Society*, Vol. VII, 1898, p. 114; Best, E., *op. cit.*, p. 29.

[9] *Education Gazette*, "Jackstones," Dec. 1st, 1942, p. 298; (Wanganui area)

ly it is peculiar that these Maori names should not contain Maori terms for this fourth movement when they do contain Maori terms for the other movements.

In order to discover whether English names are generally given by Maoris to the movements of this fourth type when they are included in their games, I collected descriptions of knucklebones from sixteen Maori students at Ardmore Teachers' Training College. Of these sixteen students only two had not played the game at all. These two students came from districts in North Auckland. Four students had played the game without the fourth type of movement. One of these students came from Parapara (North Auckland); one from Okahukura (King Country); and the other two from isolated villages in the Bay of Plenty area, namely Ruatoki and Omarumutu. The other ten students had all played a game of knucklebones (generally under the name of *huripapa*) which included the fourth movement. Of these ten students, eight students used only English terms for the fourth movements although using Maori terms for the other types of movements. The English terms they used were: "Hurdles," "Stealing Eggs," "Eggs in the Basket," "Piano." All these terms are familiar in English records of knucklebones.[10] These eight students came from the East Coast area, from Nuhaka, Whangaparoa, Whakatane, Horoera, Tekaraka, Rangitukia, Mokai, Manutahi. Two students had a Maori term for one of the movements in the fourth category of movements, but English terms for all the rest of the movements in that category. Thus "Stealing Eggs" was called alternatively by its Maori name *tahae heki*. These two students came from Tikitiki and Whakaangiangi.

When Elsdon Best made his records of knucklebones in the East Coast he did not record any of these type four movements. Yet they are there today, but under English, not Maori names. This certainly suggests that the Maoris have borrowed the type four movement from the Europeans; that they have assimilated into their own knucklebone tradition a type of Pakeha cultural phenomena of a nature analogous to their own. It is probable that they have been able to do this because the Maori tradition of knucklebones was more

---

"Koruru, Knucklebones or Jackstones," N.Z. *Physical Education Soc. Bull.,* No. 4, 1947, p. 105 (Rotorua area).

[10] Lovett, Budd and Newman, *ibid.*

vigorous than the European tradition. The vigour of the Maori tradition would be responsible both for the assimilation of the distinctive European type of movement and for the fact that knucklebones are still played today much more frequently in Maori schools than in European schools. Fourteen of the above sixteen Maoris had played the game at school, whereas the game was well known in only three European schools (Hokitika, Collingwood, Kaiata) out of the thirty-two I visited in various parts of New Zealand. And even at these three schools it was seldom played by the children at school. It was a home game rather than a school game.

There follows an account of the games which have been enumerated above. This is followed in turn by an account of the games which are played today in Maori schools, but which are adaptations of games from the European tradition.

The names of some of the *hand games* that are reported as being still played by Native school children today are as follows:[11] Hei Tama, Homai (Whakaropi); Matemate ra, Hipi Toi, Ropi, Toro Piko (Mokai, Rotorua); Homai, Ropi, Kumute (Materawa); Hei Tamatutama (Nuhaka); Hei Tama, Whakaropi (Horoera); Hei Tama, Whakaropi, Ropi, Mate ra, Hipitoetoe, Toropiko (Rangitukia); Hipitoitoi with thumbs, Toro Piko, Whakaropiropiro, Hei Tama, E Ropi (Tikitiki); Whakaropiropiro, Hei Tama, Horo Piko (Omarumutu); Homai, Tu Tama (Whangaparoa); Hipi Toi (Te Paroa). Of these games one area-organizer in *Physical Education* writes: "These games are often played in North Auckland Maori schools. I have never taught one in a Maori school nor have I met a teacher who has. Several teachers have confessed that when they have professed any interest in the hand game, the children have turned up with many varieties saying, 'Dad told me,' etc."

String games reported are the following:[12] Diamonds 1, 2, 4 (Okahukura); Mouii, Wharekehua (Whakaangiangi); Whai, Whare Kehua (Tikitiki); Cup and Saucer, Diamonds 2, 3, 4, Waewae pikaokao, Wharekehua (Horoera); Cot, Mattress, Single and Double Diamond (Te Karaka); Whai wahine, Whai tane, Mouti

[11] The names of the district or village are placed in parentheses. The hand names are recorded as they were given to me. It will be noted that there are often various forms of the same name. I have not attempted to select the correct one.

[12] For details see Andersen, J. C., *String Games*.

Mourea, Waewae pikaokao, Diamonds 1, 2, 3, 7, 11, 13 (Rangitukia); Tane, Wahine, Diamonds 1 to 13, Canoe, Moti, One Diamond
with loops, Cup and Saucer (Te Paroa); Bird's net, Bird's foot,
Diamonds 1 to 7, Mouti-Mourea (Mokai); Mauii, Wahine, Tane,
Cup and Saucer, Waewae Pikaokao, Wharekehua (Nuhaka). Other
areas which have been reported as strong centers of Maori string
games are Matauri Bay, Whakarewarewa and Kaitaia.

There are several reports of *stilts*. "We played 'follow the leader'
games on stilts made out of wineberry tree or *manuka*" (Huirau).
"We had fights and races on stilts made out of manuka or old
planks." (Horoera).

"*Whip Tops* made from pine cones or with manufactured tops
are common in North Auckland and they are invariably propelled
by cabbage tree whips." "We shaped the hardwood into a top and
then put a nail in at the point. A medium sized piece of flax was
tied on a stick to make a whip. The top was spun by winding the
flax around the tops. There were top fights." (Okahukura). "We
made tops from manuka and whips from cabbage trees." (Waitaruke). "Tops from manuka and totara." (Rangitukia). "Tops from
hinehine." (Tikitiki). "We played broad-jumping with tops, bowling another top over and jumping obstacles with them." (Horoera).

Vine-Swinging of an informal nature is still common. "We used
to swing on willow trees" (Te Paroa). "We had distance tests of
vine-swinging as a method of qualifying for entrance to our gang"
(Bay of Plenty). "This was a variation of the Maori game of
swinging on a vine and flying into a river. A good vine hanging
from a tree was selected. The player took a run back, flew through
the air and let go. The place he landed was marked. This practice
could almost be termed a long jump and some would be really long
too. The aim was to gain speed on the run up, then really fly
through the air holding the vine. The main ingredient after that
was the courage to let go in order to land many yards further on.
I can recall a number of injuries." (Kaikohe).

"*Hunting* filled a large part of our leisure time in summer. Eels
and birds were the main victims. There was a variety of methods of
catching both. Snares from flax were used to catch hawks or
pheasants. We tied down a good springy stake of *manuka*, lance-
wood or *tanekaha*. The stake was stuck into the earth then bent

over and secured by a piece of flax, to which was attached the bait. The bait for hawks was meat or fish; for pheasants a cob of corn. When the bait was moved a little it would release the flax and the stick would spring upright. At the end of the stick would be another piece of flax attached and laid on the ground about the flax in a loop. When the stick was released this loop was supposed to catch on to the bird's legs. The method was very successful with hawks, and sufficiently successful with pheasants for us to keep on trying. With smaller birds a kit or box was used. This was propped up at one end with a stick and seeds and crumbs were scattered under the box. The hunter lay concealed at a distance holding onto a string that was attached to the prop-stick. A little tug was supposed to drop the cover over the birds." (Kaikohe).

"Wax-eyes were caught on an apparatus which consisted of two poles and a cross-bar of string. A decoy wax-eye was swung on the string cross-bar. The wax-eyes were attracted by the hunter who hid in the bush next to the cross-bar. By sucking inward that part of a corn leaf which is like cigarette paper he made whistling sounds like the squeak of the wax-eye. When the birds alighted on the cross-bar, they were knocked unconscious with a flick from a supple piece of *manuka* hardened in the fire." (Huirau).

"In tidal rivers, when the tide is out the entry and exit holes of *eels* are clearly visible in the mudbanks. The method is simply that of putting a hand in each hole, feeling the eel inside and pulling it out. A grip with the middle finger over the top, and the second and fourth fingers underneath is a firm one. Very large numbers can be caught in a very short time. Where holes are very large, discretion is the better part of valour. The most suitable costume for this game is the nude and several of us would spend an hour or two roaming the tidal banks in the nude pulling out eels. We have met parties much older than ourselves similarly clad. Mud banks can be very messy. In swamps a piece of plain wire attached to a stout stick is all that is required. By frequent poking eels can be felt by the quivering of the stick. The eel is then pulled out as before. In soft muddy places they can be felt with the feet. In rivers, night time is the best. A torch made from sacking or the stalks of flax flowers provides a suitable light. A gaff is needed to pull out those attracted to the light." (Kaikohe). "We used a lighted tyre to attract

the eels." (East Coast). "We fished eels with a rod. A bait of
worms was strung on cabbage tree leaves and *wiwi* was used as a
hook." (Nuhaka).

"*Crab* fishing was done at night. A light was used to attract the
crabs and they were hooked out with a piece of wire turned up at
one end." (Whangaparoa). "We dived for *paua*, sea-eggs and crayfish. Crayfish pots (called *pouraka*) were set at night. Crowds of
families would go down at the early morning tide and fish them
out. We would compete to see how many sea-eggs we could bring
up at one time. This was done in shallow water. We felt around
with our feet first then dived to bring them up. The same was done
with crayfish. We felt round for their holes with our feet, then
dived to bring them up. The sea-eggs could be eaten raw. Some old
folks would eat the whole thing." (Horoera).

"*Putuputu* is played by cutting out from tin a piece the shape of
a horseshoe. A hole is made in the tin through which a piece of
string is threaded about a yard long. At the other end of the string
is a knot. This knot is held between the toes. Each player then has
his *putuputu* dragging behind and the idea is to give chase and to
tramp on the other fellow's *putuputu*." (Kaikohe). The same game
is mentioned as having been played with flax threaded through the
holes in shells (Omarumutu, Opotiki). Although it is not mentioned
by Elsdon Best it is probably a traditional Maori game. An informant from Waitaruke, North Auckland, speaks of threading string
through the holes in *paua* shells and walking on them like imitation horses. The two games may have had the same origin.

"*Hotaka* consists of the main stalk of a *nikau* frond. This is
almost severed at about four inches from the thick end and is so
cut that the nearly severed piece hangs by the outer bark of the
frond. The heel plate of a working shoe, which is shaped like a
small horseshoe, is attached to the swinging end of the frond. This
toy makes a very good imitation of a horse hoof in the sand or dust
and smaller children get a lot of fun playing horses with it."
(Kaikohe). In most reports of this game, which appears to be widespread, the children use the frond as a horse hoof without attaching
any shoe-plate; in others the children use flax. The flax-hoof (Okahukura, Omarumutu) or flax-capper (Te Paroa, Nuhaka) is made
by cutting a piece of flax leaf near the hoof. The stalk is cut longi-

tudinally and then bent double. Children then run along making a cracking sound like the hooves of a horse.

There is report of children making *slippers* out of giant kelp (Horoera).

Children throw *pipi* shells in the air to make them glide (Te Paroa, Huirau). They skip flat stones and the flakes of the paper rock (Horoera).

There is mention of *slings* in which an arrow lying on the ground is slung a distance by the aid of a string looped over a notch by the arrow head. The string is attached to a stick and the stick is flicked (Huirau). There is report of fern root slings which are used to throw stalks of the pampas grass (called *kakaho*). There are competitions in distance throwing (Horoera). "A piece of flax slit down the seam can be shot into the air when the seam is pulled quickly through the fingers. We aimed at each other and had distance competitions." (Ohakune).

Natural foods eaten are *tawa* berries, *miro* berries, *totara* berries, *koramu* berries and the fibre of the lace bark (Huirau). "We chewed supplejack and the flower of the *kia kia*." (Horera).

A *stick game* which is mentioned as having been played spontaneously is *tititorea* (Ruatoki).

"*Mud-slides* were very unpopular with parents, but very popular with the children in the winter. All that is required is a grassy slope. Buckets of water are poured down this slide. After a time a very slippery surface can be obtained. Skill is required to negotiate the slide at speed while remaining standing on two feet. A spill is rewarded by a patch of mud on the seat of the pants." (Kaikohe). Most of the sliding that is reported is done on the leaves of cabbage tree or on *nikau* fronds (Ruatoki) which are used as sledges (Omarumutu, Rangitukia).

Flax boats are also well known.[13] These are made out of the pointed piece at the end of the flax leaf. The flax rib is the bottom of the boat. The ends of the two sides of the flax are turned round each other and a stick is pushed through to hold them in place. Cross-bar sticks are placed in the middle of the boat to keep the sides apart. A flax sail—another similar piece of flax—can be slid

[13] See, for example, Morice, Stella, *The Book of Wiremu*, p. 16.

under these cross-bars, brought over the top and fastened by its point to the stern of the boat (Ruatoki). Boats are also made out of the dry flax sticks. These sticks are hollowed out and shaped like a boat. Smaller sticks can be used for outriggers and masts can be put in for the paper sails. A white *pipi* shell is put in for a keel (Russell).

Penny Doctor beetles, also known as "Butcher Bats" is a game widely reported by Wellington Training College students as being played in many parts of the North Island. In this game straws moistened by spittle are pushed down the hole of the appropriate beetle. The beetle seizes the end of the straw. When the player feels the straw moving he or she flicks out the beetle. The player who can catch the most beetles wins the game.

It is worth noting that I received no reports of kites, hoops or darts. Yet these are all games which had their European and Maori counterparts. It is probable that they have faded in Maori schools for the same reason that they have faded in European schools, although they may have both been confirmed and accentuated in earlier years; that is, before road traffic and organized sports became of any great importance, say, prior to 1910.

The *introduced* games which appear to have become of some importance in Maori schools are: marbles, smoking, ball-bouncing, stagknife, bow and arrows, shanghais, pop-guns, windmills and propellors, ball hop-scotch. Others which are also mentioned, but which do not seem to be so widespread, are: *Poka*, buttons, tractors, rotten egg, Toi and Whatonga, rollers, whistles, sending a message. The popularity of marbles and stagknife may perhaps be explained by the fact that the Maoris have always had more pastimes involving manual dexterity than the Europeans.[14] It is worth noting that the Maoris often fire their marbles in the "Mollybar" fashion, namely, off a straight middle finger which is held in two fingers of the other hand and then catapulted. It is of interest also that while marbles faded in many European schools during the war because there were no supplies, the supply was supplemented in many Maori schools from melted down gramophone records which were rolled into a ball shape.

---

[14] The American negroes also excel their white counterparts in games of manual dexterity.

Poka is a game played with a ball and four holes in the ground (Kaikohe). It is an adaption of the marble game of "Holey" which is still to be found among the mining settlements north of Westport in the South Island. Buttons (Kaikohe) is an adaptation of the old Scottish marble game "leggings-out" or "knock-backs." Rotten-egg (Omarumutu, Opotiki, Huirau, Ruawera) is the game of egg cap or egg cup which is still played at Alexandra in Otago.[15] Toi and Whatonga which is reported from Nuhaka. Tikitiki and Whakaan-giangi is said to be a game which is similar to draughts but played on an eight-pointed star scratched in the sand. It is said by these informants to have died out in their time (within the last ten years). The shape of the diagram and the fact that the game is not mentioned by Best, suggests it may be nothing but an adaption of Chinese checkers. Sending a message, which is played in a circle formation, and in which the message is conveyed by a squeeze of the hand, may be an adaption of the well known English parlour game of slip the button (Mataraua).

It was noticeable in all reports that there were a large number of typically rural pursuits mentioned. This was not unusual as a large number of Maori settlements are still of a predominantly rural nature. There seemed also to be more attention to games starring war parties. For example: "There were many varieties of war parties. Our weapon consisted of a *tanekaha* stick about two feet long—any supple and springy wood would do—and a ball of soft clay on the end. The stick was bent back and the ball of clay let fly. We became very accurate with these. Hits were really hits! One boy had an eye put out. But the game was not encouraged. Wet clay was not very suitable for carrying round in the pocket and the hits were severe." (Kaikohe). "One of our gang specialties was the fern fight. Two gangs stood off at about twenty yards and hit off the tops of the yellow shoots of the bracken fern with sticks. The fern tops whizzed around like spears." (Huirau). "We all used to ride to school with our bows and arrows. We would have bow and arrow gang fights on horseback. Some boys were able to stand on their horses' backs and fire the bows." (Horoera). "We had two teams at war with fern spears. Each player had about ten spears and a shield of wood or tin. Any player being hit must drop out.

[15] See *New Zealand Physical Education Society Bulletin*, Vol. 2, No. 4, 1947.

We also divided up into teams for sword fights with *manuka* sticks."
(Ruatoki).

These Maori war party games may be simply a parallel for the
European children's cowboy and Indians. Both may be stimulated
also by the influence of the films and literature. On the other hand
this type of Maori play may be an expression of something peculiar
to Maori culture. The Beagleholes, for example, have pointed out
that the Maoris tend to foster inter-tribal competitiveness as one of
the means of supporting the "basic character structure of Maori
culture."[16] If this is the case, the children's play would naturally
reflect this spirit of inter-group competitiveness, particularly in the
terms in which that competitiveness was originally expressed,
namely, in terms of war parties.

The above article has dealt almost entirely with the effects of
the European tradition of games upon the games of Maori children.
The meeting of cultures has not, however, been entirely one-
sided. There are occasional reports of European children playing at
Maori games such as humming tops and team whip tops. And also
many reports of white children building *raupo* huts and sledging
on cabbage tree leaves. It can be assumed that the Maori games
which were the same as the European games would confirm the
European children in the play of those games.

In conclusion it can be said that in the new cultural environment
provided by the meeting of these two cultures, there has been a
tendency for the unique pastimes of the submerged culture to be
cancelled out, and for the pastimes which both cultures shared to be
strengthened. But this tendency has been affected by yet another
influence which has been stronger than the re-emphasis given by
each culture to the analogous traits in the other. This other influence has been the influence of organized sport which has tended to
cancel out all the minor games of both cultures irrespective of their
nature.[17]

[16] Beaglehole, E. and P., *Some Modern Maoris*, p. 145.
[17] The incompleteness of the material I have recorded above will be only too
apparent to the experienced eye. It is my hope, however, that the documenta-
tion of this material will stimulate others to record the spontaneous play life
of Maori children today and yesterday in more detail and with more accuracy.
Further material could be sent to me c/o The Polynesian Society, Alexander
Turnbull Library, Wellington.

5. The Cross-Cultural and Psychological Study of Games

This article will be in the form of a summary statement of a series of researches which have been published or are to be published in detail elsewhere. Beginning in 1959 with an initial cross-cultural study by Roberts, Arth, & Bush, our intent has been to use cross-cultural evidence to establish hypotheses about the function of games in culture, and then to proceed to psychological studies within our own culture as a means of testing these hypotheses.

In the initial study, games were defined as competitive activities which always terminate in an outcome; namely, winning, drawing, or losing (Roberts, Arth, & Bush, 1959).* Three classes of games, games of physical skill, chance and strategy became the subject-matter of inquiry. Games of *physical skill* were defined as those in

SOURCE: *The Cross-Cultural Analysis of Games*, pp. 100–108 (Champaign, Ill., Stipes, 1970), edited by Gunther Luschen. Reprinted with the permission of the co-author, John M. Roberts, and the publisher.

*Material within parentheses refers to sources listed at the end of this article.

which the outcomes are determined by the player's motor activities (marathon races, darts, etc.); games of *chance* were those in which the outcome is determined by a guess or some external artifact such as a die or wheel (bingo, roulette); games of *strategy* were those in which the outcome is determined by rational choices (checkers, chess, go, etc.). The games with which most of us are familiar are mixtures of these elements. Thus, football involves physical skill and strategy, and poker involves chance and strategy. By and large we restricted our inquiry to the pure types of games alone.

CROSS-CULTURAL FINDINGS

Cross-cultural analyses were based on the Human Relations Area Files. While there appear to be some cultures with no games, physical skill games had the widest distribution, chance games were of intermediate distribution, and the games of strategy were the most restricted of these three classes. If we take these types of games, in turn, we may summarize our information as follows:

Cultures without games

Games are so nearly universal in culture that it was a surprise to discover that some cultures had no games. In all probability the cultures scored as lacking games fall into three groups: (1) cultures which have never had games, e.g. the Yir Yuront; (2) cultures which have lost games through a process of deculturation, e.g. possibly the Cuna; and (3) cultures which, in fact, possess games, but which have been erroneously scored as lacking them, e.g., perhaps the Hinchol.

Unfortunately, the sample of cultures lacking games is small and unsatisfactory; and so we are somewhat uncertain about the basic data. It is still profitable, however, to consider the contrast between the societies scored as possessing games and those which have been scored as lacking them. In general, they appear to be tropical groups with simple subsistence patterns, simple technology, low political organization, no class stratification, kin-homogeneous communities, no bride-price, low obedience training and low stress in child socialization. They are cultures which appear to be quite noncompetitive when compared with cultures which do have games. This is consistent with one of our earlier findings that the greater number of types of games possessed by a culture, the greater concern was shown for the induction of achievement (competitiveness) in the child training procedures (Roberts & Sutton-Smith, 1962).

Cultures possessing games of physical skill alone

This game category establishes the minimal level or baseline against which the remaining game categories can be compared. These cultures are found in tropical regions. Their subsistence economics and technologies are simple. Communities are small. The level of political integration is low. Class stratification is absent. The judicial system is undeveloped. Child socialization is easy, and anxieties and conflicts are low. Sexual satisfaction is high. They are not warlike. They give a general impression of simplicity, particularly when they are contrasted with the chance and strategy categories. As contrasted with the no game cultures, however, there seems to be increased sex segregation and more independent families (rather than extended) which suggests the possibility of greater needs for and emphasis upon masculine self-reliance in hunting, fishing, etc. The ethnographic accounts, for example, contain many records of the elders encouraging the young boys in games of spear-throwing and archery, which have an obvious relationship to the adaptive skills required of males in the adult culture.

Cultures with games of chance

In all probability all cultures possessing games of chance also possess games of physical skill. In addition, however, some of them possess games of strategy. In many ways this particular chance game category is the most complex of the three pure types considered here, and it is the least easy to understand theoretically.

In general, chance cultures display a wide range of cultural complexity varying from quite simple cultures to the most complex known today. Yet since these games are fundamentally simpler than games of strategy, and since games of strategy are known to be associated with cultural complexity, it is reasonable to assume that chance playing began in relatively simple settings. The most important conclusion is that games of chance appear to flourish in the presence of environmental, individual and social uncertainty regardless of the relative complexity of the cultures in which they occur. Only a few of the relationships which have been the basis for this conclusion can be given here. They are detailed more fully elsewhere (Roberts & Sutton-Smith, 1966). For example, if we contrast the simple chance cultures (those which lack games of strategy) with the simple physical skill cultures (those which lack both games of strategy and games of chance), these simple chance cultures in comparison with the simple physical skill cultures are found in higher latitudes where there are striking seasonal changes and greater cold. Their settlements are non-fixed. Their food supply is not secure and food shortages are frequent or annual. For subsistence they rely primarily on hunting, fishing and collecting, also uncertain procedures. The communities are small indicating a marginal subsistence base.

First cousin marriage is not permitted and to this extent there is an increased probability of an uncertain search for a spouse. The divorce rate is high. The early sexual satisfaction potential is low. Sexual socialization anxiety is high. Premarital sexual relations are not freely permitted. Child socialization also appears to be severe. Finally, religious divinatory procedures as well as games of chance are customary means of decision-making. A game of chance in such cultures appears to be a way of making up one's mind with the help of a benevolent Fate, when life conditions are sufficiently uncertain that one has no better instrumental procedures for decision-making.

Cultures with games of strategy

Cultures possessing games of strategy are at a higher level of cultural complexity than the cultures in the other game categories. Larger settlements, more complicated subsistence patterns, higher technology, higher levels of political integration, jurisdiction, social stratification, occupational specialization and many other traits confirm the fact that these cultures are complex.

Child socialization tends to be severe. There are briefer periods of nurturance, a high inferred transition anxiety, a high pain inflicted by nurturant agent, a low degree of reduction of the infant's drives, low overall indulgence and high responsibility, achievement, self-reliance and obedience training. Here the child must be obedient and responsible, but at the same time he must be achieving and self-reliant, all of this within the context of a stratified and highly organized social system.

The cultural correlates are impressive: there are political, judicial, economic, military and religious organizations in which strategic skills and strategic decisions are rewarded. It is not hard to envisage games of strategy as forms of social system learning in contexts of this character.

In a parallel study of folktales, furthermore, we have established that folktales with strategic elements flourish in the same cultural environments as games of strategy (Roberts, Sutton-Smith, & Kendon, 1963).

Cultures possessing games of physical skill, games of chance and games of strategy

These are the most complex of all of the cultures discussed. Every modern industrial society, of course, falls in this group and most, if not all, of the classic cultures known to history and archaeology. They appear to be an amalgam of the general physical skill tradition with an overlay of chance, and then, very importantly an overlay of strategy. The antecedent conditions for involvement in both chance and strategy appear to be present.

These then are a sample of the findings from a number of studies. They challenge the traditional view that games are of no functional significance. Furthermore, they suggest that at least on the empirical level, there is evidence in favor of both classic psychogenic (Freudian) and sociogenic (Groos) theories of play. Games appear to require a theoretical structure which will account both for their relationship to child-training antecedents and to their cultural outcomes. What the nature of such a theory might be has been suggested in our conflict-enculturation theory of games (Roberts & Sutton-Smith, 1962).

PSYCHOLOGICAL FINDINGS

Everyone is familiar with the weaknesses of cross-cultural research, beginning with inadequacies in the records that form the substance of the cross-cultural and human relations area files, and going on to the more fundamental question of whether you can lift traits out of a cultural context and then treat them as similar. One answer to these criticisms is to show that relationships discovered cross-culturally can be replicated intraculturally, a procedure we have termed sub-system replication.

Our earliest predictions were that the types of child-training which had been associated with the games on a cross-cultural basis should allow us to make predictions that girls and women would show greater preference for games of chance and strategy, boys and men for games of physical skill, lower status persons for games of chance; and higher status persons for games of strategy and physical skill. These predictions were borne out in several studies (Roberts & Sutton-Smith, 1962; Sutton-Smith, Roberts, & Kozelka, 1963).

Most of our earlier problems with psychological studies lay with the development of adequate measures of play and game involvement. Obviously if game playing was to be systematically related to other psychological variables in the personality of the player, it must first be of some considerable importance to the player. Studies using preference measures such as those mentioned above had obvious drawbacks. What the subjects said they did in response to such inventories did not always correspond to their actual behavior (Sutton-Smith, 1965). Measures using a temporal criterion were somewhat more useful. In an unpublished study by Sutton-Smith and Rosenberg, college students claiming to play less than five hours a week of sports recorded a depressive profile on the Minnesota Multiphasic Personality Inventory, while students reporting more than 30 hours recorded a hysterical profile. A more normal profile was reported by students with between five and 30 hours. Unpublished interview studies by Roberts and Kendon with students who were game addicts, playing more than 30 hours of chess or bridge per week, showed the former to be somewhat asocial and disputatious and the latter to be quite gregarious and to prefer avoiding argumentation (1963).

A sociometric measure was also used in an attempt to discover whether game playing was a model of more general personality characteristics. Children were asked to nominate their peers who were leaders because of: (a) their ideas for things to do (strategists), (b) their power, bravery, and courage (potents), (c) their luck (fortunists). There were various supportive findings, but the most meaningful were those for the boys distinguished as Strategists or Potents. Strategists and Potents each preferred their own type of game on a play inventory. The former were seen as good sports, but not good at sport; and the latter were seen as good at sport, but not good sports. We felt that the ability of our strategists to be seen as good sports, though not good at sport, was quite a strategic accomplishment for preadolescent boys (Sutton-Smith & Roberts, 1964). Later we also found that such boys were actually better at the games they preferred. We had thus established a construct consistency between their being seen as strategists, their preferring strategy games and their being good at them.

Still these evidences were all somewhat tenuous. What we needed was a measure of game *involvement* which would be reliable enough to provide a sufficient justification for the expectation that the player's game addiction would be an expression of his personality in general. Up to this point we had used only preference measures, measures of the number of hours per week spent game playing and the sociometric measure. It seemed that a test of game *competence* might provide a more critical measure. We began with strategy because we had already had our best results with that game variable.

To this end and with the help of Robert Kozelka, a mathematician of Williams College, we created a test of strategic competence. We began with the most elementary and the most general of all strategy games, namely Tick Tack Toe. The test was composed of six parts of six different games and in each part the player was expected to make the next move. Possible moves were scored for their probability of contributing towards a win or a draw. Each was treated separately and compared with the probability that the player would lose. The results were the most consistent and meaningful for boys who played with a high win probability. These boys tended to win in real Tick Tack Toe tournaments, to have a high I.Q. and to be especially good at problem-solving and arithmetic (Roberts, Hoffman, & Sutton-Smith, 1965). They were perceived by their peers as "strategists" (care of the previous sociometric); they were observed to persist with intellectual tasks; and to rapidly reduce intellectual tasks to a habit level. Boys who played with a high draw probability were adult dependent but high need achievers on McClelland's projective measure. Girls who were winners were aggressive, hyperactive and masculine. Girls who played for a draw were feminine and socially withdrawing (Sutton-Smith & Roberts, 1967). We would like to interpret this information as indicating that the Tick Tack Toe competence is just part of a more generalized strategic competence, manifest also in these other logically congruent ways. But, of course, other interpretations are also possible.

What is established by this series of studies at the most parsimonious level of interpretation is that game competence (of this sort, for boys and for winning) is systematically related to other psychological variables, which is somewhat the same conclusion we reached after the cross-cultural studies. That is, both lines of study converge to the view that games are functional. Furthermore, in both series of studies the games have been empirically related to variables that can be construed as their antecedents and to other variables that can be construed as their outcomes, so that a theory which embraces psychogenic as well as sociogenic explanations seems required.

Discussion

In several articles we have presented a theory of play to account for the presence of both these psychogenic and sociogenic correlates (Roberts & Sutton-Smith, 1962; Sutton-Smith & Roberts, 1964). This theory says that the individual and psychological motivation for game playing is the presence in the player of anxieties and conflicts induced by antecedent child-training processes. The game is enjoyable to the player because it consists in a symbolic statement of these conflicts, and because in the course of the buffered learning which the game provides, the player develops confidence and competence to handle the real life situations towards which the original anxieties point. A brief illustration must suffice. On the basis of an earlier symbolic analysis of children's central person games (tagging, hide and seek, red rover, etc.), we had postulated that they represent the child's anxieties about exercising independence during the transition from primary to secondary ties. In the course of the game the child can either manifest the endangering independence by running out from safe bases and tackling strange persons (The "It") or he can retreat to the safety of the home or base (Sutton-Smith, 1959). A cross-cultural test for the presence of these types of games demonstrated a significantly greater concern with independence training in those cultures where these games were present. In addition, in those same cultures there were marriage customs requiring the girl to go out from her own kin group and marry amongst relative strangers. It is this double relationship of the games both to the inducing child-training procedure and the required adult cultural performance that has led us to entitle our theory a conflict-enculturation theory of games. Such a theory is, of course, based only on empirically demonstrated correlates. It has not been actually demonstrated that the child training does induce these game proclivities or that the games do prepare the children for their role performances, though the great usage of games in social science theorizing and in war and business simulation does not make it difficult to believe that games actually do influence their players. We have, in fact, made some earlier demonstrations of that sort (Gump & Sutton-Smith, 1955).

Our work on the enculturative end of this theory has led us to the formulation that games are, among other things, models of power. Games are, we suggest, models of ways of succeeding over others, by magical power (as in games of chance), by force (as in physical skill games), or by cleverness (as in games of strategy). We have speculated that in games children learn all those necessary arts of trickery, deception, harassment, divination and foul play that their teachers won't teach them, but that are most important in successful human interrelationships in marriage, business and war. Further that boys played games of physical skill because this is the power form that they can most easily command; and that girls showed a preference for games of strategy and chance because these are the lesser power forms available to them.

RELATED LITERATURE

Gump, P. V., and Sutton-Smith, B. The "it" role in children's games. *The Group.* 17, 1955: 3–8.

Roberts, J. M., M. J. Arth and R. R. Bush. Games in Culture. *American Anthropologist.* 61, 1959: 579–2605.

Roberts, J. M., and Sutton-Smith, B. Child training and game involvement. *Ethnology.* 1, 1962: 166–185.

Roberts, J. M., Sutton-Smith, B., and Kendon, A. Strategy in games and folktales. *Journal of Social Psychology.* 61, 1963: 185–199.

Roberts, J. M., Hoffman, H., and Sutton-Smith, B. Pattern and Competence: A consideration of tick tack toe. *El Palacio.* 1965, 72, 17–30.

Roberts, J. M., Thompson, W. E., and Sutton-Smith, B. Expressive self-testing and driving. *Human Organization*. 25, 1966: 54–63.

Roberts, J. M., and Sutton-Smith, B. Cross-cultural correlates of games of chance. *Behavior Science Notes*. 3, 1966: 131–144.

Sutton-Smith, B. A formal analysis of game meaning. *Western Folklore*. 18, 1959: 13–24.

———. Cross-cultural study of children's games. *American Philosophical Society Yearbook*. 1961: 426–429.

———. Play preference and play behavior: a validity study. *Psychological Reports*. 16, 1965: 65–66.

———, Roberts, J. M., and Kozelka, R. M. Game involvement in adults. *Journal of Social Psychology*. 60, 1963: 15–30.

———, and Roberts, J. M. Rubrics of competitive behavior. *Journal of Genetic Psychology*. 105, 1964: 13–37.

———, Roberts, J. M., and Rosenberg, B. G. Sibling association and role involvement. *Merrill-Palmer*. 10, 1964: 25–38.

———, and Roberts, J. M. Studies in elementary strategic competence. (A monograph in collaboration with Vaughn Crandall and Don Broverman). *Genetic Psychological Monograph*. 75, 1967: 3–42.

Textor, R. B. *A Cross-cultural Summary*. New Haven, 1967.

6. Strategy in Games and Folk Tales

A. INTRODUCTION

Earlier publications have shown that the three major divisions of
games in culture (games of physical skill, games of strategy, and
games of chance) have specific associations with child training
practices and other cultural variables (11, 12).* In these studies
games were viewed as expressive models and both the players' involvement in them and the cultural support of them were explained
in terms of a conflict-enculturation hypothesis (12). This hypothesis
holds that conflicts induced by child training processes and subsequent learning lead to involvement in games and other expressive

SOURCE: Reprinted from the *Journal of Social Psychology*, no. 61 (1963), pp.
185–189, with permission of the co-authors, John M. Roberts and Adam Kendon, and the Journal Press. Copyright, 1963, by The Journal Press. This investigation was supported by PHS Research Grant MHO4161-03. The authors
wish to acknowledge the theoretical and practical assistance of William Lam-
bert, Marjorie Wolf, and Charles D. Hughes.

* Numbers in parentheses refer to sources listed at the end of this article.

models which in turn provide buffered learning or enculturation important both to the players and to their societies. Since all games model competitive situations it was suggested also that these three classes of games represent different competitive or success styles (12, 14). The present study continues this general inquiry into models, but it is focused on the strategic mode of competition not only as it is modeled in games of strategy but also as it occurs in folk tales with strategic outcomes.

Folk tales and games are quite different media of expression, but they are similar in that they model or represent behaviors occurring in other settings, both real and imaginary. As models they belong to an extremely important cultural category which is both ancient in human culture (models appear in the Upper Paleolithic) and universally represented (no culture lacks models). The *model array* in any one culture may include representations in such diverse forms as graphic art, sculpture, drama, literature, toys, maps, plans, folk tales, games, and many more. In most, but not all societies, folk tales and games figure prominently in the model arrays and the study of these two types is a reasonable first step in the cross-cultural study of models.

All games model competitive situations, for a game can be defined as a recreational activity characterized by organized play, competition, two or more sides, criteria for determining the winner, and agreed-upon rules (11). Other recreational activities not satisfying these requirements are "amusements." Some folk tales resemble games in that they display definite outcomes with winners and losers, but other folk tales resemble amusements in lacking such outcomes. Folk tales of the latter type are excluded from this discussion. Indeed, this inquiry is strictly limited to those games and tales which display outcomes realized through the strategic mode of competition.

It is the general hypothesis of the present study that the strategic mode in folk tales will occur in the same general cultural setting as the strategic mode in games. Before proceeding to test this hypothesis, however, it is necessary first to outline the nature of the cultural setting in which games of strategy occur. While this outline is in part a repetition of statements made earlier (11), it is required by the large amount of new material now made available as a result of the adoption of the present system of game classification in the Ethnographic Atlas (8).

B. Games of Strategy

The strategic mode of competition does not occur in all games (11). Strategy does not appear in any games of chance, pure physical skill, or physical skill and chance. Strategy is present as a minor mode in games of physical skill and strategy (e.g., football) and games of physical skill, strategy, and chance (e.g., tipcat). Strategy, however, is the *dominant* mode of competition in games of pure strategy (e.g., chess) and strategy and chance (e.g., poker). The strategic mode of competition, then, is most clearly modeled in games of pure strategy and games of strategy and chance and it is present as a minor mode in games of physical skill and strategy and games of physical skill, strategy and chance. It will be seen that while there are analogies to these game types in folk tales, there are not exact equivalents.

Not only is the strategic mode of competition limited to a few types of games, but the ethnographic distribution of games of strategy is limited. Of 141 tribes listed without qualification in the Ethnographic Atlas (8), eight were listed as having no games at all; 45 had only games of physical skill; 41 had games of physical skill and games of chance; three had games of strategy only; five had games of strategy and games of chance; 16 had games of physical skill and games of strategy; and 23 had games of physical skill, games of chance, and games of strategy. Only 33 per cent had games where strategy was a dominant mode of competition and another 61 per cent had games of physical skill with the possibility of the presence of the minor mode of strategic competition. Since the cross-cultural data do not permit the assessment of the degree of strategic competition found in the widely distributed games of physical skill, the following discussion of the cultural environment favoring the modeling of the strategic mode of competition is based on the presence or absence of games of strategy.

An earlier study has shown that games of strategy are associated with high political integration and high social stratification: societies which are low in political integration and in social stratification are unlikely to have games of strategy (11). These findings support the generalization that tribes low in social complexity lack games of strategy while tribes high in social complexity have them.

The new data presented in the Ethnographic Atlas provide further support for this generalization. Societies possessing games of strategy are characterized by a low dependence on gathering, hunting, and fishing for subsistence, a higher dependence upon animal husbandry, and a high dependence upon agriculture. Table 1 shows the association between the presence of games of strategy and the more developed types of agriculture, particularly intensive agriculture.

Over and above the subsistence base, it is clear that games of strategy are associated with relatively advanced and specialized technologies. Only three societies possessing games of strategy lack pottery and a majority possess weaving and leather working. The association with metal working, however, is most relevant (see Table 2). Metal working is often regarded as an indicator of cultural complexity. It is safe to say that every society possessing an advanced industrial organization also possesses games of strategy.

Further indication of the relationship between strategy and complexity is found in the relationship between the mean size of the local community and game types (see Table 3). Games of strategy are associated with large local communities. Only four of the 39 strategy societies were nomadic, seminomadic, or semisedentary, the others being sedentary in settlement pattern. Twenty-one strategy societies lived in compact and relatively permanent settlements and four in complex settlements.

TABLE 1
Games of Strategy and Intensity of Cultivation

	Games of strategy	
	Present	Absent
Absence of agriculture	2	32
Horticulture	0	14
Casual agriculture	1	6
Extensive agriculture	13	33
Intensive agriculture with irrigation	13	7
Intensive on permanent fields with avoidance of fallow	12	3

TABLE 2
Games of Strategy and Metal Working

	Games of strategy	
	Present	Absent
Metal working present	31	11
Metal working absent	1	58

TABLE 3
Games of Strategy and Mean Size of Local Community

Mean size of	Games of strategy	
local community	Present	Absent
50 or less	1	18
50–59	1	10
100–199	7	10
200–399	5	3
400–1000	3	4
1000+	2	0
Towns up to 50,000	5	1
Towns of more than 50,000	11	0

The societies possessing games of strategy are also distinguished by having jurisdictional levels beyond the local community:

Levels beyond Local Community	0	1	2	3	4
Games of Strategy Absent	66	26	2	0	0
Games of Strategy Present	5	10	14	9	4

Societies possessing games of strategy had high gods. Of the 36 tribes only seven lacked a high god. With 15 the high god was otiose and with four the high god was active. Finally, with 10 the high god was actively supporting human morality.

A more elaborate search of the literature would no doubt reveal other relationships. Freeman and Winch, for example, have arranged societies on a scale of societal complexity (6). With these cultures games of strategy do not tend to appear until the societies have "crimes punished by the government."

In sum, then, games of strategy are associated with high political integration, social stratification, animal husbandry, advanced agriculture, advanced technology (weaving, pottery, metal working, and industrialization), large settlements, more jurisdictional levels beyond the local community, high gods, and crimes punished by government. In associated research it is intended to scale these and other items in terms of their significance for the development of the strategic mode of competition in culture. For the present it is enough to establish the relationship between games of strategy and cultural complexity.

Another aspect of the cultural environment which favors the modeling of the strategic mode of competition is the presence of certain characteristic types of child training. It has already been demonstrated that games of strategy are positively associated with obedience training both cross-culturally and within American culture (15). Games of physical skill are associated with achievement training and games of chance are linked with responsibility training, but neither type of game is correlated with obedience training, which is associated only with games of strategy.

The strategic mode of competition as modeled in games of strategy, then, is associated with societal complexity on the one hand and with obedience training on the other. The conflict-enculturation hypothesis may account for these relationships. One element of this hypothesis is the view that complex societies can function only if a significant number of adults are socialized to life in a complex system. These are adults who have learned when and how to obey and to disobey and, very importantly, when and how to command and not to command. Obedience training involving both reward and punishment is part of the socialization procedures designed to produce such fully participating adults in complex societies. This necessary training produces psychological conflicts which heighten drive and curiosity in this area and these in turn are assuaged by play with model social systems, i.e., games of strategy. In addition the play with the models also teaches the player such appropriate skills as the discernment and foresight he will need if he is to function later as commander, obeyer, or decision-maker.

The above data concerning the cultural setting in which games of strategy occur lead to the following specific applications of the general hypothesis presented in the introduction. Namely, *that if the strategic mode in folk tales occurs in the same general cultural setting as the strategic mode in games, it will be possible to establish relationships between strategic outcomes in tales and: (a) the presence of games of strategy in the same cultures; (b) political complexity; and (c) high obedience training.*

C. METHOD

The investigation of folk tales parallels the study of games, but it is much more exploratory and preliminary in character. It is argued, however, that this is one of the situations in which work with a small sample merits a report in the scientific literature. The tales considered here were taken from a sample of folk tales prepared by Irving Child and his associates (4). Twenty-seven of the societies appearing in the folk-tale sample were also societies in which game scores existed at the time of the research. For each society the sample, except in a few instances, consisted of 12 selected tales purporting to be representative of the variety of tales found in that society. Those tales which had definite outcomes were treated as if they were games or game-like phenomena.

Three judges were used. A tale was rated as having an outcome if it was an account of a contest between two or more sides. This would be the case (a) when the fortunes of the hero are followed through, either to triumph or defeat; and (b) where one individual or a group of individuals induce or restore a state of misfortune besetting a whole group. Some stories recount happenings which may, for example, purport to explain the present state of affairs, and in these cases it is often not possible to say whether it is an outcome or not. The judges were instructed to reject such doubtful tales. Still only one judge excluded a significant proportion of the tales. One judge scored 100 per cent of the tales as having outcomes, a second scored 92 per cent, and the third scored only 56 per cent. This marked difference in the number of tales scored between the third judge and the other two probably accounts in part for the somewhat unreliable results produced. Only the tales agreed upon by two judges were used for this analysis.

While the present paper is concerned solely with strategy, it was a part of a more general inquiry into all games and their analogous outcomes in tales. The other two outcomes (physical skill and chance) are, therefore, referred to here for purposes of contrast, although they are not central to this paper. It should be mentioned,

however, that the findings for the physical-skill and chance outcomes were largely nonsignificant. Important theoretical issues
were raised by this fact, but these are sufficiently complex to merit
separate treatment in a later paper. The first judge used a set of
definitions of the three categories, *physical skill, strategy*, and
chance, first with a set of tales not included in the sample and secondly with the tales in the sample. The following definitions established by the first judge were used by the two other judges:

Physical Skill: any form of motor activity which is instrumental in
furthering the outcome, including killing by physical means, *being
eaten* or *eating, running* in flight or pursuit, skill in *dancing* or *singing*, etc. Physical skill takes primary place where it is the means by
which the outcome is achieved. Even when physical skill immediately
precedes the outcomes, if its importance is merely incidental, it still
takes a secondary or tertiary place.

Strategy can be said to occur whenever someone makes a decision to
act in a certain way; whenever someone engages in devices to deceive
another; whenever he evaluates a situation, weighs up one set of considerations against another; whenever he outwits an opponent as in a
fight where, for example, he tries to gain advantage by an intelligent
use of the physical terrain. Discount instances where the terrain re-
arranges itself for the convenience of the subject in question. Only
instances of someone using his wits to further his ends in the real world
are considered. Magical strategies are not included, but real strategies
which lead the hero to a magical being or fetish are included. In terms
of the analogy between games and folk tales, strategy in a folk tale has
an analogy to moves in a chess game.

Chance: The actual definitions given two of the judges differed from
those worked out and used by the first judge in that an attempt was
made by the latter to distinguish magic from guessing, casting lots,
and pure chance happenings. In the present study, however, all the
ratings that refer to any of the magic or chance categories used by the
two judges have been taken together and they have thus become equivalent to the category employed by the first judge, who considered as
chance any instance of magic, whether it was magical ritual, the gra-
tuitous intervention of a magical or supernatural being, or the intervention of animals as people into the world of people. Also included
in this category were instances of guessing, casting lots, and pure
chance events.

Each tale was judged in terms of the relative extent to which the three outcome categories of physical skill, strategy and chance were involved in it. A weight of three was assigned to the competitive mode which was primary, a weight of two to the secondary mode, and a weight of one to the tertiary mode. When two of the categories seemed to be equal in importance, the same weight was assigned to each. The weights for each category were added together and a score for the total sample of tales for each tribe for each judge was thus obtained. An overall score for each tribe for the three judges taken together was obtained simply by adding these totals together. The rank-order correlation coefficients for the outcome ratings for the three judges are presented in Table A. These show that such judgments can be made with significant if modest reliability, which is probably due to the great variability in the tales themselves. Other investigators using similar methods of analysis with folk tales have encountered very similar results (7).

In addition to scoring folk tales as if they were games, it was decided to score them for the presence of themes expressive of the child-training variables used in the earlier game studies. It was thought that such themes (which are not obvious in games) might be more explicit in tales and, if they were, would add confirmation to the present inquiry. The child-training themes studied included responsibility, obedience, achievement, nurturance, and independence. These themes are described in more detail elsewhere (1). Although two judges made a thematic classification of the tales in these terms, these judges were not found to be consistent to an ac-

TABLE A
Reliability of Three Judges on Outcome Ratings

Outcome	Judges	Rho	P
Physical skill	A & B	.64	.01
	A & C	.52	.01
	B & C	.30	.05
Strategy	A & B	.42	.05
	A & C	.56	.01
	B & C	.52	.01
Chance or magic	A & B	.68	.01
	A & C	.56	.01
	B & C	.32	.05

ceptable degree. The authors incline to the view that this was largely due to the inadequacy of the training of one of the judges. The other judge did yield two findings of relevance to this article which because of their exploratory value are listed here: Tribes with many games of physical skill tend to have folk tales emphasizing independence ($p<.01$). Tribes with games of chance tend to have tales of nurturance ($p<.05$).

In sum: (a) tales with outcomes were selected for study; (b) these outcomes were classified as due to physical skill, strategy or chance; (c) the presence of folk tales with strategic outcomes was related to the presence of games of strategy; (d) folk tales with strategic outcomes were related to an index of political complexity; (e) folk tales with strategic outcomes were related to the child-training ratings on obedience, responsibility, nurturance, self-reliance, achievement and independence which had been used in the earlier study of games; and (f) the tales themselves were subjected to a thematic content analysis for episodes indicative of some of the same child-training themes as were scored in the Barry, Bacon and Child child-training ratings. In this latter study (f) tales were analyzed for their child-training analogues, whereas in the preceding step (e) the tale outcomes were related to separately rated child-training practices.

D. RESULTS

Table 4 demonstrates that societies possessing games of strategy tend to have folk tales in which the outcome is determined or partly determined by strategy.

It is not enough, however, to establish a relationship between folk tales and games. It is necessary to show that the strategic mode in folk tales occurs in the same general cultural setting as the strategic mode in games. Table 5 shows that the strategic mode of competition tends to be modeled in the folk tales of tribes which are politically complex. The strategic mode may appear in the tales of simpler societies, but it is less likely to be prominent in the tales of such groups. Other relationships are directional. If the sample had included a larger number of truly complex societies (e.g., American), the relationship would have been stronger.

Games of strategy are associated with high obedience training in children (12). If the strategic mode modeled in folk tales is psycho-

TABLE 4
Games of Strategy and Strategic Outcomes in Folk Tales

Games of strategy present	Strategy outcome score rank	Games of strategy absent	Strategy outcome score rank
Ashanti	12	Aranda	1
Mbundu	14	Crow	2
Zuni	16	Woleaians	3
Thonga	19.5	Baiga	4
Hopi	22	Pukapuka	5
Chagga	23	Nauru	7
Azande	25	Lepcha	7
Masai	27	Marquesan	7
		Muria	9
$N_1=8$	$R_1=158.5$	Chukchee	10
		Kwakuitl	12
		Koryak	12
		Mandan	15
		Kurtachi	17
		Comanche	18
		Navaho	19.5
		Ojibwa	21
		Ainu	24
		Kaska	26
		$N_2=19$	$R_2=219.5$

$U=29.5$
$P<.01$ (one-tailed).

logically similar to the strategic mode modeled in games, the same relationship should hold. Table 6 shows that there is a relationship between strategic outcomes in tales and reward for obedience. There were also directional relationships between strategic outcomes and anxiety about "nonperformance of obedience" (rho= .24, $p<.05$). These are the same two child-training relationships previously associated with games of strategy. It is this high emphasis on *both* reward and anxiety (punishment) that forms the cross-cultural empirical basis for the theoretical stress on conflict in the present series of studies.

In the case of folk tales there is the possibility of an internal check. If the strategic mode of competition bears a relationship to obedience training, there should be an emphasis on obedience

TABLE 5
Levels of Political Integration and Strategic Outcomes in Folk Tales

Political integration	Strategic outcome low (24 or less)			Strategic outcome high (25 or more)
Absent	Arapesh (16)	1	1	Kaska (40)
Autonomous local communities	Tenetahara (21) Zuni (21) Koryak (20) W. Apache (18) Paiute (18) Pukapuka (16) Nauru (15) Jicarilla (14) Chukchee (14) Aranda (10) Baiga (10) Chenchu (9) Crow (9)	13	5	Kurtachi (48) Chiracahua (38) Navaho (29) Hopi (27) Ojibwa (26)
Peace groups	Klamath (24) Teton Dakota (16)	2	1	Masai (47) Comanche (34)
Dependent societies	Lepcha (17)	1	1	Ainu (44)
Minimal states	Marquesan (19) Cheyenne (12) Crow (9)	3	3	Mandan (43) Arapaho (42) Chagga (36) Winnebago (31)
Little states		0	3	Azande (41) Mbundu (37) Thonga (25)
States		0	3	Yoruba (39) Zulu (37) Ashanti (36)

themes in the tales themselves. This relationship did appear at least directionally (see Table 7).

It should be noted that the independent relationship between cultural complexity and obedience training is either directional or confirmed in this study, and has been observed also in other independent investigations. Barry, Child and Bacon (3) state:

Pressure toward obedience and responsibility should tend to make children into the obedient and responsible adults who can best ensure the continuing welfare of a society with a high accumulation economy, whose food supply must be protected and developed gradually through the year.

The same paper by Barry, et al., shows a relationship between

TABLE 6
Strategic Outcomes in Tales and Rewards for Obedience

Tribes in order of strategy outcomes		Reward for obedience score	
		(Girls)	(Boys)
Masai	82	12	12
Kaska	72	8	8
Azande	70	13	13
Ainu	69	14	13
Chagga	67	14	13
Hopi	56	13	13
Ojibwa	53	11	10
Thonga	51	10	10
Navaho	51	10	10
Comanche	50	—	5
Kurtachi	48	6	6
Zuni	47	11	9
Mandan	43	—	10
Mbundu	37	11	11
Ashanti	36	13	12
Kwakuitl	36	10	10
Chukchee	35	12	12
Muria	34	11	10
Marquesan	33	4	4
Lepcha	33	9	9
Nauru	33	12	12
Pukapuka	32	9	9
Woleaians	28	11	9
Crow	25	10	10
Aranda	12	9	8
		$N=23$	$N=25$
		rho$=.49$	rho$=.41$
		$p<.05$	$p<.05$

obedience training and animal husbandry and agriculture. The greater the reliance on domestication, the higher the obedience. Obedience training also figures in a combined score which is positively associated with such variables indicative of complexity as size of settlement, degree of political integration, and complexity of social stratification (3).

In sum, the constellation of variables required by the conflict-enculturation hypothesis is virtually complete, though all the relationships found are not equally convincing.

The principal findings of this inquiry were: (*a*) the strategic mode of competition is modeled in both games and folk tales in a number of cultures; (*b*) where the strategic mode of competition is modeled in one medium (i.e., games) it is likely to be modeled in the other (i.e., folk tales); and (*c*) the strategic mode of competition as modeled in games and in folk tales is associated with both obedience training and cultural complexity. It was also noted that games of strategy were associated with obedience themes in tales and that obedience training is associated with cultural complexity.

E. Discussion

The constellation of relationships which are either significant or directional and which have been explored in the previous articles and in the present paper can be described simply. Within the full

TABLE 7

Obedience Themes in Folk Tales and Games of Strategy

Games of strategy Present	Obedience theme score rank	Games of strategy Absent	Obedience theme score rank
Mbundu	7.5	Ainu	2.5
Azande	12	Navaho	2.5
Chagga	17	Lepcha	2.5
Hopi	17	Kurtachi	2.5
Masai	21	Kaska	5
Thonga	21	Chukchee	7.5
Zuni	23	Woleaians	7.5
Ashanti	27	Muria	12
$N_1 = 8$	$R_1 = 145.5$	Ojibwa	12
		Pukapuka	12
		Comanche	12
		Marquesan	12
		Baiga	17
		Koryak	17
		Mandan	17
		Kwakiutl	21
		Nauru	24
		Aranda	25
		Crow	26
		$N_2 = 19$	$R_2 = 237.5$

$U = 32.5.$

scale realm of actual competition, cultural complexity and obedi- ence training are associated. Within the model realm, games of strategy and strategy in tales are associated and games of strategy are also associated with obedience themes in tales. Between the model realm and the full-scale realm, games of strategy and strat- egy in tales are associated with cultural complexity and obedience training. In sum these relationships constitute a consistent and meaningful configuration in terms of the conflict-enculturation hypothesis.

It has been argued that obedience training is necessary if adults are to function in a complex social system. This training produces conflict, which leads to heightened curiosity and drive, which in turn favor involvement in strategic models. Involvement in the models, in turn, assuages the conflict-induced drive and provides supplementary training which further enables game participants to meet the demands of a complex social system.

It is difficult to say much about the enculturation side of the hypothesis until more is learned about the psychology of strategic competence in individuals. While there is little direct research on the development of strategic abilities in children, some evidence suggests that such abilities appear relatively late. Although chil- dren play games of strategy such as checkers and tic-tac-toe in a routine fashion in early childhood, ongoing research suggests that they do not show the ability to execute deceptive strategies until about the age of 10 or 11 years or later. Piaget has contended that children achieve the theoretical capacity that strategic thinking implies at these ages and that children demonstrate this ability in the way they recodify their own games systematically and vari- ously in pursuit of more exciting play (9). Perhaps it can be said that individuals must reach certain advanced levels of social and intellectual maturation before they can appreciate the strategic mode in models.

It is probable, too, that cultures must reach an advanced level of organization before strategy in models becomes salient. If historical depth can be inferred from cross-cultural distributions and as- sociations, then games of strategy are most likely a relatively late invention appearing no earlier than Steward's period, "Formative Era of Basic Technologies and Folk Culture," or Coon's Level III, and no later than Steward's "Era of Regional Development and

Florescence" (13) or Coon's Level IV (5). The specific association between games of strategy and the presence of metal working is informative. This is not to say that there is a direct relationship in a causal sense, but rather that a culture which has metal working is almost certain to be sufficiently complex to warrant a game of strategy. The highest development of games of strategy appears at much later periods. Folk tales, however, are less specialized and the strategic elements in them may have appeared at an earlier cultural period. Tales may have had their strategic elements derived from the expression of the minor mode of strategic competition, as in games of physical skill and strategy which are linked with achievement rather than with the major mode—the games of strategy— obedience training—cultural-complexity association. Well-developed tales of strategy with clear outcomes are probably no earlier in appearance than games of strategy.

These various speculations are based on the underlying assumption that child-training practices themselves and their associated models are cultural adaptations and inventions with their own culture histories. If we can conclude with a final speculation, the probable order of the appearance of the cultural inventories of child-training procedures and models is as follows: (a) nurturance and self reliance with no games; (b) independence, responsibility, and achievement with games of physical skill and games of chance; and (c) obedience with games of strategy. The full culture history of models such as games and their associated conflicts, however, must be studied much more systematically than it has been to this time if the above order is to be regarded as being anything more than speculative. Perhaps the time will come when types of tales can be arranged in analogous fashion.

Finally, it would appear that the strategic mode of competition is modeled more sharply in games than in tales and that, in general, game associations are stronger than tale associations. The relative weakness of these associations in tales may be a result of work with a limited sample, unsatisfactory content analysis, and poorly translated tales, but it must be noted that tales, unlike games, are not confined to the modeling of competition and that in general they constitute a more flexible medium than games. In an earlier article, games were labeled *behavioral models* and tales were called *vicarious models* (12). In this frame of reference, tales appear to be more general and less specialized, while games of strategy appear to model the strategic mode of competition in particularly powerful and direct ways. Thus, the strategic mode is not modeled with equal strength in games and tales; games are the favored medium. The present discovery of linkages between both tales and games, and other cultural variables, however, is a first step in the more general study of the nature of model involvement in human culture.

F. Summary

Earlier cross-cultural work with games of strategy has demonstrated linkages with obedience training and cultural complexity. These linkages were supported by further cross-cultural analysis in the present investigation. In addition, it was hypothesized that folk tales with strategic outcomes would be found in the same cultural setting as games of strategy. This hypothesis was confirmed. The results were explained in terms of a conflict-enculturation hypothesis, which seeks to locate the origins of model involvement in psychological conflicts induced by child training, but explains the culturally adaptive value of these models (in this case games and tales), in terms of the learning which arises out of this same model involvement.

REFERENCES

1. Bacon, M., Barry, H., III, and Child, I. L. Raters' instructions for analysis of socialization practices with respect to dependence and independence. Mimeographed paper, Yale University, New Haven, 1952.
2. ————. Cross-cultural ratings of certain socialization practices. Mimeographed paper, Yale University, New Haven, 1955.
3. Barry, H., Child, I. L., and Bacon, M. K. Relations of child training to subsistence economy. *Amer. Anthropologist*, 1959, 61, 51–63.
4. Child, I. L., Storn, T., and Veroff, J. Achievement themes in folk tales related to socialization practice. In J. W. Atkinson (Ed.), *Motives in Fantasy, Action, and Society*. Princeton, N.J.: Van Nostrand, 1958.
5. Coon, C. S. A Reader in General Anthropology. New York: Henry Holt, 1948. Pp. 611–614.
6. Freeman, L. C., and Winch, R. F. Societal complexity: An empirical test of a typology of societies. *Amer. J. Sociol.*, 1957, 62, 461–466.
7. McClelland, D. C., and Friedman, G. A. A cross-cultural study of the relationship between child-training practices and achievement motivation appearing in folk tales. In Swanson, Newcomb, and Hartley (Eds.), *Readings in Social Psychology*. New York: Holt, 1952. Pp. 243–249.
8. Murdock, G. P. Ethnographic atlas. *Ethnology*, 1962, 1, 113–134, 265–286, 387–403, 533–545; 1963, 2, 109–133.
9. Piaget, J. The Moral Judgment of the Child. Glencoe: Free Press, 1948.
10. ————. The Growth of Logical Thinking. New York: Basic Books, 1958.
11. Roberts, J. M., Arth, M. J., and Bush, R. R. Games in culture. *Amer. Anthropologist*, 1959, 61, 597–605.
12. Roberts, J. M., and Sutton-Smith, B. Child training and game involvement. *Ethnology*, 1962, 1, 166–185.
13. Steward, J. H. Theory of Culture Change. Urbana: Univ. Illinois Press, 1955.
14. Sutton-Smith, B., and Roberts, J. M. Rubrics of competitive behavior. *J. Genet. Psychol.*, 1964, 105, 13–37.
15. Sutton-Smith, B., Roberts, J. M., and Kozelka, R. M. Game involvement in adults. *J. Soc. Psychol.*, 1963, 60, 15–30.

Department of Anthropology
Cornell University
Ithaca, New York

7. Studies of an Elementary Game of Strategy

BRIAN SUTTON-SMITH AND JOHN M. ROBERTS
with the collaboration of
Robert M. Kozelka, Vaughn J. Crandall, Donald M. Broverman,
Abraham Blum, and Edward L. Klaiber

Acknowledgments 360

I. Introduction 361

II. An elementary game of strategy: Tick Tack Toe . . 362

III. Description of Tick Tack Toe Test 365

IV. Study 1: Normative data 370

V. Study 2: Achievement correlates 379

VI. Study 3: Cognitive and physical correlates . . . 383

VII. Discussion 388

VIII. Summary 397

References 398

SOURCE: Reprinted from *Genetic Psychology Monograph*, no. 75 (1967), pp. 3–42, with permission of the co-author, John M. Roberts, the collaborators, and The Journal Press. Copyright, 1967, by The Journal Press.

ACKNOWLEDGMENTS

Although the formulation of the research problems and the interpretations in the present monograph are the responsibility of the principal authors, the studies included would not have been possible without the willing support of the other collaborators. For example, Robert Kozelka was chiefly responsible for the mathematical derivation of the present test of strategic competence. Vaughn Crandall, Donald Broverman, and his collaborators, Abraham Blum and Edward Klaiber, showed an open-minded and exploratory willingness to test out the device in their own extensive research projects, the first concerned with achievement in children and the second with cognitive styles. Dr. Crandall's death prior to final formulation of the results was a great loss to the project and to us. We owe a special debt of gratitude to Virginia Crandall for her many subsequent contributions.

The work of John M. Roberts, Brian Sutton-Smith, and Robert M. Kozelka was supported by PHS Research Grant MH-04161-03. John M. Roberts and Brian Sutton-Smith received further support from PHS Research Grant MH-08161-01. Brian Sutton-Smith and Vaughn Crandall received support from PHS Research Grant M-2238. Brian Sutton-Smith, Donald Broverman, Edward Klaiber, and Abraham Blum received support from PHS Research Grant M-8996. Abraham Blum was a Special Research Fellow, NIMH.

The investigators are thankful to Harlan Lehtooma, Principal of Kenwood School, Bowling Green, Ohio; and to the teachers and children for their cooperation in this project. Gratitude is also expressed to the principal, teachers, and children of South School and the Junior High School, Bowling Green; and to the principal, teachers, and children of Columbus Park School, Worcester, Massachusetts. This research was also supported by released time for B. Sutton-Smith by Bowling Green State University, 1962–1963.

Brian Sutton-Smith
John M. Roberts

Department of Psychology
Bowling Green State University
Bowling Green, Ohio 43402

Department of Anthropology
Cornell University
Ithaca, New York 14850

I. Introduction

The present study owes its immediate origin to the discovery in cross-cultural research that games are systematically related to other cultural variables (25, 26, 29).* It is maintained in that earlier research that games have a modeling and enculturative role in human culture, and that this role varies with the type of game being considered. Thus it is argued that games of physical skill train in competitiveness, games of chance train in divination, and games of strategy train in warlike command. The present series of studies is concerned to test the hypothesis, derived from this earlier research, that competence in a particular game should therefore be associated with distinctive psychological characteristics. It is contended that if games do in fact model various success styles (35, 38, 39), then those who are competent at these games should also reveal their type of success orientation in other forms of behavior. The particular types of games that are the subject-matter of this inquiry are games of strategy. The particular game is Tick Tack Toe.

While it is the logic of this argument that the game is a representation of a more generalized success style, it is necessary in this investigation to reverse the direction of the implied relationship. The study thus commences with the defined game skills and then proceeds, as it were backwards, to explore their psychological correlates. That is, the study deals directly with skill at an elementary game of strategy as an indirect means of inferring an hypothesized and underlying *elementary strategic competence*.

The hypothesis that skill at the game of strategy represents an underlying and generalized strategic competence should receive support if the systematic relationships established between competence at a game of strategy and the other social, physical, and cognitive variables studied have sufficient logical coherence to suggest the existence of a generalized strategic competence underlying the particular game successes. Preliminary support for this position has already been gained in an earlier study in which it was

* Numbers in parentheses refer to sources listed at the end of this article.

demonstrated, using a sociometric device, that boys nominated by their peers as strategists (those whose leadership is due to their good ideas) do indeed show a greater preference for games of strategy than do boys nominated by their peers as potents (those whose leadership is due to force or strength). In that study such strategists were shown to be of high intellectual and social status; and also to demonstrate what is a rather subtle social ability for preadolescent boys, the ability to be popular, while not preferring the stereotypically popular games, and the ability to be seen as a "good sport," while not being perceived as good at sports (35). This earlier study gives some confidence that strategic competence is indeed a general factor in human personality and that, while it may be expressed most purely in strategic games, it is by no means restricted to them. While the foregoing results bias us toward the view that strategic competence will involve leadership through ideas and subtlety in social relationships, and game theory predisposes us to the view that such a competence should involve rational decision-making processes, the approach that follows is, in the main, inductive.

II. An Elementary Game of Strategy: Tick Tack Toe

The game chosen for this preliminary inquiry into success at a particular game of strategy, and the existence of a generalized strategic competence, was the game of Tick Tack Toe, or Noughts and Crosses. Although most adults, if not children, regard this game as being trivial and uninteresting, the game of Tick Tack Toe nevertheless presents intricate scientific problems and provides a point of entry into the consideration of strategic competences in general.

At the outset it should be stated that, while Tick Tack Toe is unquestionably simple, it is, none the less, a true game. It is a recreational activity characterized by (a) organized play, (b) competition, (c) two or more sides, (d) criteria for determining the winner, and (e) agreed-upon rules (25). More specifically, Tick Tack Toe is a game of strategy in contrast with games of physical skill or chance. Within games of strategy—a class that includes checkers, chess, bridge, poker, and many other games—Tick Tack Toe falls into the category of games of pure strategy, which lack the attribute of chance.

The specific reasons for the present choice of the game are as follows. First, Tick Tack Toe is a systemic pattern and as such it is particularly suitable for cross-cultural research. As a nonverbal interaction device, the game provides opportunity for testing cross-cultural theses about the distribution and associations of strategic competence in human culture. Second, it is the most widely known game of strategy among children and adults within American culture. Of all the common games of strategy, this is chronologically the first to be played with competence and certainty by young children. Interest and involvement in the game diminish in later years as the players exhaust its apparently trivial nature, but some knowledge of Tick Tack Toe tends to persist throughout life. Table 1 indicates the strategy items ranked in order of preference (out of the first 30 preferences) by 2700 Ohio children in grades 3 through 8 in response to a play inventory. Tick Tack Toe does not achieve sufficient mention in the early grades to be ranked in the first 30, although it ranks in the first 30 items from grade 3 onwards, when an overall total of 70 per cent of the children indicate that they play it. Table 1 also includes, for comparative purposes, the one other item of pure strategy that appears in the first 30 rankings (checkers) and the two items involving both chance and strategy, cards and Monopoly.

Tick Tack Toe has been described by a number of authors, the most authoritative of whom is Murray (23). He states:

Noughts and Crosses. . . . the players who make the board afresh for each game, form it by drawing two parallel lines vertically and horizontally across them. A children's game played in Britain, some parts of Europe, and by European settlers in America. The board is drawn on paper, slates, or on the ground. Two players. The game is one of entry only and the men have no power of movement; their positions on the board are marked by one player with an "O" and by the other with an "X" in Britain and an "I" in Sweden. The aim is to make a row in any direction. When a player succeeds in making a row, he draws a line through the three men, exclaiming in Britain, "Tit Tat Toe, Here I go, Three jolly butcher boys all in a row." . . . In England, drawn games are scored to Old Nick or Old Tom. Nothing is known as to the an-

TABLE 1
Ranked Preferences of Children for Games of Strategy

Grade and sex		Number	Tick Tack Toe	Checkers	Cards	Monopoly
Kindergarten	boys	130				
	girls	142				
1	boys	295				
	girls	276				
2	boys	167				
	girls	175				
3	boys	153	13th			
	girls	137	15th			
4	boys	252	14th	12th		
	girls	260	19th	10th		
5	boys	278	18th	19th		
	girls	245	19th	13th		
6	boys	227	23rd	9th	16th	
	girls	286	8th	4th		20th
7	boys	227		10th	14th	
	girls	223	27th	5th	13th	22nd
8	boys	170		8th	11th	
	girls	168	15th	5th	12th	16th

tiquity of this game. It was more frequently played in the days when slates were used in schools than at present day (23, p. 40).

The descriptions of other authors are in substantial agreement (3, p. 91; 6, pp. 229–230; 15, pp. 420–421; 32, p. 110). The game may be of relatively recent origin but falls into an ancient and widely distributed class of games of strategy, described by Murray as the "three in a row" category of games, or games of "alignment and configuration," or games of position. It is a reasonable guess that the game is derived from Three Men's Morris (15, p. 418), a game of great antiquity and wide distribution, and is a child's adaptation to the fact that permanent alignment boards could not exist in the nineteenth-century schoolroom under the master's

vigilant eye, but that transitory forms of the game involving only
a slate or a paper and pencil could.[1]

III. Description of the Tick Tack Toe Test

The practical problem facing the investigators was that of developing a quantitative device for the quick determination of competence
at playing Tick Tack Toe.[2] The device developed is illustrated down
the left-hand side of Figure 1. The solutions with probabilities are
indicated on the right-hand side of the figure.

In each game the subject is to make one move and that is all.
The six separate parts have no connection with each other. It was
found necessary to emphasize this latter point in the instructions,
as pilot studies indicated that there was a tendency on the part of
subjects to think of the parts as a connected series. Administration
of the instrument takes about five minutes. With few exceptions all
children already know how to play the game itself. The instructions
are as follows:

These are six parts of six games of Tick Tack Toe. In each game you
make only one move. You always use an X as your mark. Look at the
first diagram. There is no mark on it. You make the first move. Put
your X wherever you think it should go. Put it where you would put
it if you were playing this game against someone else. Now look at the
second diagram. The other person has already made one move. Now
it is your turn to make a move. Put the X wherever you think it should
go. (Repeat instructions for third diagram.) Now look at the fourth
diagram. You have both had one move. Now it is your move again.
(Repeat for fifth diagram.) In the last diagram you have already each
had two moves. Put in your X wherever you think it should go.

The six sample parts of the game of Tick Tack Toe illustrated in
Figure 1 were picked to illustrate standard situations in the game.

[1] Peter Opie, author of *The Language and Lore of Schoolchildren*, Oxford
University Press, 1960, concurs in this interpretation (personal communication).
[2] This section was written in collaboration with Robert M. Kozelka, Williams
College, Williamstown, Massachusetts.

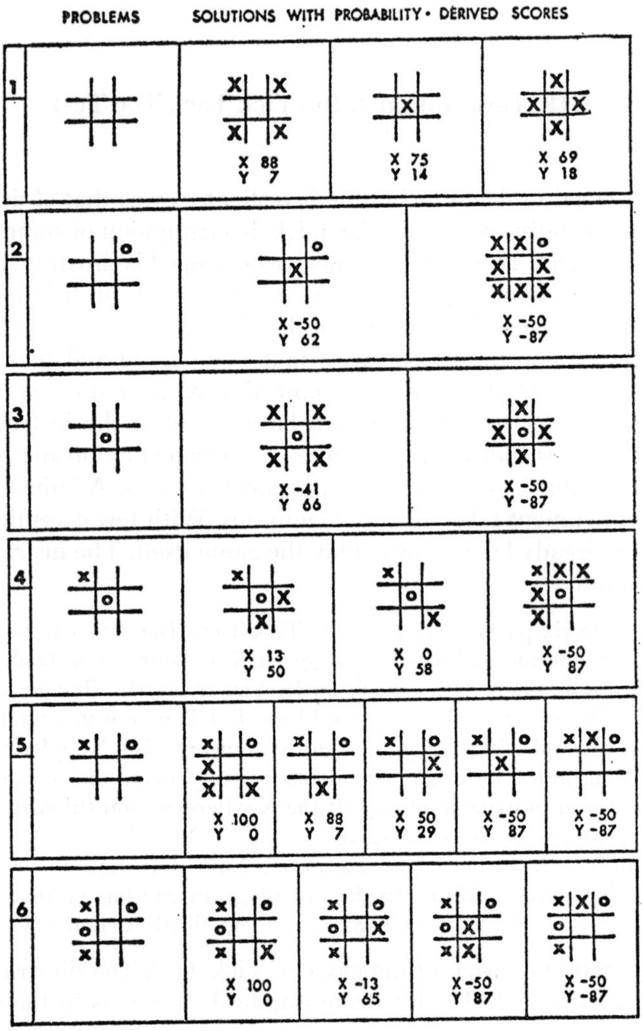

Figure 1: Tick Tack Toe: Problems and Solutions with Probability-Derived Scores

Items one to four represent situations in which the respondent indicates by his opening moves the type of game that he is likely to play, whether it be to win, to draw, or to lose. Items five and six are rather like chess problems in which the player must cross to win in a minimum number of moves. These assumptions about moves, of course, assume familiarity with the game, and do not follow if the player does not understand the game as a whole.

Scores are attached to item responses according to the probabilities of that response leading to a win, to a draw, or to a loss. This probability model depends upon the following two assumptions: (a) that the nought player will play at random except that (b) any player will force a win if he can (after the first response) or will block two in a row of the opposing mark. It may appear that these assumptions are contradictory in the sense that an opposing player who could recognize situations leading to a forced win would *never* play at random. However, a totally intelligent player would result in all items having Pr (draw) $= 1$. On the other hand, total randomness would make a response like that shown in Figure 2(A) have a winning score when it is clear that such a response is not as satisfactory from the point of view of the respondent as the response shown in Figure 2(B). Both of these responses are possible alternatives to diagram 4 in Figure 1. From a rational point of view the game is trivial, so that to get discrimination of responses certain semiintelligent behavior must be postulated. The above assumptions take into account such semiintelligence. The scoring of the 720 distinct possibilities resulting from possible responses to the six items of the test is indicated in Figure 1.

Since the three probabilities of each response (for a win, a draw, or a loss) must sum to unity, only two scores, the X and Y scores appearing on Figure 1, are necessary for each item. In order to make a graphical representation on axes, the probabilities were

 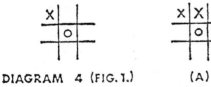

DIAGRAM 4 (FIG. 1.)   (A)   (B)

Figure 2: Responses

transformed by using the usual formulas for the rotation of axes. Since only two probabilities are independent, a two dimensional space is sufficient. Assume that Pr (win) is plotted along the horizontal axis. Then it is reasonable to represent Pr (draw) and Pr (lose) scores along axes inclining respectively 120° and 240° from this axis, to divide the space into equal parts. Then if Pr (win) = x' and a y'-axis is taken in the usual fashion perpendicular to the x'-axis with a positive $y' = 90°$ around from positive x', the Pr (draw) and Pr (lose) scores can be broken up into x' and y' components. This gives a negative win (x') component to a draw strategy, and a negative x' *and* y' component to a losing response. The transformation formulas are

$$x' = 1\text{-}\{3 \; [Pr \; (\text{draw}) + Pr \; (\text{lose}) \;] \; /2\};$$
$$y' = \sqrt{3} \; [Pr \; (\text{draw}) - Pr \; (\text{lose}) \;] \; /2.$$

In plotting and analyzing, the sum of the x' and y' scores over the six items is used. From here on, then, we write

$$x = \Sigma 100x' \qquad\qquad y = \Sigma 100y'$$

over the six items. Due to the finite nature of the game, not all points in the (x, y)-space are possible. In fact a complete analysis of the 720 distinct possibilities resulting from the possible responses to the six items shows that the scores divide into five distinct stripes, each easily distinguished from the others (see Figure 3). For convenience, the possible stripes can be taken as given by the equation

$$x + 2y = k, \; k = \pm 600, \pm 300, 0.$$

Not every point falls exactly on one of these lines, but if the value $x + 2y$ is rounded to the nearest of the above five values, the proper stripe will result. Sometimes it will be convenient to number the stripes; this will be done by starting from the top. Thus a player in the first stripe had a score $x + 2y$ closer to 600 than to 300. and so on. Figure 3 indicates schematically the position and breadth of the five stripes, while the number in each section indicates the possible number of responses. The divisions at $x = 0, \pm 100$ are arbitrary.

To illustrate how the scores are computed, consider problem 6 in Figure 1, which has been renumbered for reference purposes in Figure 4. In this diagram another cross is called for. Thus (a) if the response is in cell 2, the nought can force a win by playing in cell 9, so we have Pr (lose|2) = 1. (b) If the response is in cell 4, a nought following in cells 5, 6, or 7 will result in a draw according to the assumption that a two-in-a-row will always be blocked by

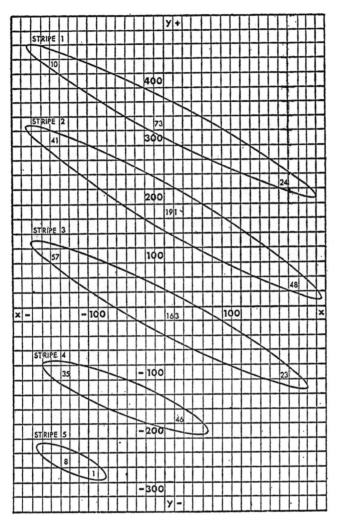

Figure 3: Distribution of Possible Test Scores

the opponent. A nought following in cell 2, however, allows the cross to play in cell 9 and force a win. By the randomness assumption, since the nought cannot force a win immediately after the cross response, we get Pr (win|4) $= \frac{1}{4}$, Pr (draw|4) $= \frac{3}{4}$. (c) If

Figure 4: Problem 6

the response is in cell 5, a win can be forced, so Pr (win|5) $= 1$.
(d) If the response is in 6 or 9, Pr (draw|6) $= Pr$ (draw|9) $= 1$.

An example of the x' and y' scores resulting from the rotation equations would be

$$x' = 1 - \{3[Pr(\text{draw}|4) + Pr(\text{lose}|4)]/2\} = -\tfrac{1}{8} \doteq -0.13;$$
$$y' = \sqrt{3}[Pr(\text{draw}|4) - Pr(\text{lose}|4)]\tfrac{1}{2} = \sqrt{3}(\tfrac{3}{8}) \doteq 0.65.$$

All x' and y' scores were rounded to two decimals. Computations for item six are necessarily easier than the others, since there are few possibilities, but the procedure for each item is the same as in the illustration.

It is clear that the two assumptions made up about behavior do allow us to discriminate among responses in a useful way. One may care to argue that this simple probability model does not fit with the way children actually play the game, but the analysis clearly shows that the game can be played in different ways. The model is not claimed to be normative, in the sense of game theory, but only such as to allow distinctions to be drawn among the three types of behavior: play to win, play to draw, and play to lose. It remains to be seen whether play of these sorts on Tick Tack Toe does indeed model similar attitudes toward winning, losing, and drawing in larger life.

IV. Study I: Normative Data

A. Introduction

Normative data on test performance were sought in order to discover the particular age periods at which examination of strategic competence through this game might be appropriate. The earlier preference data led to the expectation that this would be between the third and the sixth grades. In this preliminary inquiry, intelligence test, achievement test, and sociometric data were also available for some of the pupils, and these data were explored to discover if there were any relationships between Tick Tack Toe Test scores and the social and cognitive competences assessed by these other measures.

The test described in the previous section was administered to 582 subjects ranging from grade 1 pupils to college sophomores and distributed by grade and sex as indicated in Table 4. All subjects were drawn from two elementary schools (Kenwood and South), the junior-high school, and the university in the midwestern town of Bowling Green (population 12,000). Children from grades 1 to 3 were from one of the elementary schools, children from grades 4 to 6 were from the two elementary schools. The sample was extended at this latter age level owing to the prediction that this would be the critical age period at which Tick Tack Toe competence would make a difference in terms of other skills. The four junior-high school classes were chosen at random (classes were not homogeneously grouped by intelligence) from the eight available at each level, two from the seventh grade, and two from the eighth grade. The university sophomores were from two sophomore psychology classes at Bowling Green State University. Their average age was 19, with 95 per cent of all subjects ranging in age from 18 to 20 years inclusive.

B. Additional Measures

The results from group intelligence test data (the California Test of Mental Maturity) and group achievement test data (Iowa Test of Basic Skills) were available for all children in grades 4 through 8. In addition, scores from a sociometric device for testing success styles were available for the fifth- and sixth-grade children at one of the elementary schools (35).

C. Reliability of the Tick Tack Toe Test

Although the investigators were not primarily interested in the use of the test for individual diagnosis, its reliability was checked as follows: One of the classes at each of the second-, fourth-, and sixth-grade levels was readministered the test one week after the original administration. In addition, a second reliability test was taken three months after the first testing with three other classes (not used for the first check) from the fourth-, fifth-, and sixth-grade levels. The results that are derived from rank correlations between scores on each of the X and Y axes are presented in Table 2. The rank correlation was used owing to the lack of normality of distribution along these axes. Boys' and girls' scores were combined. The results indicate that adequate reliability on this measure is approached only at the sixth-grade level in the groups tested and only on the X axis. The test is, therefore, not useful in this form for individual assessment. In subsequent usage the test has been administered twice with more promising results (see next sections).

D. Validity

As the investigators were also interested in measuring real competence in playing Tick Tack Toe with this test, it was thought desirable to check whether the children who scored highly on the Tick Tack Toe Test were actually those who could win games of Tick Tack Toe against their opponents. Results for a total group of 20 boys and 30 girls in the sixth grade playing games against each other *and* taking the test were significant only for the boys and only for X scores. Relationships between winning games and X scores for boys were rho $= .549$ $(p < .05)$.

E. Results
1. *Shifts between Stripes*

Table 3 indicates the number of children at each age level that are to be found on the X positive and X negative segments of each

TABLE 2
Rank Order Reliability Measures on Tick Tack Toe Test

Grade	Number	One week period		Three month period	
		X axis	Y axis	X axis	Y axis
2	25	.387	.524		
4	24	.489	.345		
6	31	.712	.570		
4	25			.341	.317
5	38			.529	.553
6	25			.815	.445

TABLE 3
Distribution by Grade and Sex on Stripes

Grade and sex		X	1	2	Stripes 3	4	5	N
1	boys	X−	6	7	9	1	2	26
		X+	0	1	0	0	0	
	girls	X−	2	14	10	2	0	29
		X+	0	0	1	0	0	
2	boys	X−	2	9	5	0	0	24
		X+	1	5	1	1	0	
	girls	X−	4	16	3	0	0	31
		X+	0	4	3	0	0	
3	boys	X−	4	6	7	0	0	21
		X+	2	1	1	0	0	
	girls	X−	2	17	5	0	0	29
		X+	0	2	3	0	0	
4	boys	X−	10	14	7	1	0	44
		X+	1	8	3	0	0	
	girls	X−	6	15	8	0	0	35
		X+	1	4	1	0	0	
5	boys	X−	4	15	5	0	0	33
		X+	3	5	1	0	0	
	girls	X−	10	12	6	0	0	36
		X+	1	6	1	0	0	
6	boys	X−	12	24	2	0	0	56
		X+	2	16	1	0	0	
	girls	X−	10	4	5	0	0	29
		X+	0	9	1	0	0	
7	boys	X−	8	7	2	0	0	26
		X+	1	7	1	0	0	
	girls	X−	11	9	0	0	0	31
		X+	3	7	1	0	0	
8	boys	X−	7	3	1	0	0	25
		X+	3	10	1	0	0	
	girls	X−	4	5	2	0	0	27
		X+	7	8	1	0	0	
College	males	X−	6	0	1	0	0	38
		X+	15	13	2	1	0	
	females	X−	10	3	0	0	0	41
		X+	14	14	0	0	0	

of the stripes illustrated in Figure 3. Examination of these frequencies indicates that there is clear evidence of a shift in scoring positions from the first grade through the eighth grade. The change is even more marked for the college group, but as the latter is a less representative group it will not be considered further in the analysis. The graphical movement from the earlier grades onwards is toward the upper stripes and the X positive area of those stripes. For example, for data involving only stripes one, two, and three, a contingency table test for independence of grade and stripe number produces a chi square significant at $p < .001$. The direction of dependence is away from the third stripe and the bulk of the shift is in grades 7 and 8 and is into stripe one. Stripes four and five have too few frequencies to indicate anything. The same shift across stripes one, two, and three is significant at $p < .01$ for grades 1 to 6 only, but not for grades 1 to 5, suggesting once again that grade 6 is a critical age for performance on this test.

2. *Shifts along Stripes*

Along a given stripe, a right-hand tendency $(X+)$ should indicate a greater strategy potential than does a left-hand $(X-)$ tendency. Each of the first three stripes was tested for independence of $\pm X$ with grade. Because of the small values for stripe one, the comparison was made between grades 1 to 4, and 5 to 8. The resulting chi square was significant at $p < .02$. For stripe two, grades 1 to 3 were combined in order to accumulate $X+$ values and compared with grades 4 to 8. The resulting chi square was significant at $p < .001$. For both stripes one and two, the shift was from $X-$ to $X+$. There was no significant shift on stripe three when grades 1 to 4, and 5 to 8 were compared, but this may have been due to the small number of cases especially in the upper grades.

Regardless of stripe, $X+$ is more desirable in terms of winning potential than is $X-$. Table 4 shows the distribution of X scores by grade. The scores tend to cluster, and the groupings in Table 4 show these observed clusters. This clustering is not in proportion to the hypothetical distribution of all possible results stated in Figure 3, but no particular meaning has been adduced from the observed clustering, although it has served as a convenient way to group the data. Since rather small numbers occur in some of the groups for a given grade, further groupings can be considered on

TABLE 4
Distribution by Grade Along X Axis

Grade and sex		<-160	$-40/-160$	$0/-40$	$0/120$	$120/190$	>190	N
1	boys	7	9	9	1	0	0	26
	girls	5	12	11	0	0	1	29
2	boys	2	7	7	6	2	0	24
	girls	7	9	8	4	2	1	31
3	boys	6	3	8	2	2	0	21
	girls	9	4	11	4	1	0	29
4	boys	12	5	15	7	3	2	44
	girls	10	7	12	2	3	1	35
5	boys	9	2	13	2	7	0	33
	girls	12	5	11	4	4	0	36
6	boys	22	9	7	4	9	6	57
	girls	4	2	13	2	8	0	29
7	boys	8	0	7	2	7	2	26
	girls	7	5	8	1	7	3	31
8	boys	3	2	6	1	6	7	25
	girls	4	0	7	1	12	3	31
College	males	4	1	2	4	17	10	38
	females	2	1	10	3	19	6	41

the total X axis. One such grouping is to test $X+$ against $X-$ regardless of particular location on the stripe. In this comparison, using the eight grades again, grades 1 and 2 are combined in order to get sufficient representation in the X positive area. The results for boys are significant at $p < .02$, while for girls they are significant at $p < .001$. Apparently girls make slightly more dramatic changes from earlier to later grades than do the boys, but no significant differences for the sexes within grades were found. Another comparison made possible by Table 4 is to group the two columns of extreme $X+$ scores, the two columns of extreme $X-$ scores, and the middle two columns. Independence of these groupings from grade can then be tested for each sex. The results were significant at $p < .02$ for boys but nonsignificant for girls. That is, there is a tendency for boys' scores to be heterogeneous and for girls' scores to be homogeneous; the boys are overrepresented at the extremes and the girls in the middle of the distribution along the X axis. A similar comparison between sexes within a given grade showed no significant results except in grade 6, where results of the same character led to a difference between the sexes significant at $p < .001$.

3. *Responses to Tick Tack Toe Test Diagrams*

It is possible to examine the frequency with which the children place their X's in each of the cells in the Tick Tack Toe diagrams by grade and by sex. When such an examination is carried out these frequencies confirm what has been mentioned above, that a shift to more strategic responses becomes most marked at about the sixth grade. In the earlier grades, responses to some of the problems tend to cluster irrelevantly (from the point of view of winning) in particular cells. While it is probable that some positional orientations are dominant at these early age levels, the logic of these is not clear-cut. At the first grade, for example, responses to the first diagram certainly demonstrate such a bias in favor of the left side upper line cell which is due perhaps to the placing of that problem at that spot on the test sheet, or perhaps to a "reading set" on the children's part. The preference for the other upper line pockets in problems 3 and 4, however, is not equally intelligible, except in terms of a general upper line set. On the other hand, the high choice of the center pocket in diagrams two, five, and six is in game terms quite rational, though it may not have that significance for the grade 1 players.

If there is any response tendency in the first two grades it seems to lie in a tendency toward adjacent responses—that is, a tendency to put one's X's adjacent to the X that is already on the page regardless of whether a player can win that way. This is clearest in diagrams four, five, and six in grade 1. After grade 2 in these same problems alignment responses prevail. The player now places X adjacent to the X already on the board only if it will put him in a position to add a third X and thus get three in a row.

Responses in the center which are most likely to lead to a drawn game tend to dominate throughout the early elementary grades (diagrams one, two, four, and six). The more strategic corner responses by and large do not obtain sizeable frequencies until the fifth and sixth grades. In sum, it seems that earlier orientations are dominated by upper line responses, and adjacent responses, but that from the second grade onwards these give way increasingly to rational responses that dictate the value of an alignment or a safe central cell response. After the fourth grade an increasing number of players learn that success may also come by a less obvious method: that is, by putting X's in the corners. Apart from six children in grade 1 who said they did not know how to play the game and whose papers were eliminated, all other children claimed to know how the game was played, so it may be presumed that all the children *felt* that they were doing the right thing to win. As a partial test of this presupposition, small groups of children in the second, fourth, and sixth grades were interviewed and asked, "How do you try to win in these games? Do you have any special ways of winning?" Of the 20 children asked this question in the second grade, 15 said that you win by getting three X's in a row; three said that you win by blocking the other person; one by putting your X in the center; and one said you win by cheating (by which he meant putting them in when the other person was not looking). Of the 20 persons asked the same question in grade 4, six said you win by putting three in a row, four by blocking the other player, four by putting your X in the center, and six by putting your X in the corners. Of the 20 asked in grade 6, four said you win by putting three in a row, six by putting your X in the center, nine by putting it in the corners, and one by waiting for others to make mistakes. These verbal responses correspond closely to the observed trends in the positional responses to the test. If the erratic single responses across these grades are ignored in these interviews and blocking and alignment responses combined and contrasted with center and corner responses in grades 2 and 6, there is a significant change toward the latter across these grades $(p < .01)$.

One final way of considering developmental changes is to take into account only the percentage of persons at each grade level that receive very high probabilities of winning scores on the Tick Tack Toe Test—for example, who receive scores of $X \geq 134$ and $Y \geq 190$. This puts the scorers in the extreme positive segment of the first stripe. When we use this cutting-off point (which is not the most extreme that could be used), no children in grades 1 through 4 are to be found, 6 per cent are in grade 5, 3 per cent in grade 6, 7 per cent in grade 7, 19 per cent in grade 8, and 30 per cent are college sophomores. It is perhaps surprising to find that in a game that is so often quoted as being trivial mathematically (24, p. 137), a majority of college students are not able to make the moves that show highest probability of success given the assumptions stated in the method section above. A sample of Cornell undergraduate students ($N = 30$) likewise yielded only about 30 per cent capable of the highest scores on this Tick Tack Toe Test. These results suggest that most of the data showing change at the sixth grade have to do with the improvement in Tick Tack Toe responses at an intermediate level because, in the present data, the striking upsurge of this highest level of competence does not occur until the eighth grade.

4. *Tick Tack Toe Success Correlates*

Results were nonsignificant for intelligence and achievement data with X and Y scores for both boys and girls separately across grades 4 to 8. It should be mentioned that, in subsequent research to be reported more fully elsewhere (26), when actual successes (wins and draws) at games played in Tick Tack Toe contests have been used instead of the present paper and pencil test, substantial relationships have been discovered. This latter research conducted only with sixth-grade children demonstrates that, in boys, winning games of Tick Tack Toe rather than losing them correlates significantly with intelligence and achievement with highest correlations between winning and nonlanguage competences, such as arithmetical problem solving. By contrast, drawing rather than losing, in boys, correlates with the perception of spatial relations. Winning and drawing in girls also correlate significantly with intelligence and achievement tests, but without the special differences noted in the case of boys.

The sociometric test (35) had been given the previous spring (a year before) and included the categories of strategic success style and a failure style ("Children who are never able to get anyone to follow them whatever they do"; "Who give up and do not try to get over difficulties"). All scores were compared with both X and Y scores separately using a median test. No relationships were found for the fifth grade. In the sixth grade there was a negative relationship for boys and girls ($N = 52$) between scoring high on X and being seen as a failure ($\chi^2 = 4.93$; $p < .05$). There was a slight relationship for sixth-grade boys between X scores and attributions on the strategy question in the sociometric test (see above Introduction, p. 362) ($\chi^2 = 3.67$; $p < .10$).

F. SUMMARY

In sum, in this first study, the majority of changes in Tick Tack Toe competence occur at the sixth grade. The majority of correlates are for X scores only, and are for boys. Perhaps the only consistent picture at this point is that boys who are seen as idea leaders on the earlier sociometric study both say they play games of strategy (35) and get high X scores on the Tick Tack Toe Test. In the results that follow in the subsequent studies, it is important to remember that only the correlates of winning responses for boys have a demonstrated connection with winning in actual games of Tick Tack Toe.

V. Study 2: Achievement Correlates

A. INTRODUCTION

Being able to avoid a loss at Tick Tack Toe by forcing a draw or a win is clearly a form of achievement. The preceding section demonstrates that this competence changes with age. If the competence at this game is a part of a more general strategic competence, which is the major hypothesis of this monograph, there should be systematic relationships between such success and achievements of a nongame character.[3]

The opportunity for such a test was provided by the Achievement Development Project at the Fels Research Institute, which has for the past six years been investigating interrelationships between a variety of motivational and ability variables, achievement performances, and other variables observed in children's free play behaviors (11, 13).

B. METHOD

The Tick Tack Toe Test was administered individually to the 50 elementary-school-age children (grades 1 through 6) of the Fels Institute Longitudinal Study, who attended the Institute's Day

---

[3] This section was written in collaboration with the late Vaughn C. Crandall, Fels Research Institute, Yellow Springs, Ohio.

TABLE 5

Variables Associated with X Scores (Winning) on the Tick Tack Toe Test

Variable	Boys ($N=25$)	Girls ($N=25$)
A. Status variables		
Age	.10	.38
Intelligence	.08	—.19
Socioeconomic	.15	—.51**
B. Motivational variable		
Need achievement	.11	—.17
C. Behavior variables		
Achievement		
Concern with fine motor mastery	.20	—.37
Amount of time spent alone on tasks	.18	—.48*
Task persistence	.43*	—.46*
Independent achievement efforts	.34	—.33
Aggression		
Instigation of physical aggression	—.08	.54**
Instigation of verbal aggression	—.22	.47*
Activity-passivity		
Associative play	—.08	.55**
Dominance of same sex peers	—.01	.53**
Uncontrolled motoricity	—.05	.50*
Concern with mastery of gross motor skills	—.03	.41*
Withdrawal from social environment	—.01	—.64**
Withdrawal from aggressive attacks	—.16	—.60**

* $p < .05$.
** $p < .01$.

Camp during the summer of 1962. This population is described elsewhere (14). The six problems were presented one at a time on separate strips of paper, rather than altogether on one sheet as in the earlier study involving the development of normative data through group administration of the test. This procedure was adopted to control for the confusion that sometimes arose from children believing that the six separate problems were all part of the same game. As the earlier statements on the rotation of axes would lead one to suspect, a two-tailed rank order test revealed that scores on drawing and winning were negatively and significantly correlated both for boys ($-.49$) at the 5 per cent level and girls ($-.53$) at the 1 per cent level.

The variables against which drawing and winning at Tick Tack

Toe were compared are itemized in Tables 5 and 6. Briefly, they include the status variables of age, intelligence, and socioeconomic status. In addition a measure of n Achievement derived from an analysis of responses to TAT pictures was included. Most important, however, were the variables derived from ratings made of the children's free play behaviors in the Fels Day Camp.[4] These included ratings of the child's concern with fine motor mastery, the amount of time that the subject spent alone on tasks, the subject's task persistence, and the subject's independent achievement efforts. In addition, there were two ratings of aggression: instigation of physical aggression and instigation of verbal aggression. Other

TABLE 6

Variables Associated with Y Scores (Drawing) on the Tick Tack Toe Test

Variable	Boys ($N=25$)	Girls ($N=25$)
A. Status variables		
Age	−.03	.05
Intelligence	.37	−.00
Socioeconomic	.07	.51**
B. Motivational variable		
Need achievement	.40*	.41*
C. Behavior variables		
Achievement		
Concern with fine motor mastery	−.05	.20
Amount of time spent alone on tasks	.14	.23
Task persistence	.05	.08
Independent achievement efforts	.11	.16
Aggression		
Instigation of physical aggression	−.03	−.43*
Instigation of verbal aggression	−.18	−.26
Activity-passivity		
Associative play	−.15	.10
Dominance of same sex peers	.13	−.26
Uncontrolled motoricity	.17	−.18
Concern with mastery of gross motor skills	.04	−.42*
Withdrawal from social environment	.09	.37
Withdrawal from aggressive attacks	.06	.33

* $p < .05$.
** $p < .01$.

[4] A copy of the rater's manual used by Mrs. Alice Rabson in this study is available from Fels Research Institute, Yellow Springs, Ohio.

play attributes rated were the amount of associative play, the dominance over same sex peers, uncontrolled motoricity, the subject's concern with mastery of gross motor skills, withdrawal from the social environment, and withdrawal from aggressive attacks. An elaborated complete description of these measures is to be found elsewhere (10, 11). Several additional measures were added for exploratory purposes. One was a measure of the sex appropriateness of play and game choices, which was derived from responses to a self-report inventory of play and games, the items of which had earlier shown differentiating power (30, 33). Each child was given a sex-appropriate score on this inventory by subtracting his opposite sex choices from his or her same sex choices. Several other Fels measures of the children's relationships with adults at the Day Camp and with their mothers were also included (14).

C. Results

The results for boys and girls separately as these correlated with a tendency to make winning or drawing responses to the Tick Tack Toe Test are to be found in Tables 5 and 6. Correlations were Pearson Product moment r's.

Results for the *status variables* of age, intelligence, and socioeconomic status are significant only for socioeconomic status and only for girls. Y scores (drawing) are positively related to socioeconomic status for girls. X scores (winning) are negatively related to socioeconomic status for girls.

The *motivational* measure of n Achievement derived from responses to TAT pictures was significantly and positively related to Y scores (drawing) on the Tick Tack Toe Test for both boys and girls.

Many of the *free play variables* were also associated with winning and drawing scores on the Tick Tack Toe Test. More significant relations were discovered for girls than for boys. These results will be discussed in turn for winning scores in girls (X), winning scores in boys (X), drawing scores in girls (Y), and drawing scores in boys (Y).

Girls' X (winning) scores are the most salient in this study. Ten of the 12 free play variables are significantly related to X scores; there are significant relations between X responses and associative play, dominance of same sex peers, uncontrolled motoricity, a concern with mastery of gross motor skills, and instigation of physical and verbal aggression. In addition there are negative relations with withdrawal from aggressive attacks or from the social environment, time spent alone on tasks, and persistence.

X scores for boys, by contrast, relate positively and significantly to task persistence, but unlike the girls no other free play behavior is significantly correlated with Tick Tack Toe Test performance.

Y scores for girls are negatively and significantly correlated with a concern for mastery of gross motor skills and with instigating physical aggression. There are also relationships with withdrawal from the social environment and from aggressive attacks which are of a similar character as these significant correlates, but these relationships do not reach conventional levels of significance. There are no significant free play concomitants for Y scores with boys.

D. SUMMARY

In sum, in these results, the girls are fairly clearly characterized, but the boys are not. Winning scores (X) for girls give the picture of a girl who is hyperactive, dominating, and masculine. Drawing scores (Y) give a picture of a girl who comes from a high-social-class home, has a high n Achievement, and is not concerned with gross motor skills or prone to express aggression. Winning in boys correlates with task persistence, and drawing in boys with n Achievement.

These various interrelationships clearly show that competence on this test is systematically related to other aspects of personality. Whether the relationships therefore justify the view that success at the game is one part of a more generalized strategic competence is a question best reserved for the final discussion.

VI. Study 3: Cognitive and Physical Correlates

A. INTRODUCTION

In the previous section it has been demonstrated that winning and drawing at Tick Tack Toe are systematically related to a variety of free play achievement and interpersonal variables. It has been the general argument of this series of studies that if games do have the enculturative function attributed to them, then competence at games should be systematically implicated with the rest of personality. It was also argued, however, that this implication should make coherent sense. It should be possible to say that the strategic game competence is a part of a more generalized strategic style manifested in areas other than games—more specifically, that games of strategy which are, among other things, exercises in decision making should be representative of decision-making processes in general.

The opportunity for testing the relationships of success on the Tick Tack Toe Test against other measures of decision making was made possible by the cognitive style project of Donald Broverman and associates of Worcester State Hospital and Clark University Heinz Werner Institute of Developmental Psychology.[5] This project has for the past six years been investigating the behavioral correlates of various cognitive styles. One of these cognitive styles, termed "Strong *versus* Weak Automatization," showed particular promise of relevance in the present case. Strong Automatizers are individuals who are able to perform simple repetitive tasks more rapidly than can be expected from their general level of ability. Strong Automatizers seem to be more efficient individuals than are Weak Automatizers, since normal adult Strong Automatizers achieve higher level occupations than do Weak Automatizers of the same age, education, and intelligence (7).

A clue as to what may underlie the greater effectiveness of the Strong Automatizers is Caffrey's finding that Strong Automatizers make decisions with greater confidence than do Weak Automatizers.

Strong Automatizers have also been reported to differ from Weak Automatizers physically in a manner suggesting that the Strong Automatizers have higher levels of androgen (8). Androgens have been frequently correlated with aggressive behavior in ani-

[5] This section was written in collaboration with Donald M. Broverman, Worcester State Hospital, Worcester, Massachusetts; Abraham Blum, Clark University, Worcester, Massachusetts; and Edward L. Klaiber, Worcester Foundation for Experimental Biology, Worcester, Massachusetts.

mals (2). Thus, if the androgen hypothesis of Broverman *et al.* is correct, and if androgens have similar effects in humans, then the Strong Automatizers may be described as assertive, self-confident, effective individuals. It is quite likely that such an individual would play to win in games as well as in life situations.

Accordingly, the present study examines the relationships of the automatization cognitive style and the physical development of children to game strategy in Tick Tack Toe.

B. Method

The measures of automatization that were used in the present study were the speed of naming objects, the speed of naming repeated color hues, and the speed of reading repeated color names. The first of these tasks requires the subject to name, as fast as possible, 70 pictures of a cup, a tree, and a fly, 10 pictures to a line in random order. The time taken to complete the task was taken as the automatization score for the test. The other tasks were of a similar character and are described more fully in the major project, of which this is a derivative study (8). In addition, a number of tests of restructuring ability were administered. These are tests which in previous studies had been found to be reliably opposed to the automatized tasks. The restructuring tasks require that the individual's initial automatized responses to obvious stimulus attributes be set aside in favor of a response to less obvious hidden stimulus relations. The tasks included selected items from the Thurstone-Gottschaldt figures, the Porteus mazes, and the WAIS Block Design subtest. These tasks are also described fully in the parent project (8).

The physical measures included the child's standing height, weight, leg length (from the most lateral point of the right iliac crest to floor) and arm span. The height and weight of both parents were also obtained, as parental stature has been shown to be systematically related to the child's height (19). In addition, the physical dimensions predicted for each child by multiple regression equations based on the parents' height and weight were subtracted from each child's actual physical dimension. This is a method of correcting the child's actual size for his parents' size. The remaining differences are interpretable then as indices of the child's rate of

386   ANTHROPOLOGICAL APPROACHES

maturation. Thus, a child who is larger than one would expect from
his parents' stature is presumed to be maturing more rapidly than
expected; a child who is smaller than expected for his parents' size
is presumed to be maturing at a slower rate than expected.

The subjects were 40 boys in two fourth-grade elementary classes
of middle-class status. The Tick Tack Toe Test was administered
individually twice, each problem being presented on a separate
strip of paper. All the results that follow refer to the second administration. There were few significant results for the first administration, but a large number for the second administration.
Scores on X and Y axes were treated separately as in the previous
study.

C. Results

Table 7 indicates that high-scoring X or winning boys are Strong
Automatizers, at least as indicated by the object-naming task ($L =$
.345, $p < .05$). They tend also to be poor at restructuring tasks (all
of the correlations are negative, although not statistically significant), as is also typical of Strong Automatizers. None of the raw
measures of height, weight, leg length, or arm span is significantly
related to the Tick Tack Toe measures. However, the physical
measures corrected for the physical size of the parents yield large
significant correlations with both the X and Y axes. Specifically,
Table 8 shows that high-scoring X boys tend to be taller and heavier

TABLE 7
Correlations Between Scores on Tick Tack Toe Test
and Other Cognitive Variables

| | Males ($N=40$) | |
Normative scores	X scores	Y scores
Automatization tasks		
Naming objects	.345*	−.066
Naming color hues	.157	.069
Reading color names	.142	−.038
Restructuring tasks		
WAIS block designs	−.210	.167
Thurstone-Gottschaldt	−.076	.103
Porteus mazes	−.002	−.244

* $p < .05$.

TABLE 8
Correlations Between Scores on Tick Tack Toe Test and Physical Measures

Variable	X scores	Y scores
Raw physical dimensions		
Height	.218	−.231
Weight	.222	−.185
Leg length	.005	.101
Arm span	.119	−.005
Physical dimensions corrected		
for parental stature		
Height	.513***	−.393*
Weight	.409**	−.207
Leg length	.122	.123
Arm span	.292	−.085

* $p < .05$.
** $p < .01$.
*** $p < .001$.

than can be predicted from their parents' size, with the reverse true of low-scoring X boys.

Similar relations occur between automatization and physical dimensions corrected for parental size: i.e., Strong Automatizers tend to be larger than predicted, while Weak Automatizers tend to be smaller.

The above results suggest, then, that the cognitive competences of high automatization and strategy are both related to each other and are both related in turn to a large preadolescent body build. It also follows, therefore, of high X scoring as it does of Strong Automatization that, in view of what is known about the relationships of physique at this stage of development and early and late maturation, it is likely that Strong Automatizers (and high X scorers) are earlier maturing individuals than are Weak Automatizers (and low X scorers).

There are also positive relationships between the X scores and the mother's and father's ages (respectively, r's = .484 and .450, $p < .01$). That is, high X scorers tend to come from older mothers and fathers than do low X scorers.

High Y scoring or drawing boys tend to contrast with high X boys on most characteristics. There are not, however, significant relationships with automatization or restructuring tasks. The significant relationships are of a physical sort. Y scorers, like Weak Automatizers, tend to be shorter than expected from parental stature, indicating that high Y scorers are probably late maturers. Their relationships with mother's and father's ages ($r = -.302$, $p < .05$; and $r = -.302$, $p < .05$) respectively imply that they have relatively young parents.

In sum, X and Y scoring in boys is obversely related to the physical measures, and directionally so to the cognitive measures.

VII. Discussion

A. INTRODUCTION

It was the original thesis of this series of studies that if games have the function that has been claimed for them in the earlier cross-cultural studies then within this culture and intrapersonally they should be systematically related to other aspects of the player's behavior. The results of the foregoing studies show that this is the case. Whether or not the results of these studies support all the assumptions from which they were derived may still be an open question. At the very least they support the view that an empirical inquiry into the psychological functioning of games is a fruitful research undertaking.

It was further argued, however, that if competence at games of strategy is systematically related to personality in general, which it would have to be if an enculturative function were to be claimed for games, there should be an internal coherence to the various interrelationships that have been found. The rest of this discussion is given to an examination of this possibility. All the results from the three studies are brought together and each sex is dealt with separately in relation to the two scoring possibilities in the game: that is, X scores and Y scores. It is a convenient simplification to discuss the results in terms of winning boys, drawing girls, etc., though what is actually meant when discussing, say, winning boys is the correlation between boys' X scores and whatever other variable is being considered.

B. Types of Player
1. *The Winning Girl*

Practically all the results for this girl derive from the Fels study of grades 1 to 6. This girl is shown to be hyperactive, impulsive, aggressive, and masculine in her free play behavior. One other measure was available in the Fels study which complements this picture. This was a questionnaire of everyday play activities scored for the sex appropriateness of play choices (33). There was a significant negative relationship between sex appropriate choices and winning scores. That is, girls who gain high winning scores tend *not to choose* items which differentiate in favor of females, but rather to prefer masculine activities. Their "masculinity" is thus reflected both in their observed free play behavior (gross motor skills, etc.) and their reported play preferences. Table 9 indicates that relationships between the play-preferences scale and Tick Tack Toe strategies hold only for girls, but not for boys. It is interesting to note that other studies dealing with subjects of various ages and using various assessment devices have found intercorrelations for girls which are at least partially similar to those presented in Table 6 (16, 17, 22, 31, 37). As far as the evidence goes, it seems to suggest that a win-oriented strategy in a competitive intellectual game is an aggressive ("masculine") manifestation in girls.

Past child-training research permits inquiry into the probable child-training origins of these aggressive strategically competent girls. In a number of studies, positive associations have been established between aggressive characteristics in girls and perceived or real distance, rejection, or punishment by their mothers (4, 17, 18, 31). Moreover, it has been suggested that it is because of negative mother-daughter relationships that these girls express themselves aggressively and tend to behave like males (18). Several antecedent

TABLE 9

Correlations Between Scores on Tick Tack Toe Test
and Sex-Appropriate Play Choices

Subjects	X scores	Y scores
Boys	.20	−.21
Girls	−.47*	.41*

* $p < .05$.

variables were available for the present sample that allowed a test
of the hypothesis that strategically competent girls experience negative relations with their mothers. Relevant results, presented in Table 10, indicate that high winning responses in girls on the Tick
Tack Toe Test are associated with past experiences of receiving
more severe penalties from the mothers than occurs for girls who
are less win-oriented. The linkage between this child-training procedure (severe penalties) and the cognitive function (winning at
Tick Tack Toe) may be envisaged as follows. By their use of severe
penalties these mothers provide a model of aggression or power assertion for their daughters. The girls in consequence can be expected to express such responses themselves where opportunity offers,
and indeed we have seen that they do so through their same sex
dominance and instigation of aggression. In addition, when these
winning girls attempt to generalize power responses to peer situations, they readily find scope for these responses in the "tomboyish"
(gross motor sports) activities that are permitted and even popular
for girls at some points in preadolescence (40). Although we are not
particularly impressed with any need for subtlety in these high winning girls, it might well be that games of strategy are also favored
by them because girls, in general, prefer such games more than boys
do, so that involvement in the games is sex appropriate (25). At the
same time these games rationalize aggressive winning within a sex
appropriate context. The ludic model of strategy may thus provide
reconciliation for a sex-appropriate desire to prefer feminine activities (board games, conceptual games, etc.) and a less sex-conven-

TABLE 10
Correlations Between Scores on Tick Tack Toe Test
and Relationships with Adults

Variable	X scores		Y scores	
	Boys	Girls	Boys	Girls
A. Observations free play at camp				
Recognition: Approval seeking from adults	−.05	.38	.46*	.06
B. Home observations				
Accelerational attempts by mother	−.39	−.21	.58**	−.29
Severity of actual penalties by mother	.04	.47*	−.20	−.23

* $p < .05$.
** $p < .01$.

tional (it is not strictly inappropriate) desire to win in overt competition.

On the basis of the evidence presented here, however, it would appear that winning at Tick Tack Toe is not an isolated competence in the lives of these winning girls. It is instead one manifestation of a more general drive to win, as indicated by such associated terms as "dominance," "aggression," "independence," and "masculinity." Thus, the data about these girls do support the hypothesis that strategy in games is a part of a more generalized competence. Nevertheless, it is hard to resist the conclusion that, in the case of these girls at least, it is so only because strategic competition has been subsumed to a more generalized and powerful drive for victory in all areas of competence, whether physical or intellectual. In the earlier study of strategy using a sociometric device (35), it was also found that girls who are seen as outstanding in strategic leadership were generally seen as outstanding in all other respects also. In sum, with these girls it is legitimate to say that strategic competence is but one manifestation of a general expression of interpersonal power, and judging by the inconsistencies in girls' responses across Studies 1 and 2, not a very central expression at that.

2. *The Winning Boy*

In the first study above, high X scoring by boys is associated with superiority on arithmetic, language, and intelligence, and being chosen as leaders more often than are losing boys at the sixth-grade level. In the Fels study, X scores are associated with high task persistence, and independent achievement efforts are directional. In the Worcester study these boys are the Strong Automatizers. There is, it would seem, a construct consistency between the task persistence of these boys (Fels), their ability to carry out routine tasks quickly (Worcester), and their ability to carry a strategic game through to a successful conclusion. This is particularly so in the light of another investigation, carried out by these investigators and reported elsewhere (28), which shows that boys who win in games of strategy tend to be superior both in arithmetic and in the pattern velocity of their game playing. Pattern velocity is a cognitive competence which refers to the relationship between the number of paths open to a player and the number of moves he actually takes. High velocity players tend to take fewer moves to terminate the games in which they play than do other players. The ability of these players to persist with intellectual tasks (task persistence), to subordinate such tasks to rapid responses (Strong Automatization), and to make economical decisions (pattern velocity) about their intellectual responses as well as to be good at arithmetical problem solving would seem to imply a certain construct congruence throughout. It is natural that we would prefer to think of these interrelated cognitive competences as subaspects of a general strategic competence, which elsewhere we have sought to relate to child training and cultural functioning in general. Whether or not this be a legitimate construction, however, the evidence certainly supports the hypothesized interrelationships between competence at games of strategy and competence in analogous general intellectual performances. The case is made much stronger because of the other demonstrated relationships between boys' X scores, actual success at Tick Tack Toe contests, preference for games of strategy (35), and selection on sociometrics as idea-leaders.

In the case of the winning girls there was evidence for believing that strategic competence had much to do with their forced independence from the mother. Such high independence training has been found to be regularly associated with analytic abilities in girls (20). Independence of the mother appears to be important for winning boys also. Table 10 indicates, at least directionally, that the mothers of the winning boys do not make accelerational attempts upon them. This distinguishes the winning boys markedly from the drawing boys, whose mothers do make such attempts, and seems to imply that the winning boys are given more independence by their mothers than are the drawing boys. Other research showing relationships between independence training for boys and excellence at quantitative skills seems to be of confirming import (5). It has been noted above, for example, that quantitative skills are found to be associated regularly with winning at Tick Tack Toe. In sum, both winning boys and winning girls show evidence of independence or psychic distance from the mother, although both the character of the independence and the sex role conventionality of their subsequent behavior varies markedly.

In the Worcester study the winning boys had larger bodies than expected from the size of their parents and, presumably, were early maturers. It would be natural for such mature boys to be given independence by their parents and to demand it for themselves.

The finding that winning in boys is associated with parents of older age levels cannot be simply explained in this paper and will be taken up elsewhere. For the present it must suffice to say that we associate this condition with the production of independence, decision making and, therefore, strategic competence in boys.

3. *The Drawing Girl*

In the Fels study, Y scoring by girls is associated with correlates that provide a picture of sex-appropriate orientations and actions. These girls report preferring feminine games in everyday life (Table 9) and their observed behaviors (Table 6) indicate that they are neither aggressive nor interested in gross motor (traditionally masculine) activities. They are also of high socioeconomic status and demonstrate high need achievement. In sum, they are conventional and ladylike. Playing for a draw in Tick Tack Toe would appear to mirror their appropriate and conventional sex-role behavior in everyday life: that is, if we can assume that making draw responses is analogous to "playing it safe," or playing with intent not to fail or lose. There is a consistency between being "feminine" on the various measures and making draw responses in Tick Tack Toe. Perhaps these results imply that in yet another way this particular ludic microcosm (Tick Tack Toe) models realities that extend beyond the sphere of play.

4. *The Drawing Boy*

Boys who play for a draw, like girls who play for a draw, display high *n* Achievement as this is reflected in a preoccupation with achievement on responses to TAT stimuli. Results in Table 10 also indicate that these boys have experienced high accelerational pressures from their mothers and that they seek approval from adults. Winterbottom (41) found that high *n* Achieving boys, as compared with low *n* Achieving boys, were subject to more accelerational pressure by their mothers; and, according to their teachers, these boys showed more pride in their schoolwork, expressed more concern for success, but, in contrast to low *n* Achievers, were not more successful in the objective terms of school success. It seems a legitimate inference, although the details are not all clear, that we have here a group of boys encouraged by their mothers to show a concern for achievement, but at the same time made unduly dependent on adult structured situations in the demonstration of such a concern. In some unascertained way, although there is a parallel in Bing's work (5), the mother's accelerational attempts appear to have had a constrictive effect upon the boy so that he plays it cautiously when the situation is not clearly structured for him by adults. Both the boys and girls who display draw responses in high degree thus have in common a great reliance on adults, the girl showing this by being conventional, the boy through making direct bids for adult attention.

The Worcester data complement this picture by demonstrating that these drawing boys are late maturers. It is not unlikely that such late maturation would lead to a continued dependence upon the parents, nor unlikely that their younger more inexperienced mothers would fuss over them and expect more of them than would the older, presumably maturer, mothers of the winning boys. The relationship between drawing by these boys and high scores on the spatial relations subtest of the California Test of Mental Maturity (mentioned in the section on normative data) tends to confirm this inference. Several studies have indicated relationships between high scores on such spatial relationship subtests and dependency or femininity in boys (20).

The present association between drawing and high n Achievement is of particular interest in respect to current personality theory concerned with achievement. Many studies have shown that persons of all ages scoring high on n Achievement tend to have a preference for intermediate level risks in a variety of achievement situations (1). Successfully playing for a draw on Tick Tack Toe is not, in the probabilistic sense, equivalent to an intermediate level risk. On the contrary, in Tick Tack Toe the draw player, one whose cautiousness ensures that he will not fail, has little likelihood of winning, but most probably will draw. His is only an intermediate level risk in the sense that he prefers to play for a draw rather than to risk either losing or winning. One possible explanation for the difference between the present status of the high need achiever and the status ascribed to him in McClelland's work lies in the differential nature of the situations involved (21). Most n Achievement studies have been carried out using games of physical skill in which the goals and probabilities have been clearly structured for the subjects. Even the chance situations which have been used have involved an impersonal setting forth of the probabilities before the subject. But in the present Tick Tack Toe Test, which is derived from a game, the situation is considerably less structured. The high n Achievers may play cautiously at this game because in it the situation is interpersonal rather than impersonal, and it involves competition with others, rather than competition with a standard which is clearly defined. In a study of high n Achievers in a gambling situation involving competitive bidding and ambiguity as to the competitor's moves, Littig also found that high n Achievers played an extremely cautious game (21). McClelland interpreted this latter finding as due to the dislike of high n Achievers for chance situations in which they could not influence the outcome through their own skills and abilities—"In games of pure chance they normally prefer the safest odds they can get" (21, p. 214). But it has been shown here that these same high n Achievers also play it safe when strategic skills are involved. As both chance and strategy have in common a relative lack of structure with respect to outcomes, we might conclude that the critical variables in explaining high n Achieving behavior are not alone the influence of the skills and abilities of the players, but also the cognitive structuring of the field in which these skills are to be made manifest. When both paths and outcomes are made clear by adults or authorities, and not made ambiguous by social or chance contingencies and competition, then the high n Achiever may be the one who feels safe enough to state a high expectation of success. When these conditions are not guaranteed he pursues more cautious play. This hypothetical sketch of the high n Achiever who plays for a draw on Tick Tack Toe is confirmatory of McClelland's position insofar as it demonstrates that high n Achieving does not go with losing. But in terms of Tick Tack Toe such persons are only intermediately successful; a finding which casts some doubt on McClelland's more general contentions concerning his measure of achievement.

Once again, therefore, we reach the conclusion that the strategy of play in the game is a model of the generalized behavior of the player. In this case a somewhat immature, dependent boy, motivated by his mother's accelerational attempts, expresses high verbal aspirations with respect to his performance; but when in situations which are not clearly structured for him, he chooses a low-risk strategy.

C. Conclusion

In conclusion, these accounts of the various types of play appear to justify the assumption that the game of Tick Tack Toe and the strategies adopted within this game do indeed model related characteristics in the players. For each of these "types" of players the game has a different value or "utility," and this determines the type of strategy that they use while in the game. However, it would seem that only in the case of X scoring by boys can we talk securely of an underlying and general "elementary strategic competence." It is only with X scoring by boys that we find consistency between scores on the test and successes in Tick Tack Toe game contests; a preference for games of strategy (35), sociometric selection as idea leaders; and an association with the related constructs of automatization, task persistence, pattern velocity, and problem-solving ability. Here it does seem that a case can be made for the view that strategic (winning) play at Tick Tack Toe models an underlying style of life in which strategic qualities find general manifestation.

With the other types of scoring, it is safe to conclude that, while the data seem to indicate that the players approach the game in ways characteristic of general life styles, the games are nevertheless less relevant to these life styles than is the case with winning boys. For winning in girls, the expression of interpersonal power seems to be relatively undifferentiated and their play at games of strategy is just one, and probably a not very central, manifestation of that power. Playing for a draw, on the other hand, appears to be preferred by feminine girls and conforming boys, both of whom seem particularly dependent upon the adult world to structure the nature of achievement for them. Once again, while they perhaps reveal themselves in their play, it is unlikely that these particular games are of much importance to them.

In sum, while the general view that games are buffered learning devices with an important role in individual development and in cultural history cannot be fully established by this investigation (34), there does seem some support for the view that such games may be of importance in the development of elementary strategic competence by some individuals.

VIII. Summary

A series of studies with elementary-school-age boys and girls, using a test of strategic competence based on the game of Tick Tack Toe, inquired into relationships between competence at this game and parallel cognitive, social, and physical processes. It was discovered that winning at this test by boys was related to a variety of other social and cognitive characteristics of an analogous nature. Results are interpreted in terms of a modelling and enculturative theory of games.

REFERENCES

1. Atkinson, J. W. Motivational determinants of risk taking behavior. *Psychol. Rev.*, 1957, 64, 359–372.
2. Beach, F. A. Hormones and Behavior. New York: Hoeber, 1948.
3. Bell, R. C. Board and Table Games from Many Civilizations. London: Oxford Univ. Press, 1960.
4. Bing, E. Effect of childrearing practices on development of differential cognitive abilities. *Child. Devel.*, 1963, 34, 631–648.
5. ———. Childrearing antecedents of perceptual cognitive functions. Paper delivered at the Society for Research in Child Development, Berkeley, California, April, 1963.
6. Brewster, P. G. Malomjatek and related three-in-a-row games. *Acta Ethnographica*, 1957, 6, 225–231.
7. Broverman, D. M. Generality and behavioral correlates of cognitive styles. *J. Consult. Psychol.*, 1964, 28, 487–500.
8. ———, Vogel, W., Broverman, I. K., Palmer, R. D., and Klaiber, E. L. The automatization cognitive style and physical development. *Child Devel.*, 1964, 35, 1343–1359.
9. Caffrey, C. B. Flexibility of cognitive control as a factor in decision making. Unpublished Master's thesis, Catholic University of America, Washington, D.C., 1962.
10. Crandall, V. J. Achievement. In H. Stevenson (Ed.), *Child Psychology: The Sixty-Second Yearbook of the National Society for the Study of Education*. Chicago, Ill.: Univ. Chicago Press, 1963. Pp. 416–459.
11. ———, and Sinkeldam, C. Children's dependent and achievement behaviors in social situations and their perceptual field dependence. *J. Personal.*, 1964, 32, 1–22.
12. ———, Katovsky, W., and Preston, A. A conceptual formulation of some research on children's achievement development. *Child Devel.*, 1960, 97, 161–168.
13. ———. Motivational and ability determinants of young children's intellectual achievement behaviors. *Child Devel.*, 1962, 33, 643–661.
14. ———, Preston, A., and Rabson, A. Maternal reactions and the development of independence and achievement behavior in young children. *Child Devel.*, 1960, 31, 243–251.
15. Gomme, A. B. The traditional games of England, Scotland, and Ireland. In G. L. Gomme (Ed.), *A Dictionary of British Folklore (Vols. 1 and 2)*. London: Nutt, 1894, 1898.

16. Kagan, J., and Moss, H. A. Birth to Maturity. New York: Wiley & Sons, 1962.

17. Lansky, L. M., Crandall, V. J., Kagan, J., and Baker, C. T. Sex differences in aggression and its correlates in middle-class adolescents. *Child Devel.*, 1961, 32, 45–48.

18. Levin, H., and Sears, R. R. Identification with parents as a determinant of doll play aggression. *Child Devel.*, 1956, 27, 135–153.

19. Livison, N., McNeill, D., and Thomas, K. Pooled estimates of parent-child correlations in stature from birth to maturity. *Science*, 1962, 138, 818–820.

20. Maccoby, E. E. Sex differences in intellectual functioning. Unpublished manuscript, Stanford University, Palo Alto, California, 1964.

21. McClelland, D. C. The Achieving Society. New York: Van Nostrand, 1961.

22. Milton, G. A. The effects of sex role identification on problem solving skill. *J. Abn. & Soc. Psychol.*, 1957, 55, 208–212.

23. Murray, H. J. R. A History of Board Games Other than Chess. Clarendon, Texas: Clarendon Univ. Press, 1952.

24. Rapoport, A. Fights, Games and Debates. Ann Arbor: Univ. Michigan Press, 1961.

25. Roberts, J. M., and Sutton-Smith, B. Child training and game involvement. *Ethnology*, 1962, 1, 166–185.

26. ———. Games: Models of Power. New York: McGraw-Hill, in preparation.

27. ———, Arth, M. J., and Bush, R. R. Games in culture. *Amer. Anthrop.*, 1959, 61, 597–605.

28. ———, Hoffman, H., and Sutton-Smith, B. Pattern and competence: A consideration of Tick Tack Toe. *El Palacio*, 1965, 72, 17–30.

29. ———, Sutton-Smith, B., and Kendon, A. Strategy in game and folk tales. *J. Soc. Psychol.*, 1963, 60, 15–30.

30. Rosenberg, B. G., and Sutton-Smith, B. The measurement of masculinity and femininity in children. *Child Devel.*, 1959, 30, 373–380.

31. ———, ———, and Morgan, E. The use of the opposite sex scales as a measure of psychosexual deviancy. *J. Consult. Psychol.*, 1961, 25, 221–225.

32. Sutton-Smith, B. The Games of New Zealand Children. Berkeley: Univ. California Press, 1959.

33. ———. Play preference and play behavior: A validity study. *Psychol. Rep.*, 1965, 16, 65–66.

34. ———. Piaget on play: A critique. *Psychol. Rev.*, 1966, 73, 111–112.

35. ———, and Roberts, J. M. Rubrics of competitive behavior. *J. Genet. Psychol.*, 1964, 105, 13–37.

36. ———, and Rosenberg, B. G. Peer perceptions of impulsive behavior. *Merrill-Palmer Quart.*, 1961, 7, 233–238.
37. ———. Impulsivity and sex preferences. *J. Genet. Psychol.*, 1961, 98, 187–192.
38. ———, Roberts, J. M., and Kozelka, R. M. Game involvement in adults. *J. Soc. Psychol.*, 1963, 60, 15–30.
39. ———, ———, and Rosenberg, B. G. Sibling associations and role involvement. *Merrill-Palmer Quart.*, 1964, 10, 25–38.
40. ———, Rosenberg, B. G., and Morgan, E. Development of sex differences in play choices during preadolescence. *Child Devel.*, 1963, 34, 119–126.
41. Winterbottom, M. R. The relation of need for achievement to learning experiences in independence and mastery. In J. W. Atkinson (Ed.), *Motives in Fantasy, Action and Society.* Princeton, N.J.: Van Nostrand, 1958. Pp. 453–478.

SECTION III

PSYCHOLOGICAL APPROACHES

Games not only have a history and parallel other cultural phenomena as the previous sections have sought to demonstrate, but they also have an importance in the lives of individuals. For the most part, the treatment of games in psychology, including my own long-standing collaboration with B. G. Rosenberg, at Bowling Green State University, has meant using games chiefly to illustrate supposedly more important things about the psychology of their players. While legitimate as a method of obtaining information, this particular focus does not tell us a great deal about the games themselves. The first two articles in this section, whose concern is with the development of sex and sibling differences in play choices, illustrate the more common individual-oriented approach.

However the significance that I have derived from historical and anthropological studies, and exemplified by the article on elementary strategic competence, is that games are formative and not merely epiphenomenal. They cause things to happen; they do not merely *express* what has already happened. Games are independent as well as dependent variables. This stance is illustrated in the remaining two studies in this section III by two experimental field studies. The first, coauthored with Paul Gump, grew out of my work as a Fulbright Research Fellow while at Wayne State University in 1953–1954. Fritz Redl, director of that project, was at the time concerned with the formative effect that particular games have on the psychology of the disturbed children who play them.

The second manipulative study was derived from the general point of view that if games are functional we should be able to demonstrate their effects in terms of other psychological variables. The large amount of study and effort on game simulation in contemporary social science has sprung from this same point of view; indeed it has provided the basis for the proliferation of war and business games for the past two centuries. However the implication of this article, "The Game as a School of Abstraction," is that there can be a developmental psychology of games in which different games are shown to be useful for promoting psychological functions of various sorts, although a great deal of experimental work and correlative assessment would be required to fully implement that psychology.

8. Development of Sex Differences in Play Choices during Preadolescence

This paper is one of a series in which the differences between the preferences for play activities of preadolescent boys and girls have been studied. Two of the papers have contrasted the play preferences of children today with those of children 30 and 60 years ago (10, 16).* Other papers have dealt with a masculinity-femininity scale (9) which is derived from this preference data and which predicts a variety of psychosocial correlates (11, 14, 15). While in previous papers the preadolescent period has been treated as a whole, the present paper is concerned with developmental changes in preference patterns of boys and girls which take place within that period itself, in particular, the changes occurring between the third and sixth grades.

SOURCE: Reprinted from *Child Development* 34 (1963): 119–126, with permission of the co-authors B. G. Rosenberg, E. F. Morgan, Jr., and the Society for Research in Child Development Inc. Copyright, 1963, by the Society for Research in Child Development Inc. This study was facilitated by a grant from the Scholarly Advancement Committee. Special appreciation is due the following persons for their assistance in analyzing the data of this study: Mr. P. Schneider, Mr. C. Barker, and Miss P. Finn.

* Numbers in parentheses refer to sources listed at the end of this article.

Earlier research with the game and play preferences would lead to the expectation that girls should show increased responsiveness with age to the items on this scale (10); that girls' preferences would become increasingly like those of boys across these grades (16); that, at the fifth grade, girls' preferences might tend again to become more feminine, although the evidence in the literature is somewhat inconsistent on this point (1, 2, 17, 18); and that the changes in girls' preferences may be an indication of sex role confusion, though here again, there are differences of opinion (1, 3).

PROCEDURE

In order to investigate these questions concerning girls' increased responsiveness, their increased preference for masculine items, their changes in preference patterns at the fifth grade, and their sex role confusion, a play scale composed of 180 items (13) was administered to 928 boys and 973 girls in grades 3 through 6 in 12 midwestern townships. The samples were obtained from small towns, varying in population from 300 (New Middleton, Ohio) to 24,000 (Findlay, Ohio). The schools sampled were predominantly of lower and middle socioeconomic classification. The number of children responding to the inventory in each grade was as follows:

	3rd Grade	4th Grade	5th Grade	6th Grade
Boys	137	260	245	286
Girls	153	252	278	290

Children respond to this play scale by ignoring items which they do not play or by indicating like or dislike for the items which they do play. Their responses were analyzed for sex differences and age changes. First, the like and dislike choices for the 180 items were subjected to a chi square analysis for the differences *between* the sexes at each grade level. Secondly, the same choices were analyzed *within* each sex for differences between grade levels .

RESULTS

Only items to which 30 per cent of the children responded in at least one grade level were included for analysis. One hundred and forty-six items of the 180 met this criterion. Of this 146, 33 showed no significant sex differences throughout, i.e., they did not distinguish between the sexes ("neutral" items).

TABLE 1
Play and Game Items which Differentiate Boys from Girls
at Several Levels of Significance

Differentiating Level	Items
All Grade Levels	
$p = .001$ ...	bandits, soldiers, cowboys, cops and robbers, spacemen, bows and arrows, throwing snowballs, wrestling, football, boxing, hunting, using tools, model aeroplanes, toy trains, work machines, build forts
$p = .01$ ...	cars, marbles, darts, baseball, shooting, fishing, make radio, climbing
$p = .05$ ...	baseball
*Some Grade Levels**	
$p = .05$ ...	blackman (3), fly kites (3), king of the mountain (3,6), bowling (3), soccer (3,4,6), boating (3), ghosts (4), inventors (4), horseshoes (4,6), racing (4,6), tug o war (5), capture the flag (5,6), skiing (5), horse riding (5,6), pool (6), dice (6), handsprings (6)

* The grade level(s) are indicated in parentheses after each item.

The first and most important finding is that, if only those items differentiating at the $p = .01$ level or better are considered, girls and boys have approximately equal numbers of items differentiating between them at all grade levels: the boys have 24, and the girls have 24 (Tables 1 and 2). When the number of items differentiating between the sexes is extended to the $p = .05$ level, greater differences between the sexes begin to appear. These differences do not show themselves, however, until after the third grade level, for at that grade the number of items favoring each sex, even at the .05 level, is approximately equal. It is at the fourth grade level that the girls suddenly appear much more responsive to the items on this scale than the boys (i.e., more items differentiate in favor of girls than boys). The numbers of items differentiating between the sexes at the .05 level during these grades are as follows:

	Masculine Items	Feminine Items
Third grade	31	37
Fourth grade	30	52
Fifth grade	29	60
Sixth grade	34	59

TABLE 2

Play and Game Items which Differentiate Girls from Boys
at Several Levels of Significance

Differentiating Level	Items

All Grade Levels

$p = .001$ ... dolls, dressing-up, houses, store, school, church, actresses, stoop tag, ring around rosy, London bridge, farmer in dell, in and out the windows, drop the handkerchief, mulberry bush, hop scotch, jump rope, jacks, Mother, may I?, dance, sewing, cooking, knit

$p = .01$ ... actors, crochet

$p = .05$ ... red rover, follow the leader, poor pussy, cartwheels

Some Grade Levels*

$p = .05$ ... I've got a secret (3,5,6), roller skating (3,4,5), pom pom pull-away (3), muffin man (3,4,6), spin the bottle (3,4,6), red-light (3,5,6), skating (3,4,5), draw or paint (3,5,6), seesaw (3,4,6), cat & mouse (4,5,6), puss in corner (4,5), fox & geese (4,5), frozen tag (4,5,6), huckle buckle (4,5,6), hoops (4,5,6), crack the whip (4,5), leap frog (4,5,6), name that tune (4,5, 6), hide the thimble (4,5,6), musical chairs (4,5,6), statues (4,5,6), here I come (4,5,6), what time is it (4,5,6), pick up sticks (4,6), scrapbook (4), collections (4,5), build snowmen (4,5,6), clay modeling (4,5,6), blindman's bluff (5), wood tag (5,6), squirrel in tree (5,6), post office (5), checkers (5), puzzles (5), black magic (5,6), doctors (6), hide & seek (6), colors (6), dog and bone (6), tiddley-winks (6)

* The grade level(s) are indicated in parentheses after each item.

When the same preferences are analyzed within the sexes for age level differences, it becomes apparent that the fourth grade is a period of greatly increased responsiveness for both sexes. Examining those items which differentiate the sexes at the .05 level or better, there are 69 significant item increases between the third and fourth grades and only seven significant decreases (Table 3). While the boys show 28 of these item increases, girls show 41. Girls' greater responsiveness, then, is a condition presumably produced by changes that occur between the third and fourth grades.

Inspection of the present data reveals that various types of

changes are taking place at this time. The play items in this inventory can be divided into two levels of maturity. At the immature level are the simple pastimes, such as singing games, make-
believe, and tagging games which predominate in the play of
children up until the age of about 9 years (12). At the more mature
level are the more complex adult recreations (shooting, fishing),
hobbies, games, and sports. Games and sports are recreational activities governed by definite rules of procedure. They have stable sides
and definite outcomes, which is to say there are winners. Pastimes,
by contrast, although governed by rules of procedures, do not have
definite outcomes as both the competition and the winners are epi-
sodic, and the sides are unstable (7, 8). Inspection of the responses
of the girls which increase significantly between the third and the
fourth grades reveals that these responses involve both levels of maturity and are divided almost equally between masculine and feminine items. Thus, the girls show increased preference for the immature masculine items (bandits, soldiers, cowboy, cops and robbers,
bows and arrows, toy trains). At the same time, they show increased
preference for the relatively mature masculine items (marbles,
basketball, boxing, soccer, baseball, skiing, boating). Again, during
this period, girls show not only increased preference for the simple
feminine pastimes (pom pom pullaway, hoops, black magic, I spy,
statues, here I come, what time is it?), but also for the more mature

TABLE 3

Number of Items Showing Significant Increases or Decreases in
Preference Between Grades for Each Sex*

	Boys				Girls			
Grades:	3–4	4–5	5–6	3–6	3–4	4–5	5–6	3–6
Increases in masculine items	8	..	3	8	15	3	1	18
Decreases in masculine items	..	4	3	5	..	1	..	..
Increases in feminine items	6	..	..	5	14	1	..	6
Decreases in feminine items	4	5	19	29	3	6	16	19
Increases in neutral items	14	1	2	16	12	..	1	17
Decreases in neutral items	..	..	..	..	..	..	..	2
Totals								
Increase	28	1	5	29	41	4	2	41
Decrease	4	9	22	34	3	7	16	21

* $p \leq .05$.

and complex feminine games and activities (bingo, crochet, skating). There are indeed some masculine items for which the girls show increasing preference (bandits, cowboys) at the very time the boys are showing decreasing preference for the same items. Though it should be pointed out that, while the trends for the preferences are in opposite directions, there are still great differences between the sexes in their respective percentages of interest. For example, from the third to the sixth grade, the percentage of boys expressing a liking for bandits drops from 87 to 61 per cent, whereas the percentage of girls liking bandits increases from 29 to 39 per cent. For cowboys, likewise, boys' preferences decrease from 94 to 73 per cent, while the girls' preferences increase from 34 to 52 per cent. As these continued differences between the boys and girls are typical, we should not exaggerate the extent to which girls become like boys, even though they do become more like them than before. Boys' increases from the third to fourth grade, on the other hand, are without exception for male items of only the second and more mature game and activities categories (e.g., shooting, horse riding, boating, soccer, darts) and for a few feminine items also of the more mature level (e.g., dance, skating, checkers). In sum, the greater responsiveness of girls in the fourth grade is produced by their choice of both masculine and feminine items on both levels of maturity.

In the fifth and sixth grades there is a reversal of the trend which occurred between the third and fourth grades. Instead of a marked expansion of preferences for items on the scale, there is a marked contraction. Between the fourth and fifth grades, there are 16 significant decreases and only five increases. Between the fifth and the sixth grades, there are 38 decreases and only seven increases. For boys there are no great changes in their preferences for the male items already established in the fourth grade, but there are 19 significant decreases in their preferences for female items. For girls also, changes through the fifth and sixth grades involve mainly decreases of interest in female items. There are 16 such decreases. Thus, while the pattern of girls' choices was dissimilar to that of boys in the fourth grade, in the fifth and sixth grades it shows considerable similarity. A further test of these changes was made possible by a two-phase longitudinal study involving the masculine-feminine scales derived from the play scale (10). Scores were available for a group of children in the fourth grade and for the same children in the fifth grade. Similarly, there were scores available for a group in the fifth grade and subsequently in the sixth grade. In this study, there was a significant decrease in the girls' scores on the femininity scale between the fourth and fifth grades ($t = 2.59$, $p = .05$), but no other significant changes for boys and girls. This finding is consistent with the present inquiry, but limited by the much smaller number of items used in the Mf scale and the fact that it was standardized only on the fourth through sixth grades. This study is reported more fully elsewhere (6).

The present data do not show the fifth grade or the sixth grade as a turning point towards greater femininity as some writers have suggested. If there is such a trend, it is not revealed by any changes in children's responses to play items. There is rather an accelerated decrease in responses to feminine items. As we shall note in the discussion, this lack of change towards increased preference for feminine items at the fifth grade is most probably attributable to the nature of the items.

DISCUSSION

While the results of this study document the changes that occur in children's play and game preferences, there are certain important limitations to drawing broader conclusions from them. From puberty onwards, playing games and sports is predominantly a masculine phenomenon in this culture. Boys proceed from pastimes into games, but girls by comparison do not. Games and sports are positively associated with the male sex role, but negatively associated with the female sex role (4). The marked changes in play preferences at the age of 8 to 9 years which have been recorded here are an indication, we believe, of children's dawning awareness of this fact. The boys' shedding of pastimes and their increased interest in sports would seem to indicate such a change in attitude. The generalized choices of the girls are, however, something of a puzzle. If, at the age of 9, they perceive that games are not to be of great importance in their future feminine role, the reasons for their increased responsiveness to many items on this scale are not immediately apparent. While this undirected responsiveness can be interpreted as a sign of confusion, it can be argued with some cogency that this responsiveness is rather an indication of greater role flexibility. Thus, the boys' specialization can be seen as a response to a clear-cut role prescription, the girls' diversity as a response to a lack of such prescription. The girls are free to choose in whatever way they wish, and they do so in much more idiosyncratic terms than the boys. It can be argued, for example, that those girls who increase their responses to the more immature Mf items may well be expressing a response to the domestic aspects of the female role, which involve playing with younger children, being interested in them and nurturing them, or at the very least, not being defensive about this when called upon to do it. It can be argued also that girls who show greater interest in mature masculine items may be merely more active, for which only masculine items are appropriate; or that they may be acting as tomboys which girls are free to do; or that they may be showing an awareness that, although girls may not be as generally participants in boys' sports, they are expected to be interested in them as a part of their adolescent sex partner role.

Yet despite all these arguments, there is evidence from associated research by these authors (5) that the fourth grade period is one of peak anxiety for girls (as measured by the Children's Manifest Anxiety Scale) and that this is significantly related to girls' perceiving themselves as "tomboys" rather than "little ladies" at this age level (items from the Tuddenham sociometric [18]). After the fourth grade, however, those girls who show a trend away from tomboyish sociometric attributions towards ladylike attributions are the ones who show a decrease in anxiety. This is perhaps not an unnatural finding as relations have earlier been demonstrated between the CMAS and sex role identification (14). This evidence certainly raises the question as to whether the girls' more generalized responsiveness at the fourth grade level is a product of greater role flexibility or is actually a defense against a sex role anxiety that occurs at that time. Such anxiety would presumably have its source in the lack of prescription for girls' activities and in the greater prestige given to the activities of boys (1).

Summary

A play inventory of 180 items was administered to approximately 1900 children in 12 midwestern townships in grades 3 to 6. The responses were subjected to chi square treatment for sex differences and differences between the grades. The results indicate that girls are more responsive to the items on this inventory than are boys and also show an increasing interest in masculine items throughout these grades. The major part of these changes occur between the third and fourth grades. At this time, boys show an increasing interest mainly for the more mature items, whereas girls show an increased interest in both immature and mature masculine and feminine items. There is no evidence of a change back towards an increased preference for feminine items during the fifth grade. It is suggested that, if this occurs in other aspects of girls' behavior, it may not occur with play activities because these are negatively related to the female sex role. The present paper does not contribute definite evidence as to whether or not the generalized responses of the girls at the fourth grade are an index of sex role confusion at that time, although this possibility is indicated.

REFERENCES

1. Brown, D. G. Sex role preference in young children. *Psychol. Monogr.*, 1956, 70, No. 14.
2. Gray, S. W. Perceived similarity to parents and adjustment. *Child Develpm.*, 1959, 30, 91–107.
3. Hartley, R. E. Children's concepts of male and female roles. *Merrill-Palmer Quart.*, 1960, 6, 83–91.
4. Moss, H. A., and Kagan, J. Stability of achievement and recognition seeking behaviors from early childhood through adulthood. *J. abnorm. soc. Psychol.*, 1961, 62, 504–513.
5. Morgan, E., Rosenberg, B. G., and Sutton-Smith, B. Anxiety as a function of change in sex role. Paper presented at Midwest. Psychol. Ass., Chicago, May 5, 1961.
6. ———, Sutton-Smith, B., and Rosenberg, B. G. Age changes in the relation between anxiety and achievement. *Child Develpm.*, 1960, 31, 515–519.
7. Roberts, J. M., Arth, M. J., and Bush, R. R. Games in culture. *Amer. Anthrop.*, 1959, 61, 597–605.
8. ———, and Sutton-Smith, B. Child training and game involvement. *Ethnology*, 1962, 1, 166–185.
9. Rosenberg, B. G., and Sutton-Smith, B. The measurement of masculinity and femininity in children. *Child Develpm.*, 1959, 30, 373–380.
10. ———, and ———. A revised conception of masculine-feminine differences in play activities. *J. genet. Psychol.*, 1960, 96, 165–170.
11. ———, ———, and Morgan, E. The use of opposite sex scales as a measure of psychosexual deviancy. *J. consult. Psychol.*, 1961, 25, 221–225.
12. Sutton-Smith, B. *The games of New Zealand Children.* Univer. of California Press, 1959.
13. ———, and Rosenberg, B. G. Play and game list. Bowling Green State Univer., I.B.M. Form I.T.S. 1100 A 6140.
14. ———, and ———. Manifest anxiety and game preferences in children. *Child Develpm.*, 1960, 31, 515–519.
15. ———, and ———. Impulsivity and sex preference. *J. genet. Psychol.*, 1961, 98, 187–192.
16. ———, and ———. Sixty years of historical change in the game preferences of American children. *J. Amer. Fokl.*, 1961, 74, 17–46.

17. Tryon, C. M. Evaluations of adolescent personality by adolescents. *Monogr. Soc. Res. Child Develpm.*, 1939, 4, No. 4 (Serial No. 23).
18. Tuddenham, R. D. Studies in reputation: III. Correlates of popularity among elementary school children. *J. educ. Psychol.*, 1951, 42, 257–276.

9. Role Replication and Reversal in Play*

The present investigations grew out of an intensive analysis of two day-long specimen records on the same boy, one at home and one at camp (Gump, Schoggen and Redl, 1963).[1]

It was apparent in these records that the central character, Wally, who was the oldest in his family, nearly always dominated his younger siblings whether playing with them or not. His play status replicated his sibling status. Yet, when playing with his neighborhood and camp friends, Wally often took an egalitarian

SOURCE: Reprinted from the *Merrill-Palmer Quarterly of Behavior and Development* 12, no. 4 (1966): 285–298, by permission of the publisher. This investigation was supported in part by Grant MH 07794-02 from the National Institute of Mental Health.

* The author wishes to express his appreciation to Paul V. Gump of the Department of Psychology, University of Kansas, for permission to review these day studies, and to E. F. Morgan, Jr., and Linda Brandt of Clark University for their participation in the analysis of the studies.

[1] Names within parentheses refer to authors whose works are listed at the end of this article.

or low status role and in some cases even showed remarkable passivity in the face of the playful teasing of his best friend (Gump, Schoggen, Sutton-Smith, Schoggen, and Goldberg, 1955, p. 117). His play status with friends was the reverse of his status with his siblings. It was the purpose of the present study to inquire whether such changing status relations occurred more generally among children—in particular, whether the play with siblings systematically replicated sibling status relationships while play with friends systematically reversed the relations which might be predicted from knowledge of the sibling status order. The case study permitted the specific hypothesis that first-borns would dominate their siblings in play but be of equal or lower status with their friends.

The more general significance of this hypothesis is that it is one expression of a recurrent problem in the interpretation of children's play. This problem centers on the nature of the relations between variables antecedent to the play (motivational variables, child training variables, or status variables as in the present case), and variables which are a part of the play structure itself (acts of mock aggression, strategy, or being boss as in the present case). (See Roberts and Sutton-Smith, 1962; Levin and Wardell, 1962.)

The classic position on the relations between antecedent social status and formal play status is that presented by William F. Whyte in *Street Corner Society* (1933). In the young adult group that he studied, Whyte discovered that performance in a favorite game did not depend solely on the player's skill at that game. On the contrary, if that person was playing along with the members of his own gang or clique, his score was determined primarily by his status in that gang. Thus, the leader of the group would tend to get the highest score in the game and the gang member of the lowest status would tend to get the lowest score. This would occur whenever the gang played together even though other tests indicated that from the point of view of pure skill, the players of lower status should have been capable of doing better.

This case study evidence of Whyte's was subsequently paralleled by Harvey (1953) in an investigation of dart playing among well-defined groups of adolescents, in which the expectations that were held for success in game performances were shown to be largely determined by the subject's previous social standing in the friendship group. There are other studies also which indicate that sociometric status outside of a game may interfere with performance, for example, in marksmanship (McGrath, 1962) and basketball (Fielder, 1954). In addition, there are anecdotal materials about children's play which are of similar import. Gesell (1946, p. 121) mentions children who willingly accede to domination in order to be accepted into the play group. And Jones (1943, p. 55) describes a boy who "in spite of almost daily humiliations . . . showed a persistent eagerness to 'belong,' to be a member of groups, and take part in group activities . . ." so always took a lower status in play.

Against such evidence that play status directly replicates sociometric status, it is possible to cite other less well documented evidence which suggests that play status may sometimes have a reverse relationship to sociometric status. Thus Redl and Wineman (1951, p. 288) cite the case of a high-powered boy who took lower powered roles in play: "For him to yield his power in fantasy seems to be acceptable since he is achieving enjoyment out of the other elements of the game, perhaps even his essentially despotic yielding of power." Sometimes because sociometric leaders are of the unassertive and congenial sort mentioned by various investigators (Jennings, 1947, p. 15; Tryon, 1944, p. 227; Tuddenham, 1951, p. 257), other low status children are permitted to take higher status roles in play. As a grade three boy said of one such sociometric leader in a pilot study carried out by the present investigator:[2] "He does what I like doing. He does anything the other guys want him to do."

Alternatively, there are children of lower sociometric status who so arrange the circumstances of their play that they can reverse the roles within it. Valentine (1948, p. 188) cites the case of the younger sister in a large family compensating for her henpecked family status by exercising an iron control over her peer play group. Lehmann and Witty (1927, p. 146) cite the case of a lower

[2] In the pilot study, 34 grade-three children (19 boys and 15 girls) were given a sociometric to rate them on playmate acceptance, and were observed in their free noon-hour play in order to discover relationships between their group status and their play status. This was done in a Berkeley, California, elementary school while the investigator was a Smith-Mundt research fellow at the Institute of Child Welfare, University of California, 1952–53. A belated appreciation is here expressed for the interest and help of Dr. H. E. Jones, at that time the Director of the Institute.

status group of children who were unsuccessful in school achievement playing persistently at a game of high status content, namely, "schools." In the pilot study referred to above, the girl with the lowest sociometric ranking in her class was observed to spend the greater part of her lunch hour playing with children of a lower grade level whom she could dominate. She claimed to have invented the game she played with them, which she called "Witch Pie" and in which she herself took the important role of mother (Gomme, 1964, p. 396).

There are additional reasons for believing that children may sometimes reverse their usual sociometric status in play. These are inherent in the structure of the games themselves, particularly those played by children between the ages of 6 and 12 years. These games usually involve a variety of counting-out, turn-taking, and role-reversal devices which so vary the allocation of status within the game that it would be difficult for children not to get some experience of differential status through playing them (Sutton-Smith and Gump, 1955).

In sum, the literature suggests both that persons may have experiences of status within play which replicate their status with associates outside of play, and that they may have play experiences that are reversely related to their status outside of it. From the above evidence we may derive either that different persons have different types of relations between their status in and out of play, some replicative and some reversed, or what seems more likely, that the *same* persons sometimes have direct and sometimes reversed relations.

In this literature survey a variety of inter- and cross-group relations have been involved. In the present study, the questions being asked refer only to play status within the family and to play status with playmates. The major hypothesis is that first-borns will tend to dominate their play with siblings and be of equal or less power in play with others. While it is not possible to speak with great confidence about the later-borns except to say that they will be dominated in play by their older siblings, there are some indications in the literature to suggest that they may attempt to dominate their best friends. Several studies have indicated that later-borns tend to be more power striving in general (Harris, 1964; Krout, 1939; Veroff, Atkinson, Feld, Gurin, 1960).

METHOD

Subjects

The question of the relations between status in and out of play with siblings and friends was investigated by submitting five copies of a play inventory to 95 children (44 boys and 51 girls) in two fifth grades at Kenwood School, Bowling Green, Ohio.[3] Children in this school are from an upper sociometric housing area and are of predominately middle-class families.

Inventory

The inventory used was an 180-item play inventory (Sutton-Smith and Rosenberg, 1959) which has previously been used extensively in testing masculine-feminine difference (Rosenberg and Sutton-Smith, 1964), age changes in play preference (Sutton-Smith, Rosenberg, and Morgan, 1963), and relations between play preferences and play behavior (Sutton-Smith, 1965).

Procedure

The children were asked to write on the first inventory the name and age of their nearest sibling. If they were oldest in the family, this should be the next sibling below them in age; if they were a younger sibling, this should be the sibling immediately older than themselves. Children were asked to check on this 180-item play inventory the games that they had played with that sibling over the past year. They were told also to indicate in each case who had been usually the boss in the play, or whether they were usually equal when they played together. They did this by writing in *me*, *sib*, or the *equal sign* (=) after the play. Being boss was defined as being in charge of the game, taking the better positions in the game, and being better at the game. The same instructions were followed for the other inventories—only this time the children were instructed to write in respectively, the name of their best friend (*B. F.*), the person in their own class with whom they played most while at school (class playmate: *C. P.*), the person outside of their own class with whom they played most at school

[3] A special note of appreciation is also in order here for the assistance provided by Harlan Lehtooma, principal of the Kenwood School, and teachers Mrs. Shaddix, Slebos, Maurer, and Benham.

(school playmate: *S. P.*), and the person in their neighborhood with whom they played most at home (neighborhood playmate: *N. P.*). They were to fill in the names and the ages of these persons regardless of whether the identity of the various playmates was the same or different.

The forms were administered on two separate occasions, with the sibling and best-friend forms administered on the first occasion and the other three forms three weeks later. This double administration resulted in slight differences in the size of the N on the separate occasions. In addition, not all the children filled in all the forms properly (omitting names, etc.) which similarly contributed to minor changes in the N (see Table 1). The number of children in each of the eight ordinal groupings is indicated in Table 1. Children were only retained who were in a two-child or larger family and who were within five years of their sibling's age. There was no significant difference in average age difference between first-borns with their younger siblings (2.48 years) and later-borns with their older siblings (2.72 years). First-borns were equally distributed across the two-child, three-child and larger-than-three-child families (11: 13: 10), but the later-borns tended to come more often from the larger size families (10: 26: 38).

These similarities and differences in family size, however, showed no relation to the results that follow. Results for first-borns were uniform irrespective of family size, and results for later-borns varied by type of later-born positions but not by family size. A check for overlap of persons responded to across the inventories indicated that friend and class playmate were the same in 27% of the cases; friend and schoolmate were the same in 9% of the cases; friend and neighborhood playmate were the same in 23% of the cases; classmate and neighborhood playmate were the same in 9% of the cases; and schoolmate and neighborhood playmate were the same in 9% of the cases.

Reliability

In one grade the sibling form was administered again after the three-week period as a check on the reliability of responses. The form scored as to whether the subject said he or sib was more often the boss ($N = 24$) yielded a 79% agreement between the two occasions.

As an intra-subject check on the reliability of the children's responses to the play inventory, they were also given an open-ended questionnaire (at the end of the second administration of the play scales) in which they were asked the questions: "When playing with your sibling, who gets to be the boss?" "Why?"; "When playing with your friend, who gets to be the boss?" "Why?" Results are to be found in Table 2 and are consistent with those derived from the play inventories in Table 1.

RESULTS

Table 1 shows the number of subjects by ordinal position who say they see themselves or the sibling as more often the boss or equal in the games they play. The determination in a particular case was arrived at by counting the *me* and *sib* references on each play scale (ignoring the "=" references), then deciding whether there were more of the me or sib references or whether these were equal in number. The same procedure was followed for *B. F., C. P.,* etc. The numbers in Table 1 therefore refer to the gross power outcome in each case rather than the frequency within cases. This technique had the virtue of eliminating the effects of different frequencies of response to each inventory by different individuals. There were, however, no significant differences in response frequency of first- or later-borns as a whole, though females as compared with males checked approximately a third more items.

The hypothesis that first-borns would take high power roles with siblings and equal or low power roles with friends was tested by comparing the totals of first-born responses to siblings and to friends across *High Power, Equal,* and *Low Power* (31, 0, 3: 9, 10, 15)—that is, the upper section of the first two columns in Table 1. The data offers overwhelming support ($\chi^2 = 30.10$, $p < .001$). That is, first-borns see themselves more often as boss when playing with siblings and more often as equal or not boss when playing with friends. For later-borns, the situation is neatly reversed with later-borns seeing themselves as not being the boss with their older siblings but more often as boss with their friends (22, 11, 41: 30, 25, 19) ($\chi^2 = 14.74$, $p < .025$).

Results for answers to the questionnaire on who gets to be boss when playing with siblings or friends are similar to those derived from the play inventory, as can be seen from Table 2. First-born

TABLE 1
Play-scale Relations Between Ordinal Position and Power in Play

Ordinal Position	N	Sibling			Best Friend			Classroom Playmate			School Playmate			Neighborhood Playmate		
		High Power	Equal Power	Low Power	High Power	Equal Power	Low Power	High Power	Equal Power	Low Power	High Power	Equal Power	Low Power	High Power	Equal Power	Low Power
First-borns																
M1M	(13)	12	0	1	3	4	6	2	6	5	3	7	2	2	9	2
M1F	(5)	4	0	1	1	1	3	0	4	1	0	4	1	1	3	1
F1F	(9)	9	0	0	3	3	3	0	6	2	1	6	1	2	4	2
F1M	(7)	6	0	1	2	2	3	3	3	1	1	3	2	0	5	1
Totals	*(34)*	*31*	*0*	*3*	*9*	*10*	*15*	*5*	*19*	*9*	*5*	*20*	*6*	*5*	*21*	*6*
Later-borns																
MM2	(20)	3	2	15	10	6	4	1	8	4	0	12	1	6	7	1
FM2	(11)	7	3	1	4	4	3	2	6	2	0	9	0	4	5	1
FF2	(24)	10	4	10	12	6	6	6	8	3	6	9	2	11	5	2
MF2	(19)	2	2	15	4	9	6	3	10	2	4	9	2	4	7	2
Totals	*(74)*	*22*	*11*	*41*	*30*	*25*	*19*	*12*	*32*	*11*	*10*	*39*	*5*	*25*	*24*	*6*

responses to siblings and friends (26, 2, 3: 5, 5, 18) yield $\chi^2 =$ 26.12, $p < .001$. Responses of the later-born (16, 2, 39: 22, 17, 16) yield $\chi^2 = 22.38$, $p < .001$. In short, verbal responses to this questionnaire follow along lines expected from the play scales.

Another way of contrasting firsts and later-borns is by directly comparing their respective play with friends. On the inventory, first-borns have a tendency to see themselves as less powerful than friends to a greater extent than do later-borns (9, 10, 15: 30, 25, 19) ($\chi^2 = 3.94$, $p < .20$). The results for the questionnaire are much more clear cut, resulting in a significant difference between the two groups in their statements about play with friends. Firsts see themselves as bossed, non-firsts as bossing a little more than they are bossed (5, 5, 18: 22, 17, 16) ($\chi^2 = 9.74$, $p < .01$).

In response to the question "Why?", the majority of first-borns who give reasons (and not all do) say they are the boss of their siblings because they are older or bigger. The majority of later-borns say they are not the boss for the same reason, i.e., that the sibling is older or bigger. The responses to the friend question, however, appear to have a more "projective" character and are interesting because of that. While there is less similarity of answers

TABLE 2

Questionnaire Relations Between Sibling Position and Power in Play

Ordinal Position	Sibling			Friend		
	High Power	Equal	Low Power	High Power	Equal	Low Power
First-borns						
M1M	11	0	1	2	5	6
M1F	4	1	1	0	0	4
F1F	7	0	1	1	0	4
F1M	4	1	0	2	0	4
Totals	*26*	*2*	*3*	*5*	*5*	*18*
Later-borns						
MM2	3	1	11	8	2	2
FM2	4	1	3	3	2	3
FF2	4	0	16	6	6	8
MF2	5	0	9	5	7	3
Totals	*16*	*2*	*39*	*22*	*17*	*16*

than with respect to the sibling question, the largest single category of responses from the first-born is that their friend is boss because he is older. Firsts also indicate more compliance with the friend by answers such as: the friend "is bigger," "is bossy," "says things and gets to be boss," "is older," "I do whatever he says," "if my friend doesn't get his own way he won't play," "give the friend a chance," "I let him have his own way," "to be polite," "he knows more." By contrast, the later-borns say they are more often boss with their friends because more often they are older than the friend. But in addition, there are other statements made by the later-borns which are of an assertive character or indicate compliance with them by their friend. For example: "I can play better," "I think of most games," "I know more," "I do most things right," "the friend doesn't care," "the friend doesn't get mad," "I like to be boss," "the friend lets me be boss," "I am more firm and convincing."

As indicated in Table 1, relations of firsts and later-borns with classmates and schoolmates seem to be less indicative of power relationships. The characteristic pattern appears to be an egalitarian one with equality of relations predominating. This outcome may be due to the intrinsically egalitarian nature of play structure (built-in role reversal, etc.), as indicated in the introduction. Or it may perhaps be due to the nature of game controls existing in the school situation where the play with class playmate and school playmate occurs. That is, it may be understood that everyone is expected to get a turn and bossing is not permitted. The same egalitarianism holds for neighborhood playmates, at least for first-borns. The later-borns persist with their dominating friendship pattern; that is, they claim a higher power over their neighborhood playmates in the same way as they did over their friends. If their sibling and neighborhood playmates are contrasted (22, 11, 41: 25, 24, 6) again there results a $\chi^2 = 28.92$, $p < .001$.

If the particular ordinal positions within the larger set are examined, it is clear that results are much more consistent for firsts than for later-borns. Later-borns with older and presumably more powerful brothers (the MM2 group) follow the trends observed above most perfectly. The younger child with an older female sibling, however, does not fit the trend. If the younger is a male (FM2) he claims more bossing than his older sister; if a female (FF2), she claims an equal amount. There is a conflict in the evidence here, because the reciprocal older siblings also claim to boss the younger ones. On the direct questionnaire as compared with the game inventory, however, both the younger siblings concede superiority to the older siblings, though this is more marked for the later-born girl. Perhaps it makes sense that the later-born boy with the older sister should be the one most unwilling to concede her superiority.

In all the above computations, power or equality is based on the balance of claimed power between subjects and the other player. Equality by that system of reckoning was derived from a balance of claims made for self and other. But the subjects were also asked in the play inventory to indicate the number of games in which they felt relations were equal. If all protocol is rescored for the number of power attributions (*me* or *sib*) as compared with the number of equal attributions, and each protocol then classified as concerned mainly with power or equality, it is clear that equality dominates throughout most of the play, with one exception. That exception is play with siblings, where power counts at least as much as equality with first-borns and even more so with later-borns. If firsts and later-borns are combined, and their relations in which power is dominant are compared with those in which equality is dominant and comparisons then made between their responses to siblings and friends (57, 45: 29, 78), the first two columns of Table 3—there results a $\chi^2 = 17.86$, $p < .001$. In sum, power is the major concern in play with siblings and a minor concern in play with friends. Power is also a minor concern in play

TABLE 3
Power and Egalitarian Relations with Different Associates

Relations	Sibling	Best Friend	Classroom Playmate	School Playmate	Neighborhood Playmate	Totals
First-borns						
Power	18	9	6	12	5	50
Egalitarian	16	24	36	30	40	156
Later-borns						
Power	39	20	5	7	13	84
Egalitarian	29	54	41	40	34	198

with class playmates, school playmates and neighborhood play-mates, as is clear from Tables 1 and 3.

Yet, another road to the same conclusion is simply to count the total frequency of games over all protocol in which the self is mentioned, the other is mentioned, or equals is mentioned. The totals are: for *me*, 1833; for *other*, 1315; for *equal*, 5375. These totals again show an overwhelming concern with equality rather than with power relations in the responses to these scales.

Discussion

It was the major intent of this paper to investigate the possibility of systematic relations existing between sibling-status and play-status (with siblings and friends), with a view to examining the replicative or reverse character of play structure in general. While results are based only on the children's perception of their own play, the agreement across and between ordinal positions suggests that these responses have consensual validity. Whether real behavior follows the course of these agreements is not dealt with directly. Taken together, however, the self-evidence of the view that older siblings boss younger ones, the case study data cited in the introduction, and the corroborative studies and sociometric references cited below, seem to imply that it does.

The results show that the first-borns' perception of their play with siblings replicates their actual position in the sibling power structure, but that their perception of their play with friends reverses that position. That is, though high powered in the sibling structure, first-borns take equal or lower power positions with friends. Among the later-borns the same duality between replication and reversal of roles in play holds, but with the opposite effect. The later-borns show low power in relation to siblings but high power in relation to friends. In both cases, therefore, replication of sibling power occurs in play with siblings but reversal of sibling power occurs in play with friends.[4]

---

[4] It was judged that these effects were not produced by a response reversal phenomena on the first administration. It might be argued, for example, that the first-born having said that he was powerful over his sibling might select from among his best friends one who was more powerful than he; or, vice versa, the later-born having said he was less powerful than the first, might

Within sibling relationships where the sociometric relations are fairly rigidly established by age and size differences (and probably long standing differences in parent treatment as well), the current situation parallels that described by Whyte (1933), mentioned in the introduction. The family-group hierarchy is reproduced in the play hierarchy. In the friendship play relations, however, where the engagement in play is presumably of a more voluntary nature, play status relations take on a character which, on the surface, reverses the sibling relations within the family. By implication the methodological usage of relations with "friends" as a "projective" technique is an incidental finding worthy of further investigation.

Nevertheless, it is open to question whether the non-bossiness or compliance of first-borns with their friends is a reversal of relationships with the siblings, or whether it is actually a replication of their existing relationships with the parents. Given the extensive data on the first-borns' compliance, conformity, dependence (Sampson, 1962; Sears, et al., 1957; Goodenough and Leahy, 1927; Becker and Carroll, 1962), the latter interpretation may be the more likely alternative. If so, the conclusion may be that while the firsts strive to keep non-firsts in lower status positions on all possible occasions, thus preserving their own status in the family hierarchy, when in a more voluntary situation among friends they prefer the behavior of being dependent or conforming with another person, which is the relationship they have had with their parents. Thus, their friendship play behavior may be a replication of their responses to their parents rather than a reversal of their attitudes towards their siblings.

Later-borns, on the other hand, who have been characterized in other studies as aggressive and power-striving (Harris, 1964; Krout, 1939; Veroff, et al., 1960), look as if their play relations are a reversal of their responses in sibling relationships. It is not an unreasonable thesis that the power they exercise over friends is a manifestation of the power they seek but cannot obtain with their

---

select from among his best friends one who was less powerful than he. Both sets of subjects would thus balance out their responses in the direction of an overall socially desirable response. The neighborhood friend responses given on the second administration, however, are similar in direction to the best friend responses, particularly for the later-born, which suggests that the substantive interpretations being made here are the most parsimonious.

older siblings, and that their model in this is the power exercised over them by those older siblings. If this is true, it might account for the stronger power-seeking of later-borns. It is a well-established finding in the ordinal literature that firsts tend to be relatively more influenced by their parents than do later-borns, and that later-borns in turn tend to be relatively more influenced by their older siblings (Rosenberg and Sutton-Smith, 1964). As older children are relatively inexperienced and presumably harsher yielders of power than are their parents, it follows that behavior modeled after theirs by the younger children may have a more assertive character also. It is noticeable in the above results that the later-born claim to assert their power not only over best friends, but also over neighborhood friends. This is not the case with first-borns, although the percentage of overlap between B. F. and N. F. is approximately the same in both cases. That this bossiness of the later-born is of a more general nature is supported by a finding in a parallel sociometric study which has shown that classmates more often perceive later-borns, than first-borns, as bossy (Sutton-Smith and Rosenberg, 1965).

In sum, while firsts and later-borns replicate their sibling relationships in their play status relations with siblings, their reversal of these status relationships in play behavior with friends appears to be of a quite different origin. The following hypotheses, therefore, seem worthy of further investigation. Namely, that firsts generalize to their play with friends relationships analogous to those they maintain with their parents, but that later-borns generalize to play with friends behavior modelled after the power exercised over them by the first-born.

The present finding that the uses of status in play vary by ordinal position, as well as by play associate and presumably by play ecology (neighborhood, school, etc.), contributes towards an understanding of the complexity of the findings in the literature with respect to status and play.

From the finding that about five-eighths of the games checked were characterized as ones of equality not power, a further conclusion may be drawn. That is, normatively speaking, it is not the function of play to systematically replicate or reverse the status relationships found in the family. If we may extrapolate this finding to other dimensions which have been studied in relation to play (aggression, sex, dependency, etc.), and which have been said to bear possible replicative or reverse relations with play, the present data appear to suggest that, again normatively speaking, these matters will not dominate the play behaviors. The fact, however, that they can dominate those behaviors for a considerable portion of the time (three-eighths in the present estimate) helps to explain the predictive power of those play theories which subsume play to concepts which do not derive directly from play phenomena as such. One example in point can be found in psychoanalytic theory, in which play is often explained in terms of affective conflict (Waelder, 1933). Another example is Piaget's play theory, in which play is explained in terms of cognitive disequilibrium (Piaget, 1962; Sutton-Smith, 1966). The present finding that, normatively speaking, children do not perceive their play status relations as dominated by status relations outside the intrinsic economy of play, gives some support to those who view play as a behavior system with a formal character that must be understood in terms of its own intrinsic dimensions (Huizinga, 1949).

REFERENCES

Barker, R. G. and Wright, H. F. *Midwest and its children.* New York: Row Peterson, 1955.

Becker, S. W. and Carroll, Jean. Ordinal position and conformity. *J. abnorm. soc. Psychol.,* 1962, 65, 129–131.

Fielder, A. E. Assumed similarity measures as predicters of team effectiveness. *J. abnorm. soc. Psychol.,* 1954, 49, 381–388.

Gesell, A. *The child from five to ten.* New York: Harper, 1946.

Goodenough, F. L. and Leahy, A. M. The effect of certain family relationships upon the development of personality. *J. genet. Psychol.,* 1927, 34, 45–72.

Gomme, A. B. *The traditional games of England, Scotland, and Ireland.* New York: Dover, 1964.

Gump, P. V., Schoggen, P. H., Sutton-Smith, B., Schoggen, M. and Goldberg, T. *Wally O'Neill at camp.* Wayne State University ms., 1955.

———, ———, and Redl, F. The behavior of the same child in different milieus. In R. G. Barker (Ed.), *The Stream of Behavior.* New York: Appleton-Century Crofts, 1963.

Harris, I. D. *The promised seed: a comparative study of eminent first and later sons.* Glencoe, Ill.: Free Press, 1964.

Harvey, O. J. An experimental approach to the study of status relations in informal groups. *Amer. sociol. Rev.,* 1953, 18, 357–367.

Huizinga, J. *Homo Ludens: a study of the play-element in culture.* London: Routledge and Kegan Paul, 1949.

Jennings, H. H. *Leadership and isolation.* New York: Longmans, Green & Co., 1947.

Jones, H. E. *Development in adolescence.* New York: Appleton-Century, 1943.

Krout, M. H. Typical behavior patterns in 26 ordinal positions. *J. genet. Psychol.,* 1939, 54, 3-29.

Lehmann, H. C. and Witty, P. A. *The psychology of play activities.* New York: Barnes, 1927.

Levin, H. and Wardwell, E. The research uses of doll play. *Psychol. Bull.,* 1962, 59, 27–56.

McGrath, G. E. The influence of positive interpersonal relations on adjustment and effectiveness in rifle teams. *J. abnorm. soc. Psychol.,* 1962, 365–375.

Piaget, J. *Play, dreams, and imitations in childhood.* New York: Norton, 1962.

Redl, F. and Wineman, D. *Children who hate.* Glencoe, Ill.: Free Press, 1951.

Roberts, J. M. and Sutton-Smith, B. Child training and game involvement. *Ethnology*, 1962, 1, 166–185.

Rosenberg, B. G. and Sutton-Smith, B. The measurement of masculinity and femininity in children: an extension and revalidation. *J. genet. Psychol.*, 1964, 104, 259–264.

———, and ———. Ordinal position and sex-role identification. *Genet. Psychol. Monog.*, 1964, 70, 297–328.

Sampson, E. E. Birth order, need achievement, and conformity. *J. abnorm. soc. Psychol.*, 1962, 64, 155–159.

Sears, R. R., Macoby, Eleanor E. and Levin, H. *Patterns of child rearing.* Evanston, Ill.: Row Peterson & Co., 1957.

Sutton-Smith, B. Play preference and play behavior: a validity study. *Psychol. Reports*, 1965, 16, 65–66.

———. Piaget on play: A critique. *Psychol. Review*, 1966, 73, 111–112.

———, and Gump, P. Games and status experience. *Recreation*, 1955, 48, 172–174.

———, and Rosenberg, B. G. Sibling perceptions of power styles within the family. Paper presented at A.P.A. Chicago, September, 1965.

———, and ———. Play and game list. Bowling Green, Ohio: Bowling Green State University, 1959 (I.B.M. Form I.T.S. 1100 A 6140).

———, ———, and Morgan, E. The development of sex differences in play choices during preadolescence. *Child Develpm.*, 1963, 34, 119–126.

Tryon, C. M. *The adolescent peer culture.* In the 43rd yearbook of the National Society for the Study of Education, Chicago, 1944.

Tuddenham, R. D. Studies in reputation: III. *J. educ. Psychol.*, 1951, 42, 257–276.

Valentine, C. W. A study in the beginnings and significance of play in infancy. *Brit. J. educ. Psychol.*, 1948, 8, 188–200.

Veroff, J., Atkinson, J. W., Feld, S. C. and Gurin, G. The use of thematic apperception to assess motivation in a nationwide interview study. *Psychol. Monogr.*, 1960, 74, No. 12.

Waelder, R. The psychoanalytic theory of play. *Psychoanalyt. Quart.*, 1933, 2, 208–224.

Whyte, W. F. *Street corner society.* Chicago: Univer. Chicago Press, 1933.

10. The "It" Role in Children's Games

The present experiment was part of a larger research effort on the problem of how the ingredients of different children's activities and programs affect participants' individual and group behavior and experience.[1] The aim of the research is to develop concepts and findings which will assist the practitioner in selecting, inventing, and managing activities so that children's experiences in these activities will be beneficial.

Among the most prominent activities used in group work with children are games. Also, games are relatively coercive activities since they specify the roles persons shall take, the goals they shall seek, and other areas of behavior which many non-game activities leave to the choice of participants. Because games are coercive, they may be expected to determine behavior in a relatively pre-

SOURCE: Reprinted from *American Association of Group Workers* 17, no. 3 (1955): 3–8, with permission of the publisher and the co-author Paul V. Gump.

[1] This investigation was supported by research grant M-550 from the National Institute of Mental Health, of the National Institutes of Health, Public Health Service. Its original title is "The Relationship of the Power of the *It* Role to Experience in the *It* Role."

dictable fashion. The prominence and the coerciveness of games suggested that they be given special study.

The ingredients of games differ widely and these differences may be expected to generate parallel variations in the experience and behavior of their participants. Such variations go beyond differences in game-required acts to differences in response to these acts. For example, the games of Tag and Beater-Goes-Around obviously differ in that one requires tagging and the other beating; however, the response to tagging (and being tagged) may be expected to be different from the response to beating (and being beaten).

Since a large proportion of all active games for children are *It* games, these games were selected for study. *It* games contain a central person who acts in opposition to the rest of the playing group or the "pack." One aspect of these games which seemed important in determining the experience of the *It*—and the reaction of the group or pack to him—was the *game-determined power* of the *It* role. This power is shaped by a number of game provisions: *It's* prerogatives in determining which pack member he will engage in competitive encounter and when this encounter will begin; his "trappings," for example, his game name *or* his power symbols; his protection against the combined efforts of pack members against him; and so forth. Power of this type resides entirely in the *It* role and is separate from the skill of the player occupying the *It* role.

The study investigated how behavior and experience of players in the *It* role were affected by the amount of power of the *It* role. One supposition was that a high-power *It* role would expose its occupants to *fewer* competitive failures in the game than would a low-power *It* role. A second related supposition was that relatively unskilled players could be protected from too frequent failure by enabling them to occupy a high-power, rather than a low-power, *It* role. The problem of helping the unskilled participant in situations in which he can become the focal person is a real and a practical one. Readers are doubtless aware of the difficulties which arise when unskilled players are put into certain *It* positions. Their failure to find, catch, or tag skilled members of the pack leads to discouragement for themselves and boredom for the pack. The pack's derision of *It* for his failure intensifies his frustrations. Since a group worker can do nothing immediately to change skill, selecting or managing games so that lack of skill becomes less crucial is a potential solution. The study tested the supposition that lack of skill in *It* games can be partially compensated for by opportunity to occupy a high-power *It* role.

The experiment reported below, then, checked two basic suppositions which are closely related:

1. High-power *It* roles result in fewer game failures for *It* players in general than do low-power *It* roles.

2. High-power *It* roles result in fewer game failures for unskilled *It* players than do low-power *It* roles.

Since number of game failures might be expected to affect *It*'s feeling about himself and the pack's feeling toward *It*, data relevant to these issues were also collected.

EXPERIMENT
Games Played

Two games were employed which met the following criteria: the games significantly differed only with respect to the power of the *It*; they required the same basic skill—running speed; they permitted reliable measurement of amount of failure; and they were representative of a popular kind of children's game.

The games were Black Tom, and Dodge the Skunk; both are similar to Pom-Pom-Pullaway.[2] A field was lined with boundaries and with safe or "home" areas at either end. *It* was required to tag pack members as they ran from one home area to the other. Any player tagged was out; when *It* had tagged two of the three pack members, that game session was over and another *It* took over. Each *It* was given a handkerchief tail to wear as a symbol of *It*.

Black Tom, involving a high-power *It* role, differed from Dodge the Skunk, involving a low-power *It* role, in the following ways: The Black Tom *It* called a series of names the last one of which (Black Tom) was the signal that required the pack members to run to the opposite home. In actual play, Black Tom could come fairly close to players at home and then call the running signal when he thought he could tag a particular player. The Dodge the Skunk *It* called no signal and chased players as they ran, at will, from one home to the other. In actual play, *It* ranged about from the middle

---

2 Bancroft, J. H., *Games*, New York, Macmillan, 1952, p. 184.

of the field in order to be able to choose runners from either home. In Black Tom, *It* had the opportunity to choose the time, place, and opponent for a competitive encounter; in Dodge the Skunk, *It* had no such choice; the pack members decided if and when they would attempt the dash across the unsafe field to the opposite home area.

Population Employed

Forty boy campers,[3] seven to ten years old, were divided into ten four-person playing groups. Boys of similar age but who differed in running speed[4] were put into each group. One skilled boy, i.e., a fast runner, two semi-skilled boys, and one unskilled boy were placed in each group. Data were collected on *It* role behavior for only the fast or skilled and the slow or unskilled boys. Boys of medium skill were included to enlarge the playing group and to screen the fact that the observers were focussing only on skilled and unskilled boys. These semi-skilled boys were *It* in games which observers considered practice sessions but which, to the playing groups, looked like the "real thing."

Administration

One experimenter taught the games using demonstrations and practice sessions so that the limitations and privileges of the *It* and pack roles were clarified. Ordinarily, each game session was over when *It* made two successful tags. However, in eight of the twenty game sessions, the unskilled *It* experienced such obvious and complete failure that further play would have been painfully discouraging. When both experimenters agreed that further play would not result in tagging success for the *It*, the game session was terminated and a new *It* assigned.

A total of forty game sessions were included in the experiment: ten skilled boys were *It* once in Black Tom and the same ten were *It* once in Dodge the Skunk; the ten unskilled boys went through this same regime.

[3] We wish to thank Mr. Bob Luby, Director of the Fresh Air Camp, Brighton, Michigan, for his help in the research. Counselors Al Camiener, Sherman Hesselman, Leonard Rachmiel, and Jerry Wolberg contributed time, effort, and ideas to our research.

[4] A series of foot races were held several days before the experiment in order to identify fast, medium, and slow runners.

Data Collection

The following data were collected: (1) the number of unsuccessful tag attempts made by each skilled or unskilled *It* before he tagged out two pack members, (2) the number and quality of verbal expressions made by *It* players, and (3) the general behavior of the pack toward the *Its*.

RESULTS
Tagging Success

It players were eventually successful in tagging two other members in 32 of the 40 game sessions. The average numbers of tag attempt failures for these 32 games were as follows:

All players in high-power *It* roles: 1.7 tag failures;

All players in low-power *It* roles: 3.7 tag failures.

In general, then, boys endured markedly fewer tagging failures in high-power *It* roles than in low-power *It* roles. When these gross results were broken down to show differences for skilled and unskilled players, the following averages were obtained:

Skilled players in high-power *It* roles: 0.6 tag failures;

Skilled players in low-power *It* roles: 2.2 tag failures;

Unskilled players in high-power *It* roles: 4.4 tag failures;

Unskilled players in low-power *It* roles: 6.7 tag failures.

The above numbers show two results: skilled players had fewer failures than unskilled ones, regardless of the power of the *It* role occupied; and both skilled and unskilled players had fewer failures when in the high-power role. The tendency of the high-power role to help unskilled boys is indicated by one further fact. In 8 of the 40 game sessions, unskilled *Its* completely failed to make the required two tags. However, only three unskilled *Its* so failed in the high-power *It* role, while these same three plus *two more* unskilled players failed completely in the low-power *It* role.

Game Actions and Attitudes

The number of tag failures yields an objective picture of the intensity of the *It*'s success-failure situation. The response of *It* to his role and the responses of others to him gives a psychological picture of this situation. Observations recorded of taunting and other expressive "side play" justified the following conclusions:

1. *The pack combined against "It" most frequently when he was in a low-power role.* In six of the twenty game sessions, pack members intrigued together against *It*; for example, "Same plan! When you put your hand down, all three of us run." These alliances occurred *only* in the game sessions of Dodge the Skunk (low-power *It*).

2. *The pack disparaged "It" most frequently when he was in the low-power "It" role.* Disparaging remarks were made before the game began to six unskilled *Its*; this happened equally frequently in Black Tom and in Dodge the Skunk. For example, before Dodge the Skunk, it was said of one unskilled boy about to be *It*, "Oh, Peter's easy to beat." Before Black Tom, one unskilled *It* was called "Spaghetti Balls." No skilled *It* received such pre-game disparagement.

Once the game began, however, it was the *game*, as well as the players' more abiding attitudes toward each other, which dictated the targets of taunts. There were nine occasions of marked taunting of the low-power *It* in Dodge the Skunk—seven times to unskilled and twice to skilled *Its*. "C'mon you chicken. Lay an egg." "This skunk really smells" were typical disparagements of low-power *Its*. Unskilled boys in this low-power It role of Dodge the Skunk suffered other humiliations. Pack members began to *walk* past them, to run circles around them, to jeer in their faces, and to pull off their tails.

No comparable taunting was directed to either skilled or unskilled players in the high-power "It" role. Although it is the unskilled boy who suffers the most disparagement, this occurs mainly in the game role which offers him the least power.

3. *With unskilled players, a sense of failure occurred more often in the low-power "It" role than in the high-power "It" role.* In Dodge the Skunk, three of the ten unskilled boys expressed their sense of failure and powerlessness by sighs and by complaints directed towards the experimenters; they wanted "out." The same boys did not make similar appeals in Black Tom. As it happened they were only slightly more successful in Black Tom, but, apparently they *felt* less failure as a Black Tom *It*.

The tendency for *felt* power to be greater in a Black Tom *It* role was demonstrated also by results from post-game interviews. All of the unskilled boys (and all but one of the skilled boys) preferred to be *It* in Black Tom. Their reasons were that *It* has an easier job and that *It* has more power over players in Black Tom. Sample remarks were: "In Black Tom you can fool people," or "It's like a mystery. They don't know when you're going to say it."

DISCUSSION
Relation of It *Power to Experience in the* It *Role*

The above results demonstrate that the game-given power of a role is an important determiner of game experience. Power affects the amount of objective failure endured by the occupant of a game role, it affects the way this occupant is treated by the rest of the playing group, and it affects how he feels about himself and his situation.

The results also reveal that unskilled players are particularly likely to endure failure and derision in *It* roles. For most of the unskilled boys, failure and derision were less frequently encountered when they played a high-power, rather than a low-power, *It* role.

Relation of Personality to Experience in an It *Role*

Although skill of participants and power of the role were two important factors determining success or failure in the *It* role, it appeared that a personality factor which might loosely be described as "drive" was also important to success. Unskilled boys who gained some success in a high-power *It* role differed from unskilled boys who failed in the following respects:

1. *Successful boys focussed on a target pack member and they used strategy.* In contrast, the unsuccessful unskilled boys *let* things happen instead of *causing* things to happen. They would stand timidly in the middle of the field and call "Black Tom" and then chase one, then another fleeing player. Concentration of effort and exploitation of the high-power of the *It* role were not employed by unsuccessful unskilled boys.

2. *Successful but unskilled boys sustained effort at climax points.* In contrast, there were those instances in which both observers were sure than an unskilled *It* was about to tag—only to watch a failure. The *It* would hesitate slightly at the crucial moment; he would slow down, or he would *drop*, instead of raise his tagging hand. Whether these "climax failures" were due to simple fear of falling while extending oneself or to an emotional "tagging

inhibition" could not be determined. It seemed possible that the aggression or assertion symbolized by the tagging act was sufficiently feared to create a momentary inhibition resulting in tagging failure.

The following game record is an example of a successful, yet unskilled boy using strategy, establishing focus, and maintaining effort at climax points.

Harry, a fat, awkward boy, is *It* in Black Tom. At first he has little success as he proceeds up and down the field after his fleet playmates. Then he begins to call "Black Tom" just as soon as the runners are safely home and so forces them to come out again immediately. A half-dozen such rapid calls fatigues the runners and they are now more in Harry's speed class. (Harry doesn't have to run as far as they do since they must go all the way home to be safe.) Harry then centers his efforts on one skilled boy: he chases him home calling, "Black Tom!" as he rushes up to the home line. The call forces the tired runner to leave home and Harry lunges and tags him as he comes out.[5]

Relation of It *Rotation Procedures to Experience in the* It *Role*

Another factor significantly affects the intensity of negative experience in the *It* role. The factor is *time* spent in the role. Amount of time spent in *It* roles is determined partly by the game prescribed arrangement for rotation of *It* players. For example, in the game I Got It, the *It* is chased and when he fails—when he is tagged—he becomes a member of the chasing pack. Although the *It* role in I Got It is one of relatively low power, prolonged failure in the role is impossible. On the other hand, in Dodge the Skunk, the failure of *It* to tag leaves him in the *It* role and subject to an extended failure experience. Thus, although low-power *It* roles are likely to result in failure for the *It*, the *extent* of failure in the *It* role is significantly determined by the game-prescribed arrangements for rotation of occupants in the *It* role.

---

[5] The possibilities inherent in *It* games for diagnoses of personality qualities —as opposed to qualities of sheer skill— seem worthy of systematic research. For example, observers also noticed that boys differed widely in terms of their desire to taunt the *It* and in their zest for the fleeing and anonymous pack role as contrasted to the more responsible and limelighted *It* role.

SUMMARY

The ingredients of children's programs and activities were assumed to have important effects upon the behavior and experience of participants. One type of activity—*It* games—was selected for experimentation. One supposition tested was that high-power *It* roles—as contrasted to low-power *It* roles—lead to less failure for *Its*, to fewer negative reactions of the playing groups toward *It*, and to more positive feeling of *It* about himself and his situation. Results showed this supposition to be generally correct. A second and related supposition was that unskilled players could be helped to more frequent success and to a less negative experience if they were placed in high-power, rather than in low-power, *It* roles. Results generally favored this supposition; however, it was found that unskilled boys who also lacked the ability or the personal drive to exploit game advantage were not materially helped by such game role manipulation. The importance of game-prescribed *It rotation procedures* in determining the intensity of failure of unskilled players in the lower-power *It* role was also pointed out.

The present study investigated specifically the effect of the power of an *It* role upon the experience of game participants. However, this factor of *It* power is just one of many game factors which shape the experience of players. For example, the extent to which game arrangements sharpen and centralize competition may be expected to affect the intensity of hostile and other "combative" impulses felt and expressed by participants. The factor of chance, as opposed to skill, is also important in game structure. It is *probable* that the gratifications and frustrations accompanying appeals to chance differ from those accompanying appeals to skill; it is *certain* that the generally unskilled player will have more success in games of chance than in games of skill. Factors inherent in games—such as power of game roles, sharpness of competition, and chance determination of success—are deserving of serious attention from both the practitioner and the researcher. Once these factors are identified and their effects upon various types of participants are known, the way is open for the strategic use of games in work with children. Games then may be employed in a conscious and deliberate fashion so that participants enjoy the maximum of beneficial experience in game play.

11. The Game as a School of Abstraction*

In *Science and the Modern World,* A. N. Whitehead makes the point that "the habit of definite and exact thought was implanted in the European mind by the long dominance of scholastic logic and scholastic divinity" (1946, p. 15).[†] In *Studies in Cognitive Growth,* Bruner *et al.* contend that children who have gone to school in one country are more similar (in logical competences) to children who have gone to school in another country, than are either to children who have not gone to school in those countries. Bruner says of the school goer: "He early shows the effect of learning to use language outside a context in which his reference is sup-

* My appreciation to Mrs. Sheree MacDonald for carrying out the game-playing phase of this study, and to Mr. Gordon Schofield, Headmaster of the Maumee Valley Country Day School, for encouraging the use of the school for experimental purposes. The project received partial support from Grant MH 07994-04 of the National Institute of Mental Health.
  † Material set within parentheses refers to the list of sources found at the end of this article.

ported either by pointing or by the structure of the situation. . . . School forces him to rely on linguistic encoding as a way of communicating, because by remoteness from direct action it robs him of contextual and ostensive reference as a mode of carrying meaning" (1956, p. 323).

One might say that Whitehead is talking about the university as a form of abstraction, and Bruner about the elementary school as a form of abstraction. In both cases, the separation of thought from everyday concerns and contingencies makes possible the development of those internal consistencies in thinking itself, which Piaget has labelled as concrete and formal operations. From such a broadly functionalist point of view, the "ivory tower" and the "Latin grammar school" may have been successful because of their unrelatedness to life, and the transfer of training they effected may have occurred in a much more fundamental way than was generally considered when such matters were moot at the turn of this century. From this point of view, the apparent sterility of these grammar schools, with their studies of syntax and rhetoric, has to be contrasted with the surgent "paleologic" (Arieti, 1967) with which mankind has traditionally surrounded most of its concerns. Just as conversion experiences are sometimes most effective when preceded by a period in the wilderness, or by fasting, or some other radical behavioral separation, so apparently the step from a preoperational to an operational level of logic has been aided historically by such institutional forms of severance. It is no accident that when many of the major Head Start programs attempt to deal with an even more elementary level of logic, that is with the distinction between *as is* and *as if*, they spend much of their time talking about things not seen, not heard, and not touchable. In some of his current work, a colleague, Gilbert Lazier of the Drama Department at Teachers College, found it difficult to induce just such an "as if" response set in fourteen-year-old functional illiterates. When the students were asked to imagine that one of the statues in Central Park was about to fly off, some of them reacted with profound cynicism; others wished to rush down to see it happening. In neither case was there a recognition of the abstractive or "as if" nature of the suggestion.

Games, I would suggest, like universities, grammar schools, Head Start programs, drama classes, and we might add, art, music, and poetry, are schools in abstraction. Like these other institutions and processes they also involve the fundamental assumption that one cannot learn enough by direct experience; that the regularities within experience (whether those of human interaction, language, or logic) require concentrated focus if the user is to master, not merely be affected by, or transmit in a partial way, their formal characteristics. Such regularities usually impinge upon us deeply embedded in regularities of other orders, as well as obscured and distorted by the contingencies of momentary survival. Furthermore, the regularities that guide our behavior usually arrive, themselves, in multi-dimensional clusters, which may well defy individual analysis. One has to think only of the amazing regularities underlying social interaction that currently are being revealed in systematic studies labelled variously as kinesics, proxemics, and so forth, to realize the great difficulty anyone would have in mastering the "elements" of his own interactive responses. What appears to be more typical is that one learns these relationships in packaged forms that do not require an awareness of their molecular supports. Unfortunately, such forms of holistic functioning and learning have not been extensively documented outside the domains of perception and logic. We might well assume that games are an example of a form of holistic learning through which participants acquire a wide variety of competences that normally function in an interactional context. Games abstract and present a crystallization of human relationships, particularly those that have to do with asserting power over others. In an extensive series of studies, John M. Roberts and I have presented information on the functioning of games, both cross-culturally and intraculturally, and have sought to show that they are models of power; or, in other words, games are buffered learning situations through which the child gains acquaintance and experience at the power strategems relevant to some of the major parameters of influence within his own culture (1962, 1963, 1963, 1964, 1967). The results of these studies have been presented and assessed in a number of publications. We dealt in the main with games that were pure expressions of physical skill, strategy, or chance. It so happens, however, that most games are mixtures of these elements.

It is among the games of young children (six to nine years old) where we find a high proportion of chance games as compared with those of strategy. Neither the chance factor nor the strategy factor is pure. The first lacks a controlling artefact (a die, roulette wheel, etc.), and the second, a clear pattern of rational choice. Both appear in the form of a more or less well informed *guess*; a guess made partly at random and partly by observing characteristics of the situation involved. In fact, we might hazard the statement that *guessing* is historically and developmentally a major type of pre-operational structure; one in which both magic and insight are fused into one form of power. What the child gains through his guessing, this argument would continue, is an education in "shrewdness"—the compound virtue that seems to derive from this schooling in chance and strategy. We might speculate that such games arose historically as institutionalized forms of abstraction through which the arts of shrewdness could be practised and learned.

A Game of Number Conservation

The present paper deals, in particular, with one game of shrewdness and seeks to show that practise at this game is as effective as direct teaching for some of the elements involved. More specifically, the game involves shrewdness in the guessing of numbers and, as such, is directly related to current attempts to measure and facilitate number conservation in cognitive psychology. Attempts to induce number conservation in children by using specific training procedures have not been particularly successful (Flavell, 1963). Piaget's theory which provides models for the character of logical operations, such as numeration, gives little guidance with respect to the acquisition of such operations.

The game of "How Many Eggs in My Bush?" (Sutton-Smith, 1959) was chosen as requiring the processes involved in number conservation. In this game, the children take turns at guessing how many counters (usually between one and six) the other player is holding in his hand. Players alternate turns, and a correct guess wins the counters from the other players. The game is finished when one player has all the counters. Each player begins with ten counters. It was hypothesized that play at this game would encourage the development of number conservation, because unless he has acquired this skill a player cannot know if he is winning and he can be cheated.

Procedure

All children were tested for number conservation using the procedure of matching a row of blocks from a pile near at hand (Flavell, p. 313). The conservation test was given before and after the game training sessions which lasted for six weeks. These involved one explicit game training session, which lasted for an hour each week, and much more informal play by the children without the teacher. Conservers played the game eagerly from the beginning. Nonconservers had to be encouraged and instructed by the teacher on how to pay attention to the counters and, in some cases, on how to count and how to guess; training procedures that in themselves had not been previously effective in inducing conservation; i.e., training in counting and similar skills (Flavell, 1963, p. 377). Within six weeks all nonconservers were playing the game with considerable enjoyment. The control group was taken from the same kindergarten in the following year, at the same time of year. Children in both experimental and control groups were between the ages of five to five-and-a-half years, but were advanced, on the average, one to one-and-a-fourth years in mental age. In mental age terms, therefore, they were at an age when average children normally begin to acquire conservation.

Results

The chi square analysis of Table 1 indicates that the experimental group with the game training changed significantly in the direction of conservation, but that the control group without the game training did not. The two exceptions in the experimental group were both extremely immature boys, one of whom was subsequently retained in the kindergarten for a further year.

TABLE 1

Changes in Number Conservation as a Result of Game Playing

Subjects	Pretest		Posttest		P
	Con.	Non/Con.	Con.	Non/Con.	
Experimental Group (1965)	10	14	22	2	<.01
Control Group (1966)	7	11	9	10	ns

Discussion

The effectiveness of this game in inducing the change is clearly of considerable pedagogic importance and parallels the use of games by others for similar pedagogic ends (Humphrey, 1966). The success of the game in inducing conservation does not, however, illuminate the psychological processes involved in number concept acquisition, though it does seem to imply that such acquisition occurs more readily when there is an interaction of influences working in its favor as typically occurs in a game.

We may perhaps theorize that when children acquire conservation there is a mutual dependency of processes as follows. On the one hand, there are such operations and performances as class equivalence, seriation, counting, matching, etc., some or all of which are apparently contributory towards the development of number conservation, but not sufficient in themselves to bring it about (Dodwell, 1960). On the other hand, there is the child's intention of using this information effectively in order to overcome a difficulty of which he has become aware; an intentionality which might be considered a key factor in the implicit or explicit feedback procedures successfully used in several studies of number conservation (Wallach and Sprott, 1964; Beilin, 1966). Alternatively, when a game is used, as in the present study, there are a variety of superordinate motives introduced: to win the game, to acquire counters, to have fun, to guard against being cheated, and so forth. Such motivation may facilitate in turn the acquisition of the above operations and performances, which apparently then transfer to the test of number conservation. We are thus confronted with the possibility that conservation concepts may be built into the child in an elementaristic way providing there is sufficient incentive, or in a hierarchical way as in the present case of game playing. It would make sense, should the two methods be compared, that the more rapid learning would occur in the second case where the conservation concepts had been acquired within the broader hierarchical context of the game. There is some evidence that this is the case (Humphrey, 1966). It follows that if this is the way in which children "normally" have learned such skills through enculturation, as the very existence of such a traditional game seems to imply, then we are also in a better position to understand the considerable difficulties experienced by a succession of researchers in attempting to induce conservation by more elementaristic means. Number conservation in service of the school of shrewdness comes easier than number conservation in service of the grade school teacher.

In sum, I have argued that the game is a school of abstraction. But it is a school of the holistic variety, apparently evolved during cultural evolution as a way of imparting knowledge of the processes of social power. The game of "How Many Eggs in My Bush?" has been presented as an example of number conservation, though it might have been more to the point to test for the derived learning of shrewdness rather than for number. The latter could be regarded as merely incidental to that larger end.

REFERENCES

Arieti, S. *The Intrapsychic Self*. New York: Basic Books, 1967.

Beilin, H. "Feedback and Infralogical Strategies in Invariant Area Conceptualization." *Journal of Experimental Child Psychology* 3 (1966): 267–278.

Bruner, J. S. *et al. Studies in Cognitive Growth*. New York: John Wiley & Sons, Inc., 1967.

Dodwell, P. C. "Children's Understanding of Number and Related Concepts." *Canadian Journal of Psychology* 14 (1960): 191–205.

Flavell, J. *The Developmental Psychology of Jean Piaget*. New York: Van Nostrand, 1963.

Humphrey, J. K. "An Exploratory Study of Active Games in Learning of Number Concepts by First Grade Boys and Girls." *Perceptual and Motor Skills* 23 (1966): 341–342.

Roberts, J. M., and Sutton-Smith, B. "Child Training and Game Involvement." *Ethnology* 1 (1962): 166–185.

———, ———, and Kendon, A. "Strategy in Folktales and Games." *Journal of Social Psychology* 61 (1963): 185–199.

Sutton-Smith, B. *The Games of New Zealand Children*. Berkeley: University of California Press, 1959.

———. "Novel Responses to Toys." *Merrill-Palmer Quarterly* 14 (1968): 159–160.

———, and Roberts, J. M. "Game Involvement in Adults." *Journal of Social Psychology* 60 (1963): 15–30.

———, and ———. "Rubrics of Competitive Behavior." *Journal of Genetic Psychology* 105 (1964): 13–37.

———, and ———. "Studies in an Elementary Game of Strategy." egy." *Genetic Psychological Monographs* 75 (1967): 3–42.

Wallach, L., and Sprott, R. L. "Inducing Number Conservation in Children." *Child Development* 35 (1964): 1057–1071.

Whitehead, A. N. *Science and the Modern World*. Cambridge: Cambridge University Press, 1946.

SECTION IV

UNIFIED APPROACHES

The attempts to consider games historically, anthropologically, and psychologically indicate a persistent search for more comprehensive explanations. The articles in the following section represent a sequence of such attempts. In the first article on play seasons, the focus is on a classic concern of folklore, along with a psychologist's attempt to apply some mildly quantitative thinking to the problem. The paper on kissing games consists of a fairly familiar combination of game categorization and psychological inference. However in the 1959 paper, "A Formal Analysis of Game Meaning," the descriptive set of categories that refers to actors, purposes, performances, space, and time is set forth for the first time. These categories are the familiar pentad from Kenneth Burke's dramatistic analysis, *A Grammar of Motives*, and I have found them most useful. As presented in this article they are much influenced by the thinking of Fritz Redl and Paul Gump, both of whom have been mentioned earlier.

In 1963–1964 I was a visiting professor at Clark University and to some extent came under the spell of Ernst Cassirer through the developmental psychology of Heinz Werner. In particular, the direct effect of Bernard Kaplan, of that university, was to reinvoke the importance of structural considerations in the analysis of behavior. While this is not a point that any literary scholar or folklorist is likely to forget, it is one that could be easily overlooked by a psychologist in his enthusiasm for causal or manipulative studies. In addition, through Werner and Kaplan's *Symbol Formation* the necessity of considering games as one among many varieties of expressive forms became apparent to me. It appeared that the understanding of games might be facilitated by an approach that took a variety of expressive forms into account at the same time. The last two papers in this section, "The Sporting Balance" and "The Expressive Profile," provide accounts of some of my first attempts in that direction.

The student of folklore will note that my use of game categories in Section I is traditional and ad hoc. The game categories in the anthropological section are likewise traditional within the field of the social sciences. Games of chance are the basis for probability theory, and games of strategy for mathematical game theory. In the present section, my use of Burke's pentad is a stop-gap decision rather than a final one. At the descriptive level it is necessary to be sure that one deals with all the essential data, and Burke's categories help in accomplishing that task. But determining the intent of their use and their comparative linkage with the arts is to go beyond these descriptive terms to structural categories that illustrate laws of relationship and laws of development. However, a delineation of that type is a challenge for the future and not the subject matter of this book.

12. Marbles Are In

Some Observations on the "Seasonal" Nature of
Children's Games in New Zealand

This article is based on historical and psychological research carried out in the years 1949–1950 into the unorganized or folk games of New Zealand elementary school children. The subjects of the investigation were children between the ages of seven and twelve years in a sample of thirty-five rural and urban schools. One of these schools was observed intensively over a two-year period. In addition, reminiscence material, referring to the games played between 1870 and 1950, was received from some 250 persons in various parts of New Zealand. For this particular phase of the study further information was taken by questionnaire from forty teachers' college students.

The supposedly mysterious way in which children's games come and go, wax and wane; the unusual rapidity with which a season arrives, and, as if by magic, all the children are playing only

Source: Reprinted from *Western Folklore* 12, no. 3 (1953): 186–193 by permission of the California Folklore Society.

marbles, or tops, or skipping has been remarked upon at great length by the romanticist of children's games. It is a favorite theme, and the complexity of the factors involved lends itself easily to mysticism. In my presence a teacher marveled at the way in which, overnight, throughout the whole country, the games were transformed and the seasons changed as if by some widespread general intuition upon the part of the children. But if the complexity of this question lends itself easily to mysticism it does not lead so easily to scientific investigation. Nevertheless, in a general way, it is possible to build up a reasonably clear picture of the manner in which it happens that today a game is "timely," it is "in season" and tomorrow it is not. It can be shown that children's play seasons result from the interaction of children's groups with a variety of influences in their environment. The influences likely to be of importance are those arising from the nature of the physical environment, its flora, fauna, and climatic changes, and those which arise from the activities of adult groups of an economic and social nature. These influences interacting with the psychology of the children's groups as determined by age, sex, and dominant interests, produce the play seasons as we know them.

In this article it is proposed to select only one facet from this complex picture; to note some of the observations which were made during the investigation about the effects of "climatic" seasons on children's games today. The aim is mainly negative; to dispel the romanticist illusion referred to above. The romanticist, it should be mentioned, seldom makes it clear whether he is talking about a climatic season or a play season, meaning by the latter a group play craze or habit. Here the focus is on the climatic season.

For a start it must be stated that in modern New Zealand playgrounds, the effects of the changing climatic seasons are obscured by the existence of other influences brought into being by the organization of sport by teachers and community.[1] Thus Rugby football begins at an arbitrarily chosen date in the autumn around about Easter, not when the feeling arrives that, "Ah! this is Rugby weather." Minor unorganized games have to adapt themselves to the conventions of this and other organized sports, in particular,

---

[1] It will be realized that in New Zealand, in the Southern Hemisphere, the seasons are the reverse of what they are in the United States.

cricket, hockey, soccer, tennis, basketball, and softball. Either the
minor games fit into the interstices of these organized sports or they
fall into desuetude. At a certain date, for example, the first football
practice is arranged. There is a craze for football which affects
everybody for a few weeks and the chosen teams for the rest of the
fixed "season." It is only when this initial craze has died down that
the younger children and the disappointed sportsmen are sufficiently free from the group enthusiasm to turn elsewhere to some other
novelty. At this point climatic change may have an influence upon
a dissentient group sated with the current organized game. But the
influence of climatic change is of a general nature only, not of the
specific nature indicated by some folklorists when they have said:
"The feeling of spring in the air which made the children spin, the
lambs dance, and flowers rise from the earth, brought the gay little
wooden tops to the villages."[2] Spring "brings the gradual lengthen-
ing daylight which is put to good use in the seasonal urge to hop,
leap, and move the arms and legs to rhythmic games."[3] Allowing
for the fact that these are the reports of English writers, and that in
Europe the spring sometimes has "seemingly miraculous"[4] effects,
from the New Zealand point of view, these statements express half-
truths only. It may be as Huntington has claimed at some length,
that the spring seasonal change does increase human vitality.[5] That
in itself, however, is no indication of just what type of reaction
human beings will take when this seasonal change arrives. In New
Zealand, at least, there is no narrow determinism. To link the
somewhat anthropomorphic "feeling of spring" and "seasonal
urge" together with the specific games of tops, hopping, leaping,
and jumping and rhythm as Uttley and Daiken have done is hardly justifiable in New Zealand. This, apparently, is also the position
in parts of the United States. And here the abruptness of the
climatic changes in many places more nearly approximates the
conditions in Europe. And yet, Lehmann and Witty, after an ex-
haustive investigation, claimed that "the bulk of the play life of the
child is not subject to marked variation effected by seasonal

[2] A. Uttley, *Country Things* (London, 1946), p. 96.

[3] L. Daiken, *Children's Games throughout the Year* (London, 1949), p. 22.

[4] L. Spence, *Myth and Ritual in Dance Game and Rhyme* (London, 1947), p. 28.

[5] E. Huntington, *Mainsprings of Civilization* (New York, 1945), p. 315.

TABLE 1
Games, Seasons, and Number of Players

Seasons	Marbles	Tops	Kites	Skipping	Hopscotch	Hoops	Tires
Autumn	18	..	5	4	..	..	..
Autumn-winter	..	..	1	3	2	..	..
Winter	5	10	2	15	7	3	2
Winter-spring	..	2	1	1	2	..	..
Spring	..	4	7	1	1	..	..
Spring-summer	1	1	1	1	1	..	..
Summer	3	4	4	..	3	2	6
Summer-autumn	2	..	..	..	2	..	..
All year	..	1	1	2	4	..	..

change."[6] In fact, in the game of marbles, which is generally reckoned to be the most "seasonal" of games, Lehmann and Witty found children playing at all parts of the year. "Marbles was being played with considerable frequency in at least one of the neighbourhoods studied during each of the three seasons of the year, but at no one time was marbles being played generally in every neighbourhood studied."[7] From this they concluded that "playing marbles appears to be not so much a product of seasonal change as of the whims of the community."[8]

Nevertheless it would be wrong if the impression was conveyed that the changing climatic seasons have no influence whatsoever on game "seasons." They do make a contribution. In some cases it is highly specific, as for example when boys make bows and arrows with spring willow shoots, play conkers in the autumn with horse chestnuts, which are only mature at that time, play soldiers with the heads of spring plantain grass, go swimming and fishing in the summer, and snowballing and skating in the winter. Usually, however, the influence is of a more general nature. Consider, for example, Table 1. Forty students from Wellington Teachers' College, New Zealand, including twenty men and twenty women, were asked to indicate in what seasons, autumn, winter, spring, or summer, they had played marbles, tops, kites, skipping, hopscotch, hoops, and tires. In every case the activities were spread

[6] H. C. Lehmann and P. A. Witty, *The Psychology of Play Activities*, p. 201.
[7] *Ibid.*
[8] *Ibid.*

throughout the year, although there were certain modes for each activity. In some cases, of course, the students had either not played the games, or had forgotten the season in which they were played. In these cases they made no report.

The details on the play of each of the above games are as follows:

MARBLES

The majority of the students' reports state that autumn and winter were the marble seasons. In addition to this information, seventeen historical reports[9] indicated that marbles were played in autumn (eight of these in connection with May 1); sixteen, that it was played in winter, and nine, that it was played in spring. Overseas writers vary as to the time of the year with which they associate marble playing. Daiken and Spence associate it with autumn; Norman Douglas places it in winter;[10] A. B. Gomme, at the end of winter;[11] Lehmann and Witty, in the spring.[12] The Woolworth's toy buyer of Wellington, New Zealand (the largest chain store), corroborated the autumn-winter emphasis. The peak sales for marbles, he said, were between the football (autumn) and cricket (summer) seasons. The toy buyer for McKenzies (the next biggest chain store in New Zealand) claimed that peak sales for marbles were in winter. Their statements, however, applied to those prewar years when marbles were freely available. At present (1949–1950) marbles, which are always in short supply, tend to sell as soon as they come into the shops. The shortage plays havoc with the "normal" seasons. The fact that most New Zealand play has been carried on in the autumn is nevertheless commemorated by a rhyme which has been widely used, namely,

> The first of May,
> Is Smugglers' Day.

This rhyme is not reported by British folklorists, though the term and practice of smuggling (that is, thieving marbles) are well known.[13] Several other New Zealand references with dates are:

[9] Reports derived from reminiscences mentioned in introduction.

[10] N. Douglas, *London Street Games* (London, 1916).

[11] A. B. Gomme, *Traditional Games of England, Scotland and Ireland* (London, 1894).

[12] Lehmann and Witty, *op. cit.*

[13] Gomme, *op. cit.*, 11, 302.

> May 24th is Smugglers' Day.

But this was the Queen's birthday and in this case the solitary informant may have been confusing the marble rhyme with the traditional holiday rhymes which said:

> Hip hip hooray
> For the Queen's birthday
> On the 24th of May.

Other rhymes with dates were:

> The first of September,
> Marbles are out,
> Flicks are in
> And smuggles about.

> First of May, Smuggling day,
> Tops are in, marbles are out.

But although ten historical reports were received in which dates were cited, as in the above rhymes, ten reports were also received in which no dates were mentioned. For example:

> Marbles are out
> Smuggles about.

> Marbles are out
> Smugglers are about.

> Marbles are out
> Smuggin's about.

> Marbles are out
> Smugglers are out
> Dubs when the bell goes.

> Marbles are out
> Kick 'em about.

The seasonal emphasis of overseas reports (mentioned above) seems to be on the winter and the spring. Overseas, marbles flourished through the winter and terminated in the spring, that is, round about May. In New Zealand marbles began about May (autumn) and carried on through the winter. So that the two halves of the world had in common their marbles in winter. They also had in common the month of May as a limit of the season. In England it was the end limit. In New Zealand, the beginning. In England marbles traditionally terminated on May 1, or thereabouts, and then tops came in. The one New Zealand reproduction of this situation is to be found in the rhyme above where marbles finished on September 1 (New Zealand spring) and flicks (cigarette card game) came in. But a customary New Zealand practice was to smuggle marbles on May 1 (if that was smugglers' day), and then, instead of going on to tops, to resume normal marble playing again the next day, for, after all, the season had only just begun. It looks as if New Zealanders brought from England the habit of playing marbles in the winter and also the association with the month of May. In England, May finished the season. In New Zealand, May started it off.

The question naturally arises, why should marbles be played mainly in winter? It is clear that it can be and often is played at any time in the year. In favor of the winter one could point to the pliability of the soil and its susceptibility to marble markings and holes; to the joy children get from chasing their marbles in and out of puddles. But this could be countered in turn by reference to the dampness of the ground and the inappropriateness of this relatively inactive pastime to a wintry climate. The favorableness of summer and autumn warmth could, in their turn, be offset by reference to the hardness of the ground. Again, what might be said in favor of spring could be countered by reference to chilblains. In fact, as long as marbles were freely available there does not seem to have been any good climatic reason why they should have been played in one season rather than another. Almost the only valid generalization that can be made is that marbles were not very frequently played in the summer and that they were in consequence associated more with climatic coolness than with heat. Possibly it was preferable to play the game when the temperature was cool and the ground pliable than to play it when the ground was hard out in the midday sun.

There is, however, an additional factor which may have contributed its bias toward the winter season. We know, for example, that marbles have only been manufactured during the last few hundred years; and where they were not manufactured, that the game was often played with nuts and berries.[14] In fact, Daiken suggests that this is how the game originated. If this was the case, then at one time the origin of each new marble craze would have to wait on the season of "autumnal fruitfulness."[15] When the autumn nuts and berries were to hand, the game could commence and the season continue from late autumn into winter. Further, the termination of this winter season with May Day "smuggling" may have been associated with rapacious May-Day customs.[16] What would it matter if one's "Taws," one's nuts and berries, were stolen, and probably eaten by others. Next season the trees would be laden with new ones.

The habit of playing marbles in winter, then, may have come down from those early times preserved by nothing but the fact that groups, having a group tradition of when and where to play, tended to play each year in the same fashion as they had in the last. But such a tradition would be a light bond—a bond easily interfered with by the commerce of marbles, the migration of peoples, and the dominance of organized sports. The present varied distribution of marble playing may be a reflection of all these and many other factors, operating on the basis of this archetypal "season."

Tops

Authorities on tops overseas almost universally place top playing in the spring and associate it with ancient spring rituals.[17] There can be little doubt, however, that in New Zealand it was played mainly as a winter game. In most cases its onset followed the flagging of interest in cricket. A New Zealand toy buyer stated that the commercial peak was in early winter. There were three historical reports of the season being in autumn; seventeen in winter, and five in spring. Two reports specified that whip tops were played in the winter and peg tops in the summer. The other reports referred to peg tops.

---

[14] J. Strutt, *The Sports and Pastimes of the People of England* (London, 1801), p. 304.

[15] Daiken, *op. cit.*, p. 167.

[16] Spence, *op. cit.*, p. 31.

[17] A. C. Haddon, *The Study of Man* (London, 1898), p. 255.

SKIPPING

This is a warming activity and takes its place fairly decisively in the cooler months of winter. Wet weather, however, acts prohibitively on it as wet ropes are likely to have a punishing effect upon the imperfect player. The New Zealand commercial peak is in winter. Overseas authorities again place its occurrence in the spring.[18] One historical report placed it in autumn, ten in winter, and one in spring.

HOPSCOTCH

This game has also a tendency to flourish in winter but this is a modal tendency far less marked than with the other games. Hopscotch, with its waiting players, is a game which has its leisurely aspects. Children often report playing it at home irrespective of the fact that it is not "in" at school. Hopscotch is generally placed in the spring by overseas writers. There is one New Zealand historical report of it being played in autumn, five in winter, and four in summer.

KITES

At first sight kite flying might appear to provide the clearest example of seasonal influence amongst the games being discussed here. Most reports state that kites was played in March and September and many informants claimed that playing with kites at these times was connected with the equinoctial winds of March and September. However, Kimble and Bush in *The Weather* state that "nowhere will you find much support for the popular idea that strong winds and gales are particularly common round the spring equinox. . . . Or the autumnal one for that matter."[19] It is probable then that the flying of kites at these times has been due in New Zealand as much to the existence of school holidays in May and September as to any particular windiness at those times of the year. This was brought out clearly in the students' lists. Many students explicitly mentioned making their kites in the May, August,

[18] H. Bett, *Origin and History of the Games of Children* (London, 1924), p. 55.

[19] G. Kimble and R. Bush, *The Weather* (Middlesex, 1943), p. 93.

TABLE 2
Peak Kite Sales

Town	Months	
Wellington	April	September
Palmerston North	April	
Hamilton	March	September
Wanganui	March	
Hastings	March	
Timaru	May	
Gisborne	March	
New Plymouth	March	
Greymouth		August
Whangarei	March	September
Hawera	March	
Dunedin	May	
Auckland	March	September
Christchurch		Spring

and December vacations. An investigation into the sale of kites was carried out throughout New Zealand in 1946. All the Woolworth shops in the main centers were approached to find out at what times in the year they sold the greatest number of kites. Their replies show very clearly the holiday appearance of the games.

CONCLUSION

This study of the effects of climate on children's play seasons or group crazes has sought to show that in general climatic influence on these activities is essentially limited; and, in consequence, that there is little merit in the romanticist's claim that spring or any other climatic season has a magical effect upon children's games.

13. The Kissing Games of Adolescents in Ohio

There do not appear to be any English language folklore collections which include kissing games within one special category. In general, these games are to be found under the titles of "Courtship" "Marriage" "Forfeits" and "Play-Party" games. In this century, however, the explicit and formalized elements of courtship, marriage, forfeiture and play-party dancing have been practically discarded in adolescent play, while kissing has continued and increased in importance as a formal element in many games. The primary aim of the present study, therefore, is to record a collection of the contemporary kissing games of adolescent children. Subsidiary aims are to note the origins of these games and the reasons for the changes that have come about in the way in which they are played.

Source: Reprinted from *Midwest Folklore* 9, no. 12 (1959): 189–211, with permission of the publisher.

METHOD

Games, game descriptions and accounts of the circumstances of play were collected by questionnaire from 246 children (135 boys and 111 girls) in a northwestern Ohio rural high school (Sandusky County), and from 100 college students (50 men and 50 women) in a state university also in northwestern Ohio (Wood County). The high school children were in the fifth to twelfth grade classes with approximately thirty children in each class. The college students were mainly sophomores of eighteen and nineteen years of age. The items in the questionnaire are those listed in the table. These items were derived from previous lists made out by the college students. High school and college students were requested to check only those games that they had played themselves, indicating whether or not they liked or disliked the game. The great majority of these students came from towns in Ohio.

The games appeared in the questionnaire list as follows:

Kiss in the Ring   L   D
Post Office   L   D

The percentage of each group, high school and college students checking the games and the rank order of preference is indicated in the table. This table includes only the twenty-two games listed on the original questionnaire. It does not include the thirty-two other game names discovered in the course of the investigation. These are mentioned in the alphabetical collection below. All of these games have been played at some time during the 1950's. A smaller group of students in another rural high school also contributed descriptions of some of their games.

THE COLLECTION

The games collected are listed alphabetically below. Where there is more than one name for the game, the description of the game is given under that name most commonly used. Some of the following games are played more often without kissing but are included here because kissing is occasionally a part of the game. Games of this nature are "Chew the String" and "Pass the Orange." There are other games which do not contain kissing, but for which much of the fun consists in the close contact of the partners, and the near

TABLE

Name of Game	Rank Order in High School Gp. (N=246)	Percentage of High School Gp. check. item	Rank Order in College Group (N=100)	Percentage of Coll. Gp. check-ing Item
Spin the Bottle	1	57	1	91
Post Office	2	38	5	70
Winks	3	32	12	23
Mistletoe Kissing	4	26	3	83
Chew String	5	25	10	34
Necking	6	22	2	89
Biting the Apple	7.5	21	11	25
Truth and Consequences	7.5	21	13	22
Endurance Kissing	9.5	20	9	39
Flashlight	9.5	20	7	49
Hayride Kissing	11	18	6	69
Passing the Orange	12	17	8	45
Musical Circle	13	14	15.5	9
Kissing Tag	14.5	13	15.5	9
Chase and Kiss	14.5	13	17.5	8
Perdiddle	16	12	4	72
Numbers	17.5	10	17.5	8
Kiss in the Ring	17.5	10	19	6
Sardines	19	7	20	5
Clap In, Clap Out	20	6	21.5	0
This or That	21	5	14	10
Minx	22	4	21.5	0

kissing they experience, for example "Biting the Apple" and "Pass the Lifesaver."

When the information was derived from the major high school sample this is indicated by the reference in parentheses to "Thompson." Descriptions derived from the minor high school sample are indicated by the reference "Woodville." References to other places in Ohio or elsewhere indicate that the information was derived from the college sample. Where the game was reported by only one person and is probably an ephemeral pastime, this is indicated. It will be noticed that while the majority of the games have not appeared before in earlier collections, some elements of most of them are traceable to earlier games.

Base Kiss

The boy stands on the pitcher's base. He covers his eyes. The girls run from the home base around the diamond. When he shouts out "base" they must stop. If any girl is on a base he kisses her. This also is called "Baseball Kissing" (Thompson). This appears to be a unique adaptation of baseball to more romantic ends.

Biting the Apple

This is a relay race in which couples compete against couples. The apples hang from the roof on a piece of string and the couples, hands behind their backs, endeavor to be the first to get the apple eaten. It is played throughout the year although some still report it as played only at Halloween which is the traditional time for it (Toledo).[1] "Kissing occurs only by accident and is something to avoid" (Swanton). The game may be played also with doughnuts (Rossford) or candy bars (Southington).

Boys Catch Girls

There are two sides. The ones who are caught are kissed. The boys may catch the girls or the girls may catch the boys (Thompson). Informal activity of this type appears to be practically universal throughout the Western World. I have observed it most often in eight- and nine-year-old children, but it is certainly not restricted to that age level. Children often engage in activities of this sort without giving a name to them.

Bridge

This is played the same way as Perdiddle, but bridges are used instead of motor car headlights. Naturally, this has the effect of increasing the number of occasions on which the game may be played (Thompson).

Candy, Cigarettes

Girls and boys in two teams take the names of, say, cigarettes (boys) or candy (girls). Each group then takes turns at calling out

[1] Alice B. Gomme, *The Traditional Games of England, Scotland and Ireland*, I (London, 1894–98), 42 ("Bob Cherry").

any example of the category of nomenclature chosen by the opposite sex ("Lucky Strike"). If this happens to be someone's name, that person is kissed (Industry, Penn.). This is one of a group of games which emphasize the chance element in the selection of partners. Other games of this sort which follow are: "Draw and Kiss," "Dynamite," "Five Minute Date," "Heavy Heavy Hang Over the Head," "Musical Circle," "Numbers," "Post Office," "Professor," "Spin the Bottle" and "This or That." There is precedent for this chance selection of partners in traditional games.[2]

The Card Game

This game is known also as Hearts (Cleveland). The players go round in a circle, and take turns to pick a card from a pack. Having picked a card they then pick a person of the opposite sex. If they pick a spade they slap the person they have chosen on the back. If a club, they shake hands. If a diamond it is a public kiss. If a heart, a private kiss (Woodville). There are variations in the interpretation of these suits. From the same locality, for example, another version was: club = slap; spade = shake hands; heart = kiss in public; diamond = kiss in private. Yet another interpretation from Cleveland had it that a club = a kiss on the hand; a diamond = a kiss on the forehead; a spade = a kiss on the cheek; and a heart = a kiss on the lips. Here again we have a game which emphasizes the fortuitous choice of partners although the "chance" element is here provided by a pack of cards, rather than some traditional game performance. The game of "Hearts," and "Kings and Queens" are of the same sort.

Chase

The girls snatch the boys' hats and in order to get them back the boys have to kiss the girls (Ohio).

Chase and Kiss

One person sits on a chair, all the rest take numbers (odd for boys, even for girls). The person on the chair calls out two numbers (an odd and an even). If it is a girl on the chair, then the boy

---

[2] Gomme, II, 255 ("Three Flowers").

called out tries to kiss her before he is kissed by the girl whose number was also called. If he succeeds he takes the player's place on the chair. If he fails and is kissed first, then the chair player calls out again (Monclova). There are traditional games which are similar to this, all involving couples who chase each other for kisses.[3]

Chew the String

This is a relay race in which couples compete against each other. There is a long piece of string. The partners chew from each end until they meet in the middle. In most cases this is simply a race to see which couple can get all the string out of sight first. But it may be played to see who can be first to eat a lifesaver (Summit, N.J.) or marshmallow (Thompson) in the middle. Or it may be a race to see which partner can eat the most (Whittier, Cal.). In some cases the partners are reported as finishing the ordeal with a rather clumsy kiss (Celina, Cincinnati, Chicago, Dayton, Portage).

Clap In, Clap Out

No description reported in this research but it is a traditional game frequently mentioned in the literature.[4]

Choo Choo

This is a variant of "Pony Express." A couple go into another room. They ask a third person to join them. These three then run all around the house like a train. When they stop in the secluded room, the first kisses the second, who kisses the third. A fourth person is asked to join them and the game proceeds as before and so it goes on with chain kissing at the end of each episode. The train alternates boys and girls. When the last person is chosen, and the kissing commences, the second to the last person instead of kissing the final player, gives him a slap (Ohio). This victimization of a player also occurs in "Pony Express" and is a familiar element in

---

[3] Edwin F. Piper, "Some Play Party Games of the Middle West," *JAF*, XXVIII (July, 1915), 266 ("Chase That Squirrel").

[4] Gomme, I, 215 ("Kiss and Clap"); *The Frank C. Brown Collection of North Carolina Folklore*, I (Durham, 1952) 123; Paul G. Brewster, *American Non-singing Games* (Oklahoma, 1953), 154.

children's games.[5] Players holding on behind each other is of course familiar in "Fox and Goose."[6]

Draw and Kiss

All the players' names are placed in a dish. All the players place their hands in together and draw a name. They must kiss the name drawn out as well as be kissed by the person who has drawn their name. As soon as they have kissed and been kissed they may run to take their place in a line of chairs. There is one chair short, and the person who is left over must kiss everyone (Thompson). This game, which appears to be a new one, combines elements of "Musical Chairs" and "Forfeits."[7]

Dynamite

All the boys leave the room. Each girl selects a magazine and lays it on the floor. There are several magazines placed on the floor but belonging to no one. These are known as "dynamite." The boys come in one at a time and step on a magazine. If they step on one belonging to someone, they must kiss that person. If they step on one belonging to no one, then dynamite—they must kiss everyone in the room. Sometimes a small magazine is placed inside a large magazine. If someone steps on these, they have a double dynamite, kissing everyone twice (Ohio).

Like the traditional game of "Clap In, Clap Out" and the game of "'Winks," this is a game so contrived to make the boys play out their choices in front of the girls.

Endurance Kissing

This has been reported as a game played by a few couples together, or by a group of couples at a party. It is essentially a comical endurance test, in which a couple sees how long they can hold a kiss without breathing. A watch is used. The bystanders laugh at the competitors. It is done usually only with one's steady date. On a double date the losers might be expected to buy a coke for the

[5] B. Sutton-Smith, "The Historical and Psychological Significance of the Unorganized Games of New Zealand Primary School Children." (Ph.D. Thesis: Univ. of New Zealand, 1954), p. 718 (Microfilm copy of typescript, 2 reels, positive, Ball State University, Muncie, Indiana).

[6] Gomme, I, 139.

[7] Gomme, I, 137 and 148.

winners. The endurance kissing may also occur with breathing allowed, in which case it is a contest to see which couple can keep their mouths together for the longest period of time. Under the name "Football" it is described as follows: "About three or four couples would start kissing at the same time and the couple who held out the longest would score a touchdown. They would then go for the extra point, gaining this by again out-enduring their competitors. If a game was played for long a score would be kept. Sometimes a couple could hold out for 45 minutes" (Burgoon).

Fiddle Diddle

This is another name for the game of "Perdiddle" (Woodville).

Five Minute Date

One player sits on a chair blindfolded. On each side of him sits a member of the opposite sex. He takes their hands in his, and drops the one he doesn't want. He takes off his blindfold and goes on a five minute date with the one he has chosen (Woodville). The blindfolding of the players who must then exercise a guess is a familiar element in games.[8]

Flashlight

This is known also under the names of "Willpower" and "Spotlight." The game is played in a number of different ways. In the most common, couples sit around the edge of a dark room. One person sits in the center with a flashlight. If he flashes it onto a couple that is *not* kissing, then he joins the opposite sex member of that couple, and the other member takes his place in the center with the flashlight. In only one or two reports did the It character in the center escape his position because he found a peripheral couple that *was* kissing. In short it was normal in this game to be kissing, not normal to be caught unembraced. In another type of flashlight game the central character is blindfolded. He is then spun around. When his light falls on someone, if it is a person of the opposite sex, she kisses him. If a person of the same sex, he is spun again. If he can guess who it is that has kissed him, he may leave the center. If not the game continues as before.

This is clearly a new game, but even so contains several elements

[8] Sutton-Smith, p. 507.

that are quite traditional. It is very normal in the It games of adolescence for the central person to be a left-over character or scapegoat.[9] He is like the "Jolly Miller" who can't get himself a wife.[10] It is traditional too for a torch to be a dangerous possession.[11]

Football

Another name for "Endurance Kissing."

Freeze Tag

"When the It kisses you, you stay frozen to the spot and cannot move until some other player comes and unfreezes you with a kiss" (Thompson). This is a variant of the well known chasing game of the same name.

Hayride Kissing

In most cases hayrides are occasions which may or may not include kissing, not strictly speaking a game in themselves. For example, there are reports of playing "Flashlight" and "Endurance Kissing" while out on hayrides. However, there is at least one report of kissing proceeding sequentially around the conveyance in the order of sitting (Rockford).

Hearts

All players have cards and take turns at turning them up. If hearts are matched the two players involved kiss while the light is turned out momentarily (Erie, Penn.).

Heavy, Heavy, Hang over the Head

An object is taken from each player as a means of identification. These objects are put in an ash tray and held over the head of a person called the teacher. The holder lifts out an object and indicates whether it belongs to a boy or girl.

Holder: "Heavy Heavy hang over the head. What should this boy do to get back his ring?"

Teacher: "He must sit on the couch with —— and kiss her everytime I tell him to do so" (Rossford).

[9] Sutton-Smith, p. 718.
[10] Brown collection, p. 111.
[11] Gomme, I, 256 ("Jack's Alive"); Henry Betts, *The Games of Children* (London, 1929), p. 75.

In a briefer version, everyone simply puts objects in a hat, takes out an object and kisses the owner (Cleveland). This is a classic element in "Forfeits."[12]

Kings and Queens

Children stand in a circle around a deck of cards. One by one they turn up the cards. If a girl turns up a king she may choose a boy and go off into another room with him. If a boy turns up a queen he goes into another room with his choice (Willoughby).

Kissing Tag

This game is also called "Kissing Tab" (Woodville).

The person who is It catches and kisses someone who is then It and must also pass it on by kissing (Lorain). In another game with the same name a person in the center is blindfolded. The others circle around him. When he calls "Kissing Tag" he chases the others, and the person he catches he kisses for five minutes (Thompson). These are again variations on the traditional games of "Chase" and "Blindman's Buff."

Kiss under Water

Players try to kiss each other while swimming under water. One report only (Woodville).

Minx

One player is It and tries to catch the other players without their fingers, arms or legs crossed. If the It so catches anyone he "minxes" that person which means simply he kisses them, and that person takes his place in the center (Ohio). This crossing of fingers, limbs, etc. is a common way in which children symbolize being "safe" in game terms.[13] Safety tag games are numerous.

Mistletoe Kissing

A Christmas and New Year custom, not usually regarded as a game, but made into one in some cases. For example, the mistletoe is hung in the doorway under which the couples march. The couple

[12] William Wells Newell, *Games and Songs of American Children* (New York, 1883), p. 143.
[13] Sutton-Smith, p. 501.

under the mistletoe when the whistle blows must kiss (Fostoria). There are reports in which boys struggled to drag girls under the mistletoe in order to kiss them, or took the mistletoe to the girls and held it over their heads as a pretext for kissing them (Lorain, Anna).

Murderer and Detective

Two versions are mentioned. One person is appointed the detective and he leaves the room. Another is appointed the murderer, but the detective does not know who this child is. The lights are turned out and the murderer kisses someone. The detective is called in and he must guess the name of the murderer (Woodville). This is a kissing version of another game of the same name.[14] In another variety, the game has a "Spin the Bottle" pattern. Someone spins the bottle. The person it points to becomes the detective. The detective spins the bottle. If it points to a person of the opposite sex, that person is a murderer. The detective then chases the murderer and attempts to kiss her (Woodville).

Musical Circle

The boys are in a circle and the girls form a circle around them. The music is played and the boys walk around; when it stops, they kiss the girl facing them (Ohio). Circle forms of courting games were common in earlier days, though not this particular form.[15]

Necking

This is not normally considered a game, but in some reports elements of ritual show up that approximate it to play. "This was done in a car at some spot well frequented by teenagers. One of our favourite spots was the Pumping Station overlook, Presque Isle Bay on Lake Erie. Our favorite expression at that time was that we were going to watch the 'submarine races.' " Or, "We usually went to the park that closed at 11 p.m. But soon the park police found out and would quietly pull up along side the car and shine their spotlight on you. Then it became a fad to be caught necking like this. Many times a bunch of us would park the car and just wait for the

[14] E. O. Harbin, *The Fun Encyclopedia* (New York, 1940), p. 145.
[15] Brown collection, pp. 89–133.

police. When they pulled up and shone their flashlights we would just sit there laughing" (Cleveland).

Numbers

A boy or girl goes into another room which is in the dark. This is preferably a bedroom. The members of the opposite sex are assigned numbers. The first person calls out a number and the chosen one enters the room and "necks" for a period of one minute. The same number cannot be called for more than three times. When all numbers have been called, a member of the opposite sex goes into the room (Dayton).

Pass the Kiss

Players stand in a circle and pass around a kiss (Thompson). A traditional form though usually it is a whisper or a button that is passed round the periphery.[16]

Pass the Lifesaver

A relay or couple game in which each player holds a toothpick in the mouth, and then players endeavor to pass the lifesaver from one toothpick to another without dropping it. A game which brings faces into proximity though it does not necessarily result in kissing (Elmore).

Pass the Orange

This is usually played as a relay. The orange is placed under the chin and then the next player, a member of the opposite sex, endeavors to get it under his chin without use of hands (Berea). Or it may be played with the members of each sex alternating around in a circle (Lorain). In another version the partners stand with faces close together with the orange supported between their foreheads. The competition is to see which couple can keep it there the longest (Warren). In a number of reports the couple must kiss if they drop the orange while passing it from one chin to the next (Poland, Cleveland, Westlake). In one, they kiss if they pass it on successfully (Green Bay, Wis.).

[16] Newell, p. 151.

Perdiddle

This game is known also as "Fiddle Diddle," "Popeye" and "Rinky Dink." A boy and girl are riding in an automobile. If a car with one light goes by, then if the boy says "perdiddle" first he can claim a kiss from the girl. "It used to give us the nerve to take a kiss," says one report (Middletown). But if the girl sees the light first and says "perdiddle" she can slap the boy. It is played in other ways also. Sometimes the couples save up their "perdiddles" throughout the evening and have a reckoning before departure. "In this way we didn't get all messed up on our way to the function" (Findlay). Other versions ignore the slapping and either partner may take a kiss when the one light provocation appears (Toledo, Elmore). According to some, a truck light is good for an extra long kiss (Berea).

Photography

"The lights are turned out to see what develops" (Findlay). This is just a pretext for kissing between couples in the group setting. However, as such it is a more obvious example of a characteristic of so many of these games.

Pony Express

This is similar to the game of "Choo Choo." A boy leads a girl out, with her hands on his waist, into a secluded and darkened room and kisses her. They return and a second boy couples on behind the girl. They depart once more, and once again the first boy kisses the first girl, and she turns and slaps the second boy. They return to the group and a second girl couples on behind the second boy. A kisses B, B kisses C and C slaps D. And on the game goes until all are kissed. The pairs are usually made up of couples going steady with each other. There is much laughter, astonishment and some annoyance (Bascom). It is reported also as being the same game as "Post Office" but played much faster (Woodville). In addition there is an expression relating to this game, which is not actually a game in itself, but rather game-like in that it has become a conventional smart saying. The question is asked:

"Do you want to play 'Pony Express'?"

"What is that?"

"The same as 'Post Office,' but a little more horsing around" (Thompson).

Popeye

Another name for "Perdiddle" (Painesville).

Post Office

There are several versions. One is similar to those found in the collections of traditional games.[17] In this version there is a player in another room (the postman) who sends a message via the intermediary that he has a letter for such and such a person. He may nominate the value of the letter, that it has a three-cent stamp or a six-cent stamp, etc., and this is meant to indicate the number of kisses he intends to give that person. The elected person goes to the postmaster, kisses, and then replaces him as postmaster (Newton Falls). In another version, more frequently reported, the boys choose odd numbers and the girls choose even numbers, or vice versa. The postman then calls out any number without knowing who has that number. They kiss, and the number called becomes the new postmaster (Toledo, Oregon, Poland, Industry, Penn.). In yet other versions, the postman writes a number (one to five) on a piece of paper. The girl who guesses his number kisses him that many times (Toledo). Or the postman is out of sight and the opposite sex persons do not know who it is. They come one at a time and ask for a given number of stamps. They get that many kisses (Cleveland). Or the couples simply line up and have turns at going into another room to kiss for one minute (Vienna). In a number of reports there was indication that the rules were not well known and the many variations in the game seem to confirm that position. It is of interest that the main change from the traditional to the modern form is from an explicit selection of partners to kiss, to a chance selection. Most versions, however, retain the private kissing, and the giving of the couple a limited time to go ahead with it, say, one or two minutes. If they take longer there will be much banter and laughter when they finally appear. "Usually after the first kiss the couple sat on the edge of the bed and made the springs squeak. This was always a big hit with those in the other room

[17] Gomme, I, 404 ("American Post"); Brewster, p. 154.

when it could be heard" (Ohio). The expression "Dog Sled" is used in connection with this game.

"Do you want to play 'Dog Sled'?"

"What is that?"

"The same as 'Post Office,' only a little more mush" (Thompson).

Pretty Please

This is more of a ritual than a game. Every time the boy says, "Pretty Please" to his girl she must kiss him. One report only (Thompson).

Professor

Numbers are written on pieces of paper, then cut in two. The boys receive one half, the girl the other half. Players see if they can match their pieces. Those whose papers match go to some private place to kiss. After they have kissed, the boy says to the girl, "Do I pass?" If she liked the kissing she says, "No," and he continues to kiss her until she says he passes (Thompson).

Rinky Dink

Another name for "Perdiddle" (Ginn).

Sardines

One couple goes and hides, then another couple finds them and hides in the same place; in the end everyone is hiding together. This game can be played with or without kissing, though usually it is played without kissing.[18]

Serve It in the Dark

"The boy should raise her chin to the right level, then bake her in the young man's arms for fifteen minutes, and finally beat it before her old man gets home." One report only (Thompson).

Show Kiss

A boy and a girl go to a movie which is according to this report a

[18] Jessie H. Bancroft, *Games for the Playground, Home, School, and Gymnasium* (New York, 1909), p. 172.

"Love Show." Every time the screen characters kiss, the boy and girl kiss too. Only one report (Thompson).

Spin the Bottle

All versions have the traditional circle of players with one player in the center spinning the bottle, though in two reports it was a flashlight in the center with the room in darkness[19] (Toledo, Poland). Generally, the center player must kiss the peripheral player pointed out by the bottle. Usually the kissing is done in public, but the couple may go off and do it in private (Payne, Lancaster). If it points to a player of the same sex that player may go into the center, or it may be spun again, or the person to the right may be kissed, or this situation may be avoided by having two sexually segregated circles with an opposite-sex person spinning the bottle. Usually, however, the sexes alternate around the circle. Sometimes when the bottle points between two of them, those two have to kiss (Chicago). There is much report of pretending to avoid the bottle, and of cheating so that it ended up pointing toward the pretty or the handsome, and not towards the unattractive. This is an interesting application of the sociometric determination of game behaviors first described by Whyte.[20]

Spotlight

Another name for "Flashlight" (Thompson). But used also for the practice of shining a spotlight on a group of dancing couples. The couple on whom the spot alights must stop dancing and kiss.

This or That

One child goes out of the room. Two other children of the opposite sex are named "This" and "That." The outside child returns and nominates "This" or "That," without knowing who they are, and kisses the one he thus ignorantly chooses. The other child ("This" or "That") then goes out and the game carries on (Upper Sandusky). In another similar version a girl goes into another dark room; a person who has been out before names two boys "This" and "That." The girl outside calls back, "This" (or "That") and

---

[19] Gomme, II, 312 ("Turn the Trencher"); Brewster, p. 32 ("Spin the Plate").

[20] W. H. Whyte, *Street Corner Society* (Chicago, 1943).

the person named goes into the room with her. She can kiss him if she likes or she can shake hands with him if she doesn't want to kiss him. She comes back and he remains behind. The process is repeated. However, if the boy tries to shake hands with a girl, she can either shake hands with him or slap his face (Upper Sandusky).

Games of fortuitous choice like this have forerunners in traditional game collections.[21]

Truth or Consequences

An It person asks embarrassing questions of group members in turn. If the member will not tell the truth, then he must take the consequences. Questions asked are of the nature of: "Do you like Johnny?" Whether he or she is telling the truth depends upon group decision. Consequences vary. They may involve kissing, singing a song, proposing, running around the block, etc. (Rossford).[22]

Turtle Climb

One member of the couple starts telling the story of how the poor little turtle tried to climb the hill. He uses his arms to demonstrate the turtle climbing. When the turtle finally reaches the top, the two arms are clear around the partner's neck. The person narrating says: "What are we talking about turtles for?" and gives the other a kiss. One report only (Findlay).

Willpower

Another name for "Flashlight." But used also for a pursuit type of "Flashlight." There are several versions. In one, the person with the flashlight comes into a dark room, turns on his flashlight and kisses the person upon whom it alights, if of the opposite sex (Newton Falls). In another version, the boys as a group have flashlights and they pursue the girls who hide. They kiss the girl whom they catch in their light beam (Toledo, Dayton), or they stay with the girl they catch in the light beam (Willoughby).

Windshield Wiper

Two couples stand with the same sexes opposite each other, and

[21] Gomme, II, 255 ("Three Flowers").
[22] Brewster, p. 37 (forfeits but no kiss).

arms about each other's shoulders or waists. They turn heads from side to side like windshield wipers, kissing as they do so. One report only (Cleveland).

Winks

This game is known also as "Popeye" (Chicago). Members of one sex, more usually the boys, stand in a circle behind chairs, all of which contain girls, except one. The boy with the empty chair tries to entice the girls in the other chairs to come over to his chair. They may come only if he winks at them. When he winks they try to rush over to his chair, but the boy behind them tries to prevent them from doing this by taking hold of their shoulders and arms, or perhaps simply by tagging them. There may be no kissing. More usually they are kissed by the boy who has winked at them when they succeed in getting to his chair. Occasionally they are also kissed by the boy behind them when he succeeds in holding them (Upper Sandusky). This is a traditional game.[23]

CIRCUMSTANCES OF PLAY

For the purposes of this discussion the games are grouped into three sections:

I. *Chasing Kiss Games; which includes, "Base Kiss," "Boys Catch Girls," "Chase," "Chase and Kiss," "Freeze Tag," and "Kiss in the Ring."*

The first group of games are most typical of the preadolescent age group of thirteen years. This investigation did not provide much information about these games except that they are mostly played out of doors or in school grounds, and are limited to small numbers of children. That is, many children do not mention them. The games are mentioned mainly by the high school sample and there is some evidence that rural children are sometimes precocious in these respects.[24] Kinsey-type data would lead to the hypothesis that this sort of precocious aggressive osculatory play would be more marked amongst lower class children.[25] However, this thesis requires further investigation.

[23] Brown collection, I, 154; Brewster, p. 153.
[24] Sutton-Smith, p. 664.
[25] H. J. Eysenck, *Uses and Abuses of Psychology* (Middlesex, 1953), pp. 184ff.

II. *Mixing Kiss Games: which include: (a) "Candy-Cigarettes," "Card Game," "Clap In Clap Out," "Draw and Kiss," "Dynamite," "Five Minute Date," "Hearts," "Kings and Queens," "Heavy Heavy Hang Over the Head," "Minx," "Murderer & Detective," "Numbers," "Post Office," "Spin the Bottle," "This or That," "Truth or Consequences," "Winks." (b) "Bite the Apple," "Chew String," "Musical Circle," "Pass the Lifesaver," and "Pass the Orange."*

The mixer games of group II (a) are the kissing games of the junior high school period. The games of group (b) are played at the junior high school age level, at the senior high school age level and by older persons. They are frequently reported as games played on fraternity-sorority visits. Their main appeal is their ludicrous nature. In all the games of group II the couples are not paired off before the game begins; pairing occurs in the games but it is characteristically of a momentary sort.

III. *Couple Kiss Games: which include (a) "Choo Choo," "Flashlight," "Hayride Kissing," "Mistletoe Kissing," "Pass the Kiss," "Photography," "Pony Express," "Sardines," "Spotlight," "Willpower"; (b) "Bridge," "Endurance Kissing," "Necking," "Perdiddle," "Pretty Please," "Serve It in the Dark," "Show Kiss," "Turtle Climb," "Windshield Wipers."*

The couple games of group III are most characteristic of the senior high school years. Here the couples are usually matched off beforehand and the games permit them to continue their interest in each other. Type (a) are games played at group events such as parties. Type (b) usually take place amongst a few couples or between one couple in a motor car or other suitable place.

A child's experience of these games may be extensive or limited. There are varying degrees of acquaintance and varying types of occasions on which the games are played. Some of the varieties of experience are as follows: (1) There are those who have never played these games. In the high school group 42% of the children did not check any games in grades 5, 6, and 7. From the 8th grade on, however, only 8% failed to check any items. In short while most children have some experience of these games during childhood, a small minority records no experience of them. One informant explained that he had attended a boys' boarding school and was unacquainted with these games. (2) A few explained that they had never played games like "Spin the Bottle" and "Post Office" on formal occasions, but had played them clandestinely in the daytime out of doors, or inside only when their parents were absent from home. (3) A considerable group indicated having played the games only occasionally at birthday or New Years parties, or, for example, in a recreation hall when a school picnic had been abandoned because of wet weather. On these occasions adults were usually supervising the games. (4) For another considerable group these games constituted an important part of their social life throughout the high school years. These are the children who report playing these games at all their regular parties, which might be held every few weeks, on birthday parties, class parties, or following special occasions such as football games, music recitals, shows, plays, or as a precursor to slumber parties. The games generally took place in a recreation room or basement; but only occasionally out of doors in a backyard. Parents were generally in the house but not directly supervising activities. A game like "Spin the Bottle" might go on for over an hour, before another of a similar nature such as "This or That" was taken up. One report mentions a father who took motion films of the activities then showed them at the next meeting of the group. Although the evidence is not clear cut, it seems probable that more frequent participation in these activities is a part of an upper-middle socioeconomic course of events.[26]

Origins

The basic collections of Gomme and Newell demonstrate that in the nineteenth century, kissing occurred mostly in the games of marriage, courtship and lovemaking, or in their play-party equivalents. "Forty years ago half the play-party amusements were built about some ceremony for kisses."[27] The above alphabetical list contains no games of that sort with the exception perhaps of "Kiss in the Ring." Examination of the present collection shows that it is composed largely of what Gomme termed "Forfeits and Amusements." Yet kissing was not as typical of the forfeits and amuse-

[26] Harold R. Phelps and John E. Horrocks, "Factors Influencing Informal Groups of Adolescents," *Child Development*, XXIX, 78.

[27] Edwin F. Piper, "Some Play Party Games of the Midwest," *JAF*, XXVIII (July, 1915), p. 262.

ments cited by Gomme as it is of these games as played today. Gomme classifies sixteen games as forfeits, and kissing occurs in only two of them. Furthermore, the kissing in Gomme's games was more often a penalty than it is today. "I command yee to kiss the crook . . . his naked lips must kiss the sooty implement."[28] For the greater part the forfeit games of today do not contain very unpleasant consequences; at the worst a slap ("Perdiddle" and "Pony Express"). Newell supplies stronger precedent for the present position when he says, under the heading "Redeeming Forfeits":

The following are examples of old penalties, which usually involved kissing, with infinite variety of method: *To go to Rome.* To kiss every girl in the room. *Flat-irons.* The lad and lass lay their hands on the wall and kiss. *Measuring yards of tape, and cutting it off.* To kiss with arms extended. *"I'm in the well." "How Many Fathoms Deep?"* (Any number is answered.) *"Whom will you have to take you out?"* (Someone in the company is named.)[29]

Each fathom represents a kiss. The basic inventiveness in these expressions is very near in kind to that in our alphabetical list above. The rather surprising way in which so many games have been turned to kissing purposes in the above collection was clearly forecast in this record published by Newell in 1883.

Analysis of the formal pattern of the marriage games of yesterday in one of the most comprehensive collections[30] shows that the commonest procedure was for the central player to choose the partner that he would kiss. That is, at the end of an appropriate verse, the player in the center of the dancing circle chose a player from the periphery, kissed him and was then replaced by that person in the center. Yet in the largest number of forfeit games of today, and those played most frequently [the mixer group II (a)] the choice of kissing partner is made fortuitously.

In short, two major changes have occurred in kissing games. First kissing takes place in forfeit type games rather than in marriage games. Secondly, it takes place less often by the explicit choice of one person for another and more often by chance. Some of the reasons that can be advanced to explain these changes are as follows.

[28] Gomme, II, 325 ("Wadds and Wears").
[29] Newell, p. 143 (No. 88).
[30] Brown collection, pp. 89–133.

The first change is due to the fact that modern parents and the church are no longer averse to the fiddle and no longer restrict their children to the play-party game; it is due to the rise of the modern dance; to the fact that forfeit and amusement games are still as suitable to the indoor parlor and party setting as they were in the last century; to the large amount of freedom given modern children to develop these games in accordance with their own interests. The second change from choice of kissing partner to chance allotment of kissing partner is probably due to the fact that the play-party games of yesterday were designed to suit late adolescence (although they were played by younger children also). An older age group is certainly implied in Dulles' statement. "The violin (fiddle) was taboo, but we sang songs and danced to them and hugged the girls until they would often grunt as we swung them clean off the floor or the ground, in the barn or house or on the green."[31] The equivalent of these games today are the couple games of Group III above. The forfeit games of the mixer group today are played mainly by children of early teen age who are most of the time not yet mature enough to risk such explicit choices. As far as can be judged, the emergence of these kissing games from forfeits and amusements is a spontaneous "folk" occurrence. An examination of a number of "Party" and "Indoor" game books dating from early in the century does not give any indication of adult encouragement for the type of games being discussed here. In fact, the reverse is the case. Great lengths are traversed in order to avoid the introduction of kissing, even in an event such as St. Valentine's Day. There are games with the titles of "Proposals," "Famous Lovers," "Flowery Romance," "Cupid's Carnival of Hearts," "Heart's Desire," "Heart's Fate," but no kissing. There are games of "Chew the String," "Bite the Apple," "Spin the Platter," "Postman," "Forfeits" and "Heavy Heavy Hang Over Your Head," but no kissing. The only mention of kissing in all the books cited below is kissing a stone. Kissing the Blarney Stone! Clearly these party books continue the puritan tradition of the play-party.[32]

[31] Foster Rhea Dulles, *America Learns to Play* (New York, 1940), p. 275.

[32] J. H. Bancroft, op. cit., pp. 80, 254, and 257. Mary J. Breen, *The Party Book* (New York, 1939), pp. 23–24. Arthur M. Depew, *The Cokesbury Party Book* (New York, 1932), pp. 82 and 178. George Draper, *School, Church, Home and Gym Games* (New York, 1927), pp. 180 and 203. Helen and Larry Eisen-

Discussion

The picture of developmental change represented by these games must be taken into consideration briefly in order to explain why these games have persisted and increased in the modern world, a world not generally propitious to the persistence of ancient pastimes. Although the role of games in development cannot be dealt with fully here, the general position taken is that a game performs something of a bridge function in development. It allows for the expression of given impulses but at the same time safeguards the players by putting limits on the way in which those impulses can be expressed.[33] That is, the game allows the player to grow along the lines that he desires, but it safeguards him against the danger of risking too much. The game is essentially an adventure of a non-hazardous kind.

In group I, for example, the players are at the preadolescent age level which is characterized by indifference and hostility between the sexes. When boys and girls of this age level begin to show an interest in each other, they often do so in a rough, clothes-pulling, and arm-twisting manner. Their embryonic heterosexuality is aggressively displayed. They move into adolescent relationships in terms of the feelings they have learned in their preadolescence. The games of group I, boisterous though they are, place limits on these appetites at the same time as gratifying them. In "Freeze Tag," for example, you are permitted to kiss, and to chase, but only according to the rules. Although kissing in Western Culture is a symbol of the mature intimate relationship, in these games it is but a frenetic approximation to the form, with little of its spirit.

In the games of group II, thirteen-, fourteen-, and fifteen-year-old children show less hurly-burly in their play but not much more

---

berg, *The Omnibus of Fun* (New York, 1956), pp. 375 and 336. Edna Geister, *Geister Games* (New York, 1930). E. O. Harbin, *The Fun Encyclopedia* (New York, 1940), pp. 245, 254, 820 and 821. William Ralph La Porte, *A Handbook of Games and Programs* (New York, 1922), p. 54. Sidney Lear and M. B. Mishler, *The World's Best Book of Games and Parties* (Phil., 1926), p. 106. Snyder Madelin, *My Book of Parties* (New York, 1928). Bernard S. Mason and E. D. Mitchell, *Social Games for Recreation* (New York, 1935), pp. 71, 85 and 216. Theresa Hunt Wolcott, *The Book of Games and Parties* (Boston, 1911).

[33] B. Sutton-Smith, "A Formal Analysis of Game Meaning," *Western Folklore*, XVIII (Jan., 1959), 13–24.

expertise in handling their relationships with each other. These games provide a socially structured means by which they can be brought into relationship with each other, even to the extent of taking partners and kissing, but without responsibility for the partner choices that are made. The fortuitous elements in these games provide the youngsters with a form of trial-and-error partnership, but without the danger of being taken too seriously. They are able to indulge their own general interest in the opposite sex, but are defended against its outcome ("Could I help it if the bottle pointed my way!"). We need to remember that this is the age of tongue-tied and incompetent early dating. By playing these games the children can be with the other sex and by following the rules they can act fairly competently. At the same time they are *protected from a commitment to another person* for which they may not yet be ready. Not unnaturally, most of the kissing is described by the participants as a "peck" rather than a kiss. During the games the manner of the play will vary with the maturity of the players. Some will be eager for the kissing. Some will be reluctant. The virtue of the games is that they allow some to reach quickly towards their heterosexual goals and others to drag their feet, and yet by participating still to remain members of their social group. In general, girls show an earlier interest in promoting these games than do boys. The greater physiological maturity of the girls and the greater cultural interest of women in romance is probably sufficient explanation for this. This earlier interest is demonstrated in the figures from the high school sample. The average number of games checked per child for the 5th, 6th and 7th grades was; boys: 2.9 and girls: 2.7. For the 8th and 9th grades; boys: 2.7 and girls: 6.6. For the 10th, 11th and 12th grades; boys: 7.1 and girls: 6.6. In sum, girls showed a marked increase in checking these games at the age of 13. Boys did not show an equivalent increase until the age of 15. These ages parallel closely the average ages for the onset of puberty. Total figures for likes and dislikes by boys and girls show that while girls check an average of five games, boys check only four. However, there is no significant tendency for girls to like these games more than boys do. Both sexes show approximately the same ratio of likes to dislikes (2:1).

In the group III stage there were girl informants who talk of getting together after the party to discuss which of the boys were the best kissers, but also reports in which boys were said to favor the more advanced games of Group III while the girls were trying to stay with the more guarded Group II games and thought of games such as "Flashlight" and "Endurance Kissing" as "quite disgusting." These differences are, however, simply further evidences of the varying levels of maturity and perhaps varieties of moral attitude involved. The important question to be asked of the games of the Group III stage, is why, if the couples are chosen, should there be any need for games? And in some reports indeed it was mentioned that parties would break up early so that each couple could go off on its own way for some time before the required hour of arrival at home. However, when couples of sixteen, seventeen and eighteen years are not able to go off on their own, or have a social reason for staying together such as a birthday party, it is not unnatural that they develop these group games of unabashed indulgence. Once again, of course, there will be less-mature children present who are happier holding the flashlight than cuddling in the corners of the room. Or, perhaps more important, there will still be children who prefer the relatively public nature of these games to the face-to-face intimacy of being alone with their date. Paradoxically as it may seem the public and funful nature of "Flashlight" and "Endurance Kissing" may be less anxiety provoking for some than the total and serious intimacy of necking in private. Just as "Spin the Bottle" provides a defense against the responsibility of choice, so "Flashlight" provides a *defense against the possibility of intimacy* which is, according to dynamic theory, quite a hurdle for the maturing child.[34] This is to say again that these games, like the others, serve a bridge function. They provide a guarantee of certain gratifications, in this case relationship with the opposite sex, but they place limitations upon excess. One may enjoy a kissing relationship, but be protected from a more total and intimate commitment. The uncertainty of what "might" happen is removed by the structure of the game. It may, for example, be safer to "perdiddle" all the way home than to venture into the other unknown possibilities of an immature relationship.

Here then are a number of psychological reasons why the kissing

[34] E. H. Erikson, *Childhood and Society* (New York, 1950), p. 229.

games have not decreased as have so many other games but have prospered in the freer society of the young and immature.

SUMMARY[35]

This article describes approximately fifty kissing games collected from between three and four hundred persons. The games are categorized into the three classes of chasing-kiss, mixing-kiss and couple-kiss games. Various modes of play are described. It is shown that the kissing games of today are related historically to forfeit and amusement games, and that they have taken the place of the older marriage and courting games. It is suggested that they have prospered and developed in the modern world because they are appropriate to the parlor settings in middle- and upper-middle-class homes, and because they satisfy the desire of adolescents for increasing heterosexual experience, but at the same time safeguard them against too open a commitment to, or too much intimacy with, the other sex. Thus these historically derived forms are changed and sustained by particular sociological and psychological circumstances of the present day.

[35] I wish to acknowledge the assistance of David W. Smith in collecting the high school sample and Judy Trumbell in preparing the manuscript.

14. A Formal Analysis of Game Meaning

As complex group behaviours, games ideally lend themselves to multilevel historical, sociological, psychological and ludic analysis. Paucity of information, however, often prevents gaming behaviours from getting the rich consideration they deserve. This article proposes to take one game and show some of the factors that must be taken into consideration in the analysis of its meaning. It cannot be claimed that every relevant statement will be made about this game, but it is hoped that, by implication, the relative inadequacy of more meager approaches to the explanation of games will be exposed.[1]

The game chosen is one that has been played in New Zealand from 1840 until the present day. The name of the game is "Bar the Door," and its American counterparts are games known variously

SOURCE: Copyright 1959 by the California Folklore Society. Reprinted from *Western Folklore* 18, no. 1 (1959): 13–24, by permission of the Society.

[1] Consider in this light the unhappy preface in Lewis Spence's *Myth and Ritual in Dance, Game and Rhyme* (London, 1947), pp. i–v.

as "Blackman," "Pom Pom Pullaway," "Black Tom," "Anty
Over," "Sheep Sheep," "Goosie Goosie Gander," "Red Rover,"
"Colors," "Uncle Sam May I Go By," and "Johnny Can't Cross
My River."[2] In general this game is played by children running
between two bases. A central player (called a "He") stands in the
middle. The He calls the name of one child who runs from the base
on which he has been standing to the far base, endeavouring at the
same time not to be tagged by the He. If tagged, that runner stays
in the middle with the He and helps him to catch other players that
run across. If a player succeeds in running right across without being tagged, the player shouts "Bar the Door," and the other players
run across, the He and his assistants catching all they can. The
game continues until one player is left untagged. This player becomes the He in the center for a new game. We can speak with
some certainty when we say that either this or some analogous
form of the game came originally to New Zealand from the British
Isles, for 93 per cent of the inhabitants of New Zealand have come
from, or are descended from children who have come from, the
British Isles. Another 6 per cent of New Zealand's two million population are Maoris, a Polynesian people who first settled in New
Zealand some six hundred years ago. But they did not have this
particular game in their folk repertoire and could not very well
have given it to the British immigrants.[3] The responsibility of the

[2] Sources for these American counterparts are as follows: "Blackman" has
been reported to me as played in Oskaloosa, Kansas. Paul G. Brewster, *American
Nonsinging Games* (University of Oklahoma Press, 1953), p. 56, reports the
game as being played in Indiana. H. C. Lehmann and P. A. Witty, *The Psychology of Play Activities* (New York, 1927), p. 112, report that the game is
played by rural children in Kansas. "Pom Pom Pullaway" is reported by Brewster, *op. cit.*, p. 76, in Maine and Indiana. "Red Rover" and "Red Rover Let
Johnny Come Over" I observed myself in New York and in Berkeley, California,
in 1953. "Uncle Sam May I Go By," observation, Berkeley, 1953; "Colors," observation, Berkeley, 1953; "Johnny Can't Cross My River," observation, Berkeley, 1953; "Anty Over," Lehmann and Witty, *op. cit.*, p. 113, Kansas; "Goosie
Goosie Gander" is noted in Z. McGhee, "A Study of the Play Life of Some
South Carolina Children," *Pedagogical Seminary*, VII (1900), 459–478.

[3] Elsdon Best, *Games and Pastimes of the Maori* (Dominion Museum Bulletin, No. 8, Wellington, New Zealand, 1928). See also, B. Sutton-Smith, "The
Meeting of Maori and European Cultures and Its Effects upon the Unorganized
Games of Maori Children," *Journal of the Polynesian Society*, LX (1951),
93–107.

immigrants for bringing the game with them is further attested by the fact that in various forms and under a variety of names the game has been played in all the provinces of New Zealand in all historical periods from the beginning of settlement in 1840 until the present day. It has been the most widely known and the most popular of children's games.[4]

In order to provide any comprehensive analysis of this game, it is necessary first to have some systematic way of describing it. Unfortunately no generally accepted system of ludic analysis is available. Games are usually classified and described in a great variety of fashions. I cannot go into a full account of what I think such a descriptive system should contain, but I will indicate a few of the major game features that I believe require consideration and apply them to this game of "Bar the Door." These features, which will be dealt with in turn throughout the rest of this article are: 1. The Game Challenge; 2. Player Participation; 3. Performances; 4. Spatial Scene; 5. Temporal Structure.

1. The Game Challenge

First there has to be some statement of the game purpose. This is a statement of the game-contained goals of the players. In competitive games, these statements of the basic game purposes can be thought of as challenges. In "Bar the Door" the challenge presented to the players is primarily that of a "Chase." Other common game challenges include the "Hunt," the "Rescue," the "Capture," the "Seduction," the "Attack," the "Race," and the "Harrassment." These eight challenges are believed to cover most of the basic situations of reciprocal opposition which are to be found in games. In addition every game carries with it certain response-qualities which go along with all basic challenges and seem to be a part of their essential nature. First, each challenge brings with it an element of uncertainty or chance. The players are not certain whether or not they will be caught, or will capture. Secondly, players experience these challenges as fun.

---

[4] B. Sutton-Smith, "The Historical and Psychological Significance of the Unorganized Games of New Zealand Primary School Children" (Ph.D. Thesis, University of New Zealand, 1953). A copy is in the library of Victoria University, Wellington, New Zealand, and a microfilm copy is in the library of Ball State Teachers' College, Muncie, Indiana.

The view is taken here that despite the fact that these challenges are never expressed except in terms of the patterns of player participation and performance, these ludic challenges are the primordial and integrating factors in these games. As a consequence it is assumed that "Bar the Door" evolved gradually from simpler forms of the Chase over long periods of time. This means, in effect, that there is no ultimate and final historical origin for the chase element in this or any other game, though there will be historical origins for some of the other elements that the game contains (categories 2–5 below). This is an elaboration of the thesis presented by Huizinga.[5]

2. PLAYER PARTICIPATION

(a) The challenge has to be represented in terms of some statement of the participation of the players. We want to know something of the actor and counteractor roles which constitute the two sides of the challenge. In our game, the actor and counteractor roles are the chaser and chasee.

(b) We need to know also about the organization of the players as a group. Whether it is in pairs, in a Central Person game, or in teams. There must be some statement of the relationship of the other players to the actors in the central game challenge. Are they merely waiting or are they potential actors or counteractors themselves. Further, when referring to the organization of the players we have to know how they are deployed over the game territory, whether they are in lines, in circles, or, as in this case, in groups at one end of the territory facing a central player in the middle. We want to know also how the players move when the game starts. Do they converge on the central player or do they disperse from him. These various patterns of participation, organization, deployment and movement are not easily explained. Sometimes the circles, lines, etc., appear to have almost as much universality about them as the basic challenges, at other times close examination suggests a certain relativity to local culture patterns. "Bar the Door" has the organization of a Central Person game. The analysis of all the games played by children in the first three school grades shows that

[5] J. Huizinga, *Homo Ludens, or The Play Element in Culture* (London, 1944).

approximately three quarters of these games are Central Person games. These are games in which one central player plays in opposition to the rest of the group. There are only two roles, the central role and the group-member role. No doubt their simple organization is at least part of the reason for the success of these games with the young children who play them. We have to remember that children between the ages of six and nine have only a partial understanding of the reciprocity of rule behaviours. Simple role organizations of this type are suitable to their fairly elementary level of social maturity. At the same time one can hardly overlook the fact that the organization of these games in a sense parallels other social organizations of which the children have had a great deal of experience, namely the organizations of the family and the school. In both these situations children are constantly acting as group members in relation to a Central Person—the parent or teacher—who has the initiating or controlling power. In Central Person games, the central player has similar initiating and controlling powers. It is interesting to note that as the game is now played only by younger children it persists only in this Central Person form; in the nineteenth century, when the game was played by early teenagers, it was often played as a team game. A game played in Timaru in 1880 is described as follows:

There were two sides with a captain for each side. Each team lined up on opposite sides of a space with boundaries marked with stones. The captain of one side would go into the middle and call one person from the other side. That person would run across and attempt to avoid capture. If he succeeded the whole team would come after him. Everybody caught joined the team of this captain in the middle. Now the other captain would have his turn and see how many he could catch for his side.

Sociological changes in recreation have determined that teenagers now spend their time with forms of organized sport, so that team forms of "Bar the Door" no longer persist. The younger children who do play the game today are not socially mature enough to maintain team forms spontaneously.

(c) In discussing the nature of player participation we must consider role-clothings, such as animal names applied to players, or symbolic cries made by them. It will be clear that such role-clothings are directly influenced by events in the surrounding culture, as when small boys play as G-men or spacemen. One way to study this aspect of a game is through a description of game names and game terms. "Bar the Door" has had approximately fifty names during its life history in New Zealand, and these can be divided into ten groups. (I) First there is the term "Bar the Door" and variants and corruptions of this term, viz., "By the Door," "Barbadoor," "Father Door," "Bar the Gate," and, not strangely in socialist New Zealand, a game called "Labor Door." Of these terms "Bar the Door" and "Bar the Gate" seem to be the only original names. They are the only terms in this group reported by informants of the nineteenth century. All the other terms derive from the play of youngsters during the past twenty years. Despite the efforts of their mentors, children of the young age group that now plays the game frequently mix up and mispronounce even the written word. It is hardly strange that they corrupt the oral tradition. (II) There is another group that begins with the word "King," and includes: "King Seenie," "King O Weenie," "King O Seenie," "King Caesar," "King Seize-Her," "King's Den," "Punch King Seenio" and "Punch King." (III) "Red Rover" and "Red Rover All Over." (IV) "Horney." (V) "Barley," "Barley Goats," "Broken Barley." (VI) "Blackthorn," "Black Bull Bee," "Black Peter." (VII) "Goosey," "Goosey Up and Down." (VIII) There is a group in which the name is suggested by the action. Here presumably the original name has been forgotten, although some of these names were once the calls or "nominys" that went with the game under other names, viz., "Holding," "Last Over Call," "All Over," "Last Man Over," "Pass Over," "Free Pass," "Running Through the Middle." (IX) There is a large group of "Bar the Door" variants played only by girls that includes: "Sheep Sheep," "Colors," "Vegetables," "Fruits," "Initials," "Please Jack," "Nigger Boys," "Cross the Bar," "Charley Over the Water," "Chase the Leader," "Farmer and the Lion," "Fishes and Whales." (X) There is a group of invented names from modern gymnastic books: "Chinese Wall," "Great Wall of China," and "British Bulldog."

Many of the game names that are mentioned above are to be found in British folklore sources, sometimes in connection with "Bar the Door," and sometimes in connection with games of a different sort.[6] The only source in which both game and name are the same as "Bar the Door" is MacLagen's *Games of Argyleshire* (Scotland), 1900. The term "Bar the Door" was first used in New Zealand by the Scottish settlers in the Province of Otago in the bottom portion of the South Island. Some of these settlers may well have come from Argyleshire. From Otago this name has spread throughout the country, following in the wake of those many Scottish schoolteachers who have had such an effect upon the New Zealand education system. In her *Traditional Games of England, Scotland and Ireland* (1894–1898), Lady Alice Bertha Gomme described a game similar to the one reported above, but known as "King of Cantland," "King's Covenanter," "Kings," and "The King and Queen of Cantland." Gomme considers that these and other games of a similar nature are degenerate forms of a dramatic dialogue game called, "We are the Rovers" which she suggests, "owes its origins to the border warfare which existed on the marshes between England and Scotland and England and Wales."[7] Evidence of the universality of similar games throughout Europe, however, shows that in fact only the role-clothing of the game has been affected by these historical events in England.

As in many chasing games the central figure sometimes takes upon himself the role-clothing of a fearful character, of a bogeyman or a hairy man. We will discuss this aspect of the games when considering the part that the emotion of fear has to play in the player performances.

---

[6] Parallels for some of these terms that are to be found in British sources are as follows: "Bar the Door" and "Bar the Gate"—R. C. MacLagen, *The Games of Argyleshire* (London: Nutt, 1900), p. 210; "Get Up and Bar the Door"—Francis James Child, *English and Scottish Popular Ballads*, eds., H. C. Sargent and G. L. Kittredge (Boston: Houghton-Mifflin, 1904), No. 275, pp. 602–603; "King Caesar"—A. B. Gomme, *Traditional Games* (London, 1894), I, 299, and II, 482; see also N. Douglas, *London Street Games* (London: Chatto and Windus, 1931), p. 83; "Red Rover"—Gomme, *op. cit.*, I, 286; "We are the Rovers" and "Johnny Over"—*Ibid.*, II, 343–356; "Horney"—H. Bett, *Origin and History of the Games of Children* (London, 1924), pp. 78–79; "Barley"—H. Bett, *op. cit.*, p. 4; see also Gomme, *op. cit.*, I, 21; "Blackthorn"—*Ibid.*, I, 34; "Sheep Sheep"—*Ibid.*, II, 187; "Bar"—*Ibid.*, I, 18; "Lamploo"—*Ibid.*, I, 325; "Chickidy Hand"—*Ibid.*, I, 67; "Stag Warning"—*Ibid.*, II, 213; "Hunt the Staigie"—*Ibid.*, I, 242; "Whiddy"—*Ibid.*, II, 212; "Warney"—*Ibid.*, II, 342.

[7] *Op. cit.*, II, 343–356.

3. PLAYER PERFORMANCE

In the analysis of a game there must be some discussion of the nature of the performances demanded by that game (and sometimes implemented with material objects) in order to resolve the challenges. In "Bar the Door" the performances involve running, tagging, calling, dodging, etc. Performances also involve the type of control the players have over the game action. In this game the central player has a great deal of control because he may choose which player has to run across and, by that choice, when he must run across.

An examination of early forms of this game in New Zealand reveals that not only was the organization often more complex (team forms), but that performances were often of a different nature. Many of the older forms used to contain crowning ceremonies. For example in one such ceremony called "Kinging" the captive was patted on the head while he lay on the ground with the other players sitting astride him. While they sat they shouted the rhyme below, and if he moved during the recital they had to begin again:

> King Seenie, one, two, three,
> You're the very man for me,
> Keep him quiet, hold him down,
> Pat him thrice upon the crown.
> Blackball, blackball, one, two, three,
> Joseph Jackson, you are He.

The game was also much rougher in those days because the tackling performance of rugby football carried over into this game. And in many schools where the grounds were suitable rather unorthodox forms of tackling were substituted for tagging. It was often a general practice in these games to let some disliked player run across last; then the whole crowd of players in the middle would "down" him and pile on top like "Sacks on the Mill." Thus, if a running player fended off tacklers too hard on his earlier trips, he would generally meet a time of reckoning later on when the mass of players combined to return the injuries. In some cases, the tagging was done with three punches. This is said to have led to many fights, especially when running players felt that they had been punched too exuberantly. Tackling forms of the game were often known as "Scragging" or "Collaring," and by the boys' mothers as the "clothes tearing game."

Sociological changes have led to the abandoning of these performances.[8] First changes in recreation which we have already mentioned have meant that only younger children play the game, and they cannot execute complex crowning ceremonies or accept games of such a high degree of roughness. In addition, the hard surfacing of playgrounds, together with teacher supervision, have forced children to give up such rougher forms and channel their more aggressive play releases into the accepted times and places for organized sports. Like many other games this one has suffered a whittling down of its traditional folklore role-clothing and performances. Games, it appears, now have a more specialized motoric role to play in childhood than previously. Presumably their animal symbolism, their rhymes, and their reference to odd characters have been replaced by the modern symbolisms of the mass media.

However, one sociological change that has worked to the advantage of "Bar the Door" has been the change in attitude towards the sexes and the increasing prevalence of coeducational policies in schools. In the more enlightened elementary schools of today boys and girls are free to play together or apart as they wish; they used to be kept strictly separate and seldom ever played the same games. The modern policy has not only meant that girls today play "Bar the Door," but also that characteristically feminine variants have developed. For example, in a game called "Colors," the runners at the end of the ground pick colors and the He player in the middle calls out the name of any color at random. The player who has chosen the color which is thus called, then runs across and tries to avoid the He in the center. Other games of a similar nature go under the names of "Vegetables Fruits," and "Initials." In a version called, "Please Jack May We Cross Your Golden River?" Jack, who is the He in the middle, replies to the players who ask that question, "Yes, you may cross my golden river (which is a crack in the playground), if you have red on you." Jack may mention any color. Those wearing that color walk across freely. Those without it run across and the He attempts to tag them.

---

[8] B. Sutton-Smith, "Traditional Games of New Zealand Children," *Folk-Lore*, LXIV (1953), 411–423.

The running and dodging performances have not changed throughout time. Clearly they are necessary to implement the basic nature of the challenge. But we can assume as well that additional gratifications accrue to the players from these performances in themselves, quite apart from the fact that they are necessary to the execution of the game. It is said, for example, that the years between six and twelve constitute "a period of general growth of muscle and bone, with possibly some neural maturation to make muscular coordination easier. In general large muscle coordination precedes that of the small muscles and, therefore, the refinements of neuro-muscular skill come at the end rather than the beginning of the period."[9] Our game is a good example of such large muscle activity and presumably meets the growth needs of the players very appropriately.

Another performance which is of importance in this game is the act of tagging. This is both a symbolic expression of the act of capture and a vehicle for aggressive release. As we have seen, in historical times boys often made this aggressiveness quite explicit by punching or tackling the captured player. When children are merely tagging each other such aggressive motives are not so obvious. Children are characteristically action-oriented in their games and do not clearly show at all times the psychological states that may underlie their actions. Occasionally however, the extreme behaviour of a few individuals provides us with a clue to the feelings of the rest. Thus we sometimes encounter children who seem completely unable to tag other children, even though they can run just as fast as those other children and it is within their competence actually to touch them. They will run right up to or alongside the other player but at the last moment will seem to draw back from the act as if they have some inhibition about the actual tagging itself. We can perhaps infer that for these children the tagging represents an aggressive act which for a variety of possible psychological reasons that need not concern us here they fear to perform. We can infer also that for those who are not troubled by such inhibitions tagging represents a guilt-free act of aggression; gratifying because it provides a release for aggressive feeling, guilt-free because it is limited and symbolic.

[9] J. Havighurst, *Development Tasks and Education* (University of Chicago Press, 1952), p. 15.

Yet another performance in the game which is made apparent by the extreme behaviour of some individuals is the expression of the emotion of fear. In this game one often sees children running hard to get away from the He and shrieking with mock, but almost real, fear just as they are about to be caught or to escape. And from such an observation it is possible to hypothesize that one of the psychological sources of the children's satisfaction in the chase in this game is the playful sensation of fear which it affords them. In the game fear may be experienced and yet it is not limitless. It exists within a controlled setting. The players control the fear, the fear does not control the players. In other words it is symbolic only, though once again the borderline between play and reality is often a fine one. I have witnessed the game played by children when a too-realistic He (generally an older boy) reduced the smaller players to real terror and ultimately tears. In normal circumstances, however, we may assume that the enjoyment of the expression and mastery of fear is one of the game performances which is a source of satisfaction to the players.

Another important performance is the type of control that the players have over the game action. "Bar the Door" is a Central Person game in which the central player has much choice over the actions of the game. He chooses which players shall run, and he chooses when they shall run. In one piece of game research the question of whether or not the possession of these controls makes any difference to the players has been investigated.[10] Two types of game were compared. In one game like "Bar the Door" the central player exerted the usual controls. In another game of a similar sort, the players were not controlled by the central player but could run backwards and forwards whenever they chose. There were ten groups of children, each group composed of low-skilled, intermediately-skilled and highly-skilled runners. The experiment was arranged so that all the low- and the highly-skilled runners had experience at the central positions in both games. The success and failure of these children was then measured by the number of successful tagging attempts and subjective expressions of success and failure that the children made in these positions. The results showed that the low-skilled runners gained a much more gratify-

[10] P. V. Gump and B. Sutton-Smith, "The 'It' Role in Children's Games," *The Group*, XVII (1955), 3–8.

ing and successful experience in the central position when they had more game control. Lack of these controls led to expressions of failure and a desire to quit. The highly-skilled children were successful in both games. The implication is that games like "Bar the Door" are more suitable for less mature players; that Central Person games which provide "controlling" power for the He players bring satisfaction to young players. It is noticeable that in the games of older children it is a straight test of skill that is important rather than any special controlling influence that one player has. In "Bar the Door," it is as if the younger players agreed to take turns at the positions of importance. One of the gratifications inherent in the game must lie in its provision of such special controls.[11]

4. THE SPATIAL SCENE

Another necessary consideration is that of the spatial scene. This is the terrain upon which the players or their representatives (e.g., chessmen) are deployed and upon which the game action takes place. This spatial scene has external limits (boundaries) and internal differentiations (goal regions, taboo zones, etc.). In "Bar the Door" there is a safety zone at each end for the runners and a danger area in the middle for all but the chaser. Interpretation of these characteristics has varied throughout history.[12] In Europe in the Middle Ages the game is reputed to have been connected with the dances of death, the idea being that the "blackman" in the middle represented the God of Death and would catch his victims and lead them off to hell.[13] In the same vein, the game has been associated with the old demonic cult figures of a lower European mythology.[14] There is a Swiss version of the game called "Running the Bar" that is the same as "Bar the Door," though in this case the

[11] B. Sutton-Smith and P. V. Gump, "Peer Status and Play Status," *Recreation*, XLVIII (1955), 172–174.

[12] E. L. Rochholz, *Alemannisches Kinderlied und Kinderspiel* (Leipzig, 1857), No. 26, pp. 408–409; No. 32, pp. 414–415. These are closely allied to the examples from Gomme, *op. cit.*, I, 21–23 and 376.

[13] F. M. Böhme, *Deutsches Kinderlied und Kinderspiel* (Leipzig, 1897), No. 379, pp. 565–566.

[14] For discussion of the demonic figures in children's games see Samuel Singer, "Deutsche Kinderspiele," *Zeitschrift des Vereins für Volkskunde*, XIII (1903), 49–64. There is some incidental mention of the subject in the continuation of the article; see pp. 167–179.

Swiss word *Bâr* appears to stand for boundary, whereas the term bar in "Bar the Door" seems to mean "to block" the door, that is, to prevent others from running through.[15] However, it would not be straining the imagination to believe that the bar of "Bar the Door" was originally derived from some term signifying boundaries, and that the name of "Bar the Door" referred to players' attempts to run between boundaries and through a door that might or might not be open. Perhaps we may speculate that the middle territory was sometimes known as hell, and the end bases represented heaven and earth. In this case the runner would be defying the devil by a skilled flight from earth through purgatory to heaven. It is an idea not alien to the Christian conception of the cosmological scheme and an idea already quite explicitly embodied in the historical accounts of "Hopscotch."

The question next arises as to what relevance such a spatial conception has to the young players of today. Is there any parallel in their lives for such a spatially represented series of behaviours. You will have noticed that in this game the children first advance outwards from a safe and secure base or "home." They adventure across a dangerous space in the face of a hostile adversary, and then once more seek safety in the home on the other side. There is a parallel for this in other children's activities. Gesell speaks of the way in which young children often identify one part of their house as being "safe" and another part as being "dangerous." "The upstairs becomes inhabited with lions and tigers but oddly enough these creatures do not invade the mother's room."[16] Or we might parallel this spatial representation with the process of growing up and leaving home, an evolution that children accustom themselves to by successively venturing out from their own homes and then returning to them once more.[17] The He player, it appears, stands for all the dangerous powers of the unknown world against which the child is asserting himself when he makes his dangerous ventures from home and back again. The base—or the touchline, or the home —stands for the secure place. Players manifest their independence

[15] Kurt Ranke, "Meister Altswerts Spielregister," *Schweizerisches Archiv für Volkskunde*, XLVIII (1952), 165. I am indebted to Professor Archer Taylor of the University of California for his assistance with references 12 through 15.

[16] A. Gesell, *The Child From Five to Ten* (New York, 1949), p. 114.

[17] E. Fromm, *The Fear of Freedom* (London, 1942), p. 23.

by venturing forth and challenging the He, but then fly back to the home again to escape him. Why should danger be represented by a single He player? We know that many of children's real and imaginary fears center around parent figures.[18] It may be that the central figure in this game is a representation of fears of this sort. The devil of yesteryear is the dangerous adult of today; the cosmological scene of the Middle Ages is the developmental scene of the modern child. Such parallels, while only speculative, suggest that the meaningfulness of this game in its various details may well be due to its ability to meet the multiple needs of the players.

5. The Temporal Structure

The last game feature requiring consideration is the structure by which the time for the beginning and ending of the game and the game phases is determined. There is usually a clear correspondence between such space and time structures and the physical abilities and attention-span of the players. This game guarantees justice to the young by controlling the alternation of central players. The last player tagged becomes the He for the next game. It continues throughout in a loosely organized form which allows players to come and go, to join and quit, more or less at will. This fluidity suits the needs of young children well in their school playtimes.

There is as well the external temporal relations of the game, or its seasons.[19] In the brisk but temperate climate of New Zealand this running game is suitable for playing at almost any time in the year. In the main, the play seasons for "Bar the Door" are interstitial. The first summer enthusiasm for cricket and softball is over. The first winter enthusiasm for rugby will not begin until May. In the interstices of these major seasons, younger children who show at least a peripheral interest in these major sports when they first appear, can return to their minor pursuits of more perennial interest, namely marbles, tops, and "Bar the Door."

Summary

(a). It has been suggested that sociological changes have led to a decrease in the team forms and the rougher elements in "Bar the

---

[18] A. Freud, *The Ego and the Mechanisms of Defence* (London, 1932), p. 119.
[19] B. Sutton-Smith, "Marbles Are In," *Western Folklore*, XII (1953), 186–193.

Door" games and to an increase in feminine variants of these games.

(b). That the role-clothings are the most transient of the games' features and that game names show evidence of historical "survivals" as well as current symbolism.

(c). That the Central Person organization of "Bar the Door" corresponds to the social immaturity of the children who play it.

(d). That the Central Person role parallels the nature of the players' conception of the adult figures in their lives.

(e). That the game plot parallels the development of independence in these children.

(f). That the game's motor performances, its allowance for controlled expression of fear and aggression, its spatial arrangements and temporal successions are all appropriate to the age-level needs of seven- to nine-year-old children.

In short, sociological factors operate externally to determine who shall and who shall not play the game and to place limits on how they play it. Historical factors operate symbolically to determine the meaning that the players attach to their own activities. Psychological factors operate internally to determine the range of gratifications that the players will get from the activity and the needs that it will meet. And finally, the desire to chase and be chased, is due to the inherent ludic nature of mankind.[20]

[20] No one has yet proven that these game challenges are universal, although it is usually assumed by those who study games that they are. For example, see H. Marshall, "Children's Play, Games, and Amusements," in C. Murchison (ed.), *Handbook of Child Psychology* (London, 1933), p. 518; S. E. Hunt and E. Cairn, *Games the World Around* (New York, 1941), p. 4; N. Miller, *The Child in Primitive Society* (London, 1928), p. 144.

15. The Sporting Balance

In this article I wish to review some of the studies in play and games with which I have been associated in order to draw some implications for the study of sports. I should begin, however, by setting forth some important limits to this enterprise. I am a developmental psychologist by vocation and an artist by inclination. This means that I will talk mainly about the reality of imaginative structures and the importance of motivations, and have very little to say about sport as an institutionalized game or as a social institution. It means also that I will over-emphasize the origins of sports and the symbolic elements in them. I will ask what play has to say about sport, and what games have to say about sport, but neglect what sport has to say about sport. Whether this is a wise or a futile approach depends upon whether the relationships between the three are more like those that occur between the dreams of children and adults, or more like those that occur between the logic of children and adults. In the first case, adults continue to dream in the same way as children, merely adding new crises; but in the second case, the logic of adults is quite different from that of children, and doesn't require a knowledge of the earlier forms for its own understanding. Naturally, I am presupposed to the view that it is the dreams rather than the logic which provide the best model for understanding the interrelationships of play, games and sports. That's the risk I take.

To deal with these interrelationships and remain somewhat clear about one's procedures it is helpful to have an explicit frame of reference. I find it useful in these matters to ask three formal and three functional questions. The formal questions focus on the sequence of forms of which a given game is a member, so necessarily deal with *precursors* and *sequelae*. The most important formal question has to do with the chosen *grammar*, for the example being considered, and in this matter I take a page from Kenneth Burke's *Grammar of Motives* (1945) and have terms for actors and counter-actors, actions, agencies, the spatio-temporal context and the purposes of the players.* Thus, formal questions have to do with precursors, the grammar and the sequelae. In parallel fashion, functional questions have to do with *antecedents* (biological, psychological, sociological) from which we derive the meaning of the games' symbolism; *rhetoric*, in terms of which we understand the situational or contextual factors instigating the current performances; and the *telos* from which we derive the non-game intentionalities and cultural values of the event. Diagrammatically, the following discussion is guided as follows:

Formal Questions	*Functional Questions*
Precursors	Antecedents
Grammar	Rhetoric
Sequelae	Telos

PLAY AND SPORTS

There is no adequate structural (formal) treatment of play. There are indeed the descriptive systems of Huizinga and Caillois, but they may fall short of the operational specificity required to encourage research. Piaget's efforts, which are based on his theory

---

* Material enclosed within parentheses refers to sources listed at the end of the article.

of cognitive development, also fall short of adequacy—partly because he is really more interested in cognition than he is in play (Sutton-Smith, 1966). In another paper I have attempted to indicate how a structural system based on Burkian analysis might apply at different age levels (Sutton-Smith, 1971). In this paper I want to stress only what is implicit in these efforts, namely, that they take seriously the view that play is indeed a separate behavioral system. Most psychologists have, unfortunately, approached play as a sub-category of some other form of adaptation (as a defense mechanism, as a type of exploration, or as a form of intelligence) so have tended to emphasize the way in which its formal characteristics have imitated those of other "more serious" forms of adaptation. This has led both to a neglect of play analysis sui generis, and to an emphasis on the repetitive or conservative quality of play. By seeing play as merely a mirror of antecedent events, its own specific qualities, transformations and novelties have been neglected. This is like analyzing sports for the "aggressions" they contain with little attention to the rule systems within which aggression is constrained.

Current efforts to grapple with the reality of play as a separate behavioral system derive from explorations of the relationships between exploration and play in early childhood, and from studies of play in lower species. Thus Eibl-Eibesfeldt writing about the transformational character of animal play says that the action patterns are not carried through to their usual ends, they are combined in play in ways that are not found outside of it. "Play may even combine behavior patterns of functional cycles that normally operate in mutual exclusion, for example, hunting, fighting, and sexual behavior" (1967, p. 138). And Welker writes that play involves "The novel variation of the subjects' own responses, more or less irrespective of the variation of the stimulus qualities of the objects with which he is engaged" (1961).

Definitions of this nature not only suggest that play is a quite distinctive behavioral system, but contrary to our earlier conservative descriptions, also suggest that play's essence may lie in its radical character. The player's purpose may be to make things differently, to move events away from their customary cognitive and affective equilibria. For this reason the player requires the freedom, separateness and make-believe character of play as preconditions. It could be argued similarly that sports are systems that strive to produce eventual inequality. While we usually recognize this disequilibrial character of sports, we tend, perhaps, to mask its significance with equal emphasis on the underlying cooperation involved in the "cooperative antagonism." Our problem here may be the difficulty we all encounter when dealing with open systems. Language systems and logic are structured to make sense. Whereas it may well be that play and sports are structured to make nonsense out of ordinary expectations. Like the Mardi Gras and cocktail parties, they require a paleologic for their comprehension, and the problem with our systematic descriptions may lie in our own inability to develop this logic of nonsense. It seems likely that it is only by focusing on the unique transformations that occur in play (and sports) that we will begin to accumulate the empirical data that such a theory of play as a disequilibrial phenomenon would require. As I will indicate later, there are ways in which play is disequilibrial in its own terms and ways in which it is disequilibrial in terms of interrelationships with other forms of experience. But it's not easy to think about disequilibrating phenomena or even to take seriously that they exist. It is like supposing that Caillois' "vertigo" is a general experiential phenomenon as well as a physical possibility. In formal terms, we are not accustomed to focusing our grammars on non-sequiturs.

In raising this question about play's grammar, I am, of course, speaking only to the matter of its purpose. I do not have anything else to say at this point about the other grammatical issues raised above, nor anything about formal precursors and sequelae.

Let me move now to some functional issues. One of the paradoxes with play is that within the work ethic of Western culture, it has been perceived as "trivial" and as not contributing in any obvious way to human adaptation. At the same time the paradox exists that biologists have demonstrated that phylogenetic evolution is accompanied by the increasing playfulness of the higher species members. One way out of this dilemma is to revise the notions of adaptation which have prevailed in the life sciences these past 100 years, and concede that behaviors formally called expressive may actually be useful to the adaptation of the higher species. It would make sense to argue, for example, that play is primarily an exercise of the voluntary control systems. Voluntary control implies various forms of mastery such as the anticipation of outcomes, the choice of instrumental behaviors, freedom from immediate sensory controls, a capacity to sustain the direction of behavior over a number of responses, sequential organization and skill in mobilizing resources. A deterministically oriented social science has tended to underemphasize the importance of these voluntary control systems in human behavior, though play theorists have traditionally pointed to them for their play definitions (the pleasure of being a cause, etc.). Given the view that there are such systems then play is obviously a sphere where they could most readily receive exercise. This would satisfy the functional paradox, that play seems to be nonproductive, but is associated with higher order functioning phylogenetically. The particular outcomes of play may not be of value, but the general exercise of systems would be. This argument has been presented more fully elsewhere (1967).

In turn, such an approach would imply that the major antecedents for play would be the existing voluntary system competences, just as the major outcome would be a general increase in competence at exercising these systems. An analysis of such systems used at any age level, and for that matter in sports, might permit us to pose the question of transfer of training in a more specific and empirically testable fashion.

In saying this, however, I do not intend to reduce play to an exercise of antecedent voluntary control systems. I wish to provide it with a more general set of biological antecedents than are usually provided. Such antecedents may well sustain, they do not explain the formal matters discussed above.

A second functional system of some consequence has to do with the sequential relationships of play and sports. Does the one lead to the other? Is there continuity or discontinuity? Some have supposed, for example, that play is a particularly infantile activity which is displaced in adults by constructive thought and by organized recreation (Piaget, 1962). But recent work on adolescent and adult fantasy and dreams suggests strongly, on the contrary, that play continues in the adult but through internalized forms (Singer, 1966). The adults' ruminations, daydreams and reveries appear to be the counterpart of the child's solitary motor and imaginative play. The adult, no less than the child, continues to assimilate, react to and rehearse his experiences through his own unique, if silent, ludic discourse. Perhaps more pertinently, just as the majority of childhood dreams place the dreamer in the passive position of victim (90%), so too a substantial percentage of adult dreams continue to portray the dreamer as undergoing misfortune (30%) (Hall and Van De Castle, 1966). We frequently describe the child's play as turning passivity into activity, that is, as a form of compensation for his passive-like life status. We say in his play, at least, he can master his experience. His dreams indicate to us that in these states of low awareness (dreams) he customarily feels overwhelmed by that experience. As adult dreams continue to contain similar elements and adult sports (like children's play) deal with contests between those who are victors and those who are victims, it is arguable that the play and the sports are similarly concerned to redress the balance of unconscious life. Each exercise is a dialectical relationship with the dreams and fantasies of the involved subjects whether they are children or adults. To be a victim and suffer misfortune is both an unconscious (dream) and conscious (fantasy) apprehension that unites child and adult. To oppose this state and assert on the contrary that victory and success are possible similarly unite the child and adult content of daydreams, fairy tales, cartoons, movies and sports.

In sum, I am making the argument that much of the symbolism of the child's play and the adult's sport is the same. While one part of play and sport gives expression to voluntary control systems, another part uses these very freedoms to deal with the pains of involuntary psychic experience. From this point of view the sporting counter balance, which is disequilibrial with the unconscious misfortune, engenders a larger equilibration. Things are put right and the moral order is restored, which is, I believe, one of the less well known interpretations of what Aristotle really meant by *catharsis*.

GAMES AND SPORTS

Because of the license taken by many writers, we have come to use the term game in so many ways it is almost impossible to reach an adequate formal definition. Games are dealt with as authentic cultural phenomena, as representations of distinct social and psychological behaviors and as conceptual models for thinking about human behavior. Etymologically, the word game has diverse roots, including: *ghem*: to leap joyfully, to spring; gam: a leg, especially a woman's leg; gamba: a musical instrument; gambado: a leap of a horse; gambit: an opening move; gambol, gammon, etc. The term is applied diversely to Hide and Seek, Solitaire, Bingo, Chicken, Zero-sum, Simuload Alcoholic and Frigid Woman (Avedon and Sutton-Smith, 1971). Any definition must attempt to encompass all these.

A baby of about four months old, sitting on his mother's lap while he is being fed with a bottle, grasps the mother's finger. The mother pulls it away, and the baby grasps it again, sometimes interrupting the feeding process because of the pleasure of these alternations. We say in this instance that the baby is playing a game with his mother. It is not purely play because each is to some extent controlled by the reaction of the other. Each has a certain goal in mind in this case to capture or to avoid the capture of the finger. Perhaps this simple incident provides us with a lead towards a formal definition. From a cultural point of view it is usual to emphasize that play is unique and individual but ephemeral; whereas a game is sufficiently systematic that it may be repeated by others in other places. The finger game could be repeated and instigated by mothers with babies in almost any culture. Games are, therefore, repeatable because they have systematic patterns and predictable outcomes. Play on the other hand is less systematic and is open ended with respect to outcomes. In a game the participant's voluntary control over procedures has been subordinated in anticipation of, but without guarantee for, a given goal.

Again games imply some opposition or antithesis between players. Even in solitary games (puzzles) it seems this same sense of opposition is present. That is, the player contends against impersonal obstacles or against fortune. In games that do not seem to have opposition, such as the kindergarten "mulberry bush," opposition is present in the children's attempt to have their bodies and impulses obey the rhyme and rhythm of the song. The stylized movements may not be a challenge to an older child or adult, but they are to the preschooler.

Even in an elementary game, therefore, we have repeatable pattern, opposition and outcome. At this level then we can define a game *as an exercise of voluntary control systems in which there is an opposition between forces, confined by procedure and rules in order to produce a disequilibrial outcome.*

With a little revision this definition can be expanded to cover the central person games of early childhood (hide and seek, tag, etc.) with which I have dealt extensively elsewhere (1959) and the games of physical skill, strategy and chance with which Roberts and I did our major cross-cultural work (1962, 1963a. 1963b, 1964, 1965, 1966a, 1966b). Central person games deal essentially with ascriptive power just as the other triad deals with achieved power. In the first, status is given arbitrarily or by counting out procedure whereas in the latter it is obtained by prowess. In the first relationships between actors and counter-actors are hierarchically patterned whereas in the latter they are patterned in egalitarian terms. I have presented the argument elsewhere that this is an historical as well as a developmental separation (1969).

A game definition, however, must not only take into account the purpose of the players (to obtain or retain power) it must also deal with types of interaction patterns, prescribed performances, procedures for action and the spatio-temporal contexts. If all of these various facets be epitomized by the term *rules*, then it becomes possible to restate the definition above with specific application to formal games. A game is an exercise of voluntary control systems in which there is a *contest between powers*, confined by rules in order to produce a disequilibrial outcome.

The precursor "opposition between forces" has now become a "contest between powers." Clearly this definition should do for sport also, except that compared with sports, games are relatively less often institutionalized nor themselves a social institution. But these latter matters have to do with the context within which the game is played, rather than with any essential formal difference between games and sports' rules themselves. As Gregory Stone suggests, sport adds display to play, and yet has to ignore display if play is to continue true to itself. Perhaps we can cover this position by adding to our above definition as follows: A sport is an exercise of voluntary control systems, in which there is a contest between powers, confined by rules in order to produce a disequilibrial outcome *with rhetorical effect*. By adding the latter phrase we take into account, that despite their concentration on the game, the sportsmen, unlike the games' players customarily, are part and parcel of a larger communication or contextual situation which affects them greatly before the play, during the play (the rooting section) and after the play. In turn their performance affects this audience of promoters, managers, gamblers and vicarious participants. Recollecting the earlier statements on play, we can stress that many others are also involved in the disequilibrial outcome; these others have a psychic or economic stake. So great in fact is this stake, that it is hard to resist the inclination to suggest that the reason a sport has rhetoric whereas a game usually does not, is because the sport is part of a larger mythic game being played by a segment of people in the culture concerned. In the game the dream is restricted to the participants. But in the sport, the dream is exercised both through the game and its rhetoric.

I have been dealing with formal questions, though in part by connecting sport, play, myth and dreams, I seem also to have implied answers to functional questions. Whether or not this is true any such generalities have to be explicated for particular cultures, particular sports and particular sportsmen.

There are various approaches. One can seek to trace the antecedents, outcomes and rhetoric of games in terms of cross-cultural constancies. Thus Roberts and I sought to show, that games of physical skill, chance and strategy always have a certain cultural context; that the games of physical skill are associated primarily with forms of physical survival; that the games of chance are associated with economic uncertainty and divinatory decision making; that the games of strategy are associated with high command training and cultural interaction complexity. But this search for constancies could draw inferences only about psychological antecedents and cultural outcomes (from correlational materials); there was no dealing with the rhetoric itself, nor with the fact that within complex cultures all these game phenomena exist, though perhaps not necessarily for the same reasons.

A second step, therefore, was to seek for subcultural constancies. We attempted to make predictions from the cross-cultural to the sub-cultural, and established that games of chance and strategy (of the lower risk variety) are more common with females than males, and that the situation is reversed for games of physical skill. In addition games of low risk chance are commoner in lower socioeconomic groups and games of strategy and physical skill in higher socioeconomic groups. These predictions were made on the basis of cross-cultural information about the association between child training variables and particular games. Although the approach was at best tangential, it did support the view that complex cultures contain embedded within themselves sub-cultural patterns which parallel those seen in simpler form in tribal cultures.

Along with these materials we advanced the conflict-enculturation hypothesis in terms of which we hoped to reconcile the psychogenic interpretations of psychoanalysis and the sociogenic interpretations more familiar in sociology. We suggested that our cross-cultural material implied that child training processes led to states of conflict, which were appropriately represented in the games of different types. The children were drawn into these games because the games then structured their own experience. Once in the games, however, the exigencies of play led to a real rehearsal of strategies of power. The game we contended was a model of power, and the rehearsal of bluffing, deception, agility, etc. in the game, was probably useful in subsequent life. Whether or not the latter was true, military game theories, business game programs and educational simulation games have for many years been based on the same assumption. Current evidence is that students can learn as much through games as through lessons (Boocook and Schild, 1968).

Looking at these speculations in terms of what was said earlier about dreams, one might regard them as specifications of that more general conflict between victim and victor which the dreams so clearly manifest. For example, in a high command culture the child is made victim of complex symbolic and social demands, and exercises his redress through martialing his own forces in games of strategy. Again, in cultures where the child is victim of outer circumstances and where personal achievement and inner resources are penalized, the child and adult may exercise redress with lady luck. At the same time each type of player presumably develops prowess in strategies or probabilities.

What this general framework still lacks are more precise ways of measuring the antecedent conflicts, the steps towards involvement, the character of the learning that occurs in the model, and finally the transfer of training to other spheres. We would suppose, as mentioned earlier for play, that the learnings are general rather than specific; that they become resources for potential use, and that transfer depends on the exigencies of subsequent occasions rather than upon the game experience itself.

As a third step in this program we sought for individual constancies (within culture, within subculture) across games. We have not much to report here. But we did find game players in general (at least at the college level) to be less depressive than non-game players; and moderate game players to be more normal (in clinical terms—the M.M.P.I) than game addicts (more than 40 hours of play per week). Again chess players turned out to be more disputatious and solitary individuals than bridge players—who were more gregarious and avoiding of argumentation.

A yet more important and fourth step in the search for game antecedents and consequents was to look for variation across individuals (rather than constancies across culture, sub-culture and normative game playing). Some of our recent research has shown for example that bridge players are not always gregarious and "hysterical." It depends on the type of bridge. Contract Bridge players are more often recruited from management and professional classes, and play their game very much like chess, with little intrusion by other facets of personality. With these players Contract Bridge can be a concentrative intellectual occupation. In Auction Bridge, however, the players are more often members of middle status and female, and there is a great intrusion into the game of the player's personality characteristics. A dominant player exercises a great influence on the course of the game. Or to move to sports in High School, there is recent evidence to show that the significance of the same sports varies with the social class of the player. Sports played by middle and upper status individuals do not show positive relationships with school achievement, but when played by lower status individuals, they do. The game may be model of achievement for some players, but not for others.

Our most extensive studies with the elementary game of strategy: Tick Tack Toe, also show that even when playing the same game, players enter it with different styles of play. There are those who play for a win, and those who play it safe; and these stylistic characteristics furthermore vary by sex; the winning girl is dominant and hoydenish, whereas the winning boy is intellectual and non-physicalistic. The boy who plays it safe is a conformer, the girl is feminine.

Finally, one can talk about the game player in intra-individual terms. Here we are concerned with the role that his games have in his total psychic economy. What relationship do they have to his dreams, his drawings, his music, his dramatizations? Does he find parallel or complementary expression through these many vehicles? Unfortunately, there is very little data on matters of this sort. By and large, it looks as if the general rule is that of consistency. A strategic person will tend to approach all expressive forms in the same way. But there are numerous exceptions. Psychoanalysis is replete with examples of quietness in one realm and braggadochio in another. Football likewise has many examples of athletes who are most quietistic off the field and a terror when on it. In some of my own current research in drama (which I see as in the same general category as sport), we have observed children who are most expressive in those terms and yet quite inhibited in normal conversation; and alternatively those who express themselves poorly in mime or rhythm but who are most loquacious in conversation.

To one concerned with individual motivation in sports these intra-individual relationships might well become a central issue in future inquiry into the nature of sports. It is clear from the various constancies accounted above, that normative data, while of general interest and value in understanding cultural parameters, does not alone explain what the games or sports mean to the individual players. For this we need the subject's full expressive profile. How similar is he across expressive forms (music, art, drama, sport, play, humor, poetry, etc.)? Or, to what extent does one balance against the other? We might call this the question of intra-balance amongst expressive forms.

CONCLUSION

This has been a selective approach to some of the interrelationships between play, games and sports. The general effect has been to reduce the differences between them, at least insofar as they are seen as hierarchically arranged members of a similar order. Play was defined as an exercise of voluntary control systems for disequilibrial effects. Elementary games added to this the provision that there be opposition between forces and control by rules. In formal games it was suggested that the opposition is between powers governed by arbitrary, strategic physical or fortunistic agencies. Sports were defined as containing all these together with the production of rhetorical effects.

On the functional level the argument was made that there is continuity of underlying motivation between player and sportsman. Certain basic crises of development are celebrated and counteracted in both. Mastery in both play and sport is part of the same mythos, that one must overcome the giants and monsters of the inner life; though the cross-cultural, subcultural and normative studies of game players show clearly that there are multiple ways and styles within which this conquest can be rendered.

Emerging from these various considerations, however, the central emphasis of this paper has been upon various types of balance and imbalance within the forms of play, games and sports, and between these and other segments of reality. We have suggested that as against the rest of the world they are all forms of imbalance, all forms of nonsense, and that this is a principle of human behavior insufficiently investigated in human affairs.

But within each form there are the dialectical tensions, oppositions and struggles of powers which constitute a balance in themselves. The player who doesn't handle these equilibria is no sportsman, is not sufficiently playful, etc.

Or again, though defined as disequilibria, our discussion suggested that there is a balance between them and other realities. The antecedent misfortune of dreams, and the compulsion of involuntary behavior is here balanced by mastery and voluntary display. Furthermore, a style of expression in one media may be counterbalanced by a style in another.

From all of which we conclude that a useful line of study for the future of sport's sociology or psychology, is the role that sports play, not just by themselves, but as part of this web of imbalances and counterbalances in the individual's life. A notion which we may capture as the *sporting balance*.

REFERENCES

Avedon, E., and Sutton-Smith, B. *The Study of games*. New York: Wiley (in press, 1970).

Boocock, S. S., and Schild, E. O. *Simulation games in learning*. California: Sage Publications, 1968.

Burke, K. *A grammar of motives*. New York: Prentice-Hall, 1945.

Eibl-Eibesfeldt, I. Concepts of ethology and their significance in the study of human behavior. In Stevenson, H. W., *et al.*, *Early behavior*. New York: Wiley, 1967, 127–146.

Hall, C. S., and Van De Castle, R. L. *The content analysis of dreams*. New York: Appleton–Century, 1966.

Piaget, J. *Play, dreams and imitation in childhood*. New York: Norton, 1962.

Roberts, J. M., and Sutton-Smith, B. Child training and game involvement, *Ethnology*, 1962, Vol. I, No. 2, 166–185.

——, ——, and Kendon, A. Strategy in folktales and games, *Journal of Social Psychology*, 1963, 61, 185–199.

——, Hoffman, H., and Sutton-Smith, B. Pattern and competence: A consideration of Tick Tack Toe, *El Palacio*, 1965, 72, 17–30.

——, Thompson, W. E., and Sutton-Smith, B. Expressive self-testing and driving, *Human Organization*, 1966, 25, 54–63.

——, and Sutton-Smith, B. Cross-cultural correlates of a game of chance, *Behavior Science Notes*, 1966, 3, 131–144.

——, and ——. The cross-cultural and psychological study of games, *International Journal of Sports Sociology* (in press).

Singer, J. L. *Daydreaming*. New York: Random House, 1966.

Sutton-Smith, B. The syntax of play. In R. Herron and B. Sutton-Smith. *Child's play*. New York: Wiley (in press, 1970).

——. The games of two cultures. In G. Kenyon (Ed.), *Sociology of Sport* (in press).

——. The folkgames of the children. In T. Coffin (Ed.), *Our living traditions*. New York: Basic Books, 1968, 179–191.

——. Games, play and daydreams, *Quest*, 1968, 10, 47–58.

————. Novel responses to toys, *Merrill-Palmer Quarterly*, 1968.

————. The role of play in cognitive development, *Young Children*, 1967, 6, 361–370.

————, and Roberts, J. M. Studies in an elementary game of strategy, *Genetic Psychological Monographs*, 1967, 75, 3–42.

————. Piaget on play: A critique, *Psychological Review*, 1966, 73, 111–112.

————, and Roberts, J. M. Rubrics of competitive behavior, *Journal of Genetic Psychology*, 1964, 105, 13–37.

————, and ————. Game involvement in adults, *Journal of Social Psychology*, 1963, 60, 15–30.

————. *The games of New Zealand children*. Berkeley: University of California Press, 1959.

16. The Expressive Profile

In an earlier article, titled "The Psychology of Childlore," I have suggested that one who is both psychologist and folklorist has the unique problem of conjoining these two disciplines without subordinating the one to the other.[1] If he is a developmental psychologist, moreover, he must also deal with the fact that juvenile folklore has traditionally handled games, rhymes, jokes, riddles and other such lore, while developmental psychology has handled dreams, play, fantasies, humor, and comics. It would seem to make sense that the conjoint treatment of both—say games and play, jokes and humor—would be likely to provide more explanatory power than their treatment separately. In part, this division of function seems to have been based on the mutual suspicion of both

SOURCE: *Journal of American Folklore* 84, no. 331 (1971): 80–92, reprinted by permission of the American Folklore Society.

[1] Brian Sutton-Smith, "The Psychology of Childlore," *Western Folklore*, 29 (1970), 1–8.

parties, on the one hand, that the folklorist would be concerned with the accumulation of endless forms without reference to their functional significance and, on the other, that the psychologist would persist in his psychogenic reductionism without respect to the meaning of the formal expression he was attempting to explain.

In this article I will act as if no such scholarly boundaries need exist, and proceed to look at a variety of expressive forms such as dreams, stories, folktales, rhymes, cartoons, and games as if they could all be part of the same conceptual domain. It is assumed that the understanding of any one of these will be increased by a study of its parallels and interactions with the others. There are four different categories of expressive forms to be dealt with here: (1) the imaginative phenomena such as dreams, stories, and fantasies whose normative character can be traced; (2) the folk forms such as games, tales, rhymes, and jokes; (3) the mass media forms, particularly those found in cartoons, comics, and movies; and finally (4) the art forms of drama, art, music, dance, and poetry. Although the term "childlore" applies only to the second of these categories, the point to be established is that childlore is best explicated within the context of all four, if all four indeed have a unity as expressive forms.

By expressive forms it is meant that these are all ways of presenting or representing human experience, sufficiently consistent across individuals to permit functional and formal analyses. Given such unity, then, it might follow that analyses appropriate to one form would be illuminating when applied to another, or again, that within the experience of a given individual or group the forms may function in related and perhaps complementary ways. The system of analysis to be used here involves three formal questions and three functional questions. The formal questions to be applied to each example are (1) what are formal precursors, the genetically prior forms? (2) what is the present structure, the grammar? (3) what are the normatively expected sequels? The functional questions are (4) what are the psychogenic or sociogenic antecedents (the symbolism)? (5) how does the form function in its present context (situational, contextual and rhetorical variables)? (6) what is the player's intentionality; how does the involvement profit the participant in terms of future functions (the *telos*)? As an illustration of the present system of analysis, consider some of the earlier studies and theorizing on games of strategy by Roberts and Sutton-Smith.[2]

Our answers to the above six questions were, in order:

1) Within American culture, games of strategy evolve from tick-tack-toe through checkers to chess.

2) The act of strategy involves the rational choice of alternative courses of action. The actors and counter-actors compete. The purpose is winning. The agencies are the moving pieces, and the spatio-temporal scene usually involves a playing board and sometimes special playing times and arrangements.

3) The sequels involve more complicated game theory and computer applications of the same formal patterns.

4) Interest in these games is engendered psychogenically by obedience conflicts and sociogenically by complex cultures requiring competence in intergroup strategies.

5) In pure games of strategy the context and audience seem to be a relatively unimportant part of the contest (unlike physical sports, where it can be critical).

6) Empirical relationships between competence at games of strategy and other psychological variables (arithmetical competence, task persistence and social subtlety) argue for the view that the game rehearses for subsequent skills of the bargaining or diplomatic sort.

When these questions have been answered for each expressive form, presumably a network of relationships between forms and functions will then become apparent, yielding a sounder understanding—among other things—of the meaning of childlore. Obviously in the present state of the science, no one is going to give adequate answers to these questions which cover four types of expressive form for anyone given population of subjects. What is necessary is the undertaking of a comprehensive study with some representative groups.

2 John M. Roberts and Brian Sutton-Smith, "Child Training and Game Involvement," *Ethnology*, 1 (1962), 166–185; also: "Strategy in Folktales and Games," *Journal of Social Psychology*, 61 (1963), 185–199; and "Cross-Cultural Correlates of a Game of Chance," *Behavior Science Notes*, 3 (1966), 131–134. See also Brian Sutton-Smith and John M. Roberts, "Game Involvement in Adults," *Journal of Social Psychology*, 60 (1963), 15–30; and "Rubrics of Competitive Behavior," *Journal of Genetic Psychology*, 105 (1964), 13–37.

This paper will attempt to explore these matters across a heterogeneous group of studies that are currently a part of the available literature. Subjects within the age range of five through seven years have been chosen for the analysis because this is the age group in which childlore materials first begin to take on a fairly substantial existence. We will look at studies of five-year-old dreams, stories, games and tales, and give some minor attention to books, rhymes, and art. These materials do not always lend themselves to the six-point system of analysis outlined above, so the analysis will usually be of a partial character in terms of that system.

It should be pointed out that the system of analysis clearly owes much to the preoccupations of a developmental psychologist with formal and functional sequences; but it is derived in part also from the dramatistic analyses of Kenneth Burke, whose description of qualitative progressive structures seems most applicable to the type of forms under consideration.[3] Obviously other systems of structural analysis are possible; logical categories, mathematical categories, or syntactic categories might also be applied. In the following presentation each form is handled at first only in terms of the formal questions, with functional questions postponed for inquiry afterwards.

FORMAL QUESTIONS
Dreams

The material discussed here is from the doctoral dissertation of Beverly Elkan.[4] It includes dreams collected from males matched at each of three age levels (five, ten, and fifteen years), and analyzed in terms of a system based on Erikson's categories of psychosexual development.[5] While there are no pre-five-year-old materials available in this study, the general Freudian point of view is that prior to the age of five years there is no distortion in dreams, so manifest and latent content are the same.[6] In his interviews, Piaget reported

---

[3] Kenneth Burke, *A Grammar of Motives* (Englewood Cliffs, N.J., 1945).

[4] Beverly Elkan, "Developmental Differences in the Manifest Content of Children's Reported Dreams," Ph.D. dissertation, Columbia University, 1969.

[5] Erik H. Erikson, *Childhood and Society* (New York, 1951).

[6] Sigmund Freud, *A General Introduction to Psychoanalysis* (New York, 1964), 132–133.

that children up to this age perceive dreams as visiting them from outside and watch them as they would a movie.[7] By the age of seven or eight, although the child still sees the dream as a picture, it has moved inside his head. Later the child conceives of it as similar to thinking. Those who have reported age changes in dream content indicate that prior to the age of five most dream content is domestic, including daily play, playmates, and animals; but at five, wolves, bears, and strange people chasing and punishing the child begin to predominate.[8]

A Burkian grammatical analysis of the twenty dreams of twenty five-year-olds in Elkan's collection gives us the following results. While the subject is in the dream on all occasions and while there are occasionally other actors (parents = five; siblings = six; peers = one; relatives = one), the predominant counter-actor is a monster figure in seventeen out of twenty dreams (lion, ghost, tiger, witch, animal, murderer, monster). Where sex is attributed to these figures, females predominate over males, seven to two. In fifteen out of twenty dreams the dreamer is the passive recipient of another's actions. The monster chases, captures, bites, hurts, scares, and injures the dreamer bodily. In only five out of twenty dreams does the dreamer counteract by screaming, saving a sibling, calling for help, or slapping a monster. Half the time the situation is domestic (bed, home, house, or room). Temporal relations are either present or not explicit. The agency through which the acts are effected does not have any consistent shape in this sample. Predominant, however, are monsters coming through doors or in and out of water. The experience also differs: drowning or falling through holes, clothes being removed, being put in machines, being bitten, and so forth. The fact that most dreamers report being scared and yet do not do anything suggests a predominantly "freezing" reaction to fear, which is also the most familiar elementary fear response reported in animal and human literature.

The dreamer's purpose in the dreams is not always clear. Escape seems most important but is mentioned by only two out of twenty, though in ten out of twenty cases the dreamers reported feeling scared. If this analysis is contrasted with the twenty dreams of the

[7] Jean Piaget, *The Child's Conception of the World* (New York, 1960).
[8] Arthur Jersild, *Child Psychology* (Englewood Cliffs, N.J., 1968).

ten-year-olds, all the same elements are present but with slight changes in emphasis. Monsters are slightly less frequent (thirteen to twenty), siblings are less frequent (two to twenty), parents retain the same frequency (six to twenty), and friends appear more often (seven to twenty). The dreamer is somewhat less passive, though he is still scared (thirteen to twenty) and counteracts a little more (eight to twenty). There are more acts involving exploration, building, and searching; and there are more helpers, an important change from a fairytale perspective. Home spaces are less frequently mentioned (four out of twenty); places away from home now figure predominantly (fourteen to twenty). Past and future are more explicit (ten out of twenty). Elkan using a different scoring system highlights some of the changes in table 1.[9]

In sum, at age five years, the subject is characteristically a defenseless victim of a monster in a domestic setting. Time and agencies are not systematically differentiated. At age ten, the setting is less often domestic, the subject is less often a victim and even occasionally a victor, particularly with the help of friends.

Stories Told by Children

The material to be discussed is from Ames' work on children's stories which deals with the tales of 270 children between the ages of two and five years.[10] The analysis relies perforce on Ames' categories, which do not match too suitably with the ones from Burke, adopted above. In general, the stories told by these children were not unlike the dreams reported above, except that the children seemed to see themselves somewhat less as victims at this level of awareness. Parents played stronger supporting roles and the harm more often than not occurred to others (siblings and animals) rather than to the narrators. The actors were predominantly people or animals in a ratio of about four to three.

Contrary to what happens in dreams, mothers predominate, though their positive roles decrease and their negative roles increase over this age span. An appreciable number of mothers are seen as

[9] Elkan, 47.

[10] Louise Bates Ames, "Children's Stories," *Genetic Psychological Monographs*, 73 (1966), 337–396; Evelyn G. Pitcher and E. Prelinger, *Children Tell Stories* (New York, 1963).

TABLE 1
Frequency by Age of Positive Scores for Items from Empirical
Checklist with Highest Power of Discrimination

Items	Age Groups		
	4–5	8–9	14–15
Animal chasing dreamer	3	0	0
Authority	0	5	5
Communication	2	6	11
Enemy	15	9	5
Getting hurt	8	1	0
Introspection	0	1	9
Projectiles	0	0	5
Speaking	1	5	9
Monster	9	4	0
Terror, fear	11	8	4

disappearing or as punishing, hurting, or ignoring the child characters (38% girls, 16% boys). The mother is the most active in the story relationship at the age of two, while the child is the most active at the age of five years. The fathers' negative roles at age five are 17 percent for girls and 29 percent for boys. Even so, unlike dreams, positive roles predominate for both mothers and fathers (power figures) at age five. Monsters do not predominate in these tales. Again, however, the major act is that of violence (72% of all stories), and it is again mainly passively incurred, especially at the age of two years. Age-two stories are more like age-five dreams in that the children are often victims. The violence occurs through accident (41%), aggression (35%), and harm to people (34%), to animals (22%), or to objects (25%). Things are broken (15%), there is punishment (11%) and death to people (9%) or animals (9%). Most two-year-old stories take place in the home (60%), but this decreases markedly by five years (20%).

There are clearly strong formal parallels between this collection of stories and the collections of dreams discussed above. In both, passivity in the face of violence is pronounced, but these samples (which are not by any means matched) give us the impression that in stories the development of initiative and protective devices is more advanced than in the dreams experienced at the same age.

Folktales

There is little systematic information on the folktales regularly told to five-year-olds. The nearest we can get is Lanham's and Shimura's recent study of tales told to American and Japanese children, which lists twenty tales that eighty-three parents said they told their children, though the ages of the children were not supplied.[11] The first ten in rank order were "The Three Bears," "Three Little Pigs," "Little Red Riding Hood," "Cinderella," "Snow White," "Jack and the Beanstalk," "Sleeping Beauty," "Hansel and Gretel," "Rumplestiltskin," and "Rapunzel." In a questionnaire study of fifty-nine children in a fourth grade, a somewhat similar list was arrived at by the present investigator.[12] The rank order preferences for girls were "Cinderella," "Sleeping Beauty," "Snow White," "Rumplestiltskin," "Hansel and Gretel," "Elves and Shoemaker," "Beauty and the Beast," "The Three Pigs," "The Princess on the Glass Hill," and "Jack and the Beanstalk." For boys the preferences were "Jack and the Beanstalk," "Sleeping Beauty," "Uncle Remus," "The Golden Touch," "Cinderella," "The Three Bears," "The Tortoise and the Hare," "Snow White," "Rumplestiltskin," and "The Gingerbread Man." Only "Cinderella" and "Sleeping Beauty" were responded to by half the girls and only "Jack and the Beanstalk" by half the boys. Other frequencies were quite low, being responded to by only four out of nine children. We are thus not in a good data position to talk about the folktales of five-year-olds, though the correspondence between the two lists shows that these are probably the current tales for many children between the ages of three and ten years.

Without making any detailed analysis of the tales it is immediately clear that the major features of the dreams and stories are repeated, but now with the significant difference that the victim becomes victor and actually escapes or overcomes the monster. Apart from the heroes themselves (bears, pigs, Cinderella and

[11] Betty B. Lanham and Masao Shimura, "Folktales Commonly Told Japanese and American Children," *Journal of American Folklore*, 80 (1967), 34–48.

[12] At Kenwood School, Bowling Green, Ohio. Respondents were thirty-three girls and twenty-six boys in the fourth grade. Our thanks to Harlan Lehtooma, principal.

Jack), the leading counter-actor is some sort of monster figure who is usually feminine (bear, wolf, giant, stepmother, witch) in all ten tales. By Lanham and Shimura's count, female figures dominate the Western sample (thirteen to five), which corresponds to the stories children tell where the ratio of mothers to fathers is about four to two. The victor and the monster-figure engage each other through a variety of agencies unmatched in dreams, though hinted at in children's stories: flight, tasks, trickery, magical aid, strategy, skills, poison, robbery, daring, and guessing. Females prefer magical assistance (Cinderella, Sleeping Beauty); males prefer personal prowess (Jack and the Beanstalk). Though these tales are, in general, not dominated only by female figures, they are preferred by females. The locales throughout are surprisingly domestic. Houses or castles dominate. The purposes are more explicit than in the stories and dreams. In most cases the intent is clearly to escape from or to overcome the dangerous creature. Not that these purposes should be overemphasized. Propp remarks that motivations are not generally explicit in folktales.[13] The inner life and intents of the victors and villains are not revealed. Like Piaget's children of this age, the concern is with consequences, not with intentionality.

What is perhaps most noteworthy about the tales is that they seem an extraordinary complement to the dreams. In both cases there is a moratorium on ethical and religious concerns. The dreams provide what Propp might call a lack or deficiency, "a sudden emergence of misfortune,"[14] and the folktales provide a response. In the tale the victor overcomes the villain. The oft-noted way in which children spend months of their lives glued to the pursuit and victories of cartoon heroes (Superman, Cool McCool, Superboy and Marine Boy) indicates a dynamism of a most powerful sort. Apparently the same dynamism penetrates more conventional stories written for children. In their content analysis of third- and fourth-grade readers, psychologists Child, Potter, and Levine complained of the unrealistic optimism of the stories, of

13 V. Propp, "Morphology of the Folktale," *International Journal of American Linguistics*, 24 (1958), 1–135.
14 *Ibid.*, 25.

their presentation of life where reward is stressed and failure never mentioned, of unsocialized adults who were aggressive and acquisitive and of animals and fairies who were also aggressive.[15] The stories did not contain constructive suggestions as to how to handle this aggression; they overemphasized physical activity at the expense of the intellect; they overemphasized dependence on authority as a way of succeeding. Here again we see, in effect, the monsters, protective parents, magical helpers, and physicalistic initiatives of fairy tales. One striking difference in this analysis, however, was the more "adult" emphasis on male characters and male superiority (seven to three) with women shown as relatively helpless and inferior.

Nursery Rhymes

These rhymes, like the stories made up for children, have a mixed character. An unpublished analysis of the Opies' collection of 550 nursery rhymes yields a male to female ratio of four to two,[16] which is more like the ratio in grade school readers than in fairy tales. The predominant behaviors were classified as amusement (14%), riddles (10%), violence (9%), death (8%), love (5%), sex and courtship (10%). In 43 percent these actions had no consequences. In 19 percent they were punished and in 15 percent rewarded. Unlike the grade-school readers mentioned above, the characters in nursery rhymes do meet with failure, which makes them more like dreams and less like tales. They also use unsocialized techniques of gaining their way, which makes them more like fairy tales and less like grade-school readers. Men and women are both aggressive, again more like the tales than the readers. Any tentative developmental sequence, then, might present an arrangement ordering dreams before children's stories, children's stories before nursery rhymes, rhymes before fairy tales, and tales before conventional grade-school reader material.

[15] Irving L. Child, Elmer H. Potter, and Estelle M. Levine, "Children's Textbooks and Personality Development," *Psychological Monographs*, 60 (1946), 1–53.

[16] Karen Neely, "A Content Analysis of the Oxford Dictionary of Nursery Rhymes," M.S. thesis, Bowling Green State University, 1966; Peter and Iona Opie, *The Oxford Dictionary of Nursery Rhymes* (Oxford, 1951).

Play and Games

Table 2 indicates the rank-order play and game preferences of 561 five- to six-year-old children in an unpublished sample of Ohio school children.

Hide and Seek and Drop the Handkerchief are in some ways analogous to the previous materials. There are "It" (or monster-like) figures who "tag" (or kill) the fleeing children. At this level one counteracts "It" by hiding or by flight. "It," by agency of reconnaissance or tagging disposes of the subject. From tagging games at later age levels, we know that—over time—the monster is increasingly counteracted. The chased players begin to harass him, to defend and rescue themselves. At five years, however, there is a continuing emphasis on "home" and safe places, where one can escape the "It." The major purpose seems to be flight. At later age levels it will be to fight.

The latter activism is perhaps prefigured by the other play in the list above, where there is an emphasis on sex-role competences. The boys say that they are playing at the conventional and legendary roles and sports of men, though we suspect they do it in a fairly routine and simple way. The actors are sex-role types, the actions involve expression of power and competence (males), routine care and choosing (females). The girls—with their houses, dolls, and schools—focus on the actions of the females. In the Farmer in the Dell and London Bridge, the issues of choosing and being

TABLE 2
Play Preferences of Five- to Six-Year-Old Children

Males (N=285)	Females (N=276)
1. Tag	Tag
2. Cowboys	House
3. Baseball	Dolls
4. Hide and Seek	Hide and Seek
5. Pretend games	Farmer in the Dell
6. Marbles	Drop the Handkerchief
7. Football	London Bridge
8. Ball	Draw and Color
9. Trucks, cars, trains	Schools
10. Swinging	Swinging

chosen as central persons, which is a key female concern, are also apparent.[17]

Interestingly, the play and games contain parallels to the passivity of the dreams, stories, rhymes, and tales; but at the same time they provide, like the tales, some scope for active redress. This latter element is even more strongly emphasized in the television representations made for children.[18]

In an unpublished study of ten television programs in which parent-child relationships predominated, the majority were centered on comic relationships (Donna Reed, Rifleman, Littlest Hobo, Everglades, Voyage to the Bottom of the Sea, My Three Sons, Lucy Show, Andy Griffith, Shindig). The very clear result was that the children showed more independence than the parents did control. The child asserts independence, accepts responsibility, and manipulates the parents. This is an entirely different order of behavior from that we have been exploring so far in the other forms.

Summary

We may sum up as follows these various approaches to the grammar of the expressive form in dreams, stories, folktales, nursery rhymes, and games. In all of these forms as used by children at the age of five, the "flight syndrome" is the key imaginative structure. Furthermore, it is predialectical. It is possible to envisage defeat and failure without adequate counterbalance, although in fully developed folktales there is usually such redress. Even in Tag —which involves both—the actor and the counter-actor are not equally balanced. One never overcomes the "It" figure. At this age level he is only eluded. He is all-powerful, and the other players can only escape. In an unpublished study of children's art, Rand and Wapner have shown that when young children of age seven or less are asked to portray an event such as looking for a lost coin, they also tend to emphasize only one side of the event.[19] They

[17] Brian Sutton-Smith, Benjamin G. Rosenberg, and E. F. Morgan, "The Development of Sex Differences in Play Choices during Preadolescence," *Child Development*, 34 (1963), 119–126.

[18] Rebecca Thompson, "A Content Analysis of Parent-Child Relations in Television Programs," M.S. thesis, Bowling Green State University, 1965.

[19] George Rand and Seymour Wapner, "Graphic Representations of a Motivated Act: An Ontogenetic Study," Unpublished paper, 1967.

may emphasize the lostness of the coin, or the impenetrability of the grass. It is defeat of action that is represented, rather than a balance between the lostness of the coin and the action of the searcher. In mythic terms, we are perhaps discussing an attitude of "fatefulness." Things happen to one. There are consequences, but they have an asymmetrical nonreciprocal character.

Judging by the examples in this present study, when the dominance of feminine figures (dreams, stories, folktales) gives way to an equal differentiation of the sexes or predominance of males (play, readers, cartoons), the flight pattern gives way to a fight-flight pattern. To the five-year-old, however, only the active agent (monster or parent figure) and a submissive counter agent (child) seem differentiated. Actions involve being attacked, being chased, and escaping; but they do not involve as yet the reciprocals of adequate defense, rescue and capture.[20] Agencies are mainly physical (hitting and biting), and although magical assistance and strategy are employed in the tales, the latter are not developed as clear instrumentalities. It may require the development of clearer intentionality for such agencies to become differentiated. When power attitudes become more conscious and actively pursued, then such instrumental behaviors presumably become more clearly delineated as useful or nonuseful tactics.

The complementary interrelatedness of the forms is perhaps the most important conclusion to be derived from the present study. The balance of passive participation (dreams), audience participation (fairy tales), vicarious involvement (stories), and actions (games) permits various parallel expressions using different human functions. At the same time the modal emphasis on passivity in some media (dreams and stories) is complemented by a contrary stress on action in the others (folktales and games). The present study can only partially demonstrate these interrelated balances, but it does strongly suggest the incompleteness of accounts dealing with only one expressive medium. There is, clearly, room for a transstructural study of expressive media. In individual terms the importance of the total profile of expressive forms is indicated. Is the individual further advanced in some expressive media than in

[20] These reciprocals are outlined in a paper, "The Sporting Balance," presented at the International Workshop in Sports Sociology, Maglingen, Switzerland, September, 1969.

others? Are certain types of development (say, spatio-temporal)
facilitated by some forms rather than others?

Paucity of data has led to an emphasis in the present analysis on
the grammar of these forms. There has been little attention either
to formal precursors or to formal sequels, though these are equally
important matters in a formal analysis. Even so, we should point a
finger to the fact that we are dealing here with quite different
types of structural sequences. In games, earlier forms are hierarchically subordinated to more complex later forms (chasing and
rescue become elements in football). In dreams, however, old crises
never die; new ones are added. Elkan argues that "at least in the
dream world, development consists of the expansion of the repertoire of crisis themes encountered rather than a sequence of conflicts met, overcome, and abandoned in due time."[21] Elkan did find
that when the earlier crises were represented at later age levels,
they were more often associated with a wider variety of competent
responses than at an earlier age when the crises first appeared.
However, if an older subject dreamed only of earlier crises, then he
dreamed like a younger child. As a part of a transstructural study,
therefore, there is a need for sensitivity to the differences between
the developmental parameters within each expressive type. On the
other hand, all these forms have in common the imbalanced emphasis on "flight" reactions (with the complementary "fight" reactions coming at the next developmental level, around seven
years). Perhaps growth from one structural phase to the next
proceeds by overdelineation of one of the polarities of what will
later be called a reciprocal system, though both poles of the system
are there from the beginning. Even in "It" games—as in dreams—
though escape may be more clearly adumbrated than attack, there
still is alternation with the other role. The "It" is buttressed in his
role by game-given power, which partly carries him in that "autonomous" role despite his own incompetence. Similarly in even
less developed games, the Farmer in the Dell, for example, there
is also role alternation, although only the central role receives much
differentiation (the farmer chooses a wife, a child, etc.). The principle may be that development proceeds lopsidedly towards reciprocal systems, but that there is at least a ritualistic presence of the

[21] Elkan, 51.

two required polarities, even in the beginning. Thus though the dreamer does little to escape the monster, the counterpoise between victim and victor is there at the beginning.

Functional Questions

Finally we have come to the questions of function that have to do with antecedents (symbolism), rhetoric, and consequences. The emphasis on flight throughout these forms would prompt a comparative psychologist to stress the similarity between these phenomena and the agonistic (fight-flight) behavior across many species. It might be argued that at the time of emergence from maternal dependence, flight reactions become critical forms of response for the young of most species. A social psychologist might note that the child, at about this time, increases the number of secondary ties to his peers and consequently his escape reactions and concern with home bases may well be elicited by his required independence among relative strangers.[22] To the psychoanalyst this age period involves the oedipal crisis with attendant fears of danger from rivalrous parents.

According to Erikson, at this age level children should show various expressions of initiative. This is only partially evident in the present material. There is little initiative in the dreams and stories, though there is more in the folktales and games. In the dreams there is a strong hint of earlier psychosexual crises, particularly in the lack of autonomy that flight implies. In "It" games, as in dreams, we have a subject represented whose boundaries and territories are not secure. He is exploited by foreign or arbitrary control. On the level of dependent rather than antecedent variables, there are the data in the achievement literature indicating that up until the age of about seven, children tend to give up under the stress of failure. After that age there is an increasing tendency, particularly in boys, to fight back against experimenter-induced failure in an attempt to overcome it.

Perhaps what is required in order to understand antecedent events that may give rise to the flight reactions noted in the formal material is some theory of motivational overlay. The comparative,

[22] A theme dealt with in detail in Brian Sutton-Smith, "A Formal Analysis of Game Meaning," *Western Folklore*, 18 (1959), 13–24.

psychological and psychoanalytic arguments presented above appear to be discussing the same phenomena in slightly different languages, each of which calls attention to selective aspects of the total situation. How one proceeds from such domains to the symbolism of the formal structures outlined above is, of course, quite a problem. Roberts and I have proposed that the psychological conflict induced by antecedent events induces a readiness to be involved in structures (fantasied, thematic, group psychological, and so forth) in which the polarities of the conflict are configured. But this is at best a general proposition. Even if true, the many mediating steps from the psychological state to the involvement in the expressive media have not yet been spelled out, any more than have the folk processes that lead to the invention of these "peremptory metaphors" in the first place.[23]

Empirical data on the antecedents of these various expressive forms is sparse. There are various studies relating dreams and play to antecedent events of the prior day as well as to long-standing needs for compensation. The children's own story themes of sibling rivalry, violence, and castration imply the presence of anxieties about these subjects. Since these states are well known in the clinical literature about young children, there is good reason to believe that there should be a connection between such antecedent psychological states and involvements in the expressive forms. In a cross-cultural study of preliterate groups, tagging games were shown to be related to independence training.[24] It was argued that the anxiety about independence induced by high independence training manifests itself in involvement in games that symbolize the assertion of independence and the obtaining of security in the face of dangerous strangers. The same study also revealed that this relationship between child training and games existed only for females and was correlated with the presence of marriage customs requiring the girl to marry away from her own immediate kin group. The games were thus constructed both as a representation

---

[23] See also Georges Klein, "Peremptory Idealism," in *Cognition, Personality and Clinical Psychology*, ed. Richard Jessor and Seymour Feshbach (San Francisco, 1968).

[24] Elliott M. Avedon and Brian Sutton-Smith, eds., *The Study of Games* (New York, 1971), 436.

of anxieties about such independence and a preparation for more independent behavior among strangers.

Functional analysis must deal not only with the transformation of antecedent states into thematic material; it must be done in terms of an analysis of the contemporary situation in which that transformation both occurs and has life. That is, contextual situational or "rhetorical factors" must also be spelled out. In fact, there has been very little of this done with the materials here under study, though a beginning has been made with other folk materials.[25] There are no systematic studies of the contexts in which children tell dreams to others, but it is not unreasonable to suppose that the predominance of "unpleasant" dreams in such settings is in part itself a social gesture. It could be that the predominance of monster dreams noted in the Elkan study manifested an appeal for reassurance, intended to evoke a sympathetic or interested response from others. An older child, on the contrary, might use a dream report to prove something about himself rather than as an appeal for help. This is also the case with reports of play participation.[26] We know that more pleasant dreams are reported when subjects are awakened during their sleep. Not that this gainsays the importance of the above structural analyses. It does, however, hold in abeyance any reckoning of the proportionate importance of monster dreams in the child's total dream experience.

Again there is little evidence about parent reactions to children's storytelling, though we can get a clue from Wolfenstein's study, "The Impact of a Children's Story on Mothers and Children."[27] In this study a fantasy story was presented to both mothers and children. The mothers were found to be much more troubled by the fantasy elements than were the children. They felt they were superfluous. "Underlying this belief there seems to be the assumption that the child has no wishes that cannot be satisfied in real-

[25] Roger D. Abrahams, "Introductory Remarks to a Rhetorical Theory of Folklore," *Journal of American Folklore*, 81 (1968), 144–158.

[26] Brian Sutton-Smith, "Play Preference and Play Behavior: A Validity Study," *Psychological Reports*, 16 (1965), 65–66.

[27] Martha Wolfenstein, "The Impact of a Children's Story on Mothers and Children," *Monographs of the Society for Research in Child Development*, 11 (1946), 1–54.

ity."[28] We might, therefore, draw the implication that most homes are not particularly hospitable either to children's fantasy story-telling or to their fantasy story listening, an attitude which in these days is most often masked as protesting the violence depicted in the ubiquitous cartoons.

Elsewhere I have discussed a similar adult uneasiness about children's play and games in terms of the "triviality barrier."[29] The amazing persistence of all these expressive phenomena despite the general context of adult indifference or hostility, speaks to their importance as crucial imaginative structures. But it is clear that in dealing with rhetoric, one has to deal with the conflicts between the participants and the peripheral audience, as well as with the immediate audience of supporting fellow enthusiasts and players. The various circumjacent groups vary across cultures and quite differentially show support for the children's imaginations of the sort displayed in this article. We are also emphasizing that in dealing with these phenomena we approach conflict on a number of levels: in terms of antecedent conflicts (for example, dependence-independence), structural conflicts (victor-victim), and between the form and the adult ideology (important-trivial).

Instigated by antecedent events, sustained or repressed by surrounding circumstances, the imaginative structures carry an intentionality and have consequences, which must also be considered as part of any functional analysis. Unfortunately, intentionality theory is in its infancy. There is no elaborated theory of mastery conation, competence, or striving that is really apt for the present materials. How limited are the participant's purposes? Are his fantasy-linked actions attempts to produce in his current life situation replicas of unconscious prototypic themes? Are life circumstances and actions improvised to recreate perceptually the contradictions of unconscious fantasy with respect to both wish and danger, as Klein suggests? Or, not inconsistently, are there certain implicit human interpersonal structures (flight-fight, escape-capture, chase-elude, etc.), which because they are the syntax or shape of human interpersonal experience—supported by current cues as well as antecedent, unconscious ones—exercise their own

[28] *Ibid.*, 49.
[29] Sutton-Smith, "Psychology of Childlore," 1.

intrinsic lure, their challenge, their tension enhancement, their disequilibrial inducement to human involvement? Does the participant pursue these, partly at least, as he exercises his other competences for the implicit enjoyment of voluntary control?

The notion that the child's pursuits have useful consequences has long been a standard argument in sociological theories of play, as well as in more recent theories of fantasy as a form of problem solving or preparation.[30] Roberts and I have presented the argument that games are models of power through which the child learns the power tactics of his culture.[31] It is important, however, to stress that involvement in fantasy, play, or games appears to have a generalized and probable pay-off rather than any specific usefulness.[32] The higher species play more, as do the more complex human cultures. The involvement of the player in the imaginative structure—while instigated by antecedent events, sustained by fellow participants, and having a value beyond the present moment— functions primarily as a consummatory experience of voluntary function. At least this is the way I have preferred to conceptualize function as applied to expressive phenomena.[33] The virtue of giving functional primacy to the player's celebration of the expressive form (which means that functional analysis is devoted primarily to the "arousal jag" effects of particular formal tension systems) is that the long standing hiatus between formal and functional analyses is dissolved. That hiatus was based on formal analyses that were not focused on the dramatics of the event, and on functional analyses giving primary attention to extrinsic rather than intrinsic motivation.

Conclusion

This paper has attempted to show some of the complexities and results that ensue when a large segment of expressive behavior is

30 Jerome Singer, *Daydreaming* (New York, 1966).

31 Brian Sutton-Smith and John M. Roberts, "The Cross-Cultural and Psychological Study of Games" in *The Folkgames of Children* (in press).

32 This argument is presented in more detail in Brian Sutton-Smith, "Novel Responses to Toys," *Merrill-Palmer Quarterly*, 14 (1968), 159–160.

33 See Elliott Avedon and Brian Sutton-Smith, *The Study of Games* (New York, 1971) and Robin Herrin and Brian Sutton-Smith, *Child's Play* (New York, 1971).

subjected to analysis. Although the data were only partly appropriate to the purpose, they were sufficient to suggest that there are patterns of parallel and complementary involvement running across a child's expressions in dreams, stories, and games. It is possible to talk about the normative expressive profile of a particular age group, though undoubtedly it is even more profitable to talk about the unique profile of the particular participant. The virtue of considering folk phenomena at the same time as other expressive phenomena is that we stand to enrich our understanding of both. There may be a false abstraction in taking any particular form out of its context in the array of expressive forms used by the individual and his group. In addition, this paper suggests a conceptual tool for the analysis of these folk and other expressive forms, involving three formal and three functional questions. A knowledge of expressive profiles must be considered as just one of the outcomes of the larger-scale analysis, which we might term the social science of expressive forms.

THE PUBLISHED WORKS OF BRIAN SUTTON-SMITH
A CHRONOLOGICAL BIBLIOGRAPHY

BOOKS

1950. *Our Street*. Wellington, New Zealand: A. H. & A. W. Reed.

1959. *The Games of New Zealand Children*. Berkeley: University of California Press.

1961. *Smitty Does a Bunk*. Wellington, New Zealand: Price Milburn.

1970. (With B. G. Rosenberg) *The Sibling*. New York: Holt, Rinehart & Winston.

1971. (With E. Avedon) *The Study of Games*. New York: John Wiley & Sons.

—. (With R. Herron) *Child's Play*. New York: John Wiley & Sons.

—. (With J. P. Scott *et al.*) *Social Control*. Chicago: University of Chicago Press.

1972. (With B. G. Rosenberg) *Sex and Identity*. New York: Holt, Rinehart & Winston.

ARTICLES

1949. "Our Street." *Education* 2: 49–51.

1951. "New Zealand Variants of the Game Buck Buck." *Folklore* 52: 329–333.

1951. "The Meeting of Maori and European Cultures and Its Effects upon the Unorganized Games of Maori Children." *Journal of the Polynesian Society* 60, nos. 2/3: 93–107.

1952. "That Boy Again." *National Education* 34: 22–23.

1952. "Jottings From London: Part 1." *National Education* 34: 249.

1952. "Jottings From London: Part 2." *National Education* 34: 293–294.

1952. "Jottings From London: Part 3." *National Education* 34: 352–353.

1952. "What Is a Junk Playground?" *National Education* 34: 398–399.

1952. "The Fate of English Traditional Games in New Zealand." *Western Folklore* 11: 250–253.

1953. "Creative Writing." *Elementary English* 30: 492–499.

1953. "The Traditional Games of New Zealand Children." *Folklore* 64: 411–423.

1953. "A Postscript on Junk Playgrounds." *National Education* 35: 8–9.

1953. "Jottings From the U.S.A." *National Education* 35: 52–53.

1953. "Competitive Athletics for Primary School Children." *National Education* 35: 289–291.

1953. "The Game Rhymes of New Zealand Children." *Western Folklore* 12: 14–24.

1953. "Marbles Are In." *Western Folklore* 12: 186–193.

1954. "The Last Frontier." *National Education* 36: 134–135.

1954. "Will Boys Be Boys?" *National Education* 36: 389–391.

1955. (With P. V. Gump) "Activity Settings and Social Interaction." *American Journal of Orthopsychiatry* 25: 755–760.

1955. (With P. V. Gump) "The 'It' Role in Children's Games." *The Group* 17: 3–8.

1955. "The Psychology of Games: Part 1." *National Education* 37: 228–229.

1955. "The Psychology of Games: Part 2." *National Education* 37: 261–263.

1955. (With P. V. Gump) "Games and Status Experience." *Recreation* 48: 172–174.

1956. "Play Settings and Social Interaction: Part 1." *National Education* 38: 13–15.

1956. "Play Settings and Social Interaction: Part 2." *National Education* 38: 59–61.

1956. "On Being a Mere Teacher: Part 1." *National Education* 38: 333–335.

1956. "On Being a Mere Teacher: Part 2." *National Education* 38: 387–390.

1958. "Some Notes From the Study of Human Development." *National Education* 40: 399–400.

1959. (With B. G. Rosenberg) "The Measurement of Masculinity and Femininity in Children." *Child Development* 30: 373–380.

1959. (With B. G. Rosenberg) "A Scale to Identify Impulsive Behavior in Children." *Journal of Genetic Psychology* 95: 211–216.

1959. "The Kissing Games of Adolescents in Ohio." *Midwest Folklore* 9: 189–211.

1959. "Some Comments on the Class Diffusion of Children's Lore." *Midwest Folklore* 9: 225–228.

1959. "A Formal Analysis of Game Meaning." *Western Folklore* 18: 13–24.

1960. (With B. G. Rosenberg) "Manifest Anxiety and Game Preferences in Children." *Child Development* 31: 307–311.

1960. (With E. Morgan and B. G. Rosenberg) "Age Changes in the Relationships between Anxiety and Achievement." *Child Development* 31: 515–519.

1960. (With B. G. Rosenberg) "A Revised Conception of Masculine-Feminine Differences in Play Activities." *Journal of Genetic Psychology* 96: 165–170.

1960. "The Cruel Joke Series." *Midwest Folklore* 10: 11–22.

1961. "Cross-Cultural Study of Children's Games." *American Philosophical Society Yearbook*, pp. 426–429.

1961. (With B. G. Rosenberg) "Sixty Years of Historical Change in the Game Preferences of American Children." *Journal of American Folklore* 74: 17–46.

1961. (With B. G. Rosenberg and E. Morgan) "The Use of Opposite Sex Scales as a Measure of Psychosexual Deviancy." *Journal of Consulting Psychology* 25: 221–225.

1961. (With B. G. Rosenberg) "Impulsivity and Sex Preference." *Journal of Genetic Psychology* 98: 187–192.

1961. (With B. G. Rosenberg and E. Morgan) "Historical Changes in the Freedom with which Children Express Themselves on Personality Inventories." *Journal of Genetic Psychology* 99: 309–315.

1961. (With B. G. Rosenberg) "Impulsivity and Peer Perception." *Merrill-Palmer Quarterly* 7: 233–238.

1962. (With J. M. Roberts) "Child Training and Game Involvement." *Ethnology* 1: 166–185.

1963. (With B. G. Rosenberg and E. Morgan) "The Development of Sex Differences in Play Choices During Preadolescence." *Child Development* 34: 119–126.

1963. "The Information Culture." In *Where Now* edited by A. Webster. Wellington: Wellington Teachers' College.

1963. (With J. M. Roberts) "Game Involvement in Adults." *Journal of Social Psychology* 60: 15–30.

1963. (With J. M. Roberts and A. Kendon) "Strategy in Games and Folktales." *Journal of Social Psychology* 61: 185–199.

1964. "Why Children Play." *Education* 13: 31–36.

1964. (With B. G. Rosenberg) "Ordinal Position and Sex Role Identification." *Genetic Psychological Monographs* 70: 297–328.

1964. (With B. G. Rosenberg) "The Measurement of Masculinity and Femininity in Children: An Extension and Revalidation." *Journal of Genetic Psychology* 104: 259–264.

1964. (With J. M. Roberts) "Rubrics of Competitive Behavior." *Journal of Genetic Psychology* 105: 13–37.

1964. (With J. M. Roberts and B. G. Rosenberg) "Sibling Association and Role-Involvement." *Merrill-Palmer Quarterly* 10: 25–38.

1964. (With B. G. Rosenberg) "The Relationship of Ordinal Position and Sibling Sex Status to Cognitive Abilities." *Psychonomic Science* 1: 81–82.

1965. (With B. G. Rosenberg) "Age Changes in the Effects of Ordinal Position on Sex Role Identification." *Journal of Genetic Psychology* 107: 61–73.

1965. (With J. M. Roberts and H. Hoffman) "Pattern and Competency: A Consideration of Tick Tack Toe." *El Palacio* 72: 17–30.

1965. (With B. G. Rosenberg) "Sibling Differences in Empathic Style." *Perceptual and Motor Skills* 21: 811–814.

1965. "Play Preference and Play Behavior: A Validity Study." *Psychological Reports* 16: 65–66.

1966. (With J. M. Roberts) "Cross-Cultural Correlates of a Game of Chance." *Behavior Science Notes* 3: 131–144.

1966. "The American University in One-Eyed Perspective." *Education* 15: 17–20.

1966. (With J. M. Roberts and W. E. Thompson) "Expressive Self-Testing and Driving." *Human Organization* 25: 54–63.

1966. (With B. G. Rosenberg) "Sibling Association, Family Size, and Cognitive Abilities." *Journal of Genetic Psychology* 109: 271–279.

1966. "Role Replication and Reversal in Play." *Merrill-Palmer Quarterly* 12: 285–298.

1966. (With B. G. Rosenberg) "The Dramatic Sibling." *Perceptual and Motor Skills* 22: 993–994.

1966. "Piaget on Play: A Critique." *Psychological Review* 73: 111–112.

1966. "The Value of Dramatic Role-Playing: An Experimental Confirmation." *The SACS Bulletin* 5: 26–27.

1967. (With J. M. Roberts *et al.*) "Studies in an Elementary Game of Strategy." *Genetic Psychological Monographs* 75: 3–42.

1967. (With B. G. Rosenberg) "The Dramatic Boy." *Perceptual and Motor Skills* 25: 247–248.

1967. "The Role of Play in Cognitive Development." *Young Children* 6: 361–370.

1968. "Father-Absence Effects on Families of Different Sibling Composition." *Child Development* 39: 1213–1222.

1968. (With A. Sharples, J. Exner, and B. G. Rosenberg) "Logical Analysis and Transitivity." *Journal of Genetic Psychology* 112: 21–26.

1968. (With B. G. Rosenberg) "Sibling Consensus on Power Tactics." *Journal of Genetic Psychology* 112: 63–72.

1968. (With B. G. Rosenberg) "Family Interaction Effects on Masculinity-Femininity." *Journal of Personality and Social Psychology* 8: 117–120.

1968. "Novel Responses to Toys." *Merrill-Palmer Quarterly* 14: 151–158.

1968. (With R. Laurence) "Novel Responses to Toys: A Replication." *Merrill-Palmer Quarterly* 14: 159–160.

1968. "The Folkgames of American Children." In *Our Living Traditions: An Introduction to American Folklore*, edited by T. Coffin. New York: Basic Books.

1968. "Games, Play, Daydreams." *Quest* 10: 47–58.

1969. "The Two Cultures of Games." In *Aspects of Contemporary Sport Sociology*, edited by G. Kenyon. Chicago: Athletic Institute.

1969. (With F. Landy) "The Effect of Limited Father-Absence on the Cognitive-Emotional Development of the Child." *Child Development* 40: 941–944.

1969. (With B. G. Rosenberg) "Sibling Age-Spacing Effects on Cognition." *Developmental Psychology* 6: 661–667.

1970. "The Cross-Cultural Study of Games." In *A Cross-Cultural Analysis of Sports and Games*, edited by Günther Leschen. Champaign, Ill.: Stipes Publishers.

1970. "A Psychologist Looks at Playgrounds." *The Educational Product Report*, Fall.

1970. (With J. Exner) "Birth Order and Hierarchical Versus Innovative Role Requirements." *Journal of Personality* 38: 581, 587.

1970. "Developmental Laws and the Experimentalist's Ontology." *Merrill-Palmer Quarterly* 16: 253–259.

1970. "The Psychology of Childlore." *Western Folklore* 29: 1–8.

1971. (With G. Lazier and D. Zahn) "Age Differences in Dramatic Improvisation." *American Psychological Association Proceedings*, (Division 10).

1971. (With G. Lazier) "Psychology and Drama." *Empirical Research in Theatre* 1: 38–46.

1971. "Sex Differences." *The Encyclopedia of Education*. New York: The Macmillan Co.

1971. "The Expressive Profile." *Journal of American Folklore* 84: 80–92.

1971. "Sex Role Identity and Sibling Composition." *Journal of Genetic Psychology* 118: 29–32.

1971. "Children at Play." *Natural History* 80: 54–59.

1971. "The Playful Modes of Knowing." In *Play: The Child Strives towards Self-Realization.* Special Monograph of the National Association for the Education of Young Children: 13–25.

1971. "A Developmental Psychology of Play and the Arts." *Perspective on Education,* Spring: pp. 8–17.

1971. "Child's play." *Psychology Today* 5: 66–69.

1971. (With G. Lazier and D. Zahn) "A Systematic Analysis of Developmental Differences in Dramatic Improvisational Behavior." *Speech Monographs* 37: 155–165.

INDEX

Achievement Development Project: 379

achievement game culture: development of, 303–309

Afghanistan: and ascriptive game culture, 301–302

Alla Balla. SEE Queenie

Alley Alley Ooh, The. SEE Eely Ily Oh, The

All In: description of, 77–78

Alphabets. SEE Letters

American Jump: description of, 115

American Nonsinging Games: 215

Ames, Louise Bates: material borrowed from, 526

Animal, Vegetable, or Mineral: 147

animal play: 58

Animated Oats: description of, 124

April Fools' play: description of, 62–63

Ardmore Teachers' Training College: research data collected at, 318, 322

Ariès, Philippe: and changes in family, 3; and ascriptive game culture, 299; and the creation of childhood, 304

ascriptive game culture: description of, 299–303

Auckland: schools in, visited, 9

Auction Bridge: players of, gregarious, 516. SEE ALSO Contract Bridge

automatization: measures of, 385–386

Babbity Bowster: 42

Babes in Toyland: as source for a children's game, 160

Ball-Bouncing: description of, 117–120

Ball Hopscotch: description of, 211

Ball Tag: description of, 207

Baloo Baloo Balight: description of, 20–21

Bandits: popularity of, 265; increased preference for, among girls, 409; decreased preference for, among boys, 410

Bar the Door: fades from playground, 12; variants of, 79–80, 84–85; as most popular tagging game, 81–83; as research topic, 491–493; game challenge of, 493–494; player participation in, 494–497; alternative names for, 496, 497; player performance in, 498–502; and the spatial scene, 502–504; temporal structure of, 504; factors operative upon, 504–505; mentioned, 77

Baseball: and preference by sex, 263; increased preference for, among girls, 409

Base Kiss: description of, 468

Basketball: and preference by sex, 263; increased preference for, among girls, 409; minor sports subservient to, 456–457

Battle Games: description of, 56–57

beads: as implement of play, 59

Beater-Goes-Around: characteristics of, 434

Bedlam: description of, 80

Bellahonie, The: description of, 80

Bell Horses: description of, 19

Bells: in 1920–1950 period, 14; description of, 170

Best, Elsdon: on knucklebones in New Zealand, 321, 322

Beware the Bear: 93

Bicycle-riding: popularity of, 267

bicycles: as implement of play, 64

Big and Wee: description of, 195–196

Bingo: as feminine pastime, 410; encompassed by term "game," 512

Bird-Nesting: 57

Biting the Apple: as near-kissing game, 466–467; description of, 468

Black Magic: description of, 145; as feminine pastime, 409

Black Maria: 267

Black Peter: 93

Black Tom: employed in "It" role

test, 435–436; and "It" role test re-
sults, 438–439
Blind Hopscotch: 211
Blindman's Buff: description of, 141;
and preference by sex, 263, 264;
mentioned, 79
board games: enumeration of, 151;
changes in preference for, 265, 277–
278
Boating: increased preference for,
among girls, 409; increased prefer-
ence for, among boys, 410
Bobby Bingo: description of, 19, 31.
SEE ALSO Who Goes Round My
Stone Wall?
Bogies: 93
Bold Jolly Lads: 42
Bouncing Ball Hopscotch: 211
Bowling Green (Ohio): site of Tick
Tack Toe Test, 371
Bowling Green State University: 403
bows and arrows: as implement of
play, 57; popularity of, 265; in-
creased preference for, among girls,
409
Boxing: increased preference for,
among girls, 409
Boys Catch Girls: description of, 468
Brewster, Paul: on mechanization of
children's games, 215
Bridge: description of, 468
Broken Barley: 93
Broverman, Donald: cognitive style
project of, 384–385
Bruner, J. S.: on the nature of schools,
442–443
Buck Buck: fades from playground,
12; description of, 191–192; persists,
194–195
Buffalo Bill: popularity of, 265; men-
tioned, 267
Bull in the Ring: fades from play-
ground, 12; description of, 202; and
ascriptive game culture, 300
Bull-Roarers: as implement of play,
58
Bumble Puppy: description of, 162
Bumpers: description of, 186
Burglars: 93
Burke, Kenneth: dramatistic analysis
of, 453, 454, 524
Bushrangers: description of, 56
Bush Tiggy: 93
Busy Bees: description of, 72
Butcher Bats: description of, 58–59
Butcher's Bat: description of, 73
Button Hockey: 181

Buttons: in 1920–1950 period, 14; description of, 142, 151, 170, 181
buzkashi: description of, 301–302
Buzz: description of, 148–149

Cabbages. SEE Colours
California, University of (Berkeley):
5
California Test of Mental Maturity:
371, 394
Cameras (matchbox): 65
Camp: description of, 208–209
Candy, Cigarettes: 468–469
Cannon Balls: 73
Cap-It: description of, 190
Cap-Tag: 125
Card Game, The: description of, 469
card games: enumeration of, 151; and
preference by sex, 263, 264; changes
in preference for, 265, 277–278
Carry My Lady to London: 42
Cassirer, Ernst: author's association
with, 453
Cat and Mouse: 76
Cat's Cradle: played by girl students,
12; and artifacts of play, 14; widely
played, 184
Cauliflowers. SEE Colours
central-person games: definition of,
212–213; changes in preference for,
265, 277–278
Centuries of Childhood, The: 3, 299,
304
Chain Tag: description of, 84
chance, games of: in classification system, 16; descriptions of, 120–122;
linked to nomadic cultures, 297–
298; definition of, 332; cultural
context of, 333–334, 335; and education in shrewdness, 444–445
Changing Nature of Man, The: 3, 304
Charades: and preference by sex, 263,
264; mentioned, 140
Charlie over the Water: description
of, 92
Chase: description of, 469; mentioned,
77
Chase and Kiss: description of, 469–
470
chasing games: descriptions of, 75–99;
changes in preference for, 265, 270–
271
chasing kiss games: characteristics of,
482
Checkers: and preference by sex, 263,
264; increased preference for,
among boys, 410

Chess: and preference by sex, 263, 264

Chevvy Chase: description of, 199

Chew the String: kissing element in, 466; description of, 470

Chibby: description of, 199

Chicken: encompassed by term "game," 512

Child, Irving: prepares sample of folk tales, 347

children: improved position of, in modern society, 219–221

Children's Games in Street and Playground: 3

Children's Manifest Anxiety Scale: and sex role identification, 412

child training: effects of, on game preference, 335–336

China: girls' play in, 266

Chinese Walking: description of, 127

Choo Choo: description of, 470–471

choral games: definition of, 212

Christchurch: schools in, visited, 9

Cinematographs: 65

Clap In, Clap Out: as traditional game, 470

Clark University: author visiting professor at, 453

Clark University Heinz Werner Institute of Developmental Psychology: and cognitive style project, 384

clay-shooters: as implements of play, 57

Clothes. SEE Colours

Cobbler, Cobbler, Mend My Shoe: 29

Cockfighting: fades from playgrounds, 12; description of, 201–202

Cole's Book Arcade: 183

collections: 59

Colours: description of, 67, 91; mentioned, 93

Come and Sit in My Chair: description of, 146–147

competitive games: absent from Australia and South America, 297

Conkers: description of, 160–161

Consequences: description of, 143–144

Constantinople (game): description of, 148

Contract Bridge: as intellectual occupation, 516. SEE ALSO Auction Bridge

Cops and Robbers: popularity of, 265, 266; increased preference for, among girls, 409

Cornell University: 315

Country Cricket: 209

couple games: changes in preference for, 265, 279

couple kiss games: characteristics of, 483–484

Cowboys and Indians: description of, 56; increase in popularity of, 64; increased preference for, among girls, 409; decreased preference for, among boys, 410; mentioned, 265, 266

crab fishing: among the Maori, 326

Creeping Up: description of, 69–70

Cricket: in 1900–1920 period, 12, 13; description of, 155–156; and control of children's play, 216; minor sports subservient to, 456–457

Crochet: as feminine pastime, 410

Croquet: 161, 162

cross-cultural research: weaknesses of, 335

Crosswell, T. R.: research conducted by, 259; on roller skating, 275

culture: complexity of, linked with game patterns in, 297–298

Cunning Joe: fades from playgrounds, 12; description of, 159–160

Dancing: and preference by sex, 263, 264, 265; increased preference for, among boys, 410

Danish Rounders: 210

darts: as implement of play, 58; increased preference for, among boys, 410

Dead Man's Dive: description of, 167

Defence: 210

dialogue games: in classification system, 16; descriptions of, 46–54; changes in preference for, 265, 269–270; in achievement game culture, 303

Diggley Bones. SEE Old Lady from Botany Bay, The

Do As I Do: description of, 140

Dodge the Skunk: employed in "It" role test, 435–436; and "It" role test results, 438

Dog and Bone: 73

Dolls: and preference by sex, 263, 265; popularity of, 267

Dominoes: and preference by sex, 263, 264

Donkey: description of, 147, 208

Donkey Tag: 93

Dooking for Apples: description of, 144

Douglas, Norman: fears decline in children's creativity, 215

Down in the Valley: 21, 25
Dozens, The: and ascriptive game culture, 300
Draw a Bucket of Water: description of, 113–115
Draw and Kiss: description of, 471
dreams: formal analysis of, 524–526, 527
Dressing-up: popularity of, 267–268
Drop the Handkerchief: description of, 19, 30–31; still played, 43; and preference by sex, 263, 264, 265; analogous to other expressive forms, 531
Ducking: 125
Ducks and Drakes: description of, 167
Ducks in the Pond: 73
Duckstones: fades from playground, 12; description of, 166–167
Dumb Crambo: description of, 140
dummy parcel: description of, 125; mentioned, 129
Dunedin: schools in, visited, 9
Dunk and Davey: description of, 186
Dutch Rounders: 210
Dynamite: description of, 471

Echo: description of, 207–208
eels: fishing for, 325–326
Eely Ily Oh, The: description of, 35–36
Effects of Sociodramatic Play on Disadvantaged Pre-School Children, The: 298
Egg Cap: fades from playgrounds, 12; description of, 168–169
Eggs in the Nest. SEE How Many Eggs in the Bush?
elastic gun: as implement of play, 64
Elements: description of, 148
Elkan, Beverly: material borrowed from, 524
Endurance Kissing: description of, 471–472; participants' attitude toward, 489
Ethnographic Atlas: game classification system of, 342–343
expressive forms: explanation of, 522; study of, 524; interrelatedness of, 532–535, 539–540; antecedents of, 535–537; rhetoric of, 537–538; consequences of, 538–539

Fairy Gardens: 60
Family Coach: 143
Farmer in the Dell: still played, 43, 45; and sex roles, 531–532; mentioned, 19, 21, 25

Fels Institute Longitudinal Study: provides sample for Tick Tack Toe Test, 379–380
Fels Research Institute: 379
Fiddle Diddle. SEE Perdiddle
Fill the Gap: description of, 81. SEE ALSO Drop the Handkerchief
Find the Key. SEE Giant and His Treasure, The
Fire, Air, and Water. SEE Elements
Fire on the Mountains: description of, 41
Fishing: included in sex difference inventory, 409; mentioned, 57
Fish in the Pond: 73
Five Minute Date: description of, 472
Flashlight: description of, 472–473; attitudes of participants toward, 489
flax boats: among the Maori, 327–328
Flax-Flappers: as implement of play, 58
Flicks: description of, 211
Florida: singing games in, 269
flower games: description of, 58
Flyball: 210
Fly the Garter: fades from playgrounds, 12; description of, 190–191
Folding Arms: description of, 71
folklore: *vs.* psychology, 521–522
folk tales: resemblance of, to games, 342–343; and cultural setting of strategic mode in, 346–347; types of, 347–348; rating of, 348–349; as child training, 349–350; strategic outcome in, *vs.* games of strategy, 350, 351; strategic outcome in, *vs.* levels of political integration, 350, 352; obedience themes in, *vs.* games of strategy, 351–352, 354; strategic outcome in, *vs.* rewards for obedience, 351, 353; strategic mode in, and games of strategy, 356–357; formal analysis of, 528–530
Follow Me to London. SEE In and Out the Windows
Follow the Leader: description of, 199–200
Food Play: description of, 59
Football. SEE Endurance Kissing; Rugby Football
Foot Races: 201
Forfeit Games: 145
formal questions: nature of, 507
Fortune-Telling: description of, 65
Fox and Geese: and preference by sex, 263, 264, 265; mentioned, 77. SEE ALSO Hen and Chickens

Freeze Tag: description of, 473; limits set by, 487

French and English: fades from playgrounds, 12; description of, 198; mentioned, 77

French Cricket: description of, 209–210

French Tag. SEE Touch Touch

Frigid Woman: encompassed by term "game," 512

functional questions: nature of, 507

Gag or No Gag: description of, 83

game-determined power: importance of, 434

games: as index to culture, 3–4; method of study of, 9–10; in 1870–1900 period, 11–12; in 1900–1920 period, 12–13; from 1920 onward, 13–15; classification of, 15–17; developmental classification of, 212–214; and children's creativity, 215–219; importance of changes in, 258; research on changes in, 258–262; changes in preference for, 279–281; and theory of universality, 295–297; as indicator of particular cultures, 309; definition of, 331; absence of, from cultures, 332–333; significance of, 338–339; and cultural variables, 341–342; types of, vs. child training practices, 356; importance of, to participants, 403–404; and sex differences, 405–406; tested preference for, by sex, 406–411; associated with male sex role, 411; and flexibility of female sex role, 411–412; preference for, by sex, 412–413; abstract nature of, 443–444; facilitate learning process, 447–448; and the romanticist's illusion, 455–456; seasons, and number of players, 458–459; vs. sports, 511–517; interrelationship of, with play and sports, 517–518; formal analysis of, 531–532

Games and Pastimes of the Maori: incomplete, 317

Games of Argyleshire: 497

General Post: description of, 143

Geography: description of, 148

Get the Keys. SEE Giant and His Treasure, The

Ghost in the Garden: description of, 46–48

Ghosts: 93

Giant and His Treasure, The: description of, 70

Giant Steps. SEE Steps and Strides

Giggies: sought after by children, 58

Go, Go, Stop. SEE Creeping Up

Goals: 210

Golden Bay: schools in, visited, 9

Golden Rule, The: description of, 123–124

Gomme, Alice Bertha: folkgame theories of, 3; on Mother, Mother, the Pot Boils Over, 48; on variants of Bar the Door, 497

Goosey. SEE Punch King

Grammar of Motives, A: 453, 507

Grandmother's Footsteps. SEE Creeping Up

Grand Old Duke of York, The: description of, 19, 42

grass games: description of, 58

Green Gravels: description of, 19, 25–27

Green Grow the Leaves: 42

Guessing: description of, 71

Gump, Paul: collaborates with author, 403; mentioned, 453

Guy Fawkes Play: description of, 61–62

hand-clapping games: description of, 115–117

hand games: played in Maori schools, 323

Hand Hockey: 210

Handkerchief Hockey: 210

Hand Rounders: 210

Hand Shadows: 183

Handstands: description of, 74

Hands upon Hands: description of, 182

Hand Tennis: 210

Hanging Bailey: description of, 65

Hares and Hounds: fades from playgrounds, 12; description of, 200

Hayride Kissing: description of, 473

Heads, Bodies and Legs: description of, 144

Head Start: and abstract learning, 443–444

Hearts: description of, 473

Heave Ho: description of, 203

Heavy, Heavy, Hang Over the Head: description of, 473–474

Hen and Chickens: description of, 52; mentioned, 35

Here Come Two Nuns: description of, 72

Here I Come: as feminine pastime, 409

Here's a Prisoner. SEE London Bridge

Here's a Thing: description of, 145–146

Here's the Church: description of, 182–183

Here We Go Round the Mulberry Bush. SEE Mulberry Bush, The

Hickety Bickety: description of, 122

Hide and Seek: description of, 76, 77; and preference by sex, 263, 264; encompassed by term "game," 512; analogous to other expressive forms, 531

Hide the Thimble: 142

Hideygo. SEE Hide and Seek

Hive-Hunting: 57

Hockey: minor sports subservient to, 456–457

Hoki Toki. SEE Baloo Baloo Balight

Homaiacky. SEE Kick the Tin

Homo Ludens: The Play Element in Culture: 296

Honey Pots: description of, 51–52

Hooks and Eyes: description of, 115

Hoops: played by older children, 12; played by younger children, 14; as implement of play, 58; description of, 162; as feminine pastime, 409

Hop, Step, and Jump: 201

Hop-Peg: description of, 186

Hopping Base: description of, 184–186

Hopscotch: variations of, 187–189; and preference by sex, 263, 264, 265; seasonal occurrence of, 458, 463; metaphysical implications of, 503

Hop the Hats: description of, 186–187

Horney: description of, 85

Horse Riding: increased preference for, among boys, 410; mentioned, 60

Horses: played by older children, 12; played by younger children, 14; declining popularity of, 267

Horse's Piss: 125

Hotaka: among the Maori, 326–327

Hot Cockles: description of, 122

Hot Rice: description of, 209, 210

Houses: and preference by sex, 263, 264, 265; popularity of, 266, 267

How Many Eggs in the Bush?: description of, 121; as game of number conservation, 445

How Many Miles to Babylon?: 42

Huizinga, Johan: play theories of, 296–297

Human Relations Area Files: analyses based on, 332

hunting: among the Maori, 324–325

Hunt the Skipper: 142

Ickety Bickety. SEE Hickety Bickety

Imitations: description of, 140

imitative games: slipped down the age scale, 63–64; changes in preference for, 265–268

In and Out the Windows: description of, 34–35; still played, 43

individual skill games: definition of, 213; changes in preference for, 265, 273–274

informal games: descriptions of, 54–66

Initials. SEE Letters

insect play: description of, 58

Institute of Child Welfare: author's affiliation with, 5

intellectual games: 149

In the Pond and Out of the Pond: 73

Inventors: popularity of, 267

Iowa Test of Basic Skills: 371

Isaac and Rebecca: description of, 141–142

I Saw You: 93

I See a Ghost: description of, 144

I Spy: as feminine pastime, 409; mentioned, 93, 147

Israel: and girls' play, 266

"It" role: high-power and low-power, 434–435; experience in, vs. personality factors, 439–440, 441; power of, vs. experience in, 439, 441; rotation in, vs. experience in, 440, 441

"It" role test: participants in, 436; description of, 436–437; results of, 437–439

I've Come to See Poor Mary Jane: 42

Jack-a-balan: description of, 79

Jack a Lingo. SEE Who Goes Round My Stone Wall?

Jack of All Sorts: description of, 72

Jacks: and preference by sex, 263, 264, 265

Jenny Jones: description of, 27–28

Jingle the Penny: description of, 124–125

Jingo Ring, The: description of, 19, 21, 25

John Brown's Body: description of, 142–143

Johnny in the Inkpot: description of, 72

Jolly Miller, The: description of, 19, 40–41

Jones, Mary Cover: on game preference by sex, 262
Jump, Little Nag Tail: description of, 193–194
Jumprope: and preference by sex, 263; popularity of, 267

Kansas: singing games in, 268; dialogue games in, 270; leader games in, 270; team guessing games in, 272
Kaplan, Bernard: 453
Kat: 210
Kenwood School (Bowling Green, Ohio): site of play inventory, 420
Keys or Pads: 93
Kick, Donkey, Kick: description of, 123
Kicking Ball Hopscotch: 211
Kicking Block Hopscotch: 211
Kicks: description of, 209
Kick the Tin: description of, 76, 80
Kikeri: 93
King of the Castle: description of, 203; as central-person game, 213
King of the Golden Sword: description of, 300; mentioned, 125
King on the Mountain: and ascriptive game culture, 300
King Pin: description of, 198–199
Kings and Queens: description of, 474
kissing: as important formal element in games, 465
kissing games: changes in preference for, 265, 279; research on, conducted, 466; preference for, ranked, 467; subsets of, 482–484; origins of, 484–485; changes in, 485–486; developmental change represented by, 487–490
Kissing Tag: description of, 474
Kiss in the Ring. SEE Drop the Handkerchief
Kiss under Water: description of, 474
Kites: played by older children, 12; as implement of play, 58; and preference by sex, 263, 264; seasonal occurrence of, 458, 463–464
Kiwi. SEE Queenie
Knick Knock: description of, 124
knife, the: as implement of play, 57–58
Knock-Backs: description of, 170
Knucklebones: played by girl students, 12; description of, 176–181; as evidence of Maori-European culture mix, 320–323

Kozelka, Robert: helps create test of strategic competence, 337

Lady on the Mountain: 21, 25
Last Couple Out. SEE Race for a Wife
Lazier, Gilbert: and teaching of illiterates, 443
Lazy Stick: description of, 204
leader games: in classification system, 16; in 1870–1920 period, 66; descriptions of, 66–75; changes in preference for, 265, 270
Leap Frog: description of, 189–190; and preference by sex, 263, 264, 265
Lehmann, Harvey C.: research conducted by, 260
Letters: description of, 67
London Bridge: description of, 19, 32–33; and sex roles, 531–532
London Street Games: 215
Longball: description of, 206–207
Lore and Language of Schoolchildren: 3
Lubyloo. SEE Baloo Baloo Balight

McGhee, Zach: research conducted by, 259
MacLeod, Jean: aids author's research, 5
make-believe games: in classification system, 16
Man the Ship: 73
Maori, the: description of, 56; submergence of culture of, 317–318; games played by, 319; and games introduced by Europeans, 328; games of, played by Europeans, 330
Marble Board: description of, 121
Marbles: played by older children, 12; played by younger children, 14; games of, 174–176; as individual-skill game, 213; and preference by sex, 263, 264, 265; increased preference for, among girls, 409; seasonal occurrence of, 458, 459–462
Mark: description of, 209
Massachusetts: singing games in, 269
May I?: description of, 68–69; as central-person game, 212
Merry Go Rounds: description of, 19
Merry Go Tansy. SEE Jingo Ring, The
Michigan: singing games in, 269
Minx: description of, 474
Mistletoe Kissing: description of, 474–475
mixing kiss games: characteristics of, 483

model array: examples of, 342
Monkey on the Bridge: description of, 194
Moonlight, Starlight: description of, 78
Mother, Mother, the Pot Boils Over: description of, 47, 48–51; as central-person game, 212
Mother Mumby's Dead. SEE Mrs. Mc-Kenzie's Dead
Mousetrap: description of, 183–184
Mrs. McKenzie's Dead: description of, 140–141
Mud-slides: among Maori children, 327
Mulberry Bush, The: description of, 28–29; still played, 43
Murder: 93
Murderer and Detective: description of, 475
Musical Chairs: 147
Musical Circle: description of, 475
Musical Statues. SEE Tableaux
My Aunt Sally Has Gone to Paris: description of, 141
My Fair Young Lady: 42
My Father Has Cut My Finger Off: description of, 129–130

Names. SEE Letters
National Olympic Federation: sponsors buzkashi matches, 302
natural foods: among the Maori, 327
necking: description of, 475–476
New Zealand: settlement of, 10–11; singing games in, 269; importation of games to, 492–493
New Zealand Education Department's Infant Syllabus: and singing games, 43
Nigger Boys: description of, 92
Nivy Nivy Nick Nack: description of, 121–122
No Man Standing: description of, 203
nonsense: as play activity, 138–139
nonsense rhymes: in chasing games, 86–91, 94–99
Non-Stop Cricket: 209
North Otago: schools in, visited, 9
Noughts and Crosses: description of, 149
Noughts and Dots: description of, 149–150
number conservation test: description of, 446; results of, 446
Numbers: description of, 476
nursery rhymes: formal analysis of, 530

Nurses: popularity of, 266
Nuts and May: description of, 19, 36–37; still played, 43

Oats and Beans and Barley: 21, 25
Odd Man Out: 93
Ohio: singing games in, 269; sports in, 278; as testing site, 406; provides kissing games research sample, 466
Oka Ball: description of, 20
Old Lady from Botany Bay, The: description of, 53
Old Mother Gray: description of, 53–54
Old Tom. SEE Who Goes Round My Stone Wall?
Ooh! My Toe!: description of, 125
Opie, Iona: folkgame theories of, 3
Opie, Peter: folkgame theories of, 3
Opossum: 93
Oranges and Lemons: description of, 19, 31–32; still played, 43; combined with Draw a Bucket of Water, 114
ordinal position: vs. power in play, 423

Pakeha: games of, parallel Maori games, 319
Pakehas and Maoris. SEE Maori, the
Paper Chase: fades from playgrounds, 12; description of, 200–201
parachute: as implement of play, 64
Parchesi: and preference by sex, 263, 264–265
parlor games: in early New Zealand settlements, 11; in classification system, 16; descriptions of, 139–152; changes in preference for, 265, 271–272, 279; in achievement game culture, 303
Pass the Kiss: description of, 476
Pass the Lifesaver: as near-kissing game, 467; description of, 476
Pass the Orange: kissing element in, 466; description of, 476
pea-shooters: as implement of play, 57
Pebbles and Stones: 93
Peep Behind the Curtain. SEE Creeping Up
Peep Shows: 65
Pee Wee Some More Yet: 125
Peg Ball: 209
Pegknife: description of, 173–174
Peg Rounders: 210
Peg Top: description of, 164
Penny Doctor Beetles: played by

Maori children, 328. SEE ALSO Butcher Bats
Penny Under the Chair: 93
Perdiddle: description of, 477
Peter and Paul: description of, 182
Photography: description of, 477
Physical Education: on hand games in Maori schools, 323
physical skill, games of: changes in preference for, 265, 277; reflect cultural pattern, 297; definition of, 331–332; cultural context of, 333, 335
Pin Dips: description of, 59
pipi shells: as Maori plaything, 327
Pitch and Toss: 121, 170
play: *vs.* sports, 507–511; interrelationship of, with games and sports, 517–518; formal analysis of, 531–532
Play Horse: popularity of, 265
play inventory: description of, 420–421; reliability of, 421–422; results of, 422–427
play status: *vs.* sibling status, 416–417, 427–430; *vs.* sociometric status, 417–419
Please, Jack, May We Cross Your Golden River?: description of, 91–92
Point to the Bell: 93
Poisonous Ball: 93
Poison Tag. SEE Touch Touch
Poka: played by Maori, 329
Pole-Vaulting: 201
Policeman: popularity of, 265; mentioned, 93
Polo: 69
Pom Pom Pullaway: as feminine pastime, 409
Pony Express: description of, 477–478
Poor Old Tom. SEE Who Goes Round My Stone Wall?
Poor Pussy: description of, 145
Poor Sally Is a-Weeping: description of, 19, 21, 23–24; still played, 43
Pop 'Em Down, Gents: description of, 120
Popeye. SEE Perdiddle
popguns: as implements of play, 57
Pork and Beans: description of, 145
post cards: provide recreational activity, 13
Postman's Knock: description of, 146
Post Office: description of, 478–479
Pretty Little Girl of Mine: description of, 19, 21–23; no longer played, 45; mentioned, 24

Pretty Please: description of, 479
Prick Books: introduced into New Zealand, 13; description of, 59–60
Priest of the Parish, The: description of, 149
Prisoner's Base: fades from playgrounds, 12; description of, 197–198; revival of, 207; and preference by sex, 263, 264, 265; mentioned, 77
Professor: description of, 479
psychogenic theory: *vs.* sociogenic theory, 315–316
psychological studies: problems with, 336–337
psychology: *vs.* folklore, 521–522
Psychology of Play Activities, The: 265
Punchinello: description of, 43–44; as central-person game, 212
Punch King: description of, 83–84
Puss in the Corner: description of, 77; and preference by sex, 263, 264
Putting Out Goes In: description of, 210
Putuputu: played among the Maori, 326
puzzles: and preference by sex, 263, 265

Queen Anne's Dead. SEE Mrs. McKenzie's Dead
Queenie: description of, 70–71
Queen of Sheba, The: description of, 142, 144–145
Queen's Birthday: celebrated in rhyme, 60–61
Quoits: description of, 171

Rabbit-Hunting: 57
Race for a Wife: description of, 143
Rats: description of, 125
Rats and Rabbits: 73
Red and Blue. SEE Colours
Redl, Fritz: 453
Relievo. SEE Bedlam
rhyming games: in 1920–1950 period, 14
rhythm games: in classification system, 16; descriptions of, 99–120
Ric Tic Toe: description of, 150
Ring-a-let: description of, 120–121
Ring a Ring a Roses: description of, 19, 20; still played, 43
Rinky Dink. SEE Perdiddle
Rivelea Rounders: 210
Roberts, John M.: value of, as co-

worker, 315–316; collaborates with author, 444
Robinson Crusoe: 267
Roller-skating: popularity of, 267
Rosenberg, B. G.: research conducted by, 259; on game preference by sex, 262; collaborates with author, 403
Rotten Egg: description of, 169, 208. SEE ALSO Drop the Handkerchief
Round and Round the Village. SEE In and Out the Windows
Rounders: more popular than Cricket, 12; description of, 153–154
Rugby Football: skills utilized by, 12; improved provisions for, 13; as institutionalization of Battle Games, 64; and Bar the Door, 82–83; development of, 196–197; and control of children's play, 216; and preference by sex, 263, 264, 265; season for, begins on arbitrarily chosen date, 456; craze for, 457
Rules of Contrary: for Shinty, 155
Running Waters: 93
Run Sheepie Run. SEE Sheep, Sheep
Rushes and Reeds: description of, 35

Sack Races: 201
Sacks on the Mill: description of, 203
Saddle the Nag: description of, 192–193
Sally Waters: description of, 19, 21, 24–25
Salvation Army: teasing of, 129
San Francisco: sports in, 278
Sardines: description of, 479; mentioned, 93
Schools: description of, 55; popularity of, 266, 267
Science and the Modern World: 442
Scrag: description of, 209
scrapbooks: introduced into New Zealand, 13; as implement of play, 59
Seat Tig: 93
Serve It in the Dark: 479
Shadow Tig: 93
Shanghais: as implement of play, 57
Sharky: 93
Sheep, Sheep: description of, 92–93
Shinty: more popular than Rugby, 12; description of, 154–155
shooting: included in sex difference inventory, 409; increased preference for, among boys, 410
Shortball: 210
Shove Penny: description of, 170–171
Show Kiss: description of, 479–480
Shuttlecock: 161, 162

sibling status: *vs.* play status, 416–417, 427–430; *vs.* power in play, 424
Sides: 210
Simon Says: description of, 181; and preference by sex, 263, 264, 265
Simuload Alcoholic: encompassed by term "game," 512
singing games: in early New Zealand settlements, 11; in 1870–1900 period, 12; in classification system, 16; descriptions of, 18–45; changes in preference for, 265, 268–269; in achievement game culture, 303; included in sex difference inventory, 409
Skating: as feminine pastime, 410; increased preference for, among boys, 410; mentioned, 60
Skiing: increased preference for, among girls, 409
skill, games of: in classification system, 16; descriptions of, 152–211
skilled pastimes: changes in preference for, 265, 274–276
Skin a Rabbit: description of, 124
Skip a Basket: 115
Skipping: description of, 100–104; rhymes used in, 104–113; seasonal occurrence of, 458, 463
Skipping Stones. SEE Ducks and Drakes
Skittles: 171
slanging contests: description of, 138
sledges: as implement of play, 58
slings: as implements of play, 57; as Maori plaything, 327
slippers: made by Maori children, 327
Slip the Ring: description of, 142
Smart Answers: examples of, 136–138
Smilansky, Sara: suggests nonuniversality of play, 298–299
Smudographs: description of, 60
Smuggling the Geg. SEE Gag or No Gag
Snakes: 93
Snap: and preference by sex, 263, 264
Snory-Bones: as implement of play, 58
Snowballing: 60
Snowmen: 60
Soccer: increased preference for, among girls, 409; increased preference for, among boys, 410; minor sports subservient to, 456–457
sociogenic theory: *vs.* psychogenic theory, 315–316

sociometric status: *vs.* play status, 417–419

Softball: minor sports subservient to, 456–457

Soldiers: description of, 160; popularity of, 265, 266; increased preference for, among girls, 409

Solitaire: encompassed by term "game," 512

South Carolina: chasing games in, 265, 270–271; team guessing games in, 272

Spacemen: popularity of, 267

Space Ring. SEE Drop the Handkerchief

Spang-Weazling: description of, 161

Spiders: description of, 150–151

Spin the Bottle: description of, 480; participants' attitudes toward, 488, 489

Spin the Trencher: description of, 147

Spitting: 125

Spitting Through Crossed Fingers: description of, 127

sports: seasonal classification of, 153; changes in preference for, 265, 278; *vs.* play, 507–511; *vs.* games, 511–517; interrelationship of, with play and games, 517–518

Spotlight: description of, 480

spring: folklorists' commentary on, 457

spring guns: as implement of play, 57

Stagknife: in 1920–1950 period, 14; description of, 171–173; metaphysical implications of, 220

Statues: description of, 69; as feminine pastime, 409

Steamboat: 267

Steps and Strides: description of, 67–68

stick games: played by Maori, 327

Stick Hockey: 210

stilts: as implement of play, 58; played with, in Maori schools, 324

Stone, Scissors, and Paper: description of, 181

Stone Tag: 93

Store: and preference by sex, 263; popularity of, 266

stories told by children: formal analysis of, 526–527

strategy: and childhood development, 355; and cultural advancement, 355–356

strategy, games of: linked to technological cultures, 298; definition of, 332; cultural context of, 334–335; competence in, related to psychological factors, 337–338; cultural distribution of, 343–344; *vs.* intensity of cultivation, 344; *vs.* metal working, 344, 345; *vs.* size of local community, 344, 345; *vs.* governmental structures, 345; *vs.* religion, 345; and child training, 346; *vs.* strategic outcomes in folk tales, 350, 351; *vs.* obedience themes in folk tales, 351–352, 354; linked to strategic mode in folk tales, 354–357; traced to other variables, 361–362; children's preference for, 363, 364; and psychological make-up of participants, 388; and education in shrewdness, 444–445; subjected to analysis of expressive forms, 522–523

Street Corner Society: 302, 417

string games: played in Maori schools, 323–324

"Strong *versus* Weak Automatization": explanation of, 384–385

Studies in Cognitive Growth: 442

Surrender the Tower: description of, 38–40

Sutton-Smith, Brian: research conducted by, 259; on game preference by sex, 262; on singing games, 269

swapping games: introduced in New Zealand, 13

Swimming: and rhymes, 60; and preference by sex, 263, 264

Symbol Formation: 453

Tableaux: 147

Tag: and preference by sex, 263, 264; characteristics of, 434; inequality of actor and counter-actor in, 532; mentioned, 76

tagging games: in early New Zealand settlements, 11; in classification system, 16; included in sex difference inventory, 409

Tail on the Donkey: description of, 152

Target-Shooting: 57

Taylor, Archer: aids author's research, 5

team games: definition of, 213; changes in preference for, 265, 277

teasing expressions: examples of, 135–136

teasing games: in classification system, 16; descriptions of, 122–139

teasing rhymes: examples of, 125–129, 130–134

Teazle. SEE Twos and Threes
Telegrams: description of, 148
telephone calls: as children's prank, 129
Telephones (treacle-tin): 60
Tennis: and preference by sex, 263, 264; minor sports subservient to, 456–457
Terman, Lewis M.: research conducted by, 259, 261
Texas: singing games in, 269
There Was a Man: rhyme used with, 117
There Was an Old Woman Who Lived in a Shoe: 143
This Little Pig: description of, 183
This or That: description of, 480–481
Threading the Needle: description of, 184; mentioned, 42
Three Dukes, The: description of, 19, 37–38
Three-legged Races: 201
Throwing Block Hopscotch: 211
Throwing Hats: description of, 167–168
Tick Tack Toe: as test of elementary strategic competence, 337–338, 361; as suitable research topic, 362–363; description of, 363–364; origins of, 364–365; success in, related to characteristics of participants, 396–397; different styles of play in, 516–517
Tick Tack Toe Test: description of, 365–370; participants in, 370–371, 375, 379–380; reliability of, 371–372; validity of, 372; and shifts between stripes, 372–374; and shifts along stripes, 374–376; response to, 376–378; skills indicated by, 378–379; and variables associated with winning scores, 380–382; and variables associated with drawing scores, 380–382; results of, 382–383; related to decision-making, 383–385; and cognitive variables, 386–388; and physical measures, 386–388; and "the winning girl," 389–391; and "the winning boy," 391–393; and "the drawing girl," 393; and "the drawing boy," 393–396
Tiddleywinks: and preference by sex, 263, 264
Tiggy Tiggy Touchwood: description of, 76
Tiki Tiki Touchwood: 93
Times: description of, 72

Tip Cat: fades from playground, 12; and artifacts of play, 14; description of, 156–158, 161
Tippenny Runs: description of, 209
Tip Tap: 93
Tip the Finger: description of, 93–94
Tobogganing: 60
Toes off the Counter: 93
Tom Tiddler's Ground: 77
Toodle-em-Buck: description of, 171
Tops: played by older children, 12; played by younger children, 14; games played with, 164–166; as individual-skill game, 213; and preference by sex, 263, 264; seasonal occurrence of, 458, 462
Touch Touch: description of, 78–79
toy trains: increased preference for, among girls, 409
Tractor Cotton Reels: as implement of play, 65
Trades: description of, 73
Traditional Games: 17
Traditional Games of England, Scotland and Ireland: 497
Transfers: introduced into New Zealand, 13; mentioned, 59
Treasure Hunts: 142
Tree-climbing: 60
Tree Grows in Brooklyn, A: 27
Tree Tig: 93
Trim the Hat: description of, 144
Trip and Go: 77
Trolley Wheels: as implement of play, 64
Truth or Consequences: description of, 481
Tug-o'-War: 201
Tuppenny Catches: description of, 73–74
Turtle Climb: description of, 481
Twilight Tig: description of, 78
Twos and Threes: description of, 80–81; mentioned, 76
tyres: as implement of play, 64

undifferentiated team guessing and acting: changes in preference for, 265, 272
Ups and Downs: 93

van den Berg, J. H.: and changes in family, 3; on childhood innocence, 304
Vegetables. SEE Colours
verbal teasing tricks: examples of, 135
Vine-swinging: in Maori schools, 324

Wairarapa: schools in, visited, 9
Walk down the Path: 183
Wallflowers: description of, 28
War: popularity of, 265
war party games: played by Maori, 329–330
Wash the Dishes: description of, 115
water play: description of, 60
water-shooters: as implement of play, 57
Wayne State University: author's work at, 403
Weather, The: 463
Wellington: schools in, visited, 9
Wellington Teachers' College: research conducted at, 458
Wellington Training College: students of, report instances of Penny Doctor beetles, 328
Werner, Heinz: developmental psychology of, 453
West Coast (New Zealand): schools in, visited, 9
Wet and Dry: 93
Whales in the Ocean: 93
What Colour's the Sky?: 143
What Have the Robbers Done to You?. SEE London Bridge
What's a Ship to Do?: description of, 123
What Time Is It?: as feminine pastime, 409
Wheelbarrow Races: 201
When I Was a Lady: description of, 29; no longer played, 45
whips: as implement of play, 58
Whip Tops: description of, 162–163; played in Maori schools, 324
Whispers: description of, 143
whistles: as implement of play, 58

Whitehead, A. N.: on the nature of schools, 442, 443
Who Goes Round My Stone Wall?: description of, 52
Who Steps in the Dark?: 93
Whyte, William F.: on play in lower socioeconomic strata, 302; theory of, on play status, 417
Wiggle Waggle: description of, 181–182
Williams College: 337
Willpower: description of, 481
Windshield Wiper: description of, 481–482
Winks: description of, 146, 482
Witch's Tig: 93
Witty, Paul A.: research conducted by, 260
Wolf, Wolf, Go Home. SEE Sheep, Sheep
Wolfie: 93
Worcester State Hospital: and cognitive style project, 384
word-making: description of, 147–148
Would You Lend My Mother a Saucepan?: description of, 41
Wrestling: description of, 203–204; and preference by sex, 263, 264, 265

Yoffie, Leah Rachel Clara: research conducted by, 258–259; on singing games, 268, 269
You Have Things in Your Head: description of, 124
Young Maori Party: 318

Zero-sum: encompassed by term "game," 512